Criminalising Hate Speech

Eric Heinze
Editor

Criminalising Hate Speech

A Comparative Study

ASSER PRESS

Springer

Editor
Eric Heinze
Department of Law
Queen Mary University of London
London, UK

ISBN 978-94-6265-652-9 ISBN 978-94-6265-650-5 (eBook)
https://doi.org/10.1007/978-94-6265-650-5

Published by T.M.C. ASSER PRESS, The Hague, The Netherlands www.asserpress.nl
Produced and distributed for T.M.C. ASSER PRESS by Springer-Verlag Berlin Heidelberg

This T.M.C. ASSER PRESS imprint is published by the registered company Springer-Verlag GmbH, DE, part of Springer Nature.
The registered company address is: Heidelberger Platz 3, 14197 Berlin, Germany

Foreword

This important volume constitutes an invaluable, unique resource for exploring the increasingly significant topic of "hate speech" and its regulation all over the world, in both traditional and online media.

The quotation marks underscore a point that is highlighted in the book's illuminating Introduction by its editor Eric Heinze, drawing upon his service as General Rapporteur on the Criminalisation of Hate Speech for the International Academy of Comparative Law. As Prof. Heinze observes, there is no single, universally accepted definition of "hate speech," and there are "many uncertainties plaguing" that concept. Nonetheless, as Prof. Heinze also notes, the term itself—which "only gained currency among jurists and scholars in the 1980s"—has since then "rapidly internationalised and is now acknowledged across the globe, often in the form of directly translated neologisms." Even more fundamentally, notwithstanding differing specific definitions in various legal regimes, this term has received "a core of consistent usage… across national jurisdictions and within leading international organisations."[1]

In a nutshell, mirroring the way the term tends to be used in everyday speech, multifarious legal regimes around the world apply it to expression that conveys discriminatory views about people on the basis of various personal characteristics. Beyond *reflecting* discriminatory ideas, such speech is widely feared to *foster* such ideas, which in turn could fuel discriminatory conduct, including violent conduct. Correspondingly, widespread restrictions on such expression reflect the hope that these restrictions could promote equal rights. In contrast, those who advocate only narrow restrictions on hate speech, including US Supreme Court Justices from across the ideological spectrum throughout the past half-century, maintain that broader restrictions are the worst of both worlds: they abridge free speech rights but do not materially promote equality rights. These debates have become even more consequential in the context of burgeoning online expression, including social media, and will be enhanced by the significant information that this book presents.

[1] See this book, p. 3.

The Book's Contributions to the Ongoing Debates

This book gathers together summaries and analyses of the legal authorities governing hate speech and its regulation in more than twenty diverse countries primarily in Europe, but also representing four other continents (Africa, North America, Oceania, and South America). For each country, the book details the multiple pertinent sources of national and international law, ranging from administrative regulations to international human rights norms, and including judicial rulings that interpret and enforce the standards that other sources of law set out. The authors have responded to a comprehensive questionnaire about these matters, generating each of the country-specific chapters. The result is a treasure trove of transnational information for analyzing and comparing myriad hate speech laws and their enforcement.

In the recent past, the global power of social media and other online platforms has been paralleled by growing efforts to rein in online hate speech in national, regional, and international legal systems. As has been true of all debates about the hate speech concept since its 1980s emergence, the current debates focus on the impact of various regulations, and specifically whether their costs to free speech are justified by their benefits to equality. Essential as these philosophical debates have been, they have been marked by a paucity of systematic empirical evidence about the actual implementation and impact of various hate speech restrictions. Too often, scholars, advocates, and policymakers alike have relied solely or primarily upon assumptions about the relative importance of free speech and equality rights, and about the impact that hate speech regulations would have upon each set of rights. At a more basic level, these debates too often have been waged in the absence of specific information about the array of actual hate speech laws and their enforcement records in various jurisdictions.

Given the lack of information about various countries' hate speech laws and their implementation that have characterized the rampant hate speech debates until now, this new book makes a novel contribution. The collected materials should serve as critical resources for policymakers and scholars who are designing and studying hate speech regulations.

Significant as this book is because of its detailed information about hate speech laws in multiple countries, it also has added significance in laying a foundation for future similar studies. It should inspire future scholarship that chronicles future developments in the jurisdictions that this volume includes.

Having been intensely engaged in both research and advocacy about hate speech restrictions since their advent upon the US legal and cultural scene in the 1980s, I look forward to drawing upon the wealth of newly available source materials that this book collects, to enrich my understanding.

The Real Problem: Not *Whether* But *When* Hate Speech Should Be Restricted

Contrary to the false binary that is too often postulated in debates about hate speech restrictions—*whether* hate speech should be restricted—the real question is *when* it should be restricted. After all, even proponents of the strongest protection for hate speech—including the many US Supreme Court Justices who, since the 1960's, have consistently held that government may not restrict such speech solely due to its hateful content or message—have nonetheless recognized that government may restrict such speech consistent with what is often called the "emergency" standard: when, considered in context, the speech directly causes or imminently threatens certain specific, serious harm, such as intentionally inciting imminent violence by supportive listeners,[2] or intentionally or recklessly instilling a reasonable fear on the part of directly addressed audience members that they will be subject to imminent violence.[3]

Consistent with this book's comparative lens, it is worth underscoring that even US First Amendment law—which is often described as "exceptionalist" in its strong protection of hate speech[4]—permits government to restrict hate speech in many factual contexts, consistent with the emergency standard. For many proponents of hate speech restrictions, the paradigmatic situation in which they advocate such restrictions is when speakers deliberately aim racist epithets at members of a racial minority group. Therefore, it is noteworthy that such intentionally targeted insulting, discriminatory expression is subject to punishment under four specific First Amendment doctrines that implement the general emergency standard. Elsewhere I have described these as follows[5]:

1. First, as just noted, if the expression intentionally or recklessly makes the targeted persons reasonably fear that they will be subject to violence, it constitutes a punishable "true threat," even if the speaker did not intend to commit any violent act.
2. Second, if the expression intentionally harries or annoys the targeted persons by intruding upon their privacy or freedom of movement, it constitutes punishable harassment.

---

[2] See, e.g., *NAACP v.* Claiborne Hardware Co., 458 US 886 (1982); *Brandenburg v. Ohio*, 395 US 444 (1969).

[3] See, e.g., *Counterman v. Colorado*, 600 US 66 (2023); *Virginia v. Black*, 538 US 343 (2003).

[4] See, e.g., Jean Stefancic and Richard Delgado, "A Shifting Balance: Freedom of Expression and Hate Speech Regulation." 78 *Iowa Law Review* 737 (1992–1993); Kevin Boyle, "Hate Speech: The United States versus the Rest of the World?" 53 *Maine Law Review* 487 (2001).

[5] Nadine Strossen, *Free Speech: What Everyone Needs to Know*, Oxford: Oxford University Press, 2023, 167–168.

3. Third, if the expression intentionally provokes a retaliatory violent response, it constitutes punishable speech, commonly described by the US Supreme Court as "fighting words."[6]
4. Fourth, when such expression occurs in settings where individuals are required to be—in particular, workplaces or educational institutions—it constitutes punishable "hostile environment harassment." Accordingly:

   a. Workplace expression may be punished on this ground if it is sufficiently "severe or pervasive to alter the conditions of [the victim's] employment and create an abusive working environment."[7]
   b. In educational contexts, expression may be punished on this ground when it is "so severe, pervasive, and objectively offensive that it can be said to deprive the victims of access to the educational opportunities or benefits provided by the school."[8]

Non-emergency Restrictions on Hate Speech

The foregoing analysis explains why, in the US as well as in other countries, debates about whether government and social media companies should restrict hate speech have centered largely on whether restrictions should extend even to hate speech that does not pose an emergency (which I dub "non-emergency" speech), given the uncontroversial nature of restrictions on speech that does pose an emergency.

To be sure, non-emergency hate speech may well cause harm, perhaps by undermining equality rights.[9] Yet the problem with legal restrictions on such speech is that it cannot readily be shown to cause harm in any specific instance, let alone in the aggregate. *All* speech has both positive and negative potential impacts, with its specific impact in any situation turning on countless context-specific factors, ranging from the speaker's intent to the audience's perceptions. Given the dual positive and negative potential of all speech—even speech with heinous messages, such as hate speech—it remains uncertain whether any non-emergency hate speech restriction would have a net positive or negative impact, including on the very equality goals that are cited as justifying such restrictions.

By definition, non-emergency speech does not directly and imminently cause or threaten specific serious harm. For that very reason, such speech is not necessarily harmful in any given instance. Consider, for example, racially insulting remarks made by a powerful political figure. Members of the disparaged group, far from experiencing any lessened sense of self-respect, may lose respect for the disparaging speaker, particularly in a society where problems of racism and discrimination can

---

[6] *R.A.V. v. City of St. Paul*, 505 US 377 (1992); *Chaplinsky v. New Hampshire*, 315 US 568, 572 (1942).

[7] Meritor Savings Bank v. Vinson, 477 US 57, 67 (1986).

[8] Davis v. Monroe County Bd. of Ed., 526 US 629, 650 (1999).

[9] See Strossen, above note 4, at 39–42.

be and are robustly debated. As lifelong gay rights champion Jonathan Rauch wrote: "If someone calls me a 'fucking faggot,' I interpret her as telling me that she needs counseling, not that I am a fucking faggot."[10] By extension, other members of the public, who previously might have supported that politician, could feel alienated and vote against him due to their realization of his racist ideas, which they repudiate.

Moreover, even if non-emergency speech were in fact harmful in any specific situation, it would not necessarily have a net harmful impact in the aggregate, considering all the situations in which it had a positive impact, as well as those in which it had a negative impact. Consider, for example, the notorious Unite the Right demonstrators who marched in Charlottesville, Virginia in 2017, chanting, "You will not replace us" and "Jews will not replace us," widely understood to refer to conspiracy theories about plans to eliminate or reduce the ethnically white population.[11] Was the net impact of this speech positive or negative? Did it, on balance, recruit more white supremacist followers, or did it instead spur more antiracist government initiatives and grassroots activism?

The latter conclusion was supported by none other than Susan Bro, the mother of Heather Heyer, the counter-demonstrator who was murdered when a Unite the Right supporter ruthlessly drove his car into a crowd of counter demonstrators. In 2019, the driver was sentenced to life imprisonment plus 419 years for these crimes, and in 2021 an appellate court confirmed the conviction.[12] In a 2019 interview, Bro strongly supported the Unite the Right demonstrators' free speech rights specifically because she believed that the airing of their racist views should have a net positive impact on the anti-racism cause for which her daughter's life had been sacrificed:

> [W]e walk into the room blindly if we don't take the time to know what the other side is thinking… [H]ate groups …want a violent reaction or they want no one to oppose them at all. [N]either approach is effective… [T]he effective approach is to show up in even larger numbers, without violence, to assertively say,"… We see you, we don't like you [or] what you're saying…" And we saw this in the second Unite the Right Rally in Washington when they showed up in very small numbers and … were met with counter protesters… in… very large numbers, saying "go home, go away."[13]

Even if we assumed that non-emergency hate speech did have a net harmful impact in the aggregate, non-emergency speech restrictions would not necessarily be justified. Rather, as a logical matter, such restrictions would only be warranted if all the following questions were also answered affirmatively:

1. Do these restrictions materially reduce the harmful impact of the targeted speech?

---

[10] Jonathan Rauch, *The Constitution of Knowledge: A Defense of Truth* (2021) 202.

[11] See, e.g., Sheryl Gay Stolberg and Brian M. Rosenthal, "Man Charged After White Nationalist Rally in Charlottesville Ends in Deadly Violence." *The New York Times*, Aug. 12, 2017. https://www.nytimes.com/2017/08/12/us/charlottesville-protest-white-nationalist.html (accessed 2 Apr. 2024).

[12] "Man convicted in Virginia rally death in 2017 loses appeal." *AP News*, Nov. 17, 2021. https://apnews.com/article/sports-ohio-race-and-ethnicity-racial-injustice-virginia-05301c89ae9785b06c9e793417372fd5 (accessed 2 Apr. 2024).

[13] Transcription from Bro's remarks delivered at the *Economist*'s Open Future Festival, Chicago, 5 Oct. 2019.

2. Can these restrictions be written in sufficiently clear and precise language to avoid problems of undue vagueness and substantial overbreadth, which endanger much speech that is not harmful?
3. Do the restrictions' benefits, in terms of reducing the speech's harmful impact, outweigh their unintended costs, including: suppressing non-targeted, non-harmful speech; increasing attention to or sympathy for the targeted speech; and disproportionately silencing marginalized voices and views?
4. Are there no alternative measures, which are less speech-restrictive than the non-emergency speech restrictions, that would be as effective as these restrictions, or more so? For example, how effective is "counterspeech"—i.e., information and ideas that counter discriminatory stereotypes?

Logically, each of these questions should be answered affirmatively as a prerequisite for validating any hate speech restriction. We might well tolerate restrictions on our fundamental free speech rights in order to promote some important benefit, such as decreased discrimination. What is far less clear is whether we should tolerate such restrictions if they cannot promise such a benefit, or if the same benefit could be promoted through an alternative measure, which does not limit our free speech rights. Given this logical appeal, it is not surprising that this analysis is reflected not only in First Amendment law, but also in major United Nations proceedings on free speech, as well as the free speech law in many other countries.[14]

This Book's Answers to Some Salient Questions

This book can assist in answering some of the foregoing questions. It lays out the exact language of each country's hate speech restrictions, which can help in answering the second question above: whether such restrictions can be written in sufficiently clear, precise language to avoid problems of undue vagueness and substantial overbreadth. As for the remaining questions, much pertinent information is also provided by many contributors.

One noteworthy instance comes from George Karavokyris's chapter about Greece, discussing the landmark 2015 ruling by the first instance criminal court of Rethymno in Crete, arising from "the first time that an individual had been charged under anti-racism [hate speech] legislation introduced in Greece." The prosecutor had charged Heinz Richter, a German professor of Greek and Cypriot modern history at the University of Mannheim, with "denial of defamatory nature of the Nazi crimes committed against the Cretan people," in his 2011 book, *Operation Mercury: The Invasion of Crete*. In a number of countries, expression that questions certain widely accepted historical facts or interpretations surrounding the Holocaust and other atrocities has been outlawed as hate speech. In effect, such expression is deemed to be

[14] See Nadine Strossen, "United Nations Free Speech Standards as the Global Benchmark for Online Platforms' Hate Speech Policies," 29 *Michigan State International Law Review* 307, 339–346 (2021).

hate speech against the pertinent minority groups, meaning that Holocaust denial is treated as illegal hate speech against Jews and other victims of the Nazis. Yet the inevitably contested nature of such matters was underscored by the Richter case. On the one hand, the University of Crete had decided to celebrate Richter's work by awarding him an honorary degree. On the other hand, his critics, including the prosecutor, found the book "offensive," since it "focused[ed] on the demythification of the resistance on the island during WWII."[15]

In a thoughtful opinion, the Greek court declared the law unconstitutional for violating free speech and academic freedom, providing negative answers to two of the key questions noted above: whether the restriction could be written with sufficient narrowness to avoid endangering valuable expression; and whether the restriction's costs outweighed its benefits. Concluding that the Greek law impermissibly "habilitates the parliamentary majority to act as a body of scientific knowledge on historical facts," the court's explication of the unintended adverse consequences of this approach is worth quoting:

> [S]cientific bodies are not formed by the current parliamentary majorities and governments, but by researchers and academics… [T]he recognition that public authorities can… impose historical truths… and prohibit alternative interpretations of specific historical events inevitably leads many different groups to seek to use the power of law in order to protect their own versions from any dispute… [L]egislation that criminalises the denial of crimes against humanity can have pernicious unintended consequences for important freedoms. Although these laws are the result of collective disapproval of certain historical atrocities, they can lead down the slippery slope of threatening freedom of speech. Extreme caution is needed to control the irrational elements within the collective consciousness in a way that is compatible with the protection of important liberties such as academic freedom. Our collective search for meaning within our various communities should be open and allow for expressing interpretations of historical facts that might seem idiosyncratic or even offensive and disturbing to the collective narratives of a community in its search for self-understanding.[16]

This book also sheds light on two other questions that should be answered affirmatively to justify non-emergency hate speech restrictions. Several chapters question the efficacy of hate speech restrictions in redressing discriminatory attitudes, and point to the advantages of alternative counterspeech approaches. By way of illustration, I will briefly summarize the pertinent conclusions from three chapters.

Barbara Herceg Paksic's chapter on Croatia concludes:

> [T]he majority of citizens view the efforts to suppress [hate speech] as ineffective… Given the complexity of the social need to combat hate speech, the primary focus should not solely be on repressive solutions. Prevention, particularly through tailored education, is likely to be more impactful and effective.[17]

A similar recommendation is included in the chapter about the Czech Republic by Marek Fryšták, David Čep, and Katarína Kandová. Stressing the widespread prejudices against the Roma minority, which "can be easily turned into hateful motives

[15] See this book, p. 276.

[16] Ibid.

[17] Ibid. at p. 144.

and thus into hate speech," the chapter notes the importance of counterspeech in addressing these problematic underlying attitudes. Citing examples of constructive counterspeech that NGOs and public television spearheaded, the chapter concludes that "[s]uch activities… can shape public opinion in terms of acceptance of [the] Roma minority." For example, regarding public television, the authors write: "The very popular Czech Television series MOST!… brought a fundamental turn in the view of the Roma in a certain part of society… Broadcast in 2019… this ethnic group was not shown in a negative light at all."[18]

Another chapter that positively comments on a counterspeech, educational alternative to hate speech restrictions is the chapter about Finland, by Tarja Koskela and Riku Neuvonen. Referring to "[t]he most famous [hate speech] case in Finland," which involved a magazine that was convicted for disseminating anti-immigrant conspiracy theories, they note the multiple academic studies that have critically examined this case. One of the cited studies supports "the need for more nuanced concepts" of discriminatory "fake news" about minority groups, and instead advocates "improv[ing] media literacy skills to help readers understand various motivations behind framing and reframing processes on different platforms and increasing the ability to understand the wider context."[19]

To be sure, the above-cited passages hardly constitute conclusive evidence about the critical questions they address, yet they make significant contributions to a rigorous, evidence-based examination of the overarching issue that is of such great concern to all of us, worldwide: *Which* hate speech restrictions—as well as which counterspeech measures—will most effectively foster both free speech and equality rights?

New Milford, CT, USA
April 2024

Nadine Strossen

Nadine Strossen is a Professor Emerita at New York Law School and Senior Fellow at FIRE (the Foundation for Individual Rights and Expression). She served as national President of the American Civil Liberties Union from 1991 to 2008. Her most recent books are *Free Speech: What Everyone Needs to Know* (2023); and *HATE: Why We Should Resist It with Free Speech, Not Censorship* (2018). Strossen is Host and Project Consultant for Free To Speak, a 3-hour documentary film series distributed in 2023 on American public television. In 2023, she won the Lifetime Achievement Award from the US-based National Coalition Against Censorship.

---

[18] See this book, p. 164.

[19] See this book, p. 182.

Acknowledgments

The reports gathered in this book are based on materials provided by Special National Rapporteurs commissioned by the International Academy of Comparative Law (IACL) from 2021 to 2023. They provide nothing more than a snapshot in time, but also nothing less. Hate speech is an old problem and shows no sign of disappearing. The problem is recognised internationally yet often has distinctly local dimensions reflected in the chapters.

It was an honour for me to have had the opportunity to present these themes in my capacity as General Rapporteur on the Criminalization of Hate Speech for the IACL General Congress in Asunción, Paraguay, from 23 to 28 October 2022. I owe an enormous debt of gratitude to Prof. Diego P. Fernández Arroyo for this kind invitation, and to Dr. Alexandre Senegacnik who first approached me with this invitation and constantly offered prompt and thoughtful guidance at every phase of the project. As everyone present in Asunción will have noticed, Dr. Senegacnik performed the Olympian task of overseeing this week-long, multi-event conference with unfailing collegiality. Of course, I must also express my great thanks to the entire organising and managing committee for the 2022 conference, which ran seamlessly at all stages, bringing together scholars and jurists from around the world, and I owe an equal debt of thanks for support provided by Dr. Senegacnik's successor Dr. Philippine Blajan, as well as IACL Secretary General Professor Gary Bell.

A personal thanks goes also to Judge Vivian López Núñez of the First Instance Civil Court in Paraguay and to Francisco Segura Riveiro, formerly of the Universidad de Concepción in Chile, for so generously hosting me in a city where my acquaintances were sparse. Many thanks also to the magnificent Prof. Aida Kemelmajer, former Justice of the Supreme Court of Mendoza, Argentina, who kindly chaired one of my sessions à l'improviste. A heartfelt thanks is due also to Uladzislau Belavusau of the Asser Institute in the Hague, who offered expert feedback on the questionnaire, which ensured that the Special Rapporteurs could use it as a tool for completing comprehensive responses. Ulad's colleague Frank Bakker of T.M.C. Asser Press also deserves special mention for the interest he has taken in the book, along with copy editors Nettie Dekker and Annika Mäkinen. Of course, and most importantly, I must thank all the authors who took the time to contribute to this volume.

London, UK Prof. Dr. Eric Heinze

Contents

Editor and Contributors

About the Editor

Eric Heinze (Maitrise *distinction*, U. Paris; J.D. cum laude, Harvard; Ph.D. cum laude, Leiden), Professor of Law at Queen Mary University of London, served as 2022 General Rapporteur on the Criminalization of Hate Speech for the *Académie internationale de droit comparé*. In addition to writings on legal theory, Heinze's books on free speech include *The Most Human Right: Why Free Speech is Everything* (The MIT Press, 2022) and *Hate Speech and Democratic Citizenship* (Oxford University Press, 2016). He led the EU consortium Memory Laws in European and Comparative Perspectives in 2016–2019 and has been a Fulbright Fellow, DAAD fellow, and Chateaubriand Fellow along with grants from the Nuffield Foundation and from Harvard University, and is general editor of the *Oxford Handbook of Hate Speech* (forthcoming 2025). e-mail: e.heinze@qmul.ac.uk

Contributors

Chara Bakalis School of Law and Social Sciences, Oxford Brookes University, Oxford, United Kingdom

Gwénaële Calvès Département de droit public, Université de Cergy-Pontoise, Cergy, France

Paolo Caroli Faculty of Law, University of Turin, Turin, Italy

David Čep Department of Criminal Law, Faculty of Law, Masaryk University, Brno, Czech Republic

Ursula Cheer University of Canterbury, Christchurch, New Zealand

Javier Augusto De Luca Faculty of Law, University of Buenos Aires, Buenos Aires, Argentina

Anjalee de Silva Melbourne Law School, University of Melbourne, Melbourne, Australia

Darko Dimovski Faculty of Law, University of Niš, Niš, Serbia

Ahmed Elkahwagy Alexandria University, Alexandria, Egypt

Marek Fryšták Department of Criminal Law, Faculty of Law, Masaryk University, Brno, Czech Republic

Luc Gonin Département de droit public, Université de Fribourg, Geneva and Neuchâtel, Switzerland

Eric Heinze School of Law, Queen Mary University of London, London, United Kingdom

Tom Herrenberg Faculty of Law, Open Universiteit, Heerlen, The Netherlands

Katarína Kandová District Public Prosecutor's Office, Prague, Czech Republic

George Karavokyris University of Thessaloniki, Thessaloniki, Greece

Tarja Koskela School of Law, Criminal Law at the University of Eastern Finland, Joensuu, Finland

Jan Kulesza University of Lodz, Lodz, Poland

Joanna Kulesza Lodz Cyber Hub Research Center, University of Lodz, Lodz, Poland

Olivier Lacombe Faculté de droit, Université Laval, Québec, Canada

Koen Lemmens Faculty of Law and Criminology, KU Leuven, Leuven, Belgium

Filip Mirić Faculty of Law, University of Niš, Niš, Serbia

Boban Misoski Faculty of Law Iustinianus Primus, University of Ss. Cyril and Methodius, Skopje, Republic of North Macedonia

Ricardo Narváez Departamento de Derecho Penal y Criminología, Universidad de Buenos Aires, Buenos Aires, Argentina

Riku Neuvonen Tampere University, Tampere, Finland;
University of Helsinki, Helsinki, Finland

Barbara Herceg Pakšić Faculty of Law, University of Josip Juraj Strossmayer, Osijek, Croatia

Stephan Parmentier Faculty of Law and Criminology, KU Leuven, Leuven, Belgium

Matías Quercia Departamento de Derecho Penal y Criminología, Universidad de Buenos Aires, Buenos Aires, Argentina

Pierre Rainville Faculté de droit, Université Laval, Québec, Canada

Velimir Rakočević Faculty of Law, University of Montenegro, Podgorica, Montenegro

Florin Streteanu Faculty of Law, Department of Public Law, University of Cluj-Napoca, Cluj-Napoca, Romania

Cristina Tomuleţ Faculty of Law, Department of Public Law, University of Cluj-Napoca, Cluj-Napoca, Romania

Alexander Tsesis Florida State University College of Law, Tallahassee, United States of America

Nikola Tupancheski Faculty of Law Iustinianus Primus, University of Ss. Cyril and Methodius, Skopje, Republic of North Macedonia

Brian Valerius University of Passau, Passau, Germany

Anastasiia Vorobiova Institute of Legal Sciences, Polish Academy of Sciences, Warsaw, Poland

Jogchum Vrielink Faculty of Law and Criminology, KU Leuven, Leuven, Belgium

Chapter 1
Introduction

Eric Heinze

Contents

Abstract Hateful expression poses the newest—and oldest—of social problems. The term 'hate speech' is recent within national and international legal regimes, yet problems of hostile expression and its regulation have confronted societies throughout history. The term germinated among legal scholars in the United States in the 1980s, then progressively became international, particularly after the end of the Cold War. Yet as far back as the Genocide Convention of 1948, international law has included directives for the regulation of hateful expression, as confirmed in subsequent treaties, such as the International Convention on the Elimination of All Forms of Racial Discrimination (ICERD) and the International Covenant on Civil and Political Rights (ICCPR).

Keywords Racism · Genocide · Minority rights · History of hate speech · Law and broadcast media · Hate speech legislation

In 1948 the Convention on the Prevention and Punishment of the Crime of Genocide bound states parties to punish any '[d]irect and public incitement to commit genocide'.[1] Of course, calendrical starting points are often arbitrary in contexts of complex social forces, yet World War II marked a turning point in global understandings of hateful expression, particularly insofar as that war was swiftly followed by widespread decolonisation movements as well as an internationally publicised civil rights movement in the United States.

E. Heinze (✉)
School of Law, Queen Mary University of London, London, United Kingdom
e-mail: e.heinze@qmul.ac.uk

[1] Convention on the Prevention and Punishment of the Crime of Genocide, 78 U.N.T.S. 1021 of 9 December 1948 (entered into force 12 January 1951), Article 3(c).

E. Heinze (ed.), *Criminalising Hate Speech*,
https://doi.org/10.1007/978-94-6265-650-5_1

These and other developments sparked renewed anxieties about the role of speech[2] in the entrenchment of discriminatory attitudes, policies, and practices. Within two decades after the Genocide Convention, the International Convention on the Elimination of All Forms of Racial Discrimination (ICERD) obliged States to penalise 'all dissemination of ideas based on racial superiority'[3] and then the International Covenant on Civil and Political Rights (ICCPR) provided that '[a]ny advocacy of national, racial or religious hatred that constitutes incitement to discrimination, hostility or violence shall be prohibited by law.'[4] The present volume continues down the path first paved by these precedents. Our question is straightforward: How have these concepts internationalised and how do they continue to develop in today's world?

1.1 The Concept of Hate Speech

The specific term 'hate speech' only gained currency among jurists and scholars in the 1980s, largely through a bourgeoning critical race studies movement in the United States, as witnessed in publications such as the influential collection *Words That Wound.*[5] In those years the concept of 'hate speech' was still new in the United States and largely unknown elsewhere. Yet as those international treaties confirm, many countries had long confronted the underlying problems.[6]

Since those days the concept of 'hate speech' has rapidly internationalised and is now acknowledged across the globe, often in the form of directly translated neologisms such as *discours de haine, discurso de odio,* or *Hassrede.* The chapter on France offers one of several examples of a country that had been dealing with the problem years before 'discours de la haine' made its Parisian debut. Similarly, in Germany and the Czech Republic, the concept of militant democracy (*wehrhafte* or indeed *streitbare Demokratie*), along with related notions of inter-group hostility or incitement (*Volksverhetzung*) had been developed in law long before the newer term *Hassrede* entered the scene.

Arguably the term's currency arises, in part, through its very imprecision. Like many terms in law, what started out as an improvised catch phrase seemed to capture

[2] See, e.g., International Convention on the Elimination of All Forms of Racial Discrimination, Declarations and Reservations, United Nations Treaty Series: Multilateral Treaties Deposited with the Secretary-General, ch. 4, doc. 2; International Covenant on Civil and Political Rights, Declarations and Reservations, United Nations Treaty Series: Multilateral Treaties Deposited with the Secretary-General, ch. 4, doc. 4.

[3] International Convention on the Elimination of All Forms of Racial Discrimination, 660 U.N.T.S. 195 of 21 December 1965 (entered into force 1 April 1969), Article 4(a). Cf. Article 4(b) (enjoining States Parties to ban organisations that promote racist ideas).

[4] International Covenant on Civil and Political Rights, 999 U.N.T.S. 171 of 19 December 1966 (entered into force 23 March 1976), Article 20(2).

[5] Matsuda et al. 1993.

[6] See, e.g., Rohrßen 2009.

a range of diverse yet related problems, precisely because of its flexible contours. After all, to take just three examples, racism, sexism, and homophobia, are in many ways very distinctive kinds of problems, yet the concept of 'hate speech' seems to describe one crucial overlap uniting them. As several of this book's chapters suggest, the concept of 'hate speech' remains in flux, often responding to immediate social tensions, and seems ill-suited to any exhaustive definition.

Yet that defect is hardly unusual. Vagueness characterises some of the terms that boast the oldest vintage and greatest durability in law. After all, can any of us formulate exhaustive – let alone trans-jurisdictional – definitions even for law's meat-and-potatoes concepts such as 'constitution', 'crime', 'contract', or 'property'? On this point it is also important to note that 'free speech' and 'hate speech' have become customary terms, yet lawmakers and courts have long construed them to include non-verbal expression, such as public displays of flags, symbols, uniforms, silent vigils, and the like. Therefore, unless strictly verbal expression is at issue, these terms should be construed broadly to mean, respectively, 'free expression' and 'hateful expression'.[7]

It will come as no surprise that several of this book's authors observe ambiguities inherent within concepts such as 'hate speech' and 'hateful expression'. Any admirer of Ludwig Wittgenstein will recall that such concepts draw their meanings not from fixed, extra-linguistic realities, but within language itself, through shared usage. Importantly, then, despite the many uncertainties plaguing these concepts, their meanings remain broadly consistent from chapter to chapter. However novel the phrase may have sounded decades ago, a core of established usage has persisted across national jurisdictions and within leading international organisations.

Following in the footsteps of these post-World War II international treaties, the European Commission against Racism and Intolerance (ECRI) examined the problem in its 2015 General Policy Recommendation #15: 'On Combatting Hate Speech'. Whilst this Recommendation is non-binding it nevertheless attempts a comprehensive depiction of hateful expression, which it describes as:

> . . . the advocacy, promotion or incitement, in any form, of the denigration, hatred or vilification of a person or group of persons, as well as any harassment, insult, negative stereotyping, stigmatization or threat in respect of such a person or group of persons, and the justification of all the preceding types of expression.[8]

The Recommendation further indicates that hate speech may 'take the form of the public denial, trivialisation, justification or condonation of crimes of genocide, crimes against humanity or war crimes which have been found by courts to have occurred, and of the glorification of persons convicted for having committed such crimes'.[9] Having set forth this broad topology the Recommendation then proceeds to enumerate a list of at least fourteen identitarian traits which confirm the instances in which such expression can be described as hate speech. These traits include: '"race",

---

[7] See, e.g., Heinze 2016, pp. 18–19.

[8] European Commission against Racism and Intolerance (ECRI), General Policy Recommendation #15 (2015), preamb. para 6.

[9] Ibid., preamb. para 3.

colour, descent, national or ethnic origin, age, disability, language, religion or belief, sex, gender, gender identity, sexual orientation and other personal characteristics or status'.[10]

Some of this definition's terms – 'advocacy', 'promotion', 'incitement', 'denigration', 'vilification', 'harassment', 'insult', 'stereotyping', 'stigmatization' – are subject to divergent interpretations not only across but even within European nations, and within and across democracies more generally, which makes it impossible to imagine hate speech bans lending both complete and equal protection to so many groups. If the protection is equal then it cannot be complete, and if it is complete then it cannot be equal. After all, if it were both complete and equal then massive quantities of censorship would be required. To avoid that result states inevitably become selective, which means they end up applying bans arbitrarily[11], particularly in an age of electronic communications witnessing millions of messages posted every day with often random controls.

These inconsistencies seem confirmed in several of the chapters. For example, as we read in the chapter on Italy, an utterance counts as 'insulting' or 'defamatory' depending on whether the targeted individual is present when and where the utterance is made, a distinction not drawn in most other nations. Indeed, and rather more candidly, the late Jovan Ćirić, writing when he was a Judge in Serbia's Constitutional Court, observed:

> 'In Serbia there is widespread consciousness about the problem of hate speech. The term 'hate speech' is widely used in everyday and political life but the courts have not adopted any definition or description of hateful expression. This may be because the Serbian language, like the Croatian, Bosnian and other former Yugoslav languages (essentially the same languages) is rich in obscenities so it is difficult to set forth a clear definition. In everyday discussion, people often accuse others of using hate speech, but no one knows where the ordinary insult stops and hate speech starts. People, especially politicians, blame each other for hate speech, often having in mind nothing more than an ordinary insult. In such cases, the meaning and purpose of hate speech becomes lost because there is no clear definition.'

Despite these many ambiguities, we find agreement across chapters in acknowledging that the problem itself needs some level of resolution. Several of the chapters are submitted from longstanding or emerging democracies, which define free speech as a paramount value. Indeed, as the chapter on Australia reminds us, free speech rights appear nowhere in that nation's constitution, yet its highest court has deduced the primacy of free speech from the very fact of the constitution's democratic character. Surely many other democracies, even those boasting formally constitutionalised free speech rights, would view those rights not merely as adding to democracy

---

[10] Ibid., preamb. para 6. The authors add the following justification for printing the word 'race' in quotation marks: 'Since all human beings belong to the same species, ECRI rejects theories based on the existence of different races. However, in this Recommendation ECRI uses this term "race" in order to ensure that those persons who are generally and erroneously perceived as belonging to another race are not excluded from the protection provided for by the Recommendation.' Ibid., preamb. para 6, n. 1.

[11] See, e.g., Heinze 2009, pp. 193–209. For criticism of that view, see, e.g., Courtois 2022, pp. 249–269.

but as following necessarily from it, at least if the concept of 'democracy' is to have any serious substantive meaning. For that very reason, identifying limits poses a weighty challenge.

The constitutive importance of vibrant public discourse for any legitimate political order – let me repeat that: the constitutive importance of vibrant public discourse for any legitimate political order – means that the present volume focuses on areas of law that are concerned with constitutive questions, not only of law but of all ethics and politics. From these observations the reader will surely guess that the first major area of law to be interrogated for the present volume was the constitutional law for each of the nations that was included, and most chapters indeed confirm the primacy of free speech, again bearing in mind that most submissions have come from established or emerging democracies.

Of course, these observations can scarcely slight the more conventional areas of statutory and administrative law, which indeed feature prominently in most chapters, not least because for most nations hate speech entails breaches of criminal or civil law, or both, as most chapters confirm. Yet even those provisions, and even when they are not drafted and adopted pursuant to any constitutional mandate, constantly respond to or resonate with another, highly elevated sphere of law, namely, international human rights law. In many of the chapters we find that lawmakers and courts have adhered to their nations' ICCPR and ICERD obligations, with some authors including their nations' obligations under the Genocide Convention.

1.2 The Methodology

To explore these developments, how they have occurred, and how they are still unfolding, this book started life in the form of a questionnaire that was sent to national rapporteurs, many previously affiliated with the International Academy of Comparative Law (IACL). The reports gathered in this book are based on materials provided by special rapporteurs from the various countries in 2021 or early 2022, with several updated in 2023. Timing is crucial because, as several chapters show, the monitoring and regulation of hate speech remains an intricate and rapidly evolving problem. Although the reports in this book offer only a snapshot at that moment in time, the core problems and legal obstacles described by this book's authors have been with us for many years and will likely remain with us well into the future.

In most cases we were able to find only one author or group of authors who were able to supply information for any given country. For Serbia we also received two separate reports, one of them from Jovan Ćirić, again, at the time, a Judge in the nation's Constitutional Court. Sadly Judge Ćirić passed away in December 2022, but Darko Dimovski and Filip Mirić have generously, and masterfully, incorporated Judge Ćirić's findings into their chapter. Responses were invited in either English or French, and, whilst the former predominate, we have been delighted by the breadth of francophone analyses submitted for Canada, France, and Switzerland. Of course, the Canadian and Swiss reports admirably cover vital information arising from *non*-francophone sources in those nations. Similarly, the Belgian report, drafted in English by our Flemish colleagues, fully takes account of that nation's multilingual composition.

Some readers might wonder why a greater range of geographical locations and political systems is not represented. This is unfortunate and there is no single reply, though the reasons were mostly circumstantial. This study was undertaken within the existing IACL framework and relied largely on members and affiliates who had volunteered their participation in advance. Yet other reasons also played a role. For purposes of legal regulation, hate speech has arisen as a distinctive problem within at least reasonably functional liberal democracies in which some background sphere of free speech could be assumed, and then the primary question was about where limits should be drawn. By contrast, for politically repressive regimes where no such sphere exists, there is no serious way to treat hate speech in isolation from the very question of free speech.

That political constraint manifests in immediate practice: experts from such countries avoid publishing scholarship on free speech, particularly in a critically-minded vein, because the risks to their person, profession, family, colleagues, or acquaintances can become terrifying. Indeed, even scholars working in freer environments are subject to surveillance and remain at risk, particularly if they were to travel, or to travel back, to such countries. These obstacles tell us a good deal about what such reports might have contained. In regimes that pervasively repress public discourse, routine recitations of interests appealing to national security, public safety, public order, and public morals – if a government even bothers to recite such rationales – suffice for speakers to be wholly silenced, and for punishments or detriments to be imposed on them and even on their families, friends, and affiliates.

1.3 The Questionnaire

To explore the criminalisation of hate speech around the world, the topics featuring most prominently seemed likely to require attention from all or most rapporteurs, such as questions about basic national and international legal norms. Meanwhile, other types of questions seemed relevant or had information available only for some countries, and were therefore posed as optional. Indeed, in view of national variations and available data, even the primary (that is, non-optional) questions could not always be answered, or answered in detail, by all rapporteurs, nor did all rapporteurs adhere strictly to the questionnaire format when alternative means of presentation appeared more appropriate for explaining their national contexts.

Bearing these considerations in mind, the items appearing on the original questionnaire ran as follows, and were posed individually for each of the countries:

1. National constitutional law: Has constitutional law been applied to hateful expression in any important legislative, administrative, or case law. For example, in

addition to free speech rights, have other constitutional provisions, such as non-discrimination rights, rights to religious freedom, rights of free association, etc., been applied?

2. National statutory or administrative law: Have national statutory or administrative laws been applied to hateful expression? For example, in addition to free speech rights, have statutory or administrative laws regarding non-discrimination rights, rights to religious freedom, rights of free association, etc., been applied? Has an Ombudsman or other such administrative agency played an important role?
3. International Covenant on Civil and Political Rights (ICCPR): If your country is a party to ICCPR, then has the UN Human Rights Committee (UN-HRC) issued Concluding Observations for your country commenting specifically on hateful expression? Has your country consented to individual complaints procedures? If so then please cite and summarise any complaints relevant to hateful expression. In addition:

   3.1 How have your country's legislators, officials, or courts have applied ICCPR to hateful expression, if at all.

   3.2 If your country is *not* a party to ICCPR, are you aware of government plans or broader debates about joining?
   Optional: Additional information

   3.3 As a party to the ICCPR, has your country deposited any reservations or declarations relevant to hateful expression? If 'yes', then it would be helpful if you could provide the following, including full citations to relevant UN documents:

      3.3.1. Texts of those reservations or declarations that specifically relate to hateful expression.

      3.3.2. Texts of any comments deposited by *other* ICCPR states parties directly responding to your country's reservations or declarations.

      3.3.3. Texts of any comments deposited by your country about *other* ICCPR states parties' reservations or declarations regarding hateful expression.

      3.3.4. Texts of any comments made by the UN-HRC, e.g., in Concluding Observations within a periodic report on your country.

      3.3.5 Has any other authoritative body, such as a national court, government agency, or independent expert body, commented on your country's reservations or declarations?

4. International Convention on the Elimination of All Forms of Racial Discrimination (ICERD): If your country is a party to ICERD, then has the UN Committee on the Elimination of Racial Discrimination (UN-CERD) issued Concluding Observations for your country commenting specifically on hateful expression? Has your country consented to individual complaints procedures? If so then please cite and summarise any complaints relevant to hateful expression. In addition:

   4.1 How have your country's legislators, officials, or courts have applied ICERD to hateful expression, if at all.

4.2 If your country is *not* a party to ICERD, are you aware of government plans or broader debates about joining?
Optional: Additional information

4.3 As a party to the ICERD, has your country deposited any reservations or declarations relevant to hateful expression? If 'yes', then it would be helpful if you could provide the following, including full citations to the relevant UN documents:
4.3.1 Texts of those reservations or declarations that specifically relate to hateful expression.
4.3.2 Texts of any comments deposited by *other* ICERD states parties directly responding to your country's reservations or declarations.
4.3.3 Texts of any comments deposited by your country about *other* ICERD states parties' reservations or declarations regarding hateful expression.
4.3.4 Texts of any comments made by the UN-CERD, e.g., in Concluding Observations within a periodic report on your country.
4.3.5 Has any other authoritative body, such as a national court, government agency, or independent expert body, commented on your country's reservations or declarations?

5. Optional: Additional information on other international law and organisations

5.1 To your knowledge, have any other human rights treaties (e.g., Genocide Convention, CEDAW, etc.) or other sources of international law become relevant to your country's laws or policies on hateful expression?
5.2 To your knowledge, have any interventions by other monitoring bodies (e.g., UN Human Rights Council) or by major NGOs (e.g., Amnesty International or Human Rights Watch) had an impact on your country's laws or policies regarding hateful expression? In your opinion, have leading NGOs reported accurately on your country?

6. Regional law and organisations: If your country is a member of any regional treaty or organisation primarily concerned with human rights, such as the Council of Europe, then please indicate any rulings or findings of such organisations that have actually or potentially affected your country's laws or policies on hateful expression.

7. Comparative national law: Have national lawmakers or courts cited the law of other national jurisdictions regarding hateful expression in any important (i.e., more than just incidental) ways, either to adopt such law as precedent or to distinguish an alternative approach?

8. Judicial rulings: Has case law contributed to defining or clarifying the problem of hateful expression? Have courts adopted any definitions or descriptions of hateful expression? Please include official case citations.

9. Optional: National popular culture.
   9.1 How would you describe depictions of hateful expression within your country's state-chartered as well as independent professional media? How would you describe these sources' depictions of relevant law or policy?
   9.2 How would you describe popular understandings of hateful expression in your country, particularly as witnessed in social media? How would you describe the impact of social media on relevant law or policy?
   9.3 How would you describe attitudes towards hateful expression in your country's primary education system?
   9.4 How would you describe attitudes towards hateful expression in your country's higher education institutions?

10. Optional: Please add any further information or comments that you find relevant to your country's approaches to hateful expression. Also, please feel free to mention any scholarly writings in your country (including your own) that you feel have exercised influence or that you regard as helpful for understanding your country's approach.

References

Courtois S (2022) Are Hate Speech Laws Useless? An Appraisal of Eric Heinze's Arguments. Res Publica 28(2):249-269

Heinze E (2009) Cumulative Jurisprudence and Hate Speech: Sexual Orientation and Analogies to Disability. Age and Obesity. International Journal of Human Rights 12:193-209 (reprinted as chapter 14 in Weinstein J, Hare I (eds) Extreme Speech and Democracy. Oxford University Press, Oxford, pp 264-284

Heinze E (2016) Hate Speech and Democratic Citizenship. Oxford University Press, Oxford, pp 18-19

Matsuda M, Lawrence III Ch, Delgado R, Crenshaw K (eds) (1993) Words That Wound. Westview. Boulder, CO

Rohrßen B (2009) Von der 'Anreizung zum Klassenkampf' zur 'Volksverhetzung (§ 130 StGB): Reformdiskussion und Gesetzgebung seit dem 19. Jahrhundert. De Gruyter, Berlin

Eric Heinze (Maitrise *distinction*, U. Paris; J.D. *cum laude*, Harvard; PhD *cum laude*, Leiden), Professor of Law at Queen Mary University of London, served as 2022 General Rapporteur on the Criminalization of Hate Speech for the *Académie internationale de droit comparé*. In addition to writings on legal theory, Heinze's books on free speech include *The Most Human Right: Why Free Speech is Everything* (The MIT Press, 2022) and *Hate Speech and Democratic Citizenship* (Oxford University Press, 2016). He led the EU consortium Memory Laws in European and Comparative Perspectives in 2016-19 and has been a Fulbright Fellow, DAAD fellow, and Chateaubriand Fellow along with grants from the Nuffield Foundation and from Harvard University, and is general editor of the *Oxford Handbook of Hate Speech* (forthcoming 2025).

Chapter 2
Argentina

Javier Augusto De Luca, Ricardo Narváez and Matías Quercia

Contents

Abstract This chapter analyzes the legal framework and judicial interpretations related to hate speech in Argentina. Although the Argentine Constitution does not explicitly address hate speech, discriminatory expressions are restricted through hermeneutic interpretations and laws. The chapter explores the Argentine Supreme Court's position and key cases from Courts of various instances where the incitement of hatred based on race, religion, or nationality was a central issue, are also analyzed.Additionally, the role of international treaties with constitutional status in Argentina in shaping the legal responses to hate speech.

Keywords Argentina · Hate speech legislation · Discriminatory acts · Judicial rulings · Administrative agencies

J. A. De Luca (✉)
Faculty of Law, University of Buenos Aires, Buenos Aires, Argentina
e-mail: javieraugustodeluca@gmail.com

R. Narváez · M. Quercia
Departamento de Derecho Penal y Criminología, Universidad de Buenos Aires, Buenos Aires, Argentina

E. Heinze (ed.), *Criminalising Hate Speech*,
https://doi.org/10.1007/978-94-6265-650-5_2

2.1 National Constitutional Law

Argentina's Supreme Court of Justice has stated that the right to free speech has a preeminent position within the framework of constitutional freedoms[1] due to its importance for the functioning of a democratic republic,[2] and the development of collective self-government as outlined in the Constitution of Argentina,[3] among other reasons. Nevertheless, the Supreme Court has held that such 'special constitutional recognition of the right to seek, give, receive, and impart information and ideas of any kind does not remove the criminal liability before a court of law for the criminal offences and damages committed in its exercise'. (*Fallos* [Argentine Supreme Court Decisions], 308:789; 321:667 and 3170; 332:2559 and 335:2090).

There are no legal provisions in the Constitution of Argentina about hate speech. However, from a hermeneutic interpretation of Section 16 of the Constitution of Argentina,[4] any expression that represents a discriminatory act is prohibited. Such speech is legally restricted in several international human rights treaties which have constitutional hierarchy pursuant to the provisions set forth in Section 75, subsection 22 of the Constitution of Argentina. Therefore, the special preeminent recognition of the right to freedom of speech does not make it an absolute right.

The Law on Discriminatory Acts (No. 23592) prohibits propaganda or incitement to racial or religious hatred. This law enables the victim of a discriminatory act to be indemnified (Section 1), and raises the penalties for crimes set forth in the Penal Code of Argentina and supplementary laws (Section 2) when the act 'is committed for persecution or hatred of a race, religion or nationality, or with the aim of destroying in part or in full a national, ethnic, racial, or religious group'. The Law further punishes anyone who takes part in an organisation or carries out propaganda based on ideas or theories of racial superiority (Section 3, first para), or who encourages or incites persecution or hatred (Section 3, second para).

As to non-punitive mechanisms, Law No. 24515 established the National Institute to Combat Discrimination, Xenophobia, and Racism (INADI) [*Instituto Nacional Contra la Discriminación, la Xenofobia y el Racismo*], with the mission to create policies against hate speech, for instance, by disseminating pertinent information for the purpose of raising awareness. In addition, the Observatories of Discrimination on the Internet, Radio, Television, and Sports [*Observatorios de Discriminación en Internet, Radio, Televisión y Deportes*] were created with the aim to preserve such contexts from any kind of discriminatory violence that violates the rights of groups, communities, or individuals.

[1] *Fallos* [Argentine Supreme Court Decisions], 321:412.

[2] *Fallos*, 320:1272.

[3] *Fallos*, 340:1364.

[4] 'The Argentine Nation admits neither blood nor birth prerogatives: there are neither personal privileges nor titles of nobility. All its inhabitants are equal before the law, and admissible to employment without any other requirement than their ability. Equality is the basis of taxation and public burdens'.

2.2 National Statutory or Administrative Law

Courts of various instances and jurisdictions have applied administrative and regulatory laws to cases of hate speech. For example, in *Bonavota Liliana Graciela v. Bar Association of the City of Buenos Aires (CPACF)* [*Bonavota Liliana Graciela c/ CPACF*] (case file 3556/2000) of 18 August 2000[5], a fine was imposed by the Disciplinary Court of the Bar Association of the City of Buenos Aires on the lawyer Liliana Graciela Bonavota for having vehemently expressed her hatred against the Public Prosecutor, in the framework of a correctional trial, because of his Jewish religion.

These hateful statements were orally made in an interview that she had with the Judge and the Secretary of the court. The Judge was asked who the Public Prosecutor was and when the Judge answered, Bonavota retorted "Jewish, of course!", adding sarcastically, "I'm going to say that I am Nazi, so I can challenge him".[6] The Court of Appeals in Federal Administrative Adversary Proceedings of the City of Buenos Aires affirmed the fine imposed by the Disciplinary Court of the Bar Association of the City of Buenos Aires, finding Bonavota criminally liable under Section 22, subsection b) of the Code of Ethics for having vehemently expressed her hatred towards the Public Prosecutor because of his Jewish religion, which clearly showed a discriminatory hatred towards him, altering the sense of mutual respect that must preside during the entire judicial proceeding.

Another case to highlight is *Partido Nuevo Triunfo on qualification-City of Buenos Aires* [*Partido Nuevo Triunfo s/ reconocimiento-Distrito Capital Federal*] (case file No. P.1469.XLI) of 17 March 2009.[7] The political party "Partido Nuevo Triunfo" intended to stand in the National Elections emulating the Nazi or National Socialist German Workers' Party (*Nationalsozialistische Deutsche Arbeiterpartei*) of the 1930s. At first the party had tried to be publicly recognised with the name National Socialist Workers' Party. Next, the party used symbols such as the swastika, the Seventh of Saint Cajetan, bracelets, and banners in the same way that the Nazi regime did. The party's program, expressed orally and in writing, included "the drastic dismantling of the homosexual, drug addict and corrupt network infecting Argentina," with reference to the punishment of "vagrancy"[8] [translation by María Belén Severino] and the respect "to this rule will be doubly important in the case of foreigners."

The Supreme Court of Justice affirmed the judgment of the Federal Electoral Court, which in turn had previously affirmed the decision of the lower court dismissing Partido Nuevo Triunfo's legal and political capacity to act as a political party in the City of Buenos Aires, given that it had stirred up hatred, incited violence,

[5] Published on elDial.com—AA643.

[6] As quoted by the Court.

[7] http://www.saij.gob.ar/corte-suprema-justicia-nacion-federal-ciudad-autonoma-buenos-aires-partido-nuevo-triunfo-reconocimiento-distrito-capital-federal-fa09000013-2009-03-17/123456789-310-0009-0ots-eupmocsollaf?

[8] As quoted by the Court.

and used Nazi symbolism. The Federal Electoral Court held that Partido Nuevo Triunfo's statements and activities counted as actual discriminatory acts contrary to the principle of equality before the law, and that, for the purposes of Partido Nuevo Triunfo's qualification as a political party, such acts did not fall under the scope of Section 38 of the Constitution or under any international treaties legally recognised in Section 75, subsection 22 of the Constitution, perusant to Law No. 23298 on Political Parties or Law No. 23592 on Discriminatory Acts.

In addition, in *R. D. O. v. Province of Chubut on Adversary Administrative Lawsuit of Full Jurisdiction* [*R. D. O. c/ Provincia del Chubut s/ Demanda Contencioso Administrativo de Plena Jurisdicción*] of 15 June 2021, the Medical Examiner D. O. R., belonging to the Forensic Medical Corps of the city of Esquel, Province of Chubut, was fired for having published on Facebook:

> From Radio Insania we are informed that many people are happy because this girl "C" found her granddaughter. Wouldn't have it been better for this woman to educate her daughter at the corresponding time and in the right way to avoid what happened? Personally, I feel no empathy for her. I think this woman, along with others such as "B", should have been tortured and then executed with a shot in the back of the neck. They are not good human beings. They are malignant. They have a lot of evil and resentment[9] [translation by María Belén Severino].

These statements targeted the organisation "Grandmothers and Mothers of Plaza de Mayo", an Argentine human rights association created in 1977 with the aim of locating and restoring to their legitimate families those children who had been disappeared under the Argentine dictatorship. The Superior Court of Justice of the Province of Chubut rejected the claim filed by D.O.R. against the Province of Chubut, seeking the nullity of the court decision which convicted him for the violation of Section 10, subsection b) of the General Internal Regulations of the Judicial Branch of the Province of Chubut, on the grounds that the claimant had failed to respect the decorum required by his position as a result of certain publications made on Facebook. These publications deemed to be hate speech, which exceeded the scope of the right to criticism, and deemed to be excluded from the protection of the exercise of the rights to freedom of thought and free speech.

Finally, regarding the role of administrative agencies, the National Institute against Discrimination, Xenophobia, and Racism (INADI) is a decentralized body created in 1995 under Law No. 24515. The agency is answerable to the Ministry of Justice and Human Rights, and enforces Law No. 23592 on Discriminatory Acts. It is authorised to receive complaints about discriminatory, xenophobic, or racist acts. It is also authorised to file complaints and take legal action against individuals, branches, and officials of government. Its function is guaranteed because it turns out to be a decentralised organism, with some autonomy to act. It also takes part in the preparation of case records by publishing opinions on events within the scope of its authority.

[9] Quoted by the Court on its decision.

2.3 International Covenant on Civil and Political Rights (ICCPR)

In accordance with the ICCPR, Law No. 23592 on Discriminatory Acts was enacted in 1988. As previously stated, since the 1994 amendment to the Constitution of Argentina, and the consequent inclusion of Section 75, subsection 22 in it, ICCPR has attained constitutional hierarchy. Hate speech is firstly described in the provision set forth in Section 2 of Law No. 23592:

> The minimum of the sentencing range of the criminal offences punished by the Penal Code of Argentina and supplementary laws shall be raised by one third, whereas the maximum of the sentencing range of such offences shall be raised by one half, whenever a crime is committed for persecution or hatred of a race, religion or nationality, or with the aim of destroying in part or in full a national, ethnic, racial, or religious group. In no case may the legal maximum of the type of sentence in question be exceeded.

In this way, an aggravating circumstance is established on the sentencing range for the criminal offences that are committed for persecution or hatred of a race, religion, or nationality. With regard to hate speech, this offence would be provided for in crimes that are committed for hatred or discriminatory purposes, such as the criminal offences of calumny and defamation (Section 109 and Section 110 of the Penal Code). For example, the Federal Criminal and Correctional Court of Appeals of the City of Buenos Aires stated that the criminal prosecution of a party who spoke insults and discriminatory statements into the answering machine of a person of the Jewish faith would be constitutional. The Appellate Court held that, although such expressions did not fall under the scope of the criminal offence of simple threats (Penal Code Section 149bis), it would have been possible to institute a criminal proceeding on defamation within the framework of a private action.[10]

Penal Code Section 3(2) provides for imprisonment sentence ranging from one month to three years for anyone who 'encourages or incites persecution or hatred by any means against an individual or group of people because of their race, religion, nationality, or political ideas'. Following case law, courts have consistently held that the statutorily defined act consists of *'encouraging or inciting persecution or hatred (...). Encouraging entails persuading or instilling someone with reluctance to, in this case, persecution or hatred. Conversely, inciting entails making or persuading someone to carry out something, in the case at hand, the acts referred to by the laws: chasing or hating'*.[11]

Regarding the expression of ideas that are considered 'erroneous' or 'not valuable', it has been argued that careful consideration of the relevant circumstances is required to determine whether such expression is intended to incite or result in an

---

[10] Federal Criminal and Correctional Court of Appeals of the City of Buenos Aires, Panel I, 'Miñón Bolivar, Alicia on indictment' [*Miñón Bolivar, Alicia s/ procesamiento*], 28 May 2003.

[11] National Highest Court of Appeals in Criminal Matters, Panel II, 'Russo, Ricardo et al. on appeal to the National Highest Court of Appeals in Criminal Matterś [*Russo, Ricardo y otro s/ recurso de casación*], 12 April 1999.

imminent illegal action, and whether such illegal action is likely to be brought.[12] Guidelines for understanding this type of criminal offence have been defined, explaining that the Law on Discriminatory Acts punishes propaganda that necessarily implies *'the beginning or development of a progressive course of marginalisation and discrimination which results in a serious and direct impairment of the peaceful and harmonious coexistence of the citizens of a sector of the population, capable of culminating in the materialisation of violent behaviour'*.[13]

Accordingly, the Federal Criminal and Correctional Court of Appeals of the City of Buenos Aires, in the case captioned 'Cherashny' (2004),[14] held that Section 3 of Law No. 23592 punishes *'expressions that are likely to create an atmosphere of hostility in which the recipients of such speech may be incited to carry out discriminatory or violent acts'*. In 2006 this Court held that the Law on Discriminatory Acts punished the dissemination of information and ideas that implied *'the beginning or development of a progressive course of marginalisation and discrimination which results in a serious and direct impairment of the peaceful and harmonious coexistence of the citizens of a sector of the population, capable of culminating in the materialisation of violent behaviour'*.[15]

Finally, regarding this criminal offence, Panel I of the Criminal, Misdemeanour and Petty Offences Court of Appeals of the City of Buenos Aires stated that: *'This offence consists of an intentional crime whose wilful misconduct entails, on the one hand, the understanding that persecution or hatred is being encouraged or incited against a group of people for the aforementioned reasons and, on the other hand, the will to do so'* (excerpted from the opinion delivered by Mr. Justice Marum and Mr. Justice Vázquez).[16]

---

[12] Federal Criminal and Correctional Court of Appeals of the City of Buenos Aires, Panel II, 13 February 1993, excerpted from *Compendio de Jurisprudencia* [Case Law Collection], *Ley contra la discriminación* [Law on Discriminatory Acts] by José Luis Amadeo, LexisNexis publishing house, Buenos Aires, 2006, page 186.

[13] Federal Criminal and Correctional Court of Appeals of the City of Buenos Aires, Panel I, 'FIKZ INMEDIATA, Nicolás', 4 April 2006.

[14] Federal Criminal and Correctional Court of Appeals of the City of Buenos Aires, Panel I, 'CHERASHNY, G. on indictment' [*CHERASHNY, G. s/ procesamiento*].

[15] Federal Criminal and Correctional Court of Appeals of the City of Buenos Aires, Panel I, 'Bonafini, Hebe on dismissal' [*Bonafini, Hebe s/ sobreseimiento*], 27 April 2006.

[16] Criminal, Misdemeanour and Petty Offences Court of Appeals of the City of Buenos Aires, Panel I, 'Saboulard, Rubén Oscar on violation of Section 3 of Law No. 23592' [*Saboulard, Rubén Oscar s/ inf. Article 3 Ley 23.592*], case file No. 15.199/09, 16 July 2010.

2.4 The International Convention on the Elimination of All Forms of Racial Discrimination (ICERD)

The UN Committee on the Elimination of Racial Discrimination (CERD) has issued several Concluding Observations regarding Argentina in which the Committee has made specific comments on hate speech. In the report of 7 August 1987, the Committee commended the government for the law adopted to comply with the legal provisions set forth in Article 4 of the Convention. It stated that the amendments to the Penal Code outlined in the bill submitted to the Argentine Congress seemed to comply with the requirements established in Article 4 of the Convention. Nevertheless, the Committee stressed that the only missing element was the funding of racist organisations by people who were not members of them. The Committee also wished to know if antisemitism was still a problem in Argentina, and how the issue was being addressed.

In the report of 23 August 1991, the Committee noted that racial hatred was considered to be an aggravating circumstance in several criminal offences under the Penal Code, and inquired whether incitement to racial hatred and racist remarks were punishable offences *per se*. They also pointed out that the report gave no examples and no statistics of sentences imposed for the commission of criminal offences in connection with racism. Some members of the Committee enquired whether there were any groups or organisations referred to in Article 4(b) in Argentina and, if so, whether criminal proceedings had been brought against their members. In this respect, they noted that the scope of Law No. 23592 on Discriminatory Acts of 1988 was not entirely clear, and requested further clarification. Considering the Argentina's history of anti-Semitism, which occasionally resulted in anti-Semitic incidents, members of the Committee pointed out that no reference to this aspect had been made in the report. Members of the Committee also wished to know if any action had been taken regarding the systematic *de facto* exclusion of Jews from important institutions such as the armed forces.

In the report of 18 September 1997 (CERD/C/304/Add.39), the Committee noted with satisfaction that Law No. 23592 of 1998 regarded racial motives as an aggravating circumstance of several criminal offences punishable under Argentine criminal law. Nevertheless, the Committee regretted that Argentina failed to fully comply with the provisions set forth in Article 4 of the Convention regarding the criminalisation of racist ideas and racist propaganda, incitement to racial discrimination, racial violence, and the creation of racist organisations. The Committee urged Argentina to comply with these duties, pursuant to Article 4 of the Convention, by declaring as punishable by law the offences of dissemination of racist ideas and racist propaganda, the incitement to racial discrimination, racial violence, and the creation of racist organisations.

In the report of 10 December 2004 (CERD/C/65/CO/1), the Committee was concerned about some incidents of incitement to racial hatred and racist propaganda in the media, including on the internet. In addition, the Committee recalled that Article 4 of the Convention applies to racism in the media, including online, and that the fundamental principle of respect for human dignity required all States to combat dissemination of racial hatred and incitement to racial hatred. It recommended that Argentina take appropriate measures to combat racist propaganda in the media.

In the report of 29 March 2010 (CERD/C/ARG/CO/19-20), the Committee took note with satisfaction of the measures adopted in order to ensure that discriminatory messages were not conveyed by the media. It also took note with satisfaction the creation of the Discrimination in Radio and Television Observatory, an interinstitutional agency which coordinates the work of the Federal Broadcasting Committee (COMFER), the National Women's Council (CNM), and the National Institute against Discrimination, Xenophobia, and Racism (INADI). The Committee welcomed the Argentina's efforts to combat anti-Semitism at national and regional levels. Nevertheless, the Committee noted with concern that Argentina had failed to establish racial discrimination as a criminal offence in its domestic law pursuant to the provisions set forth in the Convention, and recommended that Argentina make every possible effort to do it.

In the report of 11 January 2017 (CERD/C/ARG/CO/21-23), the Committee raised concerns again about the fact that Argentina had not yet established racial discrimination as a criminal offence in its domestic law. Therefore, the Committee urged Argentina to legally classify as criminal offences the acts outlined in Article 4 of the Convention, taking into account General Recommendation No. 35 (2013) on combating racist hate speech.

Argentine courts have applied the provisions set forth in the International Convention on the Elimination of All Forms of Racial Discrimination (ICERD) regarding hate speech on several occasions. For example, on 16 May 2011, in the case of *Delegation of Argentine Jewish Associations v. Google Inc.* (on precautionary measures, No. 34023/11) [*Delegación de Asociaciones Israelitas Argentinas c/ Google Inc. s/ medidas precautorias*], a Buenos Aires Civil Court took into account the provisions set forth in the Convention by granting the requested measures and ruling that certain websites should be removed from the so-called 'suggested searches' that appear on the website www.google.com.ar, and search engines as well as advertisements should be modified accordingly.

On 13 July 2016, in the case of *S., R. et al.* (No. C. 18037-00-CC-15) [*S., R. y otros*], the Buenos Aires Criminal, Misconduct and Misdemeanour Court of Appeals considered the type of criminal offence that is established in Section 3 of Law No. 23592. A newspaper director had been accused of promoting racial and religious discrimination and inciting persecution and hatred against the Jewish community. The Court took into account the concept of racial discrimination set forth in the ICERD and reversed the lower court decision, which had originally ruled against the dismissal.

On 10 February 2012, in the case of *Pinelli, Edgardo Ernesto on violation of Law No. 23592* (No. C.2008/11) [*Pinelli, Edgardo Ernesto s/ av. Inf. Ley 23.592*], the San Martín Federal Court of Appeals recalled that pursuant to ICERTD Article 4(a) the propaganda of the organisation in question through the web was tended to incite third parties to commit discriminatory acts against all non-European immigration, propagating the superiority of the white race. These racist statements appeared inwriting and were published online.

2.5 The International Convention on the Elimination of All Forms of Racial Discrimination (ICERD)

The parliamentary debate which resulted in the enactment of Law No. 23592 on Discriminatory Acts took place in the Argentine Senate on 10 March 1988. Senator Fernando De la Rúa cited international laws that punished any kind of act based on intolerance, stating:

> [I]n Russia, a sentence is imposed for any kind of propaganda or disturbance aimed at inciting antagonism or racial or national discord, any direct or indirect restriction of rights, and any direct or indirect privilege in favour of any citizen for reasons of race or nationality. In Australia, incitement to racial discrimination, for example, is considered a criminal offence that is severely punished. In addition, a small island in the Antilles with no more than two hundred thousand inhabitants defines the aforementioned criminal offence as the provocation to hatred against any sector of the population for its colour, race, or beliefs.
>
> There are other important nations, such as Bulgaria, which establish that any act aimed at provoking or instigating racial or national animosity, hatred or discrimination, is a crime. Denmark goes even further since it defines such criminal offence as any statement of any kind that poses a threat to one or more groups of people who are ridiculed or humiliated for reasons of race, colour, nationality, ethnicity, or religion. In France, a law against racism that punishes any kind of incitement was enacted on 1 July 1972. Besides, the Federal Republic of Germany, in the law passed to amend its Penal Code, dated 23 November 1973, set forth that incitement to racial hatred was considered a criminal offence, whereas the German Republic, in Section 91 of its Penal Code, imposes a sentence on whoever acts intending to persecute, expel or destroy, either in whole or in part, national, ethnic, racial, or religious groups.
>
> Furthermore, Hungary has passed Executive Order No. 35 of 1970 regarding discriminatory acts, which punishes whoever commits an act in public that may incite hatred against any people. Also, we can cite the legislation of Sweden, whose law dated 27 May 1970 has introduced amendments to its Penal Code that are added to its current provisions regarding agitation against ethnic groups and the criminal offences of threatening or insulting an ethnic group publicly or through any means of communication directed to the public for reasons of race, colour, nationality, ethnicity, or religious beliefs.

2.6 Judicial Rulings

Among the judicial decisions that might be considered relevant when dealing with and defining the features of hate speech, we can mention Opinion No. 11912 of Public Prosecutor's Office No. 4, submitted before the National Highest Court of Appeals in Criminal Matters on 11 September 2018 on ancillary proceeding No. CFC13 of the case *OLEA, Alan Emmanuel et al. on violation of Law No. 23592* (Section 2)

(No. FMP 24837/2015/TO1) [*OLEA, Alan Emmanuel y otros s/ infracción ley 23.592 (Article 2)*]. This case concerned an organisation that intended to impose a neo-Nazi ideology and to combat other people's ideologies by force and fear. The organisation adopted National Socialism as its ideology, believing in the supremacy of certain races and discriminating against other people based on race, religion, nationality, sexual orientation, and/or political ideology. Its purpose was to spread hatred and based on homophobia, xenophobia, and antisemitism, inciting other people through social activism, the distribution of brochures, and the use of musical bands. Members of the organisation made death threats to several people, carried out persecution through 'hunts', and attacked, individually or in groups, several victims.

After a criminal conviction, the defendants' appealed, arguing that their mere thoughts (ideologies) were being subject to criminal punishment. In the Mar del Plata Federal Criminal Oral Court, the Prosecuting Officer of the Public Prosecutor's Office argued that the case was not about the criminalisation of mere thoughts or innocuous expressions, but the punishment of not only the acts that instilled actual public fear, but also the public message of joining the organisation. It was stated that these kinds of acts were not protected by the right to freedom of speech and, therefore, legislators had the legal authority to legislate on this matter. It was further explained that, in the exercise of the right to freedom of speech, some expressions such as hate speech, incitement to violence, or expressions that preached the imposition of ideas by force and, as a result, instilled fear, were left out the scope of the right's protection. Consequently, opinions lost their immunity when the circumstances in which they were stated were such that their expression constituted an actual instigation to some illegitimate act. Opinions were identified as stimuli to immediate, almost automatic acts.

The Anglo-Saxon term 'hate crimes' [in Spanish, *'delitos de odio'*] was defined as criminal offences committed for reasons of intolerance towards other people. The motives of hate crimes were ideological, religious, racial, and based on sexual orientation, ethnicity, political opinion, disability, etc. They were characterised by their extreme brutality and terrible impact on the victims, whom they stigmatised and subjected them to psychological-emotional issues. It was stated that in most cases the criminal offence committed on the grounds of hatred sent an alarm message to the rest of the members of the victim's community, intimidating the entire group as a consequence of the victimisation of one of them.

Nevertheless, it was held that the indiscriminate punishment of such offences should be avoided since the overprotection of people and institutions based on temporary and ephemeral interpretations might lead to legitimising the state repression against generally unorthodox discourses of certain minorities for considering them hateful or offensive to the dominant culture, which situation might lead to preventing such minorities from imparting their ideas, claims, and other expressions of their culture, religion, etc. It was concluded that the expressions that constituted stimuli, immediate acts, direct incitements to third parties' harmful acts, or created imminent dangers against other people's rights, or directly prevented their recipients from taking part in the public debate were criminally punishable.

Furthermore, when considering the aggravating circumstance provided for in Section 2 of Law 23592 outlined in the grounds of the conviction of the aforementioned case, the Court stated that the thought itself (in this case, a Nazi ideology) was not being criminalised, however blameable it was under the standards that should govern in a community of reciprocal tolerance. The Court stated that if the organisation's cults had been confined to the privacy of the defendants' homes, there would have been no criminal offence whatsoever. Besides, given that the actual facts of the case at issue were motivated by Nazis slogans that violated the rights of third parties, the aforementioned cults were outside the protection of Section 19 of the Constitution of Argentina.[17]

Finally, it should be noted that Argentine Courts have held that the swastika cross, if attached to publications, is sufficient by itself to consider the crime consummated, as set forth in Article 3 of Law No. 23592, as well as the imperial eagle that the German forces wore in the upper part of the caps and the jackets of their uniforms.[18]

Javier Augusto De Luca is Professor of Criminal Law and Criminal Procedure Law at the Faculty of Law of the University of Buenos Aires. He received his Doctor of Law from the University of Buenos Aires and has served as President of the Argentinian Group at the International Association of Penal Law. De Luca teaches in graduate and undergraduate programs at several law faculties, and has authored multiple works in Criminal Law, Criminal Procedure Law, Human Rights and Freedom of Speech. He is a member of Argentina's Penal Code Drafting Commission of 2006, and has served as General Prosecutor before Argentina's Federal Court of Cassation.

Ricardo Narváez has authored several publications focused primarily on Criminal Law and Criminology. His work explores themes such as the crime of treason and the history of public punishment, the constitutional role of the Public Prosecutor's Office, and international criminal responsibility, with a focus on crimes against humanity and genocide. Additionally, his areas of interest also cover white-collar crime and corruption.

Matías Quercia is an Interim Associate Professor for the course "Crimes in Conflict with Freedom of Speech" at the Faculty of Law, Universidad de Buenos Aires (University of Buenos Aires). He holds a Master's degree in Criminal Law from Universidad Austral (Austral University) and a specialization in the Administration of Justice from the Universidad de Buenos Aires. Quercia has authored works on Criminal Law and Freedom of Speech. He also serves as an Assistant Public Defender at the Defensoría General de la Nación (National Public Defender's Office).

---

[17] Section 19 of the Constitution of Argentina: 'The private actions of men that in no way offend public order or morality, nor injure a third party, are reserved only to God, and are exempt from the authority of the magistrates'.

[18] Federal Criminal and Correctional Court of Appeals, Panel II, 28 February 1996, 'Biondini, Alejandro'. Excerpted from José Luis Amadeo *op. cit.*, LexisNexis publishing house, Buenos Aires, 2006, page 186.

Chapter 3
Australia

Anjalee de Silva

Contents

Abstract Laws sanctioning hate speech or 'vilification' on the basis of various protected characteristics are relatively well-established aspects of Australia's legal landscape. Some such laws criminalise vilifying speech, though significant inconsistencies exist in relation to their enforcement, and there have been almost no successful prosecutions to date. As in many other jurisdictions, the most apparent gap in Australia's anti-vilification laws is the exclusion of sex-based (or gendered) vilification against women as a category of vilification. This is notwithstanding that such speech is prevalent and no less harmful than other kinds of vilification that are prohibited criminally or civilly.

Keywords Hate speech regulation · Hate speech laws · Hate speech penalties · Hate speech against women · Misogynistic speech · Online harassment

3.1 National Constitutional Law

The Australian Constitution[1] is enforced by strong form judicial review. Accordingly, courts with jurisdiction can render legislation invalid on the basis that it is unconstitutional. The Constitution does not, however, incorporate a bill of rights. In the absence of a federal bill of rights, what operates at the federal level as a free speech

A. de Silva (✉)
Melbourne Law School, University of Melbourne, Melbourne, Australia
e-mail: adesilva@unimelb.edu.au

[1] Commonwealth of Australia Constitution Act 1900 (Imp).

E. Heinze (ed.), *Criminalising Hate Speech*,
https://doi.org/10.1007/978-94-6265-650-5_3

principle is a limited protection for freedom of communication on government and political matters, commonly referred to as the 'implied freedom of political communication'.[2] The implied freedom is a principle that derives by 'necessary implication' from Australia's constitutionally prescribed system of representative and responsible government.[3] It protects communication that is required for the effective functioning of that system, specifically, communication that is required for the voting public to 'exercise a free and informed choice as electors', and operates to constrain the legislature in its law-making capacity and the executive in its rule-making capacity.

There have been no constitutional law decisions by Australian courts relating to the constitutionality or otherwise of Australian anti-vilification laws with reference to the implied freedom. Given the absence of a federal bill of rights, there have also not been any constitutional law decisions by Australian courts relating to anti-vilification laws or hateful or vilifying expression with reference to rights more generally, including non-discrimination, religious freedom, or freedom of association rights.

Racial vilification is civilly prohibited in Australia at the federal level under s 18C of the *Racial Discrimination Act 1975* (Cth) ('Racial Discrimination Act'),[4] as discussed in detail below. In *Hobart Hebrew Congregation v Scully*[5], the Human Rights and Equal Opportunity Commission (now the Human Rights Commission), the body responsible for administering the Racial Discrimination Act, considered whether Part IIA of the Act ('Prohibition of Offensive Behaviour Based on Racial Hatred')[6] unduly impinged on the implied freedom. The Commissioner noted that while the restrictions imposed by s 18C(1) of the Racial Discrimination Act may at times burden free communication about government and political matters, the exemptions available in s 18D of the Act meant that Part IIA of the Act was 'reasonably appropriate and adapted to serve a legitimate end the fulfilment of which is compatible with the maintenance of government prescribed under the Constitution.'[7] That legitimate end encompassed racial tolerance, as well as the fulfilment of Australia's international obligations pursuant to the[8] ICERD, in particular, Article 4 of the ICERD.[9]

---

[2] Cf. Charter of Human Rights and Responsibilities Act 2006 (Vic) s 15; Human Rights Act 2004 (ACT) s 16.

[3] Lange v Australian Broadcasting Corporation (1997) 189 CLR 520, 570.

[4] Racial Discrimination Act 1975 (Cth) s 18C.

[5] Unreported, HREOC, Commissioner Cavanough QC, 21 September 2000 (extract at (2000) EOC 93–109).

[6] Ibid. [12]–[14].

[7] Ibid.

[8] International Convention on the Elimination of All Forms of Racial Discrimination, opened for signature 21 December 1965, 660 UNTS 195 (entered into force 4 January 1969) ('CERD').

[9] Ibid., Article 4.

3.2 National Statutory and Administrative Law

Laws sanctioning vilifying speech on the basis of race, religion, and other ascriptive characteristics are relatively longstanding aspects of Australia's legal landscape. These laws tend to be directed at conduct on the basis of its locutionary or expressive characteristics, as well as its perceived perlocutionary or causal functions. No Australian anti-vilification law is directed at the illocutionary or constitutive harms of vilifying speech.[10]

Advocacy of genocide and incitements to violence based on race, religion, or political opinion are subject to criminal prohibitions under the *Criminal Code Act 1995* (Cth).[11] To date, there appear to have been no prosecutions pursuant to these provisions.

Several Australian state and territory jurisdictions also have in place criminal prohibitions against vilifying conduct where such conduct constitutes threats of or incitements to physical harm, violence, or property damage.[12] Penalties typically include a fine or imprisonment of up to six months. The criminal standard of proof makes it difficult to prosecute these offences successfully, and where vilifying conduct has been accompanied by threats or physical harm, prosecutions may progress pursuant to other criminal offences such as criminal damage.[13] There are also 'procedural and threshold limitations on the referral of incidents for criminal prosecution that tend to result in a reluctance to pursue criminal law options on the part of prosecutorial authorities.'[14]

Western Australia is the only state or territory that has in place only criminal, and not civil, anti-vilification laws. The *Criminal Code 1913* (WA) creates several offences covering conduct 'intended or likely to create, promote or increase animosity towards' target group members on the basis of their race,[15] possession of material

[10] That is not withstanding that s 18C of the Racial Discrimination Act 1975 (Cth), discussed in detail below, is framed to address some harms of racially vilifying speech from victims' perspectives. For a description of the constitutive harms of vilification, see de Silva 2020, p. 987.

[11] Criminal Code Act 1995 (Cth) ss 80.2A–80.2B, 80.2D.

[12] Crimes Act 1900 (NSW) s 93Z; Racial Vilification Act 1996 (SA) s 4; Racial and Religious Tolerance Act 2001 (Vic) ss 24–25. Criminal offences of vilification also exist in the Australian Capital Territory and Queensland, but they are formulated somewhat differently: Criminal Code 2002 (ACT) s 750; Anti-Discrimination Act 1991 (Qld) s 131A.

[13] Katharine Gelber, 'Hate Speech and the Australian Legal and Political Landscape' in Katharine Gelber and Adrienne Stone (eds), *Hate Speech and Freedom of Speech in Australia* (2007, The Federation Press) 2, 9. See, eg, below in relation to the position in Western Australia.

[14] For example, prosecution of the offence of serious vilification requires consent from the Attorney-General of New South Wales and carries a maximum penalty of a $10,000 fine or 6 months' imprisonment for an individual, or a $100,000 fine for a corporation: Crimes Act 1900 (NSW) s 93Z.

[15] Criminal Code Act Compilation Act 1913 (WA) ss 77–80. 'Animosity towards' is defined to mean 'hatred of or serious contempt for': at s 76 (definition of 'animosity towards') and 'harass' includes 'to threaten, seriously and substantially abuse or severely ridicule': at s 76 (definition of 'harass').

for dissemination intended or likely to do the same,[16] conduct intended or likely to racially harass,[17] and possession of material for display intended or likely to racially harass.[18] Maximum penalties range from imprisonment of up to one year to 14 years, depending on the offence and the presence or otherwise of relevant intent.

There appears to have been only one successful prosecution under Western Australia's criminal provisions, involving a graffiti attack in which swastikas and slogans including 'Hitler was right' and 'Asians out' was painted on a synagogue and Chinese restaurant in 2004.[19] One of the five men involved in the attack was sentenced to four months' imprisonment for possession of material for dissemination intended to create, promote, or increase racial animosity.[20] He was also sentenced to eight months' imprisonment for criminal damage.[21] Notably, the other four men involved in the attack were charged with, and successfully prosecuted for, criminal damage only.[22] In 2006, an Indigenous girl was charged with assault and engaging in conduct intended to racially harass for attacking another young woman and referring to her as a 'white slut'.[23] In dismissing the charges relating to racial harassment, 'the court noted that the laws were intended to counter severe abuse and not petty name calling.'[24] Katharine Gelber has written in relation to the racial harassment charges in that case that 'the criminal law has had an undesired effect in this instance, implying that the wider political context within which anti-vilification laws are enforced is crucial to determining the effectiveness of those laws in combatting hate speech effectively.'[25]

Racial vilification is civilly prohibited in Australia at the federal level under s 18C of the Racial Discrimination Act.[26] That provision makes it unlawful for a person to do a public[27] act if the act is:

a. reasonably likely, in all the circumstances, to offend, insult, humiliate or intimidate another person or a group of people; and

[16] Ibid., ss 79, 80.

[17] Ibid., s 80A.

[18] Ibid., ss 80C, 80D.

[19] Gelber 2007, p. 8, n 13.

[20] Ibid.

[21] Ibid.

[22] Ibid. See also n 13 and accompanying text.

[23] Ibid. See also n 13 and accompanying text.

[24] Tasmania Law Reform Institute 2010, p. 13, n. 77.

[25] Gelber 2007, p. 8. The particular racial context of this case aside, it also highlights the gap in existing Australian anti-vilification laws with respect to sex-based or gendered vilification. Women remain unprotected in all Australian jurisdictions against misogynistic slurs such as 'slut'. For further discussion see nn 63–72 and accompanying text.

[26] Racial Discrimination Act 1975 (Cth) s 18C.

[27] 'Public place' includes 'any place to which the public have (sic) access as of right or by invitation, whether express or implied and whether or not a charge is made for admission to the place': ibid (definition of 'public place').

b. done because of the race, colour or national or ethnic origin of the other person or of some or all of the people in the group.[28]

The broad range of conduct potentially captured by s 18C is to be viewed in light of the exemptions contained in s 18D of the Racial Discrimination Act,[29] which are directed at striking a balance between the proscription of vilifying conduct and the protection of free speech.[30] Those exemptions relate to artistic, academic, and scientific expression, as well as other expression in the public interest, provided that such expression is carried out 'reasonably and in good faith'.[31]

Under s 17 of the Racial Discrimination Act, it is also unlawful to incite the doing of an act of unlawful racial discrimination.[32] Incitement for the purposes of s 17 requires 'actively inciting or encouraging' acts of racial discrimination or promoting the doing of such acts.[33] Section 16 of the Racial Discrimination Act prohibits the publication or display of advertisements that indicate an intention to do an act of unlawful racial discrimination.[34] Vilifying conduct of the kind captured by s 18C of the Racial Discrimination Act may also constitute direct discrimination pursuant to s 9 of the Act.[35]

As mentioned, the above sections of the Racial Discrimination Act sit within Part IIA of the Act, which prohibits 'offensive behaviour based on racial hatred', and civil remedies, rather than criminal sanctions, attach to their breach. Complainants must first undergo a conciliation process through the Human Rights Commission.[36] If that is unsuccessful, they may take their complaint to the Federal Court of Australia or Federal Circuit Court of Australia.[37] A conciliated remedy at the Human Rights Commission level may comprise, for example, an apology or publication of a retraction.[38] Court orders may similarly involve the giving of apologies or retractions, as well as payments of fines or damages.[39]

The Racial Discrimination Act is Australia's enactment into domestic law of some of its international law obligations pursuant to the ICERD.[40] Section 18C was introduced to the Racial Discrimination Act in response to recommendations of major inquiries into racism and racially motivated violence, including the National

---

[28] Racial Discrimination Act 1975 (Cth) s 18C(1).

[29] Ibid., s 18D.

[30] See Eatock v Bolt (2011) 197 FCR 261, 341–2 [349]–[350] (Bromberg J).

[31] Racial Discrimination Act 1975 (Cth) s 18D.

[32] Ibid., s 17. Unlawful 'racial discrimination' is defined at s 9.

[33] Obieta v NSW Department of Education and Training [2007] FCA 86 at [232].

[34] Racial Discrimination Act 1975 (Cth) s 16.

[35] Ibid., s 9; see also, e.g., Qantas Airways Ltd v Gama [2008] FCAFC 69.

[36] Australian Human Rights Commission Act 1986 (Cth) ss 46P, 46PD, 46PJ.

[37] Ibid., s 46PO.

[38] Gelber 2007, p. 9.

[39] Australian Human Rights Commission Act 1986 (Cth) s 46PO(4).

[40] See Koowarta v Bjelke Petersen (1982) 153 CLR 168, 211–221 (Stephen J), 222–235 (Mason J), 237–242 (Murphy J), 253–261 (Brennan J).

Inquiry into Racist Violence[41] and the Royal Commission into Aboriginal Deaths in Custody.[42] Those inquiries found that racially vilifying speech may emotionally and psychologically harm those targeted by it.[43] They also found that such speech may normalise other forms of discrimination and marginalisation, including in legitimising and paving the way for harassment, intimidation, and violence.[44]

Racial vilification is also prohibited in all other states and the Australian Capital Territory, but not the Northern Territory.[45] Religious vilification is prohibited in Queensland, Tasmania, and Victoria.[46] Other Australian jurisdictions have in place protections against vilification based on sexual orientation,[47] gender identity,[48] intersex status,[49] HIV/AIDS status,[50] and disability.[51] The thresholds of conduct covered by the various state and territory laws vary and are generally higher than that contained in s 18C of the Racial Discrimination Act. For example, civil provisions in the relevant ACT, NSW, Tasmanian, Victorian, and Queensland legislation prohibit conduct that incites hatred towards, serious contempt for, or revulsion or severe ridicule of target group members on the basis of their relevant ascriptive

---

[41] McNamara 2002, p. 38.

[42] Ibid.

[43] Ibid.

[44] Ibid. For further on the legislative history of s 18C, see McNamara 2002 at ch. 1; Toben v Jones (2003) 129 FCR 515, 541–8 [114]–[131] (Allsop J).

[45] Discrimination Act 1991 (ACT) s 67A; Anti-Discrimination Act 1977 (NSW) s 20C; Anti-Discrimination Act 1991 (Qld) s 124A; Civil Liability Act 1936 (SA) s 73; Racial Vilification Act 1996 (SA) s 4; Anti-Discrimination Act 1998 (Tas) s 19; Racial and Religious Tolerance Act 2001 (Vic) ss 7–8. In September 2017, the Northern Territory Department of the Attorney-General and Justice published a discussion paper in relation to, among other things, amending the Anti-Discrimination Act 1992 (NT) to include anti-vilification laws prohibiting offensive conduct on the basis of race, religion, disability, sexual orientation, gender identity, and intersex status: Department of the Attorney-General and Justice (NT), 'Modernisation of the Anti-Discrimination Act' (Discussion Paper, September 2017).

[46] Anti-Discrimination Act 1991 (Qld) s 124A; Anti-Discrimination Act 1998 (Tas) s 19; Racial and Religious Tolerance Act 2001 (Vic) s 8.

[47] Discrimination Act 1991 (ACT) s 67A; Anti-Discrimination Act 1977 (NSW) s 49ZT; Anti-Discrimination Act 1991 (Qld) s 124A; Anti-Discrimination Act 1998 (Tas) s 19.

[48] Discrimination Act 1991 (ACT) s 67A; Anti-Discrimination Act 1977 (NSW) s 38S; Anti-Discrimination Act 1991 (Qld) s 124A; Anti-Discrimination Act 1998 (Tas) s 19. Gender identity as a category of vilification is typically addressed to vilifying speech directed at and about transgender and intersex persons: see, e.g., Anti-Discrimination Act 1977 (NSW) s 38S, and excludes vilification directed at and about women on the basis of their female sex: see, e.g., Discrimination Act 1991 (ACT) Dictionary (definition of 'gender identity'); Anti-Discrimination Act 1991 (Qld) sch (definition of 'gender identity'); Anti-Discrimination Act 1998 (Tas) s 3 (definition of 'gender identity').

[49] Criminal Code 2002 (ACT) s 750(1)(c)(iv).

[50] Discrimination Act 1991 (ACT) s 67A; Anti-Discrimination Act 1977 (NSW) s 49ZXB.

[51] Anti-Discrimination Act 1998 (Tas) s 19.

characteristics.[52] South Australian legislation creates a tort of 'racial victimisation' that captures similar conduct.[53] Broadly speaking, the state and territory civil anti-vilification laws incorporate similar exemptions for speech to those contained in s 18D of the Racial Discrimination Act.[54] The Victorian legislation has in place an additional exemption for proselytising.[55] The processes for complaints to be brought under civil provisions in the states and the Australian Capital Territory are similar to that at the federal level.[56]

In Victoria, there has been some momentum in recent years to expand the Racial and Religious Tolerance Act 2001 (Vic) ('Victorian Act'). The Racial and Religious Tolerance Amendment Bill 2019 (Vic) ('Victorian Bill') seeks to amend the Victorian Act to introduce, in addition to race and religion, disability, gender, gender identity, sexual orientation, and sex characteristics as categories of vilification.[57] If the Victorian Bill is passed, it will become unlawful in Victoria to 'engage in ... [public] conduct that is likely to incite hatred against, serious contempt for, or severe ridicule of' a person or 'class of persons' on the basis of those attributes.[58] Further, if passed, it would lower the standard of review of what constitutes vilification under the Victorian Act to conduct that is '*likely* to incite', as opposed to that which does incite, hatred, contempt, and ridicule.[59] That would bring the standard of civil review under the Victorian Act in line with the standard of review for criminal 'serious vilification' offences involving likely incitements to violence or property damage.[60]

The Victorian Bill also proposes to remove the present exemption under the Victorian Act for proselytising[61] and empower the Victorian Human Rights Commission, which administers the Victorian Act, to apply to the Victorian Civil and Administrative Tribunal for an order compelling production of information or documents that

---

[52] Discrimination Act 1991 (ACT) s 67A(1); Anti-Discrimination Act 1977 (NSW) s 20C; Anti-Discrimination Act 1991 (Qld) s 124A(1); Anti-Discrimination Act 1998 (Tas) s 19; Racial and Religious Tolerance Act 2001 (Vic) ss 7–8.

[53] Civil Liability Act 1936 (SA) s 73.

[54] Discrimination Act 1991 (ACT) s 67A(2); Anti-Discrimination Act 1977 (NSW) s 20C(2); Anti-Discrimination Act 1991 (Qld) s 124A(2); Civil Liability Act 1936 (SA) s 73(1); Anti-Discrimination Act 1998 (Tas) s 55; Racial and Religious Tolerance Act 2001 (Vic) s 11(1).

[55] Racial and Religious Tolerance Act 2001 (Vic) s 11(2). Section 11(2) was added to the Victorian Act in response to the decision in Catch the Fire Ministries Inc v Islamic Council of Victoria Inc (2006) 206 FLR 56.

[56] See Gelber 2007, p. 9.

[57] Racial and Religious Tolerance Amendment Bill 2019 (Vic) cl 1, 8. 'Sex characteristics' is defined in the Bill: cl 7 (definition of 'sex characteristics'). Oddly, 'gender' is not, though 'gender identity' is: cl 7 (definition of 'gender identity').

[58] Racial and Religious Tolerance Act 2001 (Vic) s 7; Racial and Religious Tolerance Amendment Bill 2019 (Vic) cl (2)(a), 10(1).

[59] Racial and Religious Tolerance Amendment Bill 2019 (Vic) cl 10(2)(b).

[60] Racial and Religious Tolerance Act 2001 (Vic) s 7; Racial and Religious Tolerance Amendment Bill 2019 (Vic) cl (2)(b), 10(1).

[61] Racial and Religious Tolerance Amendment Bill 2019 (Vic) cl 14(2).

are relevant and necessary for the Commission's resolution of a complaint of vilification.[62] If the Victorian Bill is passed, those powers, unprecedented at least in the context of Australian anti-vilification laws, may enable the Commission to compel online platform hosts, for example, to disclose such information or documents, including the identities of online speakers.

Significantly, as part of the justifications for the proposed amendments, the second reading speech of the then Member of Parliament who introduced the Victorian Bill refers to the 'swarms of vile harassment' that women, in particular, receive online and notes that 'we have done little to address this type of violence against women where it is most pervasive.'[63] It rightly draws attention to the particular and significant problem of sex-based or gendered vilification as manifesting as part of the cyber harassment of women, as some scholarship has also identified.[64] Further, introducing the Member's second reading speech notes that 'hate speech lives and breeds in social media feeds and the comments sections of news articles', that 'bullying in this form … causes physical, psychological and emotional harm', and that 'hate speech … if left unchecked can embed discrimination and prejudice … [and] can lead to hate crime, which does not occur in a vacuum'.[65] However, focusing, as it does, on conduct that is likely to incite hatred, serious contempt, or severe ridicule, the Victorian Bill models itself after existing Australian anti-vilification laws and prioritises causal harms, while overlooking constitutive harms. The Victorian Bill lapsed in November 2022 without receiving major party support from either the Victorian Government or the Opposition, though the recent Victorian Legislative Assembly Legal and Social Issues Committee Inquiry into Anti-Vilification Protections made recommendations broadly in line with the changes proposed in the Victorian Bill.[66]

Relatedly, the most apparent gap in Australia's anti-vilification laws is the exclusion of sex-based or gendered vilification as a category of vilification. Vilifying speech that is gendered and is directed at and about women on the basis of their actual or perceived female sex is prevalent and no less harmful than, for example, racial or religious vilification,[67] yet such speech remains unregulated in Australia.

There is only one provision under Australian law that arguably approaches a sex-based or gendered vilification law. Section 17(1) of the *Anti-Discrimination Act 1998* (Tas) ('Tasmanian Act') prohibits conduct that 'offends, humiliates, intimidates, insults or ridicules' a person on the basis of various defined attributes, including 'gender', in circumstances in which a reasonable person would have anticipated that the victim would be so affected or harmed.[68] A separate offence of 'inciting hatred' is set out in s 19 of the Tasmanian Act, which prohibits vilification on the

---

62 Ibid., cl 17.

63 Victoria, Parliamentary Debates, Legislative Council, 28 August 2019, 2726 (Fiona Patten MP).

64 de Silva 2021, ch. 3, pp. 65–119.

65 Victoria, Parliamentary Debates, Legislative Council, 28 August 2019, 2726 (Fiona Patten MP).

66 Legal and Social Issues Committee, Parliament of Victoria, Inquiry into Anti-Vilification Protections (Parliamentary Paper No 207, March 2021).

67 See, e.g., de Silva 2020.

68 Anti-Discrimination Act 1998 (Tas) s 17(1).

basis of race, disability, sexual orientation, and religion.[69] Notwithstanding that the threshold for prohibited conduct is lower pursuant to s 17(1) than s 19, s 17(1) is more limited than s 19. First, s 17(1) only covers conduct directed at and about a person, rather than a group of people.[70] Accordingly, to the extent that it covers sex-based or gendered vilification, it applies to conduct directed at and about individual, identifiable women, rather than women generally. Second, s 17(1) only applies to specified spheres of public life (for example, in connection with employment or the provision of accommodation) rather than to public conduct generally.[71] Consequently, sex-based or gendered vilification is not regulated in Tasmania to the same extent as vilification on the basis of race, disability, sexual orientation, or religion. Indeed, s 17(1) is not so much a sex-based or gendered vilification law as it is an extension of existing anti-discrimination laws to encompass harmful conduct engaged in limited contexts that would not be captured by, for example, provisions prohibiting sexual harassment.[72]

3.3 Interaction with International Law

As mentioned, the Racial Discrimination Act is Australia's enactment into domestic law of only some of its international law obligations pursuant to the CERD.[73] The CERD was ratified by Australia on 30 September 1975 subject to the following reservation with respect to article 4(a).

> The Government of Australia ... declares that Australia is not at present in a position specifically to treat as offences all the matters covered by article 4(a) of the ... [CERD]. Acts of the kind there mentioned are punishable only to the extent provided by the existing criminal law dealing with such matters as the maintenance of public order, public mischief, assault, riot, criminal libel, conspiracy and attempts. It is the intention of the Australian Government, at the first suitable moment, to seek from Parliament legislation specifically implementing the terms of article 4(a).[74]

Criminal anti-vilification laws 'specifically implementing the terms of Article 4(a)', as anticipated by the reservation, have not been enacted into federal law to date. Accordingly, the Committee on the Elimination of All Forms of Racial Discrimination has repeatedly and consistently criticised Australia's continuing non-withdrawal of the reservation and its non-compliance with ICERD Article 4 due to the Racial

[69] Ibid., s 19.

[70] Ibid., s 17(1).

[71] Ibid., s 22(1).

[72] Sexual harassment offences tend to be articulated similarly to Anti-Discrimination Act 1998 (Tas) s 17(1) but additionally require that the offending conduct be of a sexual nature: see, eg, Anti-Discrimination Act 1998 (Tas) ss 17(2)–(3). Section 17(1) is also headed 'Prohibition of certain conduct and sexual harassment'.

[73] See n 40.

[74] *Convention on the Elimination of all Forms of Racial Discrimination*, signed 13 October 1966, [1975] ATS 40 (entered into force 30 October 1975).

Discrimination Act's providing for only civil, rather than criminal, remedies.[75] The Committee has also previously requested 'information on complaints, prosecutions and sentences regarding serious acts of racial hatred or incitement to racial hatred in States and Territories the legislation of which specifies such offences'.[76] Additionally, the Committee made the following remarks in its latest Concluding Observations on these issues in 2017.

> The Committee notes the State party's definition of multiculturalism and social cohesion and appreciates the implementation of the National Anti-racism Strategy. The Committee is, however, concerned that expressions of racism, racial discrimination and xenophobia, including in the public sphere, in political debates and in the media, are on the rise. The Committee also expresses concern that migrants, notably Arabs and Muslims, asylum seekers and refugees, as well as Africans and people of African descent, South Asians and indigenous peoples, are particularly affected by racist hate speech and violence ... [The Committee urges the State party to ...]: [i]ncrease its measures to combat racist hate speech and xenophobic political discourse, and ensure that public officials not only refrain from such speech but also formally reject and condemn hate speech, in order to promote a culture of tolerance and respect; [e]nsure that anti-discrimination provisions, notably sections ... [18C and 18D] of the Racial Discrimination Act 1975 (Cth), are effectively applied by law enforcement officials, thereby conveying a clear message that manifestations of racial discrimination and racism will not be treated with impunity; [and] [p]ut an end to racist hate speech expressed in the print and electronic media and encourage the media to adopt a code of good conduct containing provisions against racism and racial discrimination.[77]

The *International Covenant on Civil and Political Rights* was ratified by Australia on 13 August 1980 subject to the following reservation with respect to article 20.

> Australia interprets the rights provided for by articles 19 [relating to freedom of expression], 21 [relating to freedom of assembly] and 22 [relating to freedom of association] as consistent with article 20; accordingly, the Commonwealth and the constituent States, having legislated with respect to the subject matter of the article in matters of practical concern in the interest of public order (ordre public), the right is reserved not to introduce any further legislative provision on these matters.[78]

The Committee on Civil and Political Rights has asked Australia to withdraw this reservation.[79] The Committee additionally made the following remarks in its Concluding Observations in 2009.

> While acknowledging the measures taken by the State party to combat Islamophobia, the Committee remains concerned at reports of an increased number of cases of discrimination of persons of Muslim background. The Committee regrets the lack of hate speech prohibitions of the form envisaged by article 20 of the Covenant.[80]

---

[75] See, eg., CERD/C/304/Add.101 (19 April 2000) [14], CERD/C/AUS/CO/14 (14 April 2005) [12], CERD/C/AUS/CO/15-17 (13 September 2010) [17], CERD/C/AUS/CO/18-20 (27 Dece,ber 2017) [9]–[10].

[76] See, eg., CERD/C/AUS/CO/14 (14 April 2005) [12]. It is unclear whether and to what extent this information was forthcoming: CERD/C/AUS/CO/15-17 (13 September 2010) [17].

[77] CERD/C/AUS/CO/18-20 (27 December 2017) [13]–[14].

[78] *International Covenant on Civil and Political Rights*, signed 18 December 1972, [1980] ATS 23 (entered into force 13 August 1980).

[79] CCPR/C/AUS/CO/5 (7 May 2009) [9]; CCPR/C/AUS/CO/6 (1 December 2017) [8].

[80] CCPR/C/AUS/CO/5 (7 May 2009) [9].

The Committee made the following remarks in its latest Concluding Observations in 2017.

> The Committee is concerned about: (a) reports of discrimination on the basis of ethnic, racial, cultural or religious background, with migrants from African countries being particularly targeted by discrimination and racial profiling; (b) attacks on places of worship and on individuals who are visibly religious or perceived to belong to a particular religion, such as Muslims, Jews and Sikhs; and (c) reported inconsistencies in anti-vilification laws across different states and territories ... The State party should strengthen its efforts, both through law enforcement activities and awareness-raising, to combat racial discrimination, hate speech and incitement to discrimination or violence on racial, ethnic or religious grounds, in accordance with articles 19 and 20 of the Covenant and the Committee's general comment No. 34 (2011) on freedoms of opinion and expression. It should, inter alia: (a) enhance funding and support initiatives aimed at promoting tolerance for diversity and at countering racism; (b) provide more training to law enforcement personnel, judges and prosecutors on the promotion of racial, ethnic and religious diversity and on the inadmissibility of racial profiling; (c) investigate hate crimes thoroughly, prosecute suspected perpetrators where appropriate and, if they are convicted, punish them and provide victims with adequate remedies; and (d) ensure the existence of adequate measures of response to instances of incitement to discrimination or violence on racial, ethnic or religious grounds, across all states and territories.[81]

3.4 Other Relevant Judicial Rulings

The leading case on Australian anti-vilification laws is *Eatock v Bolt*[82], which concerned a complaint pursuant to s 18C of the Racial Discrimination Act. The complaint was brought against Andrew Bolt, a high-profile Australian journalist, and The Herald and Weekly Times Pty Ltd in relation to a series of articles published in print and online by Melbourne newspaper the *Herald Sun* during 2009. The articles targeted prominent light-skinned Aboriginal people and criticised their decisions to identify as Aboriginal, given their mixed heritage. They also 'contained erroneous facts, distortions of the truth and inflammatory and provocative language.'[83]

In that case, Bromberg J of the Federal Court of Australia held that Part IIA of the Act aims to promote racial tolerance and protect against the dissemination of racial prejudice. Equality and dignity or 'recognition respect' are the underlying values that s 18C of the Act is directed to protect.[84] Although s 18C refers to 'offence', it is concerned with more than 'mere personal hurt'.[85] Instead, it covers conduct that is 'injurious to the public interest and relevantly, the public's interest in a socially cohesive society.'[86] Additionally, 'conduct which invades or harms the dignity of an

---

[81] CCPR/C/AUS/CO/6 (1 December 2017) [19]–[20].

[82] (2011) 197 FCR 261.

[83] Ibid., [8] (Bromberg J).

[84] Ibid., [222]–[226] (Bromberg J).

[85] Ibid., [263] (Bromberg J).

[86] Ibid., [263] (Bromberg J).

individual or group involves a public mischief in the context of [the Act] which seeks to promote social cohesion.'[87]

The assessment of whether conduct is reasonably likely to offend, insult, humiliate or intimidate a group of people is to be made by reference to an ordinary and reasonable member of the group of people concerned and the values and circumstances of those people. The reference in s 18C(1)(a) to 'in all the circumstances' needs to be firmly kept in mind. It requires that the social, cultural, historical, and other conditions attending the person or the people in the group be considered when assessing whether offence was reasonably likely.[88] General community standards are relevant, but only to an extent.[89]

Specifically, there is one sense in which community standards are relevant. The burdens created by Part IIA are not imposed for the benefit of persons whose intolerance to the points of view of others is the true cause of the offence, insult, humiliation, or intimidation that those persons experience. In those situations, it may be properly said that it is the intolerance of the receiver of the message, rather than the intolerance of the speaker that is responsible for causing the offence.[90]

The relevant group in this case was fair-skinned Aboriginal people.[91] In finding against the respondents, Bromberg J found that 'it will be of no surprise that a race of people subjected to oppression by reason of oppressive racial categorisation will be sensitive to being racially categorised by others'.[92] He found that in addition to the hurt and insult involved, the conduct was particularly likely to have an intimidating effect on young Aboriginal persons or others with vulnerability in relation to their identity.[93]

Further, no defence pursuant to s 18D of the Racial Discrimination Act was available to the respondents, essentially because the manner in which the articles were written, including that they contained errors of fact, distortions of the truth and inflammatory and provocative language, precluded a finding of good faith.[94] In this respect, Bromberg J broadly followed the approach of French J in the earlier case of *Bropho v Human Rights & Equal Opportunity Commission*[95] in relation to what acting in good faith involves.

---

[87] Ibid., [267] (Bromberg J).

[88] Ibid., [257] (Bromberg J). Racial Discrimination Act 1975 (Cth) s 18C has consistently been interpreted narrowly by the Federal Court of Australia to involve an objective test. Evidence as to the subjective reactions of target group members to the vilifying conduct in question is admissible, but is not determinative of the contravention or otherwise of the provision: see, e.g., ibid. [241]–[242] (Bromberg J); Jones v Scully (2002) 120 FCR 243, 268–9 [98]–[99] (Hely J); Creek v Cairns Post Pty Ltd (2001) 112 FCR 352, 355–6 [12]–[13] (Kiefel J).

[89] Eatock v Bolt (2011) 197 FCR 261 [253]–[256] (Bromberg J).

[90] Ibid., [254] (Bromberg J).

[91] Ibid., [280].

[92] Ibid., [171].

[93] Ibid., [296], [415].

[94] Ibid., [425].

[95] (2004) 135 FCR 105.

3.5 Conclusion

As flagged at the outset, laws sanctioning hate speech or vilification on the basis of race, religion, and some other ascriptive characteristics are relatively well-established aspects of Australia's legal landscape. Nevertheless, controversies remain both in relation to their framing and enforcement. In prioritising causal harms while overlooking the constitutive harms of vilifying speech to target group members, such laws are unideally adapted to protect target group members against the systemic subordination and silencing functions of vilification.[96] Conversely, references to 'offence', for example, such as that contained in s 18C of the Racial Discrimination Act, may be setting the bar too low with respect to the relevant harms.[97] The most glaring shortcoming in the framing of Australia's anti-vilification laws relates to their exclusion of sex-based or gendered vilification, despite hate speakers' regular targeting of women with especially vitriolic expression both online and offline.[98] While this gap is by no means unique to the Australian context,[99] given existing protections for a range of other target group members, it functions to further accommodate and thus authorise the relevant subordination and silencing harms to women.[100].

Significant inconsistencies also exist in relation to the enforcement of Australia's anti-vilification laws, particularly criminal laws as found in some Australian jurisdictions. On the one hand, criminal laws may be framed prohibitively narrowly such that target group members are rarely able to enforce them meaningfully. On the other hand, given their largely acontextual and ahistorical framing and application, such laws have the potential to be enforced counterproductively and indeed punitively against already marginalised communities.

Finally, it remains to be seen how Australia's anti-vilification regime will fare against and adapt to particular challenges presented by 'new' media. For example, it is unclear how existing statutory prohibitions against hate speech apply to social media platforms and other such content hosts. In all likelihood, the operation of existing laws will only be further problematised in the context of the ever growing and evolving digital and online speech economy.

---

[96] de Silva (n 10) 1026–9.

[97] de Silva (n 10) 1030.

[98] See, e.g., de Silva (n 64) 65–119.

[99] Some notable exceptions are *Criminal Code*, RSC 1985, c C-46, ss 318(4), 319(1)–(2), (7); *Promotion of Equality and Prevention of Unfair Discrimination Act 2000* (South Africa) s 10. See also *Strafgesetzbuch* [Criminal Code] (Germany) § 130. In June 2020, the Cologne Upper Regional Court held that 'sections of the population' for the purposes of that provision includes women: 'German Hate Speech Laws Also Cover Misogynist Abuse, Court Rules', *DW* (Web Page, 15 June 2020) https://www.dw.com/en.german-hate-speech-laws-also-cover-misogynist-abuse-courtrules/a-53819941, archived at https://perma.cc/23J4-RE4Z.

[100] de Silva (n 10) 1023–5.

References

de Silva A (2020) Addressing the Vilification of Women: A Functional Theory of Harm and Implications for Law. Melbourne University Law Review 43(3):987.

de Silva A (2021) Addressing the Vilification of Women: A Functional Theory of Harm and Implications for Law. Ph.D Thesis. The University of Melbourne, pp. 65–119.

Gelber K (2007) Hate Speech and the Australian Legal and Political Landscape. In Gelber K, Stone A (eds) Hate Speech and Freedom of Speech in Australia. The Federation Press,, pp. 2, 9.

McNamara L (2002) Regulating Racism: Racial Vilification Laws in Australia. Federation Press, p. 8.

Tasmania Law Reform Institute (2010) Racial Vilification and Racially Motivated Offences. Issue Paper No 16, p. 13.

Anjalee de Silva is a Lecturer at Melbourne Law School, The University of Melbourne. She is also an Associate Investigator at the ARC Centre of Excellence for Automated Decision-Making and Society and a Women's Leadership Institute Australia Fellow. She is an expert in administrative, anti-discrimination, and free speech and media law and theory, with a focus on harmful speech and its regulation, especially in online contexts. In particular, her work examines vilification or 'hate speech' directed at and about women, its democratic and participatory harms, and the role of law in deterring, regulating, and mitigating those harms.

Chapter 4
Belgium

Jogchum Vrielink, Koen Lemmens and Stephan Parmentier

Contents

Abstract This chapter outlines key aspects of Belgian law concerning freedom of expression and hate speech. It begins by highlighting the Constitutional provisions and their liberal roots dating back to 1831, emphasizing the traditionally exceptional protection of intellectual freedoms like freedom of speech, press, assembly, and religion, and addressing technical complexities like the concept of 'press offenses'. The chapter goes on to sketch the scope and application of national statutory law concerning hate speech, with a focus on federal legislation that penalizes incitement

J. Vrielink (✉) · K. Lemmens · S. Parmentier
Faculty of Law and Criminology, KU Leuven, Leuven, Belgium
e-mail: jogchum.vrielink@uclouvain.be

K. Lemmens
e-mail: koen.lemmens@kuleuven.be

S. Parmentier
e-mail: stephan.parmentier@kuleuven.be

E. Heinze (ed.), *Criminalising Hate Speech*,
https://doi.org/10.1007/978-94-6265-650-5_4

(to hatred, discrimination, violence) on a range of protected characteristics, denialism and sexism. The text also discusses the procedural challenges in prosecuting hate speech, especially in cases involving written materials that enjoy a special protection regime under the Belgian Constitution. The role of equality bodies like Unia and the Institute for the Equality of Women and Men is highlighted in enforcing these laws and generating court cases. Additionally, the text focuses on how international and supranational law and legal institutions have shaped the interpretation and application of the Belgian hate speech regulations.

Keywords Freedom of expression · Belgium · Censorship · Press · Incitement · Sexism · Denialism

4.1 National Constitutional Law

4.1.1 The Essential Provisions Concerning Freedom of Expression

The 1831 Belgian Constitution which resulted from the Belgian Revolution (1830) had the reputation of being a hallmark of classic liberalism. This was particularly so because of its catalogue of fundamental rights, that served as a model for many other European constitutions.[1] Typical of the Belgian fundamental rights catalogue is the attention paid to the "intellectual" freedoms: freedom of the press, freedom of speech, the right to peacefully assemble, freedom of association, the right to education, freedom of religion and the right to petition.[2]

This should not come as a surprise. The Belgian revolution against King William I of the Netherlands resulted from a coalition including Catholics, for whom religious freedom was paramount, and liberals, who insisted on freedom of consciousness and thought and the rights to freely express their ideas. Moreover, the Belgian Revolution has been characterized as an uprising of the intellectual middle class[3], and several of its leaders had had "skin in the game". Jan Velaers recalls that some of the prominent revolutionaries had been the subject of legal prosecution because of what they had written.[4]

When it comes to freedom of expression and of the press, three articles are of fundamental importance.

> Article 19: Freedom of worship, its public practice and freedom to demonstrate one's opinions on all matters are guaranteed, but offences committed when this freedom is used may be punished.

---

[1] Popelier and Lemmens 2015, p. 8.

[2] Alen and Muylle 2011, p. 944.

[3] Witte et al. 2009, p. 21.

[4] Velaers 1991, I, p. 106.

> Article 25: The press is free; censorship can never be introduced; no security can be demanded from authors, publishers or printers. When the author is known and resident in Belgium, neither the publisher, the printer nor the distributor can be prosecuted.
>
> Article 150: A jury is sworn in for all criminal matters, as well as for political and press offences, with the exception of press offences motivated by racism or xenophobia.

Other provisions also play an important role with regard to hate speech. Article 26 protects the right to gather peaceably, without any prior intervention. However, the Constitution states that open-air meetings remain subject to police regulations, which implies that they may require prior approval from local authorities. This article has been used to forbid public gatherings when there is a risk to public order. On the basis of this provision and the Statute on the municipalities, conferences featuring hateful expression can be forbidden if there is serious and well documented risk of violence.[5] Nevertheless, the Supreme Administrative Court (Council of State) is very strict and will only exceptionally accept these prohibitions. Its case law against the French stand-up "comedian" Dieudonné M'Bala offers a good example. This artist is known for his antisemitic rhetoric, has often been condemned in France, and even received an Article 17 ECHR decision in Strasbourg (his application was found inadmissible on account of the abuse of freedom). However, in most cases before the Belgian Council of State, he obtained rulings declaring the bans on his shows unlawful.[6]

Article 27 protects the freedom of association, with again a focus on the prohibition of prior intervention. The Constitution also protects more specific forms of expression, such as parliamentary freedom of speech (Article 58) and its "governmental" counterpart (Article 101), which protects freedom of expression of the members of the cabinet.

4.1.2 The Basic Principles

It follows from the various constitutional provisions, that certain fundamental principles underpin the Belgian constitutional protection of freedom of expression. They can be summarized as follows.[7]

First, the Belgian Constitution leaves virtually no room for prior restraints. Accordingly, while freedom of expression is not absolute, authorities should refrain from prior interventions. People can be sanctioned afterwards, if they overstep legal boundaries but they should be given at least the opportunity to do so.

Second, since the Belgian constitution accepts limits to freedom of expression, we must have a look at how it conceives them. It may seem odd to 21st Century lawyers, but the Belgian constitutional framers strongly believed in the capacity of elected

---

[5] Council of State, judgement nr. 227.249, 4 May 2014.

[6] E.g., Council of State, judgement nr. 146.226, 17 June 2005; judgement nr. 191.742, 23 March 2009.

[7] Voorhoof and Valcke 2014, p. 28.

bodies to protect fundamental rights. Although there are some technical discussions on the possibility for Parliament to delegate its powers in the field of criminal law to the executive, the spirit of the Constitution requires that restrictions on freedom of expression be adopted by Parliament.[8] In that respect the Belgian constitutional system is called a system of "formal" restrictions. It puts forward formal limits to freedom of expression (the freedom can be limited only by formal legislation, issued by Parliament), but does not explicitly come up with substantive limits, such as a proportionality test.

Third, in line with the idea that it must be "representatives" of the citizens that vote upon restrictions of freedom expression, the Constitution attributes the power to judge so-called "press offences" to a lay jury (the Court of Assizes). Here too, the ideal of popular sovereignty prompted the constitutional lawmaker to distrust professional judges and endow "representatives" of the people to decide upon the criminal charges on account of press offences.

Fourth, the Constitution develops a chain of liability for press offenses, regarding both criminal and civil liability. If an author is known and resident in Belgium, (s)he is the only person who can be prosecuted, excluding all others involved in the publication. If one of those conditions is not fulfilled, the editor will be prosecuted if (s)he is known and living in Belgium. If not, it will be, upon the same conditions, the printer and ultimately the distributor. This is known as "serial liability" or, as Behrendt calls it in English, "cascading liability".[9] It is usually said that the aim of this specific type of liability is to protect journalists and writers against "private censorship",[10] i.e. the mere fact that editors and all others involved in the publication process would put pressure on the writers or refuse any publication out of fear for otherwise being prosecuted themselves.

4.1.3 The Problems

The system we briefly sketched functioned fairly well for decades, yet there are important challenges, due to the fact that means of communication have greatly changed over time. Some problems have been solved, but many are still waiting for a solution. This all the more so, since the emergence and breakthrough of digital and social media. Some of the most urgent problems, especially those presenting a particular interest within the ambit of combatting hate speech, are as follows.

1. Press

Article 25 of the Constitution explicitly mentions that "the press" is free. For decades, judges, scholars and lawyers had wondered whether this meant press, as in print

[8] Velaers 1991, I, pp. 129–130.

[9] Behrendt 2019, p. 6.

[10] Though, admittedly, given the formal legal meaning of censorship, this notion of "private censorship", that is often used to describe this pressure from editors and publishers, is confusing.

media, or whether this had to be understood as also encompassing "new forms" of media, such as broadcast media. This debate arose because, in the view of some observers, if "press" referred exclusively to written media only then prior restraints pertaining to radio and television would be possible. The discussion has not yet been properly resolved on the national level, but is nevertheless closed thanks to a judgment of the European Court of Human Rights. In the case *RTBF v. Belgium*, the Strasbourg Court had to assess whether a prior restraint on the Francophone public broadcaster not to broadcast a documentary on aesthetic surgery was in line with Article 10 of the Convention. Strasbourg found a breach of that article, precisely because the legal framework was not foreseeable (cf. infra 4.1).[11] Thus, the guarantees that the Constitution offers to the press, understood as print media, must be extended to all media. However fortunate the outcome of the case is, it is regrettable that Belgian politicians failed to devise a solution through constitutional amendment, instead leaving a resolution to the Strasbourg Court.

2. Press offence

The concept of "press offense" is not defined in the Constitution. The case law of the *Cour de cassation* and scholarly writings have been decisive in interpreting this concept. Press offenses are expressions of opinions, which breach the criminal law, are spread through the press (or an equivalent technique, so print media are envisaged), and reach an audience.[12] If these conditions are met, the Court of Assizes is the only competent court, unless the offenses concern the expression of racism or xenophobia (see point 3 below).

Again, Belgian constitutional media law is not technology neutral. If the expression was spread through printed words, the Court of Assize has exclusive jurisdiction. If not, the jurisdiction falls to the ordinary courts and tribunals. Of course, the Internet has dramatically affected this situation. Whereas one could still wonder why there was a difference in prosecution between press offenses and similar offenses committed trough radio and television, the Internet adds a further question: is it still feasible to distinguish between written and spoken expression? The Supreme Court's solution manages to respect its traditional case-law while taking account of the new reality. If user-generated materials such as YouTube clips contain text (such as subtitles), then they are dealt with as if they were traditional press offenses (provided that the other conditions are met). If they do not contain text, then by definition there can be no press offense.[13] This approach has raised eyebrows, and here too the old rules should really be adapted to the 21st Century.

3. Court of Assizes

Again, a key aspect of Belgian constitutional protection for free expression was the choice to assign press offenses to the Court of Assize. This Court, presided by a professional judge, includes a lay jury of twelve citizens. Its jurisdiction is limited

[11] ECtHR, RTBf v Belgium, 29 March 2011.

[12] Jongen and Strowel 2017, p. 710.

[13] Cass., 6 March 2012, Arr. Cass., 2012, p. 558 ; Cass., 29 October 2013, Arr. Cass., 2013, p. 2260.

to press offences, crimes (i.e. the most serious offences) and political offences. The *ratio legis* of this choice is clear: the constituent power distrusted professional judges and wanted the "people" to decide these cases. Representatives of the people were assumed to be more sympathetic to critical journalists and writers than professional judges, who were seen as part of the establishment.

This attitude came at a price. Court of Assizes procedures can become highly complex. The orality of the procedure can make them lengthy, so they are often seen as time-consuming and quite demanding *qua* cost and people management. It is easy nowadays to understand why authorities are still willing to invest in these procedures as far as crimes are concerned—although there has been a constant trend to "correctionalize" crimes, that is: to attribute them to the ordinary ("correctional") courts, with professional judges—but for press offences there is far less enthusiasm to organise jury procedures. This should not come as a surprise, since the societal impact of press offences is rather limited compared to the costs of a procedure before the Court of Assizes. Moreover, because of their special status, proceedings before the Court of Assizes are highly mediatized. This phenomenon can be counterproductive for press offences: if the idea was that the opinion should be sanctioned, it is ironic that it is (again) placed at the centre of the attention. This result is reminiscent of the "Barbra Streisand effect".

For these reasons, press offences have by and large not been brought to court since World War II, with only few exceptions. Belgian lawyers call this the "*de facto* decriminalization" of press offences. They are dealt with before ordinary civil courts through the mechanism of tort law. Again, one may be surprised by the pragmatic approach of Belgian law. On the one hand, formally the existing legal rules are not changed, which can please more conservative minds. Yet on the other hand, practice completely changed. But for one reason or another, updating the constitutional provisions appeared to be impossible. As a result, we have a striking example of the difference between law in books and law in action. Sociologically speaking, it shows that using criminal law for press offences no longer seems to reflect social needs. All of this would not be very important if there was not the problem of racist and xenophobic press offences. Because of *de facto* depenalization, these offenses also benefitted from this "immunity".

This was deemed problematical given that Belgium had ratified CERD, and EU bodies (see point 4.2) equally started to enact legislation combatting hate speech and discrimination. By the 1990's, a consensus grew that something had to be done. One solution would have been to conduct legal proceedings for hate speech pursuant to existing constitutional rules, which would have required Court of Assizes proceedings. Given the importance of the values at stake (equality and non-discrimination), arguments about the costs involved (be it financial or others) could in principle be countered. One could argue that such fundamental values are at play that they outweigh arguments of costs. Yet the "Barbra Streisand effect" would still be relevant. While bringing the cases before the Court of Assize, a high degree of attention would be given to opinions that one would prefer not be in the spotlight. This argument is not merely theoretical. Empirical research showed indeed that some (Holocaust) denialists as well as apologists of far-right ideologies welcomed and actively invited for public prosecution, since it would give them public attention they craved.[14] It seems therefore, as to the expediency of prosecution a valid consideration: what if the outcome of such a proceeding is counterproductive? One could easily counter this argument as follows: if it seems counterproductive to prosecute, would it not be more appropriate to change the law, instead of upholding the criminalisation while at the same time admitting that it would be counterproductive to sanction its violation?

Be that as it may, there are reasons to believe that there was another argument, that played a key role here—although few people would openly admit it. Since the Assize jury is composed of laymen, who are supposed to represent the citizens, a correlation between the electoral results and a randomly chosen panel of citizens, i.e. the jury, could be assumed. Since, in the 1990s the radical rightwing political party Flemish Block (*Vlaams Blok,* and since 2004: *Vlaams Belang* (Flemish Interest)) was very popular, especially in the region of Antwerp, there was a genuine risk that cases brought before the Antwerp Court of Assizes on account of racist or xenophobic press offences would be concluded with acquittals.

To avoid this, a political majority wanted to bring (racist) press offences before professional judges sitting in the ordinary criminal courts. But this required a constitutional amendment. What followed was a minimalist modification of Article 150. One could have expected a principled decision on the question whether the jury had still a role to play in judging press offences, but this is not what Belgian politicians did in 1999. Instead, they came up with a compromise that is still in force today. Accordingly, press offences in general remain the exclusive jurisdiction of the Assizes jury (and therefore the *de facto* depenalization persists), with the sole exception of press offenses motivated by racism or xenophobia. Thus, the ordinary criminal courts have obtained jurisdiction, only for this specific category of press offences. The problem today is that we now have one category of hate speech by press that can be effectively prosecuted. Other categories of hate speech, to the extent that they qualify as press offences, are not prosecuted. Victims of sexist, homophobic, and other such press offences find this both unfair and upsetting. There have been several initiatives already to modify the constitution and extend the "correctionalization" to all forms of hate speech, but up until now these have not been successful.[15]

4. Cascading liabilities

As mentioned, a special mechanism of liability was put in place to avoid that writers would not find anyone willing to publish, print, and disseminate their work. By (in principle) holding only the first in line liable, excluding the next persons in the chain of communication, the constitution guarantees the free flow of expression. Whenever the author is known and lives in Belgium, (s)he will be liable and no-one else. Only if one of those conditions is not fulfilled, liability will shift to the next person in line.

[14] Vrielink 2010.

[15] On the latest initiative see: Delgrange 2022 (with contributions by E. Van den Broeck, S. Van Drooghenbroeck and J. Vrielink).

This provision does not apply to audio-visual media (radio and television). For journalists who are employed under labour law, this entails and important consequence. Whereas journalists in the print media are liable for their work themselves by exclusion of anyone else on account of the constitutional provision, this is not the case for journalists working broadcasters under labour law. If labour law applies to their situation, they will benefit from a specific protection. The employer will be held liable, as a rule, unless there was fraud, a serious shortcoming or repeated minor shortcomings. This difference in treatment may seem odd and unfair, but the Constitutional Court had to acknowledge that it stems directly from the Constitution.[16] It is for the constituent power to change it, should that be felt more equitable for today's society. Neither ordinary lawmakers nor the Constitutional Court can intervene.

Given the chain of liability and various actors involved, the "cascade" cannot be applied to radio, television or any other audiovisual media. However, lawyers continue to debate the question whether cascading liability should be extended to digital media. An author like Velaers is in favour[17], based on the underlying principles, but others seem to hesitate.[18] In fact, it is not that straightforward that the actors mentioned in the Constitution can be transposed to the functioning of the Internet. Moreover, specific (European) rules govern the liability of intermediaries in the digital environment.

5. Limitations to limitations

Belgian constitutional law clearly allows restrictions on free expression. The Constitution, however, only provides for formal conditions for limitations. It is up to the lawmaker to restrict freedom of expression without there seemingly being "substantive" limits.[19] However, a proportionality analysis is applied due to the fact the Courts, especially the Constitutional Court, integrate Article 10 ECHR in their analysis.[20] Proportionality and legitimacy assessment has become part and parcel of the Belgian judicial review.

What is distinctive of the Belgian model is the (almost) complete rejection on prior interventions. Yet, it is not always easy to distinguish prior interferences from a posteriori interventions. Often the distinction put forward by Velaers is used. Preventive measures are those that (a) not only sanction the abuse of freedom but touch upon the potential use of freedom, (b) that intervene a priori, before the freedom at stake is fully exercised and (c) are not assessed by a judge.[21]

---

[16] Constitutional Court, 22 March 2006, judgment nr. 47/2006.

[17] Velaers 2019, p. 560.

[18] See Jongen and Strowel 2017, pp. 663–666 for an overview.

[19] Velaers 1991, I, pp. 230–231.

[20] Popelier and Lemmens 2015, p. 240.

[21] Velaers 1991, I, p. 224.

4.1.4 *The Equality Provisions*

The regulation of hate speech is a matter, among other things, of reconciling free speech with non-discrimination. The major rules on anti-discrimination are of statuary nature and will be discussed below under heading 2. However, the Constitution contains some relevant provisions on equality and non-discrimination.

The general equality provision is included in Article 10 of the Constitution, which confirms that all Belgians are equal before the law. This is a traditional provision, focussed on formal equality. Although the provision is general in nature, equality based on gender has been explicitly included. In Article 11 bis, gender equality in the exercise of fundamental freedoms is highlighted, with a particular stress on the promotion of gender equality in public and elective mandates.

In 1970, the beginning of the federalisation of the then unified State, a provision was included (currently Article 11, previously Article 6bis), which states that there cannot be any discrimination on philosophical or ideological grounds. This provision was included in order to protect the secular minority in Flanders and the Catholics in the French speaking part of Belgium. These articles operate closely together with the statutory rules on non-discrimination, which we will discuss under point 2.

4.2 National Statutory or Administrative Law

National statutory law, and federal law in particular, has regularly been applied to hateful expression, and has been expressly conceived to this end as well. In the following we will discuss the main provisions and legislative acts, as well as their application.

4.2.1 *Incitement to Hatred, Discrimination, Violence and Segregation (on Protected Grounds)*

The central provisions covering "hate speech" specifically on the basis of sex, sexual orientation, age and disability, in the federal legislation are the prohibitions on "incitement to hatred, discrimination, segregation and violence." Article 20, 1°–2° of the Act of 30 July 1981 punishing certain acts motivated by racism or xenophobia[22] (Anti-racism Act, relevant for the grounds of "presumed race, skin colour, nationality, descent, national or ethnic origin"), Article 22, 1°–2° of the Act of 10 May 2007

---

[22] Act of 30 July 1981 punishing certain acts motivated by racism or xenophobia available at http://www.ejustice.just.fgov.be/cgi_loi/change_lg_2.pl?language=nl&nm=1981001359&la=N.

aimed at combating particular forms of discrimination[23] (Anti-discrimination Act, relevant for the grounds handicap, philosophical or religious beliefs, sexual orientation, age, wealth, civil status, political conviction, language, trade union membership, state of health, physical of genetic characteristics, birth, social background or situation) and Article 27, 1°–2° of Act of 10 May 2007 aimed at combating discrimination between women and men[24] (Sex discrimination Act, relevant for the grounds of sex and gender in the broad sense of the word) make it a crime, punishable "*by imprisonment of one month to one year and with a fine of 50–1000 euros*",[25] to publicly incite to discrimination, hatred or violence against a person on the basis of one of the protected criteria. Article 20, 3° and 4° Anti-racism Act, Article 22, 3° and 4° Anti-discrimination Act and Article 27, 3° and 4° Sex discrimination Act prohibit incitement to discrimination, hatred, violence or segregation against a group, a community or its members on the same grounds (with the same penalties).

The incitement must take place in the circumstances of Article 444 of the Penal Code in order to fall within these articles' scope. This means the incitement must take place: "*Either in public meetings or places; Or in the presence of several people, in a place that is not public but accessible to a number of people who are entitled to meet or visit there; Or in any place in the presence of the offended person and in front of witnesses; Or through documents, printed or otherwise, illustrations or symbols that have been displayed, distributed, sold, offered for sale, or publicly exhibited; Or finally by documents that have not been made public but which have been sent or communicated to several people.*"

The Constitutional Court has ruled in 2004 and 2009 that "incitement" under all of these Acts—presupposes actively "urging", "stimulating" or "instigating" third parties to undertake certain actions or to adopt a particular conduct. Moreover, the Constitutional Court required the presence of "specific intent" for the application of the incitement clause to be constitutional. As such, apart from the requirement that the content of words and expressions must incite or provoke hatred, discrimination, violence or segregation, it must also be demonstrated that such was the defendant's conscious intention.[26]

A practical/procedural barrier for the application of the incitement provisions (save the one concerning the racial criteria: cf. *infra*), at least where it concerns

[23] Act of 10 May 2007 aimed at combating particular forms of discrimination, available at https://www.ejustice.just.fgov.be/cgi_loi/change_lg.pl?language=nl&la=N&cn=2007051035&table_name=wet.

[24] Act of 10 May 2007 aimed at combating discrimination between women and men, available at https://www.ejustice.just.fgov.be/cgi_loi/change_lg.pl?language=fr&la=F&cn=2007051036&table_name=loi.

[25] To counter inflation, judges have to increase the nominal amounts mentioned in the statute with 7, 9 eurodecimes per euro, which amounts to a multiplication by 8 to reach the actual amount of the fine (Article 1 Act of 5 March 1952, available at https://www.ejustice.just.fgov.be/cgi_loi/change_lg_2.pl?language=nl&nm=1952030505&la=N).

[26] Constitutional Court, 6 October 2004, nr. 157/2004, https://www.const-court.be/public/n/2004/2004-157n.pdf; Constitutional Court, 12 February 2009, nr. 17/2009, https://www.const-court.be/public/n/2009/2009-017n.pdf; Constitutional Court, 11 March 2009, nr. 40/2009, https://www.const-court.be/public/n/2009/2009-040n.pdf.

written expressions, is the special protection regime that the Belgian Constitution offers to so-called "press offences" (see also *supra*, 4.1.3). In Belgium, written and published materials are subject to a special protection regime according to which they can in general only be tried by a jury.[27] In Belgium, jury trials are in the first place reserved for the most serious crimes (murder, rape, terrorism, etc.). However, several other crimes are also referred to a jury, not so much because of their seriousness, but rather because of their (politically subversive) nature: e.g. political crimes and press crimes.

In practice this arrangement means that press crimes are rarely prosecuted, given the burdensome and time-consuming procedure of jury trials. In 1999, the federal Parliament introduced an exception to the constitutional principle of the jury trial for press crimes, and allowed that press offences "inspired by racism or xenophobia" be brought before professional judges (*supra*).[28] However, for press offences on other grounds, such as sexual orientation, religion, disability, gender etc., there is no comparable exception. This makes it highly improbable that a prosecution will be brought against authors of written incitement on those grounds. For the first time in the history of the Belgian Constitution, however, a person has—in 2021—been referred to the jury by the indictments chamber because of online hate messages. More specifically, the defendant is accused of having intimidated feminists and women more generally on his Twitter account, which is punishable by imprisonment of 6 months to 5 year and with a fine of 100–500 euros[29] according to Article 327 Criminal Code.[30]

Proposals to amend the Constitution and to add other forms of hate speech to the exception have been debated in Parliament,[31] but have thusfar not managed to obtain the required 2/3 majority to effectively change the Constitution on this point.[32]

---

[27] Article 150 Constitution, available at https://www.ejustice.just.fgov.be/cgi_loi/change_lg_2.pl?language=nl&nm=1994021048&la=N.

[28] Act of 7 May 1999 concerning the amendment of the Constitution, available at http://www.ejustice.just.fgov.be/cgi_loi/change_lg.pl?language=fr&la=F&cn=1999050732&table_name=loi.

[29] All fines mentioned in the Criminal Code have to be multiplied by 8 based on the Act of 5 March 1952 in order to counterbalance the impact of inflation.

[30] Indictments Chamber Liège, 1 April 2021, not published. A press article is available at https://www.rtbf.be/info/regions/liege/detail_renvoye-en-assises-pour-des-menaces-sur-facebook-une-premiere-en-belgique?id=10732870.

[31] Parliamentary Documents 2020–21, Chamber, Proposal for the revision of Article 150 of the Constitution in order to extend the constitutional safeguards for the printing press to all information media and to ensure equal prosecution of all criminal communications inciting hatred, violence and discrimination, no. 1791/1, submitted by K. Calvo et al., available at https://www.dekamer.be/kvvcr/showpage.cfm?section=/flwb&language=nl&cfm=/site/wwwcfm/flwb/flwbn.cfm?legislat=55&dossierID=1791.

Parliamentary Documents 2020–21, Chamber, Proposal for the revision of Article 150 of the Constitution, no. 1760/1, submitted by S. Verherstraeten, available at https://www.dekamer.be/FLWB/PDF/55/1760/55K1760001.pdf.

[32] Abbeloos 2021.

Regarding the case law, the large majority of applications pertain to the racial or ethnic criteria (hundreds of cases, since 1981).[33] Perhaps the most notable case concerned the conviction of 3 organisations belonging to the radical right-wing Flemish Block (presently, Flemish Interest).[34] Concerning other criteria, cases exist in relation to sexual orientation (eight known cases),[35] religion/belief,[36] political conviction,[37] and disability.[38] Cases pertaining to the other grounds included in the incitement provisions are not known to us. Whereas this does not (necessarily) mean that there is *no* case law on other grounds,[39] it does appear to be an indication that such cases are not often brought to court. There are however a few cases of hate speech concerning gender/sex that were brought under the anti-sexism act (see below).

---

[33] For an overview, see De Prins et al. 2005, pp. 321–343; Vrielink 2010, part III.

[34] Court of appeals Ghent, 21 April 2004, available at https://www.unia.be/files/Documenten/Rechtspraak/r040421_gent.pdf. For some recent cases, see: Correctional Court Leuven, 14 July 2020, available at https://www.unia.be/files/Documenten/Rechtspraak/2020_07_14_Corr._Leuven.pdf; Correctional Court Luxembourg, 22 October 2020, available at https://www.unia.be/files/Documenten/2020_10_22_Trib._Luxembourg.pdf; correctional court Antwerp, 4 November 2020, https://www.unia.be/files/Documenten/Rechtspraak/2020_11_04_Rb._Antwerpen.pdf; Correctional Court Courtrai, 22 February 2021, available at https://www.unia.be/files/Documenten/Rechtspraak/2021-02-22_Rb._Kortrijk.pdf.

[35] More specifically: correctional court Hasselt, 19 November 2008, available at https://www.unia.be/files/Documenten/Rechtspraak/2008_11_19__Corr._Rb._Hasselt__CGKR_t._Stephan_W..pdf; Correctional court Liège, 3 march 2011, available at https://www.unia.be/files/Documenten/Rechtspraak/2011_03_03_corr_Liege.pdf; correctional court Brussels, 25 February 2014, available at https://www.unia.be/files/Documenten/Rechtspraak/2014_02_25_corr_bruxelles.pdf; correctional court Antwerp, 27 February 2014, available at https://www.unia.be/files/Documenten/Rechtspraak/2014_02_27_corr_antwerpen.pdf; correctional court Ghent, 5 May 2015, available at https://www.unia.be/files/Documenten/Rechtspraak/2015_05_05_corr._gent.pdf; correctional court Liège, 25 November 2015, available at https://www.unia.be/files/Documenten/Rechtspraak/2015_11_25_corr._liege.pdf; correctional court Leuven, 22 November 2016, available at https://www.unia.be/files/Documenten/Rechtspraak/Correctionele_rechtbank_Leuven__22_november_206.pdf; correctional court Brussels, 22 May 2018, available at https://www.unia.be/files/Documenten/Rechtspraak/Tribunal_correctionnel_Bruxelles__22_mai_2018.pdf.

[36] Correctional court Ghent, 16 November 2020, available at https://www.unia.be/files/Documenten/Rechtspraak/2020_11_16_Corr._Gent_1.pdf and correctional court Hasselt, 22 July 2020, available at https://www.unia.be/files/Documenten/Rechtspraak/2020_07_22_Rb._Limburg.pdf.

[37] Correctional court Antwerp, 3 February 2021, available at https://www.unia.be/files/Documenten/Rechtspraak/2021_02_03_Rb._Antwerpen.pdf.

[38] Correctional court Liège, 25 November 2015, available at https://www.unia.be/files/Documenten/Rechtspraak/2015_11_25_corr._liege.pdf (combining disability and other grounds).

[39] In Belgium cases are not systematically made available to the public.

4.2.2 Anti-sexism Act[40]

2014 witnessed the enactment of the Act to combat sexism in the public space, which can include a wide variety of hate speech (but also non-speech conduct). For the purposes of this Act, the concept of sexism is understood to mean "*any gesture or act that, again in the circumstances of Article 444 of the Penal Code (supra), is evidently intended to express contempt for a person because of his gender, or that regards them as inferior, or reduces them to their sexual dimension, and which has the effect of seriously violating someone's dignity*".

The Constitutional Court clarified, in a ruling from 25 May 2016 concerning a request to annul the legislation, that the provision requires a specific intent, most specifically the (malicious) "intention to express "disdain" for a person or to regard a person as inferior, in the knowledge that the gesture or action may lead to an affront to that person's dignity".[41] Furthermore, the Court required it had to concern attacks on the dignity of concrete individuals (i.e. not of "women" or "men" as an abstract group).

The number of applications of the law has been very limited up until now. The first known application concerned a female police offices that was called "dirty whore" and who was told to go do "a job suited for a woman, like bank assistant".[42] Another known application likewise dealt with a female police officer.[43] Two media figures were convicted as well.[44]

4.2.3 Racism and Denialism

In addition to the ban on "incitement" (*supra*) the aforementioned Antiracism Act contains several additional hate speech provisions as well. To begin with, Article 21 provides a prison sentence of one month to one year and/or a fine of fifty euros to one thousand euros for "*anyone who, in the circumstances referred to in Article 444 of the Penal Code, spreads ideas based on racial superiority or hatred*"

---

[40] Loi tendant à lutter contre le sexisme dans l'espace public et modifiant la loi du 10 mai 2007 tendant à lutter contre la discrimination entre les femmes et les hommes afin de pénaliser l'acte de discrimination, 22 May 2014, available at http://www.ejustice.just.fgov.be/cgi_loi/change_lg.pl?language=fr&la=F&cn=2014052240&table_name=loi.

[41] Constitutional Court 25 May 2016, available at https://igvm-iefh.belgium.be/sites/default/files/downloads/2016-072n.pdf.

[42] Correctional Court Brussels, 7 November 2018, available at https://igvm-iefh.belgium.be/nl.

[43] See Boterman 2020.

[44] A case was brought against a well-known plastic surgeon that, in a speech at a university (at the invitation of a student organisation) had uttered misogynist speech (Court of Appeals Ghent, 21 February 2023), and another case was brought against a politician belonging to a (small) Islamic party that refused to look at a female interviewer, during a television interview (Brussels Court of appeal, 2 February 2002). Both were convicted.

Article 20, point 5 renders these same sanctions applicable, since 2019, to anyone who, again in the circumstances referred to in Article 444 of the Penal Code, "*denies, grossly minimises, attempts to justify or approves acts corresponding to a crime of genocide, a crime against humanity or a war crime as referred to in Article 136 quater of the Penal Code, and established as such by a final decision of an international court, knowing or being supposed to know that this conduct might expose either a person a group, a community or its members to discrimination, hatred or violence based on*" a racial criterion or religion; in practice this concerns denial (etc.) of the genocides in Rwanda and former Yugoslavia (Srebrenica).

Both provisions require a specific intent. In addition to the aforementioned provisions, there is a (pre-existing) act specifically concerning denialism of the Nazi-genocide. The Act of 23 March 1995 sanctioning the denial, [minimisation], justification or approval of the genocide committed by the German National Socialist regime during the Second World War.[45] The Act is slightly less demanding than the denialism provision in the Anti-racism Act and requires that someone, in the circumstances provided for in Article 444 of the Penal Code, "*denies, grossly minimises, attempts to justify or approves the genocide committed by the German National Socialist regime during the Second World War*".

Concerning case law, several applications exist of the "dissemination ban", often in combination with the incitement provision. The Holocaust denial act has led to a handful of rulings since 1995 (including, notably, of a politician[46] and of the most renowned Belgian Holocaust denier), and no applications have yet been made on the basis of the "new" denialism provision in the Antiracism Act.

4.2.4 Federated Levels

Belgium is a federal state. Aside from the federal level, it consists of three communities (Flemish, French-speaking, and German-speaking). It also comprises three regions (the Brussels region, the Flemish Region, and the Walloon Region) and four language areas (the Dutch language area, the French language area, the German language area, and the bilingual Brussels-Capital area).

At the community and regional levels almost all legislatures (with the exception of the French Community Commission in Brussels, and the Brussels Region in its Public Service Ordinance and Employment Ordinance) have enacted provisions regarding hate speech. As far as sexual orientation, age, disability and gender are concerned most of these instruments contain a prohibition of incitement to hatred,

---

[45] Loi tendant à réprimer la négation, la minimisation, la justification ou l'approbation du génocide commis par le régime national-socialiste allemand pendant la seconde guerre mondiale, 23 mars 1995, available at https://www.ejustice.just.fgov.be/cgi_loi/change_lg.pl?language=fr&la=F&cn=1995032331&table_name=loi.

[46] Correctional court Brussels, 12 December 2008, available at https://www.unia.be/files/Documenten/Rechtspraak/2008_12_12_corr_Brussel.pdf; Court of appeals Brussels, 15 September 2010, available at https://www.unia.be/files/Documenten/Rechtspraak/2010_09_15_Brussel.pdf.

discrimination and violence. The German-speaking Community's Equal Treatment Decree also prohibits "dissemination of ideas based on racial superiority and hatred" (just as the federal law does).

It is legally somewhat unclear whether these additional offences of "incitement" (and in the case of the German-speaking Community also the dissemination of racist ideas) add anything to the federal incriminations, since it should be noted that in areas belonging to the competence of the communities and the regions, the (federal) prohibition of incitement is applicable, at the very least until these communities and regions enact(ed) their own provisions in this regard. In practice the criminal provisions on the federated levels have never been applied, to our knowledge; the federal ones are given (*de facto*) precedence.

4.2.5 Role of Administrative Agencies

Administrative agencies have played an important role in getting hate speech legislation applied. In the first decade after the enactment of the Antiracism Act, relatively few cases were brought before the courts by prosecutors. Largely for this reason, 1993 saw the establishment of the Centre for Equal Opportunities and Opposition to Racism (CEOOR). The CEOOR was from the outset, among other things,[47] an independent governmental equality body, responsible for enforcing much of the federal discrimination legislation. It was created by the Act of 15 February 1993.[48] At the outset, it was charged with promoting equal opportunities and combating racial discrimination only, the Anti-racism act being the only non-discrimination law in existence at the time.

In 2003 the scope of the Centre's activities was expanded to include discrimination on several additional discrimination grounds. In addition to racial discrimination, the Centre in 2003 became competent to treat discrimination and hate speech cases on the following grounds: sexual orientation, marital status, birth, fortune, age, religion or belief, current and future state of health, disability or physical characteristics. With the introduction of the new federal legislation in 2007 this list was further expanded. The Centre at the time became competent to deal with discrimination complaints on the following grounds: so-called race, colour, descent, national or ethnic origin, nationality, age, sexual orientation, marital status, birth, fortune, religion or belief, political conviction, current and future state of health, disability, physical or genetic characteristics, social origin.[49] In 2013 the Centre was "interfederalised". By means of a cooperation agreement voted by all parliaments in Belgium, the institution

---

[47] It had other competences and tasks as well, e.g. in relation to education, immigration and asylum, and the fight against human trafficking.

[48] Moniteur 19 February 1993. Amended by the Acts of 13 April 1995, 20 January 2003, 25 February 2003, 10 August 2005 and 10 May 2007.

[49] For sex discrimination the Institute remains competent. Yet another institution is to be designated to deal with discriminations on the basis of "language", a ground for which the 2007 Act also provides protection.

became competent for the federated discrimination and hate speech legislation as well.[50] The official name changed to Interfederal Equal Opportunities Center, also going by the name "Unia". The institution currently has a staff of just over 100 people.

The institution's specific functions and competences include receiving complaints from persons who believe themselves to have suffered discrimination or hate speech, and dealing with these complaints in the manner it sees fit. Unia is authorised, for example, to examine and investigate situations of (alleged) discrimination; to act as a go-between or even mediate between the defendants and plaintiffs of discrimination; or (depending upon the facts) to take cases to both civil or criminal courts. The Centre is also authorised to initiate inquiries or studies into discrimination; to publish reports and to address recommendations to the public authorities and to private individuals and institutions on issues connected with discrimination. It also provides training to magistrates, lawyers and police, on problems of homophobia and dealing with discrimination on the basis of sexual orientation. Aside from victims of discrimination, other natural and legal persons can also appeal to Unia for support and guidance, such as government institutions or private businesses with questions about the legislation, or associations and interest groups working on specific groups or issues. Unia for example maintains close relations with a number of main NGO's active in the field of discrimination on the basis of sexual orientation, some of which even act as (independent) local complaint offices for the Centre, on the basis of formal protocols.

Since the institution was created the number of discrimination and hate speech cases brought before the courts has increased drastically. It has also issued a number of reports and guidelines on the issue and entered into debate with press associations to work on deontological codes etc. In 2002 a specific equality body was founded for discrimination and hate speech on the basis of sex and transgender status, called the Institute for the Equality of Women and Men. Its tasks and competences are similar to Unia, albeit limited to sex/gender (in the broad sense of the terms). Specifically regarding hate speech it has not instigated many cases, focusing mostly on discrimination cases (and sometimes also hate crimes) instead.

[50] In 2023 Flanders withdrew from the cooperation agreement, and subsequently founded its of human rights institution (Vlaams Mensenrechteninstituut or VMRI).

4.3 International Convention on the Elimination of All Forms of Racial Discrimination (ICERD)

Belgium has been a party to the ICERD since 1975.[51] Ratification provided a critical impulse to enact the aforementioned Antiracism Act of 1981.[52] Belgium ratified the Convention with the following Interpretive Declaration:

> "In order to meet the requirements of Article 4 of the International Convention on the Elimination of All Forms of Racial Discrimination, the Kingdom of Belgium will take care to adapt its legislation to the obligations it has assumed in becoming a party to the said Convention.
>
> The Kingdom of Belgium nevertheless wishes to emphasize the importance which it attaches to the fact that Article 4 of the Convention provides that the measures laid down in subparas (a), (b), and (c) should be adopted with due regard to the principles embodied in the Universal Declaration of Human Rights and the rights expressly set forth in Article 5 of the Convention. The Kingdom of Belgium therefore considers that the obligations imposed by Article 4 must be reconciled with the right to freedom of opinion and expression and the right to freedom of peaceful assembly and association. Those rights are proclaimed in Articles 19 and 20 of the Universal Declaration of Human Rights and have been reaffirmed in Articles 19 and 21 of the International Covenant on Civil and Political Rights. They have also been stated in Article 5, subpara (d) (viii) and (ix) of the said Convention.
>
> The Kingdom of Belgium also wishes to emphasize the importance which it attaches to respect for the rights set forth in the European Convention for the Protection of Human Rights and Fundamental Freedoms, especially in Articles 10 and 11 dealing respectively with freedom of opinion and expression and freedom of peaceful assembly and association."

The Convention is not often invoked by regular courts, which usually apply the Antiracism Act or other related legislation. A notable exception concerned one of the best-known applications of the Act, in the so-called "Flemish Block case" (*supra*). Three organisations associated with this radical right-wing party were prosecuted around the turn of the century on the basis of (then) Article 3 of the Antiracism Act that prescribed punishment for "whoever belongs to a group or association that clearly and repeatedly (…) advocates discrimination or segregation (…), or who lends his assistance to any such group or association".

In its analysis of the facts and relevant legislation the Ghent Court of Appeals relied heavily on the CERD, including for its definition of discrimination, and the scope of the protected grounds. The Court also cited the existence of the Convention and its resulting obligations to underscore the conformity of the Antiracism Act with the Constitution and ECHR. [53] The Supreme Court subsequently confirmed that in light of the duties flowing from the ICERD, and the application that the Court of

[51] See act of 9 July 1975 Concerning the approval of the International Convention on the Elimination of All Forms of Racial Discrimination, made at New York on 7 March 1966, Moniteur Belge 11 December 1975.

[52] Vrielink 2010, part II.

[53] Court of appeals Ghent, 21 April 2004, available at https://www.unia.be/files/Documenten/Rechtspraak/r040421_gent.pdf.

Appeals had made of the Antiracism Act, the criminal conviction did not exceed what was permitted by the ECHR.

The Constitutional Court has also, on occasion, referred to the ICERD in its rulings concerning (the constitutionality of) anti-racist hate speech provisions. Most notably it did so in 2009, in two related rulings on the (then) newly introduced ban on the dissemination of ideas based on racial hatred and racial superiority.[54] In those rulings the Court uses the requirements contained within the Convention to conclude that the "contested provisions may be considered as measures necessary in a democratic society within the meaning of Article 10.2 of the European Convention on Human Rights, in the interest of (…) the rights of others." However, the Court also uses the declaration that Belgium made upon ratification to argue for a *restrictive* interpretation of the newly introduced ban, with additional guarantees for free speech.

The UN Committee on the Elimination of Racial Discrimination (UN-CERD) has issued several Concluding Observations for Belgium commenting specifically on hateful expression. The most notable of these concerned the report that was submitted to the General Assembly on 26 September 1997, wherein the Committee urged the Belgian state to amend its Constitution in order to facilitate a more efficient criminal prosecution of written racist hate speech. In 1999—as mentioned—the Belgian parliament acted upon this suggestion, effectively amending Article 150 of the Constitution (see above). Finally, while Belgium has consented to the competence of the Committee to receive and consider individual communications, no complaints relevant to hateful expression have been submitted up until now.

4.4 Regional Law and Organisations

4.4.1 Council of Europe

As the 'jewel in the crown' of the Council of Europe, the European Convention on Human Rights (ECHR) plays a central role in guaranteeing freedom of expression through its Article 10 and the ensuing case-law of the European Court of Human Rights (ECtHR). As an early ratifying country, back in 1955, the ECHR has become directly applicable in Belgium and can be invoked before the national courts. The following paragraphs are intended to offer some insights into the application in Belgium of the Court's case law as it pertains to hate speech.

The case-law of the ECtHR in relation to freedom of speech has always been extensive but not unlimited. Ever since the Handyside judgment v. the UK, the Court has emphasized the importance of expressions that are relevant for society, in particular "pluralism, tolerance and broadmindedness without which there is no 'democratic

[54] Constitutional Court, 6 October 2004, nr. 157/2004, https://www.const-court.be/public/n/2004/2004-157n.pdf; Constitutional Court, 12 February 2009, nr. 17/2009, https://www.const-court.be/public/n/2009/2009-017n.pdf; Constitutional Court, 11 March 2009, nr. 40/2009, https://www.const-court.be/public/n/2009/2009-040n.pdf.

society'". [55] Despite this extensive view, 'offending, shocking or disturbing' expressions can be subject to certain limits. This pertains to persons who report about certain facts and developments in society, like journalists, but even more so to politicians, who are at the centre of the societal debate and the democratic institutions. In the latter case, politicians should refrain from inciting to hatred and discrimination against certain groups of the population.

The case of Féret v. Belgium (2009) is instructive for testing the boundaries of the freedom of speech of politicians under the ECHR. The Court was asked to evaluate the criminal conviction of Mr. Féret, leader of the French-speaking radical right-wing party Front National, for incitement to racism and discrimination in some political flyers that contained highly critical information and assessments about (im)migration. It its judgment, the Court confirmed that Belgium had not violated Article 10, because Féret's criminal conviction proved necessary in a democratic society, in order to avoid incitement to hate against foreigners. The Court's judgment, however, was not reached with consensus, as 3 of the 7 judges dissented in finding that Féret's activities did not amount to hate speech.[56] The Court's broad acceptance of limitations on freedom of speech, in the context of hate speech, has been the object of academic critiques.[57]

The case law of the ECtHR has also had an important impact on the scope of the prohibition of censorship, contained in Article 25 of the Belgian Constitution. As mentioned (supra C.1), the Belgian Supreme Court (Cour de Cassation) traditionally interpreted Article 25 as applying exclusively to the written press, and not to other media like radio or television. Not all (other) courts (nor the academic doctrine) supported this interpretation. Nonetheless, based on this case law of the Court of Cassation broadcasts had in several instances been prohibited, prior to being aired.

This situation was denounced by the ECtHR, in the case of *RTBF v. Belgium* (supra C.1). In that case, the Strasbourg Court had to assess whether a prior restraint on the Francophone public broadcaster (RTBF) not to broadcast a documentary on aesthetic surgery was in line with Article 10 of the Convention. Although Article 10, in the interpretation of the ECtHR, does not prohibit prior restraints as such, Strasbourg did find a breach of that article in this case, precisely because the Belgian legal framework was not foreseeable, since it lacked a sufficient legal basis, given the vague legislative framework, along with the absence of consensus within the case law.[58] Therefore, as long as the legal situation is not clarified, the guarantees that the Constitution offers to the press, understood as print media, ought to be extended to all media.

While the level of protection of the ECHR obviously applies in Belgium, it should be noted that the Belgian Constitution provides some more extensive provisions (cf. supra). If and when the rights at both levels are not fully congruent, the highest level

---

[55] ECtRM, Handyside v United Kingdom, 7 December 1976, §. 49.

[56] ECtRM, Féret v Belgium, 16 July 2009, §. 64.

[57] Sottiaux 2022, pp. 1193–1211; in general: Cannie and Voorhoof 2011, pp. 1, 58; Lemmens 2015, pp. 143 ff.

[58] ECtHR, RTBf v Belgium, 29 March 2011.

of protection will prevail.[59] This approach of cumulative protection is of particular importance in the context of hate speech, where the protection within Belgium goes beyond the case-law of the ECtHR. It is the logical consequence of the Belgian constitutional tradition, started in 1831 as resistance against the repressive regime of the then King of Holland William I.

As a result of this cumulative protection of the ECHR and the Belgian Constitution combined, the protection level for freedom of speech is quite high in Belgium, particularly when compared to neighbouring countries. The phrase 'offending, shocking or disturbing' in the case-law of the ECtHR therefore has a wider ambit in Belgium than in some other countries.

4.4.2 European Union

The role of the European Union in the area of hate speech is limited, but should not be underestimated. We discern three important layers of legislation.

First, Article 11 of the EU Charter of Fundamental Rights protects freedom of expression. Although it is not explicitly stated, hate speech and incitement to violence are not protected by the Charter.[60] However, within the Belgian context, questions on hate speech are addressed on the basis of the statutory rules on anti-discrimination we previously commented upon, the constitutional provisions and Article 10 of the European Convention.

Secondly, there are the important European Directives, amongst which most notably Council Directive 2000/43/EC of 29 June 2000 implementing the principle of equal treatment between persons irrespective of racial or ethnic origin[61] and Council Directive 2000/78/EC of 27 November 2000 establishing a general framework for equal treatment in employment and occupation[62] Council Directive 2004/113/EC of 13 December 2004 implementing the principle of equal treatment between men and women in the access to and supply of goods and services[63] that are important and are integrated in Belgian law through the anti-discrimination acts that were discussed earlier. Since the scope of the national legislation is broader (i.e. more grounds are included in the national legislation, which protects against discrimination in a very wide area of goods and services), EU-law is important, but not necessarily decisive in the Belgian context. This will only be the case where the domestic issue is entirely covered by EU-law. Which means that the European dimension mainly comes into play in cases concerning the work floor (anti-discrimination, religious symbols in

[59] See Article 26 Special Law Court of Arbitration (amended by Law of 12 July 2009), BS 31 July 2009) and Article 53 ECHR.

[60] Woods 2014, p. 322.

[61] Official Journal L 180, 19 July 2000.

[62] Official Journal L 303, 02 December 2000.

[63] Official Journal L 373, 21 December 2004.

the workplace etc…). There are, to the best of our knowledge, no cases before the ECJ against Belgium concerning hate speech.

We also want to mention Council Framework Decision 2008/913/JHA of 28 November 2008 on combating certain forms and expressions of racism and xenophobia by means of criminal law[64], which imposes on Member States the duty to sanction, amongst others, incitement to racial hatred as well as denying, condoning or grossly trivializing the Holocaust or war crimes, genocides and crimes against humanity whenever this is done in a way likely to incite to violence or hatred and directed against a group or member of group defined by specific criteria (i.e. race, colour, religion, descent or national or ethnic origin). The already mentioned anti-racism act and bans on denialism can be considered to implement those rules.

Finally, there the rules on the audiovisual media services, in its latest version: Directive (EU) 2018/1808 of the European Parliament and of the Council of 14 November 2018 amending Directive 2010/13/EU on the coordination of certain provisions laid down by law, regulation or administrative action in Member States concerning the provision of audiovisual media services (Audiovisual Media Services Directive) in view of changing market realities.[65] Again, under this legislation audiovisual hate speech is forbidden. These Directive(s) are transposed in Belgian law through the "decrees" of the Communities (federated entities competent for amongst other culture and audiovisual media). The independent regulatory bodies can impose administrative sanctions. The Francophone *Conseil Supérieur de l'Audiovisuel*[66] and the Flemish *Regulator voor de Media* (and its predecessors) have applied these provisions in some cases.[67] It is noteworthy to stress that since the sanctions are administrative in their nature, the *dolus specialis* is not required.[68]

4.5 Comparative National Law

The federal legislator in Belgium has taken the law of other national jurisdictions regarding hateful expression as examples to adopt new legislation. Particularly the French example has been cited during the preparatory works of several pieces of legislation banning forms of hate speech. This was quite clearly the case during the introduction in 1981 of the first Belgian hate speech legislation (*supra*). At the time, the drafting of the French anti-racist legislation was taken as an example by some, but more importantly the very existence and (allegedly positive) experiences

[64] Official Journal L 328, 6 December 2008.

[65] Official Journal L 303, 28 November 2018. Similarly, hate speech is a matter of concern in the Regulation (EU) 2022/2065 of the European Parliament and of the Council of 19 October 2022 on a Single Market For Digital Services and amending Directive 2000/31/EC (Digital Services Act), Official Journal L 277, 27 October 2022.

[66] Decision of 4 May 2017, approved by the Council of State, nr. 246.047, 8 November 2019.

[67] Vlaamse Geschillenraad voor Radio en Televisie 2003, p. 310.

[68] Borghs 2019, p. 899.

with said legislation were used to justify the Belgian law and to rebut criticism.[69] Likewise, in order to "justify" the introduction of the Holocaust Denial Act of 1995, the French example (the "*Loi Gayssot*" of 1990) was used as an argument.[70] In case law references to (case law or legislation of) other national jurisdictions has tended to be incidental at most and without much immediate impact on the interpretation of the relevant Belgian provisions.

References

Abbeloos J-F (2021) PVDA begraaft dossier haatspraak. De Standaard. https://www.standaard.be/cnt/dmf20210602_97598245.
Alen A, Muylle K (2011) Handboek van het Belgisch Staatsrecht. Kluwer, Mechelen.
Behrendt Chr (2019) Freedom of Expression. A Comparative Law Perspective. European Parliamentary Research Service, Belgium. https://www.europarl.europa.eu/thinktank/en/home.html.
Borghs P (2019) Aanzetten tot discriminatie vereist niet altijd bijzonder opzet. NJW 899.
Boterman B (2020) Man weigert verklaringen af te leggen bij politieagente, omdat ze vrouw is: 7 maanden cel voor seksisme. Man weigert verklaringen af te leggen bij politieagente, omdat ze vrouw is: 7 maanden cel voor seksisme | Koksijde | hln.be
Cannie H, Voorhoof D (2011) The Abuse Clause and Freedom of Expression under the European Human Rights Convention. NQHR 1, 58.
De Prins D, Sottiaux S, Vrielink J (2005) Handboek discriminatierecht. Kluwer, Mechelen.
Delgrange X (ed) (2022) Contrer l'impunité de fait de délits de presse confiés au jury d'assises (art. 150 Const.): Quelle(s) piste(s) choisir? Cahier de CIRC, no. 5.
Jongen F, Strowel A (2017) Droits des médias et de la communication. Presse, audiovisuel et Internet. Droit européen et belge. Larcier, Brussels.
Lemmens K (2015) Hate Speech in the Case Law of the European Court of Human Rights. In: Ellian A, Mollier G (eds). Freedom of Speech Under Attack. Eleven Publishing, The Hague.
Popelier P, Lemmens K (2015) The Constitution of Belgium. Oxford Hart Publishing.
Sottiaux S (2022) Conflicting Conceptions of Hate Speech in the ECtHR's Case Law. German Law Journal 23:1193–1211.
Velaers J (1991) De beperkingen aan de vrijheid van meningsuiting, Maklu, Antwerp.
Velaers J (2019) De Grondwet. Een artikelsgewijze commentaar. Deel I. Die Keure, Bruges.
Vlaamse Geschillenraad voor Radio en Televisie (2003) Auteurs en Media.
Voorhoof D, Valcke P (2014) Handboek mediarecht. Larcier, Brussels.
Vrielink J (2010) Van haat gesproken?: Een rechtsantropologisch onderzoek naar de bestrijding van rasgerelateerde uitingsdelicten in België. Maklu, Antwerp.
Witte E, Craeybeckx J, Meynen A (2009) Political History of Belgium. From 1830 onwards. ASP, Brussels.
Woods L (2014) Article 11 Freedom of Expression and Information. In: Peers S, Hervey T, Kenner J, Ward A (eds). The EU Charter of Fundamental Rights. Hart, Oxford.

Jogchum Vrielink is Professor of Fundamental Rights and Discrimination Law at the UCLouvain Saint-Louis-Bruxelles (faculty of law) and of Law and Religion at the KU Leuven (faculty of Canon law). His research topics include discrimination law, fundamental and human rights (freedom of expression and freedom of religion in particular) and legal anthropology.

[69] See extensively: Vrielink 2010, pp. 98–99.

[70] See extensively: ibid., p. 130.

Koen Lemmens holds a Ph.D., in Law (European University Institute, Florence, Italy, 2003). He is Professor of Public Law at KU Leuven and teaches as well in Venice (European Master on Human Rights and Democratization, Global Campus). In addition, he practices as an attorney specialised in procedures before the European Court of Human Rights. Currently he is also Vice-President of the Belgian Institute for the Protection and the Promotion of Human Rights. His main areas of research and teaching are European Human Rights Law with a focus on freedom of speech, and Belgian Constitutional Law and Media Law.

Stephan Parmentier is Professor of criminology and human rights at the Faculty of Law and Criminology at KU Leuven. He is currently Secretary-General of the International Society for Criminology (Paris), Advisory Board member of the International Centre for Transitional Justice (New York and Brussels), and member of the Academia Europaea, Class of Social Sciences. He has also served on the Advisory Board of the Oxford Centre of Criminology, and was a guest lecturer and scholar in many universities across the world in the fields of human rights, justice and peace, criminology and socio-legal studies. Parmentier is founding general editor of the 'Series on Transitional Justice' (Intersentia), and founding editor of *The International Journal of Restorative Justice* (Eleven Publishing).

Chapter 5
Canada

Pierre Rainville and Olivier Lacombe

Contents

Abstract Rejecting the American approach, Canadian Courts have rightly upheld the validity of legislation on discriminatory speech and hate speech so as to foster the values linked with equality and multiculturalism. Various limits on other fundamental

P. Rainville (✉) · O. Lacombe
Faculté de droit, Université Laval, 1030, av. des Sciences-Humaines, Québec G1V 0A6, Canada
e-mail: pierre.rainville@fd.ulaval.ca
URL: https://www.fd.ulaval.ca/faculte/repertoire-du-personnel/pierre-rainville

E. Heinze (ed.), *Criminalising Hate Speech*,
https://doi.org/10.1007/978-94-6265-650-5_5

rights (freedom of religion, presumption of innocence and the like) have therefore been found to be justified. However, recent case law has been prone to draw a line: it is unconstitutional to ban speech on the mere ground that it ridicules, belittles or otherwise affronts dignity of minority groups. Such encroachment upon freedom of speech is treated as excessive. Indignation is not a proper ground for banning public discourse; only words likely to lead to discriminatory treatment deserve to be prohibited.

Keywords Discours haineux et dignité de la personne · Discours haineux et liberté de religion · Discours haineux et promotion de l'égalité · Propos offensants · Propos homophobes · Ironie, stéréotypes et liberté d'expression

5.1 Droit Constitutionnel

5.1.1 Les Dispositions Consacrées Nommément au Discours Haineux en Droit « Constitutionnel » et en Droit « Quasi Constitutionnel » Canadien

Les subtilités du droit constitutionnel canadien doivent être abordées d'entrée de jeu. Au sens formel du terme, la constitution canadienne ne se prononce pas explicitement au sujet du discours haineux. En clair, ni les différentes lois constitutionnelles adoptées depuis 1867 ni la *Charte canadienne des droits et libertés* (ci-après « *Charte canadienne* »)[1] n'évoquent comme telle cette problématique. Les textes qui composent la constitution formelle du Canada ne renferment aucune disposition interdisant ou restreignant expressément le discours haineux et la propagande de cette nature. Il serait pourtant illusoire de nier l'influence primordiale jouée par la *Charte canadienne* à l'occasion de l'édification d'un arsenal législatif destiné à combattre le propos haineux disséminé dans l'enceinte publique. La jurisprudence a mis à profit plusieurs dispositions de la *Charte canadienne* afin d'asseoir la validité de certaines prohibitions tout en invalidant néanmoins certaines formes d'interdit jugées trop hardies. Les droits constitutionnels ainsi mobilisés feront l'objet des prochains développements.

Force est cependant de signaler, dès maintenant, l'apport souvent explicite des lois fédérales, provinciales ou territoriales consacrées à la protection des droits de la personne. D'origine purement législative et abstraction faite de l'appellation retenue (« Charte des droits et libertés de la personne », « Code des droits de la personne » ou encore « Loi sur les droits de la personne »), pareille législation est érigée au rang

---

[1] Charte canadienne des droits et libertés, Partie I de la Loi constitutionnelle de 1982 (R-U), constituant l'annexe B de la Loi de 1982 sur le Canada (R-U), 1982, c 11 [Charte canadienne].

des lois fondamentales pourvues d'un statut quasi constitutionnel.[2] La primauté des droits ainsi conférés ne saurait être négligée: « ... à moins que le législateur ne se soit exprimé autrement « en termes clairs et exprès », les lois sur les droits de la personne ont préséance sur toutes les autres lois en cas de conflit ... »[3]. Or, certaines lois provinciales consacrées à la protection des droits de la personne ciblent en toutes lettres le discours haineux, alors que d'autres se consacrent plus généralement à la suppression de symboles, affiches ou déclarations discriminatoires. Cette seconde catégorie de textes à portée quasi constitutionnelle sera analysée dans le cadre de l'étude de la question 2.

5.1.2 L'arbitrage Jurisprudentiel Entre la Liberté d'expression, la Liberté de Religion et les Autres Droits Fondamentaux

Pourvues l'une et l'autre d'une large portée, la liberté d'expression et la liberté de religion sont enfreintes lorsque le législateur s'avise de combattre le propos incendiaire. La liberté d'expression du locuteur est résolument entravée. La liberté d'expression assurée par l'alinéa 2b) de la *Charte canadienne* reçoit une acception large et libérale à la faveur d'une jurisprudence constante. À deux exceptions près (la violence physique[4] ainsi que les menaces[5]) la liberté d'expression se fait garante des expressions, même impopulaires ou odieuses[6]. Comme le précise la Cour suprême du Canada: «... le mot « expression » à l'al. 2b) de la *Charte* vise tout contenu de l'expression, sans égard aux sens ou message particulier que l'on cherche à transmettre. ».[7] La suppression du discours haineux porte pareillement atteinte à la liberté de religion de celui qui professe de telles thèses en raison de sa foi:[8] l'entrave ainsi

[2] Tranchemontagne c Ontario (Directeur du Programme ontarien de soutien aux personnes handicapées), 2006 CSC 14 par. 33; B c. Ontario (Commission des droits de la personne), 2002 CSC 66, par. 44.

[3] Office régional de la santé du Nord c Horrocks, 2021 CSC 42, par 34. Voir encore Canada (Commission canadienne des droits de la personne) c Canada (Procureur général), 2018 CSC 31, par. 61.

[4] R c Keegstra, [1990] 3 RCS 697, 734.

[5] Brackens c Niagara Parks Police, 2018 ONCA 261, par. 36 et s; R. c Steele, 2014 CSC 61, par. 49.

[6] Procureur général du Québec c Gallant, 2021 QCCA 1701, par. 260; Ward c Québec (Commission des droits de la personne et des droits de la jeunesse), 2021 CSC 43, par. 60 et 109; R c Keegstra, [1990] 3 RCS 697, 730: « [l]es communications fomentant volontairement la haine contre un groupe identifiable transmettent incontestablement une signification, et telle est l'intention de leurs auteurs. Puisque l'arrêt Irwin Toy insiste sur le fait que le type de signification transmise n'a aucune pertinence pour la question de savoir s'il y a eu violation de l'al. 2b), il est dès lors sans intérêt que l'expression visée au par. 319(2) soit odieuse ou désobligeante ».

[7] R c Keegstra, [1990] 3 RCS 697, 734.

[8] Saskatchewan (Human Rights Commission) c Whatcott, 2013 CSC 11, par. 152 à 156; Ross c Conseil scolaire du district n° 15 du Nouveau-Brunswick, [1996] 1 RCS 825, par. 67 à 76.

subie n'est ni négligeable ni insignifiante.[9] La diffusion de propos haineux peut donc se réclamer, au premier abord, de l'exercice de deux droits fondamentaux. Au stade initial de l'identification des droits entravés par la répression du dire incendiaire, la Cour suprême du Canada refuse de faire intervenir, de manière précoce, un quelconque équilibrage entre les droits constitutionnels des uns et des autres.[10] Que la propagation de croyances religieuses haineuses lèse les droits fondamentaux d'autrui ou malmène les valeurs chères à la société canadienne ne suffit pas à dépouiller les paroles des droits prévus aux alinéas a et b) de l'article 2 de la *Charte canadienne.*

La protection ainsi accordée au propos haineux demeure toute relative et particulièrement friable. Le législateur a libre cours pour démontrer, par la balance des probabilités, que le droit fondamental en cause a été restreint « dans des limites qui soient raisonnables et dont la justification puisse se démontrer dans le cadre d'une société libre et démocratique ».[11] Malgré le constat d'une atteinte à la liberté d'expression ou de religion, l'article premier de la *Charte canadienne* permet donc de maintenir l'équilibre délicat entre, d'une part, les valeurs fondamentales qui sous-tendent la protection constitutionnelle de la liberté d'expression et, d'autre part, celles que les interdits frappant le discours haineux tendent à protéger. L'analyse constitutionnelle au regard de l'article premier procède en deux temps. Force est tout d'abord d'identifier un objectif se rapportant à des « préoccupations urgentes et réelles dans une société libre et démocratique ».[12] La jurisprudence de la Cour suprême du Canada aura été de tout temps unanime à cet égard: le bannissement des propos haineux répond à un objectif pourvu de l'urgence voulue. Le désaccord constaté dans ses tout premiers arrêts en la matière aura plutôt porté sur le second volet de l'analyse, soit le critère de proportionnalité de la mesure gouvernementale au regard de l'objectif poursuivi. Or, c'est précisément à cette étape que sont soupesés les divers intérêts individuels et collectifs mis en jeu par la mesure contestée.

Dans ses trois premiers arrêts de principe rendus au sujet de l'éradication des propos haineux à l'aide de sanctions pénales[13] ou bien civiles comme administratives,[14] la Cour suprême du Canada se sera foncièrement divisée: une frêle majorité d'une seule voix vient valider l'interdit pénal de la fomentation de la haine prévu

[9] Saskatchewan (Human Rights Commission) c Whatcott, 2013 CSC 11, par. 155.

[10] Saskatchewan (Human Rights Commission) c Whatcott, 2013 CSC 11, par. 152 à 156; Ross c Conseil scolaire du district n° 15 du Nouveau-Brunswick, [1996] 1 RCS 825, par. 67 à 76.

[11] Article premier de la Charte canadienne. Pour un exposé du cadre d'analyse relatif à l'article premier de même que des principes relatifs à l'application de cette disposition, voir R. c Keegstra, [1990] 3 RCS 697, 734 à 738; R. c Oakes, [1986] 1 RCS 103, 135 à 140.

[12] R. c Oakes, [1986] 1 RCS 103, 139.

[13] R. c Andrews, [1990] 3 RCS 870; R. c Keegstra, [1990] 3 RCS 697.

[14] Canada (Commission des droits de la personne) c Taylor, [1990] 3 R.C.S. 892. Dépourvue de sanction pénale, la disposition à l'étude revêt plutôt une vocation préventive. Elle se propose de mettre fin à une pratique jugée discriminatoire. Comme l'expose la Cour suprême du Canada, le cadre législatif favorise un règlement par conciliation et n'autorise l'imposition d'une amende ou de l'emprisonnement que si la personne accomplit intentionnellement les actes prohibés par une ordonnance inscrite en Cour fédérale.

au code criminel[15] ainsi que le bannissement, dans une loi fédérale d'une tout autre nature, des messages téléphoniques répétés susceptibles d'exposer une personne ou un groupe à la haine ou au mépris.[16]

L'unanimité verra le jour dans les décisions ultérieures de la Cour. Quelques années plus tard, une cour suprême affichant un tout nouvel esprit de corps valide l'atteinte à la présomption d'innocence résultant de l'un des articles du dispositif du code criminel interdisant la fomentation volontaire de la haine.[17] C'est de nouveau à l'unisson qu'elle cautionne, sur le plan constitutionnel, les mesures civiles provinciales destinées à empêcher certaines formes de communication publique qui exposent ou tendent à exposer une personne ou une catégorie de personnes à la haine.[18] Dans cette même affaire, la Cour fait également front sur une autre facette du débat constitutionnel: autant elle s'entend pour proscrire les propos haineux, autant elle estime excessive la mesure législative se proposant de pourfendre les communications publiques qui ridiculisent, rabaissent ou portent par ailleurs atteinte à la dignité de ces mêmes personnes.[19]

Dans un arrêt tout récent, cette unanimité chèrement acquise cède toutefois le pas sur un sujet somme toute connexe: un désaccord au sein de la Cour suprême éclate sur la portée de sa jurisprudence antérieure ainsi que sur la signification de la notion de « dignité » de la personne en présence de paroles outrancières raillant publiquement le handicap d'un jeune adolescent.[20] Cet aperçu des arrêts de principe fera désormais l'objet de remarques plus poussées.

Force est d'analyser les premières décisions majoritaires amenées à valider, constitutionnellement parlant, les interdits fédéraux relatifs à la prévention de l'incitation à la haine. Autant l'atteinte à la liberté d'expression (voire à la liberté de religion, selon les croyances de l'intéressé) est reconnue, autant une majorité au sein de la Cour suprême du Canada se dessine dès 1990 afin de justifier pareils interdits. Les motifs de validation sont divers et se cumulent. Il est certes fait état de l'apport négligeable des déclarations haineuses dans un contexte démocratique et des liens très émoussés qu'entretiennent de tels propos au regard des fondements propres à la liberté d'expression :

> [L]a propagande haineuse apporte peu aux aspirations des Canadiens ou du Canada, que ce soit dans la recherche de la vérité, dans la promotion de l'épanouissement personnel ou dans la protection et le développement d'une démocratie dynamique qui accepte et encourage la participation de tous. Si je ne puis conclure que la propagande haineuse ne mérite qu'une protection minimale dans le cadre de l'analyse fondée sur l'article premier, je peux néanmoins reconnaître le fait que les restrictions imposées à la propagande haineuse visent une catégorie particulière d'expression qui s'écarte beaucoup de l'esprit même de l'al. 2*b*). Je conclus donc

[15] R. c Andrews, [1990] 3 RCS 870; R. c Keegstra, [1990] 3 RCS 697.

[16] Canada (Commission des droits de la personne) c Taylor, [1990] 3 R.C.S. 892.

[17] R. c Keegstra, [1996] 1 R.C.S. 458. Le moyen de défense fondé sur la véracité des déclarations communiquées impose à l'accusé d'en convaincre le tribunal par balance des probabilités.

[18] Saskatchewan (Human Rights Commission) c Whatcott, 2013 CSC 11.

[19] Id.

[20] Ward c Québec (Commission des droits de la personne et des droits de la jeunesse), 2021 CSC 43.

qu'« il se pourrait que des restrictions imposées à des expressions de ce genre soient plus faciles à justifier que d'autres atteintes à l'al. 2*b*) ...»[21].

Les juges majoritaires repèrent pareillement les engagements internationaux du Canada en matière de répression des propos haineux afin de valider les mesures pénales ou civiles prises à cet égard[22].

Le cadre analytique déployé afin d'asseoir la constitutionnalité des mesures fédérales débattues puise aussi largement dans les autres droits constitutionnels garantis en droit canadien ainsi que dans les valeurs défendues par ces mêmes instruments. Outre la nécessité de ne point assaillir et brimer les individus en raison de leur foi en bafouant, de ce fait même, leur liberté de religion,[23] ce sont, avant toutes choses, le droit à l'égalité, la lutte contre la discrimination ainsi que la nécessaire participation de tous au processus démocratique qui sont convoqués afin de faire échec à la contestation constitutionnelle des mesures prises par le gouvernement fédéral ou certaines provinces.

Le droit à l'égalité et l'importance du multiculturalisme sont appelés en renfort à ce stade de l'analyse constitutionnelle. Deux dispositions constitutionnelles sont mises en exergue, soit les articles 15 et 27 de la Charte canadienne. Le premier consacre le droit à l'égalité, notamment sa dimension négative qui a pour effet d'interdire la discrimination fondée sur une large gamme de motifs prohibés. Pour sa part, le second pose la règle d'interprétation selon laquelle toute interprétation de la Charte canadienne doit « concorder avec l'objectif de promouvoir le maintien et la valorisation du patrimoine multiculturel des Canadiens ».

De dire les juges majoritaires, ces deux dispositions traduisent ensemble « un engagement profond envers les valeurs du multiculturalisme et de l'égalité ».[24] Cet engagement se voit cependant mis à mal par la propagande haineuse, laquelle « menace gravement tant l'enthousiasme avec lequel la valeur d'égalité est acceptée

---

[21] R. c Keegstra, [1990] 3 RCS 697, 766, un passage repris dans l'arrêt Saskatchewan (Human Rights Commission) c Whatcott, 2013 CSC 11, par. 113. L'arrêt Taylor y voit pareillement une expression qui n'a « que des liens ténus avec le fondement de la garantie de la liberté d'expression »: Canada (Commission des droits de la personne) c Taylor, [1990] 3 R.C.S. 892, 940. En somme, plus l'expression en jeu s'éloigne des valeurs centrales à la liberté d'expression, plus la capacité de justifier l'action restrictive de l'État s'accroît: Procureur général du Québec c Gallant, 2021 QCCA 1701, par. 266; Lemire c Canada (Commission des droits de la personne), 2014 CAF 18, par. 60; [2015] 2 RCF 117.

[22] Cette question est approfondie dans les réponses apportées aux questions 5.3.1 et 5.4.7 du présent rapport.

[23] Canada (Commission des droits de la personne) c Taylor, [1990] 3 R.C.S. 892, 918 et 924; Ross c Conseil scolaire du district n° 15 du Nouveau-Brunswick, [1996]1 RCS 825, 878 et 879: « Quant à la liberté de religion, toute croyance religieuse qui dénigre et attaque les croyances religieuses d'autrui mine le fondement même de la garantie de l'al. 2a), un fondement qui garantit à chaque personne la liberté d'embrasser et de manifester les croyances que lui dicte sa conscience» . De surcroît, la Cour suprême fait remarquer que les propos haineux emportent pour certaines personnes une « forte incitation à renoncer aux caractéristiques culturelles qui les distinguent des autres »: Canada (Commission des droits de la personne) c Taylor, [1990] 3 R.C.S. 892, 918. Voir encore Saskatchewan (Human Rights Commission) c Whatcott, 2013 CSC 11, par. 72.

[24] R. c Keegstra, [1990] 3 RCS 697, 755.

et mise en pratique par la société, que les rapports entre les membres de groupes cibles et leur communauté »[25]. Ce constat conforte la conclusion des juges majoritaires selon laquelle l'objectif poursuivi par le paragraphe 319(2) C.cr. est à la fois légitime et suffisamment important pour justifier une atteinte à la liberté d'expression. Même à cette étape avancée de l'analyse constitutionnelle, les tribunaux continuent en effet de veiller « au respect des droits et libertés énoncés dans les autres articles de la *Charte* ».[26] Partant, les effets délétères de la propagande haineuse sur les valeurs qu'incarnent les articles 15 et 27 de la *Charte* pèsent dans la balance. Les conclusions du juge en chef Dickson au sujet de la première de ces deux dispositions constitutionnelles mettent au jour ce raisonnement:

> Compte tenu de l'engagement envers l'égalité manifesté dans la Charte et reflété à l'article premier, l'objet visé par la disposition législative contestée prend une importance accrue dans la mesure où elle est destinée à assurer l'égalité de tous dans la société canadienne. Le message véhiculé par l'activité expressive visée au par. 319(2) est que les membres de groupes identifiables ne doivent pas avoir un statut d'égalité dans la société, et ne sont pas des êtres humains qui méritent le même respect, la même déférence et la même considération que les autres. Le tort causé par un tel message est en conflit direct avec les valeurs essentielles à une société libre et démocratique et, en restreignant la fomentation de la haine, le Parlement cherche donc à renforcer la notion de respect mutuel, indispensable dans une nation qui vénère le principe de l'égalité de tous[27].

Ces enseignements font toujours autorité. La Cour suprême du Canada les reprend et les précise en 2013 dans l'arrêt *Whatcott* rendu au soutien de la validité constitutionnelle d'une loi provinciale combattant les propos haineux:

> Si un groupe de personnes est considéré comme inférieur, sous-humain ou sans loi, il est plus facile de justifier le refus de lui reconnaître, ainsi qu'à ses membres, l'égalité des droits ou de statut. Ainsi que notre Cour l'a fait observer dans l'arrêt *Mugesera c. Canada (Ministre de la Citoyenneté et de l'Immigration)*, 2005 CSC 40, [2005] 2 R.C.S. 100, par. 147, les conclusions tirées dans l'arrêt *Keegstra* laissent entendre « qu'un discours haineux nie toujours des droits fondamentaux ». Au fur et à mesure que la majorité devient insensible aux répercussions des propos haineux, on peut craindre que certains membres de la société expriment, par leur conduite, leur rejet des membres du groupe vulnérable. Les propos haineux préparent le terrain en vue de porter des attaques plus virulentes contre les groupes vulnérables. Ces attaques peuvent prendre la forme de mesures discriminatoires, d'ostracisme, de ségrégation, d'expulsion et de violences et, dans les cas les plus extrêmes, de génocide: voir les arrêts *Taylor* et *Keegstra.*[28].

La négation des droits des individus ou de la collectivité ciblée n'est pas le seul péril occasionné par les propos haineux. S'ajoutent l'érosion même de la liberté d'expression des personnes ainsi ciblées et l'effritement de leur participation au processus démocratique:

---

[25] R. c Keegstra, [1990] 3 RCS 697, 758. Voir pareillement Ross c Conseil scolaire du district n° 15 du Nouveau-Brunswick, [1996]1 RCS 825, 877 à 880.

[26] R. c Keegstra, [1990] 3 RCS 697, 755, reprenant un passage de l'arrêt Singh c Ministre de l'Emploi et de l'Immigration, [1985] 1 RCS 177, 218.

[27] R. c Keegstra, [1990] 3 RCS 697, 756.

[28] Saskatchewan (Human Rights Commission) c Whatcott, 2013 CSC 11, par. 74.

> [L]a propagande haineuse prive les membres du groupe ciblé de la possibilité de s'épanouir en articulant des pensées et des idées. Elle a également pour effet de nuire à la capacité des membres du groupe de réagir à des idées de fond au centre du débat, ce qui constitue un obstacle majeur les empêchant de participer pleinement à la démocratie. De fait, le discours haineux comporte un aspect particulièrement insidieux en ce qu'il prive le groupe ciblé de tout moyen de riposter ou de rétorquer. C'est ce qu'il fait non seulement en tentant de marginaliser le groupe de manière à ce que ses réactions soient ignorées, mais également en employant des mots qui forcent les membres du groupe à défendre leur propre humanité fondamentale ou leur propre statut social avant même d'être admis à participer au débat démocratique.[29]

Certes, ce péril s'apprécie de manière objective[30]. L'avis des personnes mises à mal par des propos incendiaires ne permet pas, à lui seul, la suppression de ces paroles. L'indignation des membres de la communauté visée ne contribue pas à définir le préjudice visé[31]. Cela dit, une fois appréciées de manière objective, l'ampleur et la gravité des préjudices appréhendés autorisent des entorses diverses à la liberté d'expression voire à la liberté de religion du locuteur incendiaire.

La première entrave à certains droits fondamentaux se constate de par *le champ de l'interdit*. Dans un premier temps, la Cour suprême du Canada valida, en 1990, deux prohibitions. L'une, de nature proprement criminelle, intéresse l'incrimination de la fomentation volontaire de la haine[32]. La seconde, de nature civile voire administrative, a trait à la suppression des messages téléphoniques répétés susceptibles d'exposer une personne ou un groupe à la haine ou au mépris[33]. Ce second interdit fut ensuite élargi en 2001 par le législateur fédéral de l'époque pour englober l'usage d'internet[34]. Les considérations énoncées précédemment auront amené en 2014 la Cour d'appel fédérale du Canada à valider constitutionnellement l'interdit ainsi

---

[29] Saskatchewan (Human Rights Commission) c Whatcott, 2013 CSC 11, par. 75. Voir également Lemire c Canada (Commission des droits de la personne), 2014 CAF 18, par. 64 et, au par. 65: « … ces observations sont tout aussi valables en matière des [sic] messages haineux communiqués par Internet qu'en matière de discours haineux communiqués par tout autre moyen. En outre, compte tenu de la nature extrême des discours haineux prohibés, il me paraît étonnant que d'aucuns puissent imaginer que ceux qui tiennent de tels discours soient susceptibles d'être ouverts à un échange éducatif d'idées » ; Ross c Conseil scolaire du district n° 15 du Nouveau-Brunswick, [1996] 1 RCS 825, 877 et 878.

[30] Ward c Québec (Commission des droits de la personne et des droits de la jeunesse), 2021 CSC 43, par. 73; Lemire c Canada (Commission des droits de la personne), 2014 CAF 18, par. 26; [2015] 2 RCF 117; Saskatchewan (Human Rights Commission) c Whatcott, 2013 CSC 11, par. 56.

[31] Rainville 2019, p. 32 et, à la p. 62: « Autant la Cour suprême se satisfait de la création d'un risque de préjudice en raison de la diffusion des propos, *autant il n'appartient pas à la communauté visée de le définir*» [référence omise; italique dans l'original].

[32] L'article 319 (2) C.cr. voit ainsi sa validité reconnue dans l'arrêt R. c Keegstra, [1990] 3 R.C.S. 697.

[33] Est ainsi déclaré constitutionnel le par. 13(1) de la Loi canadienne sur les droits de la personne, S.C. 1976-1977, ch. 33: Canada (Commission des droits de la personne) c Taylor, [1990] 3 R.C.S. 892.

[34] Cet amendement survint par l'adjonction de l'article 13 (2): Lemire c Canada (Commission des droits de la personne), 2014 CAF 18, par. 20; [2015] 2 RCF 117.

étendu à l'emploi de l'internet[35]: loin de désavouer pareil élargissement, la cour d'appel souligne qu'une prohibition « qui ne viserait pas un moyen de communication aussi largement utilisé et puissant qu'Internet serait une démarche qui friserait la futilité »[36]. Que le législateur fédéral se soit finalement décidé à abroger la disposition en cause, savoir l'article 13 de la *Loi canadienne sur les droits de la personne*, n'altère en rien les conclusions tirées par la jurisprudence quant à l'ampleur des restrictions à la liberté d'expression ou de religion qui se révèle justifiable sur le plan constitutionnel.

La seconde entorse aux droits constitutionnels du locuteur incendiaire porte sur *l'abandon de l'exigence de la mens rea.* Des distinctions s'imposent. En droit criminel canadien, l'infraction de fomentation volontaire de la haine suppose un état d'esprit résolument blâmable. Soit que l'intéressé entende fomenter véritablement la haine, soit qu'il constate que ce résultat surviendra certainement ou quasi certainement en raison de ses propos. Cette prise de conscience est indispensable à sa condamnation ; l'intensité de la faute subjective ainsi recherchée aura d'ailleurs contribué au constat de validité constitutionnelle de l'article 319 (2) C.cr.[37].

En revanche, pareille faute subjective est évacuée en présence d'une loi, fédérale ou provinciale, consacrée à la défense des droits fondamentaux. Deux raisons ont trait à la mise à l'écart de la faute subjective. D'une part, aucune condamnation n'est prononcée et les stigmates sont donc infiniment moindres qu'en matière pénale[38]. D'autre part, l'efficacité de la lutte contre la discrimination systémique commande, de l'avis de la Cour suprême du Canada, l'occultation de l'intention du locuteur. Si cette prise de position a pu faire l'objet de critiques et aura apparemment contribué à convaincre le Parlement canadien d'abroger l'article 13 de la *Loi canadienne sur les droits de la personne*[39], il n'empêche que la présence d'un état d'esprit coupable n'est point requise en dehors de la sphère du droit criminel. La liberté d'expression du locuteur est ainsi entaillée de manière accrue sans que, constitutionnellement parlant, il y ait à redire:

> L'accent mis sur les effets, et non sur l'intention, s'explique facilement si l'on tient compte du fait que la discrimination systémique est beaucoup plus répandue dans notre société que la discrimination intentionnelle. Inclure dans des dispositions relatives aux droits de la personne l'exigence subjective de l'intention, au lieu de permettre aux tribunaux de porter uniquement

---

[35] Lemire c Canada (Commission des droits de la personne), 2014 CAF 18, [2015] 2 RCF 117.

[36] Lemire c Canada (Commission des droits de la personne), 2014 CAF 18, par. 61; [2015] 2 RCF 117 et, de manière apparentée, Dion c R., 2020 QCCS 3049, par. 5 (requête pour permission d'en appeler rejetée: Dion c R, 2020 QCCA 1658). Aux par. 57 et 68, l'arrêt Lemire se propose de relativiser l'argument connexe voulant que les fournisseurs d'accès internet puissent être amenés à retirer de manière indue certains messages offensants afin de s'éviter une publicité négative.

[37] Canada (Commission des droits de la personne) c Taylor, [1990] 3 R.C.S. 892, 931. Ce sujet est fouillé dans la partie du présent rapport consacrée à la question 5.7.

[38] Canada (Commission des droits de la personne) c Taylor, [1990] 3 R.C.S. 892, 932 à 936.

[39] L'abrogation de l'article 13 de la Loi canadienne sur les droits de la personne entra en vigueur une année après la sanction royale de la Loi modifiant la Loi canadienne sur les droits de la personne (protection des libertés), L.C. 2013, ch. 37, art. 2 et 6: Lemire c Canada (Commission des droits de la personne), 2014 CAF 18, par. 9; [2015] 2 RCF 117.

> leur attention sur les effets, ferait donc échec à l'un des principaux objectifs des lois interdisant la discrimination. ... l'objectif important visé par le législateur par le par. 13(1) ne peut être atteint que si l'intention n'est pas prise en compte. En conséquence, l'exigence de l'atteinte minimale, dans le cadre du critère de proportionnalité selon l'arrêt *Oakes*, est respectée.[40]

Un constat s'impose de manière inéluctable: l'analyse constitutionnelle est façonnée de façon à favoriser la lutte envers la discrimination systémique. La jurisprudence subséquente n'y déroge pas[41]. La Cour suprême du Canada prend d'ailleurs soin de récuser la thèse voulant que la suppression de paroles répréhensibles succombe à l'élitisme:

> M. Whatcott fait valoir que les commissions des droits de la personne ne devraient pas pousser leur analyse des propos au point où... « des citoyens moins avisés ne pourraient participer au débat public sur la moralité et l'éducation du public sans craindre pour autant d'être poursuivis » ... M. Whatcott plaide que la liberté d'expression « n'a pas pour effet de permettre seulement aux élites qui ont de la facilité à s'exprimer de participer à des débats publics » ... Avec égards, la définition du terme « haine » n'exige pas que l'écrit ou le discours soit savant, rationnel, objectif ou inoffensif. Elle n'établit aucune distinction entre les personnes qui savent lire et écrire ou s'exprimer et les autres personnes. Peu importe que l'auteur de propos haineux soit sincère dans ses convictions, ou qu'il ne soit pas suffisamment averti pour se rendre compte de l'existence d'interdictions comme celles prévues à l'al. 14(1)(b) du *Code*, le but de l'interdiction demeure la protection des groupes vulnérables. Lorsque, objectivement, des propos répondent à la définition de la haine, l'al. 14(1)(b) s'applique. Toutefois, le recours à la médiation devrait permettre de réparer les violations par inadvertance, de sorte que les publications qui ne renferment pas de propos haineux se poursuivent.[42]

Une troisième atteinte aux droits constitutionnels s'entend de l'avis de la Cour suprême du Canada. En sus de la limitation apportée à la liberté d'expression, la haute juridiction valide une *atteinte – certes mesurée – à la présomption d'innocence* en matière criminelle. L'article 319 (3) a) C.cr. exige de l'accusé qu'il établisse, s'il le peut, la véracité de ses dires afin de se soustraire à une condamnation. Non sans raison, la Cour suprême du Canada ne s'oppose point à ce renversement de la charge de la preuve à cause de l'état d'esprit blâmable déjà nécessaire à une déclaration de culpabilité: l'emploi d'affirmations véridiques dans le but de favoriser la haine ne se justifie pas au regard de la Charte canadienne[43]. Partant, la faveur accordée par le

---

[40] Canada (Commission des droits de la personne) c Taylor, [1990] 3 R.C.S. 892, 931 et 932.

[41] Saskatchewan (Human Rights Commission) c Whatcott, 2013 CSC 11, par. 58 et 59: « ... il n'est pas pertinent de se demander si l'auteur des propos avait l'intention d'inciter à la haine, à la discrimination ou à une autre conduite préjudiciable à l'égard du groupe protégé. Ce qu'il faut déterminer, ce sont les effets qu'auront probablement les propos sur l'audience, compte tenu des objectifs législatifs visant à réduire ou à éliminer la discrimination. ... lorsque le mot « haine » est employé dans une loi sur les droits de la personne pour interdire certains propos, il fau[t] l'appliquer de façon objective pour déterminer si une personne raisonnable, informée du contexte et des circonstances, estimerait que les propos sont susceptibles d'exposer autrui à la détestation et à la diffamation pour un motif de discrimination illicite ». Voir également les par 126 et 127 du même arrêt.

[42] Saskatchewan (Human Rights Commission) c Whatcott, 2013 CSC 11, par. 144.

[43] R c Keegstra, [1990] 3 RCS 697, 781 et 782 (cf. aussi les p. 791 et s.). Voir encore R. c Keegstra, [1996] 1 R.C.S. 458.

législateur au nom de l'intérêt pour la vérité peut assurément s'accompagner d'un renversement de la charge de preuve sur l'inculpé.

La jurisprudence franchit un pas supplémentaire de taille dans le cadre des lois afférentes aux droits de la personne. *Aucune défense de véracité* des dires n'est généralement prévue: la Cour suprême se déclare disposée à tolérer cette *atteinte supplémentaire à la liberté d'expression*[44]. À vrai dire, l'atteinte est alors double: le locuteur peut voir ses propos bannis lors même qu'il ne prévoyait aucunement favoriser l'incitation à la haine et il ne peut exciper d'une quelconque défense de véracité de ses affirmations.

L'analyse retenue par les tribunaux s'accompagne d'une contrepartie. Les droits constitutionnels ainsi que les valeurs fondamentales identifiés à l'appui du bannissement des propos délimitent et enserrent d'autant la marge d'action du législateur.

Trois propositions peuvent être formulées: elles constituent autant de freins à l'essor prohibitif.

1. Le droit à l'égalité des groupes vulnérables et la liberté d'expression du contempteur doivent faire l'objet d'un arbitrage et favoriser la recherche d'un point d'équilibre.
2. L'accent mis sur l'interdit de la discrimination fait en sorte que des propos outranciers dépourvus d'effet discriminatoire probable ne sauraient être censurés.
3. Si elle sert de fondement à la liberté d'expression et de clef de voûte au soutien de nombreux droits fondamentaux, la notion de « dignité de la personne » ne constitue normalement pas un motif autonome de bâillonnement du discours. Cette proposition ne souffre que d'une exception à la portée fort limitée.

Chacune de ces propositions fait l'objet des développements suivants:

(i) Les limites inhérentes à la notion d'égalité

Le droit à l'égalité des membres de la communauté ciblée par des propos désavouables sert de frein à la liberté d'expression (et, le cas échéant, à la liberté de religion) du locuteur qui use de paroles de nature à emporter des effets discriminatoires.

Voilà qui ne revient pourtant pas à dire qu'un citoyen se voit interdire de remettre en cause les droits accordés à certains groupes. La constitution canadienne ne défend pas les prises de position à connotation politique défavorables à certains segments de la société. Les garanties constitutionnelles n'ont pas vocation à supprimer l'expression de nature politique, si ce n'est sa déclinaison la plus extrême. En somme, les tribunaux conviennent d'un point d'équilibre entre le droit à l'égalité de groupes vulnérables et le droit à la liberté d'expression. L'exposition à la haine sert de seuil infranchissable à partir duquel la liberté d'expression cède opportunément le pas:

[44] Canada (Commission des droits de la personne) c Taylor, [1990] 3 R.C.S. 892, 934 à 936 et, à sa suite, Saskatchewan (Human Rights Commission) c Whatcott, 2013 CSC 11, par. 136 et s. ainsi que le par. 190. Voir pareillement Lemire c Canada (Commission des droits de la personne), 2014 CAF 18, par. 67; [2015] 2 RCF 117.

> L'interdiction frappant les propos haineux suppose la recherche d'un équilibre entre la liberté d'expression et les droits à l'égalité. Les gens sont libres de débattre des droits ou des caractéristiques des groupes vulnérables ou de les dénoncer, mais ils ne doivent pas le faire d'une façon qui est objectivement perçue comme exposant un groupe vulnérable à la haine et aux conséquences préjudiciables de la haine. Les seuls écrits et discours qui devraient être exclus par application de l'interdiction sont ceux qui, selon ce que le juge en chef Dickson a reconnu dans l'arrêt *Keegstra*, « s'écart[ent] beaucoup de l'esprit même de l'al. 2*b)* [de la *Charte*] »[45]

Cette ligne de partage prend la forme que voici:

> Les polémistes peuvent toujours prendre part au débat sur des sujets controversés que l'on peut qualifier de « moraux » ou de « politiques ». Mais il ne faut pas sous-estimer le poids des mots. Dans le contexte de la présente affaire, M. Whatcott peut exprimer sa désapprobation des comportements homosexuels et sa conviction que ce sujet ne devrait pas être abordé dans les programmes de l'école ou de l'université. L'alinéa 14(1)(b) interdit uniquement, lorsqu'on exprime ses idées, le recours à des propos qui incitent à la haine contre les homosexuels. Ainsi que l'a déclaré le juge Alito, dissident dans l'arrêt *Snyder c. Phelps*, 131 S. Ct. 1207 (2011), p. 1227:
>
> [TRADUCTION] … je ne comprends pas pourquoi des propos qui sont matière à procès devraient être jugés acceptables du simple fait qu'on les a intercalés dans des propos qui, eux, sont protégés.[46]

La Cour suprême du Canada ne renonce pas pour autant à une analyse empreinte de circonspection. La nature politique ou morale du discours ne peut donner libre cours à l'exclusion. Accroître inconsidérément la liberté d'expression des uns n'est point envisageable, si cela revient à museler l'expression des autres et à leur réserver des conséquences néfastes:

> Les lois interdisant les propos haineux visent à restreindre le recours à certains propos qui exposeront probablement des groupes protégés à la haine et à ses conséquences préjudiciables. Les écrits et les discours visés par les lois sur les propos haineux sont, de par leur nature même, extrêmes. Formuler ces propos dans un contexte « moral » ou dans le cadre d'un « débat d'intérêt public » n'a pas pour effet de neutraliser leurs conséquences préjudiciables. Certes, si l'on comprend que l'une des conséquences du discours haineux est de restreindre la capacité des personnes qu'il vise de participer au débat, le fait d'assouplir la norme dans le contexte d'un débat politique entrave sans doute encore plus la liberté d'expression. Ainsi que certains intervenants l'ont fait valoir, l'histoire nous enseigne que certains des discours haineux les plus dommageables sont des discours « moraux », « politiques » ou d'« intérêt public ».[47]

Ainsi s'opère l'équilibre entre la liberté d'expression du locuteur et le droit à l'égalité du groupe pris à parti. La recherche de ce même équilibre s'observe entre la

---

[45] Saskatchewan (Human Rights Commission) c Whatcott, 2013 CSC 11, par. 145.

[46] Saskatchewan (Human Rights Commission) c Whatcott, 2013 CSC 11, par. 119 (cf. au même effet le par. 163).

[47] Saskatchewan (Human Rights Commission) c Whatcott, 2013 CSC 11, par. 116. Voir pareillement Lemire c Canada (Commission des droits de la personne), 2014 CAF 18, par. 66; [2015] 2 RCF 117: « Bien que l'expression d'opinions politiques soit au cœur de la protection assurée par l'alinéa 2b), le discours haineux n'a pas la voie libre du seul fait qu'il porte sur un sujet qui pourrait être considéré comme politique ou d'intérêt public. ».

liberté de croyance et de religion du prêcheur et les droits de la communauté ciblée. D'une part, accorder une importance cardinale à la liberté de religion du locuteur aurait pour effet de paralyser les droits des communautés mises en cause: « … si la sincérité d'une conviction religieuse devait empêcher automatiquement de conclure à une contravention de l'al. 14(1)(b), l'analyse fondée sur l'article premier échouerait et aucune pondération des droits concurrents ne pourrait avoir lieu. »[48]. D'autre part, l'atteinte à la liberté de religion est jugée incidente et circonscrite[49].

La ligne de démarcation est assurément d'appréhension malaisée. En témoigne l'absence d'interdit prononcée par la Cour suprême du Canada à l'encontre de deux extraits des propos de M. Whatcott de pair avec la prohibition réservée à deux autres de ses prises de parole. L'arbitrage ainsi opéré se résume comme suit:

> … il était raisonnable de conclure que deux des quatre tracts en cause dans cette affaire violaient l'al. 14(1)(b)… d'une part, ces tracts répondent à la définition de la haine, puisqu'ils s'appuient sur une source respectée — la Bible — pour légitimer des généralisations péjoratives et dépeindre les homosexuels comme des êtres inférieurs, des vecteurs de maladies, des dépendants sexuels, des pédophiles, des prédateurs qui font du prosélytisme auprès des enfants vulnérables et causent leur mort prématurée … D'autre part, ils invitent expressément les lecteurs à rejeter l'homosexualité et à soumettre les homosexuels à un traitement discriminatoire … En revanche, le juge Rothstein considère qu'il était déraisonnable de tirer la même conclusion au sujet des deux derniers tracts. Aussi offensants fussent-ils, ces tracts, considérés objectivement, ne répondaient pas à la définition de la haine … Il n'a donc pas été nécessaire de déterminer s'ils étaient susceptibles de mener au traitement discriminatoire des homosexuels.[50]

(ii) Les limites inhérentes à la notion de dignité de la personne

Si elle sert de fondement à la liberté d'expression et de clef de voûte au soutien de nombreux droits fondamentaux, la notion de « dignité de la personne » ne constitue normalement pas un motif autonome de bâillonnement du discours. Cette proposition ne souffre que d'une exception à la portée fort limitée. Si ce principe se dégage de la jurisprudence canadienne la plus récente, il convient d'en éclairer les jalons et les tensions.

La notion de la dignité de l'être humain fut assurément claironnée dans les toutes premières décisions de la Cour suprême destinées à valider l'interdit des propos haineux du point de vue constitutionnel. L'humiliation ressentie fut mise en exergue tout comme l'atteinte à la dignité:

> À mon avis, il est normal qu'un individu visé par une propagande haineuse se sente humilié et avili. En effet, le sentiment de dignité humaine et d'appartenance à l'ensemble de la collectivité est étroitement lié à l'intérêt et au respect témoignés à l'égard des groupes

[48] Saskatchewan (Human Rights Commission) c Whatcott, 2013 CSC 11, par. 142.

[49] Voir les explications fournies au par. 163 de l'affaire Saskatchewan (Human Rights Commission) c Whatcott, 2013 CSC 11, tout comme Ross c Conseil scolaire du district n° 15 du Nouveau-Brunswick, [1996]1 RCS 825, 883 à 885.

[50] Ward c Québec (Commission des droits de la personne et des droits de la jeunesse), 2021 CSC 43, par. 76, au sujet de l'affaire Saskatchewan (Human Rights Commission) c Whatcott, 2013 CSC 11.

auxquels appartient l'individu (voir I. Berlin, "Deux conceptions de la liberté", dans *Éloge de la liberté* (1988), 167, aux pp. 202 et 203). La dérision, l'hostilité et les injures encouragées par la propagande haineuse ont en conséquence un profond effet négatif sur l'estime de soi et sur le sentiment d'être accepté. Cet effet peut amener les membres du groupe cible à des réactions extrêmes, à éviter peut-être les activités qui les mettent en contact avec des personnes n'appartenant pas à ce groupe ou à adopter des attitudes et des comportements qui leur permettront de se confondre avec la majorité. Ces conséquences sont graves dans une nation dont la fierté est d'être tolérante et de favoriser la dignité humaine, notamment en respectant les nombreux groupes raciaux, religieux et culturels de notre société.[51]

L'accent ainsi mis sur l'estime de soi et la mise en berne de la dignité des êtres humains ne va pourtant pas sans de nombreux aléas et tempéraments:

> Intercéder en faveur de la dignité en pareil contexte est chose malaisée. Le dualisme juridique de la « dignité humaine » accentue l'ambivalence de ce concept et l'ambiguïté de son rôle. La dignité de la race humaine peut privilégier le libre discours autant qu'elle peut en favoriser le musellement : « ... la dignité humaine possède autant la faculté de défendre que de condamner un exercice poussé de la liberté d'expression, selon qu'elle est envisagée davantage en tant que fondement de la liberté d'expression ... ou en tant que fondement du droit à l'égalité ... »[52]. S'ajoutent les indiscutables difficultés d'application de la notion de dignité humaine « [d] ès qu'elle quitte le domaine des valeurs pour entrer dans celui des normes juridiques ... »[53,54].

Il est fort difficile de s'affranchir des écueils propres à la notion de dignité. La prohibition de propos au *seul motif* de leur caractère attentatoire à la dignité d'autrui est semée d'embûches: « Force est de souligner l'imprévisibilité de cet étalon de mesure[55]; force est aussi de relater sa compatibilité discutable avec le principe de la légalité lequel prise peu ou prou l'incertitude propre aux notions polysémiques ou équivoques. »[56]. Ces aléas nombreux auront incité la Cour suprême du Canada à se retrancher, dans sa jurisprudence la plus récente, derrière une conception strictement élémentaire de la dignité humaine.

Autant la Cour suprême convient de la constitutionnalité des lois pénales, administratives ou civiles prohibant le discours haineux, autant elle tient pour invalide

---

[51] R. c Keegstra, [1990] 3 RCS 697, 746. Voir pareillement les p. 754, 769, 791 et, à la p. 764: « La propagande haineuse a précisément cet effet en préconisant une société qui subvertirait le processus démocratique et priverait des individus du respect et de la dignité en raison de leurs caractéristiques raciales ou religieuses. Cette sorte d'activité expressive est donc tout à fait incompatible avec les aspirations démocratiques inhérentes à la garantie de la liberté d'expression »; Canada (Commission des droits de la personne) c Taylor, [1990] 3 R.C.S. 892, 919, 920 et, à la p. 927: « À mon avis, il n'y a aucune incompatibilité entre le fait de donner au par. 13(1) une interprétation qui le rend efficace et la protection de la liberté d'expression garantie par l'al. 2b), pourvu que l'interprétation des mots "haine" et "mépris" repose sur la pleine conscience que l'objectif du Parlement est de protéger l'égalité et la dignité de tous les individus par la réduction des manifestations de l'expression préjudiciable» .

[52] Thériault 2020, p. 69.

[53] Ward c Québec (Commission des droits de la personne et des droits de la jeunesse), 2021 CSC 43, par. 48.

[54] Ce paragraphe est extrait de Rainville 2024.

[55] Thériault 2020, pp. 12, 52 à 63 et 84.

[56] Rainville 2024.

une loi qui élargit le champ de l'interdit au point d'englober la diffusion publique de propos qui « ridiculisent », « rabaissent » ou « portent par ailleurs atteinte à la dignité » d'un groupe minoritaire[57]. Ainsi s'en explique la Cour suprême dans un arrêt unanime :

> Ces termes ne sont pas des synonymes de « haine » ou de « mépris ». Ils renvoient plutôt à des propos dénigrants et insensibles qui, par exemple, critiquent ou ridiculisent des groupes protégés en raison de leurs caractéristiques et pratiques communes, ou de stéréotypes. Ainsi que le juge Richards l'a fait observer dans *Owens (C.A.)* [...]:
>
> Bien des propos protégés de toute évidence par la Constitution exposent dans une certaine mesure au ridicule, rabaissent ou portent atteinte à la dignité pour des motifs fondés sur la race, la religion et autres. J'ai à l'esprit, par exemple, la caricature qui ridiculise des personnes originaires d'un pays en particulier, l'article de magazine qui critique le programme des politiques sociales d'un groupe religieux, et ainsi de suite. Dans le cadre d'une démocratie saine et solide, la liberté d'expression doit faire place à ce type de discours...
>
> Je suis du même avis. Les formes d'expression qui critiquent et cultivent l'humour au détriment d'autres personnes peuvent être dénigrantes au point de devenir répugnantes. Les représentations qui rabaissent un groupe minoritaire ou qui portent atteinte à sa dignité par des blagues, des railleries ou des injures peuvent être blessantes. Toutefois [...] les idées offensantes ne suffisent pas pour justifier une atteinte à la liberté d'expression. Ces formes d'expression peuvent inspirer des sentiments de dédain et de supériorité, mais elles n'exposent pas le groupe ciblé à la haine.[58]

Partant, il n'existe pas de lien rationnel entre la suppression des mots en public qui ridiculisent, rabaissent ou portent par ailleurs atteinte à la dignité d'un groupe protégé et la lutte contre la discrimination systémique dirigée contre les groupes protégés.[59] Ce vice s'avère fatal à la constitutionnalité de la prohibition. La gravité des paroles reprochées se mesure à l'aune de leurs répercussions probables sur la collectivité d'individus ciblée. Seuls des mots de nature à induire probablement une attitude discriminatoire à l'égard d'une collectivité peuvent valider l'interdit.[60] L'objectivisation du préjudice appréhendé emporte une conséquence cardinale: le droit se désintéresse de l'avis des membres de la communauté visée ou de celui de ses porte-parole:

> Partant, les émotions et réactions des membres du groupe ... visé par les paroles litigieuses demeurent sans incidence... À elle seule, la vexation éprouvée par la cible des propos ne suffit pas à fonder leur interdit: la question est plutôt de savoir quel effet auront les affirmations reprochées sur les personnes qui ne font *pas partie* du groupe visé. Il convient donc de vérifier si les propos prononcés sont propices à la ségrégation ... Pareilles balises axées sur la vraisemblance de l'effet nuisible des paroles sur le statut social des victimes évacuent d'autant la réaction émotive de la victime qui ne sert plus de vecteur pour la détermination

---

[57] La disposition ainsi invalidée partiellement est l'alinéa 14(1)(b)du Saskatchewan Human Rights Code, S.S. 1979, ch. S-24.1.

[58] Saskatchewan (Human Rights Commission) c Whatcott, 2013 CSC 11, par. 89 et 90. Voir pareillement Hudspeth c Whatcott, 2017 ONSC 1708.

[59] Saskatchewan (Human Rights Commission) c Whatcott, 2013 CSC 11, par. 92.

[60] Saskatchewan (Human Rights Commission) c Whatcott, 2013 CSC 11, par. 48, 52, 54, 58, 116 et 129 à 135. Les mêmes enseignements sont repris par les juges majoritaires dans l'arrêt Ward c Québec (Commission des droits de la personne et des droits de la jeunesse), 2021 CSC 43.

des paroles interdites. Son intolérance propre au sujet des propos formulés ... demeure sans effet sur l'action du droit ...

Autant la Cour suprême se satisfait de la création d'un *risque de préjudice* en raison de la diffusion des propos, autant *il n'appartient pas à la communauté visée de le définir*. Cette volonté d'objectivisation n'est pas entièrement inédite. Si la Cour suprême du Canada la consacre en 2013 dans l'arrêt *Whatcott*, ce critère destiné à dépouiller d'importance l'opinion de la collectivité outragée se niche dans quelques écrits doctrinaux antérieurs à cette décision.[61]

La communauté ciblée ne saurait être érigée en interprète de la notion de dignité laquelle est d'ailleurs ramenée à sa signification la plus congrue. De telles bornes sont salutaires à plusieurs titres[62].

Les enseignements dégagés dans l'affaire *Whatcott* seront repris et approfondis dans la décision majoritaire de la Cour suprême du Canada prononcée en 2021 dans l'arrêt *Ward*. Appelés à se prononcer sur la légalité des numéros d'un humoriste raillant régulièrement le handicap physique d'un très jeune chanteur, les juges majoritaires estiment que l'article 4 de la *Charte québécoise des droits et libertés* « ne permet pas à une personne de réclamer le respect, mais uniquement la *sauvegarde* de sa dignité, c'est-à-dire la protection contre la négation de sa valeur en tant qu'être humain. ».[63] Pareille conception de la dignité élève singulièrement le degré de gravité nécessaire à la sanction d'un propos dérogatoire. L'universalisme de la notion de dignité l'emporte au détriment d'une notion de la dignité fondée sur le respect escompté par un individu ou sa communauté. L'arrêt *Ward* formule ainsi le préjudice social seul à même de fonder l'interdit:

En somme, la Cour [dans l'arrêt *Whatcott*] limite la prohibition ... aux propos qui peuvent inspirer des sentiments extrêmes de détestation de nature à compromettre l'acceptation du groupe vulnérable au sein de la société et qui, par ailleurs, possèdent une force mobilisatrice suffisante pour mener au genre de traitement discriminatoire que le législateur vise à enrayer. La Cour refuse de limiter la liberté d'expression pour conférer une protection contre les préjudices émotionnels. Le professeur Rainville résume avec justesse la nature du préjudice social qui justifiait d'imposer des limites à la liberté d'expression dans l'arrêt *Whatcott*:

Le droit canadien s'assure de la protection du *statut social de la victime* tout en délaissant la protection de sa *sérénité émotive*. Les paroles offensantes sont tolérées, tandis que sont interdits les propos de nature à engendrer la discrimination, l'ostracisme ou la violence à l'égard des [personnes].

Le mal susceptible de fonder en l'occurrence une entorse à la liberté d'expression présente donc deux caractéristiques: le préjudice appréhendé se veut de nature collective et sociale ...

Le préjudice interdit est donc social et non point moral, collectif et non pas individuel. [En italique dans l'original.] (*La répression de l'art et l'art de la répression: La profanation de la religion à l'épreuve des mutations du droit pénal au sujet du blasphème et de la protection des identités religieuses* (2019), p. 61)[64]

---

[61] Rainville 2019, p. 62 [références omises].

[62] Ibid., p. 63 et s.

[63] Ward c Québec (Commission des droits de la personne et des droits de la jeunesse), 2021 CSC 43, par. 58.

[64] Ward c Québec (Commission des droits de la personne et des droits de la jeunesse), 2021 CSC 43, par. 77.

Les juges majoritaires désavouent par le fait même le critère retenu par la Cour d'appel du Québec dans l'arrêt *Calego International inc*[65]. Il convient de reprendre ce critère de même que les motifs du désaveu formulé par les juges majoritaires de la Cour suprême du Canada:

> Dans l'arrêt *Calego*, ... le juge Morissette propose de résoudre ainsi le conflit entre la dignité et la liberté d'expression:
>
> ... un critère objectif doit d'abord nous guider dans l'interprétation de l'article 4. La pierre de touche des notions de dignité et d'honneur est une norme abstraite. Il s'agit de la perception d'une personne raisonnable qui, visée comme ici par une remarque à teneur discriminatoire, tempère sa réaction parce qu'elle est habituée aux us et coutumes d'une société pluraliste où l'on valorise la liberté d'expression et où l'on admet certains excès de langage dans l'exercice de cet autre droit fondamental. En d'autres termes, on tolère ici une liberté de ton qui n'est pas la norme partout ailleurs. Cette considération doit figurer dans l'analyse des notions de dignité et d'honneur. Aussi, avant de s'estimer atteinte dans son « droit *à la sauvegarde* de sa dignité [ou] de son honneur » d'une manière qui contrevient à l'article 10 de la *CDLP*, la personne raisonnable devra avoir essuyé un affront particulièrement méprisant envers son identité raciale, ethnique ou autre, et lourd de conséquences pour elle. Enfin, en ces matières, on devrait toujours garder présente à l'esprit la maxime *de minimis non curat lex*. [En italique dans l'original; texte entre crochets dans l'original; par. 99.]
>
> À notre avis, la perception d'une personne raisonnable ciblée par des propos identiques doit être écartée. Cette approche entraîne un glissement vers la protection d'un droit de ne pas être offensé, lequel n'a pas sa place dans une société démocratique (Dworkin (2009), p. viii; voir aussi *Whatcott*, par. 50 et 90). Le test applicable ne doit être axé ni sur le caractère répugnant ou offensant des propos, ni sur le préjudice émotionnel causé à cette personne. Autrement, cela reviendrait à censurer des propos en raison de leur contenu ou de leur effet sur une personne, indépendamment de leurs effets discriminatoires. Pareille approche a été rejetée par notre Cour (*Whatcott*, par. 50-51, 58 et 82).[66]

Le sort qu'il sied de réserver au critère formulé dans l'arrêt *Calego international inc.* oppose juges majoritaires et dissidents au sein de la Cour suprême. Les juges minoritaires épousent le seuil d'intervention fixé dans l'affaire *Calego international inc.* tout en convoquant, dans le cadre de leur argumentaire destiné à réprouver les paroles prononcées par l'humoriste lors de ses spectacles, les conventions internationales prescrivant les droits de l'enfance, l'interdiction de la violence morale et la nécessaire dignité des conditions réservées aux enfants handicapés.[67] À l'inverse, la position de la majorité se contente de bannir les seuls propos de nature à générer des effets réellement discriminatoires. La nature du préjudice combattu se trouve d'autant délimitée:

> Aussi le « préjudice émotionnel » est-il évacué des considérations de nature à valider l'interdit langagier[68]. L'insuffisance du préjudice émotionnel tient à un défaut consubstantiel: l'affront

[65] Calego International inc. c Commission des droits de la personne et des droits de la jeunesse, 2013 QCCA 924.

[66] Ward c Québec (Commission des droits de la personne et des droits de la jeunesse), 2021 CSC 43, par. 81 et 82.

[67] Les juges minoritaires citent la Convention relative aux droits de l'enfant, R.T. Can. 1992 n° 3 tout comme la Convention relative aux droits des personnes handicapées, R.T. Can. 2010 n° 8.

[68] Ward c Québec (Commission des droits de la personne et des droits de la jeunesse), 2021 CSC 43, par. 74, 77, 82, 86 et 107.

> ressenti par des propos blessants ne participe pas de la nature du mal que cherchent à combattre les lois destinées à endiguer la discrimination. En somme, il n'existe pas de lien rationnel entre « la protection des émotions d'un membre déterminé d'un groupe » et « l'objectif général de réduire la discrimination » à l'égard du groupe.[69] L'indignation ne saurait aspirer à réparation pour une seconde raison dirimante: « [...] la protection d'un droit de ne pas être offensé [...] n'a pas sa place dans une société démocratique ».[70]
>
> Ainsi conçue, la dignité « n'a pas pour horizon la protection d'une personne particulière, ni même d'une catégorie de personnes, mais de l'humanité en général »[71]. Le préjudice individuel est abandonné au profit d'un préjudice proprement social.[72]

L'accent mis sur l'interdit de la discrimination fait en sorte que des propos outranciers dépourvus d'effet discriminatoire probable ne sauraient être censurés. Le positionnement actuel de la Cour suprême oblige à jeter un nouveau regard sur la motivation retenue auparavant dans la jurisprudence au sujet de l'interdit langagier. Naguère invoquée par la Cour suprême elle-même[73], *l'indignation* de la personne outrée par les propos prononcés ne semble plus faire partie des motifs de nature à valider une limitation à la liberté d'expression[74]. Pareillement mise de l'avant dans les premières décisions rendues, *la perte d'estime de soi* en raison de propos vexatoires ne semble plus figurer au rang des justifications suffisantes à l'entrave de la liberté d'expression.[75] Autant le droit constitutionnel canadien autorise la suppression des propos favorisant l'éclosion de la haine, autant les garanties de la *Charte canadienne* ne sauraient tolérer un interdit dont la portée s'étend à des propos suscitant des réactions d'une intensité moindre, comme le ridicule et l'indignation.

---

[69] Ward c Québec (Commission des droits de la personne et des droits de la jeunesse), 2021 CSC 43, par. 74, reprenant à son compte les motifs de l'arrêt Saskatchewan (Human Rights Commission) c Whatcott, 2013 CSC 11.

[70] Ward c Québec (Commission des droits de la personne et des droits de la jeunesse), 2021 CSC 43, par. 82.

[71] La Cour suprême fait sien l'énoncé de principe formulé par la professeure Fabre-Magnan: Ward c Québec (Commission des droits de la personne et des droits de la jeunesse), 2021 CSC 43, par. 57.

[72] Ces deux paragraphes sont tirés de Rainville 2024.

[73] Canada (Commission des droits de la personne) c Taylor, [1990] 3 R.C.S. 892, 918.

[74] Pareil raisonnement rend, par la force des choses, quasi inenvisageable de proscrire des paroles ou des gestes blasphématoires. Sur le principe et les rares tempéraments possibles en la matière, cf. Rainville 2019.

[75] Il suffit d'opposer les motivations retenues dans les affaires Canada (Commission des droits de la personne) c Taylor, [1990] 3 R.C.S. 892, 918, Lemire c Canada (Commission des droits de la personne), 2014 CAF 18, par. 85 (la Cour d'appel fédérale valide l'octroi de dommages et intérêts « au titre du dommage présumé avoir été causé à leur « sentiment de dignité humaine et d'appartenance à l'ensemble de la collectivité ») et Ward c Québec (Commission des droits de la personne et des droits de la jeunesse), 2021 CSC 43. Voir encore Saskatchewan (Human Rights Commission) c Whatcott, 2013 CSC 11, par. 47: « Preventive measures should only prohibit the type of expression expected to cause the harm targeted. Since the decision in Taylor, courts have confirmed that the "harm" these legislative prohibitions seek to prevent is more than hurt feelings, humiliation or offensiveness...».

Voilà qui ne revient pas pour autant à écarter intégralement toute vocation propre à la notion de dignité de la personne. S'il est vrai que l'arrêt *Whatcott* juge inconstitutionnel l'interdit de représentations publiques au seul motif qu'elles ridiculisent ou portent autrement atteinte à la dignité des membres d'un groupe protégé, les juges majoritaires conviennent que l'acception traditionnelle du mot « haine » ne suffit pas à enrayer l'ensemble des propos pouvant vraisemblablement être porteurs d'effets discriminatoires. Aussi préconisent-ils un très léger élargissement de la sphère de l'interdit au moyen de la législation civile axée sur la protection des droits fondamentaux.

L'arrêt *Whatcott* donnait, il est vrai, à la haine une acception très limitée: les termes « haine » et « mépris » « ne s'entendent que des manifestations extrêmes de l'émotion à laquelle renvoient les termes « détestation » et « diffamation ».[76] L'arrêt *Ward* préfère donner une acception autonome au concept de « droit à la sauvegarde de la dignité » d'une personne prévu à l'article 4 de la *Charte québécoise des droits et libertés*.[77] L'élargissement finement ciselé par les juges majoritaires conserve comme clé de voûte la volonté d'enrayer la discrimination. La « sauvegarde de la dignité » d'une personne renvoie à la conjuration d'un péril, non pas à une simple entorse au respect de l'individu en cause.[78] La sauvegarde de la dignité d'un individu désigne, ce faisant, la « protection contre la négation de sa valeur en tant qu'être humain »:[79] cette notion fait office de « bouclier contre ce type d'atteintes qui ne font pas moins que révolter la conscience de la société ».[80] Il en résulte une protection très légèrement accrue par rapport à l'acception donnée au mot « haine » dans les décisions antérieures:

> À notre avis, les limites à la liberté d'expression se justifient aussi lorsque celle-ci sert à diffuser des propos qui, même s'ils ne répondent pas tout à fait à la définition de la haine donnée dans l'arrêt *Whatcott*, ont néanmoins pour effet de forcer certaines personnes « à défendre leur propre humanité fondamentale ou leur propre statut social avant même d'être admis[es] à participer au débat démocratique » (*Whatcott*, par. 75; voir aussi *Keegstra*, p. 765). Comme l'écrit le professeur Waldron:
>
> [TRADUCTION] [U]ne personne [doit pouvoir] se promener dans les rues sans craindre les insultes ou les humiliations, trouver des commerces et des marchés dont les portes lui seront ouvertes, et interagir en société avec l'assurance implicite qu'on ne le traitera pas en paria. [p. 220]

---

[76] Saskatchewan (Human Rights Commission) c Whatcott, 2013 CSC 11, par. 57. La Cour ajoute au même par. la précision que voici: « Ainsi, sont écartés les propos qui, bien que répugnants et offensants, n'incitent pas à l'exécration, au dénigrement et au rejet qui risquent d'emporter la discrimination et d'autres effets préjudiciables.».

[77] Charte des droits et libertés de la personne, RLRQ, c C-12.

[78] Ward c Québec (Commission des droits de la personne et des droits de la jeunesse), 2021 CSC 43, par. 58.

[79] Ward c Québec (Commission des droits de la personne et des droits de la jeunesse), 2021 CSC 43, par. 58.

[80] Ward c Québec (Commission des droits de la personne et des droits de la jeunesse), 2021 CSC 43, par. 58.

> La liberté d'expression ne bénéficierait pas à l'ensemble de la société si elle empêchait une personne ou une catégorie de personnes de participer réellement au processus politique et aux activités ordinaires de la société au même titre que n'importe qui.[81]

Le filtre analytique n'est pourtant pas dénué d'exigences multiples. La question première consiste à savoir si les propos visant un individu ou un groupe « incitent à le mépriser ou à détester son humanité pour un motif de distinction illicite ».[82] Cela ne saurait pourtant suffire. Les juges majoritaires formulent une exigence supplémentaire:

> Dans un second temps, il doit être démontré qu'une personne raisonnable considérerait que, situés dans leur contexte, les propos tenus peuvent vraisemblablement avoir pour effet de mener au traitement discriminatoire de la personne visée. Ce second critère prend en compte les objectifs visés par la *Charte québécoise* (*Whatcott*, par. 178 et 191). L'article 10 vise à supprimer la discrimination dans la *reconnaissance* et l'exercice des droits et libertés de la personne. Or, la reconnaissance d'un droit suppose « l'acceptation sociale de l'obligation générale de le respecter » (*Commission ontarienne des droits de la personne*, p. 554). La discrimination au sens de la *Charte québécoise* implique donc une différence de traitement ayant des effets sur l'acceptation sociale d'un individu. Ainsi, ne sont discriminatoires que les propos qui, situés dans leur contexte, peuvent vraisemblablement mettre en péril l'acceptation sociale de cet individu ou de ce groupe (*Whatcott*, par. 178 et 191). L'analyse n'est pas centrée sur le contenu des propos en tant que tel, mais sur leurs effets probables à l'égard des tiers, c'est-à-dire sur les traitements discriminatoires susceptibles d'en résulter (*Whatcott*, par. 54, 58 et 82).[83]

L'analyse retenue est donc à double déploiement dès lors qu'elle nécessite également la prise en compte des effets ultérieurs vraisemblables des propos reprochés. Cette analyse en deux temps, tout comme la timide prise en compte de la dignité de la personne comme motif autonome de musellement du discours, est de nature à rejaillir sur l'interprétation donnée aux autres lois provinciales ou fédérales vouées à l'élimination de la discrimination. Autant la Cour suprême du Canada convient du particularisme possible de certaines dispositions législatives consacrées aux droits fondamentaux, autant elle est portée à minimiser l'incidence des différences terminologiques:[84] « … dans la mesure où cela n'est pas incompatible avec les règles usuelles d'interprétation, la symétrie dans l'interprétation des divers instruments de protection des droits et libertés de la personne est souhaitable »[85].

Un différend profond oppose les juges majoritaires et dissidents dans l'arrêt *Ward*. Pareil désaccord ne saurait pourtant occulter l'autonomie certes mesurée concédée à la notion de sauvegarde de la dignité d'un individu appartenant à un groupe protégé.

---

[81] Ward c Québec (Commission des droits de la personne et des droits de la jeunesse), 2021 CSC 43, par. 63.

[82] Ward c Québec (Commission des droits de la personne et des droits de la jeunesse), 2021 CSC 43, par. 83 (à lire de pair avec l'illustration donnée aux par. 108 et 109).

[83] Ward c Québec (Commission des droits de la personne et des droits de la jeunesse), 2021 CSC 43, par. 84 (à lire de pair avec l'illustration donnée aux par. 110 et s.).

[84] Ward c. Québec (Commission des droits de la personne et des droits de la jeunesse), 2021 CSC 43, par. 67 à 69.

[85] Ward c. Québec (Commission des droits de la personne et des droits de la jeunesse), 2021 CSC 43, par. 68.

Pareille prise en compte distincte de la notion de « sauvegarde de la dignité de la personne », par-delà la seule haine, appelle quelques réflexions. L'élargissement retenu semble faire en sorte que l'intolérance, davantage que la seule haine, serve de vecteur. Ce léger déplacement du curseur semble plus en phase avec la notion même de discrimination:

> Reste les frasques à l'encontre du tissu social comme ultime forme de préjudice envisageable. L'atteinte a pour point de mire l'ordre social lui-même. Pareil préjudice revêt une acception collective et porte en son sein, l'intolérance comme fléau. La mise en exergue de cette troisième forme de préjudice alimente la jurisprudence la plus récente de la Cour européenne ... Elle n'est évidemment pas absente des considérations de la Cour suprême du Canada. ... l'arrêt *Ward* illustre la volonté de la haute juridiction canadienne d'entendre un rien plus libéralement le préjudice susceptible de façonner la discrimination. La Cour suprême abandonne l'incitation à la haine comme unique horizon de nature à bâillonner le discours. Elle convient d'un léger élargissement de la sphère de l'interdit de manière à ce que des propos n'aient pas pour résultante qu'un individu soit appelé à défendre sa « propre humanité fondamentale ou [son] propre statut social » avant même d'être admis à participer au débat démocratique[86]. Un discours avilissant ne doit pas avoir pour répercussion qu'une personne ne puisse vaquer « aux activités ordinaires de la société au même titre que n'importe qui. ».[87] Sans évoquer nommément « l'intolérance » dans sa décision, la Cour suprême semble pourtant disposée à écorner, certes très timidement, la liberté d'expression afin d'en combattre les manifestations écrites ou verbales. Cette concession est très mesurée. Elle se propose de contrer la mise au ban d'une personne ou d'un groupe: le préjudice endigué conserve une résonance collective même si les paroles réprouvées peuvent porter sur un seul individu.[88]

5.2 D'autres Interventions Législatives aux niveaux Fédéral, Provincial et Territorial

5.2.1 De l'incidence du Fédéralisme sur l'encadrement du Discours Haineux ou Discriminatoire

S'impose d'emblée le thème de l'influence du fédéralisme sur l'encadrement des propos haineux ou encore discriminatoires. Le Canada relevant d'une fédération, les fonctions législatives se trouvent réparties entre l'ordre de gouvernement central et les ordres de gouvernement fédérés. L'on dénombre pas moins de 15 lois ciblant directement ou indirectement l'expression de propos haineux. Cette multiplicité s'explique avant tout par la structure fédérale de l'État canadien. La protection des droits et libertés n'est pas l'apanage du Parlement canadien ni celui des provinces. À vrai dire, la protection de « la liberté en matière de droits de la personne ou dans un sens égalitaire [es]t ...assujettie ... au pouvoir fédéral ou au pouvoir provincial ou à

[86] Ward c. Québec (Commission des droits de la personne et des droits de la jeunesse), 2021 CSC 43, par. 63.
[87] Ward c. Québec (Commission des droits de la personne et des droits de la jeunesse), 2021 CSC 43, par. 63 (à lire de concert avec le par. 83).
[88] Ces deux paragraphes sont extraits de Rainville 2024.

ces deux pouvoirs en même temps, selon que les industries, entreprises ou activités concernées ou auxquelles ces libertés se rapportent, relèvent elles-mêmes du pouvoir législatif du Parlement ou de l'assemblée législative d'une province ».[89]

Le partage des compétences législatives entre les deux ordres de gouvernement a pour conséquence de limiter la portée tant matérielle que territoriale des mesures gouvernementales s'attaquant à l'expression haineuse ou encore discriminatoire. Il existe donc presque autant de lois portant sur ces questions qu'il y a d'ordres de gouvernement au Canada.

5.2.2 *La Diversité et l'éclatement des Mesures Législatives Destinées à Contrer l'éclosion de la Haine et l'essor de la Discrimination*

Exception faite du code criminel canadien lequel s'applique à l'échelle du pays, l'encadrement du discours haineux s'avère tributaire des prédilections législatives des différents ordres de gouvernement. D'une province à l'autre, la diversité des traits sous lesquels se présentent ces interdits témoigne de l'éclectisme des postures adoptées par les législateurs provinciaux et territoriaux dans leur lutte contre ces formes d'expression enfiellées. Puisque les approches retenues diffèrent, voire contrastent, il n'est pas aisé de brosser un portrait fidèle de la répression du discours haineux au Canada. Force est cependant de rappeler la vision harmonisatrice souvent prônée par la Cour suprême du Canada en la matière. Si le tribunal suprême tient assurément compte du particularisme et de l'ampleur des droits concédés par chaque juridiction, il n'en prône pas moins une interprétation destinée à gommer certaines distinctions de forme ou apparentes. Il convient de citer de nouveau l'extrait suivant d'un arrêt tout récent: « … dans la mesure où cela n'est pas incompatible avec les règles usuelles d'interprétation, la symétrie dans l'interprétation des divers instruments de protection des droits et libertés de la personne est souhaitable ».[90]

Aussi la Cour suprême a-t-elle repris dans l'affaire *Ward* relative à la notion de « sauvegarde de la dignité de la personne », les enseignements qu'elle avait formulés au sujet de l'inconstitutionnalité de l'interdit des propos publics qui ridiculisent ou portent autrement atteinte à la dignité d'un groupe protégé, interdit énoncé dan une loi de la Saskatchewan: la protection constitutionnelle accordée à la liberté d'expression n'étant pas appelée à varier d'une province à l'autre, les juges majoritaires façonnent la notion de « sauvegarde de la dignité » d'une personne de façon à faire concorder leur jurisprudence lors même que la notion de sauvegarde de la dignité de l'individu n'était point énoncée dans la loi saskatchewanaise. Le parallélisme ainsi décrété

---

[89] Tiré d'un article du professeur Bora Laskin (devenu par la suite juge en chef du Canada) intitulé « An Inquiry into the Diefenbaker Bill of Rights », (1959), 37 R. du B. can. 77, 104, cet extrait est fait sien par la Cour suprême du Canada: Scowby c Glendinning, [1986] 2 R.C.S. 226, par. 7.

[90] Ward c Québec (Commission des droits de la personne et des droits de la jeunesse), 2021 CSC 43, par. 68.

s'explique comme suit : « Le fait que le *Saskatchewan Human Rights Code* assure le respect de la dignité humaine au moyen d'une limitation de la liberté d'expression, au lieu de garantir deux droits positifs concurrents comme le fait la *Charte québécoise*, tient à une différence de moyens plutôt que de finalité.».[91] Les divergences perceptibles entre les différentes lois provinciales ou territoriales ne portent donc pas forcément à conséquence. Les critères constitutionnels afférents à la protection de la liberté d'expression, d'une part, et les exigences liées à l'efficacité de la lutte anti-discrimination, d'autre part, tendent, dans les deux cas, à favoriser une interprétation concordante des différents instruments législatifs en cause. Ce n'est pas nier pour autant leur particularisme dans certains cas de figure précis.

5.2.2.1 Le Droit Fédéral

En droit canadien, les interdits les plus sévères à l'endroit de l'expression haineuse sont le fait de la législation fédérale en matière criminelle. D'application uniforme à l'échelle du pays, le code criminel édicte trois infractions relatives à la propagande haineuse, savoir l'encouragement au génocide, l'incitation publique à la haine et la fomentation volontaire de la haine. Ces infractions feront l'objet de commentaires dans le cadre de la question 5.6. Qu'il suffise de mentionner qu'un élément de faute subjective est indispensable à une condamnation. Qu'il suffise aussi d'indiquer pour l'instant que la portée de ces trois infractions criminelles se voit délimitée par la notion de « groupe identifiable » à laquelle se rapporte chacune des conduites incriminées. Cette notion visée au paragraphe 318(4) C.cr. a fait l'objet d'élargissements législatifs successifs: elle englobe désormais « toute section du public qui se différencie des autres par la couleur, la race, la religion, l'origine nationale ou ethnique, l'âge, le sexe, l'orientation sexuelle, l'identité ou l'expression de genre ou la déficience mentale ou physique ». Il n'y a donc perpétration de l'une quelconque de ces infractions que si le groupe pris pour cible relève de cette définition.[92] Outre les inculpations de circonstance, les dispositions des articles 318 et 319 C.cr. sont complétées par les pouvoirs de saisie et de confiscation que prévoient le paragraphe 319(4) C.cr. et les articles 320 et 320.1 C.cr.

Cet arsenal répressif n'est pas seul en lice. L'on se doit d'ajouter à cette énumération l'article 718.2 a) (i) du Code criminel qui énonce, en tête de liste des circonstances aggravantes au stade de la détermination de la peine du délinquant, le fait que l'infraction ait été motivée « par des préjugés ou de la haine fondée sur des facteurs tels que la race, l'origine nationale ou ethnique, la langue, la couleur, la religion, le sexe, l'âge, la déficience mentale ou physique, l'orientation sexuelle ou l'identité ou l'expression de genre ».[93] Loin de se satisfaire d'en faire

[91] Ward c Québec (Commission des droits de la personne et des droits de la jeunesse), 2021 CSC 43, par. 69.

[92] R. c Krymowski,2005 CSC 7, par. 17.

[93] Voir notamment Ministère de la Justice du Canada, « La haine en tant que circonstance aggravante dans la détermination de la peine - Examen de la jurisprudence – de 2007 à 2020», Sa Majesté la

un pur critère d'alourdissement de la peine, il arrive que le législateur requalifie l'infraction lorsqu'elle participe d'un sentiment haineux. Par exemple, est coupable de l'infraction de méfait aggravé au sens de l'article 430 (4.1) du Code criminel, l'individu qui commet certains types de méfait « en étant motivé par des préjugés ou de la haine fondées sur la couleur, la race, la religion, l'origine nationale ou ethnique, l'âge, le sexe, l'orientation sexuelle, l'identité ou l'expression de genre ou la déficience mentale ou physique. ».

D'autres lois fédérales entrent parfois en scène. D'une part, les règlements d'application de la *Loi sur la radiodiffusion* interdisent aux radiodiffuseurs, aux télédiffuseurs de même qu'aux distributeurs de tels services de diffuser

> des propos offensants ou des images offensantes qui, pris dans leur contexte, risquent d'exposer une personne ou un groupe ou une classe de personnes à la haine ou au mépris pour des motifs fondés sur la race, l'origine nationale ou ethnique, la couleur, la religion, le sexe, l'orientation sexuelle, l'âge ou la déficience physique ou mentale.[94]

D'autre part, le *Tarif des douanes* proscrit l'importation au Canada « [d]es livres, imprimés dessins, peintures, gravures, photographies ou reproductions de tout genre qui [...] constituent de la propagande haineuse au sens du paragraphe 320(8) du *Code criminel* ».[95]

5.2.2.2 La Législation Provinciale et Territoriale

Des différences de nature opposent la législation criminelle et l'appareil législatif provincial ou territorial. D'une part, aucune mise en accusation n'intervient en temps normal[96]. D'autre part, la suppression des textes publics propices à la discrimination s'exerce, en droit provincial ou territorial, en faisant abstraction de l'intention du locuteur[97]. Nul besoin de scruter les pensées de l'auteur des propos reprochés, alors que le droit criminel s'en soucie au premier chef.[98]

Reine du chef du Canada, 2021, 2020 CanLIIDocs 3732 (en ligne); Lawrence et Verdun-Jones 2011, p. 28; Roberts et Harting 2001, p. 93; Vinet c R., 2021 QCCQ 3474, par. 119 à 123; R. c Leach, 2019 BCCA 451, par. 84 à 90; R. c Gray, 2013 ABCA 237; R. c Woodward, 2011 BCCA 251.

94 Règlement de 1987 sur la télédiffusion, DORS/87-49, art 5(1)b). Voir également Règlement sur les services facultatifs, DORS/2017-159, art 3b); Règlement de 1986 sur la radio, DORS/86-982, art 3b); Règlement sur la distribution de radiodiffusion, DORS/97-555, art 8(1)b) (adoptés en vertu de la Loi sur la radiodiffusion, LC 1991, c 11).

95 Tarif des douanes, LC 1997, c 36, art 136(1) renvoyant à l'Annexe, chapitre 98, numéro tarifaire 9899.00.00.

96 Voir la dépénalisation et le processus de médiation abordés dans l'affaire Saskatchewan (Human Rights Commission) c Whatcott, 2013 CSC 11, par. 150.

97 La Cour suprême s'en justifie au motif que la discrimination systémique est davantage répandue que la discrimination intentionnelle : Saskatchewan (Human Rights Commission) c Whatcott, 2013 CSC 11, par. 58, 126, 127, 143 et 190 et nos développements sur le sujet dans la partie précédente du présent rapport.

98 L'intensité de la faute morale recherchée en droit criminel est abordée dans la question 5.7 du présent rapport.

Cette précision faite, il convient d'énoncer les tendances de la législation en la matière avant d'en dessiner certains traits singuliers. À l'exception notable du Yukon, toutes les provinces et tous les territoires canadiens ont adopté une loi interdisant l'expression de propos discriminatoires, voire de propos haineux, à l'endroit de groupes protégés en vertu de motifs de distinction déclarés illicites. Comme l'a souligné le professeur Luke McNamara dans une minutieuse étude des lois provinciales encadrant le discours haineux publiée 2004, ces dernières peuvent être classées en deux catégories principales, soit les lois (plus nombreuses) s'attaquant exclusivement aux représentations discriminatoires et celles (plus rares) étendant leur emprise aux représentations haineuses.[99]. Cette taxonomie a le mérite de mettre en lumière la principale ligne de fracture traversant la masse des lois provinciales s'attaquant à l'expression discriminatoire.

Une vaste proportion des lois provinciales sur les droits de la personne appartient à la première catégorie décrite par le professeur McNamara. De fait, les dispositions adoptées par huit des douze provinces et territoires ayant légiféré en ces matières ciblent l'expression de propos discriminatoires ou encore *certaines* formes d'expression incitant à la discrimination.

Les interdits provinciaux s'attaquant à l'expression de propos discriminatoires partagent, sous une forme ou une autre, certains traits communs. Ces dispositions sont en effet caractérisées par leur portée souvent modeste, leur focalisation sur les « représentations » discriminatoires et par l'adjonction fréquente d'une disposition soulignant l'importance de la liberté d'expression.

L'affaire *Warren* c *Chapman* donne un exemple de la retenue dont ont pu faire preuve les tribunaux dans l'application de ces dispositions. Une commission est saisie à l'occasion d'une plainte formée contre la publication de deux articles dressant un portrait calomnieux des Autochtones. La commission se verra reprocher d'avoir excédé sa compétence en appliquant la disposition manitobaine interdisant les représentations discriminatoires aux articles et aux éditoriaux publiés dans un journal. Au moment de rejeter l'argument de la commission voulant qu'une loi sur les droits de la personne se doive de recevoir une interprétation libérale, le juge Morse se dira d'avis qu'en usant des termes « any notice, sign, symbol, emblem or other representation » la Législature provinciale « did not intend to cover all forms or manner of discriminatory expression. If this had been intended, the legislature could very easily have said so. The specific words chosen demonstrate, in my opinion, an intention to be selective ».[100] Cette interprétation de la portée de l'interdit manitobain recevra ultimement l'aval de la Cour d'appel du Manitoba.[101]

Cette approche est pareillement adoptée par les tribunaux de la Saskatchewan à l'occasion de l'affaire *Saskatchewan (Human Rights Commission) v Engineering Students' Society*. De nouveau, la décision favorable d'une commission des droits de la personne sera infirmée par les tribunaux judiciaires au motif que l'expression « any

---

[99] McNamara 2005, p. 1.

[100] Warren c Chapman (1984), 11 DLR (4th) 474, 479 (B.R. Man.).

[101] Warren c Chapman, (1985) 17 DLR (4th) 261, [1985] 4 WWR 75, 31 Man R (2d) 231 (C.A. Man.).

notice, sign, symbol, emblem or other representation » ne saurait fonder l'application de la disposition saskatchewanaise à la publication répétée d'écrits misogynes dans un journal étudiant. Au nom de la majorité de la Cour d'appel de la Saskatchewan, le juge Cameron s'en remettra alors au sens usuel des termes interprétés tout en concédant que « [t]he purpose of the Act pulls in one direction, the cast of the section in another ».[102]

Aujourd'hui, le dilemme qu'esquissait le juge Cameron ne se présente plus avec la même acuité. Depuis le prononcé de ces décisions, la portée de certains interdits a en effet été étendue par l'ajout de termes anglais tels que « publications », « statements » et même « articles » à l'énumération des modes de communications visés[103]. Cependant, l'énumération « any notice, sign, symbol, emblem or other representation » demeure encore aujourd'hui la formule la plus répandue parmi les lois provinciales et territoriales s'attaquant aux représentations discriminatoires.[104]

Il reste à traiter sommairement de la seconde catégorie de lois provinciales ou territoriales vouées à embrasser non seulement les énoncés propices à l'éclosion de la discrimination, mais également les propos haineux. Ce double alliage est minoritaire: seules quelques lois provinciales ou territoriales se proposent d'étendre l'interdit aux déclarations haineuses.

Deux remarques visent cette seconde catégorie législative.

D'une part, la plupart des observations précédentes s'appliquent de la même manière. Il serait trompeur de présenter la catégorisation proposée par McNamara comme une dichotomie. En effet, si les lois en question peuvent être distinguées au regard de la nature de l'expression visée, on ne saurait dire qu'elles se trouvent en parfaite opposition. Au contraire, les dispositions s'attaquant, de surcroît, à l'expression de propos haineux partagent plusieurs traits attribués aux dispositions ciblant les propos simplement discriminatoires. À dire vrai, les similitudes sont telles qu'il est possible d'affirmer que seule la nature de l'expression sanctionnée distingue véritablement ces deux catégories de lois. Comme l'illustre la disposition albertaine en la matière, la plupart des commentaires formulés antérieurement peuvent être transposés à cette seconde catégorie de dispositions:

> 3 (1) No person shall publish, issue or display or cause to be published, issued or displayed before the public any statement, publication, notice, sign, symbol, emblem or other representation that
>
> (a) indicates discrimination or an intention to discriminate against a person or a class of persons, or
>
> (b) is likely to expose a person or a class of persons to hatred or contempt

---

[102] Saskatchewan (Human Rights Commission) c Engineering Students' Society (1989), 56 DLR (4th) 604, 623 (C.A. Sask.).

[103] C'est le cas des lois de la Colombie-Britannique, de l'Alberta, de la Saskatchewan, du Manitoba et des Territoires du Nord-Ouest.

[104] Cette énumération ou une part encore plus restrictive de celle-ci se retrouve dans les textes en vigueur en Ontario, au Québec, au Nouveau-Brunswick, en Nouvelle-Écosse, à Terre-Neuve-et-Labrador et au Nunavut.

because of the race, religious beliefs, colour, gender, gender identity, gender expression, physical disability, mental disability, age, ancestry, place of origin, marital status, source of income, family status or sexual orientation of that person or class of persons.

(2) Nothing in this section shall be deemed to interfere with the free expression of opinion on any subject.[105]

D'autre part, il y a tout lieu d'indiquer le désaveu relatif dont souffrent les dispositions consacrées à l'éradication des propos haineux en marge du code criminel. Autant les dispositifs législatifs soucieux de bannir les énoncés à vocation discriminatoire semblent généralement admis, autant les élans législatifs provinciaux ou fédéraux (hors code criminel) consacrés aux propos haineux suscitent la controverse. Souvent décriées, les sanctions civiles et administratives préconisées à l'article 13 de la *Loi canadienne sur les droits de la personne* auront connu leur épilogue lors de l'abrogation de ce même article 13 dans le cadre d'une loi ayant reçu la sanction royale le 26 juin 2013,[106] lors même que la constitutionnalité de cette disposition avait pourtant été consacrée par la Cour suprême du Canada dès 1990.[107] Destinée initialement aux seuls appels téléphoniques répétés « pour aborder ou faire aborder des questions susceptibles d'exposer à la haine ou au mépris des personnes appartenant à un groupe identifiable sur la base des critères énoncés à l'article 3 », la portée de l'interdit avait été élargie en 2001 à l'usage d'un ordinateur dont l'internet. L'ancien article 13 n'interdisait pas directement les propos haineux envers les groupes protégés: le procédé juridique employé consistait à les assimiler à un « acte discriminatoire ». Dépourvue de sanction pénale, cette disposition revêtait plutôt une vocation préventive. Elle se proposait de mettre fin à une pratique jugée discriminatoire. Le cadre législatif de l'époque favorisait un règlement par conciliation et n'autorisait l'imposition d'une amende ou de l'emprisonnement que si la personne accomplissait intentionnellement les actes prohibés par une ordonnance inscrite en Cour fédérale. Partant, cette disposition se voulait une « mesure de rechange »[108] par rapport aux dispositions du code criminel. Comme nous l'avons exposé précédemment, les propos pouvaient être interdits indépendamment de l'intention du locuteur. En somme, la suppression des paroles pouvait être ordonnée même si l'intéressé n'avait pas constaté la nature potentiellement discriminatoire de ses dires.

Lors même qu'elle fut jugée constitutionnelle et que ses mérites furent reconnus par une majorité de juges de la Cour suprême du Canada dans l'affaire *Taylor* relatée précédemment,[109] cette disposition fut de tout temps contestée. La Commission canadienne des droits de la personne se fit reprocher d'avoir accepté d'analyser

---

[105] Alberta Human Rights Act, RSA 2002, c A-25.5, art 3.

[106] L.C. 2013, ch. 37. L'abrogation entra en vigueur l'année d'après: Lemire c Canada (Commission des droits de la personne), 2014 CAF 18, par. 9; [2015] 2 RCF 117.

[107] Voir l'arrêt Canada (Commission des droits de la personne) c Taylor, [1990] 3 R.C.S. 892 abordé de manière détaillée à la question 5.1.1 du présent rapport.

[108] Walker 2018, p. 10, en ligne: https://lop.parl.ca/sites/PublicWebsite/default/fr_CA/ResearchPublications/201825E.

[109] Voir l'arrêt Canada (Commission des droits de la personne) c Taylor, [1990] 3 R.C.S. 892 abordé aux questions 5.1.1 et 5.3 du présent rapport.

certaines plaintes (même si elles furent par la suite rejetées), plutôt que de les avoir repoussées d'entrée de jeu. Une étude parue à la Bibliothèque du Parlement du Canada relate les débats successifs ayant eu cours à l'époque:

> le débat au sujet de cette question a suscité une attention grandissante en 2008 à la suite d'une plainte déposée en vertu de l'article 13 par le Congrès islamique canadien (CIC) contre Rogers Media auprès de la Commission canadienne des droits de la personne (CCDP). Dans cette affaire, le CIC alléguait qu'un texte de Mark Steyn publié dans la version en ligne du magazine *Maclean's* exposait les membres de la communauté musulmane à la haine et au mépris. Cet article avançait, en s'appuyant sur des données démographiques, que le « monde occidental » risquait d'être supplanté par le « monde musulman ».

La CCDP a établi que

> certains passages de l'article de M. Steyn étaient formulés dans des termes forts, colorés, choisis pour provoquer les discussions et susceptibles de nourrir la polémique, mais qu'ils ne dépassaient pas la limite fixée par la Cour suprême [dans l'arrêt *Taylor*] concernant la haine et le mépris.

Comme elle l'a noté par la suite, la CCDP estime avoir rempli le mandat que lui confère la loi en recevant et en traitant la plainte, puis en rendant sa décision. Toutefois, « de nombreuses personnes qui avaient une perception erronée du rôle de la Commission ont critiqué cette dernière pour le simple fait d'avoir accepté la plainte au départ». Le CIC a également déposé des plaintes au sujet de ce texte et d'autres articles du magazine *Maclean's* auprès de la Commission ontarienne des droits de la personne et du Tribunal des droits de la personne de la Colombie-Britannique, qui les ont tous deux rejetées.

En 2009, la maison d'édition McClelland & Stewart a publié un livre intitulé *Shakedown: How Our Government Is Undermining Democracy in the Name of Human Rights* critiquant les commissions canadiennes des droits de la personne et préconisant en particulier l'abrogation de l'article 13 de la LCDP. Écrit par Ezra Levant, ce livre relatait l'expérience de cet avocat et journaliste qui avait fait l'objet d'une plainte pour incitation à la haine devant la Commission des droits de la personne de l'Alberta pour avoir publié de nouveau les caricatures controversées du prophète Mahomet. Grand succès de librairie au pays, le livre de M. Levant a attiré une attention considérable sur la question de la réforme de l'article 13.[110]

Même la Commission des droits de la personne du Canada convenait que des amendements législatifs étaient de mise pour contrer notamment le phénomène des plaintes abusives. Tout en reconnaissant les imperfections du processus institué par l'article 13, la Commission en suggérera la modification plutôt que l'abrogation.[111] Le Parlement canadien en aura jugé autrement en 2013. Une tentative législative de faire renaître l'article 13 dans une mouture révisée aura avorté en 2021 en raison du déclenchement d'élections générales.[112]

---

[110] Walker 2018, pp. 14 et 15, en ligne: https://lop.parl.ca/sites/PublicWebsite/default/fr_CA/ResearchPublications/201825E [références omises].

[111] Ibid., p. 15, en ligne: https://lop.parl.ca/sites/PublicWebsite/default/fr_CA/ResearchPublications/201825E [références omises].

[112] PL C-36, Loi modifiant le Code criminel, la Loi canadienne sur les droits de la personne et apportant des modifications connexes à une autre loi (propagande haineuse, crimes haineux et

Le même désamour se sera affiché récemment envers les dispositions de nature provinciale destinées à enrayer le discours haineux. Lors même qu'une loi saskatchewanaise analogue fut jugée, en 2013, conforme à la *Charte canadienne des droits et libertés* de l'avis de la Cour suprême du Canada,[113] l'Assemblée nationale du Québec remisa son projet de bannir le discours haineux en raison de l'opposition suscitée à l'encontre du projet de loi gouvernemental de l'époque. Une partie des reproches formulés à l'endroit de la mesure provinciale envisagée consistait à dire que le code criminel pourvoyait déjà à ce sujet et que l'atteinte envisagée à la liberté d'expression ne se défendait guère. Enoncée par des juristes souvent connus, cette critique taisait soigneusement l'arrêt *Whatcott* de la Cour suprême ayant opiné en sens contraire au sujet de la législation de la Saskatchewan. Cette prise de position ignorait aussi les avantages supposés d'une loi axée sur les effets redoutés de la discrimination et non pas sur les intentions du locuteur[114]. Toujours est-il que le projet de loi québécois déposé en 2015[115] tourna court: les dispositions relatives à la lutte aux propos haineux furent abandonnées.

5.2.2.3 Portée Raisonnable et Portée Excessive des Paroles Visées par la Législation Civile

Il convient d'illustrer sommairement la portée des interdits de nature civile. Dans la foulée du prononcé des arrêts *Keegstra* et *Taylor*, la violation des interdits provinciaux fut constatée à la suite de l'affichage public du *svastika* et l'autodafé de croix,[116] de la distribution d'un journal pamphlétaire contenant des diatribes ciblant des représentants des communautés juive et sino-canadienne,[117] de la vente d'autocollants incitant au rejet de certains groupes ethniques[118] ou encore de la publication d'éditoriaux antisémites dans un journal local. [119]Au demeurant, font partie des énoncés susceptibles d'être frappés d'interdit, les paroles reprochant aux membres d'un groupe d'être la cause de problèmes actuels de la société, les propos qui prétendent qu'ils constituent une menace, qu'ils complotent pour détruire la civilisation occidentale, qu'ils se livrent à des activités illicites, des affirmations les présentant comme des menteurs

discours haineux), 2e sess, 43 parl, 2021, (première lecture le 23 juin 2021) [PL C-36], en ligne : https://parl.ca/DocumentViewer/fr/43-2/projet-loi/C-36/premiere-lecture.

113 Saskatchewan (Human Rights Commission) c Whatcott, 2013 CSC 11.

114 Ce thème a été abordé aux questions 5.1.2 et 5.2.2.2 du présent rapport.

115 Projet de loi n° 59, Loi apportant diverses modifications législatives pour renforcer la protection des personnes (titre modifié), en ligne: http://www.assnat.qc.ca/fr/travaux-parlementaires/projets-loi/projet-loi-59-41-1.html.

116 Kane c Church of Jesus Christ Christian-Aryan Nations (1992), 18 CHRR 268, 1992 CanLII 14249 (AB CDP).

117 Kane c Papez, (2002) 43 CHRR 120, 2002 CarswellAlta 1821, 2002 CanLII 78265 (AB CDP).

118 Saskatchewan (Human Rights Commission) c Bell, [1994] 114 DLR (4th) 370, [1994] 5 WWR 458, 120 Sask R 122, 21 CHRR 147 (C.A. Sask.).

119 Abrams c North Shore News and Collins, 1999 BCHRT 7, [1999] BCHRTD No 5, 33 CHRR 435.

ou encore des déclarations qui emploient des termes déshumanisants en assimilant ces membres à des animaux ou à des êtres inférieurs.[120]

La portée des interdits de nature civile demeure soumise aux exigences constitutionnelles. À cet égard, les tribunaux administratifs et judiciaires sont enjoints par la Cour suprême du Canada de respecter les critères que voici:

> Premièrement, les tribunaux judiciaires doivent appliquer de manière objective les dispositions interdisant les propos haineux. ... La question à laquelle le tribunal est appelé à répondre est de savoir si une personne raisonnable informée du contexte et des circonstances dans lesquels les propos ont été tenus estimerait que ces derniers exposent le groupe protégé à la haine.
>
> Deuxièmement, les termes « haine » et « mépris » qui figurent dans la disposition ne s'entendent que des manifestations extrêmes de l'émotion ... Ainsi, sont écartés les propos qui, bien que répugnants et offensants, n'incitent pas à l'exécration, au dénigrement et au rejet qui risquent d'emporter la discrimination et d'autres effets préjudiciables.
>
> Troisièmement, les tribunaux administratifs doivent axer l'analyse sur les effets des propos en cause. Les propos sont-ils susceptibles d'exposer la personne ou le groupe ciblé à la haine d'autres personnes ? Le caractère répugnant des idées exprimées ne suffit pas, en soi, pour justifier d'en restreindre l'expression. L'interdiction des propos haineux ne vise pas à censurer les idées ou à forcer quiconque à penser « correctement ». De même, il n'est pas pertinent de se demander si l'auteur des propos avait l'intention d'inciter à la haine, à la discrimination ou à une autre conduite préjudiciable à l'égard du groupe protégé. Ce qu'il faut déterminer, ce sont les effets qu'auront probablement les propos sur l'audience, compte tenu des objectifs législatifs visant à réduire ou à éliminer la discrimination.
>
> À la lumière de ces trois principes, lorsque le mot « haine » est employé dans une loi sur les droits de la personne pour interdire certains propos, il faudrait l'appliquer de façon objective pour déterminer si une personne raisonnable, informée du contexte et des circonstances, estimerait que les propos sont susceptibles d'exposer autrui à la détestation et à la diffamation pour un motif de discrimination illicite.[121]

Une autre limitation inhérente au respect de la liberté d'expression se rapporte au traitement juridique de l'ironie. Comme l'enseigne la Cour suprême du Canada:

> Premièrement, une forme d'expression qui malmène ou ridiculise des personnes peut inspirer à leur égard des sentiments de dédain ou de supériorité, mais elle n'invite généralement pas pour autant à nier leur humanité ou à les marginaliser aux yeux de la majorité (*Whatcott*, par. 89-91). Certes, poussé à la limite, le ridicule pourrait franchir cette ligne, mais il ne le fera que dans des circonstances extrêmes et insolites.
>
> Deuxièmement, l'humour, qu'il soit de bon ou de mauvais goût, possède rarement « l'effet d'entraînement requis pour susciter chez des tiers une attitude de haine et de discrimination » (Rainville, p. 68). Il se caractérise par des procédés bien connus tels que « l'exagération, la généralisation abusive, la provocation et la déformation de la réalité » (motifs de la C.A., par. 129, la juge Savard). L'auditoire sait identifier ces procédés, quand ils sont clairs, et il faut lui reconnaître assez de discernement pour ne pas prendre tout ce qui est dit au pied de la lettre (voir, par analogie, *Bou Malhab*, par. 74; S. Martin, « Rira bien qui rira le dernier: la caricature confrontée au droit à l'image » (2004), 16 *C.P.I.* 611, p. 621-622). Cela vaut à plus forte raison lorsque les propos émanent d'une personne connue du public pour son humour

[120] Cette liste inspirée de l'arrêt Whatcott est reprise dans l'affaire Dion c R., 2020 QCCS 3049, par. 25 (requête pour permission d'en appeler rejetée: Dion c R, 2020 QCCA 1658).

[121] Saskatchewan (Human Rights Commission) c Whatcott, 2013 CSC 11, par 56 à 59 [références omises].

particulier (voir, par analogie, *Bou Malhab*, par. 89) ou lorsqu'ils prennent pour cible une personnalité publique exposée à ce genre de commentaires en raison de sa notoriété (voir, par analogie, *WIC Radio Ltd. c. Simpson*, 2008 CSC 40, [2008] 2 R.C.S. 420, par. 48; *Trudeau c. AD4 Distribution Canada inc.*, 2014 QCCA 1740, par. 21-22 (CanLII)). Sauf dans des cas exceptionnels, il serait étonnant que des propos tenus dans de telles circonstances soient suffisamment mobilisateurs pour susciter des traitements discriminatoires.[122]

La Cour suprême du Canada fut par ailleurs appelée à désavouer la propension de certains tribunaux ou commissions des droits de la personne portés à se reconnaître une compétence trop accrue. Les juges majoritaires constatent et récusent

« … une tendance jurisprudentielle suivant laquelle la Commission et le Tribunal interprètent leur loi constitutive, la *Charte québécoise*, de manière à se reconnaître une compétence à l'égard de litiges impliquant des propos prétendument « discriminatoires », prononcés par des particuliers, en privé comme en public. Avec égards, nous estimons que cette tendance s'éloigne de la jurisprudence de notre Cour et témoigne d'une interprétation erronée des dispositions en cause dans cette affaire, notamment les art. 4 et 10 de la *Charte québécoise*, lesquels garantissent respectivement le droit à la sauvegarde de la dignité et l'égalité dans la reconnaissance et l'exercice des droits et libertés de la personne, y compris dans le contexte de propos prétendument « discriminatoires ». Elle entraîne la suppression de propos dont le contenu est perçu comme discriminatoire et la condamnation de leurs auteurs au versement de sommes d'argent non négligeables.

D'emblée, il faut reconnaître que la *Charte québécoise*, qui élève la liberté d'expression au rang de liberté fondamentale, n'a pas été édictée pour encourager la censure.[123]

Dans ce même arrêt prononcé en 2021, les juges majoritaires de la Cour suprême du Canada préconisent des limitations à la compétence du tribunal des droits de la personne et récusent son acception libérale de la notion de dignité de la personne. En témoigne le grief suivant:

La *Charte québécoise* confère au Tribunal une compétence directe, quoique restreinte, sur certains types de propos, dans la mesure où elle interdit le harcèlement et la publicité discriminatoires (art. 10.1 et 11). Cette compétence directe et restreinte a toutefois été élargie indirectement au cours des dernières décennies à la faveur d'un courant jurisprudentiel jumelant des interprétations généreuses des deux principales dispositions en cause, à savoir celle relative au droit à l'égalité dans la reconnaissance et l'exercice des droits et libertés (art. 10 de la *Charte québécoise*) et celle relative au droit de chacun à la sauvegarde de sa dignité, de son honneur et de sa réputation (art. 4). Selon ce courant jurisprudentiel, des propos blessants, liés à un motif énuméré à l'art. 10 de la *Charte québécoise*, constituent de la discrimination et relèveraient de la compétence du Tribunal, même si le préjudice subi est relatif et que les effets sociaux de la discrimination, comme la perpétuation de préjugés ou de désavantages, sont absents (voir, p. ex., *Commission des droits de la personne et des droits de la jeunesse c. Filion*, 2004 CanLII 468 (T.D.P. Qc); *Tchanderli-Braham c. Bériault*, 2018 QCTDP 4; *Jied c. Éthier*, 2019 QCTDP 26; *Mirouh c. Gaudreault*, 2021 QCTDP 10; *Ayotte c. Tremblay*, 2021 QCTDP 13).

En plus de se fonder uniquement sur le contenu des propos et non sur leurs effets discriminatoires, ce courant jurisprudentiel, dans lequel s'inscrit le jugement du Tribunal, met de côté

[122] Ward c Québec (Commission des droits de la personne et des droits de la jeunesse), 2021 CSC 43, par. 88 et 89. Pour de rares exemples jurisprudentiels où l'ironie sert de dissimulation à la dissémination réelle de la haine, voir Rainville 2019, pp. 76 et 77.

[123] Ward c Québec (Commission des droits de la personne et des droits de la jeunesse), 2021 CSC 43, par. 4 et 5 (à lire de pair avec les par. 28 et s., 52 et 113 et s.).

> la juste pondération entre la liberté d'expression et la protection du droit à la sauvegarde de la dignité. Ce courant ouvre ainsi une deuxième voie de recours en discrimination, parallèle au recours en diffamation, pour forcer une personne à répondre du préjudice causé par ses propos selon un fardeau de preuve nettement moins onéreux pour le plaignant, qui n'est d'ailleurs pas tenu d'intenter lui-même son recours si la Commission accepte d'agir en sa faveur.
>
> À notre avis, ce courant jurisprudentiel soulève de sérieuses préoccupations au regard de nos précédents en matière de liberté d'expression. Le recours en *discrimination* n'est pas, et ne doit pas devenir, un recours en *diffamation*. L'un et l'autre obéissent à des considérations différentes et poursuivent des objectifs différents. Le recours en discrimination doit être limité à des propos dont les effets sont réellement discriminatoires.[124]

Cette mise au point a vocation à valoir pour l'ensemble des lois destinées à assurer la protection des droits de la personne et à pourfendre la discrimination. L'on pourrait s'étonner, au premier abord, de l'acception très restreinte donnée à la notion de sauvegarde de la dignité d'autrui. Certes, les lois consacrées à la protection des droits de la personne commandent une interprétation particulière: les garanties qu'elles offrent ne sont pas seulement législatives, mais quasi constitutionnelles, de sorte qu'elles commandent une interprétation téléologique, large et libérale, comme le veut une jurisprudence constante: « Il faut donc lui donner une interprétation libérale et téléologique, dans le but de protéger largement les droits des personnes visées ... »[125]. Cette position de principe souffre pourtant d'absolutisme lorsqu'entrent en scène des paroles attentatoires à la dignité d'une communauté de personnes. La raison en est simple: la confrontation entre la liberté d'expression des uns et le droit à l'égalité des autres suppose un arbitrage. L'atteinte à la liberté d'expression suppose un réel potentiel discriminatoire sans quoi la censure devient inadmissible.

5.2.2.4 Portée Raisonnable et Portée Excessive des Mesures Civiles ou Administratives Adoptées

L'ampleur des mesures civiles ou administratives susceptibles d'être prises en application des lois anti-discrimination ou anti-haine se sont vues délimitées par la jurisprudence.

Un premier courant jurisprudentiel attribue une large acception à la *sanction administrative*. Pour peu que la loi habilitante le permette, une commission des droits de la personne est fondée à prononcer une sanction pécuniaire qui dépasse le préjudice constaté. En somme, une loi vouée au respect des droits de la personne peut autoriser le paiement d'une indemnité monétaire de façon à inciter au respect de la loi prohibant les propos haineux. Autant la jurisprudence en la matière s'appuie sur la

[124] Ward c Québec (Commission des droits de la personne et des droits de la jeunesse), 2021 CSC 43, par. 28 à 30 [italique dans l'original; notre soulignement].

[125] Tranchemontagne c Ontario (Directeur du Programme ontarien de soutien aux personnes handicapées), 2006 CSC 14 par. 33

nature préventive (et dissuasive) d'une telle mesure monétaire,[126] autant les objectifs ainsi recherchés empruntent au droit pénal malgré les démentis des tribunaux sur le sujet.

Un second courant jurisprudentiel s'assure de départager les différentes *sanctions civiles* susceptibles d'être imposées à l'auteur de propos haineux. L'arrêt de principe de la Cour suprême du Canada rendu dans l'affaire *Ross c Conseil scolaire du district n° 15 du Nouveau-Brunswick* scrute la validité d'une ordonnance prononcée par une commission d'enquête sur les droits de la personne à la suite d'une plainte pour discrimination à propos des déclarations et les publications antisémites diffusées par un enseignant en dehors de ses heures de travail. En raison de ces prises de position incendiaires, le plaignant reproche au Conseil scolaire qui employait l'appelant d'avoir omis de prendre des mesures appropriées à l'endroit de ce dernier et d'avoir, vu cette omission, « violé l'art. 5 de la *Loi sur les droits de la personne* [du Nouveau-Brunswick] en faisant preuve de discrimination envers lui et ses enfants quant ... aux services ... pour des raisons de croyance et d'ascendance ».[127] La commission d'enquête formée pour entendre cette plainte conclut que l'appelant, par ses déclarations dénigrant « la foi et les croyances des Juifs », a contrevenu à l'alinéa 5(1)b) de la loi précitée. L'ordonnance prononcée a donc vocation à corriger certaines pratiques jugées discriminatoires dans la prestation de services éducatifs. La commission estime d'ailleurs que le conseil scolaire doit être tenu responsable de la violation de cette disposition par un enseignant demeuré à son emploi. Ce faisant, le conseil scolaire aurait lui-même contrevenu à l'article 5 (1) :

> 5(1) Nul ne doit, directement ou indirectement, seul ou avec un autre, personnellement ou par l'intermédiaire d'une autre personne, ...
>
> b) faire preuve de discrimination envers une personne ou une catégorie de personnes quant au logement, aux services et aux commodités disponibles au public,
>
> pour des raisons de race, de couleur, de croyance, d'origine nationale, d'ascendance, de lieu d'origine, d'âge, d'incapacité physique, d'incapacité mentale, d'état matrimonial, d'orientation sexuelle, de sexe, de condition sociale ou de convictions ou d'activité politiques[128].

En foi de quoi, la commission d'enquête rend une ordonnance enjoignant notamment au conseil scolaire de placer l'appelant en congé sans solde, de l'affecter à un poste de « non-enseignant »—si un tel poste devait se libérer au cours de la période de congé—et, en dernier recours, de mettre fin à son emploi s'il n'a pu être réaffecté au terme d'un délai de dix-huit mois. Le conseil scolaire se voit aussi ordonner de mettre fin à l'emploi de l'appelant si, à tout moment, ce dernier s'avisait de publier ou de diffuser, de nouveau, des écrits discriminatoires. À la suite de cette ordonnance survient un pourvoi en contrôle judiciaire à l'encontre de la décision de la commission d'enquête lequel se solde par un arrêt unanime de la Cour suprême du

[126] Lemire c Canada (Commission des droits de la personne), 2014 CAF 18, par. 90 à 93 et 102 à 104; [2015] 2 RCF 117.

[127] Ross c Conseil scolaire du district n° 15 du Nouveau-Brunswick, [1996] 1 RCS 825, 836.

[128] Loi sur les droits de la personne, LRNB 1973, c H-11, art 5(1) (remplacée par Loi sur les droits de la personne, LRNB 2011, c 171, art 6(1)).

Canada. Cette dernière valide la conclusion de la commission quant « à l'existence de discrimination de la part du conseil scolaire »[129].

Se pose ensuite la question de la constitutionnalité de l'ordonnance de la commission au regard de la liberté de religion et de la liberté d'expression de l'enseignant assurées par les alinéas 2a) et 2b) de la *Charte canadienne.* La Cour prend acte de la double atteinte constitutionnelle subie par l'enseignant ainsi écarté. Force est ensuite d'identifier le degré de justification exigé de même que les facteurs permettant de soupeser l'importance de l'objectif poursuivi par l'ordonnance[130]. Cet examen assurera la validité de la plupart des atteintes aux droits constitutionnels de l'enseignant ainsi sanctionné.

Nombreux sont les objectifs pourvus de l'importance voulue:

> … l'autre facteur déterminant en l'espèce est la nature des services éducatifs en question: il s'agit ici de l'éducation de jeunes enfants. Bien que l'on reconnaisse l'importance de l'éducation à tous les âges, celle des jeunes revêt une importance primordiale. Comme on l'a dit dans l'arrêt *Brown*, précité, l'éducation éveille les enfants aux valeurs que la société espère promouvoir et développer. Les jeunes enfants sont particulièrement vulnérables aux messages transmis par leurs enseignants. Ils sont moins susceptibles de faire une distinction intellectuelle entre les remarques qu'un enseignant fait à l'école et celles qu'il fait à l'extérieur de l'école. Ils sont donc plus susceptibles de se sentir menacés et isolés par un enseignant qui dénigre les caractéristiques personnelles du groupe auquel ils appartiennent. De plus, ils ne distingueront vraisemblablement pas ce qui est faux de ce qui est vrai et seront plus susceptibles d'accepter les opinions méprisantes d'un enseignant. La création d'un milieu d'enseignement non discriminatoire où règne l'égalité et l'instauration d'un climat d'équité et de tolérance dans la classe revêtent une importance prépondérante dans l'éducation des jeunes enfants. Cela aide à promouvoir le respect de soi et l'acceptation par autrui.
>
> C'est dans ce contexte qu'il faut établir un équilibre entre la liberté de l'intimé de faire des déclarations discriminatoires et le droit des enfants du conseil scolaire «d'être instruit[s] dans un système scolaire où ne règne aucun parti pris, aucun préjugé ni aucune intolérance», droit souligné par le par. 5.5(1) de la Loi et consacré à l'art. 15 de la Charte.
>
> Le second contexte, celui de l'emploi, est pertinent dans la mesure où l'État, à titre d'employeur, est tenu de veiller à ce que les fonctions publiques soient exercées de manière à ne pas saper la confiance du public. …
>
> Loin d'être simplement un employé de l'État, l'enseignant est aussi l'employé d'un conseil scolaire. À ce titre, ses libertés doivent être pondérées en fonction du droit du conseil scolaire de remplir son propre mandat. Compte tenu de l'énoncé ministériel du Nouveau-Brunswick, cela signifie qu'il faut établir un équilibre entre l'intérêt du district scolaire n° 15 dans le maintien d'un système scolaire où ne règne aucun parti pris, aucun préjugé ni aucune intolérance et le droit de l'intimé de manifester ses croyances religieuses et d'exprimer ses propres opinions.
>
> Le dernier contexte que la Commission des droits de la personne nous a demandé de considérer est celui de l'antisémitisme. …
>
> Pour apprécier cet argument, il est utile de se reporter à l'arrêt *R. c. Edwards Books and Art Ltd.*, [1986] 2 R.C.S. 713, où le juge en chef Dickson affirme, à la p. 779:

[129] Ross c Conseil scolaire du district n° 15 du Nouveau-Brunswick, [1996] 1 RCS 825, par. 54.

[130] Ross c Conseil scolaire du district n° 15 du Nouveau-Brunswick, [1996] 1 RCS 825, par. 90, 91, 97 et 98.

> Je crois que lorsqu'ils interprètent et appliquent la Charte, les tribunaux doivent veiller à ce qu'elle ne devienne pas simplement l'instrument dont se serviront les plus favorisés pour écarter des lois dont l'objet est d'améliorer le sort des moins favorisés.
>
> Cette directive est particulièrement applicable en l'espèce. L'ordonnance rendue par la commission d'enquête visait à remédier à la discrimination qu'elle avait constatée dans le système scolaire public du Nouveau-Brunswick et dont étaient victimes les Juifs, groupe historiquement désavantagé qui avait subi des persécutions de la plus grande envergure. Il ne doit pas être permis à l'intimé de se servir de la Charte pour écarter les progrès que les Juifs ont réalisés dans leur lutte contre la discrimination. …
>
> Dans le présent pourvoi, l'ordonnance de la commission d'enquête, tout comme la loi en vertu de laquelle elle a été rendue, porte sur les intérêts opposés de différentes personnes et tente d'évaluer l'élimination de la discrimination en fonction des droits d'autrui. En fait, en rendant son ordonnance, la commission a examiné soigneusement l'incidence qu'elle aurait sur l'intimé et a décidé que c'était là une conséquence nécessaire d'une mesure destinée à remédier à la discrimination. En l'espèce, l'ordonnance fondée sur la conclusion à l'existence de discrimination reflète cette évaluation. La commission d'enquête a évalué les libertés de l'intimé en fonction de l'aptitude du conseil scolaire à assurer l'existence d'un milieu exempt de discrimination, et en fonction des intérêts des élèves juifs.
>
> La nature des droits qui auraient été violés en l'espèce est tout aussi importante. … lorsque la forme d'expression qui aurait fait l'objet d'un empiétement s'écarte davantage des valeurs fondamentales de la liberté d'expression, on a recours à une norme moins stricte de justification au sens de l'article premier…. l'expression qui fomente la haine contre des groupes identifiables ne revêt qu'une importance limitée par rapport aux valeurs qui sous-tendent la liberté d'expression.
>
> De même, toute restriction que l'ordonnance impose à la liberté d'expression de l'intimé devrait, à mon avis, faire l'objet d'un examen moins rigoureux et être plus facile à justifier en vertu de l'article premier. …
>
> L'ordonnance de la commission d'enquête traduit un engagement à éliminer la discrimination dans la prestation de services éducatifs au public. Compte tenu de la jurisprudence, des obligations internationales du Canada et des valeurs consacrées dans la Constitution, l'objectif de l'ordonnance attaquée est nettement «urgent et réel».[131]

La Cour conclura par la suite à la proportionnalité de l'essentiel des mesures prononcées à l'endroit de l'appelant. La cessation de son poste d'enseignant se justifie en l'occurrence:

> « … la loi en cause est de nature à promouvoir la conciliation et ne prévoit aucune sanction pénale. Elle est donc bien adaptée pour encourager ceux qui ont un comportement discriminatoire injuste à s'amender. En rédigeant son ordonnance, la commission d'enquête s'est attachée à l'aspect réparateur, s'efforçant le plus possible d'éviter les effets punitifs. … Pour éviter la discrimination, le milieu scolaire doit être un milieu où tous sont traités sur un pied d'égalité et encouragés à participer pleinement ».[132]

La Cour suprême du Canada se montre par ailleurs soucieuse de « l'influence importante que l'enseignant exerce sur ses élèves, et par le statut associé à son rôle. Il

---

[131] Ross c Conseil scolaire du district n° 15 du Nouveau-Brunswick, [1996] 1 RCS 825, par. 82 à 91 et 98.

[132] Ross c Conseil scolaire du district n° 15 du Nouveau-Brunswick, [1996] 1 RCS 825, par. 100.

est donc nécessaire de retirer à l'intimé son poste d'enseignant afin d'assurer qu'il n'exerce plus ce genre d'influence sur ses élèves et que les services éducatifs soient exempts de toute discrimination ».[133]

Fait notable, le Comité des droits de l'homme rejeta, par la suite, la plainte formulée par l'appelant ainsi évincé de ses fonctions d'enseignant. Comme l'expose le présent rapport à la question 5.3, le Comité estima que les restrictions imposées à cet enseignant écarté « avaient pour but de protéger "les droits ou la réputation" des personnes de religion juive, y compris leur droit à l'éducation dans un système public d'enseignement libre de parti pris, de préjugé et d'intolérance »[134]. Pareilles restrictions s'avéraient donc justifiées.[135]

Les mesures civiles ainsi prises à l'encontre d'une personne portée à l'intolérance demeurent assujetties à des bornes. Partant, certaines sanctions ordonnées par une commission ou un tribunal administratif peuvent s'avérer excessives au regard des protections dévolues à la liberté de religion ou à la liberté d'expression du locuteur. Ainsi fut invalidée, dans l'affaire *Ross*, la portion de l'ordonnance obligeant le conseil scolaire à mettre fin à l'emploi de l'appelant si, malgré son éviction du poste d'enseignant, il publiait, de nouveau, des écrits antisémites. Le lien d'emploi ne pouvait, à lui seul, être anéanti du fait de publications futures. Vu les critères d'analyse propres au critère de l'atteinte minimale, la Cour suprême du Canada convient qu'il est en effet possible

> que le maintien de l'intimé au sein du conseil scolaire ait un effet résiduel empoisonné même après son retrait de l'enseignement, et c'est peut-être ce que la clause 2d) vise à éviter. Je reconnais qu'en raison de la grande visibilité de l'intimé et de sa longue carrière d'enseignant, le problème, au conseil scolaire, pourrait subsister pendant un certain temps. Toutefois, la preuve n'étaye pas la conclusion que l'effet résiduel empoisonné durerait indéfiniment après l'affectation de Ross à un poste de non-enseignant. Pour ce motif, la clause 2d) qui impose une interdiction permanente ne porte pas atteinte de façon minimale aux libertés constitutionnelles de l'intimé. La clause 2d) n'est pas justifiée au sens de l'article premier.[136]

Les sanctions civiles destinées à enrayer la discrimination doivent être pourvues d'une efficacité réelle, mais elles ne sauraient épouser des ambitions plus larges au risque de succomber à la démesure.

[133] Ross c Conseil scolaire du district n° 15 du Nouveau-Brunswick, [1996] 1 RCS 825, par. 101.

[134] Ross c Canada, Communication n° 736/1997, UN DOC CCPR/C/70/D/736/1997 (2000), par. 2.1, en ligne: https://undocs.org/fr/CCPR/C/70/D/736/1997, par. 11.5.

[135] Ross c Canada, Communication n° 736/1997, UN DOC CCPR/C/70/D/736/1997 (2000), par 2.1, en ligne: https://undocs.org/fr/CCPR/C/70/D/736/1997, par. 12.

[136] Ross c Conseil scolaire du district n° 15 du Nouveau-Brunswick, [1996] 1 RCS 825, par. 107.

5.3 Pacte International Relatif aux Droits Civils et Politiques (PIDCP)

Le Canada est un État partie au PIDCP à la faveur de son accession le 19 mai 1976. Le Canada n'a déposé aucune réserve ou déclaration lors de la ratification du PIDCP.[137] Au surplus, il a consenti à la procédure de communications individuelles. Aucune des observations finales formulées par le Comité des droits de l'homme depuis l'accession du Canada au Pacte ne traite de la question du discours haineux. Quatre décisions du Comité relatives à des communications individuelles ont cependant porté, entre autres questions, sur l'application de l'article 20 du Pacte au Canada:

- *JRT et le parti WG* c *Canada,* Communication n° 104/1981, UN DOC CCPR/C/OP/2 à la p. 25 (1984)
- *Ross c Canada,* Communication n° 736/1997, DOC NU CCPR/C/70/D/736/1997 (2001)
- *Zündel c Canada,* Communication n° 953/2000, UN DOC CCPR/C/78/D/953/2000 (2003)
- *Zündel c Canada,* Communication n° 1341/2005, UN DOC CCPR/C/89/D/1341/2005 (2007)

Ces quatre décisions ne revêtent pas toutes le même intérêt; elles seront reprises dans leur ordre chronologique et feront l'objet d'une présentation proportionnelle à leur importance.

- *JRT et le parti WG* c *Canada,* Communication n° 104/1981, UN DOC CCPR/C/OP/2 à la p. 25 (1984)

La communication est déposée conjointement par M. Taylor et le parti politique qu'il dirige, le *Western Guard Party*. Les auteurs de la communication opéraient une ligne téléphonique diffusant un message enregistré avertissant les personnes qui appelaient cette ligne « of the dangers of international finance and international Jewry leading the world into wars, unemployment and inflation and the collapse of world values and principles ».[138]

Consécutivement à une plainte, le Tribunal canadien des droits de la personne estime que la plupart des messages contreviennent à l'ancien par. 13(1) de la *Loi canadienne sur les droits de la personne.* Cette disposition, aujourd'hui abrogée, interdisait à titre de pratique discriminatoire le fait d'utiliser un téléphone de façon répétée pour aborder des questions susceptibles d'exposer à la haine ou au mépris des

---

[137] Les quatre objections formulées par le Canada concernaient la portée générale ou indéfinie des réserves ou des déclarations déposées par d'autres États (Maldives, Pakistan, Qatar et le Royaume du Bahreïn); aucune de ces objections ne traite du discours haineux.

[138] JRT and the WG Party c Canada, Communication n° 104/1981, UN DOC CCPR/C/OP/2 (1984) au par. 2.1, en ligne: https://www.ohchr.org/Documents/Publications/SelDec_2_en.pdf.

personnes appartenant à un groupe identifiable.[139] Partant, le Tribunal ordonne aux auteurs de cesser derechef cette pratique discriminatoire.[140] Or, les auteurs désobéissent et reprennent la diffusion de pareils messages téléphoniques; leur attitude leur vaut une condamnation pour outrage à la Cour fédérale, l'instance responsable de l'exécution des ordonnances du Tribunal canadien des droits de la personne. En raison de leurs activités, les auteurs sont également visés par une ordonnance leur interdisant l'usage des services postaux canadiens. Cette ordonnance est prononcée sur la foi de l'article 7 de la *Loi sur les postes* lequel interdit la transmission de « quelque chose [...] d'injurieux et grossier ».[141]

Les auteurs prétendent devant le Comité des droits de l'homme que l'ordonnance du Tribunal canadien des droits de la personne tout comme celle formulée en vertu de la *Loi sur les postes* violent leur « right to hold and maintain their opinions without interference, in violation of article 19 (1) of the [ICCPR], and the right to freedom of expression and of the right to seek, receive and impart information and ideas of all kinds through the media of their choice, in violation of article 19 (2) of the Covenant ».[142]

L'argument ne convainc guère. Le Comité déclare, au contraire, la communication irrecevable[143]. Entre autres motifs, le Comité constate que « the opinions which Mr. T. seeks to disseminate through the telephone system clearly constitute the advocacy of racial or religious hatred which Canada has an obligation under article 20 (2) of the Covenant to prohibit. In the Committee's opinion, therefore, the communication is, in respect of this claim, incompatible with the provisions of the Covenant, within the meaning of article 3 of the Optional Protocol »[144]. Quant à l'ordonnance rendue sous l'autorité de la *Loi sur les postes*, le Comité rejette la communication pour d'autres motifs.[145]

- *Ross c Canada*, Communication n° 736/1997, DOC NU CCPR/C/70/D/736/1997 (2001)

La communication de M. Ross se plaint de la violation des articles 18 et 19 du Pacte. M. Ross faisait office d'enseignant spécialisé au sein d'un établissement scolaire du Nouveau-Brunswick. Pendant sa période d'emploi, M. Ross a prononcé des allocutions publiques et publié plusieurs ouvrages dans lesquels il exprime des opinions

[139] Loi canadienne sur les droits de la personne, LRC 1985, c H-6, art 13(1) (article abrogé par LC 2013, c 37, art 2).

[140] Smith c Western Guard Party, 1979 CanLII 1 (TCDP), par. 43.

[141] JRT and the WG Party v Canada, Communication n° 104/1981, UN DOC CCPR/C/OP/2 (1984), par. 5.4, en ligne: https://www.ohchr.org/Documents/Publications/SelDec_2_en.pdf.

[142] Ibid au par. 1 (il était également allégué que la disposition attaquée de la Loi sur les postes constituait une violation de l'article 17 du Pacte).

[143] Ibid au par. 9.

[144] Ibid au par. 8(b).

[145] Ibid au par. 8(c).

controversées au sujet de « l'avortement, [d]es conflits entre le judaïsme et le christianisme et [de] la défense de la religion chrétienne[146]. ». Des mesures sont alors prises à son encontre par son employeur, une commission scolaire, en raison des préoccupations formulées par des membres de la communauté. L'enseignement en classe de l'auteur est ainsi surveillé et il est réprimandé à deux occasions pour avoir exprimé publiquement ses opinions.

Dans la foulée d'une plainte auprès de la Commission des droits de la personne du Nouveau-Brunswick, une commission d'enquête est désignée pour entendre l'affaire. La plainte reproche à la commission scolaire d'avoir violé l'article 5 de la *Loi sur les droits de la personne* du Nouveau-Brunswick en fournissant à la population « des services d'enseignement constituant une discrimination fondée sur la religion et l'ascendance » puisqu'aucune mesure appropriée n'aurait été prise à l'encontre de l'auteur[147]. La Commission d'enquête constate que l'auteur « a dénigré la religion et les convictions des juifs » et engagé les « véritables » chrétiens non seulement à contester la validité des convictions et des enseignements juifs, mais également « à afficher leur mépris à l'égard des personnes de religion et d'ascendance juives, qui menaceraient la liberté, la démocratie et les croyances et les valeurs chrétiennes »[148]. La Commission d'ajouter « que les déclarations publiques et les écrits de Malcolm Ross [ont] contribué d'une façon permanente au cours des ans à la création d'une "atmosphère envenimée dans le district scolaire … [et] considérablement entravé la qualité des services d'enseignement fournis au plaignant et à ses enfants" ».[149] D'avis que la commission scolaire assume une responsabilité à l'égard des actions de l'auteur, la Commission d'enquête ordonne l'attribution d'un poste de non-enseignant à M. Ross et sa suspension sans solde si un tel poste n'est pas immédiatement disponible. Dans l'éventualité du refus de ce poste de non-enseignant ou de son indisponibilité au terme d'une période de dix-huit mois, il est ordonné à la commission scolaire de mettre fin à l'emploi de M. Ross. En vertu du paragraphe 2(d) de cette ordonnance, la Commission scolaire est également tenue de mettre immédiatement fin à l'emploi de l'auteur si ce dernier devait, à n'importe quel moment, « publi[er] ou écri[re] à des fins de publication tout texte faisant état d'un complot juif ou sioniste ou prenant pour cible des adeptes de la religion juive » ou distribuer l'une quelconque de ses publications précédentes.[150]

Conformément à l'ordonnance, l'auteur est transféré à un poste d'enseignement hors classe. S'ensuivent une demande en contrôle judiciaire et une série de procédures en appel débouchant sur un arrêt de la Cour suprême du Canada (CSC). La CSC reconnaît que l'ordonnance porte atteinte à la liberté d'expression tout comme à la liberté de religion garanties par la *Charte canadienne des droits et libertés*. De dire la CSC, ces restrictions s'avèrent cependant justifiées au regard de l'article premier de la

---

[146] Ross c Canada, Communication n° 736/1997, UN DOC CCPR/C/70/D/736/1997 (2000) au para 2.1, en ligne: https://undocs.org/fr/CCPR/C/70/D/736/1997>.

[147] Ibid au par. 2.3.

[148] Ibid au par. 11.5.

[149] Ibid au par. 4.2–4.3.

[150] Ibid au par. 4.3.

Charte canadienne à une seule exception près, soit le paragraphe 2(d) de l'ordonnance lequel est jugé excessif.

L'auteur fait valoir devant le Comité des droits de l'homme que les restrictions imposées à sa liberté d'exprimer ses convictions religieuses constituent autant de violations de ses droits protégés par les articles 18 et 19 du PIDCP. L'État partie plaide en deux temps. Le Canada soutient tout d'abord la thèse de l'irrecevabilité de la communication en raison de son incompatibilité avec les dispositions du Pacte, puisque les publications de l'auteur tombent sous le coup des interdits prévus par le second paragraphe de l'article 20; il s'en remet également au précédent établi dans la décision *JRT et WG c Canada*, précitée. Les représentants du Canada estiment pareillement la plainte irrecevable au motif qu'elle ne porte pas sur l'expression de « convictions religieuses ». Au surplus, l'État partie s'appuie sur les paragraphes 2 et 4 de l'article 18 pour étayer la thèse selon laquelle il est tenu d'intervenir afin de protéger la liberté religieuse des étudiants. Sur le fond de la communication, le Canada plaide l'absence de violation des droits énoncés aux articles 18 et 19 ou, à défaut, la présence d'une justification au regard du 3e paragraphe de ces articles.

Le Comité déclare la communication recevable dans la mesure où celle-ci concerne les violations alléguées des articles 18 et 19 du Pacte.[151] S'écartant en toutes lettres de l'approche adoptée dans la décision *JRT et WG c Canada*, le Comité estime désormais « que les restrictions à la liberté d'expression qui peuvent relever des dispositions de l'article 20 doivent également être autorisées en vertu du paragraphe 3 de l'article 19 qui fixe les conditions dans lesquelles elles sont autorisées. Lorsqu'il s'agit d'appliquer ces dispositions, le fait qu'une restriction est réputée être nécessaire en vertu de l'article 20 entre naturellement en ligne de compte. En l'espèce, la mesure dans laquelle les restrictions sont autorisées est une question à étudier dans le cadre de l'examen quant au fond ».[152]

Le Comité donne cependant raison au Canada pour l'essentiel quant au fond de l'affaire. Certes, le Comité convient que l'ordonnance de la commission d'enquête comme le transfert de l'auteur dans un poste de non-enseignant imposent des restrictions à l'exercice des droits protégés par les articles 18 et 19 du Pacte. En revanche, le Comité considère que les restrictions imposées à ce dernier « avaient pour but de protéger "les droits ou la réputation" des personnes de religion juive, y compris leur droit à l'éducation dans un système public d'enseignement libre de parti pris, de préjugé et d'intolérance ».[153] Pareilles restrictions respectent toutes les conditions prévues au troisième paragraphe des deux articles du Pacte et s'avèrent donc justifiées[154].

- *Zündel c Canada*, Communication n° 953/2000, UN DOC CCPR/C/78/D/953/2000 (2003)

---

[151] Le Comité déclare irrecevable la portion de la communication voulant que l'auteur ait lui-même été victime de discrimination et que son renvoi fût une conséquence de l'arrêt rendu par la Cour suprême du Canada.

[152] Ibid au par. 10.6.

[153] Ibid au par. 11.5.

[154] Ibid au par. 12.

La communication est le fruit d'un citoyen allemand résidant au Canada et ayant fait l'objet d'une plainte pour violation des dispositions de la *Loi canadienne sur les droits de la personne*: il lui est reproché d'avoir exposé les personnes de confession ou d'ascendance juive à la haine et au mépris en publiant de nombreux articles niant l'Holocauste sur le site internet qu'il hébergeait. Le Tribunal canadien des droits de la personne lui refuse le droit d'opposer une défense de « vérité » en réponse à la plainte dont il fait l'objet. L'auteur se décide alors à tenir un point de presse dans un édifice de la Colline parlementaire. Mise au fait de l'autorisation ainsi accordée à l'auteur, la Chambre des Communes adopte à l'unanimité une motion refusant à l'auteur l'accès à l'enceinte du Parlement jusqu'au terme de la session parlementaire. Ainsi éconduit, l'auteur se résoudra à tenir un point de presse informel sur un trottoir situé à proximité des édifices du Parlement.

Les tribunaux judiciaires ontariens rejettent son action fondée sur l'atteinte à sa liberté d'expression. Est pareillement repoussée son action intentée contre les partis politiques et certains membres du Parlement au motif que la Chambre des communes a « exercé son "privilège parlementaire" en refusant à l'auteur l'entrée dans ses locaux »[155]. La Cour suprême du Canada refuse d'intervenir.

Dans sa communication, l'auteur allègue la violation de sa liberté d'expression au sens de l'article 19 du PIDCP. Il fait aussi valoir le caractère discriminatoire de la motion adoptée par la Chambre des Communes et conclut à la violation des articles 3 et 26 du Pacte.

Le Comité des droits de l'homme conclut à l'irrecevabilité de la communication. Le Comité prend acte de ce que l'auteur n'a rien produit pour étayer des affirmations qui ne semblent pas correspondre aux intentions de l'article 3 du Pacte[156]. L'argument fondé sur la violation de l'article 26 est aussi jugée irrecevable puisque les recours internes n'ont pas été épuisés comme le prévoit l'alinéa b du paragraphe 2 de l'article 5 du Protocole facultatif[157].

Le Comité se prononce comme suit au sujet de la violation alléguée de la liberté d'expression: « [b]ien que le droit à la liberté d'expression, tel qu'énoncé au paragraphe 2 de l'article 19 du Pacte, s'étende au choix du moyen, il n'équivaut pas à un droit illimité qu'aurait toute personne ou tout groupe de personnes de tenir des conférences de presse dans l'enceinte parlementaire ou de faire diffuser ces conférences de presse autrement »[158]. Partant, la plainte de l'auteur au motif qu'il n'a pas pu tenir un point de presse dans un édifice parlementaire « ne relève pas du droit à la liberté d'expression, protégé par le paragraphe 2 de l'article 19 du Pacte » et est donc « irrecevable *ratione materiae* au regard de l'article 3 du Protocole facultatif »[159]

---

[155] Zündel c Canada, Communication n° 953/2000, UN DOC CCPR/C/78/D/953/2000 (2003), par. 3.1, en ligne: https://juris.ohchr.org/Search/Details/955>.

[156] Ibid., au par. 8.3.

[157] Ibid., au par. 8.6.

[158] Ibid., au par. 8.5.

[159] Ibid.

- *Zündel c Canada*, Communication n° 1341/2005, UN DOC CCPR/C/89/D/1341/2005 (2007)

Cette dernière communication présente un intérêt mitigé. De nationalité allemande et bénéficiaire de la résidence permanente au Canada, l'auteur de la communication publie, pendant sa présence en sol canadien, des ouvrages controversés dans lesquels il met en doute l'extermination de six millions de Juifs et l'existence de certaines chambres à gaz. Il se dira victime de nombreux actes de violence et de menaces en raison de ses publications et fait grief aux autorités canadiennes de ne pas mener de véritables enquêtes sur le sujet. Sa seconde demande de citoyenneté canadienne est suspendue par le ministère de l'Immigration et de la citoyenneté au motif qu'il existe des motifs raisonnables de croire que M. Zündel représente une menace pour la sécurité nationale du Canada. Il séjournera ensuite aux États-Unis pour en être par la suite expulsé. De retour au Canada, M. Zündel est détenu et un certificat de sécurité est émis de sorte qu'il devient interdit de territoire. Plusieurs actes de procédure débouchent sur un jugement de la Cour fédérale ordonnant son maintien en détention en raison d'un danger pour la sécurité nationale du Canada et faisant état de son implication dans un mouvement raciste et violent. M. Zündel sera déporté vers l'Allemagne où il sera jugé et déclaré coupable d'incitation à la haine raciale et de négation de la Shoah.

Dans sa communication, l'auteur invoque de multiples entorses au PIDCP. Il se dit en outre d'avis que sa mise en détention résulte de ses opinions politiques comme quoi de nombreux aspects de l'historiographie concernant le sort des Juifs pendant la Deuxième Guerre mondiale devraient faire l'objet de recherches plus poussées et être révisés.

Le Comité des droits de l'homme déclare la communication « irrecevable en vertu de l'article 3 et du paragraphe 2 b) de l'article 5 du Protocole facultatif »[160]. Les allégations fondées sur les articles 7, 9, 10 18, 19 et 26 du Pacte amènent le Comité à constater que l'auteur n'a pas épuisé les recours internes[161]. Au sujet de l'article 14, le Comité prend acte de l'épuisement des recours internes tout en estimant cette portion de la communication irrecevable *ratione materiae*, puisque les allégations ne relèvent pas de cette disposition.

5.3.1 Application du PIDCP au Discours Haineux par le Législateur, l'administration ou les Tribunaux

L'ordre juridique canadien est dualiste. Les traités internationaux ratifiés par le Canada ne sont donc pas directement intégrés à son ordre juridique et n'y produisent aucun effet immédiat. Leur mise en œuvre sur le territoire canadien se fait plutôt par l'entremise de la législation adoptée par le Parlement fédéral et les législatures

[160] Ibid., au par. 7.

[161] Ibid., aux par. 6.2—6.9.

provinciales[162]. À l'instar de la jurisprudence développée naguère par le Conseil privé, la Cour suprême du Canada se fait fort de rappeler qu'il n'existe « aucun pouvoir fédéral autonome de mise en œuvre des traités » de sorte que « la compétence du Parlement fédéral de mettre en œuvre des traités signés par le gouvernement fédéral est fonction du partage ordinaire des compétences »[163].

Le Pacte n'a été ni directement ni intégralement transposé dans l'ordre juridique canadien. La protection des droits et libertés qu'il énonce est plutôt assurée par un faisceau de lois fédérales et provinciales protégeant les droits de la personne de même que des textes constitutionnels comme la *Charte canadienne des droits et libertés.* Dans le cas du discours haineux, cette protection est également assurée par des dispositions relevant du droit pénal.

Ces dernières appellent certaines précisions temporelles: les dispositions du *Code criminel* définissant les infractions relatives au discours haineux et à la propagande du même acabit, soit les articles 318 et 319 C.cr., ont été adoptées en 1970 : elles ont ainsi précédé la ratification du PIDCP par le Canada. L'avènement de ces articles au sein du code criminel canadien résulte des recommandations du rapport de 1966 du Comité spécial de la propagande haineuse au Canada (appelé « comité Cohen »)[164]. Chose étonnante, le rapport du comité Cohen ne touche mot du traité international alors en cours d'élaboration. S'il est vrai que ce n'est qu'au cours de l'année ayant suivi la publication du rapport du comité Cohen que le texte définitif du PIDCP sera adopté, il n'en demeure pas moins que l'élaboration de ce dernier fut amorcée en 1947[165].

Une tendance apparentée s'observe au sujet de l'adoption, en 1977, de l'article 13 de la *Loi canadienne sur les droits de la personne* (abrogé en 2014). En effet, un rapport de la Commission canadienne des droits de la personne citera après coup la propagande haineuse menée par James Taylor Ross comme ayant été la « source immédiate » des inquiétudes soulevées « quant aux insuffisances du *Code criminel* pour faire face à de nouvelles manifestations de la propagande haineuse »[166] et justifier l'adoption d'une disposition d'une autre facture.

S'il n'a pas été directement intégré à l'ordre juridique canadien, le PIDCP, à l'instar des autres « sources du droit international des droits de la personne », demeure, comme l'écrit dès 1987 le juge en chef du Canada, l'une « des sources pertinentes et persuasives quant [*sic*] il s'agit d'interpréter les dispositions de la *Charte* [*canadienne des droits et libertés*] »[167]. Cette approche alors formulée dans le cadre d'un jugement dissident est depuis consacrée par la Cour suprême du Canada ; il est acquis que les

---

162 En revanche, le droit international coutumier est automatiquement intégré dans le droit interne sans que le législateur n'ait à intervenir: Nevsun Resources Ltd. c Araya, 2020 CSC 5.

163 Renvois relatifs à la Loi sur la tarification de la pollution causée par les gaz à effet de serre, 2021 CSC 11, par. 149.

164 Comité spécial de la propagande haineuse au Canada 1966.

165 ECOSOC, Report of the Commission on Human Rights, 2e sess, Doc off NU E/600 (1947).

166 Commission canadienne des droits de la personne 2009, à la p 14, en ligne: publications.gc.ca/pub?id=9.636619&sl=1 (at p. 13 in the English version).

167 Renvoi relatif à la Public Service Employee Relations Act (Alb), [1987] 1 RCS 313, 348, en ligne: https://canlii.ca/t/1ftnm (motifs dissidents du juge en chef Dickson).

obligations internationales du Canada en matière de droits de la personne influent « non seulement sur l'interprétation du contenu des droits garantis par la *Charte*, mais aussi sur l'interprétation de ce qui peut constituer des objectifs urgents et réels au sens de l'article premier qui peuvent justifier la restriction de ces droits »[168].

De surcroît, la jurisprudence la plus récente de la Cour suprême du Canada se montre soucieuse des obligations internationales du pays destinées à garantir un recours utile aux victimes de violations des droits énoncés au PIDCP[169]. Au demeurant, comme l'explique la professeure Sullivan dans des propos d'ailleurs repris par la Cour suprême du Canada: « le législateur est présumé respecter les valeurs et les principes contenus dans le droit international, coutumier et conventionnel. Ces principes font partie du cadre juridique au sein duquel une loi est adoptée et interprétée. Par conséquent, dans la mesure du possible, il est préférable d'adopter des interprétations qui correspondent à ces valeurs et à ces principes »[170].

Cette position interprétative semble d'ailleurs jouir d'un rôle accru dans le domaine des droits de la personne. Les décisions les plus récentes de la Cour suprême du Canada estiment qu'il faut présumer que la *Charte canadienne des droits et libertés* « accorde une protection au moins aussi grande que les instruments internationaux ratifiés par le Canada en matière de droits de la personne »[171]. Aussi est-il arrivé à la Cour suprême d'infirmer sa jurisprudence antérieure de manière à harmoniser le droit interne et le droit international. Pareil revirement jurisprudentiel s'observe notamment dans l'affaire *Saskatchewan Federation of Labour*[172]. La Cour suprême désavoue sa propre interprétation antérieure de la *Charte canadienne* au motif que les obligations internationales du Canada militent nettement en faveur de la reconnaissance d'un droit de grève protégé par le droit d'association enchâssé dans la *Charte*

---

[168] Slaight Communications Inc c Davidson, [1989] 1 RCS 1038, 1056 et 1057, en ligne: https://canlii.ca/t/1ft6s (motifs majoritaires du juge en chef Dickson) ; voir également Renvoi sur la Motor Vehicle Act (C-B), [1985] 2 RCS 486, 512, en ligne: https://canlii.ca/t/dlp; R. c Keegstra, [1990] 3 RCS 697, 750, en ligne: https://canlii.ca/t/1fv5v; R. c Zundel, [1992] 2 RCS 731, 810 et 811, en ligne: https://canlii.ca/t/1fs9p (motifs dissidents des juges Cory et Iacobucci); Baker c Canada (Ministre de la Citoyenneté et de l'Immigration), [1999] 2 RCS 817, 860 et 861, en ligne: https://canlii.ca/t/1fqlj; R. c Sharpe, [2001] 1 RCS 45, 140 et 141, en ligne https://canlii.ca/t/523g; États-Unis c Burns, 2001 CSC 7, [2001] 1 RCS 283, par. 79 et 80, en ligne: https://canlii.ca/t/523s; Suresh c Canada (Ministre de la Citoyenneté de l'Immigration), [2002] 1 RCS 3, 31 et 32, en ligne: https://canlii.ca/t/51wg.

[169] Nevsun Resources Ltd. c Araya, 2020 CSC 5, par. 119.

[170] Sullivan 1994, à la p. 330 (cité avec approbation par les juges minoritaires dans l'affaire R. c Sharpe, 2001 CSC 2, par. 175).

[171] Saskatchewan Federation of Labour c Saskatchewan, 2015 CSC 4, par. 64 et 65; Divito c. Canada (Sécurité publique et Protection civile), [2013] 3 RCS 157, par. 23.

[172] Voir également l'arrêt Mugesera c Canada (Ministre de la Citoyenneté et de l'Immigration), 2005 CSC 40. La Cour répudie un énoncé formulé dans l'arrêt R. c Finta, [1994] 1 RCS 701 en raison de son incompatibilité avec la jurisprudence de tribunaux internationaux pénaux: « Vu la relation étroite existant entre notre droit interne et le droit international en la matière, il convient d'harmoniser le plus possible la nature et la définition des crimes contre l'humanité avec la jurisprudence des tribunaux pénaux internationaux. » (Mugesera, précité, par. 143).

canadienne[173]. Un autre enseignement digne de mention porte sur la reconnaissance, en droit interne canadien, du rôle des organismes d'application des conventions internationales. Comme le précise la Cour suprême: « Même si, à strictement parler, elles n'ont pas d'effet obligatoire, les décisions du Comité de la liberté syndicale ont une force persuasive considérable et elles ont été citées avec approbation et largement reprises à l'échelle mondiale par les cours de justice, les tribunaux administratifs et d'autres décideurs, y compris notre Cour… »[174].

Les obligations internationales du Canada, notamment celles qu'il assume en vertu de l'article 20 du PIDCP, constituent donc des sources utiles à l'interprétation du droit canadien en matière de répression de la propagande haineuse. L'illustre, de fort belle manière, l'étude des interdits énoncés dans le PIDCP par la Cour suprême du Canada dans l'arrêt *R c Keegstra.* Est alors en cause la constitutionnalité du paragraphe 319(2) du *Code criminel* lequel incrimine le fait de « foment[er] volontairement la haine contre un groupe identifiable »[175]. Constatant la double atteinte à la liberté d'expression et à la présomption d'innocence, la Cour suprême se livre à l'analyse que commande l'article premier de la Charte canadienne. Ce dernier permet la sauvegarde d'une disposition enfreignant un droit ou une liberté si l'atteinte en question constitue par ailleurs « une limite raisonnable imposée par une règle de droit et dont la justification puisse se démontrer dans le cadre d'une société libre et démocratique »[176].

Au stade de l'étude de l'importance de l'objectif poursuivi par le par. 319 (2) C.cr., la Cour suprême du Canada se montre soucieuse des enseignements tirés du PIDCP, de la CEDR et de la CEDH. Les juges majoritaires se veulent particulièrement catégoriques:

> [l]a CEDR et le PIDCP démontrent que l'interdiction de l'expression incitant à la haine est considérée non seulement compatible avec la garantie des droits de la personne dans un pays signataire, mais aussi comme un élément obligatoire de cette garantie. Ce n'est pas là nier que la question du juste équilibre entre l'interdiction de la propagande haineuse et la garantie de la liberté d'expression a fait l'objet de débats sur le plan international. Malgré ces débats, le Canada, comme d'autres membres de la communauté internationale, a pris l'engagement d'interdire la propagande haineuse et, à mon avis, notre Cour doit tenir compte de cet engagement en examinant la nature de l'objectif gouvernemental sous-jacent au par. 319(2) du *Code criminel.* Le fait que la communauté internationale ait agi collectivement pour condamner la propagande haineuse et pour obliger les États parties à la CEDR et au PIDCP à prohiber ce genre d'expression, vient souligner l'importance de l'objectif qui sous-tend le par. 319(2) et des principes d'égalité et de la dignité intrinsèque des personnes, qui se manifestent aussi bien dans les droits internationaux de la personne que dans la Charte[177].

---

173 Saskatchewan Federation of Labour c. Saskatchewan, 2015 CSC 4. Au par. 70, la même décision ne manque pas de souligner que « Le Canada est également partie au Pacte international relatif aux droits civils et politiques, 999 R.T.N.U. 171 (PIDCP), auquel sont incorporées la Convention (n° 87) et les obligations qu'elle crée ».

174 Saskatchewan Federation of Labour c Saskatchewan, 2015 CSC 4, par. 69.

175 Code criminel, LRC 1985 c C-46, art 319(2), en ligne: < https://laws-lois.justice.gc.ca/fra/lois/C-46/section-319.html?wbdisable=false>.

176 R c Keegstra, [1990] 3 RCS 697, 795.

177 Ibid., pp. 754 et 755. [Références omises]

Pareille analyse fortifie la conclusion des juges majoritaires en faveur de la constitutionnalité du paragraphe 319 (2) C.cr.: la gouverne prescrite par le PIDCP étoffe la thèse d'une limite raisonnable à la liberté d'expression.

L'arrêt *Keegstra* ne fait pas figure de cas isolé. La Cour suprême réitère l'intérêt porté au PIDCP dans un autre litige constitutionnel. Les orientations arrêtées dans cet instrument international favoriseront la thèse de la validité de l'ancien article 13 de la *Loi canadienne sur les droits de la personne* en vertu duquel il était défendu « pour une personne ou un groupe de personnes agissant d'un commun accord d'utiliser ou de faire utiliser un téléphone de façon répétée en recourant ou en faisant recourir aux services d'une entreprise de télécommunication relevant de la compétence du Parlement pour aborder ou faire aborder des questions susceptibles d'exposer à la haine, au mépris ou au ridicule[178] des personnes appartenant à un groupe identifiable pour un motif de distinction illicite »[179]. L'atteinte ainsi causée à la liberté de pensée, de croyance, d'opinion et d'expression n'empêchera pas l'article d'être sauvegardé au terme d'une analyse au regard de l'article premier de la Charte canadienne faisant appel succinctement au droit international. Les juges majoritaires de la Cour suprême du Canada prennent acte notamment de la décision rendue précisément par le Comité des droits de l'homme au sujet de la Communication présentée quelques années plus tôt par le même appelant[180] afin d'y discerner « l'importance capitale qu'il faut accorder au but de prévenir les préjudices causés par la propagande haineuse »[181]. L'article 20 du PIDCP se voit gratifié d'une brève mention en faveur de l'éradication « de la diffusion d'idées fondées sur la notion de supériorité raciale ou religieuse »[182].

Les prises de position du droit international seront de nouveau interpellées dans le cadre d'un tout autre litige constitutionnel. La Cour suprême du Canada est appelée dans l'arrêt *Zundel*[183] à décider de la constitutionnalité de l'article 181 C.cr. qui s'emploie à bannir le fait de publier « une déclaration, une histoire ou une nouvelle [que l'accusé] sait fausse et qui cause, ou est de nature à causer, une atteinte ou du tort à quelque intérêt public ». Les juges majoritaires retiennent la thèse de l'invalidité de l'article du fait que l'objectif poursuivi par cette disposition se dérobe aux exigences de l'article premier de la *Charte*, puisqu'il n'est ni « urgent » ni « réel ». Cette conclusion implacable tient compte de ce que l'article 181 C.cr. n'est aucunement

---

[178] L'exposition au ridicule ne saurait toutefois justifier une atteinte à la liberté d'expression comme en décidera par la suite l'arrêt Whatcott abordé dans les réponses offertes aux questions 5.1.2 et 5.2.2.3 du présent rapport.

[179] Loi canadienne sur les droits de la personne, SC 1976-77 c 33, art 13(1).

[180] Voir l'affaire JRT et Parti WG c Canada, Communication n° 104/1981, UN DOC CCPR/C/OP/2 à la p. 25 (1984). Cette décision est abordée à la question 5.3 du présent rapport.

[181] Canada (Commission des droits de la personne) c Taylor, [1990] 3 RCS 892, 920. L'attention accordée en la matière aux décisions du Comité des droits de l'homme se constate aussi dans les arrêts Saskatchewan (Human Rights Commission) c Whatcott, 2013 CSC 11, par. 67 et R. c Keegstra, [1990] 3 RCS 697, 752 et 753.

[182] Ibid.

[183] R. c Zundel, [1992] 2 RCS 731, en ligne: https://canlii.ca/t/1fs9p.

nécessaire « pour que soit respectée toute obligation internationale assumée par le Parlement »[184].

C'est dire l'apport—en négatif comme en positif—des prescription du droit international des droits de la personne au premier chef duquel figure le PIDCP. L'absence d'interdit en droit international façonne plus aisément la thèse de l'invalidité des dispositions du code criminel canadien dès lors dépourvues d'un objectif réel et urgent. À l'inverse, le lien de nécessité ressort avec plus d'éloquence lorsque le texte d'incrimination canadien se fait l'écho de la protection de droits fondamentaux assurée par le droit international.

Abstraction faite du champ d'application du code criminel, le même apport interprétatif se constate au regard de la législation provinciale comme fédérale. Les dispositions du Pacte ont été mobilisées par la jurisprudence lors de l'application de lois provinciales comme fédérales sur les droits de la personne destinées à pourfendre le discours haineux[185]. Le droit international sert autant à conforter la mise en œuvre des dispositions pertinentes du droit canadien qu'à en établir la validité.

5.4 Convention Internationale sur l'élimination de Toutes les Formes de Discrimination Raciale (CEDR)

Le Canada est un État partie à la CEDR de par sa ratification le 14 octobre 1970. Le gouvernement n'a déposé aucune réserve ou déclaration lors de la ratification de la CEDR.[186] Le Canada n'a toutefois pas déposé la déclaration prévue à l'article 14 et n'a donc pas consenti à la procédure de communications individuelles. Exception faite des observations formulées après l'étude du premier rapport ainsi que des neuvième et dixième rapports (combinés) présentés par le Canada, chaque rapport compilant les observations finales du Comité pour l'élimination de la discrimination raciale se compose d'interrogations quant à l'application de l'article 4. Il convient de regrouper ces interrogations de manière thématique.

---

[184] Ibid à la p 764.

[185] Voir notamment Smith c Western Guard Party, 1979 CanLII 1 (TCDP), en ligne: https://canlii.ca/t/1g8h3; Nealy c Johnston, 1989 CanLII 151 (TCDP), en ligne: https://canlii.ca/t/1g8q5; Saskatchewan (Human Rights Commission) c Bell, 1991 CanLII 7733 (SK QB), en ligne: https://canlii.ca/t/g9qsx; Warman c Warman, 2005 TCDP 36 (CanLII), en ligne: https://canlii.ca/t/1ndjg; Canada (Commission des droits de la personne) c Warman, [2014] 1 RCF 608, en ligne: https://canlii.ca/t/ft222; R c Topham, 2017 BCSC 259, en ligne: https://canlii.ca/t/gxkj0.

[186] L'unique objection formulée par le Canada concernait les réserves faites par le gouvernement de la République arabe du Yémen à l'égard de plusieurs paragraphes de l'article 5 de la Convention; cette objection ne traite pas de la question du discours haineux.

5.4.1 *Le Défaut d'interdire les Organisations à Caractère Raciste*

Une préoccupation maintes fois réitérée vise le choix du Canada de réprimer les actions que peuvent poser des organisations à caractère raciste au lieu d'interdire d'emblée de telles organisations. Ce leitmotiv transpire dans huit rapports concernant cet État partie[187]. La lacune repérée a trait au non-respect de l'alinéa b) du par. 5.4 de la Convention. Cette omission a amené le Comité à s'interroger, du moins une fois, sur l'incidence de cette absence d'interdit sur les activités d'organisations tel le Ku Klux Klan.[188]

Le Comité ne se satisfait pas de ce que le Canada bannisse les activités racistes menées par des organisations au lieu de déclarer carrément illégales les organisations elles-mêmes racistes. L'absence d'interdiction pénale au sujet des organisations racistes amène le Comité à rappeler la nature « impérative » des prescriptions de l'article 4 et à enjoindre le Canada à amender sa législation pénale ou à en adopter une qui garantisse « le respect intégral » de cet article.[189]

Force nous est de noter que cette caractéristique du droit criminel canadien transcende la seule thématique des organisations racistes. Le Parlement fédéral a fait le choix arrêté de ne point interdire les organisations criminelles pour bannir, en lieu et place, des comportements précis: (i) la participation d'individus à leurs activités « dans le but d'accroître la capacité de l'organisation de faciliter ou de commettre un acte criminel »[190]; (ii) la perpétration d'un acte criminel « au profit ou sous la direction d'une organisation criminelle, ou en association avec elle »[191]; (iii) certaines infractions connexes[192]. Les organisations peuvent prospérer, certes, mais leur habilité à mener à terme leurs basses œuvres se voit, en revanche, contrée par

---

[187] CEDR, Rapport du Comité pour l'élimination de la discrimination raciale, Doc off AGNU, 31e sess, 18e supp, Doc NU A/31/18, par. 184; CEDR, Rapport du Comité pour l'élimination de la discrimination raciale, Doc off AGNU, 34e sess, 18e supp, Doc NU A/34/18, par. 262; CEDR, Rapport du Comité pour l'élimination de la discrimination raciale, Doc off AGNU, 36e sess, 18e supp, Doc NU A/36/18, par. 315; Rapport du Comité pour l'élimination de la discrimination raciale, Doc off AGNU, 38e sess, 18e supp, Doc NU A/38/18, par. 398 ; CEDR, Rapport du Comité pour l'élimination de la discrimination raciale, Doc off AGNU, 49e sess, 18e supp, Doc NU A/49/18, par. 329; CEDR, Rapport du Comité pour l'élimination de la discrimination raciale, Doc off AGNU, 57e sess, 18e supp, Doc NU A/57/18, par. 335; CEDR, Observations finales du Comité pour l'élimination de la discrimination raciale: Canada, Doc off CEDR, 70e sess, Doc NU CERD/C/CAN/CO/18 (2007) par. 16; CEDR, Observations finales du Comité pour l'élimination de la discrimination raciale: Canada, Doc off CEDR, 80e sess, Doc NU CERD/C/CAN/CO/19-20 (2012), par. 13.

[188] Rapport du Comité pour l'élimination de la discrimination raciale, Doc off AGNU, 38e sess, 18e supp, Doc NU A/38/18, par. 398.

[189] CEDR, Observations finales du Comité pour l'élimination de la discrimination raciale: Canada, Doc off CEDR, 70e sess, Doc NU CERD/C/CAN/CO/18 (2007) par. 16; CEDR, Observations finales du Comité pour l'élimination de la discrimination raciale: Canada, Doc off CEDR, 80e sess, Doc NU CERD/C/CAN/CO/19-20 (2012), par. 13.

[190] Art. 467.11 (1) C.cr.

[191] Art. 467.12 (1) C.cr

[192] Art. 467.111 et 467.13 (1)C.cr.

un faisceau d'infractions de nature proprement criminelle[193]. C'est sans compter l'incrimination du complot à l'article 465 C.cr. : au contraire d'autres ressorts, la simple concertation afin de commettre une infraction fédérale, suivie ou non d'actes préparatoires[194], emporte la culpabilité.

5.4.2 Le Défaut d'incriminer Nommément les Actes de Violence Raciste

Tout en se disant conscient de l'existence de l'article 718.2 du Code criminel qui fait de la discrimination raciale une circonstance aggravante lors de la détermination de la peine infligée au délinquant, « le Comité demeure préoccupé ... par l'absence de législation incriminant et réprimant les actes de violence raciste, malgré les prescriptions de l'article 4a) de la Convention »[195]. Cette préoccupation sera réitérée en 2012 et mènera au rappel du « caractère préventif et obligatoire » de l'article 4 ainsi que la nécessité d'en garantir « le respect intégral »[196].

Force nous est cependant de rappeler qu'à l'égard des propos haineux comme tels, le Code criminel canadien édicte des infractions consacrées explicitement à l'incitation au génocide, à l'incitation publique à la haine et à la fomentation volontaire de la haine (art. 318 (1), 319 (1) et 319 (2) C.cr.): ces infractions sont analysées dans la partie du présent rapport consacrée à la question 5.7.

5.4.3 La Répartition des Compétences Législatives et Administratives Entre l'entité Fédérale et les Entités Provinciales

Le Comité s'est enquis, à quelques reprises, de la répartition des compétences entre les autorités fédérale et provinciales en matière de discrimination raciale[197]. La question de possibles chevauchements de compétences voire de conflits de

---

[193] R. c Venneri, 2012 CSC 33; É. Tudeau-Chassé, Délinquance collective: facteur de reconsidération des principes du droit pénal classique, mémoire de maîtrise/master, Université Laval et Université Toulouse 1 Capitole, 2017; Rainville et Desrosiers 2010-2011, p. 545.

[194] La culpabilité est acquise sitôt l'entente conclue: nul besoin que l'accord soit suivi d'actes préparatoires. Au surplus, un éventuel désistement ne saurait valoir à titre de moyen de défense. Sur ces questions, voir Rainville et Desrosiers 2010-2011, pp. 545, 548 et s.

[195] CEDR, Observations finales du Comité pour l'élimination de la discrimination raciale: Canada, Doc off CEDR, 70e sess, Doc NU CERD/C/CAN/CO/18 (2007), par. 16.

[196] CEDR, Observations finales du Comité pour l'élimination de la discrimination raciale: Canada, Doc off CEDR, 80e sess, Doc NU CERD/C/CAN/CO/19-20 (2012), par. 13.

[197] CEDR, Rapport du Comité pour l'élimination de la discrimination raciale, Doc off AGNU, 34e sess, 18e supp, Doc NU A/34/18, par. 262; CEDR, Rapport du Comité pour l'élimination de la discrimination raciale, Doc off AGNU, 42e sess, 18e supp, Doc NU A/42/18, par. 394.

juridictions a été soulevée[198] tout comme celle de savoir si une action judiciaire rapide est d'actualité en faveur des victimes de violations de droits consacrés par la Convention.[199]

5.4.4 *La Portée des Dispositions Législatives en la Matière*

Il est arrivé au Comité de s'interroger sur la portée de certaines dispositions ou d'en déplorer l'étroitesse. Ces observations concernent la législation fédérale comme provinciale. Dans un ancien rapport, certains membres du Comité s'inquiétaient des exceptions prévues dans la loi relative à la protection des droits de la personne au regard de l'article 4 de la Convention[200]. Un autre rapport constate la présence, dans la disposition du code criminel consacrée à la propagande haineuse, d'exceptions ayant été arrêtées législativement bien avant l'entrée en vigueur de la CEDR. Mention est faite par le Comité de ce que ces exceptions ne trouvent pas écho dans le libellé de l'alinéa a) de l'art. 4 de la Convention[201].

Le flou supposé de l'article premier de la *Charte canadienne* a aussi fait l'objet de commentaires: l'absence de précisions dans cette disposition quant aux critères de nature à justifier une limitation aux droits garantis a amené le Comité à se demander si des distinctions fondées sur la race pourraient intervenir et s'avérer contraires aux critères que le Comité est chargé d'appliquer; aussi des éclaircissements ont-ils été sollicités à cet égard[202]. A aussi été commentée la possibilité offerte au législateur de déroger à certaines dispositions de la *Charte canadienne* telle celle consacrée au droit à l'égalité; ce mécanisme de dérogation avalisé par l'article 33 de la *Charte canadienne* a suscité la réflexion du Comité[203].

Les mesures législatives provinciales ont parfois été jugées parcellaires au regard des exigences posées par les alinéas a, b et c de l'article 4 de la Convention[204].

---

[198] CEDR, Rapport du Comité pour l'élimination de la discrimination raciale, Doc off AGNU, 34e sess, 18e supp, Doc NU A/34/18, par. 262.

[199] CEDR, Rapport du Comité pour l'élimination de la discrimination raciale, Doc off AGNU, 42e sess, 18e supp, Doc NU A/42/18, par. 394.

[200] CEDR, Rapport du Comité pour l'élimination de la discrimination raciale, Doc off AGNU, 29e sess, 18e supp, Doc NU A/9618, par. 139.

[201] CEDR, Rapport du Comité pour l'élimination de la discrimination raciale, Doc off AGNU, 31e sess, 18e supp, Doc NU A/31/18, par. 184. L'application supposément partielle de l'alinéa a) de l'article 4 a aussi fait l'objet de demande de précisions pour d'autres raisons: CEDR, Rapport du Comité pour l'élimination de la discrimination raciale, Doc off AGNU, 36e sess, 18e supp, Doc NU A/36/18, par. 315.

[202] Rapport du Comité pour l'élimination de la discrimination raciale, Doc off AGNU, 38e sess, 18e supp, Doc NU A/38/18, par. 397.

[203] Rapport du Comité pour l'élimination de la discrimination raciale, Doc off AGNU, 38e sess, 18e supp, Doc NU A/38/18, par. 397.

[204] Voir les remarques au sujet de la législation du Nouveau-Brusnwick formulées par le CEDR, Rapport du Comité pour l'élimination de la discrimination raciale, Doc off AGNU, 42e sess, 18e supp, Doc NU A/42/18, par. 393.

Le Comité relève aussi le fait que les lois provinciales combattant la publicité discriminatoire contiennent souvent une clause voulant que leurs dispositions ne doivent pas s'interpréter comme faisant obstacle à la liberté d'expression. Certains membres saisissent mal comment ces deux objectifs sont conciliables[205]. Force nous est cependant de préciser que cette apparente antinomie a depuis été dissipée par la Cour suprême du Canada qui n'y voit pas une dérogation comme telle; loin de constituer des exceptions, pareille clause interprétative serait simplement destinée à indiquer aux tribunaux qu'il leur faut « soupeser l'objectif de l'élimination de la discrimination et la nécessité de protéger la liberté d'expression»[206].

Certaines carences d'ampleur purement provinciale ou territoriale continuent de préoccuper le Comité. Dans son rapport le plus récent, le Comité constate « avec préoccupation » que ce ne sont pas toutes les provinces et tous les territoires de l'État partie qui ont adopté de loi adéquate établissant le cadre juridique de lutte contre le racisme et répondant à tous les critères énoncés à l'article 4[207].

Le Comité s'est aussi intéressé à la portée de certains précédents jurisprudentiels. Il s'est ainsi penché sur l'arrêt de la Cour suprême du Canada invalidant l'ancien article 181 C.cr. lequel prohibait la diffusion de fausses nouvelles ainsi que sur l'arrêt de cette même juridiction délimitant la portée du crime d'incitation à la haine de manière à ne pas porter indûment atteinte à la liberté d'expression.[208]

S'est aussi posée la question de savoir si l'examen amorcé par le gouvernement fédéral au sujet de la constitutionnalité de ses textes législatifs au regard des droits consacrés par la *Charte canadienne* embrasserait aussi la question de savoir si les lois et règlements canadiens sont conformes aux dispositions de la Convention.[209]

5.4.5 La Mise en œuvre des Mécanismes de Répression

Certains rapports ont estimé peu vigoureuse l'application des dispositions législatives consacrées aux activités racistes des organisations[210] ou se sont interrogés sur le

---

205 CEDR, Rapport du Comité pour l'élimination de la discrimination raciale, Doc off AGNU, 31e sess, 18e supp, Doc NU A/31/18, par. 184.

206 Canada (Commission des droits de la personne) c Taylor, [1990] 3 RCS 892, 930. Voir aussi la jurisprudence relatée par Walker 2018, p. 10, en ligne: https://lop.parl.ca/sites/PublicWebsite/default/fr_CA/ResearchPublications/201825E.

207 CEDR, Observations finales du Comité pour l'élimination de la discrimination raciale: Canada, Doc off CEDR, 93e sess, Doc NU CERD/C/CAN/CO/21-23 (2017), par. 11.

208 Rapport du Comité pour l'élimination de la discrimination raciale, Doc off AGNU, 49e sess, 18e supp, Doc NU A/49/18, par. 307 et 316.

209 Rapport du Comité pour l'élimination de la discrimination raciale, Doc off AGNU, 38e sess, 18e supp, Doc NU A/38/18, par. 397.

210 CEDR, Rapport du Comité pour l'élimination de la discrimination raciale, Doc off AGNU, 31e sess, 18e supp, Doc NU A/31/18, par. 184; Rapport du Comité pour l'élimination de la discrimination raciale, Doc off AGNU, 38e sess, 18e supp, Doc NU A/38/18, par. 398 ; Rapport du Comité pour

taux de condamnations prononcées[211] ainsi que sur « l'application pratique » de l'article 4 de la Convention et de l'article 718.2 du Code criminel qui stipule que la discrimination raciale constitue une circonstance aggravante de l'infraction.[212]

Le rapport le plus récent du Comité en la matière égrène des inquiétudes précises. Il « note avec préoccupation que les crimes motivés par la haine raciale continuent d'être peu signalés et que l'absence de données à jour, issues d'un suivi systématique et coordonné des crimes de haine raciale dans toutes les provinces et tous les territoires de l'État partie peut signifier que le nombre réel de ces crimes est en réalité beaucoup plus élevé »[213]. Le Comité se dit également « préoccupé par l'augmentation de 61 % du nombre signalé de crimes de haine raciale visant des musulmans »[214]. Une préoccupation supplémentaire se fait jour : « bien que les données fournies par l'État partie sur la mise en œuvre des dispositions antidiscrimination indiquent le nombre ou la nature des incidents et des plaintes soumises, elles ne précisent pas le nombre de poursuites d'office, d'enquêtes et de condamnations prononcées. »[215]

Ces carences donnent lieu à une série de recommandations parmi lesquelles figurent

- La prise de mesures « pour prévenir les crimes de haine raciale contre tous les groupes ethniques et minoritaires, les migrants et les peuples autochtones dans l'État partie »[216]
- La facilitation du « signalement des incidents par les victimes » et la nécessité « de veiller à ce que les crimes de haine raciale donnent lieu à des enquêtes efficaces et que leurs auteurs soient poursuivis et sanctionnés » [217].
- L'enregistrement systématique et la conservation « des données sur le nombre de crimes motivés par la haine raciale signalés, les poursuites engagées, les condamnations prononcées, les peines et les sanctions infligées et les indemnisations accordées aux victimes. L'État partie est prié de faire figurer ces données dans son prochain rapport périodique. » [218].
- La mise en place en faveur des juges et des agents des forces de l'ordre d'une « formation obligatoire sur la reconnaissance et l'enregistrement des crimes de haine raciale et des autres crimes à motivation raciale de façon à ce que les

l'élimination de la discrimination raciale, Doc off AGNU, 49ᵉ sess, 18ᵉ supp, Doc NU A/49/18, par. 329.

[211] CEDR, Rapport du Comité pour l'élimination de la discrimination raciale, Doc off AGNU, 42ᵉ sess, 18ᵉ supp, Doc NU A/42/18, par. 394

[212] Rapport du Comité pour l'élimination de la discrimination raciale, Doc off AGNU, 57ᵉ sess, 18ᵉ supp, Doc NU A/57/18, par. 335.

[213] CEDR, Observations finales du Comité pour l'élimination de la discrimination raciale: Canada, Doc off CEDR, 93ᵉ sess, Doc NU CERD/C/CAN/CO/21-23 (2017), par. 13.

[214] Ibid.

[215] Ibid.

[216] Ibid., par. 14.

[217] Ibid.

[218] Ibid.

plaintes soient traitées de façon appropriée »[219]. L'État partie se voit enjoint « de faire figurer dans son prochain rapport périodique des données actualisées, des renseignements détaillés et des statistiques, notamment sur le calendrier de ces formations, le nombre de personnes formées, et tout effet mesurable » [220].

Cet inventaire de recommandations, les plus récentes à être formulées par le Comité, attestent un souci réel.

Les propos du Comité n'auront pas toujours affiché des préoccupations aussi vives et étayées. S'il est arrivé au Comité de souligner son souci au sujet d'informations faisant état d'actes systématiques de discrimination raciale à l'encontre d'individus d'ascendance africaine ou asiatique, de relever l'expression dans les médias de préjugés à l'égard de ces individus comme des étrangers et des réfugiés [221] et de déplorer la poussée de haine raciale envers les musulmans et des Arabes à la suite des événements du 11 septembre[222], l'occasion lui a aussi été donnée de saluer les prises de position en la matière du Premier ministre canadien[223], d'accueillir favorablement l'avènement d'amendements législatifs destinés à contrer l'incitation à la haine sur internet[224], de souligner l'institution d'une équipe antihaine composée d'enquêteurs, de juristes et de policiers spécialisés dans les enquêtes portant sur des faits d'incitation à la haine sur internet ou encore de signaler le déploiement en Ontario d'un groupe de travail communautaire destiné à enrayer les crimes de haine[225].

5.4.6 Les Interrogations de Nature Factuelle

Qu'il suffise d'ajouter que d'autres demandes de renseignements factuels ont parfois été formulées par le Comité. L'une d'elles porta sur la distribution postale de propagande raciste aux élèves d'établissements scolaires; fut posée la question de savoir si ce phénomène est le fait de secteurs isolés de la population ou, au contraire, de groupes sociaux dont les bases seraient plus larges.[226] D'autres questions ont porté sur les provinces visées par des activités du Ku Klux Klan et les mesures prises en la

[219] Ibid.

[220] Ibid.

[221] CEDR, Rapport du Comité pour l'élimination de la discrimination raciale, Doc off AGNU, 57e sess, 18e supp, Doc NU A/57/18, par. 335

[222] CEDR, Rapport du Comité pour l'élimination de la discrimination raciale, Doc off AGNU, 57e sess, 18e supp, Doc NU A/57/18, par. 338.

[223] Ibid.

[224] CEDR, Observations finales du Comité pour l'élimination de la discrimination raciale: Canada, Doc off CEDR, 70e sess, Doc NU CERD/C/CAN/CO/18 (2007) par. 8.

[225] CEDR, Observations finales du Comité pour l'élimination de la discrimination raciale: Canada, Doc off CEDR, 70e sess, Doc NU CERD/C/CAN/CO/18 (2007) par. 8.

[226] CEDR, Rapport du Comité pour l'élimination de la discrimination raciale, Doc off AGNU, 42e sess, 18e supp, Doc NU A/42/18, par. 393.

matière[227]. Un rapport souhaite un complément d'information au sujet de l'influence qu'exercent sur les jeunes les groupes motivés par la haine.[228]

5.4.7 Application de la CEDR au Discours Haineux par le Législateur, l'administration ou les Tribunaux

Les mêmes causes produisant les mêmes effets, la CEDR, à l'instar du PIDCP, n'a pas fait l'objet d'une transposition intégrale en droit canadien. La nature des liens unissant le droit international des droits de la personne et le droit interne canadien a été exposée précédemment[229].

À défaut d'une transposition directe et immédiate dans l'ordre juridique canadien, la mise en œuvre législative de la CEDR est plutôt la résultante de dispositions diverses relevant tant des champs de compétence du Parlement fédéral que de ceux des législatures provinciales.

Dans les rapports qu'il soumet au Comité pour l'élimination de la discrimination raciale, le gouvernement canadien identifie une série de mesures législatives ayant pour effet d'assurer le respect des obligations prévues à l'article 4 de la Convention. Le rapport le plus détaillé à cet égard, soit le rapport consolidé préparé dans le cadre des 19e et 20e cycles d'examen, cite en premier lieu les articles 318 à 320.1 du Code criminel.[230] Ces derniers incriminent l'incitation au génocide, l'incitation publique à la haine et la fomentation volontaire de la haine. Ces dispositions permettent, au surplus, la confiscation ou la saisie de publication de cette nature ou encore l'interdiction de l'accès à de telles publications lorsque celles-ci sont rendues disponibles en ligne.

À l'arsenal répressif décrit dans le rapport s'ajoutait, avant son abrogation en 2014, l'article 13 de la *Loi canadienne sur les droits de la personne* lequel interdisait l'utilisation du téléphone ou des services d'une entreprise de communication pour exposer un groupe identifiable à la haine ou au mépris[231]. Ledit rapport cite également l'article 8 du *Règlement sur la distribution de radiodiffusion* qui interdit la distribution d'une programmation contenant « des propos offensants ou des images offensantes qui, pris dans leur contexte, risquent d'exposer une personne, un groupe ou une classe de personnes à la haine ou au mépris pour des motifs fondés sur la race, l'origine

[227] Ibid.

[228] CEDR, Rapport du Comité pour l'élimination de la discrimination raciale, Doc off AGNU, 49e sess, 18e supp, Doc NU A/49/18, par. 307. Le même rapport s'interroge quant à l'ampleur des activités des organes de défense des droits de l'homme en fonction des provinces et la compatibilité de leurs activités avec l'article 4 de la Conventions

[229] Voir les explications fournies à la question n° 5.3 traitée dans le présent rapport.

[230] CEDR, Dix-neuvième et vingtième rapports périodiques que les États parties devaient présenter en 2009: Canada, Doc NU CERD/C/CAN/19-20 (2011), par. 78–82.

[231] Ibid., aux par. 83–85.

nationale ou ethnique, la couleur, la religion, le sexe, l'orientation sexuelle, l'âge ou une déficience physique ou mentale ».[232]

L'on se doit d'ajouter à cette énumération l'article 718.2 a) (i) du Code criminel qui énonce, en tête de liste des circonstances aggravantes au stade de la détermination de la peine du délinquant, le fait que l'infraction ait été motivée « par des préjugés ou de la haine fondée sur des facteurs tels que la race, l'origine nationale ou ethnique, la langue, la couleur, la religion, le sexe, l'âge, la déficience mentale ou physique, l'orientation sexuelle ou l'identité ou l'expression de genre ».[233] Loin de se satisfaire d'en faire un pur critère d'alourdissement de la peine, il arrive que le législateur requalifie l'infraction lorsqu'elle participe d'un sentiment haineux. Par exemple, est coupable de l'infraction de méfait aggravé au sens de l'article 430 (4.1) du Code criminel, l'individu qui commet certains types de méfait « en étant motivé par des préjugés ou de la haine fondées sur la couleur, la race, la religion, l'origine nationale ou ethnique, l'âge, le sexe, l'orientation sexuelle, l'identité ou l'expression de genre ou la déficience mentale ou physique. ».

L'application de ces diverses dispositions obéit aux principes relatés précédemment au sujet de l'incidence du PIDCP en droit canadien.[234] Les obligations internationales auxquelles est tenu le Canada en vertu de la CEDR sont de nature à rejaillir sur l'interprétation accordée aux droits garantis par la *Charte canadienne des droits et libertés* tout comme elles peuvent étayer l'existence d'un objectif réel et urgent dans l'hypothèse où le respect de ces obligations emporte la limitation d'un droit fondamental.

L'on ne saurait donc s'étonner que l'alinéa a de l'article 4 de la Convention ait revêtu un « intérêt spécial » de l'aveu même des juges majoritaires appelés dans l'arrêt *Keegstra* à confirmer la constitutionnalité de la disposition du *Code criminel* qui pourfend la fomentation volontaire de la haine[235]. Dans le contexte précis de la répression des propos haineux, la Cour suprême du Canada prend soin d'énoncer qu'un « degré élévé d'importance » doit être accordé, au moment de l'analyse constitutionnelle, à une valeur hissée au rang de droit international de la personne[236]. Le texte de la Convention et les obligations qu'elle renferme ont également été mobilisés lors de plusieurs autres décisions rendues par les tribunaux canadiens, chaque fois au soutien de la validité ou de la portée des dispositions du droit canadien permettant leur mise en œuvre sur le territoire canadien.[237]

---

[232] DORS 97-555, art. 8.

[233] Voir notamment Ministère de la Justice du Canada, « La haine en tant que circonstance aggravante dans la détermination de la peine - Examen de la jurisprudence-de 2007 à 2020», Sa Majesté la Reine du chef du Canada, 2021, 2020 CanLIIDocs 3732 (en ligne); Lawrence et Verdun-Jones 2011, p. 28; Roberts et Harting 2001, p. 93; Vinet c R., 2021 QCCQ 3474, par. 119 à 123; R. c Leach, 2019 BCCA 451, par. 84 à 90; R. c Gray, 2013 ABCA 237; R. c Woodward, 2011 BCCA 251.

[234] Voir notre examen de ce sujet à la question 5.3.1 du présent rapport.

[235] R. c Keegstra, [1990] 3 RCS 697, 751.

[236] R. c Keegstra, [1990] 3 RCS 697, 750.

[237] Voir notamment Saskatchewan (Human Rights Commission) c Whatcott, 2013 CSC 11, par. 67; Canada (Commission des droits de la personne c Taylor, [1990] 3 RCS 892, 919 et 920, en ligne: https://canlii.ca/t/1fsp1; R. c Andrews, 1988 CanLII 200 (ON CA), 65 OR (2d) 161, 28 OAC 161, 43

5.5 Droit et Organisations Régionaux

Le Canada n'est partie à aucun traité régional comportant des dispositions portant sur le discours haineux ou l'incitation à la haine. Il s'est gardé de ratifier la *Convention américaine relative aux droits de l'homme*, la *Convention interaméricaine contre le racisme, la discrimination raciale et les formes connexes d'intolérance* ainsi que la *Convention interaméricaine contre toutes les formes de discrimination*. Par ailleurs, aucune des recommandations de la Commission interaméricaine des droits de l'homme portant sur le fond d'une communication concernant le Canada n'avait trait à la propagande haineuse.

D'une manière un rien incongrue, les obligations internationales du Canada en matière d'interdit de la propagande haineuse ont été citées à titre d'exemple lorsque le ministre des Affaires étrangères exposa à la Chambre des communes les raisons pour lesquelles le Canada n'a pas ratifié la *Convention américaine relative aux droits de l'homme*:

> Avant de pouvoir ratifier une convention sur les droits de l'homme, le Canada doit être certain qu'il puisse être en mesure de respecter les engagements découlant de cette ratification. [...] Un grand nombre des dispositions de la Convention sont en effet ambiguës ou contiennent des principes inconnus ou problématiques dans la législation canadienne. Plus important encore, de nombreuses dispositions de la Convention vont à l'encontre d'autres normes internationales concernant les droits de l'homme, ce qui rend encore plus difficile au Canada de respecter à la fois la CADH et ces normes.
>
> Par exemple, la CADH interdirait la censure préalable, entrant ainsi en conflit avec les obligations internationales contractées par le Canada en vue de supprimer la propagande haineuse et la pornographie juvénile.[238]

CCC (3d) 193, 65 CR (3d) 320 aux pp. 20–21, en ligne: https://canlii.ca/t/1p786 (motifs dissidents du juge Cory auxquels ont ultérieurement adhéré les juges majoritaires de la Cour suprême du Canada); Ross c Conseil scolaire du district n° 15 du Nouveau-Brunswick, [1996]1 RCS 825, 880; Canada (Commission canadienne des droits de la personne) c Warman, [2014] 1 RCF 608, 2012 CF 1162, par. 83, en ligne: https://canlii.ca/t/ft222; R c Topham, 2017 BCSC 259, par. 25, en ligne: https://canlii.ca/t/gxkj0; Saskatchewan (Human Rights Commission) c Bell, 1991 CanLII 7733 (SK QB), 88 DLR (4th) 71, [1992] 2 WWR 1, 96 Sask R 296, 16 CHRR 52, par. 43–44, en ligne: https://canlii.ca/t/g9qsx; Canadian Jewish Congress c North Shore News and Collins, 1997 BCHRT 35 (CanLII), 30 CHRR 5, par. 160, en ligne: https://canlii.ca/t/h3w1m.

238 Comité sénatorial permanent des droits de la personne, Améliorer le rôle du Canada dans l'OEA: l'adhésion du Canada à la Convention américaine relative aux droits de l'homme, 2003, en ligne: https://sencanada.ca/Content/SEN/Committee/372/huma/rep/rep04may03-f.htm.

5.6 Droit Comparé

La jurisprudence canadienne a pris parti : le droit américain en la matière est mis en veilleuse[239] au profit des décisions européennes relatives à la *Convention européenne de sauvegarde des droits de l'homme et des libertés fondamentales*[240] et des décisions rendues par des comités internationaux[241]. La distanciation prise au Canada par rapport au droit américain ne souffre guère d'ambiguïté, comme l'énoncent les motifs des juges majoritaires dans l'arrêt de principe en la matière:

> … dans les cas où l'article premier joue pour mettre en relief une vision proprement canadienne d'une société libre et démocratique, il ne faut pas hésiter à quitter la voie tracée par les États-Unis. Loin de dicter une protection moins empressée des droits et libertés garantis par la *Charte*, cette vision indépendante les protège d'une manière différente. Comme je l'indique ci-après, l'engagement international envers l'élimination de la propagande haineuse et, plus important encore, le rôle particulier donné à l'égalité et au multiculturalisme dans la constitution canadienne exige que l'on s'écarte du point de vue assez prédominant aujourd'hui en Amérique du Nord, selon lequel la suppression de la propagande haineuse est incompatible avec la garantie de liberté d'expression. (À l'appui de ce point de vue, voir les commentaires des professeurs K. Mahoney et J. Cameron dans "Language as Violence v. Freedom of Expression: Canadian and American Perspectives on Group Defamation" (1988/89), 37 *Buffalo L. Rev.* 337, aux pp. 344 et 353 respectivement)...
>
> Si les valeurs fondamentales soutenant la conception canadienne d'une société libre et démocratique suggèrent une approche qui refuse à la propagande haineuse le plus haut degré de protection constitutionnelle, c'est cette approche que nous devons adopter.[242]

Comme l'expose la Commission canadienne des droits de la personne à l'occasion de la parution d'un rapport spécial remis au Parlement canadien:

> « Comme en témoignent les affaires Keegstra et Taylor, la Cour suprême du Canada a adopté une approche différente. Dans un article signé de sa plume, le juge Russell Juriansz, de la Cour d'appel de l'Ontario, examine l'approche américaine en matière de propagande haineuse par rapport à celle adoptée par d'autres pays, dont le Canada, et conclut : Il semble que la position américaine est en train de devenir une position minoritaire, tandis que le Canada se rallie à un nouveau consensus global en émergence qui accueille favorablement l'imposition de certaines restrictions à la liberté d'expression jugées souhaitables et nécessaires. Russell Juriansz, « La lutte contre la haine et la préservation de la liberté d'expression : où faut-il établir la ligne de démarcation? », La haine sur Internet, Thèmes canadiens, printemps 2006. »[243]

---

[239] Voir les réserves exprimées au sujet de la transposabilité du droit américain en droit constitutionnel ou pénal canadien: R. c Keegstra, [1990] 3 R.C.S. 697, 738 à 744.

[240] En témoigne le traitement favorable réservé à l'affaire Glimmerveen c Pays-Bas, Comm. Eur. D. H., Requêtes n°s 8348/78 et 8406/78, 11 octobre 1979, D.R. 18, p. 187, dans les arrêts de la Cour suprême du Canada: R. c Keegstra, [1990] 3 R.C.S. 697; Canada (Commission des droits de la personne) c Taylor, [1990] 3 R.C.S. 892.

[241] Nous renvoyons le lecteur aux réponses apportées aux questions 5.3.1 et 5.4.7 du présent rapport.

[242] R. c Keegstra, [1990] 3 R.C.S. 697, 743 et 744.

[243] Commission canadienne des droits de la personne 2009, p. 17.

5.7 Des Précisions Complémentaires sur le Régime Pénal

Il est indispensable de bien différencier les régimes juridiques selon que les sanctions sont civiles ou administratives ou bien pénales. Les précisions concernant la nature des propos de nature à engendrer des sanctions civiles ou administratives, qu'elles visent directement les propos haineux ou qu'elles s'étendent aux propos de nature à susciter la discrimination, figurent pour l'essentiel dans les réponses déjà apportées aux questions 5.1 à 5.2.2.4 du présent rapport. Qu'il suffise de rappeler l'absence de prise en compte de l'intention du locuteur et l'interprétation étroite donnée à la notion de sauvegarde de la dignité d'autrui. Qu'il suffise aussi de réitérer l'impossibilité, constitutionnellement parlant, de sanctionner des propos qui se contentent de ridiculiser ou de rabaisser un groupe vulnérable.

Les remarques suivantes viseront donc, pour l'essentiel du moins, les sanctions proprement pénales énoncées au code criminel canadien. Trois crimes seront abordés.

En premier lieu, le paragraphe 318(1) C.cr. érige en acte criminel l'encouragement au génocide. À la lumière des textes internationaux incriminant également l'incitation au génocide, la Cour suprême du Canada estime que la disposition canadienne exige la preuve d'une incitation qui soit à la fois « directe » et « publique »[244]. Ainsi, les mots employés devraient non seulement être prononcés publiquement, mais aussi « être suffisamment clairs pour être immédiatement compris par l'auditoire visé. Insinuations et propos obscurs ne suffisent pas »[245].

Autre fait notable, la portée de cet acte criminel est également restreinte par une définition tronquée du crime de génocide. En effet, la définition qu'en donne le paragraphe 318(2) C.cr ne vise que deux des cinq actes incriminés au second article de la *Convention sur la prévention et la répression du crime de génocide*, nommément le meurtre de membres du groupe et le fait de soumettre délibérément ce dernier « à des conditions de vie propres à entraîner sa destruction physique »[246]. L'incitation au génocide, telle qu'elle se voit incriminée par le code criminel canadien, doit donc tendre à provoquer la commission de l'un de ces actes dans l'intention « de détruire totalement ou partiellement un groupe identifiable »[247]. En revanche, la preuve d'un lien de causalité entre l'incitation et la commission de ces actes n'est aucunement requise puisque « l'incitation est punissable en elle-même, sans égard au résultat. Elle constitue un crime qu'elle produise ou non l'effet escompté »[248].

En deuxième lieu, l'incitation publique à la haine est pour sa part incriminée au paragraphe 319(1) du Code criminel. Suivant le libellé de cette disposition, l'infraction vise « [q]uiconque, par la communication de déclarations en un endroit public, incite à la haine contre un groupe identifiable, lorsqu'une telle incitation est susceptible d'entraîner une violation de la paix ». Cette infraction exige donc une

---

244 Mugesera c Canada, 2005 CSC 40, par. 86.

245 Mugesera c Canada, 2005 CSC 40, par. 87.

246 Code criminel, art. 318(2). Comparer Convention pour la prévention et la répression du crime de génocide, 9 décembre 1948, 78 RTNU 277 (entrée en vigueur : 12 janvier 1951), art 2.

247 Code criminel, supra note 4, art 318(2).

248 Mugesera c Canada, 2005 CSC 40, par. 85.

preuve hors de tout doute raisonnable non seulement du contexte public dans lequel les déclarations incitant à la haine ont été communiquées, mais aussi du risque de violation de la paix qu'elles font naître[249]. Cette dernière exigence est propre au paragraphe 319(1) C.cr.: ni l'incrimination de l'encouragement au génocide ni celle de la fomentation de la haine n'exigent une preuve du risque suscité par les propos d'un inculpé. Encore que l'expression possède des contours un rien flous, une jurisprudence contemporaine très clairsemée estime que la violation de la paix renvoie à « un certain degré de violence et un risque de préjudice ».[250]

L'insouciance du prévenu quant aux répercussions possibles de ses gestes est obligatoire et elle s'apprécie subjectivement:

> Section 281.2(1) [dorénavant l'article 319 (1) C.cr.], unlike s. 281.2(2) [dorénavant l'article 319 (2) C.cr.], is restricted to the incitement of hatred by communicating statements in a public place where such incitement is likely to lead to a breach of the peace. ... The general mens rea which is required ... is either the intentional or reckless bringing about of the result which the law, in creating the offence, seeks to prevent and, hence, under s. 281.2(1) is either the intentional or reckless inciting of hatred in the specified circumstances.[251]

S'il se garde de sanctionner le simple délit d'opinion[252], l'article 319 (1) C.cr. peut néanmoins assurer des déclarations de culpabilité à la suite de l'autodafé d'une croix[253], de la publication de commentaires haineux sur la page *Facebook* du service de l'information d'un diffuseur télévisuel[254] et de la diffusion sur la plateforme *YouTube* d'enregistrements vidéo contenant des propos haineux[255]. À vrai dire, emportent condamnation des propos reprochant aux membres d'un groupe identifiable « d'être la cause de problèmes actuels de la société, des propos qui prétendent qu'ils constituent une menace, qu'ils complotent pour détruire la civilisation occidentale, qu'ils se livrent à des activités illicites, les présentant comme des menteurs, des propos qui emploient des termes déshumanisants en assimilant les membres à des animaux ou des êtres inférieurs »[256].

En troisième et dernier lieu, le législateur fédéral interdit la fomentation volontaire de la haine. L'article 319 (2) C.cr. défend à quiconque de fomenter la haine contre

---

249 Dion c R., 2020 QCCS 3049, par. 20 (requête pour permission d'en appeler rejetée: Dion c R, 2020 QCCA 1658) citant R. c Rioux, 2016 QCCS 6762, par. 15.

250 Ibid., par. 48 (requête pour permission d'en appeler rejetée: Dion c R, 2020 QCCA 1658). Et le tribunal de conclure en l'occurrence que « l'appel au réveil des Québécois par le ton agressif employé et les circonstances dans lesquelles les vidéos sont publiées, soit la commémoration de la tuerie à la grande mosquée de Québec, peuvent faire en sorte que les propos publiés dans les vidéos sont susceptibles d'entraîner un risque de préjudice pour les membres du groupe cible. » (par. 58).

251 R. c Buzzanga and Durocher, 1979 CanLII 1927 (C.A. Ont.).

252 Dion c R., 2020 QCCS 3049, par. 5 (requête pour permission d'en appeler rejetée: Dion c R, 2020 QCCA 1658).

253 R. c Rehberg, 2010 NSPC 101.

254 R. c Rioux, 2016 QCCS 6762.

255 Dion c R., 2020 QCCS 3049, par. 20 (requête pour permission d'en appeler rejetée: Dion c R, 2020 QCCA 1658).

256 Cette liste inspirée de l'arrêt Whatcott est reprise dans l'affaire Dion c R., 2020 QCCS 3049, par. 25 (requête pour permission d'en appeler rejetée: Dion c R, 2020 QCCA 1658).

un « groupe identifiable » en communiquant des déclarations « autrement que dans une conversation privée ». La jurisprudence balise soigneusement le champ de la répression de sorte que seules les « formes d'expression les plus intentionnellement extrêmes »[257] sont frappées d'interdit. Ainsi, la sanction de la loi criminelle ne s'étend qu'aux propos enfiellés les plus véhéments qui, n'ayant pas été échangés dans le cadre d'une conversation privée, sont de surcroît intentionnellement destinés à promouvoir la haine contre un groupe protégé.

Plusieurs garde-fous sont ainsi institués de manière à enserrer la répression sans porter atteinte indûment à la liberté d'expression. La première balise a trait à l'élément matériel de l'infraction. Tenir un propos incendiaire en public ne suffit pas à lui seul. Encore faut-il que les paroles prononcées relèvent de la fomentation de la haine:

> Du reste, la simple formulation de propos haineux n'entrave pas l'article 319 (2) C.cr.[258]; il ne saurait davantage suffire de prouver que l'accusé a favorisé, de par ses dires, la haine envers une communauté. Des propos qui « favorisent » ou « encouragent » la haine ne sont pas punissables per se[259]. Il en est ainsi parce que la vocation des propos importe tout autant que leur teneur : il leur faut être destinés à l'éclosion de la haine. Le droit criminel s'intéresse à la finalité des paroles incriminées, non point à leur effet. Le texte d'incrimination interdit la « fomentation » de la haine. Cette expression signifie, selon la jurisprudence la plus autorisée, le fait de promouvoir activement la détestation[260]. Des propos ostensiblement haineux échapperont à la répression si le contexte de l'entretien indique que l'inculpé n'entendait pas, à ce moment, favoriser l'attisement de la haine. L'étude du contexte peut révéler un dérapage verbal, l'inculpé tenant des propos haineux sans vouloir pour autant leur dissémination : des paroles haineuses prononcées sous le coup de l'emportement, sans arrière-pensée, peuvent ainsi se soustraire à la répression[261]. La finalité des propos intéresse, au premier chef, l'élément matériel du crime puisqu'ils doivent être voués à la fomentation de la haine.[262]

Ainsi s'explique l'acquittement d'un chef autochtone interpellé par un journaliste à l'issue d'une conférence. Sous le coup de l'agitation et de l'exaspération, il prononcera des propos antisémites sans se douter qu'ils seraient repris dans les médias[263].

La seconde digue est pareillement posée par le législateur. Quatre types d'énoncés échappent à l'interdit pénal comme le veut l'article 319 (3) C.cr.:

> (3) Nul ne peut être déclaré coupable d'une infraction prévue au paragraphe (2) dans les cas suivants:

---

[257] R. c Keegstra, [1990] 3 R.C.S. 697, 783.

[258] R. c Ahenakew, (2008) 227 C.C.C. (3d) 428, par. 48 et 49 (C.A. Sask.).

[259] Mugesera c Canada, 2005 CSC 40, par. 101.

[260] Ibid.

[261] R. c Ahenakew, (2008) 227 C.C.C. (3d) 428 (C.A. Sask.). Cf. encore R. c Ahenakew, [2009] S.J. n° 105 (C. prov. Sask.).

[262] Voir les nuances de bon aloi formulées dans l'arrêt R. c Ahenakew, (2008) 227 C.C.C. (3d) 428; [2008] S.J. n° 9, par. 20, 48 et 49 (C.A. Sask.). Cf. encore R. c Ahenakew, [2009] S.J. n° 105 (C. prov. Sask.). Ce paragraphe est tiré de Rainville 2015, p. 118.

[263] R. c Ahenakew, (2008) 227 C.C.C. (3d) 428; [2008] S.J. n° 9 (C.A. Sask.) et, par la suite, R. c. Ahenakew, [2009] S.J. n° 105 (C. prov. Sask.).

(a) il établit que les déclarations communiquées étaient vraies;
(b) il a, de bonne foi, exprimé une opinion sur un sujet religieux ou une opinion fondée sur un texte religieux auquel il croit, ou a tenté d'en établir le bien-fondé par argument;
(c) les déclarations se rapportaient à une question d'intérêt public dont l'examen était fait dans l'intérêt du public et, pour des motifs raisonnables, il les croyait vraies;
(d) de bonne foi, il voulait attirer l'attention, afin qu'il y soit remédié, sur des questions provoquant ou de nature à provoquer des sentiments de haine à l'égard d'un groupe identifiable au Canada

La troisième balise est de nature proprement prétorienne. Elle a trait à l'acception très limitée donnée au vocable « haine »:

> Le procédé destiné à circonscrire l'infraction aura passé par une interprétation prétorienne très étroite du vocable « haine » figurant à l'article 319 C.cr. La Cour suprême du Canada désavoue la plupart des sens attribués à ce terme par les dictionnaires[264] pour s'en tenir à une acception très limitative[265] confinée aux formes d'expression « les plus intentionnellement extrêmes »[266]. Entailler le texte d'incrimination de la sorte réduit d'autant la gamme des propos bannis.
> Une expression d'aversion envers une religion ou ses pratiques n'est pas l'équivalent de l'incitation à la haine envers la communauté en question[267]. La dérision d'une religion ne participe pas davantage de l'incitation à la haine envers les croyants. À lui seul, le discrédit jeté sur une confession ne traduit pas la volonté de fomenter la haine contre ses adeptes. En somme, les paroles offensantes ne suffisent pas à caractériser la provocation à la haine[268]: sont seuls proscrits les propos de nature « inusitée et extrême »[269]

En proclamant sa volonté d'assujettir la répression aux seuls propos destinés à susciter « des émotions exceptionnellement fortes et profondes de détestation »[270], la Cour suprême du Canada dit à demi-mot que cette ligne de démarcation met à l'abri des œuvres littéraires tels *Les Versets sataniques* de Salmon Rushdie.[271]

Il y a tout lieu, à cet égard, de comparer le degré de gravité de la faute en matière civile et celui propre à la faute de nature criminelle. Des propos insuffisants à caractériser une faute civile ne sauraient tomber sous le coup du droit criminel en raison

[264] R. c Keegstra, [1990] 3 R.C.S. 697, 776 et 777.

[265] Saskatchewan (Human Rights Commission) c. Whatcott, 2013 CSC 11, par. 39 à 42, 48 et 57.

[266] R. c Keegstra, [1990] 3 R.C.S. 697, 783; Mugesera c Canada, 2005 CSC 40, par. 101.

[267] Saskatchewan (Human Rights Commission) c Whatcott, 2013 CSC 11, par. 39 à 42.

[268] Ibid., par. 41, 46, 47, 50, 51, 57, 58, 90, 109 et 200; Mugesera c Canada, 2005 CSC 40, par. 103; R. c Keegstra, [1990] 3 R.C.S. 697, 778.

[269] Saskatchewan (Human Rights Commission) c Whatcott, 2013 CSC 11, par. 40. Voir encore les par. 41, 48, 57 et 89. Ces deux paragraphes sont extraits de P. Rainville, La répression de l'art et l'art de la répression. La profanation de la religion à l'épreuve des mutations du droit pénal au sujet du blasphème et de la protection des identités religieuses, Québec, Presses de l'Université Laval, 2019, p. 59 et 60.

[270] Saskatchewan (Human Rights Commission) c Whatcott, 2013 CSC 11, par. 40. Voir encore Mugesera c. Canada, 2005 CSC 40, par. 101.

[271] R. c Keegstra, [1990] 3 R.C.S. 697, 783. Il convient de faire état du regard pénétrant posé sur cette œuvre par Melkevik 2010, pp. 201 à 216.

du principe de l'*ultima ratio*. Aussi peut-on s'inspirer de la jurisprudence civiliste québécoise pour saisir également la ligne de démarcation du licite et de l'illicite.

Il en va notamment ainsi de la critique véhémente d'une religion ou des pratiques de ses adeptes:

> La faute de nature criminelle présente – par hypothèse – un degré de gravité accentué par rapport à la faute civile[272]. Il en résulte que les propos tolérés par le droit civil ne sauraient guère présenter la dangerosité voulue par le droit criminel. Or, la contestation acérée et sans ménagement aucun d'un dogme religieux ou des pratiques d'une confession ne caractérise pas en soi une faute civile. Plusieurs affirmations décapantes relatives au thème du sacré échappent d'autant à la conception civiliste de la diffamation. Il en ainsi va de la déclaration selon laquelle les enseignements religieux réservés aux enfants hassidiques constituent un « gaspillage de potentiel humain » au nom d'une religion pratiquée « de façon intégriste et débilitante » par la « secte Satmar [qui] sacrifie au Québec des milliers d'enfants sur l'autel de l'ultra-orthodoxie religieuse, les estropiant socialement et les rendant inaptes à contribuer de quelque façon que ce soit au développement de la société québécoise.»[273]. La dénonciation de certaines formes d'enseignement islamique dans les écoles confessionnelles québécoises ne se prête pas davantage à la caractérisation d'une faute civile. Relève de la liberté d'expression, l'opinion exprimée à la radio par une militante de la société civile qui estime que certaines sourates enseignées aux enfants « ont un caractère extrêmement violent [...] misogyne et sexiste » ou qui professe que la séparation des sexes à l'œuvre dans un établissement scolaire relève de l'«apartheid sexuel». La faute civile n'est pas davantage accusée par son avis selon lequel il est question en l'occurrence d'un « endoctrinement digne d'un camp militaire en Afghanistan ou au Pakistan » et que le système scolaire privé en cause revient à « fabriquer des militants intégristes qui vont revendiquer, d'ici quelques années, des accommodements et toutes sortes de choses farfelues »[274]. La contestation de choix religieux assis sur un dogme ne participe pas d'une faute civile. La faute criminelle est dès lors encore plus en retrait.[275]

Une quatrième balise pareillement prétorienne vient enserrer la répression. Au contraire de l'article 319 (1), l'article 319 (2) C.cr. ne se satisfait pas de la seule insouciance (« recklessness»). L'intensité de la faute morale recherche est bien plus aiguë. La jurisprudence l'a soigneusement délimitée[276]. L'indifférence de l'accusé quant aux répercussions de ses paroles ne constitue pas, en l'occurrence, un état d'esprit suffisamment blâmable[277]. Il lui faut rechercher l'éclosion de la haine ou encore prévoir que ce résultat découlera quasi inéluctablement de ses paroles. La culpabilité

[272] R. c Zundel, [1992] 2 R.C.S. 731, 774.

[273] Rosenberg c Lacerte, 2013 QCCS 6286 (pourvoi rejeté sur requête : 2014 QCCA 557).

[274] École musulmane de Montréal c Benhabib, 2016 QCCS 6067 (appel rejeté sur requête: 2017 QCCA 775).

[275] Cet extrait est tiré de Rainville 2019, pp. 65 et 66 [certaines références sont omises ou abrégées].

[276] Nos remarques se limitent à l'infraction énoncée à l'article 319 (2) C.cr. et excluent donc l'infraction connexe prévue à l'article 319 (1) C.cr.

[277] L'insouciance (une notion apparentée au dol général du droit pénal continental) affichée à l'égard du retentissement vraisemblable des paroles prononcées ne saurait se traduire par une condamnation: Mugesera c Canada, 2005 CSC 40, par. 104; R. c Keegstra, [1990] 3 R.C.S. 697, 775; R. c. Buzzanga and Durocher, (1979) 49 C.C.C. (2d) 369 (C.A. Ont.). En revanche, l'aveuglement volontaire pourrait asseoir un verdict de culpabilité: R. c Elms, (2006) 217 C.C.C. (3d) 217, par. 21 (C.A. Ont.; requête en autorisation de pourvoi à la Cour suprême du Canada rejetée); R. c Harding, (2002) 160 C.C.C. (3d) 225 (C.A. Ont.).

est tributaire de la prise de conscience par l'accusé de la fatalité de ses propos et de leur effet: l'inculpé «doit avoir l'intention d'exciter directement et activement la haine contre un groupe identifiable ou prévoir cette conséquence comme presque certaine».[278]

En somme, de deux choses l'une. Soit que l'inculpé recherche l'éclosion de la haine envers un groupe identifiable, soit qu'il envisage cette perspective comme certaine ou quasi certaine en raison des propos qu'il formule. L'un ou l'autre de ces éléments mentaux suffit.

Le procès de l'ironie n'est pas inenvisageable pour autant encore que plusieurs distinctions s'imposent:

> Cette forme d'humour est empreinte de dissimulation quant aux intentions véritables du locuteur. L'humour se tapit derrière les paroles prononcées. Aussi la parodie expose-t-elle le rieur à l'incompréhension possible de son auditoire et à celle du juriste.[279]
>
> Les dangers réels auxquels s'expose l'ironie sont attestés dans un arrêt de principe rendu au sujet du crime d'incitation à la haine. L'affaire en cause éclate sur fond de crise linguistique à la fin des années 70. Deux Franco-ontariens, Buzzanga et Durocher, rédigent un pamphlet anonyme qui s'emploie à décrier leur propre minorité linguistique. Une poursuite leur sera intentée au motif qu'ils ont fomenté la haine contre les leurs. Ils opposent en défense la thèse de l'ironie. Les inculpés auraient supposément entendu se moquer des préjugés du conseil municipal de la ville d'Essex à l'endroit des Franco-ontariens. Des mois durant, le projet de construction d'une école secondaire francophone était demeuré dans une impasse au conseil municipal. Buzzanga et Durocher affirment avoir voulu dénoncer la chose en écrivant un pamphlet anonyme qui suggérait de réserver aux Franco-ontariens le même sort qu'aux Acadiens au moment de leur déportation. Selon les déclarations des accusés à leur procès, ils espéraient voir leur texte créer la controverse et l'indignation de manière à inciter le gouvernement ontarien à passer outre à l'opposition du conseil municipal et à faire bâtir l'école malgré les réticences des échevins. Autrement dit, Buzzanga et Durocher entendaient se moquer des préjugés anti-francophones du conseil municipal et non pas attiser la haine contre leur propre communauté.
>
> La Cour d'appel de l'Ontario casse le verdict de culpabilité et ordonne un nouveau procès. Afin de se rendre coupables, il eût fallu que les inculpés prévoient l'effet néfaste de leur pamphlet sur la minorité francophone. La culpabilité de l'accusé passe par sa connaissance de ce que son pamphlet se retournera contre les siens. Un nouveau procès s'impose puisque cette question de fait fut occultée en première instance.
>
> La thèse de l'ironie n'est donc pas celle de l'impunité. Autant l'insouciance du railleur à l'égard des répercussions possibles de ses paroles ne saurait suffire à le faire condamner, autant il en ira autrement si sa faculté d'anticipation l'amène à appréhender que son texte engendrera *certainement ou quasi certainement* la haine.[280]

---

[278] R. c Keegstra, [1990] 3 R.C.S. 697, 777. Le Code criminel se distingue en cela de la législation provinciale bannissant les propos haineux afin de mieux endiguer la discrimination. La législation provinciale destinée à lutter contre la discrimination peut combattre les expressions prononcées par une personne qui n'est pas motivée par la haine: Saskatchewan (Human Rights Commission) c Whatcott, 2013 CSC 11, par. 58, 126, 127, 143 et 190 ainsi que nos explications en la matière figurant dans les réponses aux questions 5.1.2 et 5.2.2.2 du présent rapport.

[279] Le risque d'incompréhension de l'ironie et les enjeux que pose son ambiguïté en droit pénal sont abordés dans Rainville 2015, pp. 121 à 132; Rainville 2005.

[280] Ces passages sont tirés de P. Rainville, « Dérision et religion: de l'ironie à la répression » dans *Droit pénal, culture et religion* (dir. J.-C. Saint-Pau et al.), Travaux de l'Institut de sciences

Aussi la Cour d'appel de l'Ontario ordonne-t-elle un nouveau procès afin de faire élucider des questions factuelles propres à la détermination de l'état d'esprit de l'inculpé et de son sens de l'anticipation:

> I am, with deference to the learned trial Judge, of the view that an intention to create "controversy, furor and an uproar" is not the same thing as an intention to promote hatred, and it was an error to equate them. I would, of course, agree that if the appellants intentionally promoted hatred against the French-speaking community of Essex County as a means of obtaining the French-language high school, they committed the offence charged. The appellants' evidence, if believed, does not, however, as the learned trial Judge appears to have thought, inevitably lead to that conclusion. The learned trial Judge, not having disbelieved the appellants' evidence, failed to give appropriate consideration to their evidence on the issue of intent and, in the circumstances, his failure so to do constituted self-misdirection[281].

La sphère des préjudices devant être envisagée par l'inculpé nécessite pourtant certaines précisions: l'incitation à la haine ne se cantonne pas à la seule incitation à la violence[282]. Des condamnations ont été prononcées à l'égard de déclarations antisémites faites par un professeur à ses étudiants de niveau secondaire[283], de la publication d'un magazine par une organisation de nationalistes blancs[284], de l'envoi de lettres de menaces faussement attribuées à la communauté juive afin de susciter la haine contre ce groupe[285], de la distribution de dépliants ciblant les personnes de confession musulmane et la diffusion de messages téléphoniques haineux[286], de l'hébergement d'un site Internet suprémaciste et la publication de billets haineux sur ce dernier[287], de la publication sur la plateforme *YouTube* de commentaires racistes[288], de la publication répétée de commentaires haineux dans un journal communautaire[289] et de la distribution de DVD dont les pochettes et le contenu incitaient à la haine contre les homosexuels.[290]

---

criminelles et de la justice de Bordeaux, vol. n° 6, Paris, Éditions Cujas, 2017, p. 113 [références omises].

281 R c Buzzanga and Durocher, [1979] OJ No 4345, 101 DLR (3d) 488, 25 OR (2d) 705, 49 CCC (2d) 369, par. 54 (C.A. Ont.).

282 R. c Noble, [2008] B.C.J. n° 294, par. 48 (C. sup. C.-B.).

283 R. c Keegstra, [1990] 3 R.C.S. 697.

284 R. c Andrews, [1990] 3 RCS 870.

285 R. c Safadi, (1994), 121 Nfld & PEIR 260, 24 WCB (2d) 270, 377 APR 260 (C.A. Î.-P.-É.).

286 R. c Harding (2001) 57 O.R. (3d) 333 (C.A. Ont.; demande d'autorisation de pourvoi devant la Cour suprême du Canada refusée).

287 R. c Noble, 2008 BCSC 215. Voir également R. c Topham, 2017 BCSC 551.

288 R. c Castonguay, 2013 QCCQ 4286.

289 R. c Sears, 2021 ONCA 522.

290 R. c Popescu, 2020 ONCJ 427.

References

Comité spécial de la propagande haineuse au Canada (1966) Rapport soumis au ministre de la Justice par le Comité spécial de la propagande haineuse au Canada. R. Duhamel, Imprimeur de la Reine et Contrôleur de la Papeterie, Ottawa.

Commission canadienne des droits de la personne (2009) Rapport spécial au parlement: liberté d'expression et droit à la protection contre la haine à l'ère d'internet. Ministre des Travaux publics et des Services gouvernementaux, Ottawa. https://publications.gc.ca/collections/collection_2009/ccdp-chrc/HR4-5-2009F.pdf.

Lawrence M, Verdun-Jones S (2011) Sentencing Hate: An Examination of the Application of s 718.2(a)(i) of the Criminal Code on the Sentencing of Hate-Motivated Crimes. C.L.Q. 57:28.

McNamara L (2005) Negotiating the Contours of Unlawful Hate Speech: Regulation under Provincial Human Rights Laws in Canada. UBC L Rev 38(1).

Melkevik B (2010) Philosophie du droit, vol. 1. Presses de l'UnIversité Laval, Québec.

Rainville P (2005) Les humeurs du droit pénal au sujet de l'humour et du rire (préface du professeur émérite Jean Pradel). Éditions Yvon Blais.

Rainville P (2015) Paroles de déraison et paroles de dérision: les excès de langage à l'épreuve du droit criminel canadien (2015). Revue juridique Thémis 49(35); 35–132.

Rainville P (2017) Dérision et religion: de l'ironie à la répression. In Saint-Pau et al. (eds) *Droit pénal, culture et religion*Travaux de l'Institut de sciences criminelles et de la justice de Bordeaux, vol. n° 6. Éditions Cujas, Paris.

Rainville P (2019) La répression de l'art et l'art de la répression. La profanation de la religion à l'épreuve des mutations du droit pénal au sujet du blasphème et de la protection des identités religieuses. Presses de l'Université Laval, Québec.

Rainville P (2024) En quête (spirituelle) d'un préjudice : de la protection du sacré à celle du fidèle ou des avatars de la répression du blasphème. In Bernatchez S, Legault-Laberge RM, Noël PC (eds) Droit des religions - Canada - Québec, Wilson & Lafleur, Montréal, 531–585.

Rainville P, Desrosiers J (2010-2011) Le particularisme juridique de la répression de la criminalité organisée au Canada. 89-3 Revue du Barreau canadien 545, 2011.

Roberts J, Harting A (2011) Sentencing in Cases of Hate-motivated Crime: An Analysis of Subparagraph 718.2(a) (i) of the Criminal Code. Osgoode Hall L.J. 93.

Sullivan R (1994) Driedger on the Construction of Statutes 3rd edn. Butterworths, Toronto.

Thériault Y (2020) La pénalisation de l'exercice de la liberté d'expression et la portée du principe de dignité humaine quant aux infractions d'opinion. Étude comparée des systèmes canadien et français », mémoire de maîtrise. Université Laval et Université Toulouse I Capitole.

Walker J (2018) Discours haineux et liberté d'expression: balises légales au Canada. Bibliothèque du Parlement, publication n° 2018-25-F, Ottawa. https://lop.parl.ca/sites/PublicWebsite/default/fr_CA/ResearchPublications/201825E.

Pierre Rainville is Professor of Law at Laval University (Quebec). He currently co-holds the France-Québec Research Chair on contemporary issues of freedom of expression ("Chaire COLIBEX"—https://libexpress.hypotheses.org/) (FRQ /CNRS) and serves as co-leader of the LIBEX project on "Freedom of Expression, Freedom of Conscience and Freedom of Artistic Creation" (ANR) and of the "Arts on Trial" project (SSHRC). He is also a cofounder of the International Summer School on Linguistics and the Law with D. Lagorgette et al. (Univ. Savoie Mont Blanc, Univ. Laval and UQTR). pierre.rainville@fd.ulaval.ca. For a list of publications and conferences, see https://www.fd.ulaval.ca/faculte/repertoire-du-personnel/pierre-rainville.

Olivier Lacombe is master's student in law at Laval University.

Chapter 6
Croatia

Barbara Herceg Pakšić

Contents

Abstract In Croatia, measures for criminalising hate speech have evolved over time, guided by European standards. They have been widely accepted, but the practical implementation present challenges. Although important steps have been taken, certain research indicate a high prevalence of hate speech in everyday life. Public opinion views the efforts to suppress it as ineffective. The number of convictions is rather low, so the case law is very limited to further clarify hateful expressions. Some areas, such as political speech, hate speech in sports and online hate speech are recognized as requiring tailored solutions.

Keywords Policing hate speech · Minority rights · Penalties for hate speech · Media regulation · Hate speech legislation

Similar to many other countries, hate speech incidents have been on the rise in the Republic of Croatia over the last few years. Research conducted on this issue has shown a significant increase in the perception of hate speech, particularly in its online forms. The content of such hate speech statements often includes expressions of national and ethnic intolerance, as well as homophobia. Hate speech is a complex and culturally ingrained negative phenomenon characterized by strong emotional components. Its legal regulation is intricate and challenging.

B. H. Pakšić (✉)
Faculty of Law, University of Josip Juraj Strossmayer, Osijek, Croatia
e-mail: bhercegpaksic@gmail.com

E. Heinze (ed.), *Criminalising Hate Speech*,
https://doi.org/10.1007/978-94-6265-650-5_6

In line with European standards, Croatia's legislative solutions are continually evolving. Today, addressing hate speech involves multiple legal branches. In the following paragraphs, we will outline the key features of these legislative solutions, highlight challenges observed in court practices, discuss thematic observations made by relevant organizations, and explore social perceptions and exposure to hate speech.

The limitations on freedom of expression generally depend on legal regulations, societal necessities, and desired protective goals. This is directly connected to preventing freedom of expression from serving as a safe haven for various forms of incitement to hate and intolerance based on discrimination and prejudice. Going beyond mere words and encompassing various forms of expression[1], hate speech is not particularly amenable to legal regulation due to the demanding need for specifying all its constitutive elements.[2] Despite this, in European countries, it is considered unprotected and punishable expression, albeit with numerous challenges in the enforcement of these norms in judicial practice.[3] The Croatian legal system addresses hate speech suppression through a range of provisions across various branches of law, including constitutional, criminal, misdemeanour, and civil law. These related provisions may not be explicitly titled as "hate speech" but are given various titles and contain different content based on their respective legal domains. The focal point of protection revolves around safeguarding the 'rights of others,' which encompass discrimination protection, protection from hatred and violence, privacy protection, ensuring a fair trial, safeguarding professional, market-commercial, and business interests, as well as upholding effective and unbiased democratic institutions, among others.[4]

6.1 Constitutional Law

In the Republic of Croatia, freedom of expression is a constitutional human right. It is designed to safeguard freedom of speech and public expression, the freedom of the press, and other forms of communication, as well as the freedom to establish all media institutions. However, there are certain limitations in place. Any call or incitement to war, the use of violence, the promotion of national, racial, or religious hatred, or any form of intolerance is prohibited and subject to punishment. The constitution also guarantees the respect and legal protection of personal and family life, dignity, reputation, and honour, as well as the rights to religious freedoms and free association.

---

[1] "Orally or in print, or disseminated through electronic media, including the Internet and social networking sites, as well as non-verbal forms of expression such as the display of racist symbols, images and behaviour at public gatherings, including sporting events." United Nations Committee on the Elimination of Racial Discrimination (CERD). General Recommendation No. 35: Combating Racist Hate Speech, 26. 09. 2013., CERD/C/GC/35, 3, point 7.

[2] Kambovski 2013, pp. 323, 330.

[3] Herceg Pakšić 2020, pp. 225–247, 227.

[4] Alaburić 2002, p. 52.

Freedoms and rights can only be restricted by law when it is necessary to protect the freedom and rights of others, maintain the legal order, public morality, and health.

However, every limitation must be proportionate to the nature of the restriction required in each individual case.[5] Restrictions are subject to the principle of proportionality and must not result in inequality among citizens based on race, colour, sex, language, religion, national or social origin. While there is a relatively large number of decisions from the Croatian Constitutional Court related to freedom of expression in general, there are very few decisions specifically addressing hate speech in terms of incitement to violence, hatred, intolerance, or war. These limited decisions provide valuable insights into the court's stance. In one particular decision, the Court emphasized that 'The legitimate purpose of penalizing behaviours that express or incite hatred based on racial or other affiliations in sports competitions is to protect the dignity of others and uphold the fundamental values of a democratic society.[6] In another decision, where a complaint alleging a violation of the prohibition of invoking or inciting any form of intolerance was rejected, the Constitutional Court determined that the Croatian legal system, in cases such as the applicant's (involving an unknown identity of the perpetrator and an undescribed time and content of the misdemeanour), offers protection through the competent state attorney's office[7] In addition to the rights of free speech, other constitutional provisions ensure non-discrimination rights[8], religious freedom[9], and the right to free association.[10] However, this research did not identify a direct connection between these rights and hate speech in the practice of the Constitutional Court. It's important to interpret this in the context that constitutional provisions hold the highest legal standing and are effectively enacted through legal provisions in various acts (which must align with the Constitution).

[5] Ustav Republike Hrvatske (Constitution of the Republic of Croatia), Official Gazette, 56/1990, 135/1997, 113/2000, 28/2001, 76/2010, 5/2014. Articles 35, 38, 39, 40, 43, 16, 17.

[6] Constitutional Court of the Republic of Croatia, U-III/2588/2016 of 11. November 2016.

[7] The latter is competent to establish the perpetrators identity and all the circumstances of the misdemeanour commission before filing the indictment. Constitutional Court of the Republic of Croatia, U-III-2481/2018 of 13 November 2019.

[8] Everyone in the Republic of Croatia has rights and freedoms, regardless of race, color, sex, language, religion, political or other belief, national or social origin, property, birth, education, social status or other characteristics. Everyone is equal before the law. Constitution of the Republic of Croatia, Article 14.

[9] Freedom of conscience, religion, and the free public expression of religion or other belief, pursuant to Articles 40 and 41.

[10] Free association to protect their benefits or advocate for social, economic, political, national, cultural or other beliefs and goals, pursuant to Article 43.

6.2 The Ombudsperson

Due to the necessary balance required with other legal interests deserving (criminal) law protection such as honour and reputation, prohibition of discrimination, confidentiality obligations, protection of public order, and more, the interference with freedom of expression is traditionally addressed in both the previous and current Croatian Criminal Code.[11] Racial and other forms of discrimination are punishable through two categories of criminal offenses: Violation of equality and Public Incitement to Violence and Hatred. Despite the existence of hate speech bans in criminal law[12] t was traditionally marked by a lack of judicial decisions[13] and decisions from the competent prosecutor's office.[14] This situation has hindered the establishment of judicial standards in this area. Even today, given the rarity of court decisions, this deficiency remains persistent.

As previously mentioned, the Croatian Criminal Code[15] includes an offense related to hate speech titled *Public Incitement to Violence and Hatred*.[16] It is placed

---

[11] More on general policy in: Herceg Pakšić 2020, pp. 225–247.

[12] For detailed incrimination overview from 1977 till 2013 see Herceg Pakšić and Lachner 2015, pp. 295–320, 312–316.

[13] Identifying a particular community as the culprit for certain inappropriate behaviors and proposing violent treatment (placing in a barrack and releasing gas) undoubtedly points to a discriminatory and hateful attitude. The essence of the content of hatred is manifested in the feeling of the need to do evil to others and the feelings of aversion to another that pursues the evil that should happen to another. County Court Varaždin, Kž-199/14, 24 June 2014. For committing a crime, it is not a matter of mere personal views, but a public incitement to violence or hatred directed at a particular group of people is necessary ... the perpetrator actively seeks to encourage others to express hatred or violence against a particular group. County Court Zagreb, Kž-128/14, 03 June 2014.

[14] In 2015 Zagreb Municipal State's Attorney's Office rejected the criminal complaint against the author of the online message "Fagots to the camps", on the grounds that he was influenced by "psychology of crowd", indicating a lack of intent. Later the County State Attorney's Office reversed the decision and ordered the investigation to be conducted, and the State Attorney's Office of the Republic of Croatia, issued Communication on decision-making errors and announced checking the procedure for the Article 325 CC in the last three years. Available at http://www.dorh.hr/DrzavnoOdvjetnistvoRepublikeHrvatskePriopcenje11.

[15] In effect since 2013. Kazneni zakon, Official Gazette, 125/11, 144/12, 56/15, 61/15, 101/2017, 118/2018, 126/2019, 84/2021. Further in text as CC.

[16] Article 325 (1).

(1) Whoever, through a press, radio, television, computer system or network, publicly or otherwise publicly incites or makes publicly available leaflets, images or other material that invokes violence or hatred, directed against a group or a member of a group because of their race, religious, national or ethnic affiliation, language, origin, color, gender, sexual orientation, gender identity, disability or any other characteristic, shall be punished by imprisonment up to three years.
(2) Whoever organizes or manages a group of three or more persons for the purpose of committing the act referred to in para 1 of this Article, shall be punished by imprisonment for a term between six months and five years.
(3) Whoever participates in the association referred to in para 2 of this Article, shall be punished by imprisonment up to one year.

within the section on Offenses against Public Order, specifically in Article 325. This provision aligns with the standards set forth in the Council Framework Decision 2008/913/JHA of 28 November 2008, aimed at combating certain forms and expressions of racism and xenophobia through criminal law.[17] In the Croatian Criminal Code, the prohibition of hate speech is more comprehensive than what is outlined in the Framework Decision. In addition to the characteristics mentioned in the Framework Decision, it includes language, gender, sexual orientation, gender identity, disability, and an open clause for other possible characteristics. Croatia did not utilize the possibilities provided in the Framework Decision to narrow the scope of punitive measures or adapt incriminations to its own legal tradition. In essence, any form of public incitement to violence and hatred directed towards a group or its member based on any characteristic is punishable by up to three years of imprisonment. While the provision text explicitly enumerates certain discriminatory bases, the Croatian legislator has chosen to keep open the possibility of selecting victims based on other characteristics, utilizing a general (open) clause (...or any other characteristic).

This approach can be a double-edged sword: it can enhance the protection of victims, but at the same time, it may lead to an overly expansive interpretation in jurisprudence and court decisions.[18] The text of the provision was also amended. In 2017, the category of 'language' was added following the phrase 'ethnic origin.[19] A punishment of up to three years of imprisonment is prescribed for anyone who publicly approves, denies, or significantly diminishes genocide[20], the crime of aggression, crimes against humanity, or war crimes in a manner likely to incite violence or hatred against such a group or its members. Additionally, there are specific forms of hate speech related to the incitement to genocide, the crime of aggression, and incitement to terrorism.[21] In Croatian criminal law, it is not necessary to attribute personal hatred as an element of the perpetrator's intent, which would

---

(4) The punishment referred to in para 1 of this Article shall be imposed to anyone who publicly approves, denies or substantially diminishes the criminal offense of genocide, crime of aggression, crime against humanity or war crime, directed against a group or a member of the group because of their racial, religious, national or ethnicity, origin or colour, in a manner that is appropriate to incite violence or hatred against such a group or members of that group.
(5) The perpetrator shall be punished for attempting the criminal offense referred to in paras 1 and 4 of this Article.

[17] Council Framework Decision 2008/913/JHA of 28 November 2008 on combating certain forms and expressions of racism and xenophobia by means of criminal law [2008] OJ L 328/55.

[18] In this regard, one Croatian court (Pula) has interpreted and therefore positioned the affiliation to police officials as well as veterans to protected groups in decisions K-1220/15 and K-136/15-8. Croatian authors criticized this: Munivrana Vajda and Šurina Marton 2016, pp. 435, 455.

[19] The Act on Amendments to the Criminal Code, Official Gazette 101/2017.

[20] Croatian incrimination penalizes every genocide denial. Croatian CC did not use the Framework Decision possibility to limit incrimination to crimes established by a final decision of a national court and/or an international court, or by a final decision of an international court only. See also, Herceg Pakšić 2017, pp. 229–253.

[21] Incitement to genocide and crime of aggression is criminalized as public and direct, and incitement to terrorism as public. See Articles 88 and 89 (both par. 3) and 99 of Croatian CC.

require the proof of 'hate' or hostility (the hostility model). Instead, what is required is the selection of the victim based on actual or presumed affiliation to a specific group (the discriminatory selection model).[22]

In addition to criminal law liability, Croatian law allows for the sanctioning of hate speech under misdemeanour and civil liability through a range of legislations. The cornerstone of national anti-discrimination law is the Anti-Discrimination Act[23] which ensures the protection and promotion of equality as the highest value of the constitutional order of the Republic of Croatia. Pursuant to the Anti-Discrimination Act (Article 1/1), preconditions are established for the realization of equal opportunities and protection against discrimination. Discrimination can be based on race or ethnicity, colour, sex, language, religion, political or other beliefs, national or social origin, property status, trade union membership, education, social status, marital or family status, age, health status, disability, genetic inheritance, gender identity, expression, or sexual orientation. Discrimination is defined as placing any person in a less favourable position based on the aforementioned grounds, as well as individuals related to them through family or other connections. According to Article 25, a fine ranging from 5,000 to 30,000 HRK (approximately 670 to 4000 Euros) is imposed for violations of human dignity with the intention of causing fear or creating a hostile, degrading, or insulting environment based on differences related to the grounds mentioned (race, ethnicity, skin colour, gender, language, religion, political or other beliefs, national or social background, wealth, union membership, social status, marital or family status, age, health condition, disability, genetic inheritance, gender identity or expression, and sexual orientation). The responsible person within a legal entity, state body, legal entity with public authorities, or local and regional self-government unit shall be held accountable for this misdemeanour.[24]

The Public Order and Peace Act[25] contains provisions addressing various forms of expression that could lead to a disruption of public peace. For example, it pertains to the disturbance of public order and peace in a public place through the performance or reproduction of songs, compositions, lyrics, or by wearing and displaying symbols, texts, images, drawings, or by engaging in conduct that insults or belittles the moral feelings of citizens in a public place. Sanctions for such actions include fines and, in exceptional cases, imprisonment, along with the possibility of implementing certain protective measures.

---

[22] The discriminatory selection model takes an objective approach that means that the selection of the victim does not need to involve negative emotions on behalf of the perpetrator towards an individual or a group. Office for Democratic Institutions and Human Rights (ODIHR) 2014, pp. 50–51. Munivrana Vajda and Šurina Marton A 2016, pp. 435, 451.

[23] Zakon o suzbijanju diskriminacije, Official Gazette 85/2008, 112/2012.

[24] A craftsman or a person who performs another independent activity in connection with a trade or activity he performs can also be responsible, with a fine between 10.000,00 and 200.000,00 HRK (1330–26,660 Euros) and legal persons with a fine between 30.000,00 and 300.000,00 HRK (4000–40,000 Euros).

[25] Zakon o prekršajima protiv javnog reda i mira, Official Gazette 41/1977, 47/1989, 55/1989, 83/1989, 47/1990, 55/1991, 29/1994, further in text POPA.

The Prevention of Disorder at Sporting Events Act[26] serves the purpose of preventing, suppressing, and penalizing inappropriate behaviour, riots, and violence. It can be applied before, during, and after a sports competition or sporting event to protect well-behaved spectators, other citizens, and their property, as well as the property of legal entities. Its goal is to create conditions for sports competitions and sporting events that contribute as much as possible to the quality of life for citizens, especially young people. Article 4 of the Prevention of Disorder at Sporting Events Act lists illegal behaviours, including attempting to insert, inserting, or displaying a banner, flag, or other item with text, images, signs, or features that express or incite hatred or violence based on racial, national, regional, or religious affiliation. It also applies to singing songs or expressing messages whose content expresses or incites hatred or violence based on racial, national, regional, or religious affiliation. Sanctions for such actions may include fines, imprisonment, certain protective measures, as well as educational measures for minors.

Anti-hate speech provisions also exist within media law. In accordance with Article 3 of the Media Act[27], it is prohibited to incite or glorify national, racial, religious, sexual, or other forms of inequality, as well as inequality based on sexual orientation, and ideological and state constructs formed on such grounds. It is also prohibited to provoke national, racial, religious, sexual, or other forms of hostility or intolerance, as well as hostility or intolerance based on sexual orientation, or to incite violence and war through the transmission of program content in the media.

The current Electronic Media Act[28] contains provisions that prohibit the incitement to hatred. According to Article 12, in audio and/or audio-visual media services, it is not allowed to incite, promote incitement, or spread hatred or discrimination based on various grounds. These include race, ethnicity, colour, sex, language, religion, political or other beliefs, national or social origin, property status, trade union membership, education, social status, marital or family status, age, health status, disability, genetic inheritance, gender identity, expression, or sexual orientation. Additionally, it covers anti-Semitism, xenophobia, and the ideas of fascist, nationalist, communist, and other totalitarian regimes. It's worth noting that a new Electronic Media Act has been announced at the time of writing.[29]

Pursuant the Article 6 of the Croatian Radio and Television Act[30], the national radio and television are obligated to promote national interests, contribute to the respect and promotion of fundamental human rights and freedoms, patriotism, tolerance, understanding, and respect for diversity, democratic values and institutions, civil society, as well as the promotion of a culture of public dialogue. They are also

---

[26] Zakon o sprječavanju nereda na športskim natjecanjima, Official Gazette 117/2003, 71/2006, 43/2009, 34/2011.

[27] Zakon o medijima, Official Gazette 59/2004, 84/2011, 81/2013.

[28] Zakon o elektroničkim medijima, Official Gazette 153/2009, 84/2011, 94/2013, 136/2013.

[29] https://vlada.gov.hr/vijesti/obuljen-korzinek-zakon-O-elektronickim-medijima-za-transparentno-vlasnistvo/32369.

[30] Zakon o Hrvatskoj radioteleviziji, Official Gazette 137/2010, 76/2012, 78/2016, 46/2017, 73/2017, 94/2018.

required to respect the privacy, dignity, reputation, and honour of individuals and the fundamental rights and freedoms of others, particularly children, young people, the elderly, and the infirm.

In accordance with Article 9 of the Croatian Radio and Television Act, there is an obligation to inform and educate about democracy, civil society, and the culture of public dialogue. Furthermore, there is an obligation to contribute to the suppression of discrimination on any basis in accordance with the Constitution and regulations. The act also mandates the production, co-production, and publication of programs of national interest, with the aim of preventing crime, socially unacceptable and risky behaviours, and promoting community safety. Other noteworthy acts include the Gender Equality Act[31] and the Civil Partnership of the Same Sex Act[32] both of which provide provisions on the prohibition of discrimination.

Research on the jurisprudence of the Croatian Supreme Court has revealed a connection between hateful expressions and the violation of the equality principle. For instance, when a defendant, through their statements, engaged in hate speech and justified physical confrontation and attacks on the homosexual group while directly inciting violence and hatred toward LGBT people, this constituted discrimination that is prohibited under the Anti-Discrimination Act, specifically in Article 4(1) and Article 1(1), (2), based on sexual orientation.[33] Advocating for the re-establishment of the Independent State of Croatia (NDH) and considering its racial character is not only subject to punishment under Article 325 of the Criminal Code but can also be categorized as discrimination under Article 4 and Article 1(1) of the Anti-Discrimination Act. [34] The defendant's harassment of individuals of the same sexual orientation through insults that undermine their dignity and create a hostile, degrading, and offensive environment is in violation of the provisions outlined in the Gender Equality Act and the Anti-Discrimination Act. This constitutes an instance of incitement to discrimination, particularly noteworthy due to the fact that these controversial homophobic statements were made by an individual who serves as a priest and administrator of the parish community within the Catholic Church, the largest religious community in Croatia, known for its authority and reputation in society. The defendant's actions involve hate speech, justification of physical confrontation, and attacks against a procession of individuals of the same sex. Moreover, the defendant directly incited hatred and violence against such individuals, thereby falling under the scope of discrimination based on sexual orientation as per Article 4(1) of the Anti-Discrimination Act.[35]

The provision of the Prevention of Disorder at Sporting Events Act (PDSEA), specifically Article 4(1)/7, which bans singing songs or expressing messages whose content expresses or incites hatred or violence based on racial, national, regional,

---

[31] Zakon o ravnopravnosti spolova, Official Gazette 82/2008, 125/2011, 20/2012, 138/2012, 69/2017.

[32] Zakon o životnom partnerstvu osoba istog spola, Official Gazette 92/2014, 98/2019.

[33] Supreme Court of Croatia, Gž 38/2011-2, 7 March 2012.

[34] Supreme Court of Croatia, I-KŽ 665/2014-6, 18 October 2017.

[35] Supreme Court of Croatia, Gž 38/11-2 of 7 March 2012.

or religious affiliation, was applied. This occurred in a case involving a football player who turned to the spectators with a microphone and shouted ('For home'), to which they replied ('Ready'). It was recognized that this exchange symbolizes a greeting used during a totalitarian regime (NDH). The court determined that such an act constituted a manifestation of racist ideology, contempt for individuals based on their religious and ethnic affiliation, and trivialization of the victims of crimes against humanity.[36]

Protection from Domestic Violence Act[37] (specifically Article 22/5) was applied in a case where the words spoken by the defendant to his son at the time of the incident constituted an objectively humiliating treatment of the father towards his child. This treatment involved threats, economic and status intimidation, and included hate speech with discriminatory characteristics directed at the child.[38]

In a specific case, the Anti-Discrimination Act (ADA) was interpreted, which indicated the potential presence of harassment with the aim of violating a person's dignity, thereby creating a hostile, humiliating, and insulting environment. The court considered that the position of police officers constitutes a social group, identifiable in public by certain common characteristics, which distinguish them in terms of social standing, and yet they do not belong to a defined circle as outlined in Article 1, paras 1 and 2 of the ADA.[39]

When applying the Public Order and Peace Act (POPA), the Court emphasized that any speech symbolizing hatred towards people of different religions or ethnicities has a detrimental impact, particularly on children, who are the most vulnerable group in society and should receive special protection from any discriminatory effects.[40]

The Ombudsperson serves as a plenipotentiary of the Croatian Parliament for the protection and promotion of human rights and freedoms. They function as the central body for combating discrimination, act as the national preventive mechanism for the protection of persons deprived of liberty and are responsible for reporting external irregularities. The Ombudsperson operates autonomously and independently in their role. Along with their deputies, they are elected by the Parliament for a period of eight years.[41] The intention is for the Ombudsperson to function as the central anti-discrimination body.[42]

In the Republic of Croatia, there are three Ombudspersons: The General Ombudsperson, the Ombudsperson for Children, and the Ombudsperson for Gender Equality. They are all appointed by the Parliament and serve as independent human rights institutions that operate autonomously in their role. They examine cases of human rights violations and issue recommendations for their resolution. The most recent report from the Ombudsperson, covering the year 2020, was submitted to

36 Decision of Misdemeanour Court, PpJ-4877/13 of 8 December 2015.

37 Zakon o zaštiti od nasilja u obitelji, Official Gazette, 70/17, 126/19, 84/21.

38 High Misdemeanour Court, Jž-1155/2020 of 17 September 2020.

39 High Misdemeanour Court, Jž-1394/2016 of 21 September 2017.

40 High Misdemeanour Court, Jž-657/2017 of 23 September 2019.

41 https://www.ombudsman.hr/hr/sto-radimo/.

42 Pursuant to Article 12 of ADA.

the Croatian Parliament in February 2021.[43] The report includes a chapter on 'Hate crimes', highlighting the continuous growth of hate crimes in general throughout 2018, 2019, and 2020. The most frequent criminal offenses in this context were property damage and threats (as mentioned on page 91). Hate speech is not specifically detailed in this chapter. Related to this topic are the chapters on 'Rights of national minorities' and 'Discrimination based on race, ethnicity, or skin colour and national origin.' In the latter chapter, it is noted that '...unfortunately, after the outbreak of the epidemic in the Republic of Croatia, there was an increase in public expressions of discrimination against the Chinese, refugees, Roma, and instances such as graffiti with threats of death targeting Novak Djokovic appeared in Split.' [44] Some of the training sessions for the police, judges, state prosecutors, and lawyers received support from the Ombudsperson's office as part of its projects aimed at raising awareness about anti-discrimination. During these training sessions, gaps were identified in the knowledge and understanding of certain provisions of the Anti-Discrimination Act, such as the shifting of the burden of proof.[45] It has also been observed that there is an educative response to exposed cases of hate speech. For example, in a recent case involving the expression of hatred towards a journalist, the official Ombudsperson website conveyed the message that at least three conditions must be met in order to suppress hate speech on the Internet. These conditions include the need for competent authorities to react within their powers, for users of social networks to exercise personal responsibility in their communication, and for the media and profile administrators on social networks to promptly remove all unacceptable messages.[46]

6.3 International Covenant on Civil and Political Rights (ICCPR)

Croatia became a party to the International Covenant on Civil and Political Rights (ICCPR) on October 12, 1992, without making any declarations or reservations upon its accession[47]). The Government of the Republic of Croatia, under Article 41 of the ICCPR, declared its recognition of the competence of the Human Rights Committee to receive and consider communications alleging that a State Party is not fulfilling its obligations under the ICCPR. Croatia has also consented to individual complaints

---

[43] https://www.ombudsman.hr/hr/download/izvjesce-pucke-pravobraniteljice-za-2020%20godinu/?wpdmdl=10845&refresh=6038a8291f2261614325801.

[44] Ibid., pp. 104–105.

[45] ECRI Conclusions on the Implementation of the Recommendations in Respect of Croatia, adopted on 19 March 2015, published on 09 06. 2015, CRI(2015)22, https://rm.coe.int/interim-follow-up-conclusions-on-croatia-4th-monitoring-cycle/16808b57d0, p. 5.

[46] https://www.ombudsman.hr/hr/svi-imamo-ulogu-U-borbi-protiv-prijetnji-I-govora-mrznje-na-internetu/.

[47] The former Yugoslavia had signed the ICCPR on 08.08.1967 and ratified it on 02.06.1971.

procedures for the Optional Protocol to the International Covenant on Civil and Political Rights, effective as of October 12, 1995.[48] No individual complaints were found.[49]

The most recent Concluding Observations for Croatia, as issued by the Human Rights Committee, were published in 2015[50] did not include specific observations regarding hateful expression. In the previous set of Concluding Observations from 2009[51] it was noted that State party "…should strengthen measures to combat discrimination and to combat physical and *verbal attacks* against members of ethnic minorities".[52]

ICCPR in Article 20 states that law prohibition should cover war propaganda and any advocacy of national, racial or religious hatred that constitutes incitement to discrimination, hostility or violence. The article relates to incitement that includes intent[53] so it does not have a direct reference on hate speech.

At the Croatian legislative level, Article 325 of the Criminal Code incriminates actions made through the press, radio, television, computer systems or networks that publicly incite or enable publicly available leaflets, images, or other materials that invoke violence or hatred directed against a group or a member of a group because of their race, religious, national, or ethnic affiliation, language, origin, color, gender, sexual orientation, gender identity, disability, or any other characteristics. Violation of this provision is punishable by imprisonment for up to three years. In essence, any form of public incitement to violence and hatred directed towards a group or a group member based on any characteristic is subject to punishment. It is important to note that it is not necessary to prove that the perpetrator personally held hatred or hostility (hostility model). Instead, it suffices that the victim was selected based on their affiliation with a specific group (discriminatory selection model). Additionally, there are specific legal provisions addressing hate speech related to incitement to genocide, crime of aggression, and terrorism. Furthermore, many other legal acts also include bans on hateful expressions.

---

48 "The Republic of Croatia interprets article 1 of this Protocol as giving the Committee the competence to receive and consider communications from individuals subject to the jurisdiction of the Republic of Croatia who claim to be victims of a violation by the Republic of any rights set forth in the Covenant which results either from acts, omissions or events occurring after the date on which the Protocol entered into force for the Republic of Croatia." "With regard to article 5, para 2 (a) of the Protocol, the Republic of Croatia specifies that the Human Rights Committee shall not have competence to consider a communication from an individual if the same matter is being examined or has already been examined under another procedure of international investigation or settlement."

49 https://tbinternet.ohchr.org/_layouts/15/treatybodyexternal/TBSearch.aspx?Lang=en.

50 International Covenant on Civil and Political Rights, Human Rights Committee, Concluding observations on the third periodic report of Croatia, adopted by the Committee at its 113th session (16.03.–02.04.2015), CCPR/C/HRV/CO/3.

51 International Covenant on Civil and Political Rights, Human Rights Committee, Concluding observations on the second periodic report of Croatia, 04.11.20091, CCPR/C/HRV/CO/2.

52 Ibid., point 5.

53 https://www.ohchr.org/Documents/Issues/Expression/ICCPR/Santiago/TobyMendel.pdf.

6.4 Convention on the Elimination of All Forms of Racial Discrimination (ICERD)

Croatia became a party to the International Convention on the Elimination of All Forms of Racial Discrimination (ICERD) on October 12, 1992, without making any declarations or reservations upon accession.[54] The Committee on the Elimination of Racial Discrimination (CERD) may consider individual petitions alleging violations of the International Convention on the Elimination of All Forms of Racial Discrimination by States parties that have made the necessary declaration under Article 14 of the Convention. However, in the case of Croatia, the individual complaints procedure is marked as N/A.[55]

The most recent Concluding Observations for Croatia, received from the Committee on the Elimination of Racial Discrimination were in 2009.[56] There was no specific comment on hateful expressions, but regarding prohibition of racial discrimination, it was stressed "that the State takes concrete measures to ensure full implementation of the non-discrimination legislation and policies".[57] The Committee on the Elimination of Racial Discrimination expressed concern about the absence of a law prohibiting racist organizations in Croatia. It encouraged the State party to reinforce its measures for the prevention and prosecution of all cases of hate crimes and other ethnically motivated violence, with a particular focus on providing victims with effective and fair remedies. The Committee found it necessary to declare illegal and prohibit organizations that promote and incite racial discrimination. [58] At that time, current CC was being drafted, so the remarks obtained were taken into account and implemented in the text.

In the previous Concluding Observations made in 2002[59], the Committee expressed concerns about the absence of legislative measures prohibiting incitement to racial discrimination and violence in Croatia. The Committee also expressed concerns about the adequacy of the efforts by the State party to investigate and prosecute individuals responsible for fomenting ethnic hatred, especially in localities affected by war. It was noted that there had been no convictions by the courts for incitement to racial discrimination and violence, despite a significant number of allegations. As a result, the Committee recommended that the State party fully comply with its obligations under Article 4 of the Convention and take the necessary legislative measures to give full effect to the provisions of that article. It was

[54] The former Yugoslavia had signed the Convention on 15.04.1966 and ratified it on 02.10.1967.

[55] https://tbinternet.ohchr.org/_layouts/15/TreatyBodyExternal/Treaty.aspx.

[56] International Convention on the Elimination of all Forms of Racial Discrimination, Concluding observations of the Committee on the Elimination of Racial Discrimination, CERD/C/HRV/CO/8, 24.03.2009.

[57] Ibid., point 11.

[58] Ibid., point 12.

[59] International Convention on the Elimination of all Forms of Racial Discrimination, Concluding observations of the Committee on the Elimination of Racial Discrimination, CERD/C/60/CO/4, 21.05.2002.

recommended that the State party declare illegal and prosecute incitement to ethnic hatred and racial violence. These recommendations underscore the importance of addressing incitement to ethnic and racial hatred and violence through both legal and enforcement measures.[60]

Article 4 of the International Convention on the Elimination of All Forms of Racial Discrimination (ICERD) outlines six categories of activities that should be punishable by law. These include the dissemination of ideas based on racial superiority, dissemination of ideas based on racial hatred, incitement to racial discrimination, acts of racially motivated violence, incitement to acts of racially motivated violence, and assistance to racist activities.[61] In the context of hate speech provisions, it can address four of these categories: the dissemination of ideas based on racial superiority and hatred, incitement to racial discrimination, and incitement to racially motivated violence. It is important to note that these provisions do not always require proof of intent.[62] Propaganda activities as well as organizations promoting racial discriminations should be punishable. Furthermore, ICERD defines racial discrimination to encompass race, colour, descent, or national or ethnic origin (Article 1).[63] As elaborated above, Croatian hate speech provisions in the criminal law (Article 325, Public Incitement to Violence and Hatred) essentially cover various forms of public incitement to violence and hatred directed towards a group or group member based on any characteristic. This aligns with the modalities of incitement mentioned in Article 4(a) of ICERD. It's considered an intentional criminal offense related to public expressions of hate and violence, which can be qualified as incitement. Other categories of hate speech may be subject to various forms of misdemeanour law responsibility, depending on the specific circumstances and legal provisions.

6.5 Regional Law and Organisations and Comparative Law

Croatia has been a member of the Council of Europe since 1996.[64] Various acts of the Council of Europe, and especially judgments from the European Court of Human Rights, have had a significant impact on Croatian legislation and practice.

---

[60] Ibid., point 12.

[61] https://www.ohchr.org/Documents/Issues/Expression/ICCPR/Santiago/TobyMendel.pdf.

[62] https://www.ohchr.org/Documents/Issues/Expression/ICCPR/Santiago/TobyMendel.pdf.

[63] In this Convention, term "racial discrimination" menas any distinction, exclusion, restriction or preference based on race, colour, descent, or national or ethnic origin which has the purpose or effect of nullifying or impairing the recognition, enjoyment or exercise, on an equal footing, of human rights and fundamental freedoms in the political, economic, social, cultural or any other field of public life.

[64] Croatia became the 40th Member State of the Council of Europe on 06.11.1996.

The European Commission against Racism and Intolerance (ECRI) conducted its fifth report on Croatia in 2018 and published its conclusions in May 2021.[65] In this report, ECRI recommended that the authorities introduce compulsory human rights education as part of civic education in all school curricula, with a specific focus on the right to equality and the prohibition of discrimination. State authorities have informed ECRI that several teaching materials and handbooks covering human rights topics, such as the prevention of violent extremism, combating antisemitism and other forms of discrimination, and learning about the Holocaust, have been translated into the Croatian language and incorporated into available educational resources. Therefore, ECRI considers this recommendation to have been implemented.[66]

ECRI conducted its fourth report on Croatia in 2012 and published its Conclusions in June 2015.[67] In the report, it was recommended that the authorities increase their efforts to provide appropriate initial and continuous training to judges, prosecutors, lawyers, and police on the application of the new provisions in the Criminal Code for combating racism and racial discrimination, as well as the Anti-Discrimination Act.[68] After receiving information from the authorities regarding training for judges, state prosecutors, lawyers, and police on topics such as LGBT discrimination, the application of the Anti-Discrimination Act, combating hate crime, and the Gender Equality Act, it was concluded that the recommendation has been only partially implemented.

In its third report, which was issued in 2004 when the old Croatian Criminal Code from 1997 was in effect, some recommendations were made. They included the suggestion that the law should criminalize the creation or leadership of a group that promotes racism and that it should specify that racist motives constitute an aggravating factor in regular offenses.[69] These recommendations were taken into consideration and implemented in the current criminal law provisions on hate speech.

---

[65] ECRI Conclusions on the Implementation of the Recommendations in Respect of Croatia, CRI(2021)15. Adopted on 30.03.2021 and published on 18.05.2021. https://rm.coe.int/ecri-conclusions-on-the-implementation-of-the-recommendations-in-respe/1680a277b2.

[66] Due to information gathered from several organizations on only partial introduction of civic education across the country, and lack of systematic approach, ECRI encouraged Croatian authorities to ensure comprehensive and consistent initial and continuous training with a view to providing the members of the teaching profession the necessary sensitivity to and skills on human rights education and to make topics such as the right to equality and prohibition of discrimination a priority in practice. https://rm.coe.int/ecri-conclusions-on-the-implementation-of-the-recommendations-in-respe/1680a277b2.

[67] ECRI Conclusions on the Implementation of the Recommendations in Respect of Croatia, adopted on 19.03.2015 and published on 09.06.2015, CRI(2015)22, https://rm.coe.int/interim-follow-up-conclusions-on-croatia-4th-monitoring-cycle/16808b57d0.

[68] According to ECRI's General Policy Recommendation (GPR) No. 7 on national legislation to combat racism and racial discrimination, "racism" means the belief that a ground such as race, colour, language, religion, nationality or national or ethnic origin justifies contempt for a person or a group of persons, or the notion of superiority of a person or a group of persons. "Racial discrimination" shall mean any differential treatment based on a ground such as race, colour, language, religion, nationality or national or ethnic origin, which has no objective and reasonable justification.

[69] https://rm.coe.int/third-report-on-croatia/16808b57b8 p.8, point 25.

Specifically, the mentioned modality became a criminal offense under Article 325, para 2[70] and the request for hate to be considered an aggravating circumstance is in accordance with Article 87, para 21, of the Criminal Code.

The European Convention on Human Rights has been binding in Croatia since 1997.[71] Article 10 of the Convention proclaims the right to freedom of expression, which includes the freedom to hold opinions and to receive and impart information and ideas without interference by public authorities, regardless of frontiers, with possible subjection to formalities, conditions, restrictions, or penalties. Restrictions, which must be prescribed by law and necessary in a democratic society, can take seven different forms based on three primary needs: protection (of health or morals, the reputation, or rights of others), interests (national security, territorial integrity, or public safety, maintaining judicial authority and impartiality), and prevention (of disorder or crime, or the disclosure of confidential information).[72]

Up until mid-March 2020, the European Court of Human Rights had made 17 decisions related to freedom of expression in Croatia.[73] In nearly 30% of these cases (5 cases), violations were established.[74] Since then, decisions have been made in an additional 6 cases. [75] In its reasoning, the ECtHR examines the limitations outlined in Article 10(2) as well as the prohibition of the abuse of rights, a clause regulated under Article 17 (often in relation to Article 14, which prohibits discrimination).[76]

Although there is no standardized hate speech mechanism in Croatia, the Court has provided valuable perspectives. In a landmark decision in the case of Rujak v. Croatia, it was determined that lewd and obscene speech using vulgar and offensive language holds no essential role in the expression of ideas and falls outside the protection of freedom of expression, as it "amounted to wanton denigration, and its sole intent was to insult."[77] In the Šimunić case, the Court declared that speech

---

70 Turković et al. 2013, p. 400. Also, Herceg Pakšić 2020, p. 234.

71 The Convention for the Protection of Human Rights and Fundamental Freedoms was signed on 06.11.1996 and ratified on 05.11.1997, when the Act on Ratification of the ECHR came into force (Official Gazette-International Treaties 18/97).

72 Restrictions on the right to freedom of expression must be considered in the context of the case as a whole, including the content of the statements and the context in which they are made. European Court of Human Rights, Case of Europapress holding d.o.o. v Croatia, Application no. 25333/06, 22 October 2009, § 54.

73 The first was case of Želimir Jovanović v. Croatia, no. 599109/00, 18 February 2002.

74 Narodni list d.d. v. Croatia, no. 2782/12, 08 November 2018; Slava Jurišić v Croatia, no. 79584/ 12, 08 February 2018; Marunić v Croatia, no. 51706/11, 28 March 2017; Radobuljac v Croatia, no. 51000/11, 28 June 2016; Stojanović v Croatia, no. 23160/09, 19 September 2013.

75 Bon v Croatia, no. 26933/15, 18 March 2021; Prpić v Croatia, no. 19425/15, 16 February 2021; Tölle .v Croatia, no. 41987/13, 10 December 2020; Bilan v Croatia, no. 57860/14 , 20 October 2020; N.Š. v Croatia, no. 36908/13, 10 September 2020; Miljević. v Croatia, no. 68317/13, 25 June 2020.

76 Herceg Pakšić 2020, p. 232.

77 Rujak v Croatia, no. 57942/10, 02 October 2012. Croatian soldier (previously convicted of Tarnishing the Reputation of Republic Croatia), in quarrel with other soldiers used obscene and insulting language regarding religion and origins of Croats. § 29, 30. See also, Schabas 2015, p. 456. Đurđević 2019, pp. 9, 11.

incompatible with the values proclaimed and guaranteed by the Convention is not protected by Article 10, and Article 17 was used only as an aid to interpretation.[78]

Croatia became an EU Member State on July 1, 2013. Within the primary sources of EU Law, the Treaty on the Functioning of the European Union (TFEU) stipulates that, in accordance with Article 10, the EU is obligated to combat discrimination based on various factors, including sex, racial or ethnic origin, religion or belief, disability, age, or sexual orientation. Article 19 of the TFEU further advocates for taking appropriate actions to combat discrimination based on these same criteria, while Article 67(3) addresses the obligation to ensure a high level of security to prevent and combat crime, racism, and xenophobia. This entails the harmonization of criminal law provisions among Member States. The Charter of Fundamental Rights of the European Union reinforces the non-discrimination principle in Article 21 and includes an extensive list of protected grounds.

As for secondary sources of EU law, there is the Council Framework Decision 2008/913/JHA, dated November 28, 2008, which addresses the combatting of certain forms and expressions of racism and xenophobia through criminal law.[79] Article 4 of the Council Framework Decision 2008/913/JHA urges Member States to take measures ensuring that racist and xenophobic motivation is considered an aggravating circumstance or, alternatively, that courts take such bias into account when imposing penalties. Directive 2012/29/EU of the European Parliament and the Council on establishing minimum standards on the rights, support and protection of victims of crime[80] specifically in Article 22, para 3, pertains to victims who have suffered crimes committed with a bias or discriminatory motive related to their personal characteristics. According to the *Framework Decision on Racism and Xenophobia* it can be interpreted that hate speech, incriminated within Article 325 of the Croatian CC, should not be considered as hate crime in terms of Article 87 para 21 of the CC.[81]

---

[78] A football player, convicted for shouting, at a football match, "For Home" several times. While the original meaning was literary and poetic, it had also been used as an official greeting of the Ustashe movement, which had originated from fascism, and of totalitarian regime. The Court did not find it necessary to address the applicability of Article 17 because it considered it should only be resorted to on an exceptional basis and in extreme cases. Šimunić v Croatia, no. 20373/17, 29 January 2019. Also, Guide on Article 17 of the European Convention on Human Rights, Prohibition of abuse of rights (2019), p. 25.

[79] Council Framework Decision 2008/913/JHA of 28 November 2008 on combating certain forms and expressions of racism and xenophobia by means of criminal law and replacing Council Framework Decision 2001/220/JHA [2008] OJ Union, L 328/55 from 6 December 2008. In Croatian CC hate speech is criminalized on more widely grounds- apart from those mentioned in the Framework Decision—it includes language, gender, sexual orientation, gender identity, disability and other characteristics. The Framework Decision possibilities on narrowing punitive zone and adapting incrimination to own legal tradition were not used. This decision has replaced the first law against hate speech made in 1996¥ Joint action to combat racism and xenophobia (Joint action/96/443/JHA of 15 July 1996).

[80] Directive 2012/29/EU of the European Parliament and of the Council of 25 October 2012 establishing minimum standards on the rights, support and protection of victims of crime, and replacing Council Framework Decision 2001/220/JHA.

[81] A hate crime is a criminal offense committed because of race, skin colour, religion, national or ethnic origin, language, disability, gender, sexual orientation or the gender identity of another

Framework decision in Article 4 stipulates that racist and xenophobic motivation should not be considered an aggravating circumstance in criminal offenses covered by Articles 1 and 2 (public incitement to violence and hatred, denial international crimes and participation in them in the form of incitement, aiding and abetting) in that act the fact that the crime was committed because of some of the protected features should not be taken as aggravating circumstance.[82]

German-speaking countries have traditionally held significant influence on legal solutions within Croatian law, particularly in the realm of criminal law. Recent changes and innovations in the general part of Croatian criminal law are closely aligned with legal principles from Germany, Austria, and Switzerland. While it's not typical to cite comparative legal solutions in Croatian court decisions, it's relatively common for these solutions to be mentioned in public debates, comments within Croatian legal circles, or scientific papers. For instance, comparative solutions were referenced in challenges related to the regulation of online hate speech in recent years.

The German Act on the Improvement of Law Enforcement in Social Networks[83], which holds social networks responsible for specific content, has been examined and viewed as a good practice example.[84] The enhancement of national regulation concerning online hate speech is anticipated through specialized provisions in the new Electronic Media Act. This process of deliberation and seeking the best solutions has been ongoing in the Republic of Croatia.

By the end of July 2021, the final draft of the Act was adopted during a government session, and its adoption in parliament is expected soon.[85]

European standards have significantly influenced the current national framework. For instance, European law serves as a crucial source of anti-discrimination legislation for EU Member States. The adoption of the Anti-Discrimination Act was a result of harmonizing Croatian legislation with European Union laws, among other factors.[86]

---

person. Such conduct shall be taken as an aggravating circumstance if this Act does not explicitly prescribe a more severe punishment.

[82] The project "IRIS—Improving the fight against intolerance through research, development of recommendations and training", Munivrana Vajda et al. 2020, p. 14.

[83] Gesetz zur Verbesserung der Rechtsdurchsetzung in sozialen Netzwerken; Netzwerkdurchsetzungsgesetz: NetzDG.

[84] Roksandić Vidlička and Mamić 2018, pp. 329–357.

[85] Article 94 of EMA contains a clearly prescribed obligation of the electronic publication provider responsible for all published content, including content generated by the user, if he fails to register the user and if he has not warned the user in a clear and easily observable manner of commenting rules and violations of prescribed provisions. If the publisher acts in accordance with the law, ensures the registration and publication of the warning, the responsibility for possible illegal content will be on the person who published the comment, and not on the publisher. https://min-kulture.gov.hr/vijesti-8/na-71-sjednici-vlade-rh-usvojen-nacrt-konacnog-prijedloga-zakona-o-elektronickim-medijima/21269.

[86] https://pravamanjina.gov.hr/UserDocsImages/dokumenti/Nacionalni%20plan%20za%20borbu%20protiv%20diskriminacije%20za%20razdoblje%20od%202017.%20do%202022..pdf, p. 5.

6.6 Conclusion

While hate speech poses a complex challenge for legal regulation, many countries are navigating this terrain while respecting the limitations on freedom of expression. Croatia's legal framework has evolved over time, guided by European standards, to address hate speech through various branches of law. The current legal provisions consider observations from European bodies. The Croatian constitution, criminal law, and misdemeanour law contain solutions that align with European standards. However, the practical implementation of these laws presents challenges. Despite research indicating a high prevalence of hate speech in everyday life, the majority of citizens view the efforts to suppress it as ineffective.[87] The low number of convictions, regardless of the regulatory approach, can be attributed to factors such as the imprecise demarcation of relevant criminal and misdemeanour law provisions, inconsistencies in case law (where similar factual situations may be treated differently under distinct legal mechanisms), and a low number of criminal accusations, partly due to citizens' reluctance to report incidents.[88] This implies that case law is limited in its ability to significantly contribute to defining or clarifying the issue of hateful expression. Areas such as political speech, hate speech in sports, and online hate speech are recognized as requiring tailored solutions.

In 2018, the Office for Human Rights and Rights of National Minorities of the Government of the Republic of Croatia launched a campaign featuring recommendations on combating hate speech in the political arena. The campaign appealed to politicians to condemn every form of hate speech.[89] The National Anti-Discrimination Plan for the period 2017–2022[90] lists the suppression of discriminatory practices and hate speech in sports as one of its priority goals. It also addresses the issue of speech that incites violence and hatred toward individuals or groups based on certain traits. A new Electronic Media Act is expected to be adopted soon, which should enhance the sanctioning of online forms of hate speech. While the normative aspect of prohibiting hate speech can be considered satisfactory, its practical implementation presents significant challenges. The repressive measures outlined in various Croatian legal acts are relatively seldom applied in practice. Given the complexity of the social need to combat hate speech, the primary focus should not solely be on repressive solutions. Prevention, particularly through tailored education, is likely to be more impactful and effective.

---

87 Herceg Pakšić 2020, pp. 239–241.

88 Ibid., p. 241.

89 https://ljudskaprava.gov.hr/vijesti/odrzan-javni-skup-na-temu-govor-mrznje-U-javnom-prostoru-povodom-obiljezavanja-medjunarodnog-dana-ljudskih-prava/8488.

90 https://pravamanjina.gov.hr/UserDocsImages/dokumenti/Nacionalni%20plan%20za%20borbu%20protiv%20diskriminacije%20za%20razdoblje%20od%202017.%20do%202022..pdf.

References

Alaburić V (2002) Sloboda izražavanja u praksi Europskog suda za ljudska prava. Narodne novine, Zagreb, p. 52.
Đurđević Z (2019) Odluke ESLJP-a o nedopuštenosti zahtjeva podnesenih zbog povrede slobode izražavanja u RH. Informator: poslovno-pravni magazin 6600:9, 11.
Herceg Pakšić B (2017) Tvorba novih standarda u slučajevima teških oblika govora mržnje: negiranje genocida pred Europskim sudom za ljudska prava [New Standards in Cases of Severe Hate Speech Forms: Denial of Genocide at the European Court of Human Rights]. Zbornik Pravnog fakulteta u Zagrebu 67:229–253.
Herceg Pakšić B (2020) Holding All the Aces? Hate Speech: Features and Suppression in Croatia. In: Meškić Z, Kunda I, Popović DV, Omerović E (eds) Balkan Yearbook of European and International Law. Springer, Cham. pp. 225–247, 227.
Herceg Pakšić B, Lachner V (2015) Hate speech as a Violation of Human Rights: The Meaning, Implications and Regulation in Criminal Law. In: Vinković M (ed) New Developments in EU Labour, Equality and Human Rights Law. Josip Juraj Strossmayer University, Faculty of Law, Osijek. pp. 295–320, 312–316.
Kambovski V (2013) Hate Crime and Criminal Aspects of Hate Speech: Macedonian Approach. Megatrend Review 10(1):323–330.
Munivrana Vajda M (2016) A Šurina Marton 'Gdje prestaju granice slobode izražavanja, a počinje govor mržnje? Analiza hrvatskog zakonodavstva i prakse u svjetlu europskih pravnih standarda. Hrvatski ljetopis za kaznene znanosti i praksu 23:435, 451.
Munivrana Vajda M, Šurina Marton Z (2016) Gdje prestaju granice slobode izražavanja, a počinje govor mržnje? Analiza hrvatskog zakonodavstva i prakse u svjetlu europskih pravnih standarda. Hrvatski ljetopis za kaznene znanosti i praksu 23:435, 455.
Munivrana Vajda M, Sučić I, Maršavelski A, Eterović I (2020) Hate Crime in Croatia-Empirical Case Research in the Period from 2013 to 2018. http://www.hpc.hr/wp-content/uploads/2020/10/ZiM_izvjesce.pdf.
Office for Democratic Institutions and Human Rights (ODIHR) (2014) Prosecuting hate crimes. A practical guide, OSCE, Poland, pp. 50–51.
Roksandić Vidlička S, Mamić K (2018) Zlouporaba društvenih mreža u javnom poticanju na nasilje i mržnju i širenju lažnih vijesti: potreba transplantiranja njemačkog Zakona o jačanju provedbe zakona na društvenim mrežama? Hrvatski ljetopis za kaznene znanosti i praksu 25:329–357.
Schabas WA (2015) The European Convention on Human Rights. Oxford University Press, Oxford.
Turković K et al. (2013) Komentar Kaznenog zakona, Narodne novine, p. 400.

Barbara Herceg Pakšić is an associate professor at Faculty of Law, University of Josip Juraj Strossmayer in Osijek, Croatia. She completed her doctoral dissertation *Grounds of Excuse in Criminal Law* in 2014 *summa cum laude.* Her fields of interest include Criminal Law, Juvenile Justice, Criminology and Victimology, Freedom of Expression in the Legal Context, Law and Bioethics, Children in Conflict with the Law. She received a Research fellowship at the Europa Institute, Saarbrücken, Germany in 2019. In 2022 she won the Award for Scientific Achievements of the Osijek-Baranja County.

Chapter 7
Czech Republic

Marek Fryšták, David Čep and Katarína Kandová

Contents

Abstract In the Czech Republic, measures for criminalising hate speech have been developing throughout the past three decades. Steps taken by the government, legislators, police, Prosecutor General's Office, high courts and the Constitutional Court, as well as NGOs, have provided considerable improvement. International bodies and their monitoring of situations have played a significant role. The cases connected with members of the National Resistance movement, several members of Parliament and selling of items connected with Nazi ideology, led to positive changes. Mass media have played an important role, especially in connection with Roma minority situation, migration crisis and the current war in Ukraine.

Keywords Fundamental Rights and Freedoms · Minority rights · Hate speech legislation · ICCPR · ICERD · Hate speech by public officials

M. Fryšták (✉) · D. Čep
Department of Criminal Law, Faculty of Law, Masaryk University, Brno, Czech Republic
e-mail: marek.frystak@law.muni.cz

D. Čep
e-mail: David.Cep@law.muni.cz

K. Kandová
District Public Prosecutor's Office, Prague, Czech Republic
e-mail: kkandova@osz.pha1.justice.cz

E. Heinze (ed.), *Criminalising Hate Speech*,
https://doi.org/10.1007/978-94-6265-650-5_7

7.1 National Constitutional Law

Czech constitutional law is enshrined in two major constitutional acts, the Constitution of the Czech Republic and the Bill of Fundamental Rights and Freedoms. The Constitution does not enumerate fundamental rights and freedoms (such as free speech or non-discrimination rights) because these are stated in Bill of Fundamental Rights and Freedoms (hereinafter FRF). FRF sets forth numerous fundamental rights and freedoms relevant to hateful expression, including:

(a) the prohibition of discrimination on basis of sex, race, colour of skin, language, faith, religion, political or other conviction, ethic or social origin, membership in a national or ethnic minority, property, birth, or other status (FRF Article 3 para 1),
(b) the right to private and family life and its protection (FRF Article 10)
(c) freedom of thought, conscience and religious conviction (FRF Article 15 para 1)
(d) freedom of speech (FRF Article 17 para 1)
(e) the right of petition (FRF Article 18 para 1)
(f) the right to peaceful assembly (FRF Article 19 para 1)
(g) the right to associate freely (FRF Article 20 para 1)
(h) the national or ethnic identity of any individual shall not be used to his or her detriment (FRF Article 24)
(i) the right to judicial and other legal protection (FRF Article 36)

Freedom of speech, the right of petition, the right to peaceful assembly, and the right to associate freely are not absolute. FRF Articles 17 para 4, 18 para 3, 19 para 2 and 19 para 3 state in general that these rights can be limited by law when necessary for protecting the rights and freedoms of others, such as those mentioned above. The criminal law limits freedom of speech, by act No. 40/2009 Coll., Criminal Code, as amended (hereinafter "Criminal Code", see Section 2).

The collision between freedom of speech (FRF Article 17 para 1) and freedom to associate freely (FRF Article 20 para 1) on one side and public interest on protection of rights of the others as well as democracy itself on the other side was subject of judgment of the Constitutional Court of the Czech Republic from 28. 11. 2011, IV. ÚS 2011/10. In this case the Constitutional Court assessed six complaints filed by individuals who had prepared and organized or participated in meeting of movement "Národní odpor" (*National Resistance*) on 1. 5. 2007. National Resistance was known for its far-right ideas and open propagation of hateful, racist and xenophobic action against others' fundamental rights and freedoms, and the declaration of intolerance against minorities. The lower courts found the defendants guilty of criminal offence of Support and Promotion of Movement Aimed at Suppression of Rights and Freedoms of Men according to Section 260 para 1 of the act No. 140/1961 Coll., Criminal Act, as amended (hereinafter the "Criminal Act") [today Section 404 of the Criminal Code].

The Constitutional Court ruled (because *inter alia* the key idea of this judgment was to present the concept of "militant democracy") that both the right to free speech and the right to associate freely had not been breached. First, the Constitutional Court found that freedom of speech involves not only information and ideas that are accepted positively, but also those that are offensive, shocking, or disturbing. Second, the Court pointed out that *these conclusions cannot be applied to completely extreme and hateful expression (hate speech) and such expression can be restricted or even subjected to criminal proceedings.* Accordingly, criminal proceedings might be necessary if such expressions contain (explicitly or implicitly) calls for violence or for denial, questioning, approval or justification of crimes against humanity committed in the past, as well as for the support and promotion of movement aimed at suppression of fundamental human rights and freedoms, especially in relation to some minorities.

Another important and recent case where constitutional law was applied to hateful expressions is presented in the decision of the Czech Supreme Court from 12. 2. 2020, 8 Tdo 81/2020. J.S., a former member of the Chamber of Deputies of the Czech Parliament Republic had been prosecuted for criminal offences of Incitement to Hatred Against a Group of Persons or to the Restriction of Their Rights and Freedoms according to Criminal Code Section 356 para 1 as well as Deyning, Questioning, Approving and Justifying Genocide according to Criminal Code Section 405. According to the law enforcement authorities the defendant committed these offences while visiting a restaurant of the Chamber of Deputies in 2017 where he said loudly, clearly, and in front of at least three other people: "Faggots and lesbians are a disease and they should be shot right after they are born" and "Faggots, Jews and Gipsies—should all be gassed".[1] The defendant was found guilty and sentenced to imprisonment for one year on a suspended sentence, along with a fine of 70 000 CZK (approx. 2.600 EUR).

In his extraordinary appeal to the Supreme Court, the defendant cited his freedom of speech according to Article 17 para 1 of the Bill. The Supreme Court stressed that according to the Constitutional Court and the European Court of Human Rights "the Holocaust and Nazi genocide aimed against Jewish population are notorious and undeniable historic fact and its questioning is in contradiction with basic ideas of (European) Convention for the Protection of Human Rights and Fundamental Freedoms" (decision of the Czech Supreme Court from 12. 2. 2020, 8 Tdo 81/2020, § 30). Such behaviour thus cannot be according to the Supreme Court excused even by existence of fundamental freedom of speech, which is not boundless, but reducible precisely for the purpose of protecting the rights and freedoms of others, or for the purpose of protecting public security. Another important conclusion of this decision was that such public statements cannot be tolerated, regardless of when they are made or who makes them. It is important to bear in mind that statements of politicians (even in relatively restricted Parliamentary premises) send a message of possible behaviour of elites and form publicly perceived patterns of behaviour.

This case mentioned was not the only one involving a Czech public politician expressing racist, xenophobic, or homophobic statements. In 2013 another former

---

[1] A quotation from the decision of the Supreme Court of the Czech Republic of 12 February 2020, file number 8 Tdo 81/2020, translation by the authors (available via https://nsoud.cz/ but only in Czech language).

member of the Chamber of Deputies of the Parliament of the Czech Republic O. CH., while sitting in Parliament, published on his public Facebook profile: "Very clever from g. [Gypsy] leader. They definitely do not lack arrogance and self-esteem. But the people are on edge and if more of such g. provocations occur the rodeo will begin. And then even the police will not protect them." and "The pinnacle of arrogance of the g. leader. But go on, doves, push a little bit harder and it will break somewhere. The people are on the edge, so push harder and let the wild thing happen. I can hear the screams right now. No matter how fast you will run."[2] Later, he was prosecuted and found guilty of criminal offence of Incitement to Hatred Against a Group of Persons or to the Restriction of Their Rights and Freedoms according to Section 356 para 1, para 3 of the Criminal Code.

The letter "g." in his statement stood for "Gypsy" which was clear because he was reacting to a physical attack of a group of Roma on a married couple in city of Duchcov. The attackers were later tried and sentenced to conditional and unconditional punishments of imprisonment. In this case imprisonment with a suspended sentence was imposed to O.CH. Another important level of this case was that both the Supreme Court (decision from 25. 6. 2014, 3 Tcu 33/2014) and Constitutional Court (decision from 16. 6. 2015, I. ÚS 3018/14) were concerned with the limits of legitimate political speech in Parliament. Their decision, that statements of members of Parliament must address exclusively participants of parliamentary discussion and only in such cases the freedom of speech of members of Parliament (that is necessary for open parliamentary discussion) is covered by constitutional indemnity (thus the members of Parliament cannot be criminally liable for their statements), was considered crucial when discussing freedom of speech.

7.2 National Statutory and Administrative Law

Czech statutory law concerning hateful expression (when considering criminal or administrative liability) is contained in the Criminal Code and the Act on Some Administrative Offences. The Criminal Code sets forth numerous criminal offences based on hate speech. We will focus only on verbal attacks and not on physical attacks or attacks on property with hateful motives.

One offence is referred to as Violence Against a Group of People and Individuals, under Criminal Code Section 352 paras 1, 2 and 3. This offence is based on threatening a group of people with death, physical injury or large scale damage (para 1), or using violence against group of people or individual or threatening them with death, physical injury or large-scale damage because of their actual or perceived race, ethnicity, nationality, political beliefs, religion or because they are genuinely or allegedly without religion (para 2). In case of association or gathering to commit criminal offence according to para 2, or in case of committing such offence via print,

[2] Two quotations from the decision of the Supreme Court of the Czech Republic of 26 June 2014, file number 3 Tcu 33/2014; translation by the authors.

television, radio, the Internet etc. the offender shall be punished by imprisonment from six months up to three years (para 3).

Another criminal offence connected with hate speech is referred to as Defamation of a Nation, Race, Ethnic or Other Group of People under Criminal Code Section 355 paras 1 and 2. This offence is based on public disgrace of a nation, its language, race or ethnic group or of a group of individuals because of their actual or perceived race, ethnicity, nationality, political beliefs, religion or because they are genuinely or allegedly without religion (para 1). In case of committing this criminal offence with at least two more persons, or via print, television, radio, the Internet etc. the offender shall be punished by imprisonment for up to three years (para 2).

The offence of Incitement to Hatred Against a Group of Persons or to the Restriction of Their Rights and Freedoms according to Criminal Code Section 356 paras 1, 2 and 3 was mentioned above. This offence is based on public incitement to hatred against a nation, race, ethnic group, religion, class or other group of persons or to restrict rights and freedoms of their members (para 1), or association or gathering towards committing such criminal offence (para 2). In the case of committing an offence according to para 1 via print, television, radio, the Internet etc. or when the offender actively participates in activities of group, organization or association that declares discrimination, violence or racial, ethnic, class, religious or other hatred, then he or she shall be punished by imprisonment from six months up to three years (para 3). As of 2021 a new bill in the Czech Parliament aims to repeal Section 356 of the Criminal Code because some members of the Chamber of Deputies assume that it is vague and incomprehensible, and that freedom of speech should prevail over the concept of hate speech. The bill was not adopted before the October 2021 election to the Chamber of Deputies. In the new parliamentary term from October 2021, this bill was not renewed.

Another criminal offence based on hate speech is Establishing, Support and Promotion of a Movement Aimed at Suppressing Human Rights and Freedoms according to Criminal Code Section 403 paras 1, 2 and 3. This offence is based on establishing, support or promotion of movement which is demonstrably aimed at suppressing human rights and freedoms, or on proclamation of racial, ethnic, national, religious or class resentment or resentment against another group of persons (para 1). If the offender commits such act via print, television, radio or the Internet etc., or if he or she commits such act as member of organized group or as a soldier or in state of threat to the state or during the state of war, then he or she shall be punished by imprisonment from three to ten years (para 2). The preparation of this offence according to Section 403 para 2 is punishable as well. This offence is the only case of hate speech based criminal offences when preparation is punishable—on contrary, the attempt of criminal offence is always punishable according to Criminal Code. In addition, the offence of Expression of Sympathy for a Movement Aimed at Suppressing Human Rights and Freedoms according to Criminal Code Section 404 relates to this preceding one and is based on public expression of sympathy to a movement as referred to in Section 403 para 1. This offence is punishable by imprisonment from six months to three years.

In 2022 a new criminal offence based on hate speech called Spreading of Items for Purpose of Promoting Movement Aimed at Suppressing Human Rights and Freedoms was adopted under Section 403a of Criminal Code. This offence is punishable by up to three years' imprisonment. It was added to the Criminal Code because of situations in which cups and t-shirts with pictures of Adolf Hitler, or, for example, a calendar with other representatives of the former Nazi regime, were sold for commercial purposes. It was highly problematic to prove the existence of an intention to support or promote a movement aimed at suppressing human rights and freedoms, which is a necessary element of a criminal offence under Section 403. This new offence complements protections provided by Section 403 in cases when the offender spreads a greater range of items that depict symbols such as logos, flags, badges, uniforms or their parts, slogans, or forms of greetings, or representatives or the speeches of the movement referred to in Section 403 para 1. Paragraphs 2 and 3 of Section 403a authorize a longer term of imprisonment when the offender commits such an act (a) as a member of an organized group, (b) via print, television, radio or the Internet, (c) to obtain substantial benefit for himself or for another (para 2, imprisonment from one up to five years), or (d) to obtain a large benefit for himself or for another (para 3, imprisonment from two up to six years).

Finally, there is the offence of Denying, Questioning, Approving and Justifying Genocide according to Section 405 of the Criminal Code. This crime is based on public denial, questioning, approving or seeking of Nazi, communist or other genocide or of Nazi, communist or other crimes against humanity or war crimes or crimes against peace. The offender shall be punished in this case by imprisonment from six months to three years.

We assume that this list of criminal offences based on hate speech represents the scope of criminal law limitation of freedom of speech, right of petition, right to assembly peacefully and right to associate freely. But a list of offences itself does not represent the current state of hate speech in the Czech Republic and thus we would like to present some current data on criminally relevant hate speech.

> For example, police statistics note that in 2021 there were 165,525 criminal offences committed in the Czech Republic, which currently holds a total population of apx. 10.5 million inhabitants. If we focus on the criminal offences mentioned above, the Czech police registered 23 cases under Section 352 (of which 11 were clarified[3] and 11 of them were accused), 29 cases under Section 355 (of which 15 were clarified and 13 of them were accused), 34 cases under Section 356 (of which 15 were classified and 11 of them were accused), and 39 cases under Sections 403, 404 and 405 (of which 15 were clarified and 15 of them were accused).

The Police statistics also tell us that in 2021 there were 37 criminal offences that had antisemitic background, 33 with anti-Roma background, 7 based on anti-Muslim and 1 on anti-Arab background. However, this involves also other criminal offences based on hateful motive, such as intentional bodily harm under Section 145 para 2(f) and Section 146 para 2(e) of the Criminal Code or damaging of foreign

[3] According to terminology used by Czech police authority, a case is deemed to be "clarified" when enough evidence has been compiled to bring a credible accusation.

property according to Section 228 para 3(b). In addition, according to judicial statistics from 2021, 30 offenders were found guilty of a criminal offence under Section 352, 20 offenders were found guilty under Section 355, 10 were found guilty under Section 356, 10 were found guilty under Section 403, 23 were found guilty under Section 404, and 2 were found guilty under Section 405. In 10 cases the offenders were sentenced to unconditional imprisonment, but this latest information also involves other offences based on hateful motives.

The Ombudsman (Public Defender of the Rights—hereinafter "Public Defender") played no important role in these cases. The Public Defender has no powers against law enforcement authorities when considering criminal proceedings (see Section 1 para 9 of act No. 349/1999 Coll., on Public Defender of Rights, as amended) and cannot enter into ongoing criminal proceedings or file remedies for example. However, the Public Defender has standing to enter proceedings before the Constitutional Court, but only in case of general review of statutory law (for example when group of senators or members of Chamber of Deputies or even Public Defender her/himself files motion on dismissing of such law because of its incompatibility with constitutional law).

7.3 International Covenant on Civil and Political Rights (ICCPR)

The UN-HRC has issued four Concluding Observations for the Czech Republic (CCPR/CO/72/CZE, CCPR/C/CZE/CO/2, CCPR/C/CZE/CO/3, CCPR/C/CZE/CO/4). The first and fourth Concluding Observations contain recommendations for combatting hate speech. In the first one (2001), the Committee stated its concerns about violence and harassment by some groups with respect to the Roma minority, and the failure on the part of the police and judicial authorities to investigate, prosecute and punish hate crimes. The Committee recommended that the Czech Republic should take all necessary measures to combat racial violence and incitement, provide proper protection to Roma and other minorities, and ensure adequate investigation and prosecution of cases of racial violence and incitement to racial hatred. In the second Concluding Observations (2007) the Committee did not mention its concerns about investigation, prosecution and combat hate crime.

The third Concluding Observations (2013) mention an anti-Roma climate that remains prevalent among the Czech population. The Committee also stated its concern about the use of discriminatory remarks against the Roma by politicians and in the media and at the extremist demonstrations, marches, and attacks directed against members of the Roma community. According to these findings the Committee recommended the Czech Republic to redouble its effort to combat all forms of intolerance against the Roma.

In the fourth (2019) Concluding Observations the Committee noted that the Czech Republic has taken measures to address racism, hate speech and other forms of intolerance, including the annual Concept for Combating Extremism and Prejudiced Hatred and the Campaign against Racism project and Hate Free media campaign. However, the Committee was concerned about a reported high level of hate speech against Roma, asylum seekers, refugees and migrants, Muslims, Jews, and lesbian, gay, bisexual, transgender, and intersex persons, including by politicians and high-level officials and in the media and online, and attacks motivated by hatred. The Committee was also concerned that senior officials in the Czech Republic reportedly encourage the public perception of migration as a threat to public security and that the media has been used to instil fear of migrants and asylum seekers and to strengthen stereotypical prejudices based on ethnicity or religion. According to these findings the Committee recommended that the Czech Republic should redouble its efforts, through both law enforcement and awareness-raising activities, to combat racial discrimination, hate speech and incitement to discrimination or violence on racial, ethnic or religious grounds.

Notably, the Committee recommended that the Czech Republic should take effective measures to prevent hate speech, particularly by politicians and high-level public officials, firmly and publicly condemn such speech and intensify efforts aimed at addressing online hate speech (see cases mentioned above). The Committee also recommended a strengthening of awareness-raising efforts, and conduct campaigns aimed at promoting respect for human rights and tolerance for diversity and revisiting and eradicating stereotypical prejudices based on ethnicity or religion. Another recommendation was to investigate hate crimes thoroughly, prosecute suspected perpetrators where appropriate and, if they are convicted, punish them and provide victims with adequate remedies. Finally, the Committee put emphasis on ensuring that adequate training continues to be provided to law enforcement officials, judges and prosecutors on addressing hate crimes and to media workers on promoting racial, ethnic and religious diversity. Note also that the Czech Republic has consented to individual complaints procedures, but no individual complaint relevant to hateful expression has been filed as of the present publication.

In field of the criminal law the Czech Parliament reflects the ICCPR in the context of hateful expression by criminal law legislation (see verbal criminal offences containing hateful motive mentioned above). However, we must emphasize that some legislators disparage this issue and have presented a bill that aims to repeal Section 356 of the Criminal Code. The bill was not adopted before the October 2021 elections for the Chamber of Deputies. In the new parliamentary term from October 2021, the bill to repeal Section 356 was not renewed.

Another statutory law where criminal law protection against hate speech can be tracked is act No. 45/2013 Coll., on Victims of Criminal Offence and on Change of Other Laws (Act on Victims of Criminal Offences), as amended. According to Section 2 para 4, letter d), an especially vulnerable victim is also a victim of criminal offence that was committed because of victim's belonging to a nation, race, ethnic group, religion, class or other group of persons. Especially vulnerable victims enjoy some special rights as for example free specialized aid, right to ask to prevent contact between such victim and accused, right to be questioned by person of same or different sex and are subject to numerous duties of law enforcement authorities. All victims of criminal offences (including hate speech) are entitled to damages in case of material or immaterial damage and they can claim damages during both civil or criminal proceedings.

Following a recommendation of the Committee, the Czech Ministry of the Interior creates a Conception of Struggle Against Manifestations of Extremism and Bias Hatred (hereinafter "Conception"). The latest Conception was adopted for the period from 2021 to 2026. Its implementation is evaluated annually and submitted to the Parliament of the Czech Republic. It presents three strategic targets for 2023–2024 that are connected with specific measures developed for their fulfilment.

The first target ("Protection of victims of crime") emphasizes the specificities of victims of hate crime. The priority is to provide them with protection and assistance while respecting the specificities of vulnerable social groups. Emphasis is placed on unifying the activities of the police, the prosecution, and the courts to make them more predictable, since it is necessary to create good conditions for them to carry out their activities. Regular and comprehensible information to the public also facilitates the fulfilment of this target.

The second target ("Protection of democracy") focuses on protecting the pillars of Czech democracy, including active defence against groups that attack it and seek to destroy the safeguards that democracy guarantee. In order to achieve this target, the capacity to combat disinformation with xenophobic elements, the ability to detect radicalized persons, the maintenance of the ability to manage violent gatherings, the continuation of measures against the infiltration of extremists into the security forces and the armed forces, and the paralysis of anti-democratic militias are being pursued.

The third target ("Strengthening trust in democracy in a transparent and comprehensible way") focuses on creating defences against the influence of extremists and xenophobic populists. This goal is mainly achieved through activities aimed at the reintegration of (re)radicalized people and prevention of recidivism, education, and awareness raising, and transparent and mutually beneficial integration policies.

Each of these targets has its means of financing and a responsible agent who will secure its fulfilment (mainly ministries and law enforcement authorities, but also other bodies whose activities are connected with each target—such as Republic Committee for prevention of Criminality, Agency for Social Inclusion, Government's Council for Matters of Roma Minority, Probation and Mediation Service, Prison Service of the Czech Republic or Police Presidium). It should also be mentioned that in 2019, a methodological tool for police officers and prosecutors to prosecute hate speech (not only) on the Internet was created by the Prosecutor General's Office in accordance with the Ministry of the Interior of the Czech Republic [hereinafter "Methodological Tool"].

This Methodical tool focuses on online hate speech. Its main goal is to educate police officers and public prosecutors on how to assess problematic statements and how to prosecute hate speech. It provides general information about current development in hate speech and extremism, points out specifics connected with rules of criminal proceedings in such cases (including securing of online evidence), interpretation of terms constituting body of each of criminal offences (such as ethnic group, race, political belief and so). One of the greatest benefits for law enforcement authorities is that this Methodical Tool provides lists of statements that were assessed as hate speech, which promotes general knowledge about criminalizable statements and examples of judgments when such cases were decided (including description of statements of offender).

Hate crime in general is the subject of specialized units of Police of the Czech Republic and Public Prosecutor's Office that work within workgroups called "EXTREM". Each local Public Prosecutor's Office has their expert on criminal offences committed because of racial, national or other kind of hatred. At Prosecutor General's Office, there is National Correspondent for Struggle Against terrorism, Extremism and Criminal Offences Committed Because of Hateful Motive whose tasks are to guarantee intra- and interdepartmental cooperation and cooperation with foreign countries, to analyse judiciary and expert articles, to participate on educational activities organized mainly by the Justice Academy or to attend local and foreign conferences. The Czech Police also operate a special hotline for reporting problematic content and activities on the Internet, including hate crime and hate speech.

A large amount of energy is targeted to prevention as secured by the local police authority and Czech Police. A Strategy for work of the Police of the Czech Republic Towards Minorities presents contact officers for minorities and working groups of such officers, or assistants for prevention of criminality, and local prevention liaisons. Assistants for prevention of criminality and local prevention liaisons are chosen from a local minority, usually Roma, and work for local police to prevent criminality in certain locations.

Finally, we must mention the education of judges, public prosecutors and police officers focused on detection and prosecution of hate crime. In 2018 cooperation between the Justice Academy and OBSE-ODIHR (Office for Democratic Institutions and Human Rights) began in this field. Since then there have been several seminars on cybercrime, hate speech committed online and others current issues. The cooperation continues and other seminars, focused mainly on specialists on bias criminality, will follow.

7.4 International Convention on the Elimination of All Forms of Racial Discrimination (ICERD)

The UN-CERD has issued seven Concluding Observations for the Czech Republic (CERD/C/304/Add.47, CERD/C/304/Add.109, CERD/C/63/CO/4, CERD/C/CZE/CO/7, CERD/C/CZE/CO/8-9, CERD/C/CZE/CO/10-11, CERD/C/CZE/CO/12-13).

In the first Concluding Observations (1998) the Committee expressed its concern at the persistence of racial hatred and acts of violence, particularly by skinheads and others, towards persons belonging to minority groups, especially Roma and people of African or Asian origin. Reports of anti-Semitic incidents were further source of concern. Additional sources of concern were also the presence of organizations and publications which promote racist and xenophobic ideas, and reports that the Czech Republic has not been sufficiently active in countering racial violence against members of minority groups. Another source of concerns of the Committee were facts that political party represented in Parliament promoted racial discrimination and disseminated a magazine which promoted racist propaganda and ideas of racial superiority aimed at the ethnic minorities residing in the country.

In the second Concluding Observations (2001), the Committee welcomed measures taken by the Czech Republic for the promotion and the protection of the human rights of the Roma minority, in particular the ones included in the "Concept of Government Policy Towards Members of the Roma Community" (June 2000). Yet the Committee remained concerned by the fact that some organizations, including political parties, promoting racial hatred and superiority were hidden behind legally registered civic associations whose members were promoting xenophobia and racism. Concerns were also expressed at the ineffective implementation of existing legislation to prosecute the perpetrators of incitement to racial hatred and support to racist movements. In light of Article 4 of the ICERD, the Committee recommended that the Czech Republic should strengthen law enforcement to ensure that such organizations were dismantled and their members prosecuted.

In the third Concluding Observations (2003), the Committee appreciated efforts undertaken by the Czech Republic to counter racially motivated violence and discrimination. On the other side, the Committee remained concerned at the continuance of acts of racially motivated violence and incitement to hatred and the persistence of intolerance and *de facto* discrimination, in particular with regard to the Roma minority. Because of this, the Committee recommended that the Government shall pursue and intensify its efforts to achieve more effective application of existing legislation. The Committee also noted that the Czech Republic has only declared punishable active participation in organizations promoting and inciting racial discrimination [Section 356 para 3 letter b) of the Criminal Code] and thus urged the Czech Republic to consider reviewing this provision and to declare punishable any participation in organizations that promote and incite racial discrimination, in accordance with Article 4(b) of the ICERD.

The fourth Concluding Observations (2007) mentioned the question of interpretation of Sections 260, 261 and 261a of the Criminal Act (today of the Sections 403, 404 and 405) when the Czech Republic explained the application of those provisions on Nazi or Communist genocide. Such an interpretation that mixes up the ideas of hate crimes, racist propaganda and genocide with that of class struggle is, according to the Committee, incorrect and recommended an interpretation that would follow the objective of fighting racial discrimination. In our oponion, the distinction between "genocide," "hate crime," and "class struggle" in Czech jurisprudence is clear and the application of Sections 403, 404 and 405, e.g., to a neo-Nazi movement that is connected with both racial discrimination and genocide, or to a Communist movement that is connected with both class struggle and genocide, is unobjectionable. The Committee also noted that that efforts undertaken by the Czech Republic to encourage recruitment of members of Roma communities into the police have not enjoyed great success and recommended that the government enhance its efforts to improve the relationship and mutual understanding between the Roma and the police.

In the fifth Concluding Observations (2011) the Committee welcomed the 2010 decision of the Supreme Administrative Court to the Workers' Party for its advocacy of neo-Nazi ideology and expressions of opposition to immigrants and minorities. The court concluded that it was necessary to clearly name the values promoted by the party, to state unequivocally that the ideology following the totalitarian construction of national socialism constitutes evil, and that the existing system of legal values of the Czech Republic is incompatible with such an ideology. The Workers' Party has stood for freedom of expression and the right of association. However, no one, not even a political party, can effectively invoke the protection of its own fundamental rights and freedoms, exercised with the aim of threatening or violating the fundamental rights and freedoms of others. The Committee regretted that Czech legislation refers only to persons but does not prohibit organizations and other propaganda activities inciting racial discrimination and thus recommended including prohibitions of racist propaganda, organizations and activities in legislation, along with participation in such organizations or activities as offences punishable by law. The Committee also expressed concern about manifestations of hatred, hate crime, racist and xenophobic discourse in politics and the media, including reports of statements by senior political figures (the Committee has received reports of a growing number of incidents of incitement to hatred and acts of violence such as setting Roma dwellings alight with Molotov cocktails, some of which incidents allegedly have involved sympathizers of the former Workers' Party). The Committee was also concerned by information alleging that former members of extremist political parties serve as governmental advisors, including in the Ministry of Education, Youth and Sports. Because of this the Committee urged the Czech Republic to ensure that hate crime and violence, racist and xenophobic discourse, wherever they take place, are thoroughly investigated and that perpetrators, whoever they are, are effectively prosecuted. The Committee additionally urged the Czech Republic to ensure that former members of extremist political parties are not hired as governmental advisors or officials.

In the sixth Concluding Observations (2015), the Committee welcomed the launch of the Campaign against Racism and Hate Violence (2014). In the field of racial hatred, racist hate speech, and racially motivated violence, the Committee expressed its concerns at the continuing racial hatred and racially motivated violence against Roma. Particularly spreading of prejudice and stereotypes about refugees and asylum seekers among the general public (through websites and social media), increased attacks through e-mails or on social networks on people who defend the rights of foreign nationals, including activists from non-governmental organizations, increase of Islamophobia by anti-Muslim groups such as "No to Islam in the Czech Republic!" (which is openly supported by some politicians, including members of Parliament), increase in racially motivated violence against Muslim communities and media's excessive highlighting of the ethnic origin and the nationality of non-citizens in the reporting of criminal offences.

In order to change these negative aspects the Committee recommended the Czech Republic to firmly condemn hate speech by public officials and politicians, effectively investigate racist hate speech and racially motivated violence, and prosecute perpetrators, where appropriate, also to raise the awareness of the public of respect for diversity and elimination of racial discrimination and finally to adopt appropriate legislation for the media, in accordance with international standards, to promote informed, ethical and objective media and to encourage the public and private media to adopt codes of professional ethics or press codes that incorporate respect for the principles of the Convention and human rights standards.

Most recently, the Concluding Observations of 2019 again expressed concern about the prevalence of hate speech in the Czech Republic. The main problems were dissemination of racist hate speech, prejudices and stereotypes directed towards minority groups, in particular asylum seekers, refugees, Roma and Jews (via the Internet and social media), use of racist hate speech, anti-migrant and anti-Roma rhetoric by politicians and public figures, including members of the parliament, mayors and members of the Government, role of the media in the propagation of racist stereotypes and prejudices regarding minority groups and a fear of migrants and finally existence of reports on intimidation of, and a growing hostility towards, journalists who attempt to cover issues related to migration independently and impartially. In order to deal with these detected issues, the Committee recommended to the Czech Republic once again to firmly condemn any form of hate speech and xenophobic rhetoric against minority groups and distance itself from racist hate speech expressed by politicians and public figures and ensure that such acts are investigated and adequately punished. Other recommendations were to intensify public awareness-raising activities, including in schools, in order to promote a better understanding of the situation of minority groups and to decrease prejudices and stigmatization against those groups and to make media outlets and journalists disseminating hate speech more accountable, and provide journalists with training on the rights of minority groups and on the legislation prohibiting racist hate speech. Final recommendation was pointed at protection of journalists who cover issues related to migration and ensure they can perform their work without fear of reprisals or intimidation.

The Czech Republic has consented to individual complaints procedures, but to date no individual complaint relevant to hateful expression has been filed.

7.5 Regional Law and Organisations

The Czech Republic is member of various regional organizations such as EU, OSCE, Council of Europe. The legislation referring to hate speech is usually involved by EU law or conventions of Council of Europe. Yet we were not able to find any other rulings or findings that have actually or potentially affected laws or policies on hateful expression in the Czech Republic except the case mentioned below.

Section 196 Article 2 of Criminal Act (now Criminal Code Section 356 Article 2) was amended in 2002 according to standards set by Council Directive 2000/43/EC of 29 June 2000 implementing the principle of equal treatment between persons irrespective of racial or ethnic origin. Thanks to this amendment public initiation to hatred against group of individuals or individual for their ethnic group (not only because of their nationality, race, religion or lack of it) constitutes such criminal offence.

7.6 Judicial Rulings

In its statement from 13. 12. 2006, Tpjn 302/2005, published under No. 11/2007 of Collection of judicial decisions and statements (hereinafter "the Statement"), the Supreme Court provided a definition of "movement" which constituted one of the elements of criminal offence according to Section 260 para 1 of the Criminal Act (today Section 403 para 1 of the Criminal Code). The reason for adoption of the Statement was that the Supreme Court found out discrepancies in its own decision-making practice when interpreting this term. In one case an accused was found guilty of this offence because of publishing Adolf Hitler's *Mein Kampf*. His extraordinary appeal against conviction was successful before the Supreme Court when the court pointed out that a movement aimed at suppressing of human rights and freedoms must be necessarily an existing one (meaning that support or promotion of non-existing movement, such as Nazi movement or Italian Fascism could not constitute criminal offence according to Section 260 para 1 of the Criminal Act, only in case that offender would support or promote for example neo-Nazi movement). Another deciding chamber of the Supreme court did not agree with this idea (but it did not explained his reasons) and dismissed extraordinary appeal of accused who was found guilty of criminal offence according to Section 260 para 1 of the Criminal Act because of selling military badges, decorations, equipment parts and patches and flags of the criminal organizations such as SS and Hitlerjugend and other things containing Nazi symbols.

The Supreme Court ruled that term "movement" within the meaning of § 260 para 1 of the Criminal Act stands for group of persons at least partially organized, even if not formally registered, aimed at suppressing human rights and freedoms or proclaiming national, racial, religious or class resentment or resentment against another group of persons. In order to fulfil the body of crime of this criminal offence it is necessary for the movement to exist at a time when the offender supported or promoted it, even in its modified form (e.g. neo-fascist or neo-Nazi movement, etc.). The promotion of a movement demonstrably aimed at suppressing human rights and freedoms, which did not exist at the time of its promotion by the perpetrator, may, depending on the circumstances of the case, fulfil the body of attempted of criminal offence according to Section 260 para 1 of the Criminal Act, if the offender by his actions intended to initiate the establishment or renewal of such a movement, or signs of a criminal offense of Support and Promotion of Movement Aimed at Suppressing of Human Rights and Freedoms according to Section 261a of the Criminal Act (today Section 404 of Criminal Code).

7.7 National Popular Culture

If we want to look at this issue in more detail and as comprehensively as possible, it is impossible not to mention the influence of the media represented by periodicals, regardless of whether it is published in printed or online form. Periodicals are intended to inform the public. Given the scope of individual contributions and the reader's interest, they necessarily contain certain simplifications. In today's world each of us is an active or passive recipient of large amounts of information, which spreads quickly and we are often lack the time or means to process and evaluate it. Related to this, however, is the great power that the media have in that the publication of certain information, even if it turns out to be false.

The Internet also has a significant influence. Anyone with a computer and a connection to a public data network can publish information. The control authority for publishing is missing and the volume of data is constantly growing. One of the key questions when using information from the Internet is its credibility, i.e. whether it is objectively correct and true. It is also general knowledge that identification of erroneous information is relatively difficult, and the concept of credibility of information thus becomes even more important. On the other hand, the fact that a source contains incorrect information does not necessarily mean a problem if users are able to distinguish the correct information.

One of the common issues that occurs on the Internet is the spread of alarming, dangerous and unnecessary chain messages, so-called hoaxes (these were very popular in the Czech Republic during the beginning of so-called "migration crisis" in 2015). A hoax is an alarming or chain message designed to give the impression to be true. It is often a shocking or emotional message passed on without verifying both its source and verity. Exceptionally, the statement is also true, but outdated. Unauthorized information, the source of which is not mentioned anywhere, is also a great risk. It is not always clear from such webpages whether the author submits his own statements or whether it is a copy of a foreign text. For serious information, the author, the source of the information is given, and at the same time the reason why this information is published is clear.

Knowing this, it is necessary to consider question, why in the European area, including the Czech Republic, politicians and political entities supporting moods of Euroscepticism and anti-immigration moods have stable support among citizens, and in some cases this popularity continues to grow. At the same time, it is not possible to argue with the introduction of the cliché that we very often encounter in the Czech Republic, that their voters belong to lower social classes and often have lower education. In the context of the 2015 migration crisis, the European public was initially sympathetic to refugees and in fact welcomed them with almost open arms, but this trend gradually reversed. As mentioned above, this was also reflected in the fact that political parties and movements in the EU are beginning to gain in popularity, building their policies precisely on Euroscepticism, opposition to migration quotas and the reception of refugees in EU countries, i.e. anti-migration or anti-Islamic sentiments in society. We can mention well known examples such as Rassemblement National in France or Alternative für Deutschland in Germany.

In the Czech Republic such a political party is "Freedom and Direct Democracy Tomio Okamura" that received 10.64% of votes from 538 574 voters in elections into Chamber of Deputies of the Parliament of the Czech Republic in 2017. With regard to the election result, the chairman of this political party also became the vice-chairman of the Chamber of Deputies. The political program of this party states for example: "We support the traditional values of our society and consider a functioning family to be its essence. The family deserves protection and support. We consider the traditional union of a man and a woman to be the basis of the family. We refuse to promote and support opinions and behaviors that threaten the functioning of families and the upbringing of children in the family. The project of current European integration will also directly threaten freedom and democracy in Europe. Part of this process is the controlled Islamization of Europe. The ongoing illegal immigration is the initial phase of the conflict, which will ultimately threaten freedom, democracy and the very existence of the Czech Republic and our nation. We do not declare hatred for any nation, race, culture, or religion. Our society has a national tradition based on the roots of Jewish, ancient and Christian culture and civilization. We will protect these values. They are the foundation of democracy, freedom and human rights. The ongoing Islamization of European countries is incompatible with these values. We consistently reject the multicultural ideology that is the tool of Islamization. We say out loud that it is not our duty to open the door to anyone who says they will settle down with us, but that staying in our home is a privilege for foreigners. If someone wants to work and live with us, they must respect our values and adapt." In the elections to the Chamber of Deputies of the Parliament of the Czech Republic, which took place in October 2021, this political party won 9.56% votes.

7.8 Additional Observations

The Czech state and society have been based on ethnic, national and religious homogeneity in the last few decades. Generations of Czechs in the post-war period, between 1950 and 1990, lived with a consciousness of civil society where they themselves occupied a majority of the population and minorities or ethnic groups made up only a negligible fraction of the population scattered in the majority society, within local or regional contacts.

This situation changed during the period of changes brought about by the so-called Velvet Revolution on November 17, 1989. After 1990, there was a gradual change in interethnic contact in our territory, multiple migrations came in various waves already known but also new ethnic groups that came to our territory not only as a result of political changes, but also in connection with the opening of new economic and social activities. The migration crisis also played a significant role when a total of 5 260 people arrived in the Czech Republic as part of this crisis on 31 December 2016.

Since 1989, the Czech Republic has become more of a destination country for many foreigners, although in the past it had been more of a transit state. The numbers of foreigners are slowly increasing, and thanks to the stable political situation and rising living standards, they can be expected to continue to rise. If we look at the population of the Czech Republic, it is very ethnically homogeneous. Foreigners from various national minorities make up only about 6% of the total population, specifically as of March 31, 2019 it was 568 904 people. However, the question is the real number of members of these and other national minorities in our territory, as the numbers given may not correspond to reality. At the last census in 2011, in which the indication of nationality was a voluntary issue, 64.3% of the population declared their Czech nationality, but almost a quarter of respondents (25.3%) did not comment on this question.

Regarding the historical context, the predominant minorities include the Slovak national minority. Other national minorities did not exceed the required 1% of the population to be included in the census statistics. Even so, in the Czech Republic there are also Bulgarians, Croatians, Hungarians, Germans, Poles, Roma, Ruthenians, Russians, Greeks, Slovaks, Serbians, Ukrainians and Vietnamese. Inevitably some minorities enter the field of view of the majority society more often than others. The most discussed in the Czech Republic are Albanians, Ukrainians and Vietnamese.

In recent years, however, the greatest attention has been drawn to the Roma minority, which arouses the greatest interest, emotion and need to express itself among members of the majority. The Roma in the Czech Republic are among the groups most affected by social exclusion, with all the negative consequences of this phenomenon, which is often noted by the UN Human Rights Committee. Specifically, these are: low educational attainment, high unemployment and crime. In addition, many citizens have a prejudice that the Roma rob people on public transport or steal in department stores. Many of them react intuitively to the presence of Roma in these areas with increased vigilance. Society also has a negative perception that Roma do not work and live on social benefits. On this account, unemployed Roma are not motivated to look for work and gradually become accustomed to contributions and benefits and become dependent on the support system. The inability to find a job is related to their education and minimal work habits. Almost half of the Roma in working age do not have a job. However, often educated Roma also have difficulties finding employment, mainly due to the prejudices of future employers.

Politicians, with their often very unflattering statements in relation to this part of society, have a decidedly negative effect on the perception of the Roma. According to a survey conducted by the Center for Public Opinion Research (hereinafter "the Center") conducted in 2019, that concerned the coexistence of the Roma and non-Roma sections of society, 72% of respondents evaluated coexistence with the Roma as bad. On the other hand, the number of those who do not perceive coexistence with the Roma as a negative is slowly growing.

In the period from the end of April to the end of June 2021, the Center collected data within the framework of the international survey Research on the Situation of the Roma in 2020–2021. The research was commissioned by the European Union Agency for Fundamental Rights (FRA). 8,400 Roma from 10 European countries took part in the survey: the Czech Republic, Croatia, Italy, Hungary, Portugal, Romania, Greece, Spain, Northern Macedonia and Serbia. The aim of the survey is to understand the life of the Roma, to take a thorough look at their current life situation and everyday experiences in their country. The survey covers issues related to the current life situation and quality of life of Roma, health, jobs, awareness of rights and trust in institutions. The data from the Roma Survey 2021 is interesting because it allows not only to compare the situation with other EU countries where large Roma minorities live, but also to monitor trends. The results of the survey can help answer the question of why Czech society has such a negative view of the Roma ethnic group.

A positive view of Roma issues can be, for example, the activities of the ROMEA organization, which has been supporting Roma students since 2016 and has awarded 525 scholarships with a total value of 8,594,500 CZK since that year. The aim is for talented Roma students to have the opportunity to successfully graduate and continue their studies at universities. The aim is to further increase the number of educated Roma men and women, who will then become full citizens of society and who will change its view of the Roma. There are many people who do not trust Roma students and write hundreds of hateful comments on social media every day. But they do not lose motivation and work to show these people how wrong they are one day. Based on the above scholarship program, a Roma student has been attending the Faculty of Law of Masaryk University since the academic year 2021/2022.

The very popular Czech Television series MOST! also brought a fundamental turn in the view of the Roma in a certain part of society towards them. Broadcasted in 2019, when one of its main representatives was the Roma, where this ethnic group was not shown in negative light at all (although various stereotypes still occured in this series). Such activities of both NGO and public television can shape public opinion in terms of acceptance of Roma minority.

According to a survey conducted by the Center in 2015, which tested public attitudes towards foreigners, 70% of respondents still believed that foreigners should adapt to our habits as much as possible, 27% of respondents and only 2% of the Czech population were in favour of only partial adjustment. Such outcomes points to the high degree of intolerance of Czech society and could explain why hate speech is such issue in the Czech Republic.

The research of the Center, again from 2015, shows that the greatest sympathy is shown by citizens to the Czechs (88%) and Slovaks (84%) and Poles (followed by a certain distance), who are sympathetic to the majority of the public (54%), followed by Germans (38%), Greeks (37%), Jews (31%), Hungarians (30%) and Bulgarians (27%). In the case of Vietnamese (26%), Serbs (19%) and Chinese (17%), antipathy already prevails over sympathy, although the largest proportion is neutral "neither sympathetic nor unsympathetic". For Russians (19%), Ukrainians (15%), Romanians (10%), Albanians (6%) and Arabs (5%), the already declared antipathies form the relatively largest part of the answers, in the case of Albanians and Arabs even the absolute majority. Citizens declare the worst relationship with the Roma, to whom more than four-fifths (82%) of the respondents expressed dissatisfaction.

In 2015, the Center also conducted a survey in which respondents were asked who we would not like to have as neighbors. The respondents had the greatest distance to people addicted to drugs, alcoholics and people with a criminal history, which gradually 91, 78 and 76% said they would not want to have as neighbours. There is a relatively large distance even in the case of mentally ill people, who would not want to have as neighbours more than two thirds (70%) of the respondents. Others in the list of the population are no longer rejected to such an extent. A certain distance can still be noted in the case of people of different skin colour (38% of citizens said that they would not want to have them as neighbours), foreigners living in the Czech Republic (31%), people with homosexual orientation (23%) and people with other religious beliefs. (20%). It is also worth noting that 18% of respondents expressed a negative attitude towards smokers. Sharing neighbourhood with rich people was rejected by 10% of respondents (with the poor ones by 6%).

According to this data Czech society lacks tolerance towards various groups of inhabitants and the level of intolerance differs quite a lot. Such intolerance can be easily turned into hateful motives and thus into hate speech or physical insults based on hateful motive.

Finally, we must mention the international situation in Central Europe connected with Russian aggression against Ukraine, which led to sizeable westward migrations of Ukrainians. Due to false news and war propaganda, to non-negligible pro-Russian sentiments in Czech society, to massive disinformation in the wake of the Covid pandemic, much public sentiment turned to hatred against Ukrainians and international organizations such as NATO. As of this writing, several criminal cases are pending before Czech courts connected with hate crimes against Ukrainians.

Marek Fryšták Prof. JUDr. worked from 1997–2009 in positions at the Police of the Czech Republic, Regional Police Directorate of the South Moravian Region in Brno. Since 2002 he has been a member of the Department of Criminal Law at the Faculty of Law of Masaryk University in Brno. Fryšták is currently a professor of Criminal Law at this faculty (2021). He specializes in substantive and procedural criminal law and related issues of linking theory and practice.

David Čep has worked since 2015 in various positions in judicial system of the Czech Republic (2015–2016 assistant of judge of the Supreme Court, 2016–2019 assistant of judge of the Constitutional Court, 2019–nowadays assistant of judge of the Supreme Court). Since 2018 he has been a member of the Department of Criminal Law at the Faculty of Law of Masaryk University in Brno. In his scientific research he specializes on corporate criminal liability, drug crime and modern trends in criminality.

Katarína Kandová has worked since 2015 in various positions in judicial system of the Czech Republic (2015–2019 assistant of judge of the Supreme Court, 2019–2022 assistant at Prosecutor General's Office, 2022-nowadays public prosecutor at District Public Prosecutor's Office Prague 1). From 2015 to 2020 she has been a member of the Department of Criminal Law at the Faculty of Law of Masaryk University in Brno. She specializes on hate crime, crimes of communism, the role of public prosecution and subsidiarity of criminal repression.

Chapter 8
Finland

Tarja Koskela and Riku Neuvonen

Contents

Abstract The Finnish Constitution protects freedom of speech. It entails e.g. the right to express opinions without prior restraints. In Finland, hate speech is not criminalised in legislation as such, but as incitement to hatred against an ethic group is criminalised. Racial motivation is also a ground for aggravating punishment. Unlike most of European countries, blasphemy is still criminalised. Prosecutors have also brought charges of breach of sanctity of religion in courts. This has been justified by the freedom of religion. International covenants has played a significant role in regulating hate speech in Finland.

Keyword Anti-refugee speech · Blasphemy · History of hate speech · Hate speech legislation

---

T. Koskela (✉)
School of Law, Criminal Law at the University of Eastern Finland, Joensuu, Finland
e-mail: tarja.s.koskela@uef.fi

R. Neuvonen
Tampere University, Tampere, Finland

University of Helsinki, Helsinki, Finland

R. Neuvonen
e-mail: riku.neuvonen@helsinki.fi

E. Heinze (ed.), *Criminalising Hate Speech*,
https://doi.org/10.1007/978-94-6265-650-5_8

8.1 National Constitutional Law

8.1.1 The Freedom of Speech Doctrine in Finland

Finland is a member of the Council of Europe, the United Nations and the European Union. These factors significantly determine Finland's doctrine of freedom of speech and attitude towards hate speech. In its current form, the Finnish doctrine of freedom of speech is relatively new.[1] This chapter focuses on the relationship between free speech and the regulation of hate speech in Finland. These questions stem from Finnish history. Therefore, this chapter begins with a view to Finnish constitutional law and the history of freedom of speech.

Fundamental rights are covered by the second chapter of the Finnish Constitution Act. The Constitution Act was enacted in 1919 and was completely reformed in 2000. The second chapter was partially modified in 1995 after Finland joined the Council of Europe in 1990.[2] Membership of the Council of Europe requires commitment to the European Convention on Human Rights. This and the membership of the European Union in 1995 had a significant impact on changes in the Finnish legal system.

Section 12 of the Finnish Constitution (731/1999, 11.6.1999) protects freedom of speech and stands as follows:

> Freedom of expression and right of access to information. Everyone has the freedom of expression. Freedom of expression entails the right to express, disseminate and receive information, opinions and other communications without prior prevention by anyone. More detailed provisions on the exercise of the freedom of expression are laid down by an Act. Provisions on restrictions relating to pictorial programmes that are necessary for the protection of children may be laid down by an Act. Documents and recordings in the possession of the authorities are public, unless their publication has for compelling reasons been specifically restricted by an Act.
>
> Everyone has the right of access to public documents and recordings.

The structure of the Section consists of:

(a) General clause, which confirms freedom of speech as a fundamental right of everyone;
(b) A clause that specifies the rights covered by freedom of speech;
(c) The prohibition of prior restraints;
(d) The reservation that the use of free speech must be precised by an Act of Parliament; and
(e) The qualified reservation for legislation restricting pictorial programmes.

The 1995 reform of fundamental rights changed the general principles governing fundamental rights. The reform made it easier for private individuals to invoke their

[1] See Neuvonen 2012a, 2012b. Also short introduction in English, Neuvonen 2023.

[2] For more on the Finnish constitution in English, see Saraviita 2012.

fundamental rights.[3] The significance of fundamental rights in the courts, administration and other applications of law has increased. The reform expanded the scope of the application of fundamental rights. Before 1995, the focus in Finnish Constitutional Law was on how laws are enacted, that is, as a normal law or as an exceptive law.[4] After the reform, the focus was placed on the restriction of fundamental rights.

In order to understand the Finnish doctrine of freedom of speech, an idea of the basis of constitutional law in Finland is necessary. Understanding the Finnish freedom of speech doctrine and debates requires also acknowledgement of the central position of the Constitutional Law Committee in Finnish constitutional law. The Constitutional Law Committee of the Finnish Parliament ex ante reviews the constitutionality of government legislative proposals.[5] If there is doubt regarding inconsistency with the Constitution in the passing of an Act in Parliament, the Constitutional Law Committee must be consulted. The Constitutional Law Committee consists of 14 Members of Parliament (MPs). Unlike the members of other parliamentary committees, the members of the Committee see themselves as legal decision makers, not politicians.[6] It is very rare for the Committee to vote, and almost all statements it issues are unanimously agreed upon by its members.[7]

The secretariat of the Committee is composed of experts in constitutional law and the drafting of legislation. They write the statements, but the decision rests with the members. The Committee hears experts in constitutional law and other areas. These expert statements have a significant influence. Parliament is not legally obliged to follow the statements of the Committee. The Speaker of Parliament is responsible for making sure that the Constitution is observed in plenary sessions and that the Committee is consulted if necessary. However, it is possible that constitutional issues are not addressed in Parliament, and the statement of the Constitutional Law Committee may not be available in certain cases. Lastly, the Speaker of Parliament ensures that the Constitution is complied with in the plenary session.

The influence of statements is significant in the interpretation of fundamental rights and human rights. In addition, there is a reciprocal relationship between academic research and the Constitutional Law Committee. Experts on constitutional law influence the practices and hearings of the Committee and interpret the statements in their academic work. The Committee itself tends to observe its previous statements.[8] The monopolistic position of the Committee when it comes to interpretations of the Constitution means that the courts and administration must give primacy to the Constitution. In particular, Section 106 of the Constitution directs the courts to give precedence to the provisions of the Constitution if they are in evident conflict with the provisions of ordinary laws in particular cases.[9] The proposals that

[3] Lavapuro 2011, p. 505.

[4] Jyränki and Husa 2012.

[5] Husa 2020, pp. 1–26.

[6] Husa 2019, pp. 41–60.

[7] How the Constitutional Law Committee actually funcions see Dalberg 2021. Dahlberg 2022.

[8] Koivisto 2017, pp. 40, 22.

[9] Hautamäki 2007, p. 133.

have been brought to the Committee and passed the review are constitutional and they cannot be in evident conflict. Still, the courts may not strike down Acts or give pronouncements on their constitutionality. Furthermore, the statements of the Constitutional Law Committee are not legally binding on the courts and administrative authorities. The decision granting primacy to the Constitution does not affect the validity of an Act and whether it should be repealed by Parliament.

The test for the restriction is the most applied doctrine within the fundamental rights doctrine.[10] The test consists of seven elements: (1) the restriction must be based on an Act of Parliament; (2) the restriction must be precise and defined in sufficient detail; (3) the grounds for the restriction must be legitimate in the context of the system of fundamental rights, and the restriction must be necessary for the realisation of an important societal interest; (4) a restriction going to the core of a fundamental right cannot be enacted by a regular Act; (5) the restriction must adhere to the principle of proportionality; (6) the right to justice must be arranged; and (7) the restriction must comply with the international human rights obligations binding Finland.

Freedom of speech extends to all forms of expression. It includes the right to acquire, transmit, prepare, express, publish, deliver and receive information, opinions and other messages. However, the Constitutional Law Committee has stated that industrial and commercial expressions do not constitute the core of freedom of speech;[11] the Committee has instead considered the core of freedom of speech a political expression.[12] However, this doctrine has had little practical effect and it is disputed in legal literature.[13] Freedom of speech covers all kinds of expressions, regardless of their content, and applies to all communication technologies. In addition, Section 16.3 of the Constitution protects artistic expressions and freedom of science—freedom of art and freedom of science are not significant rights in Finnish constitutional doctrine. Lastly, the Finnish freedom of speech doctrine and Section 12 cover all kinds of expressions in practice.[14]

The prohibition of prior restraints means immunity against the interference of state actions. The prohibition has not been regulated or accomplished in private horizontal relations. Furthermore, regulations on the use of free speech must be provided for by specific legislation. If, according to the proposal or Parliament's view, a proposal affects freedom of speech, the opinion of the Constitutional Law Committee will be sought. The Committee defines the scope of freedom of speech. Therefore, media laws and the penal code are constitutional.

---

[10] Viljanen 2001.

[11] Manninen 1995, pp. 571–606.

[12] PeVL 3/1976 vp, PeVL 4/1976 vp, PeVL 2/1986 vp, PeVL 23/2000 vp p. 6, PeVL 60/2001 vp pp. 3–4, PeVL 19/2002 vp pp. 2–3, PeVL vp p. 7, PeVL 37/2005 vp p. 4 and PeVL 54/2006 vp pp. 2–3.

[13] Neuvonen 2012a, 2012b.

[14] Neuvonen and Rautiainen 2013, pp. 1011–1031. Government Bill HE 309/1993 vp: Hallituksen esitys eduskunnalle perustuslakien perusoikeussäännösten muuttamisesta, p. 57.

In Finland, there is no such doctrine as the abuse of rights. Theoretically, all fundamental and human rights are protected until the Committee excludes specific expression outside constitutional protection. This approach has been called the theory of external restrictions.[15] All kinds of expression are protected as freedom of speech by the Constitution. In addition, the government and Parliament have the competence to enact laws that restrict freedom of speech. The Finnish doctrine of the political core of freedom of speech combines the theories of internal and external restrictions. The Committee has stated that extreme expressions, such as extreme hate speech, are outside the scope of freedom of speech.[16] However, Finland has not yet criminalized Holocaust denial or enacted other so-called memory laws.

Compared to other Nordic countries, there have been many freedom of speech cases filed against Finland in the European Court of the Human Rights (ECtHR). The issue until the 2010s was that the Finnish courts did not apply ECtHR case law and failed to balance freedom of speech and competing rights, especially privacy. Several legislative amendments and new ways to justify cases have resolved this problem.[17] Finland has not received decisions from the European Court of Human Rights regarding hate speech. In general, the impact of rulings on freedom of speech on the reasoning of the courts also affects hate speech cases.

8.1.2 Historical Background

The Finnish freedom of speech doctrine must be seen against its historical background.[18] While Finland was under Swedish rule (circa 1200–1809), freedom of the press was established in 1776. The Finnish priest Anders Chydenius was a key figure in this process.[19] However, this period of freedom lasted only six years. Anders Chydenius was a member of the clergy at the Swedish *Riksdag* (Estates). Anders Chydenius and other influential thinkers of that era, such as Anders Nordencranz and Peter Forsskål, were in favour of classical liberalism and the Enlightenment.[20]

---

[15] Gardbaum 2014, pp. 387–405.

[16] For example, Government Bill HE 317/2010 vp in which Finland implemented European Union of Council Framework Decision 2008/913/JHA on combating certain forms and expressions of racism and xenophobia by means of criminal law into the Finnish Penal Code was not reviewed by the Constitutional Law Committee. The reasons for this are unknown.

[17] Neuvonen et al. 2018, pp. 59–77.

[18] Riku Neuvonen have wrote on the history of freedom of speech in his doctoral thesis and in a book intended for larger academic audiences. The latter one is peer-reviewed by three referees and the publisher is a very prestigious Finnish publisher. Thesis: Neuvonen 2012a. The actual book on the history of freedom of speech in Finland: Neuvonen 2018.

[19] Björkstrand 2018, pp. 89–109. This book is also available in Swedish and Finnish for free at the website of the Parliament of Sweden.

[20] Nokkala 2018, pp. 61–76. Magnusson 2018, pp. 77–88.

In 1772, the young King Gustav III forcefully usurped power and installed an absolute monarchy. The censorship system was restored and made stricter than before. Sweden lost Finland to Russia during a war that lasted from 1808 to 1809.

Finland became an autonomous grand duchy in the Russian Empire. This period was characterised by strict censorship, but also the rise of Finnish nationalism and culture. Russian rule had several effects on the Finnish freedom of speech doctrine. First, censorship was perceived as the biggest threat to freedom of speech. Second, laws and the constitution were seen as political tools. The biggest change was the establishment of Parliament and the Freedom of Speech Act in 1906. Russia was defeated in the Russo-Japanese War (1904–1905). The defeat spurred the First Russian Revolution of 1905. The revolution took the form of a national general strike in Finland. The Unicameral Parliament was established on 9 May 1906. One of the few laws, the Act of 1906 on Freedom of Speech, Assembly and Association, was passed as a constitution. However, the emperor did not approve the freedom of press law.

The February Revolution of 1917 removed the emperor. Finland declared independence after the Russian Revolution of October 1917. The social unrest escalated between the Whites and Reds and a Civil War was fought from January to May 1918. After the Civil War, freedom of speech was guaranteed in the Constitution of 1919. The Freedom of Press Act of 1919 upheld the ability to suppress newspapers if the content constituted treason or incitement for an offence or defamation of the government, Parliament, a public authority or legal order. In particular, communist activities were practically forbidden by restrictive laws in 1930.[21] During wartime (1939–1944), censorship was established. Ultimately, the peace treaty between Finland and many of the Allies was signed in Paris in 1947.

The regulation of freedom of speech in the years 1918–1945 and the period of 'Finlandization' that took place after the Second World War have influenced the Finnish debate on hate speech.[22] After the civil war, criticizing the victory of the Whites was criminalised, which can be considered a kind of memory law. During the Finlandization period from 1945 to 1991, any kind of criticism of the Soviet Union could lead to unofficial consequences and intervention by the Soviet Union. For example, Finland did not dare to talk openly about the wars with the Soviet Union. This has led to insider-related criminalisation still being avoided in Finland. Thus, freedom of speech has justified exceptions to the criminalisation of the Holocaust ban and similar obligations based on international agreements.

The regulation of the media since the war was a combination of restrictive orders and self-censorship.

During that period, Finnish constitutional law was subordinate to political goals and consensus. The Constitution of 1919 allowed the possibility of enacting an 'exceptive law'. Instead of amending or changing the constitution, the exception was passed as an Act.[23] Exceptive laws were used extensively, but since the Constitution

[21] Björne 1977, pp. 220–242.

[22] Berndtson 2001, pp. 21–33.

[23] Jyränki 1989, pp. 492–500. Lavapuro 2011, p. 505.

of 2000, their use has been limited. Exception laws were also utilised in media regulation, while in many areas there were no laws at all—mainly practices and administrative regulations. Fundamental rights and freedom of speech were taken seriously after the 1990s, when Finland joined the European Convention of Human Rights in 1990 and the EU in 1995.[24] After ascending to ECHR and EU membership, practically all media laws were enacted or renewed.[25]

During the period of autonomy in Finnish politics at the end of the 19th century, the main dividing line was the language strife. Finnish nationalism was developing, and its central element was the Finnish language. The language of the Finnish administration and the upper classes was Swedish; however, intellectuals in particular tried to push the Finnish language to be the main language of Finland. The debate that took place during the language strife was very similar to today's debate on hate speech.[26]

Another characteristic feature of the development of Finnish society is the relationship with Russia.[27] Novgorod and Russia had been at war with Sweden for centuries and Finland had remained a battlefield. Finland was destroyed in wars twice, especially in the 18th century. However, during Russian rule from 1809–1917, Finland gained autonomous status and developed as a state and as a society. After gaining independence, the idea of historical Russophobia (ryssäviha) was created in Finland, the purpose of which was to create a Finnish counterforce to the Soviet Union.[28] Later research has shown that Russophobia was a politically engineered project, the core of which was opposition to Bolshevism. The idioms and titles aimed at Russians survived, especially after the Second World War, when Finland lost amount of land to the Soviet Union. During the Second World War, Finland was an ally of Germany, but German racial doctrine or anti-Semitism did not gain a large foothold in Finland. Russophobia can very well be considered the first form of Finnish ethnic hate speech.

As a third factor, Finland was a relatively poor and isolated country after the Second World War. Apart from port cities, there were not many foreigners in the country before the 1970s. After this, two significant groups came to Finland—first, the Vietnamese in the 1970s and then the Somalis in the 1990s. These, combined with the other opening up of society, have changed Finnish society significantly.

[24] Neuvonen 2018.

[25] The Act on Telephones (1889) was renewed by the Communications Market Act (1927); the Decree on Radio Equipment (1927) was renewed by the Act on Radio Activities (1988); the Freedom of Press Act (1919) and the Broadcasting Responsibility Act (1971) were renewed by the Act on the Exercise of Freedom of Expression in Mass Media (2003); both the Act on Scrutiny of Films (1965) and the Act on Scrutiny of Video and Other Motion Picture Programmes (1987) were renewed by the Act on Pictorial Programmes (2000). New legislation included the Act on Yleisradio Oy (1993, Yleisradio is name of the Finnish Broadcasting Company) and the Act on Television and Radio Activities (1998). Neuvonen 2019, pp. 97–98.

[26] Neuvonen 2015a, 2015b, pp. 267–281, pp. 271–273.

[27] Tepora 2014, pp. 69–130.

[28] Vihavainen 2013.

8.2 Hate Speech in the Criminal Code

8.2.1 *Hate Speech as a Concept*

The obligation to criminalise expressions and acts that can be classified as hate speech in Finland is based on international regulations.[29] For example, Finland is under a binding obligation of the European Union of Council Framework Decision 2008/913/JHA to combat certain forms and expressions of racism and xenophobia by means of criminal law. It obliges each Member State to take the necessary measures to ensure that, for example, intentional public incitement to violence or hatred directed against a group of persons or a member of such a group on grounds of race, colour, religion, descent or national or ethnic origin is punishable.

Finland has voiced reservations (among other Nordic countries) regarding Article 20 of the International Covenant on Civil and Political Rights (ICCPR) and has not banned (war) propaganda in legislation. Finland has also shared its reservations on an Additional Protocol to the Convention on Cybercrime concerning the criminalisation of acts of a racist and xenophobic nature committed through computer systems (ETS 189) and the Council of European Union Framework Decision 2008/913/JHA on combating certain forms and expressions of racism and xenophobia by means of criminal law. These treaties require the criminalisation of Holocaust denial, but in Finland (and other Nordic countries), this is seen as a violation of freedom of speech.[30] It is said that the Finnish government issued these reservations in the ICCPR in the 1970s due to pressure from the Soviet Union. It is unknown why other Nordic countries made similar reservations. This highlights the problem that almost all regulation of content is a sign of Finlandization. However, the current Finnish government has issued a statement on promoting equality, gender equality and non-discrimination. The statement is based on entries in the Government Programme on combating racism and hate speech. These initiatives include the criminalisation of Holocaust denial.[31]

Finnish legislation does not include a concept of hate speech as such, nor is hate speech defined in the legislation. Actions that can be considered to constitute hate speech is covered by several criminalisations stated in the Criminal Code of Finland

[29] See more details Neuvonen 2015a, 2015b, pp. 20–21; Suomalainen 2020.

[30] Government Bill HE 317/2010 vp: Hallituksen esitys eduskunnalle Euroopan neuvoston tietoverkkorikollisuutta koskevan yleissopimuksen lisäpöytäkirjan, joka koskee tietojärjestelmien välityksellä tehtyjen luonteeltaan rasististen ja muukalaisvihamielisten tekojen kriminalisointia, hyväksymisestä ja laiksi sen lainsäädännön alaan kuuluvien määräysten voimaansaattamisesta sekä laeiksi rikoslain ja tietoyhteiskunnan palvelujen tarjoamisesta annetun lain 15 §:n muuttamisesta, p. 20. Statement by the Legal Affairs Committee of Finnish Parliament LaVM 38/2010 vp.

[31] The Programme and statement were the result of one minister's connections to a neo-Nazi organization and two other ministers' old racist writings. A minister associated with a neo-Nazi organization resigned from his post, while two other ministers continued to work.

(39/1889), later CC). A central principle of criminal law, the principle of legality[32], requires that no one can be held guilty of an act for which essential elements have not been written into law.[33] Nevertheless, it is impossible to give a precise definition of when messages cross the boundaries of freedom of expression and become punishable hate speech. The interpretation of the legal terms used in the provision depends, in part, on the prevailing and changing moral concepts in society. The problem with value-based criminalisation is the formation of an objective perception of the values prevailing in society. This perception is therefore subjective.[34]

The Finnish Criminal Code was originally provided in 1889, although it has been amended several times since. Freedom of expression is considered one of the most important principles of a democratic society.[35] The criminalisation of incitement to discrimination and discrimination against an ethnic group was enacted in the CC in 1970 when the International Convention on the Elimination of All Forms of Racial Discrimination was implemented.[36] The article was thus considered to also apply to the category based on the colour of the skin, although this was not explicitly mentioned in the provision.[37] In 1995, the crime of incitement was given its current form and was named incitement against an ethnic group. A clause was added to the provision stating that the crime of incitement also applies to hate crimes other than those motivated by racist motives. The motive behind the offence is one of the factors to be taken into account when measuring the penalty. The offence of

---

[32] The principle of legality is also reflected in Article 7 of the European Convention on Human Rights, and it also has an important role in EU law. For more details, see, for example, Klip 2021, pp. 245–257. Melander 2016, pp. 43–49. Melander 2015, pp. 157–163.

[33] Nuotio argued that the human rights assessment of hate speech is not necessarily compatible with the criminalisation of hate speech in Finnish national criminal law. According to him, uncertainty relates in particular to the extent to which speech such as hate speech, which is required by international human rights instruments, will be punishable in Finland. Nuotio 2015, pp. 139–164, 163. An article by Hannonen and Hyttinen that analyses the district court legal praxis on incitement offences shows that incitement convictions are not as problematic from a freedom of expression point of view as has suggested. They also argued that the assessment of penalties does not take sufficient account of whether the offender is guilty of hate speech that threatened a particular group or whether the offence is more likely to be defamatory and insulting. They concluded that the legal praxis of the district courts did not fully recognise the particular harmfulness and danger of threatening and inciting hate speech as compared to defamatory and insulting hate speech. Hannonen and Hyttinen 2023, pp. 307–330.

[34] Mantila 2020, pp 154–171, 169.

[35] Government Bill HE 317/2010 vp, p. 5.

[36] The Convention was implemented in Finland on 5 August 1970 (SopS 37/1970). See details about the International Convention of the Elimination of All Forms of Racial Discrimination: https://www.ohchr.org/sites/default/files/cerd.pdf. Incitement against an ethnic group has been a rare offence in Finnish legal praxis: the first Court of Appeal ruling on the 1970 regulation was only issued in 1990. Illman 2012, pp. 208–225, 209). In the early 2000s, only few individuals were convicted of incitement against an ethnic group per year (Government Bill HE 317/2010 vp, p. 6). In the 2010s, the offence of incitement started to become more important. In a study by Hannonen and Hyttinen, from 2015 to 2021 an average of twenty people per year were convicted of incitement against an ethnic group in the district courts. Hannonen and Hyttinen 2023, p. 313.

[37] Government Bill HE 241/1973 vp: Hallituksen esitys eduskunnalle ihmisyyttä vastaan tehtyjen rikosten rankaisemista koskevaksi lainsäädännöksi, p. 13.

incitement was transferred in its current place, Chapter 11, Section 10, in 2008. In 2011, a provision on 'making available to the public' was added to clarify the scope of the provision, in particular with regard to distribution on the internet.[38] Making available means, for example, posting on an internet discussion platform, but also linking to material that otherwise constitutes an offence. Availability may also extend to the site administrator, who has not produced the material but who technically contributes to the dissemination of the material.[39]

In addition to incitement against an ethnic group, the focal criminalisations related to hate speech are aggravated incitement against a particular ethnic group (CC Chapter 11, Section 10a), ethnic agitation (CC Chapter 11, Section 11) and violation of the sanctity of religion (CC Chapter 17, Section 10). Acts of hate speech can also constitute other crimes, such as public incitement to an offence (CC Chapter 17, Section 1), distribution of sexually offensive pictures (CC Chapter 17, Section 10a), dissemination of information violating personal privacy (CC Chapter 24, Section 8 and 8a) and defamation (CC Chapter 24, Sections 9 and10).

Vepsäläinen et al. examined the sociodemographic and socioeconomic background factors of Finnish individuals convicted of hate crimes. According to their research, those convicted of hate crimes differed from the population as a whole in terms of their background factors, but were not much different from those convicted of other crimes. Hate crime offenders were more likely to live in urban areas and 85% of them were male. They were also most often (67%) under the age of 40. More than half of the perpetrators had no more than the minimum level of primary education. They were less likely to live in a relationship and less likely to have children than the overall average for the population as a whole.[40]

In this article, we focus on the criminalisations of incitement against a particular ethnic group and violation of the sanctity of religion. In addition, the report covers the grounds for increasing punishment. According to Finnish legislation, a racist motive for committing a crime constitutes a reason to increase the perpetrator's punishment (CC Chapter 6, Section 5).

Public incitement to commit a crime and breaching the sanctity of religion are offences against public order, while incitement to hatred is classified as a crime against humanity. The common feature of crimes against public order is that they do not usually directly affect or endanger the rights and interests of some people as

[38] See more details on the amendment Hannula 2015, pp. 165–190; Illman 2012, pp. 210–211.

[39] LaVM 39/2010 vp: Lakivaliokunnan lausunto hallituksen esitykseen Euroopan neuvoston tietoverkkorikollisuutta koskevan yleissopimuksen lisäpöytäkirjan, joka koskee tietojärjestelmien välityksellä tehtyjen luonteeltaan rasististen ja muukalaisvihamielisten tekojen kriminalisointia, hyväksymisestä ja laiksi sen lainsäädännön alaan kuuluvien määräysten voimaansaattamisesta sekä laeiksi rikoslain ja tietoyhteiskunnan palvelujen tarjoamisesta annetun lain 15 §:n muuttamisesta, p. 4. See more about the responsibility of the administrator Forss 2018, pp. 14–16; Neuvonen 2015a, 2015b, pp. 95–103. Hannula and Neuvonen 2011, pp. 527–548.

[40] Vepsäläinen et al. 2023, pp. 26–27. https://julkaisut.valtioneuvosto.fi/bitstream/handle/10024/164987/OM_2023_26_SO.pdf?sequence=1&isAllowed=y.

such, but cause annoyance, irritation and resentment.[41] The violation of the sanctity of religion protects individual religious beliefs and the freedom of worship in society, not specific groups of people.[42]

8.2.2 Incitement Against Ethnic Groups

As stated above, hate speech can be punishable in certain cases, such as incitement against a particular ethnic group or aggravated incitement against an ethnic group. In assessing whether it is a matter of freedom of expression or an incitement against a particular ethnic group, the starting point is that in a liberal democracy, provocative allegations must be tolerated even if they are demeaning or offensive to their target.[43] According to Chapter 11, Section 10 (511/2011) of the CC, incitement against a group of people occurs when someone makes available to the public or otherwise disseminates or makes available to the public information, opinions or other messages that threaten, slander[44] or insult[45] a group on grounds of race, colour, descent, national or ethnic origin, religion or belief, sexual orientation, disability or other comparable grounds. The offence is punishable by a fine or imprisonment for up to two years.

The essential elements of the offence of incitement against a particular ethnic group must be precisely interpreted in accordance with the principle of criminal law legality and respect for the limits the wording of the statute. In addition, the particular importance of freedom of expression must be considered, which may require a restrictive interpretation. Freedom of expression includes the right to a certain degree of exaggeration and provocation but not to slander or insults. The right of freedom of expression does not include threats to individuals or groups, nor is there a corresponding argument in favour of a restrictive interpretation. The essential elements of the penal provision do not require the occurrence of a consequence. Moreover, the essential element is not written in the form of an abstract offence of endangerment, so the punishability of statements under the constituent element is not affected by whether they are capable of producing certain types of consequences. In other words, the wording of the criminalisation is a pure prohibition.[46]

According to preparatory work on the provision of ethnic agitation, the object of its legal protection is ultimately the inviolability of human dignity by protecting individuals from racist and other violations committed for the reasons specified under

---

[41] Government Bill HE 6/1997 vp: Hallituksen esitys eduskunnalle oikeudenkäyttöä, viranomaisia ja yleistä järjestystä vastaan kohdistuvia rikoksia sekä seksuaalirikoksia koskevien säännösten uudistamiseksi, p. 104.

[42] Government Bill HE 6/1997 vp, p. 127.

[43] Nuotio 2022, pp. 308–314, 310.

[44] Slander is defined as the alleged commission of crimes or similar despicable acts by a group of people. Mantila 2020, p. 165.

[45] The term "insult" is used when a group is characterised by derogatory insults. Mantila 2020, p. 165.

[46] Illman 2012, p. 215.

Section 6, Subsection 2 of the Finnish Constitution.[47] The International Covenant on Civil and Political Rights, accepted by Finland in 1966, also included a prohibition of discrimination against people. In 1995, the expression 'or a comparable basis' was amended to the provision on ethnic agitation; in consequence, the provision also applies to the type of hate crimes not committed with racist motives.

Incitement against a group of people involves not only the dissemination of information, but also making it available to the public. This includes not only placing the material on, for example, an internet discussion board or other website, but also creating and compiling links to make the material more easily accessible to others. Copyright can therefore be held by several parties: the author of the text, the person who made the text available to the public and other persons.[48] According to Section 1, Subsection 2 of the Act on the Exercise of Freedom of Expression in Mass Media (460/2003), no more interference with communication is allowed than is necessary in view of the importance of freedom of expression. Freedom of expression is of utmost importance in the fields of social and political debate as well as in science and art, and the regulation does not restrict the freedom to discuss matters of social importance. Typical offences include the dissemination of information, opinions or other messages that consider violence or discrimination against a group to be acceptable or desirable, compare people to animals or make general allegations of criminality or inferiority.[49]

The crime of incitement requires intent. The degree of intent is sufficient to be circumstantial.[50] This means, for example, in the case of linking, that the offender must therefore be aware at the time of the act that the website to which the link is made contains racist or similarly inflammatory material. The crime of incitement is considered a continuing offence, which has an effect on the offence's statute of limitations.[51] According to legal praxis and literature, in order for the crime of ethnic agitation to be committed intentionally, the perpetrator must possess an understanding or belief that: (1) they are making certain information available to the public, whether through dissemination or other means; (2) this information, opinion or message meets objective standards of being threatening, defamatory or insulting towards a specific group of people; and (3) the targeted group of people can be identified as a group provided for in CC Chapter 17, Section 10.[52]

[47] Government Bill HE 317/2010 vp, p. 49.

[48] Government Bill HE 317/2010 vp, p. 39.

[49] Government Bill HE 317/2010 vp, p. 42.

[50] According to CC Chapter 4, Section 1, an offence is not intentional if the offender does not know or is mistaken as to the existence of the elements necessary to establish the constituent elements of the offence. For more details, see the intent requirement in Illman 2012, pp. 222–223 and the references cited therein.

[51] Government Bill HE 317/2010 vp, p. 40.

[52] Valtakunnansyyttäjänvirasto: Rangaistavan vihapuheen levittäminen Internetissä. Rangaistavan vihapuheen määrittäminen ja rikosoikeudellisen vastuun kohdentuminen erilaisiin Internetissä toimiviin toimijoihin. Työryhmän raportti 21.12.2012. Dnro 17/34/1123. See also Illman 2005, p. 284.

The term 'publicly available' referred to in the essential elements of an offence is not appropriate in situations in which private communications among a group of acquaintances all outside the scope of the provision. It has been held in the legal literature that, in the case of the distribution of a communication to persons belonging to an association, the act can be considered as making it available or accessible to the public. The material may consist of writings, pictures or speech.[53] The regulation is not limited to hate speech directed at a particular ethnic group by a member of the majority population; it also applies to incitement of hatred against another ethnic minority group by a member of a particular ethnic minority group. In order for the act to be punishable, the speech must threaten, defame or insult the group referred to in the section.[54]

Two primary factors are essential for determining where the offence has been committed: the physical location where the materials were disseminated and the intended recipient audience. In practical terms, the most common scenario involves the offender utilizing their personal computer at a residence or office within Finland to make the materials accessible to a Finnish audience. In such instances, determining the location of the crime is straightforward. However, it is worth noting that the mere possession of such materials is not subject to punishment. The actual location where the materials are made available or distributed is significant. When identifying the intended recipient audience of the materials, the language in which they are presented plays a central role. If the materials are presented in Finnish, the typical assumption is that the target audience is also the Finnish public.[55]

The inclusion of religion in the criteria for the offence of incitement shows that the offence also fits some other criteria, in addition to the racist criteria proper, which can be included in the broader hate crime criteria. These include sexual orientation, gender minorities (such as transgender and intersex people) and immigrants. This underlines the fact that the incitement article provides broad protection against hate crimes. It also extends protection to persons with disabilities[56] and people of a particular religion or belief, including, for example, atheist groups.[57]

In Hannonen's and Hyttinen's study, only one ethnic group was targeted in about half of the cases of the offence of incitement against a group of people. Almost without exception, the channel of offence was the internet and its various platforms. Their study showed that the type of incitement against a group of people is not reduced to the prevailing perception in society that politically active people are the ones who are screened out as perpetrators of incitement crimes. Based on the legal praxis, the authors defined the type of incitement offence as follows: 'a politically inactive Finnish man belonging to the majority population (who identifies as a representative

[53] Government Bill HE 317/2010 vp, p. 40.

[54] Government Bill HE 317/2010 vp, p. 42.

[55] Valtakunnansyyttäjänvirasto, pp. 25–26.

[56] The disability referred to in the provision can be either physical or mental. Disability is also mentioned in the provisions of the CC criminalising discrimination (Chapter 11, Section 11) and torture (Chapter 11, Section 9a).

[57] Government Bill HE 317/2010 vp, p. 41.

of the majority) either threatens, defames or insults a victim group identifying as a minority on Facebook'.[58] One of their conclusions from the legal praxis was that the freedom of expression argument was mainly taken into account when assessing the culpability of an act. In contrast, the freedom of expression dimension of the offence of incitement is not sufficiently considered when the penalty is assessed. In contrast to the legal praxis of the European Court of Human Rights, Finnish legal praxis is not deeply aware of the particular harmfulness and danger of threatening and inciting violence through hate speech compared to slanderous and abusive hate speech, which means that the threshold for prosecuting slander and abusive hate speech is higher than that for prosecuting threatening hate speech.[59]

Chapter 11, Section 10a (511/2011) provides for aggravated incitement against an ethnic group. An offence shall be deemed to be an aggravated offence if it involves incitement against a group of persons or involves exhortation or enticement (1) to genocide or the preparation thereof, a crime against humanity, an aggravated crime against humanity, a war crime, an aggravated war crime, murder or manslaughter with terrorist intent; or (2) to serious violence other than that referred to in paragraph 1, in such a way that public order and security are clearly endangered. It also requires that the incitement against an ethnic group is aggravated when assessed as a whole. The overall assessment is made based on factors such as whether the activity was organised, whether the act actually reached a large audience, the degree of fear it is likely to cause and whether the content of the disseminated material is particularly offensive[60]. Aggravated incitement against an ethnic group is punishable by imprisonment for a minimum of four months and a maximum of four years.

The aggravated incitement against an ethnic group requires that the material disseminated must contain incitement or inducement to commit serious violence. However, incitement to discrimination or defamation is not sufficient to constitute a serious offence. If the public threat of violence does not include incitement or inducement, the basic form of incitement or unlawful threat will apply. Incitement or inducement does not require that it take place during war, armed conflict or large-scale attacks on a civilian population. The aggravated form of the offence of incitement may only be committed when the threat of serious crime is directed against a specific group of people within the meaning of Section 10. However, the application of the first qualification criterion does not require that the incitement or inducement create a risk that the offence or an attempt to commit the offence would be carried out.[61]

[58] Hannonen and Hyttinen 2023, pp. 317–319. English translation by the author.

[59] Ibid., p. 330.

[60] Government Bill HE 317/2010 vp, p. 45.

[61] Government Bill HE 317/2010 vp, p. 43.

The second qualifying criterion requires a concrete threat[62] to public order and security. For example, this is the case, when solicitation or inducement poses an imminent danger of a crime being committed or attempted. The danger may be inferred, inter alia, from the fact that someone or some persons are preparing to commit an offence; alternatively, from their statements or conduct, it may be inferred that they are about to commit the offence. Public safety is deemed endangered when the solicitation or enticement in question arouses fear or disquiet among the public. The same applies when the persons who may be the subject of an offence are obliged to take special measures to protect themselves from the offence. The criminal nature of the invitation or inducement presupposes that the persons to whom it is addressed are informed of it. The invitation or inducement must also be sufficiently specific to make it clear what type of offence the invitation or inducement is aimed at committing.[63]

It is sufficient that the perpetrator is aware that his or her message incites or calls for serious violence for his or her act to constitute aggravated incitement against an ethnic group. In other words, punishability does not require the perpetrator to have intentionality, i.e., an actual intention to incite or provoke serious violence. Incitement against an ethnic group is considered particularly dangerous during a social conflict or armed conflict or when there is a threat of such a conflict. In assessing the seriousness of the act as a whole, attention should be paid to whether the activity was organised and whether the information, opinions or other messages presented actually achieved widespread dissemination.[64]

8.2.3 Electronic Communications

In addition to sanctions in the criminal code, The Act on Electronic Communications Services contains several competition rules relating to granting licences. The common feature in all licences is that transfer of the licence must be informed to the authority and the licence may be cancelled if the transfer threatens competition or national security. The licence can be revoked from a company that is guilty of disseminating hate speech. Likewise, a licence cannot be granted to a company that is likely to disseminate hate speech. The criteria for a licence is that there is no justifiable reason to suspect that the applicant will violate the provisions of this Act, Section 6 of the Act on Audiovisual Programmes, or that they had committed ethnic agitation (CC Chapter 11, Sections 10 and 10a).

---

[62] A concrete threat to public order and security may arise if incitement has taken place in a locality where there have recently been attacks on groups in need of protection and the risk of further violent confrontations between different groups is high. As a general rule, public order and security means order or security on Finnish territory. Exceptionally, a serious armed conflict or an attack against the civilian population in another state may also be involved and the material disseminated by the perpetrator concerns these events. Government Bill HE 317/2010 vp, p. 44.

[63] Government Bill HE 6/1997 vp, p. 111.

[64] Government Bill HE 317/2010 vp, pp. 44–45.

The most famous case in Finland is *MV Magazine*. The magazine was anti-immigrant and disseminated conspiracy theories. The Helsinki District Court identified the founder of *MV Magazine* as editor-in-chief, Ilja Janitskin, and convicted him of 16 offences and sentenced him to a 22-months prison sentence.[65] One lesser-known activist of *MV Magazine* was accused of incitement to hatred and the defamation of Aro. The founder of *MV Magazine*, Ilja Janitskin, was convicted at Helsinki District Court of several offences, including multiple ethnic agitations, copyright infringements and so on.

Ilja Janitskin's defence argued that he was not responsible for the content of *MV Magazine*'s articles or comments because he had not personally written them. The District Court considered that as editor of *MV Magazine* from 2014 until at least January 2018, Janitskin was the person responsible for its content. Janitskin ultimately decided on all the material published and disseminated in the online publication, regardless of who wrote for the magazine. Janitskin died during the process and his heirs dropped the complaint.

The Helsinki District Court refers to freedom of speech and the case law of the ECtHR. The court stated that the defendant spread false information about Aro, and even though some information was correct, the intent was malicious. In the case of Janitskin, the articles in *MV Magazine* were completely inappropriate and did not contain any editorial (news) content. Most of the articles contained incorrect and offensive information and claims. Therefore, the criminal charges were not a violation of freedom of speech. The Helsinki Appeals Court upheld the conviction.[66] *MV Magazine* was very good at optimising search algorithms, both on the internet and in social media. This was proved during the case.

In Finland, a member of Parliament has extensive freedom of speech when speaking in Parliament. A charge against a member of parliament must be approved by a majority constating of five-sixths of the MPs to support the removal of this immunity. In 2019, MP likened asylum seekers to an invasive species in a speech before the legislature. Four separate complaints regarding his statements were filed with police, which prompted a preliminary investigation into suspicions of inciting hatred against an ethnic group. The Constitutional Law Committee recommended that Parliament should remove MP's immunity. Finland's Prosecutor General announced that incitement charges should be filed against the MP. The proposal to lift his immunity was supported by 121 MPs, with 54 voting against and 24 legislators absent. Therefore, immunity was not removed.

[65] Helsinki District Court, Helsingin käräjäoikeus on 18 October 2018 nr 18/144694.

[66] Helsinki Appeals Court, Helsingin hovioikeus on 14 July 2020 nr 20/124654.

8.3 Violation of the Sanctity of Religion

In most European countries, blasphemy has been decriminalised, but in Finland, criminalisation is still in force.[67] Between 2000 and 2020, 40 cases of breaches of religious peace were considered by courts in Finland.[68] However, there have been no convictions for breaches of religious peace in recent years.[69] The criminalisation has been criticised for making it difficult to justify how public debate on issues of worship could, even at its height, threaten social peace in a society steeped in democracy and human rights.[70] Nonetheless, the criminalisation of crimes against religion and religious beliefs can be justified by the protection of everyone's fundamental and human rights, such as the freedom of religion and conscience guaranteed in Section 11 of the Finnish Constitution.[71]

The elements for the violation of the sanctity of religion is provided for in Chapter 17, Section 10 of the CC. The essential elements of the offence are as follows: a person who (1) publicly blasphemes against God or, for the purpose of offending, publicly defames or desecrates what is otherwise considered sacred by a church or a religious community to in the Act of the Freedom of Religion; or (2) by making noise, acting threateningly or otherwise disturbing a church service, a religious ceremony, another similar form of worship or a funeral.[72] The violation of the sanctity of religion is punishable by imprisonment for at most six months.

The violation of the sanctity of religion encompasses several essential elements. These elements include acts such as public blasphemy, defaming or desecrating sacred objects, and the perpetrator's explicit intention to offend. Understanding these key components is crucial in comprehending the gravity of such breaches and their impact on religious communities.[73] The object under protection through the criminalisation of the violation of freedom of religion in criminal law is religious freedom in society, not religion itself.[74] Instead, criminalisation is understood as protecting people's religious beliefs and feelings by prohibiting the deliberate desecration or defamation of religion and its sacred objects. The provision also explicitly prohibits blasphemy against God. The object of the provision is the protection of the

[67] However, even if blasphemy is criminalised, the law implementing its ban is longer applied in practice in all countries. Äystö 2019, p. 40.

[68] Mantila 2021, p. 4.

[69] Statistics Finland. Sentences by district court and offence (distict courts and courts of appeal as first court instance), 2017–2021. https://pxdata.stat.fi/PxWeb/pxweb/en/StatFin/StatFin__syyttr/statfin_syyttr_pxt_13r7.px/.

[70] Nuotio 2015, pp. 155–156 and 163. Rautiainen 2011, pp. 1152–1171, 1161–1162; Mantila 2021, p. 16. Moreover, freedom of worship only applies to registered religions, which means that some religions are excluded. Nuotio 2009, p. 24.

[71] Neuvonen 2015a, b, p. 66.

[72] Unofficial translation from Finnish. https://www.finlex.fi/en/laki/kaannokset/1889/en18890039_20210433.pdf.

[73] Henttonen et al. 2014, pp. 175–225.

[74] Government Bill HE 6/1997 vp, p. 129.

peace of society as a whole.[75] The provision specifically addresses the defamation or desecration of what a religious community considers sacred[76].[77] The term 'sacred' refers to something that is revered by members of a religious community, which may vary among different religious communities.[78]

The concept of publicity refers to the dissemination of a statement to an indeterminate group of individuals to make it widely known.[79] The act of blasphemy can be defined as the act of ridiculing or degrading the values held by others.[80] However, the protection of religious freedom is not unlimited. The criminalisation of the violation of sanctity of religion prohibits defamation and slander with intent to insult. Criticism must therefore go beyond a certain level of offence: the offensive nature of the expression is understood even by those who do not themselves consider the object of the defamation or insult to be sacred but who appreciate the convictions of those who think differently.[81]

To be considered an offence, an act must be committed with intent. This requirement is fulfilled when the offensive nature of the act in question is also understood by persons who do not personally hold the object of defamation or desecration sacred but who nevertheless respect the beliefs of others.[82] In contrast to acts of defamation or desecration, a greater degree of intent is necessary for an act to be considered blasphemy. For a perpetrator to face punishment for blasphemy, it is essential that they have a clear understanding that their action is highly likely to be offensive.[83] Providing factual criticism of a religious community does not violate the principles of religious freedom. Similarly, criticism delivered in a satirical manner, as long as it is based on factual foundations, does not satisfy all the essential elements of violation of the sanctity of religion.[84]

The accusation of incitement against Päivi Räsänen, Member of Parliament in Finland, received international publicity. The case concerned, among other things, Räsänen's old religious pamphlet in which she defended marriage as a relationship between a man and a woman and made statements about homosexuality based on biblical texts that were considered discriminatory. These writings were made available to a small group of people and only later became widely publicised. In its

[75] Government Bill HE 6/1997 vp, p. 128; Mantila 2021, pp. 9–10.

[76] The term 'sacred' is not very precise, but it is considered to denote something for which members of a religious community feel a great reverence. Government Bill HE 6/1997 vp, p. 129.

[77] Tulkki 2010.

[78] Government Bill HE 6/1997 vp, p. 128. The concept of 'sacredness' is considered to have acquired a sufficiently well-established meaning in practice. Government Bill HE 6/1997 vp, p. 129. See also Tulkki 2010.

[79] Government Bill HE 6/1997 vp, p. 129.

[80] Tulkki 2008, p. 92.

[81] Government Bill HE 6/1997 vp, p. 128; Mantila 2021, p. 11.

[82] Government Bill HE 6/1997 vp, p. 128.

[83] Tulkki 2008, p. 95.

[84] Government Bill HE 6/1997 vp, p. 128.

judgment,[85] the district court and court of appeal found that Räsänen's writings were defamatory, but that they did not violate the equality and dignity of homosexuals and were not likely to arouse contempt, intolerance or even hatred towards homosexuals. The prosecutor appealed the verdict to the Supreme Court; therefore, the decision is not yet legally valid judgement.[86]

8.4 Grounds for Aggravating Punishment

The grounds for increasing the punishment are stipulated in Chapter 6, Section 5 of the CC. This provision has a substantive link with the penal provision on incitement against ethnic groups.[87] Racial motivation was introduced as a ground for aggravating the sentence in the reform of the general part of the CC in 2002, which came into force on 1 January 2004. The scope of this aggravating circumstance was broadened in 2011, when other reprehensible motives were added to the list of explicitly racist motives. Previously, the provision referred to the offence of targeting a person belonging to a national, racial, ethnic or other such group on the grounds of membership of that group.[88] According to the provisions of paragraph four, the aggravating circumstance involves 'commission of the offence for a motive based on race, colour, birth, national or ethnic origin, religion or belief, gender, sexual orientation or disability or another comparable motive'.[89]

Racist motives constitute an aggravating circumstance, regardless of who or what the crime is against. The target could therefore be a person genuinely belonging to a particular group based on race, national or ethnic origin, etc., known or assumed by the offender. This aggravating circumstance could also apply, for example, where the offence is committed against a member of the staff of a refugee centre carrying out his or her duties, against a lawyer of the majority population defending a victim of a suspected offence or against a person defending a victim of a violent racist attack.[90]

The provision does not limit the offences it covers. As with the other general criteria, this aggravating criterion covers, in principle, all types of offences. Given its background and objectives, its most natural scope is limited to violent crimes and crimes that endanger the safety or livelihood of persons belonging to a minority (e.g. criminal damage and destruction).[91]

---

[85] Helsinki Court of Appeal on 14 November 2023.

[86] KKO VL:2024-29. For more about the case, see Nuotio 2021, pp. 47–63. Karkkulainen 2021, pp. 386–395. Korpi 2022, pp. 1117–1125.

[87] Government Bill HE 317/2010 vp, p. 13.

[88] However, racist motives had already been considered in determining guilt before the amendment. Lappi-Seppälä 2000, p. 336.

[89] Unofficial translation from Finnish. https://www.finlex.fi/en/laki/kaannokset/1889/en18890039_20210433.pdf. Gender was added to the provision on 1 January 2023 (1129/2022).

[90] Government Bill HE 317/2010 vp, p. 38.

[91] Government Bill HE 44/2002 vp: Hallituksen esitys eduskunnalle rikosoikeuden yleisiä oppeja koskevan lainsäädännön uudistamiseksi, p. 193.

Aggravating circumstances can affect both the measurement of the penalty and the choice of the type of sentence.[92] For the aggravating circumstance to apply, it is not sufficient that the offence be committed against, for example, a member of a particular racial group; it requires that the specific race is the motive for committing the offence. However, racial motives need not be the only motive.[93]

The Finnish Supreme Court has assessed the racist motive as grounds for increasing the sentence in KKO 2020:32. In its judgment, the Supreme Court stated that in assessing the elements invoked to support the application of the aggravating circumstance, it is justified in applying a standard of proof similar to the sentencing threshold required for criminal liability. According to the Supreme Court, a racist motive may be revealed by the defendant himself; often, however, it must be assessed in light of the behaviour of the perpetrator before, during or after the act. The Supreme Court cited as an example the offender's insulting references to the ethnic origin of the injured party.

The Supreme Court concluded that defendants had not provided an alternative plausible explanation for their conduct. Thus, the evidence adduced in support of the grounds for aggravation supported the conclusion that the complainant had been targeted because of his skin colour and ethnic origin. On this basis, there was no reasonable doubt as to the facts relied on to support the application of the aggravating circumstance. The Supreme Court held that the name calling and the circumstances of the offence together constituted strong evidence of a racist motive beneath the act. The prosecutor's evidence strongly suggested that the offence was committed with racist motives, so in the view of the Supreme Court, the assessment of the evidence had to consider whether the defendants had presented credible evidence of other motives for the offence. In this context, the Supreme Court referred to its previous decisions[94] in which the defendant in a criminal case had been required, despite the prosecution's burden of proof, to establish the facts relied on in his defence.

8.5 Hate Speech in the Supreme Court's Legal Praxis

The definition of "hate speech" implemented at the national level in Finland has led to numerous convictions for ethnic agitation. It is therefore reasonable to assert that a legally enforceable definition is feasible at the national level, at least in the manner in which it has been adopted in Finland. However, considering that public authorities have limited resources and that online hate speech is a prevalent issue, there is a legitimate question regarding whether all ethnic agitation can be thoroughly investigated and prosecuted. Nonetheless, this does not diminish the inherent legally

[92] Tapani et al. 2021, p. 72. Matikkala 2021, p. 223.

[93] Government Bill HE 317/2010 vp, p. 38. The legal literature has found that the police, prosecutors or courts do not pay sufficient attention to the hate crime motive during the criminal proceedings, or that they do so incorrectly. Forss 2018, pp. 9–10.

[94] KKO 2019:2, paragraph 10 and KKO 2018:3, paragraph 15.

binding nature of the definition itself.[95] In terms of legal practice, the term 'hate speech' has been mentioned in four Finnish Supreme Court rulings (KKO 2012:58, KKO 2013:50, KKO 2022:8 and KKO 2022:63), primarily in reference to judgments by the European Court of Human Rights.[96]

In the case of KKO 2012:58[97], a Finnish politician faced charges of ethnic agitation and violating the sanctity of religion for publishing content on his website that contained offensive statements directed at Islam and the Somali community. The politician wrote on a website: 'The Prophet Muhammad was a pedophile, and Islam is the religion that sanctifies pedophilia, the religion of pedophiles. Pedophilia is the will of Allah,' and 'Looting passers-by and living by tax revenue is a national, perhaps even a genetic characteristic of Somali'.[98] The prosecutor charged the politician with both violation of the sanctity or religion and incitement against a particular ethnic group. The defendant denied the charge, arguing that the sentences had been taken out of context. He said that he did not intend to slander and defame what Islamic religious communities hold sacred, nor to slander and insult a national or similar group of Somalis. He also said that stating the facts could not be offensive, even if they insult someone. Although Muhammad was a holy figure, he was not immune to criticism, and as a historical figure, he can be criticised.

The Supreme Court held that the allegations against the Prophet Muhammad were highly defamatory and slanderous, both in their content and especially in the way they were expressed, and therefore the politician must be convicted of violating religious peace. The Supreme Court also found that the defendant's statement describing Somalis was defamatory and insulting to a group of people. The Supreme Court held that defamatory and slanderous statements, such as the one in question, are likely to arouse intolerance, contempt and even hatred towards the group of people to which they refer. Therefore, they can be understood as hate speech, which does not enjoy the constitutionally protected freedom of expression. Criminal sanctions against the author of such statements are justified. Consequently, the defendant was also convicted of incitement against an ethnic group.

In the case of KKO 2013:50, the limits of freedom of expression were questioned. The defendant posted a message on an internet discussion board containing serious threats against the Prime Minister, the finance minister and members of Parliament. The defendant denied the charge and pleaded in his defence that his post had been a piece of the causerie in which he had expressed his dissatisfaction with the political line taken. The persons who had been subjected to the serious violence mentioned in the writing were not aware of the text. The Supreme Court stated that if they had been aware of the writings, they might have feared that their personal safety would

[95] Henttonen et al. 2014, p. 209.

[96] Henttonen et al. 2014, p. 184.

[97] The Court's ruling is analysed in greater detail in the following article: Hyttinen 2013, pp. 940–950.

[98] Quotations from the Finnish Supreme Courts Decision number 2012:58. It can be found in the Internet (https://www.finlex.fi/fi/oikeus/kko/kko/2012/20120058), but only in the Finnish language. The translation from the Finnish by the authors.

be at risk. In its judgment, the Supreme Court concluded that the defendant had not committed the offence (illegal threat) for which the prosecutor charged him.

In the case of KKO 2022:8, the defendant posted a significant number of insulting and degrading messages about the plaintiff, a journalist, on his Facebook public pages and Twitter (nowadays called X) profile, questioned her professionalism as a journalist, made derogatory comments about her appearance and distributed degrading and distorted material about her. In addition, the defendant repeatedly approached the complainant on Facebook, inter alia, with various invitations and proposals for meetings, which the complainant had rejected. Furthermore, the defendant published a number of derogatory posts about the complainant in certain Facebook groups and provided the complainant with a plaster cast of a bronze warrior statue, which the latter had found threatening and distressing given the symbolism of the statue. The elements described in the indictment formed a coherent whole based on a single motivation, in which the defendant's activities were long-lasting and wide-ranging.

The Supreme Court found that although the defendant's public posts were motivated by public concern, his publications had little to do with the information manipulation under discussion or the article written by the plaintiff. The posts focused on the person of the complainant, such as her appearance, and the use of gender-specific expressions and derogatory names. According to the Supreme Court, personal and offensive comments were not even necessary to express negative opinions or attitudes. The Supreme Court considered that the content of the messages showed that the defendant's publications were not so much a contribution to the general debate or a contribution to the assessment of the public conduct of the complainant, but rather an attempt to limit the debate and to silence the complainant and other authors of information manipulation. The defendant's freedom of expression therefore did not entitle him to repeated publication of messages and writings that violated the complainant's privacy and freedom of expression. The procedure was therefore unlawful. The Supreme Court found the defendant guilty of charge.

The case of KKO 2022:63 concerned a charge of incitement against an ethnic group. The defendant published 24 videos on his YouTube channel, which included a speech in English given by a person in Helsinki during a demonstration, translated into Finnish, Swedish, French, Italian, Arabic and several Finnish dialects with subtitles. The defendant had also published the same speech in Finnish (with subtitles) on his own Facebook account under his name. The speaker had insulted immigrants and people of Islamic faith by calling them brutal, arrogant, stupid, worthless and sick. The speaker threatened the group by saying that (1) they should not even exist; (2) they should be banned in every civilised society; (3) one day they would all be thrown out, including the young; and (4) one day they would be defeated. The versions of the video in different languages had a large audience.

The Supreme Court found that expressions such as those described in the indictment are typical examples of defamatory and insulting messages within the meaning of Chapter 11, Section 10 of the CC. Such expressions are likely to incite intolerance and even hatred towards the target group. The Supreme Court held that the statements threatened, defamed and insulted immigrants and Muslims. The messages did not provide a factual and neutral background to historical events, and the references contained in the messages were used in a most obviously deliberate manner to make a generalised claim or insinuation about the barbarity of the ethnic groups concerned. It was therefore a false and misleading statement that stigmatised the group as a whole. The Supreme Court found that the speaker implied that immigrants and Muslims would be removed from the country and that violence would readily be resorted to if necessary.

It was therefore an expression of intolerance that was offensive to the dignity and hostility of the targeted group and questioned the right of immigrants and Muslims to live in Finland. The Supreme Court held that the expressions used in the speeches could be understood as hate speech, which in principle does not enjoy the protection of freedom of expression. The defendant was held liable for the material he made available to the public, even if it was not entirely produced by him, and he was convicted of incitement against a group of people.

8.6 Hate Speech in Academic Research

Hate speech has been the most significant research topic in Finland in the 21st century. It has been approached from the perspectives of journalism, law and history.[99] Hate speech has been interlinked with fake news and populism. The phenomenon of fake news, in turn, has been compared to alternative media and radical media. The argument, from this view, is that older alternative media is committed to journalism and truth, while new forms are not based on journalistic methods and intend to spread disinformation as well as hate speech.[100]

In particular, the MV *Magazine* case has been the subject of several academic studies. The subject matter of these studies has varied, from the history and development of the magazine to a comparative study of how similar the rhetoric of the magazine was with that of MPs from the Finns Party during the refugee crisis.[101] The latter study demonstrated how populist politicians use the same language as *MV Magazine* and that this discursive style can be found internationally. Another study examined the sources *MV Magazine* used.[102] This article proved that *MV Magazine* disseminated disinformation and hate speech from various sources. One of the articles examined the users of Finnish populist counter-media websites with the aim of exploring their motives for consuming and engaging with populist online media content and hate speech.[103] These websites, along with populist political movements, challenged the status quo of Finnish elites during the 2010s.[104] In another remarkable

99 Neuvonen 2015a, b; Vuorinen 2021; Pöyhtäri et al. 2013.

100 Neuvonen 2016, pp. 1–20.

101 History of *MV Magazine*: Mattila et al. 2019, pp. 29–49; Ylä-Anttila et al. 2019, pp. 1–8. See also Tuomola 2018, pp. 171–191.

102 Haasio et al. 2017, pp. 100–121.

103 Noppari et al. 2019, pp. 23–37.

104 Noppari and Hiltunen 2018, pp. 236–272.

article, the writers analysed the position of five counter-media outlets, which are, in common daily discussion, labelled fake media. The authors' conclusion was that these outlets are an integral part of the hybrid media environment, which challenges the concept of 'fake media' and creates the need for more nuanced concepts.[105]

In Finland, research has been conducted on online hate, especially on those who are guilty of such hate.[106] Several of these cases involve hate speech. In addition to academic research, public authorities, NGOs and foundations in Finland have financed several projects on hate speech and its interventions. These projects have produced various reports, recommendations and action programmes. The racism scandal caused by the writings of the members of the current government (Orpo I) will probably fuel even more discussion, and the government's anti-racism programme will result in the production of new policy papers.

References

Äystö T (2019) Tuomas: Religious Insult as a Societal in 21st Century Finland. Turun yliopiston julkaisuja. Sarja B.

Berndtson E (2001) Finlandization: Paradoxes of External and Internal Dynamics. Government and Opposition 1(26):pp. 21–33.

Björkstrand G (2018) Anders Chydenius. In: Örtenhed K, Wennberg B (eds) Press Freedom 250 Years. Sveriges riksdag, Vällingby, pp. 89–109.

Björne L (1977) "...syihin ja lakeihin eikä mielivaltaan...". Suomalainen lakimiesyhdistys, Vammala, pp. 220–242.

Dalberg M (2021) Perustuslakivaliokunnan valiokuntaneuvosten rooli perustuslainmukaisuuden valvontajärjestelmässä -valiokunnan työrukkanen vai merkittävä vallankäyttäjä? Lakimies 5.

Dahlberg M (2022) Asiantuntijainstituutio perustuslakivaliokunnassa -valtiosääntöoikeudellisen asiantuntijavallan taustaa, muotoja ja kipukohtia. Lakimies: 7–8.

Forss M (2018) Rangaistava vihapuhe internetissä–Miten kansanryhmän suoja eroaa yksilön suojasta?. Edilex 23:14–16.

Gardbaum S (2014) The Structure and Scope of Constitutional Rights. In: Ginsburg T, Dixon R (eds) Comparative Constitutional Law. Edward Elgar, Cheltenham, pp. 387–405.

Haasio A, Ojaranta A, Mattila M (2017) Valheen Lähteillä–Valemedian Lähteistö Ja Sen Luotettavuus. Media & viestintä 40(3–4):100–121.

Hannonen J, Hyttinen T (2023) Kiihottaminen kansanryhmää vastaan alioikeuskäytännössä. Defensor Legis 2:307–330.

Hannula I, Neuvonen R (2011) Internetin keskustelupalstan ylläpitäjän vastuu rasistisesta aineistosta. Lakimies 3:527–548.

Hannula I (2015) Vihapuhe ja sananvapaus rikoslakiin vuonna 2011 tehtyjen muutosten valmistelussa. In: Neuvonen R (ed) Vihapuhe Suomessa. Edita Publishing, pp. 165–190.

Hautamäki V-P (2007) Novel Rules in the Finnish Constitution–The Question of Applicability. Scandinavian Studies in Law 52:133.

Henttonen S, Kivinen T, Rasila T, Sammalmaa J, Vihavainen J, Neuvonen R, Honkanen M (2014) Legal Research Group on Online Hate Speech, ELSA Finland. In an International Legal Research Group on Online Hate Speech Final Report, pp. 175–225.

---

[105] Toivanen et al. 2021, pp. 1–26.

[106] Teo et al. 2016.

Husa J (2019) Constitutional Mentality. In: Letto-Vanamo P et al (eds) Nordic Law in European Context. Springer, Cham, pp. 41–60.
Husa J (2020) Locking in Constitutionality Control in Finland. European Constitutional Law Review 16(2):1–26.
Hyttinen T (2013) KKO 2012:58–Kokiko Jussi Halla-aho oikeusmurhan?. Defensor Legis 6:940–950.
Illman M (2005) Hets mot Folkgrupp. Suomalainen Lakimiesyhdistys, Helsinki.
Illman M (2012) Uudistunut säännös kiihottamisesta kansanryhmää vastaan. Oikeus 2:208–225.
Jyränki A, Husa J (2012) Valtiosääntöoikeus. Lakimiesliiton kustannus, Helsinki.
Jyränki A (1989) Lakien laki. Lakimiesliiton kustannus, Helsinki, pp. 492–500.
Karkkulainen J (2021) Raamatun siteeraaminen? Rangaistavaa? Oikeus 3:386–395.
Klip A (2021) European Criminal Law. 4th edn. Intersentia, pp. 245–257.
Koivisto I (2017) Experts and Constitutionality Control in Finland: A Crisis of Cognitive Authority? Retfaerd 40, 22.
Korpi A (2022) Räsäsen vapauttava tuomio lopputulokseltaan EIT:n linjan mukainen–Uskollisen puheen erityisasema Suomessa vielä tunnistamatta. Defensor Legis 4:1117–1125.
Lappi-Seppälä T (2000) Rikosten seuraamukset. WSLT.
Lavapuro J (2011) Right-Based Constitutionalism in Finland and the Development of Pluralist Constitutional Review.International Journal of Constitutional Law 9:505.
Magnusson L (2018) Anders Nordencrantz. In: Örtenhed K, Wennberg B (eds) Press Freedom 250 Years. Sveriges riksdag, Vällingby, pp. 77–88.
Manninen S (1995) Sananvapaudesta ja mainonnasta. Lakimies:571–606.
Mantila A (2020) Saako myös tämän sanoa? Milloin puhe muuttuu rangaistavaksi vihapuheeksi. Oikeus 2:154–171.
Mantila A (2021) Usko pilkan kohteena. Edilex 24:4.
Matikkala J (2021) Rikosoikeudellinen seuraamusjärjestelmä. Edita Publishing.
Mattila M, Haasio A, Ojaranta A (2019) Vihapuhetta valemediassa. Tiede & edistys 1(44):29–49.
Melander S (2015) EU-rikosoikeus. Talentum Media, pp. 157–163.
Melander S (2016) Rikosvastuun yleiset edellytykset. Tietosanoma, pp. 43–49.
Neuvonen R, Viljanen J, Hoikka M (2018) Finland. In: Susi M, Viljanen J, Jónsson E, Kücs A (eds) Human Rights Law and Regulating Freedom of Expression in New Media. Lessons from Nordic Approaches. Routledge, New York, pp. 59–77.
Neuvonen R, Rautiainen P (2013) Perusoikeuskonkurrenssi Suomen perusoikeusjärjestelmässä. Lakimies 6:1011–1031.
Neuvonen R (2012a) Sananvapauden sääntely Suomessa. Lakimiesliiton kustannus, Helsinki.
Neuvonen R (2012b) Sananvapauden historia Suomessa. Gaudeamus, Helsinki.
Neuvonen R (2015a) Vihapuheen kehitys Suomessa. In: Neuvonen R (ed) Vihapuhe Suomessa. Edita Publishing, Helsinki.
Neuvonen R (2015b). Vihapuhe Suomessa. Edita Publishing, Helsinki, pp. 20–21.
Neuvonen R (2016) Vastamedia sananvapauden ja journalismin rajoilla. In: Korpisaari P (ed) Viestintäoikeuden vuosikirja 2015: Oikeus, tieto ja viesti. Helsingin yliopiston oikeustieteellinen tiedekunta, Helsinki, pp. 1–20.
Neuvonen R (2018) Sananvapauden historia Suomessa. Gaudeamus, Helsinki.
Neuvonen R (2019) Viestintä- ja informaatio-oikeuden perusteet. Kauppakamari, Helsinki, pp. 97–98.
Neuvonen R (2023) Freedom Of Speech and Regulation of Fake News in Finland. In: Pollicino O (eds), Freedom of Speech and the Regulation of Fake News. Intersentia.
Nokkala E (2018) Peter Forsskål–the Freedom to Write and the Principle of Public Access to Official Documents. In: Örtenhed K, Wennberg B (eds) Press Freedom 250 Years. Sveriges riksdag, Vällingby, pp. 61–76.

Noppari E, Hiltunen I, Ahva L (2019) User Profiles for Populist Counter-Media Websites in Finland. Journal of Alternative and Community Media 4(1):2337.
Noppari E, Hiltunen I (2018) Populistinen vastamedia eliittejä haastamassa. In: Niemi M, Houni T (eds) Media & populismi – Työkaluja kriittiseen journalismiin. Vastapaino, Tampere, pp. 236–272.
Nuotio K (2009) Jumalanpilkasta viharikoksiin. Uskonnon asema rikosoikeudessa arvioitava uudelleen. Haaste 1:24.
Nuotio K (2015) Vihapuheen rikosoikeudellinen sääntely. In: Neuvonen R (ed) Vihapuhe Suomessa. Edita Publishing, pp. 139–164.
Nuotio K (2021) Sananvapausrikosten sääntelyn ja soveltamisen kehitystrendejä ja kehittämiskohtia eräiden kotimaisten oikeustapausten valossa. In: Korpisaari P (ed) Viestintäoikeuden vuosikirja 2021, pp. 47–63.
Nuotio K (2022) Kiihottaminen kansanryhmää vastaan. In: Lappi-Seppälä T, Hakamies K, Helenius D, Melander S, Nuotio K, Ojala T, Ilkka Rautio, Rikosoikeus. Oikeuden perusteokset. Alma Talent, pp. 308–314.
Pöyhtäri R, Haara P, Raittila P (2013) Vihapuhe sananvapautta kaventamassa. Tampere University Press, Tampere.
Rautiainen P (2011) Moninaisuudessaan yhtenäinen Eurooppa: konsensusperiaate ja valtion harkintamarginaalioppi. Lakimies:152–1171, 1161–1162.
Saraviita I (2012) Constitutional Law in Finland. Kluwer Law, Alphen aan den Rijn.
Suomalainen (2020) Sami: Vihapuheen rikosoikeudellisesta määrittelystä. ELSA Finlandin kansallisen esseekilpailun 2019–2020 voittajaessee. Julkaistu Edilexissä.
Tapani J, Tolvanen M, Kemppinen H (2021) Rikosoikeus-rangaistuksen määrääminen ja täytäntöönpano. Alma Talent.
Teo K, Näsi M, Oksanen A, Räsänen P (2016) Online Hate and Harmful Content. Routledge, United Kingdom.
Tepora T (2014) Heimoveljiä, valkobandiitteja ja punikin perkeleitä. In: Näre S, Kirves J (eds) Luvattu maa. Johnny Kniga, Helsinki, pp. 69–130.
Toivanen P, Nelimarkka M, Valaskivi K (2021) Remediation in the Hybrid Media Environment: Understanding Countermedia in Context. New Media & Society:1–26.
Tulkki KR (2008) Uskonnonvapauden rikosoikeudellinen suoja. University of Turku, Finland.
Tulkki K-E (2010) Uskonnonvapauden ja sananvapauden keskinäisestä suhteesta rikosoikeuden kannalta arvioiden. Edilex 28.
Tuomola S (2018) Pakolaiskeskustelu MV-lehdessä: Merkityksellistämisen mekanismit ideologisissa puhuttelutavoissa. Media ja viestintä 3(41):171–191.
Vepsäläinen J, Kaakinen M, Vauhkonen T, Näsi M, Kirjonen A (2023) Viharikosten tekijät. Oikeusministeriön julkaisuja, Selvityksiä ja ohjeita 26:26–27.
Vihavainen T (2013) Ryssäviha–Venäjän pelon historia. Minerva, Helsinki.
Viljanen V-P (2001) Perusoikeuksien rajoitusedellytykset. WSLT.
Vuorinen M (ed) Vihapuheen, viholliskuvien ja disinformaation historiaa: vallan ja vastarinnan välineitä. Turun Historiallinen Yhdistys, Turku.
Ylä-Anttila T, Bauvois G, Pyrhönen N (2019) Politicization of Migration in the Countermedia Style: A Computational and Qualitative Analysis of Populist Discourse. Discourse, Context & Media 32:1–8.

Tarja Koskela is a Doctor of Laws and Associate Professor of Criminal Law. She works as a Senior University Lecturer and researcher at the University of Eastern Finland, teaching Criminal Law and supervising theses in Criminal Law and Criminology at masters and doctoral levels. Her research has slargely focused on the vulnerable, including domestic violence, minors, environment and animals.

Riku Neuvonen is a Doctor of Laws (Helsinki) and Senior Lecturer of Public Law at the Tampere University. He is also Associate Professor of Media Law at the University of Helsinki, Principal Investigator of subproject of the research project The Democratic Epistemic Capacities in the Age of Algorithms (DECA) funded by the Strategic Research Council, and author of several books and articles in Media Law, Constitutional Law and Administrative Law.

Chapter 9
France

Gwénaële Calvès

Contents

Abstract This chapter, relying on examples drawn from higher courts' case law, presents the current state of French hate speech legislation. It stresses its broad reach, in criminal as well as in administrative law. It shows that most of its provisions were held compatible with constitutional requirements and European human rights law.

Keywords Apology for terrorism · Associations · Holocaust denial · Media regulation · Places of worship · Racism

---

G. Calvès (✉)
Département de droit public, Université de Cergy-Pontoise, Cergy, France
e-mail: gwenaele.calves@icloud.com

E. Heinze (ed.), *Criminalising Hate Speech*,
https://doi.org/10.1007/978-94-6265-650-5_9

9.1 Droit constitutionnel

En droit constitutionnel français, la répression pénale du discours de haine ne soulève pas de difficulté de principe. Bien sûr, « la liberté d'expression est d'autant plus précieuse que son exercice est une condition de la démocratie et l'une des garanties du respect des autres droits et libertés ».[1] Mais le législateur n'en est pas moins fondé à ériger en délits « les abus de l'exercice de la liberté d'expression et de communication qui portent atteinte à l'ordre public et aux droits des tiers », deux objectifs systématiquement mis en avant dans le contentieux du discours de haine.[2]

Quels abus (ou usages préjudiciables)? Comment les définir, jusqu'où les réprimer ? Les limites que le législateur ne doit pas franchir découlent de trois ensembles de normes issues de la Déclaration des droits de l'homme et du citoyen de 1789 (DDHC):

- *la liberté d'opinion* (art. 10 DDHC: « nul ne doit être inquiété pour ses opinions, même religieuses pourvu que leur manifestation ne trouble pas l'ordre public établi par la loi ») et *la liberté d'expression et de communication* (art. 11 DDHC: « la libre communication des pensées et des opinions est un des droits les plus précieux de l'homme: tout citoyen peut donc parler, écrire, imprimer librement, sauf à répondre de l'abus de cette liberté dans les cas déterminés par la loi »).
- *les grands principes du droit pénal* énoncés par la DDHC, ou déduits de ses dispositions: le principe de légalité des délits et des peines (les textes d'incrimination doivent être suffisamment clairs et précis pour garantir contre le risque d'arbitraire) ; le principe de nécessité et proportionnalité des peines (art. 8: « la loi ne doit établir que des peines strictement et évidemment nécessaires »).
- *l'égalité devant la loi et devant la justice* (art. 6 DDHC: la loi « doit être la même pour tous, soit qu'elle protège, soit qu'elle punisse [...] »).

Ces principes constitutionnels n'ont pas entravé le développement d'un droit de la liberté d'expression (pénal et administratif) destiné, à partir de 1972, à lutter contre le racisme et les formes analogues de rejet d'autrui, puis, à partir de la fin des années 1980, à parer une menace terroriste inspirée par une idéologie de haine (de l'Occident, du libéralisme, des juifs, des mécréants *etc.*).

Dans sa dimension pénale, la notion de discours de haine repose aujourd'hui sur quatre piliers, qui ont donné lieu à des débats constitutionnels d'intensité variable.

---

[1] Cette formule rituelle est apparue (sous une forme un peu différente qui se référait à la souveraineté nationale plutôt qu'à la démocratie), dans la première « grande décision » du Conseil en matière de liberté d'expression, rendue en 1984 (CC, 84-181 DC des 10-11 octobre 1984, *Entreprises de presse*).

[2] CC, 2012-647 DC du 28 février 2012, *Loi visant à réprimer la contestation des génocides reconnus pas la loi*, cons. 5.

9.1.1 Le triptyque provocation/diffamation/injure aggravées

Depuis la loi Pleven du 1er juillet 1972,[3] adoptée (notamment) pour transcrire en droit français les exigences de l'article 4(a) de la Convention internationale sur l'élimination de toutes les formes de discrimination raciale (*infra* Sect. 9.4), la loi du 29 juillet 1881 sur la liberté de la presse incrimine trois types de discours qui peuvent être considérés comme des « discours de haine » (même si ce label n'apparaît pas dans la loi). Il est important de souligner que dans le cadre de la loi de 1881, la notion d'infraction de presse désigne une très large gamme d'usages publics de la liberté d'expression: les « discours, cris ou menaces proférés dans des lieux ou réunions publics » aussi bien que les « écrits, imprimés, dessins, gravures, peintures, emblèmes, images ou tout autre support de l'écrit, de la parole ou de l'image », dès lors qu'ils sont « vendus ou distribués, mis en vente ou exposés dans des lieux ou réunions publics, soit par des placards ou des affiches exposés au regard du public, soit par tout moyen de communication au public par voie électronique ».[4]

Ces infractions sont assorties de peines pouvant aller jusqu'à un an d'emprisonnement et/ou 45 000 euros d'amende (depuis 2021, trois ans d'emprisonnement et/ou 75 000 euros d'amende lorsque les faits sont commis par une personne dépositaire de l'autorité publique ou chargée d'une mission de service public[5]). Elles recouvraient, en 1972:

- La provocation à la discrimination, à la haine ou à la violence à l'égard d'une personne ou d'un groupe de personnes à raison de leur origine ou de leur appartenance ou de leur non-appartenance à une ethnie, une nation, une race ou une religion déterminée (art. 24 al. 7 de la loi du 29 juillet 1881 sur la liberté de la presse).
- La diffamation, c'est-à-dire l'allégation ou l'imputation d'un fait qui porte atteinte à l'honneur ou à la considération, envers une personne ou un groupe de personnes à raison de leur origine ou de leur appartenance ou de leur non-appartenance à une ethnie, une nation, une race ou une religion déterminée (art. 32 al. 2 de la loi du 29 juillet 1881).
- l'injure, c'est-à-dire l'expression outrageante, les termes de mépris ou l'invective qui ne renferment l'imputation d'aucun fait, envers une personne ou un groupe de personnes à raison de leur origine ou de leur appartenance ou de leur non-appartenance à une ethnie, une nation, une race ou une religion déterminée (art. 33 al. 3 de la loi du 29 juillet 1881).

---

[3] Loi n° 72-546 du 1er juillet 1972 sur la lutte contre le racisme.

[4] Art. 23 de la loi du 29 juillet 1881 dans sa rédaction actuelle.

[5] Loi n° 2021-1109 du 24 août 2021 confortant le respect des principes de la République. Ce renforcement du quantum de la peine vaut pour les faits de provocation aggravée, contestation de crime contre l'humanité et injure aggravée.

Depuis 2004,[6] ces mêmes faits sont réprimés s'ils visent « une personne ou d'un groupe de personnes à raison de leur sexe, de leur orientation sexuelle ou identité de genre[7] ou de leur handicap » (art. 24 al. 8 pour la provocation, art. 32 al. 2 pour la diffamation et art. 33 al. 4 pour l'injure).

Le Conseil constitutionnel n'a examiné ce triptyque que pour répondre à des questions relativement mineures:

- Le législateur pouvait-il, en 2004, étendre à un an le délai de prescription de ces infractions, alors que pour les autres délits de presse, il restait fixé à trois mois ? Oui. Ni l'égalité devant la loi et devant la justice, ni les droits de la défense ne sont lésés par ce double régime, car il est loisible au législateur de tenir compte de la *nature particulière* des discours de haine, et de chercher à faciliter la poursuite et la condamnation de leurs auteurs.[8]
- Le législateur pouvait-il, en 2017, autoriser les juridictions à requalifier, lors du procès, des faits poursuivis sous le chef de provocation, diffamation ou injure aggravées, alors qu'une telle requalification est normalement proscrite en matière d'infraction de presse ? Oui. La différence de traitement ainsi créée ne revêt pas un caractère disproportionné au regard de l'objectif poursuivi (faciliter la poursuite et la condamnation des auteurs de propos haineux).[9]
- La notion controversée d'«identité de genre » est-elle imprécise ? Non, car « il résulte des travaux parlementaires qu'en ayant recours à la notion d'identité de genre, le législateur a entendu viser le genre auquel s'identifie une personne, qu'il corresponde ou non au sexe indiqué sur les registres de l'état-civil ou aux différentes expressions de l'appartenance au sexe masculin ou au sexe féminin. Les termes 'identité de genre', qui figurent d'ailleurs à l'article 225-1 du code pénal dans sa version issue de la loi du 18 novembre 2016 [...], sont également utilisés dans la convention du Conseil de l'Europe du 12 avril 2011 et dans la directive [2011/95/UE du Parlement européen et du Conseil du 13 décembre 2011]. Dans ces conditions, les termes d''identité de genre' utilisés par le législateur sont suffisamment clairs et précis pour respecter le principe de légalité ».[10]
- Le législateur pouvait-il, en 2017, rendre *automatique* la peine d'inéligibilité que le juge peut prononcer à l'encontre des auteurs de propos racistes, en complément de la peine d'emprisonnement ou d'amende ? Non, car « la liberté d'expression revêt une importance particulière dans le débat politique et dans les campagnes électorales. Dès lors, pour condamnables que soient les abus dans la

[6] Loi n° 2004-1486 du 30 décembre 2004 portant création de la *Haute Autorité* de lutte contre les discriminations et pour l'égalité.

[7] Loi n° 2017-86 du 27 janvier 2017 relative à l'égalité et à la citoyenneté, substituant l'expression « identité de genre » à celle « d'identité sexuelle » qui avait été introduite dans la loi de 1881 par la loi n° 2012-954 du 6 août 2012 relative au harcèlement sexuel.

[8] CC, 2013-302 QPC du 12 avril 2013, *M. Laurent A.* [Délai de prescription d'un an pour les délits de presse à raison de l'origine, l'ethnie, la nation, la race ou la religion]), examinant une disposition issue de la loi n° 2004-204 du 9 mars 2004 adaptant la justice aux évolutions de la criminalité.

[9] CC, 2016-745 DC du 26 janvier 2017, *Loi relative à l'égalité et à la citoyenneté,* cons. 95.

[10] CC, 2016-745 DC du 26 janvier 2017, *Loi relative à l'égalité et à la citoyenneté*, cons. 89.

liberté d'expression visés par ces dispositions, en prévoyant l'inéligibilité obligatoire de leur auteur, le législateur a porté à la liberté d'expression une atteinte disproportionnée».[11]

Pour tout le reste, la discussion a eu lieu devant la seule Cour de cassation. Depuis 2010, il est en effet possible de demander à la cour suprême de l'ordre judiciaire de transmettre au Conseil constitutionnel une « question prioritaire de constitutionnalité » (QPC) portant sur une disposition législative qui aurait échappé au contrôle exercé par le Conseil constitutionnel avant la promulgation de la loi. Tel est le cas de la loi Pleven de 1972, comme de la loi du 30 décembre 2004 qui en a élargi la portée à l'expression sexiste, homophobe, ou handiphobe. La répression du « discours de haine » organisée par ces lois heurte-t-elle, à un titre ou autre, les droits et libertés garantis par la Constitution ? La Cour de cassation a décidé de répondre elle-même à la question. Elle a jugé que l'atteinte portée à la liberté d'expression par ces dispositions « apparaît nécessaire, adaptée et proportionnée à l'objectif de lutte contre le racisme et de protection de l'ordre public »,[12] ou à « l'objectif de protection de la réputation, de la dignité, des droits d'autrui, et de défense de l'ordre public».[13] Elle a également estimé que les textes applicables « sont suffisamment clairs et précis pour que [leur] interprétation, qui entre dans l'office du juge pénal, puisse se faire sans risque d'arbitraire » (mêmes arrêts).

Sur le triptyque provocation/ diffamation/injure aggravées, pierre angulaire du dispositif français de répression pénale des discours de haine, le débat constitutionnel en est resté là.

9.1.2 La contestation de crimes contre l'humanité

Situation initiale

La loi du 13 juillet 1990 tendant à réprimer tout acte raciste, antisémite ou xénophobe (dite « loi Gayssot ») a introduit dans la loi de 1881 sur la liberté de la presse un article 24 bis incriminant le négationnisme de la Shoah.[14] Le texte avait échappé au contrôle du Conseil constitutionnel, qui ne pouvait à l'époque être saisi qu'avant

[11] CC, n° 2017-752 DC du 8 septembre 2017, *Loi pour la confiance dans la vie politique*, cons. 13.

[12] Cass., crim., 16 avril 2013, n°13-90.008 (provocation à la discrimination ethnique, nationale, raciale ou religieuse).

[13] Cass., crim., 16 avril 2013, n°13-90.010 (provocation à la haine ou à la violence en raison de l'orientation sexuelle).

[14] Art. 24 bis de la loi du 29 juillet 1881: « Seront punis d'un an d'emprisonnement et de 45 000 € d'amende ceux qui auront contesté, par un des moyens énoncés à l'article 23, l'existence d'un ou plusieurs crimes contre l'humanité tels qu'ils sont définis par l'article 6 du statut du tribunal militaire international annexé à l'accord de Londres du 8 août 1945 et qui ont été commis soit par les membres d'une organisation déclarée criminelle en application de l'article 9 dudit statut, soit par une personne reconnue coupable de tels crimes par une juridiction française ou internationale ».

promulgation de la loi (par le Président de la République, le Premier ministre, le Président de l'une des deux chambres, 60 députés ou 60 sénateurs).

Après la création du mécanisme de la QPC, il a fallu attendre un certain temps avant que la Cour de cassation ne se décide à transmettre au Conseil constitutionnel la question de la conformité de cette disposition à la Constitution. L'incrimination, a-t-elle d'abord affirmé, ne contrevient pas au principe de légalité des délits et des peines, car elle définit « de façon claire et précise l'infraction de contestation de crime contre l'humanité », en se référant à des textes de droit international régulièrement introduit en droit interne.[15] Porte-t-elle atteinte à la liberté d'opinion et d'expression ? Non, asséna la Cour (même arrêt), avant d'admettre que si, mais que l'atteinte est justifiée: elle « apparaît nécessaire, adaptée et proportionnée à l'objectif poursuivi par le législateur: la lutte contre le racisme et l'antisémitisme ainsi que la protection de l'ordre public ».[16]

L'objection tirée de l'égalité devant la loi a toutefois fini par convaincre la Cour de transmettre la question au Conseil constitutionnel:[17] pourquoi la loi incrimine-telle *uniquement* la contestation de certains crimes contre l'humanité, commis pendant la seconde guerre mondiale ? N'est-ce pas contraire au principe d'égalité devant la loi et la justice ?

Non, répondit le Conseil constitutionnel.[18] La répression du négationnisme de la Shoah est une restriction nécessaire, adaptée et proportionnée à la liberté d'expression, parce qu'elle vise des discours qui « constituent en eux-mêmes une incitation au racisme et à l'antisémitisme » (cons. 7). Tous les antisémites ne sont pas négationnistes, mais tous les négationnistes sont antisémites. Aucune négation d'un autre crime contre l'humanité ne revêt le même contenu systématiquement et intrinsèquement raciste. D'où le rejet de l'argument tiré de la violation du principe d'égalité: « en réprimant pénalement la seule contestation des crimes contre l'humanité commis [pendant la seconde guerre mondiale] le législateur a traité différemment des agissements de nature différente ; [...] cette différence de traitement est en rapport avec l'objet de la loi du 13 juillet 1990 qui vise à réprimer des actes racistes, antisémites ou xénophobes ; le grief tiré de l'atteinte au principe d'égalité devant la loi pénale doit [donc] être écarté » (cons. 10).

Extension progressive

Le délit de contestation de crimes contre l'humanité n'est pas resté cantonné au négationnisme de la Shoah. Une première tentative d'extension, qui visait pour l'essentiel

[15] Cass., crim., 7 mai 2010, n° 09-80.774.

[16] Cass., crim., 5 décembre 2012, n° 12-86.382 et Cass. crim. 6 mai 2014, n° 14-90.010.

[17] Cass., crim., 6 octobre 2015, n° 15-84.335.

[18] CC, 2015-512 QPC du 8 janvier 2016, *M. Vincent R.* [Délit de contestation de l'existence de certains crimes contre l'humanité].

à permettre de sanctionner pénalement les auteurs de propos niant la réalité du génocide des Arméniens, s'est heurtée à la censure du Conseil constitutionnel, au motif – un peu étrange – que la loi ne saurait qualifier de « négationniste » la contestation d'un crime qu'elle aurait elle-même reconnu et qualifié comme tel.[19]

La seconde tentative a tenu compte de cet avertissement: la loi *Égalité et citoyenneté* du 27 janvier 2017 a érigé en délit le fait de tenir publiquement un propos qui aura « nié, minoré ou banalisé de façon outrancière » l'existence d'un crime de génocide, d'un crime contre l'humanité, d'un crime de réduction en esclavage ou d'un crime de guerre, lorsque ces crimes « ont donné lieu à une condamnation prononcée par une juridiction française ou internationale ».[20] Le Conseil constitutionnel ne s'est pas opposé à une telle extension, de sorte qu'il est désormais possible de poursuivre, par exemple, les auteurs de propos qui nient, minorent ou banalisent les crimes contre l'humanité commis en ex-Yougoslavie dans les années 1990, ou le génocide des Tutsis.

Le Conseil constitutionnel a en revanche censuré (d'office) une seconde hypothèse que voulait ouvrir la loi *Égalité et citoyenneté*: celle de la négation, minoration ou banalisation d'un crime qui n'a *pas* fait l'objet d'une condamnation judiciaire, dès lors que les propos en cause constituent « une incitation à la violence ou à la haine à l'égard d'un groupe de personnes ou d'un membre d'un tel groupe défini par référence à la prétendue race, la couleur, la religion, l'ascendance ou l'origine nationale». Une telle incrimination, a-t-il jugé, porterait à l'exercice de la liberté d'expression une atteinte « qui n'est ni nécessaire ni proportionnée ».[21] Elle n'est pas « nécessaire », parce qu'elle fait double emploi avec l'incrimination classique de provocation à la haine ou la violence raciale, religieuse, nationale *etc* (Sect. 9.1.1). Elle n'est pas « proportionnée », parce qu'elle fait peser une incertitude sur la licéité d'actes ou de propos portant sur des faits qui, n'ayant pas été qualifiés par une juridiction, « sont susceptibles de faire l'objet de débats historiques ».

9.1.3 L'apologie du terrorisme

L'apologie consiste à inciter autrui à porter un jugement favorable sur un des crimes énumérés à l'article 24 al. 2 de la loi du 29 juillet 1881 d'une part (« les atteintes volontaires à la vie, les atteintes volontaires à l'intégrité de la personne et les agressions sexuelles », lorsqu'elles présentent un caractère criminel), à l'art. 24 al. 5 d'autre part (crimes de guerre, crimes contre l'humanité, crimes de réduction en esclavage ou d'exploitation d'une personne réduite en esclavage, crimes et délits de collaboration avec l'ennemi, y compris si ces crimes n'ont pas donné lieu à la condamnation de leurs auteurs). L'apologie n'est pas nécessairement formulée sous

[19] CC, 2012-647 DC du 28 février 2012, *Loi visant à réprimer la contestation de l'existence des génocides reconnus par la loi.*

[20] Art. 24 bis al. 2, de la loi du 31 juillet 1881.

[21] CC, 2016-745 DC du 26 janvier 2017, *Loi relative à l'égalité et à la citoyenneté.*

la forme d'un discours argumenté. Relève par exemple de ce délit le fait de dire, à propos d'un journaliste dont le patronyme est Cohen: « Quand je l'entends parler, je me dis que les chambres à gaz... quand même... dommage.... ».[22]

La liste des apologies prohibées par la loi sur la presse incluait les « actes de terrorisme », jusqu'à ce qu'une loi du 13 novembre 2014[23] transfère cette incrimination vers le code pénal. Un ancien membre du groupe terroriste Action directe, condamné pour avoir affirmé qu'il trouvait « très courageux » les auteurs des attentats commis à Paris en janvier et novembre 2015, obtint de la Cour de cassation – qui s'y jusqu'alors était refusée[24] - qu'elle transmette au Conseil constitutionnel une QPC.

Mais le Conseil a rejeté tous les griefs d'inconstitutionnalité soulevés devant lui.[25] il n'y a pas d'atteinte au principe de légalité des délits et des peines, car les dispositions en cause ne revêtent pas un caractère équivoque, et sont suffisamment précises pour garantir contre le risque d'arbitraire. Les peines prévues (cinq d'emprisonnement et/ou 75 000 euros d'amende) ne sont pas disproportionnées, même lorsqu'elles sont portées à sept d'emprisonnement et/ou 100 000 euros (apologie du terrorisme commise « en ligne »), compte tenu de « l'ampleur particulière de la diffusion des messages prohibés que permet ce mode de communication, ainsi que son influence dans le processus d'endoctrinement d'individus susceptibles de commettre des actes de terrorisme » (cons. 14). Enfin, la transformation de ce délit de presse en délit de droit commun, même si elle prive ses auteurs des garanties procédurales prévues par la loi du 29 juillet 1881, est justifiée par l'objectif de protection de l'ordre public contre des infractions d'une particulière gravité. « Par conséquent, l'atteinte portée à la liberté d'expression et de communication par les dispositions contestées est nécessaire, adaptée et proportionnée à l'objectif poursuivi » (cons. 23).

Le Conseil constitutionnel s'est en revanche opposé, à trois reprises, à ce que la répression de l'apologie du terrorisme s'étende aux *récepteurs* de ces propos.[26] L'atteinte à la liberté d'accéder à des services de communication en ligne, qui est une composante de la liberté de communication,[27] a été jugée excessive: excessive parce qu'inutile, les pouvoirs publics disposant déjà de très nombreux moyens de surveillance des individus en cours de radicalisation ; excessive, également, parce qu'elle omettait de retenir l'*intention terroriste* comme élément constitutif de l'infraction.

---

[22] TGI Paris, 17e ch., 4 mars 2015, *Dieudonné*, n° 325-01.

[23] Loi n° 2014-1353 du 13 novembre 2014 renforçant les dispositions relatives à la lutte contre le terrorisme.

[24] Cass., crim., 1er décembre 2015, n° 15-90.017.

[25] CC, 2018-706 QPC du 18 mai 2018, *M. Jean-Marc R.* [Délit d'apologie d'actes de terrorisme]. Jean-Marc Rouillan a ensuite porté l'affaire devant la Cour européenne des droits de l'homme (*infra*, note 68), mais le constat de violation prononcé par la Cour concerne uniquement l'application à l'espèce de la disposition législative, dont la conventionnalité n'est pas remise pas en cause.

[26] CC, 2016-611 QPC du 10 février 2017, *M. David P.*, 2017-682 QPC du 15 décembre 2017, *M. David P.* et 2020-845 QPC du 19 juin 2020, *M. Théo S.*

[27] Composante identifiée par la décision 2009-580 DC du 10 juin 2009, *Loi favorisant la diffusion et la protection de la création sur internet*. Le versant dit « passif » de la liberté d'expression (c'est-à-dire le droit d'accéder aux discours rendus publics par autrui public) est particulièrement bien protégé en droit français.

La seule condition d'adhésion à l'idéologie diffusée par des sites qui se livrent à l'apologie du terrorisme (condition ajoutée par le législateur après la première censure du dispositif par le Conseil constitutionnel) ne suffit pas à déduire un risque de « passage à l'acte ». Le délit de consultation habituelle de sites terroristes ou faisant l'apologie incriminait donc exclusivement des pensées et des opinions, ce que prohibe l'article 10 DDHC.

9.1.4 La question de la haine en ligne

En matière de lutte contre la haine en ligne, le législateur français intervient dans un cadre fortement contraint par le droit dérivé de l'Union européenne.[28] Les dispositions législatives qui se bornent à tirer les conséquences nécessaires des dispositions inconditionnelles et précises d'une directive échappent en effet au contrôle de constitutionnalité (sauf si elles vont à l'encontre d'une règle ou d'un principe inhérent à l'identité constitutionnelle de la France). Le Conseil constitutionnel ne peut donc intervenir qu'à la marge. Mais il l'a fait de manière spectaculaire, dans une décision du 18 juin 2020 qui consacre la liberté pour chacun, non plus seulement d'accéder aux services de communication en ligne, mais de « s'y exprimer ».[29] L'invocation de la liberté des utilisateurs, conjuguée à celle des opérateurs, a amené le juge à déclarer inconstitutionnelle, dans sa quasi-totalité, la « loi Avia » qui entendait lutter contre la haine en ligne.

Adopté le 13 mai 2020, ce texte voulait imposer aux hébergeurs ou aux éditeurs d'un service de communication en ligne de retirer certains « contenus haineux », à la demande de l'autorité administrative, dans des délais très brefs et sous peine de lourdes sanctions pénales: délai d'une heure pour les contenus à caractère pédopornographique ou provoquant à des actes de terrorisme ; délai de 24 heures pour des contenus relevant des qualifications pénales de provocation, diffamation ou injure aggravées (Sect. 9.1.1), négationnisme (Sect. 9.1.2) et harcèlement sexuel. Il n'était pas requis que ces contenus soient *manifestement* illicites. Or dans des délais aussi courts, comment envisager qu'un opérateur puisse examiner l'ensemble des contenus qui lui sont signalés, alors même (aveu du Conseil constitutionnel dont on appréciera la franchise !) « que les éléments constitutifs de certaines [des infractions de presse

[28] La loi qui gouverne la matière (loi n° 2004-575 du 21 juin 2004 pour la confiance dans l'économie numérique, plusieurs fois modifiée) transpose la directive n° 2000/31/CE du Parlement et du Conseil du 8 juin 2000.

[29] CC, 2020-801 DC du 18 juin 2020, *Loi visant à lutter contre les contenus haineux sur internet*, cons. 4 (« En l'état actuel des moyens de communication et eu égard au développement généralisé des services de communication au public en ligne ainsi qu'à l'importance prise par ces services pour la participation à la vie démocratique et l'expression des idées et des opinions, ce droit implique la liberté d'accéder à ces services et de s'y exprimer »).

concernées] peuvent présenter une technicité juridique ou [...] appeler une appréciation au regard du contexte d'énonciation ou de diffusion des contenus en cause »[30] ? Dans le doute, et pour éviter de s'exposer à une sanction pénale, l'opérateur ne risquait-il pas de procéder massivement à des retraits de contenus ? Cette inquiétude, inspirée de la théorie du *chilling effect*, a conduit le Conseil constitutionnel à juger que le dispositif prévu par la loi portait à la liberté d'expression et de communication une atteinte qui n'est pas « nécessaire, adaptée et proportionnée ».

À la suite de cette censure, le législateur a changé de stratégie. La loi n° 2021-1109 du 24 août 2021 confortant le respect des principes de la République renonce à une approche par la sanction pénale,[31] au profit d'une obligation de vigilance et d'auto-régulation mise à la charge des opérateurs, sous le contrôle d'une nouvelle autorité administrative indépendante, l'Autorité de régulation de la communication audiovisuelle et numérique (ARCOM) qui a succédé, le 1er janvier 2022, au Conseil supérieur de l'audiovisuel (CSA). Ces dispositions – qui n'ont pas été contrôlées par le Conseil constitutionnel – anticipaient l'entrée en vigueur du *Digital service Act*, un règlement européen adopté le 19 octobre 2022 entré en vigueur le 17 février 2024.

9.2 Droit administratif

Hors champ pénal, trois ensembles de dispositions législatives méritent d'être présentées, car elles permettent à l'autorité administrative de sanctionner des abus de la liberté d'expression qui ont un air de famille avec les « discours de haine » dont le juge répressif peut être saisi. Pour autant, les qualifications retenues en droit administratif sont juridiquement autonomes: une mesure de police peut ainsi frapper un discours qui n'a pas été sanctionné pénalement. On présentera ici trois exemples de polices administratives de l'expression publique.

9.2.1 La Communication audiovisuelle

Depuis la fin du monopole public dont elle faisait l'objet, « la communication audiovisuelle est libre ».[32] Le pouvoir d'émettre par voie hertzienne (radio et télévision) reste toutefois soumis à autorisation, compte tenu de la rareté des fréquences disponibles. Dans ce contexte, les chaînes doivent respecter un certain nombre d'obligations, fixées par les conventions qu'elles concluent avec l'organe de régulation, le Conseil

[30] CC, 2020-801 DC du 18 juin 2020, *Loi visant à lutter contre les contenus haineux sur internet*, cons. 15.

[31] Elle est maintenue pour le manquement à l'obligation de retirer, après injonction de l'administration, des contenus à caractère terroriste (loi n° 2022-1159 du 16 août 2022 portant diverses dispositions d'adaptation au droit de l'UE en matière de prévention de la diffusion de contenus à caractère terroriste en ligne).

[32] Loi n° 82-652 du 29 juillet 1982 sur la communication audiovisuelle, art. 1er.

supérieur de l'audiovisuel (CSA, aujourd'hui ARCOM – Sect. 9.1.4). Cette autorité administrative indépendante assure, sous le contrôle du Conseil d'État, la « police des discours » diffusés à la radio et la télévision. En vertu de la loi du 30 septembre 1986 plusieurs fois modifiée, elle veille notamment:

- au respect, dans les programmes, de la dignité de la personne humaine (art. 1er al. 2)
- à l'absence, dans les programmes, de toute « incitation à la haine ou à la violence pour des raisons de race, de sexe, de mœurs, de religion ou de nationalité » (art. 15). Cette énumération a été élargie en 2020, pour satisfaire aux exigences du droit de l'Union européenne. L'incitation à la haine ou à la violence est désormais interdite lorsqu'elle est « fondée sur l'un des motifs visés à l'article 21 de la Charte des droits fondamentaux de l'Union européenne » ou – ajout du législateur français – sur « l'identité de genre ».[33]

Ces obligations sont réitérées et précisées dans les conventions signées par les chaînes. Certaines prévoient par exemple que le titulaire de l'autorisation d'émettre veille « à promouvoir les valeurs d'intégration et de solidarité qui sont celles de la République [et] contribue aux actions en faveur de la cohésion sociale et à la lutte contre les discriminations » (le Conseil d'État a heureusement précisé que « cet engagement ne saurait être interprété comme imposant à l'éditeur du service de prohiber sur son antenne toute critique des principes et des valeurs républicains »[34]).

La gamme des sanctions que peut prononcer le CSA/ARCOM est assez large: sanction pécuniaire, suspension d'un programme ou d'une partie d'un programme pendant un mois au plus, interdiction de diffuser des séquences publicitaires pendant un mois au plus, réduction de la durée de la convention, ou retrait pur et simple de l'autorisation d'émettre.[35] La Cour européenne des droits de l'homme a jugé qu'une chaîne frappée par une sanction financière qui atteignait presque 9% de son chiffre d'affaire annuel n'était pas fondée à se plaindre d'une violation de son droit à la liberté d'expression (les séquences litigieuses portaient atteinte, pour l'une d'entre elles, à l'image des femmes et véhiculait, pour l'autre, des stéréotypes de nature à stigmatiser les personnes homosexuelles, sans contribuer en aucune manière à un débat d'intérêt général).[36]

---

[33] Ord. n°2020-1642 du 21 décembre 2020 portant transposition de la directive 2018/1808 du Parlement et du Conseil, modifiant la directive « Services de média audiovisuels ». Les motifs visés par l'article 21 de la Charte sont le sexe, la race, la couleur, les origines ethniques ou sociales, les caractéristiques génétiques, la langue, la religion ou les convictions, les opinions politiques ou toute autre opinion, l'appartenance à une minorité nationale, la fortune, la naissance, un handicap, l'âge ou l'orientation sexuelle ».

[34] CE, 15 octobre 2018, *Société RTL France radio*, n° 417228, cons. 4 (annulant la sanction prononcée par le CSA en raison de propos tenus par Éric Zemmour qui dénonçait le « fétichisme de la non-discrimination », cette « machine à désintégrer la nation, la famille, la société, au nom des droits d'un individu roi »).

[35] Pour un exemple de retrait (rare), v. CE, 6 janvier 2006, *Société Lebanese Communication Group*, n° 279596, sanctionnant une série d'émissions à caractère antisémite sur la chaîne de télévision *Al Manar.*

[36] Cour EDH, *C8 (Canal 8) c. France* du 9 février 2023, n° 58951/18 et 1308/19.

Ce genre de sanctions – dont le principe n'a pas été jugé contraire à la Constitution[37] - ne font pas peser une chape de plomb sur le paysage audio-visuel français. En 2020, par exemple, le CSA a prononcé 24 mises en demeure (préalables à une sanction) et 4 sanctions. Une partie d'entre elles seulement concernaient des manquements aux exigences formulées par les articles 1er al. 2 et 15 de la loi de 1986.

9.2.2 *La fermeture de lieux de culte*

Dans le contexte de la lutte contre des actions terroristes inspirées par une idéologie religieuse, le droit français s'est doté, en 2017, d'un dispositif qui permet à l'autorité administrative d'ordonner la fermeture temporaire d'un lieu de culte.

À l'origine,[38] la mesure de fermeture ne pouvait être prononcée qu'« aux seules fins de prévenir la commission d'actes de terrorisme » (art. L. 227-1 du code de la sécurité intérieure). C'est dans cette perspective que devaient être appréciés « les propos qui sont tenus, les idées ou théories qui sont diffusées ou les activités qui se déroulent » dans le lieu de culte, lorsqu'ils « provoquent à la violence, à la haine ou à la discrimination, provoquent à la commission d'actes de terrorisme ou font l'apologie de tels actes ». Seuls pouvaient donc tomber sous le coup de la loi des discours de haine réellement et immédiatement dangereux, ce que le juge administratif vérifie en s'appuyant sur un faisceau d'indices,[39]

L'administration n'étant pas toujours en mesure d'établir un lien entre les propos haineux et le risque terroriste, le législateur a volé à son secours en créant un dispositif parallèle, intégré dans la loi du 9 décembre 1905 concernant la séparation des Églises

---

[37] CC, 88-248 DC du 17 janvier 1989, *Loi modifiant la loi n° 86-1067 du 30 septembre 1986 relative à la liberté de communication,* cons. 26 à 32.

[38] Loi nº 2017-1510 du 30 octobre 2017 renforçant la sécurité intérieure et la lutte contre le terrorisme. Le mécanisme de fermeture administrative d'un lieu de culte était créé par cette loi à titre provisoire et expérimental mais le provisoire est rapidement devenu définitif. La loi n° 2021-998 du 30 juillet 2021 relative à la prévention d'actes de terrorisme et au renseignement a en effet pérennisé et élargi la disposition initiale, puisque la mesure de fermeture peut désormais viser, en même temps que le lieu de culte, tout local dépendant du lieu de culte. Le Conseil constitutionnel a estimé qu'au regard de l'objectif de lutte contre le terrorisme et des garanties dont le dispositif est assorti, celui-ci ne méconnaît ni la liberté de conscience et le libre exercice des cultes, ni la liberté d'expression et de communication, le droit d'expression collective des idées et des opinions, la liberté d'association ou le droit à un recours juridictionnel effectif (2017-695 QPC du 29 mars 2018 *M. Rouchdi B. et autre* [Mesures administratives de lutte contre le terrorisme]).

[39] Voir par exemple CE, ord., 31 janvier 2018, *Association des musulmans du boulevard National*, n° 417332 (« il résulte de l'instruction et d'une note blanche du 3 novembre 2017, précise et circonstanciée, qui a été versée au contradictoire, que la mosquée As Sounna a diffusé, à travers les prêches de son imam, [...] dont certains sont publiés sur son site internet, des appels à la haine et à la violence contre les Chrétiens, les Juifs, les Chiites et les personnes adultères, en des termes particulièrement explicites [...]; que, de même, dans ces prêches, l'iman légitime et glorifie le 'djihad' ; que, par ailleurs, il n'a pas été sérieusement contesté que la mosquée prônait un islamisme radical dont l'influence s'étendait à l'ensemble de la vie locale, en particulier sur les plus jeunes, et qu'au moins cinq fidèles sont partis rejoindre la zone irako-syrienne pour faire le 'djihad' »).

et de l'État.[40] La durée de fermeture qu'il autorise est plus courte (deux mois au lieu de six), mais le préfet peut se fonder - indépendamment de tout lien avec le risque terroriste - sur le seul constat de la diffusion, au sein du lieu de culte, de « propos », « idées ou théories » qui « provoquent à la haine ou à la violence envers une personne ou un groupe de personnes ou tendent à justifier ou à encourager cette haine ou cette violence ». Le Conseil constitutionnel, lors de son examen de la loi, n'a rien trouvé à redire à cette disposition.[41]

9.2.3 La dissolution administrative des associations

L'article L. 212-1 du code de la sécurité intérieure (CSI) permet de dissoudre, par un décret adopté en conseil des ministres, des associations ou groupements de fait qui « soit provoquent à la discrimination, à la haine ou à la violence envers une personne ou un groupe de personnes à raison de leur origine ou de leur appartenance ou de leur non-appartenance, à une ethnie, une nation, une race ou une religion déterminée, soit propagent des idées ou théories tendant à justifier ou encourager cette discrimination, cette haine ou cette violence ».

Ce motif de dissolution administrative d'une association a été introduit, dans une loi de 1936 dirigée contre les milices d'extrême-droite,[42] par la loi Pleven de 1972 sur la lutte contre le racisme (Sect. 9.1.1). Les deux hypothèses envisagées par le texte (« soit provoquent », « soit propagent ») sont distinctes l'une de l'autre, car la propagation d'idées « peut parfaitement ne pas inciter ouvertement les destinataires à se livrer aux agissements visés, et se distinguer ainsi nettement de la provocation directe ».[43] La simple diffusion d'idées ou théories « haineuses » expose ainsi une association à être dissoute par décret en conseil des ministres.

Le problème est qu'en démocratie, les opinions sont libres. Pour éviter d'apparaître comme un censeur politique, le gouvernement s'efforce donc, en général, de combiner ce fondement – énoncé au 6° de l'article L. 212-1 CSI - avec un des six autres motifs de dissolution prévus par cet article. Les plus fréquemment invoqués sont le fait de provoquer à des manifestations armées (« ou à des agissements violents à l'encontre des personnes ou des biens », depuis la loi du 24 août 2021 confortant le respect des principes de la République), de présenter le caractère de groupes de combat ou de milices privées, ou de se livrer « sur le territoire français ou à partir de ce territoire, à des agissements en vue de provoquer des actes de terrorisme en France ou à l'étranger » (motif ajouté par la loi n° 86-1020 du 9 septembre 1986 relative à la lutte contre le terrorisme).

---

[40] Loi n° 2021-1109 du 24 août 2021 confortant le respect des principes de la République, art. 87.

[41] CC, 2021-823 DC du 13 août 2021, *Loi confortant le respect des principes de la République*.

[42] Loi du 10 janvier 1936 sur les groupes de combat et milices privées.

[43] Concl. A. Lallet sur l'arrêt CE, 2 juillet 2021, *Association Génération identitaire*, n° 451741.

Une dissolution fondée uniquement sur le discours et l'idéologie « haineuses » de l'association est longtemps restée très rare,[44] même si elle était admise par le Conseil d'État.[45] Depuis le milieu des années 2010, cette pratique tend toutefois à se banaliser, sous l'effet d'une double évolution.

D'abord, le Conseil d'État semble désormais encourager le gouvernement à oser fonder sa décision sur ce seul motif. Lorsque les éléments invoqués par le ministère de l'Intérieur pour combiner le 6° de l'article L. 212-1 CSI à d'autres motifs de dissolution apparaissent excessivement artificiels, le Conseil d'État indique au gouvernement qu'il n'était pas nécessaire de se donner tant de peine: la décision de dissolution est *tout de même légale*, car « le Président de la République aurait pris la même décision s'il n'avait retenu que le motif de dissolution » énoncé au 6°.[46]

Ensuite, le législateur a élargi le périmètre des discours de haine qui peuvent être imputés à l'association. La loi du 24 août 2021 confortant le respect des principes de la République a en effet posé que l'association est comptable des propos tenus par ses dirigeants, mais aussi par ses membres « agissant en cette qualité », ou par quiconque apparaît « directement lié » à ses activités. Ce sera le cas d'un abonné à ses comptes sur les réseaux sociaux, par exemple, dès lors que l'association avait connaissance de ses propos et qu'elle s'est abstenue d'y mettre un terme, ou de s'en désolidariser explicitement. La loi réécrit aussi un peu le 6° de l'article L. 212-1 CSI, qui se lit désormais ainsi (les ajouts sont en italiques): « soit provoquent *ou contribuent par leurs agissements* à la discrimination, à la haine ou à la violence envers une personne ou un groupe de personnes à raison de leur origine, *de leur sexe, de leur orientation sexuelle, de leur identité de genre* ou de leur appartenance ou de leur non-appartenance, *vraie ou supposée*, à une ethnie, une nation, une *prétendue* race ou une religion déterminée, soit propagent des idées ou théories tendant à justifier ou encourager cette discrimination, cette haine ou cette violence ».

Dans l'immense majorité des cas, le juge administratif admet (au visa de l'article 11 DDHC et/ou des articles 10 et 11 CEDH) que si la dissolution contestée devant lui porte atteinte à l'exercice des libertés d'expression et d'association, l'atteinte est justifiée par la gravité des dangers que l'association fait peser sur l'ordre public.

---

[44] Voir toutefois le décret de dissolution du groupe Unité radicale (2 août 2002), qui énonce sans ambages que « pour des raisons inhérentes aux nécessités de l'ordre public, il convient de réprimer les manifestations d'une idéologie raciste et discriminatoire ».

[45] CE, 17 novembre 2006, n° 296214, *Capo Chichi* (à propos de Tribu Ka, un groupe qui « se livre à la propagation d'idées et de théories tendant à justifier et à encourager la discrimination, la haine et la violence raciales, notamment à l'encontre des personnes qui ne sont pas de couleur noire, [qui] prône également l'antisémitisme et [qui] a organisé des actions menaçantes à l'égard de personnes de confession juive »).

[46] Pour des exemples, qui concernent tous des associations d'extrême-droite ou islamistes: CE, 30 décembre 2014, *Association jeunesses nationalistes*, n°372320 ; CE, 15 décembre 2017, *Association des musulmans de Lagny-sur-Marne*, n°401378 ; CE, 26 janvier 2018, *Association Rahma de Torcy-Marne-la-Vallée*, n°412312 ; CE, 2 juillet 2021, *Génération identitaire*, n° 451741 ; CE, 24 septembre 2021, *Barakacity*, n° 445979, CE, 24 septembre 2021, n° 449215, *Collectif contre l'islamophobie en France.*

9.3 Pacte international relatif aux droits civils et politiques

La France a ratifié le PIDCP le 4 novembre 1980, sans formuler de réserves relatives à l'article 20-2 (« Tout appel à la haine nationale, raciale ou religieuse qui constitue une incitation à la discrimination, à l'hostilité ou à la violence est interdit par la loi »). Son dispositif de lutte contre le discours de haine, en tant que tel, n'a jamais fait l'objet de critiques de la part du Comité des droits de l'homme.

Celui-ci, en 2015, a toutefois jugé « préoccupante » « la recrudescence de discours racistes et xénophobes dans la sphère tant publique que politique », et a incité la France à « rappeler régulièrement et publiquement que tout appel à la haine qui constitue une incitation à la discrimination, à l'hostilité ou à la violence est interdit par la loi et [à] agir promptement pour traduire les auteurs en justice ».[47]

La France a adhéré au protocole facultatif le 17 février 1984, mais la procédure de communication individuelle n'a été utilisée qu'une seule fois par une personne condamnée par les juridictions internes pour « discours de haine ». Il s'agissait du négationniste Robert Faurisson, qui avait déclaré: «j'ai d'excellentes raisons de ne pas croire à cette politique d'extermination des Juifs ou à la magique chambre à gaz... Je souhaite que 100 % des Français se rendent compte que le mythe des chambres à gaz est une gredinerie ». Le Comité a estimé que la condamnation de Robert Faurisson n'avait pas porté atteinte à sa liberté d'opinion et d'expression, car elle sanctionnait une atteinte aux droits et à la réputation d'autrui. Il a affirmé que la loi Gayssot (Sect. 9.1.2), « telle qu'elle a été lue, interprétée et appliquée dans le cas de l'auteur par les tribunaux français, est compatible avec les dispositions du Pacte ». Plus largement, il a « noté l'argument de l'État partie qui a fait valoir que la promulgation de la loi Gayssot s'inscrivait dans la lutte contre le racisme et l'antisémitisme. Il a également noté la déclaration d'un membre du Gouvernement français, le Ministre de la justice de l'époque, pour qui la négation de l'holocauste était le principal vecteur de l'antisémitisme ».[48]

L'article 20-2 PIDCP ne semble pas être d'application directe en droit interne. Le Conseil d'État a toutefois admis, au moins une fois, qu'il pouvait être invoqué par des requérants, en l'occurrence contre l'enseignement à l'école de *La Marseillaise*, hymne national qui contient les phrases « Qu'un sang impur abreuve nos sillons » et « Quoi, ces cohortes étrangères feraient la loi dans nos foyers ! ». La requête a évidemment été rejetée.[49]

[47] Comité des droits de l'homme, Observations finales concernant le 5e rapport périodique de la France, adoptées le 21 juillet 2015, CCPR/C/FRZ/CO.5, pt 23.

[48] *Robert Faurisson c. France*, Communication No. 550/1993, U.N. Doc. CCPR/C/58/D/550/1993 [1996].

[49] CE, n° 350541, 23 décembre 2011, *Association DIH-Mouvement de protestation civique.*

9.4 Convention internationale sur l'élimination de toutes les formes de discrimination raciale

La France a adhéré à la Convention internationale sur l'élimination de toutes les formes de discrimination raciale par la loi du 28 mai 1971. En déposant l'instrument d'adhésion, le gouvernement a formulé une observation sur l'article 4(a), qui impose aux États de « déclarer délits punissables par la loi toute diffusion d'idées fondées sur la supériorité ou la haine raciale »: « en ce qui concerne l'article 4, la France tient à préciser qu'elle interprète la référence qui y est faite aux principes de la Déclaration universelle des droits de l'homme ainsi qu'aux droits énoncés dans l'article 5 de la même convention comme déliant les États parties de l'obligation d'édicter des dispositions répressives qui ne soient pas compatibles avec les libertés d'opinion et d'expression, de réunion et d'association pacifiques qui sont garanties par ces textes ».[50] S'agit-il d'une « réserve » ? Le Comité onusien chargé du suivi de la convention l'affirme avec constance, mais le gouvernement français le nie depuis l'origine.[51]

Quoiqu'il en soit de cette « réserve » ou « déclaration interprétative », la France a mis son droit interne en conformité avec les exigences de l'article 4(a) de la Convention, en tant que celui-ci impose également aux États de sanctionner l'incitation à la discrimination raciale, ainsi que la provocation à la violence ethnique ou raciale. La loi du 1er juillet 1972 (Sect. 9.1.2) a en effet décidé:

- d'incriminer la provocation à la haine raciale
- de modifier la définition de la diffamation et de l'injure raciales, qui jusqu'alors n'étaient punissables qu'à la condition que les propos incriminés aient eu « pour but d'exciter à la haine entre les citoyens ou les habitants »[52]
- d'ouvrir aux associations habilitées la faculté de se constituer parties civiles
- de prévoir un mécanisme de dissolution administrative des groupements provoquant à la discrimination raciale

Le terrain de la dissolution des associations est le seul qui relaie l'interdiction formulée par l'article 4(a) de « toute diffusion d'idées fondées sur la supériorité ou la haine raciale ». En dehors de cette hypothèse d'expression *collective* d'une idéologie raciste, l'expression publique du racisme n'est pas interdite en tant que telle. Elle ne peut être réprimée qu'à la double condition de relever d'une des trois catégories instituées par la loi (provocation, diffamation, injure) et de viser une personne ou un groupe de personnes à raison de leur origine ou de leur appartenance ou de leur

---

[50] Décret n° 71-901 du 2 novembre 1971 portant publication de la Convention internationale sur l'élimination toutes les formes de discrimination raciale, ouverte à la signature à New York le 7 mars 1966, *JORF* du 10 novembre 1971.

[51] Décret préc.: « En réponse à une demande du secrétaire général des Nations Unies, il a été précisément ultérieurement qu'en formulant une déclaration concernant l'article 4, l'intention du Gouvernement français n'est pas de réduire la portée des obligations prévues par la Convention en ce qui le concerne, mais seulement de consigner son interprétation dudit article ».

[52] Décret-loi Marchandeau du 21 avril 1939.

non-appartenance à une ethnie, à une nation, une race ou une origine *déterminée*. Il est donc impossible de poursuivre l'auteur d'une phrase comme « oui, je crois à l'inégalité des races » (prononcée en 1996 par un homme politique d'extrême-droite, et qui avait fait scandale).

Face à ce constat, un projet de loi avait envisagé d'incriminer la parole raciste *en général*.[53] Mais les protestations – au nom de liberté d'opinion et d'expression – furent d'une ampleur telle que le projet ne fut jamais examiné par le parlement. Le Comité pour l'élimination de la discrimination raciale reproche encore à la France cette « lacune » dans sa législation.[54]

9.5 La Convention européenne des droits de l'homme

La France a ratifié la Convention européenne des droits de l'homme le 3 mai 1974. Elle a admis le droit de requête individuelle le 2 octobre 1981.

9.5.1 L'application de l'article 10 de la Convention EDH par le juge national

Toutes les juridictions françaises – à l'exception du Conseil constitutionnel - veillent à ce que les prescriptions de l'article 10 soient respectées dans l'ordre interne. Lorsque des plaideurs invoquent devant elles une ingérence dans leur droit à la liberté d'expression garanti par l'article 10 de la Convention, elles sont tenues d'appliquer les standards de contrôle européen, même si elles s'y emploient avec un zèle variable (il n'est pas rare de voir le triple contrôle de légalité, légitimité et proportionnalité d'une mesure litigieuse ramassé en une phrase lapidaire).

Certaines notions issues de la jurisprudence européenne jouent désormais un rôle non négligeable dans l'analyse juridictionnelle des discours de haine. Tel est surtout le cas de la notion de « contribution à un débat d'intérêt général », qui peut conduire à écarter, au cas par cas, la qualification d'injure ou de provocation à la discrimination raciale.[55] Mais l'avancée la plus spectaculaire a été réalisé en 2020, lorsque

---

[53] Projet de loi « Toubon » relatif à la lutte contre le racisme, n° 3045, déposé sur le bureau de l'Assemblée nationale le 16 octobre 1996. La Commission nationale consultative des droits de l'homme, chargé du suivi, en France, de l'application de la Convention ERD, avait approuvé le projet, en soulignant que la France parachèverait ainsi l'exécution de ses engagements au titre de l'article 4(a).

[54] Observations finales concernant les 20e et 21e rapports périodiques de la France, adoptées les 8 et 11 mai 2015, CERD/C/FRA/CO/20-21, § 7.

[55] Par ex Cass., crim.,7 juin 2011, n°10-85.179, (jugeant que des propos violemment hostiles aux Roms « portant sur une question d'intérêt public relative aux difficultés d'intégration de la communauté rom, ne dépassaient pas les limites admissibles de la liberté d'expression ») ou Cass. crim., 11 décembre 2018, n° 18-80.525 (replaçant les paroles de la chanson « Nique la France » dans le

la Cour de cassation a adopté un nouveau contrôle de proportionnalité inspiré des méthodes du juge de Strasbourg. Ce contrôle dit concret, ou de balance des intérêts *in casu,* consiste à atténuer, voire paralyser, l'application de la loi pénale lorsque la condamnation de l'auteur de l'infraction lèserait, de manière disproportionnée, son droit à la liberté d'expression. Avant de condamner une militante Femen pour délit d'exhibition sexuelle,[56] ou des militants écologistes pour vol en réunion du portrait du Président de la République,[57] le juge du fond doit désormais s'assurer que son incrimination, si le comportement des prévenus « s'inscrit dans une démarche de protestation politique», que son incrimination, « compte tenu de la nature et du contexte de l'agissement en cause », ne constitue pas une ingérence disproportionnée dans l'exercice de la liberté d'expression.

9.5.2 Le contrôle par la Cour EDH du respect par la France de l'article 10

Pour la Cour de Strasbourg, «la tolérance et l'égale dignité de tous les êtres humains constituent le fondement d'une société démocratique et pluraliste. Il en résulte qu'en principe, on peut juger nécessaire, dans les sociétés démocratiques, de sanctionner, *voire de prévenir*, toutes les formes d'expression qui *propagent, incitent à, promeuvent ou justifient* la haine fondée sur l'intolérance ».[58] Cette appréhension très large du « discours de haine », reprise d'une Recommandation formulée par le Comité des ministres en 1997, ne pouvait pas conduire la Cour à accueillir avec bienveillance les auteurs de propos haineux sanctionnés par des juridictions françaises. Leurs victoires se comptent sur les doigts d'une seule main.

Propos antisémites

À deux reprises, la Cour a fait jouer le mécanisme de l'article 17 (abus de droit) à l'encontre de personnes condamnées en France pour propos antisémites: propos négationnistes[59] et injure à l'égard de l'ensemble des personnes d'origine ou de confession juive.[60] La Cour a par ailleurs jugé irrecevable la requête d'un requérant

contexte d'un « débat d'intérêt général » relatif au racisme de la société française, qu'elle aurait hérité de son passé colonial). En sens inverse, la Cour de cassation a censuré l'arrêt d'une cour d'appel qui avait estimé que la vente sur Internet d'un tract affichant le slogan « Islam assassin, Islam dehors » pouvait s'inscrire dans le cadre d'un débat d'intérêt général relatif à la critique d'une religion (Cass. crim. 16 mars 2021, n° 20-83.325).

[56] Cass. crim., 26 février 2020, n° 19-81.827.

[57] Cass. crim., 18 mai 2022, n° 20-87.272.

[58] CourEDH, *Erbakan c. Turquie*, 6 juillet 2006, req. n° 59405/00, § 56. Souligné par nous.

[59] CourEDH, *Garaudy c. France* du 24 juin 2003, req. n° 65831/01 (soulignant que « la contestation de crimes contre l'humanité apparaît comme l'une des formes les plus aigües de diffamation raciale envers les Juifs et d'incitation à la haine à leur égard »).

[60] CourEDH, 20 octobre 2015, *M'Bala M'Bala c. France*, req. n°25239/13 (« dès lors que les faits litigieux, tant dans leur contenu que dans leur tonalité générale, et donc dans leur but, ont un

relaxé par le juge judiciaire mais frappé par une sanction administrative pour avoir tenu des propos négationnistes.[61]

Provocation à la discrimination, à la haine, à la violence envers une personne ou un groupe de personnes, à raison de leur origine, ou de leur appartenance ou de leur non-appartenance à une ethnie, une nation, une race ou une religion déterminée.

La Cour a jugé à diverses reprises qu'une condamnation prononcée sur le fondement de l'article 24 al. 7 de la loi de 1881 répondait aux exigences de prévisibilité de la loi, de but légitime (protéger la réputation ou les droits d'autrui), et de nécessité « dans une société démocratique ».[62] D'autres requêtes ont été rejetées comme manifestement mal fondées.[63] La Cour a toutefois réservé un sort moins favorable à l'appel au boycott.

En droit français, l'appel au boycott s'analyse comme une provocation à la discrimination ethnique, raciale, nationale ou religieuse s'il incite le public à ne pas acheter des marchandises (ou des services) proposés par des membres d'un groupe ethnique, racial, national ou religieux. Cette incrimination, dans l'ordre interne, avait été jugée conforme à Constitution par la Cour de cassation.[64] La Cour de Strasbourg elle-même, dans un arrêt du 16 juillet 2009, avait admis qu'un maire condamné pour avoir appelé les services municipaux à ne plus acheter de produits alimentaires israéliens n'avait pas été condamné pour ses opinions politiques, mais pour une incitation à commettre un acte discriminatoire à l'égard de ressortissants d'une nation.[65] Mais elle s'est ravisée par un arrêt du 11 juin 2020, qui affirme que « l'appel au boycott constitue une modalité particulière d'exercice de la liberté d'expression en ce qu'il combine l'expression d'une opinion protestataire et l'incitation à un traitement différenciée, de sorte que *selon les circonstances qui le caractérisent*, il est susceptible de constituer un appel à la discrimination d'autrui »[66]. Quel genre de circonstances ? La Cour européenne est restée elliptique sur ce point, ce qui fera

caractère négationniste et antisémite marqué, la Cour considère que le requérant tente de détourner l'article 10 de sa vocation en utilisant son droit à la liberté d'expression à des fins contraires au texte et à l'esprit de la convention et qui, si elles étaient admises, contribueraient à la destruction des droits et libertés garantis par la Convention », § 40).

[61] CourEDH, 7 juin 2011, *Bruno Gollnisch c. France*, n°48135/08 (« la contribution éventuelle de ses propos aux thèses négationnistes et le désordre qui pouvait en résulter, et qui en est d'ailleurs résulté, au sein de l'université de Lyon III et, plus généralement de l'université française, était incompatible avec les devoirs et responsabilités qui incombaient au requérant en tant qu'enseignant »).

[62] CourEDH, 10 juillet 2008, *Soulas c. France*, req. n° 15948/03 (condamnation des deux auteurs d'un ouvrage dénonçant l'invasion de la France par les immigrés, notamment musulmans) et *Sanchez c. France* du 6 juillet 2021, req. n° 45581/15, confirmé par la gde chambre le 15 mai 2023 (condamnation d'un homme politique qui n'avait pas retiré du mur de son compte Facebook le propos d'un tiers provoquant à la haine ou la violence ethnique, nationale, raciale ou religieuse).

[63] CourEDH, *Seurot c. France* du 18 mai 2004, n° 57383/00 (condamnation pénale et sanctions administratives à l'égard d'un professeur qui avait publié dans le journal du collège un texte évoquant « des hordes musulmanes inassimilables ») et *Le Pen c. France* du 20 avril 2010, req. n° 18788/09 (condamnation de propos sur les musulmans tenus dans deux organes de presse).

[64] Cass. crim., 7 juin 2011, n° 10-88.315 (non-renvoi de QPC).

[65] CourEDH, 16 juillet 2009, *Willem c. France*, req. n° 10883/05.

[66] CourEDH,11 juin 2020, *Baldassi et al. c. France*, req. n° 15271/16, pt 64.

sans doute hésiter les juridictions françaises à entrer en voie de condamnation. Ce débat rejoint celui qui entoure le nouveau contrôle de proportionnalité pratiqué par la Cour de cassation (Sect. 9.5.1).

Délit d'apologie

La Cour a jugé compatibles avec la Convention des condamnations prononcées en France pour apologie d'actes de terrorisme (attentats du 11 septembre 2001 à New York[67]), sauf dans un cas où la peine prononcée lui a semblée disproportionnée.[68]

Elle s'est montrée nettement plus circonspecte à l'égard de l'apologie des crimes ou délits de collaboration avec l'occupant nazi. Tout en rappelant qu'il ne lui appartient pas de juger une disposition législative *in abstracto*, elle a jugé disproportionnée une amende (d'1 Franc) infligée aux auteurs d'un encart publicitaire à la gloire du maréchal Pétain: « même si des propos tels que ceux des requérants sont toujours de nature à ranimer la controverse et à raviver des souffrances dans la population, le recul du temps entraîne qu'il ne conviendrait pas, quarante ans après, de leur appliquer la même sévérité que dix ou vingt ans auparavant. Cela participe des efforts que tout pays est appelé à fournir pour débattre ouvertement et sereinement de sa propre histoire ».[69] La même nécessité de protéger le « débat historique d'intérêt général » a justifié un second constat de violation, dans une affaire relative à l'apologie de crimes de guerre commis par la France en Algérie.[70]

Dissolution Administrative d'associations

Dans le prolongement d'arrêts confirmant que la dissolution d'associations de supporters « hooligans » était compatible avec la Convention,[71] la Cour a rejeté les requêtes d'associations d'extrême-droite dissoutes sur le fondement de l'article L. 212-1 CSI (Sect. 9.2.3), opposant même à deux d'entre elles l'effet « guillotine » de l'article 17.[72]

---

[67] CourEDH, 2 octobre 2008, *Leroy c. France*, req n°36109/03 (dessin des attentats du *World Trade Center* accompagné de la légende « Nous en avions tous rêvé, le Hamas l'a fait ») et CourEDH, 2 septembre 2021, *Z.B. c. France*, req. 46883/15 (enfant habillé d'un T-shirt portant dans le dos l'inscription « Jihad, né le 11 septembre » et sur la poitrine « je suis une bombe »).

[68] CourEDH, 23 juin 2022, *Rouillan c. France*, req n° 2800/19 (lourde peine de prison pour un ancien membre d'Action directe qui avait jugé « très courageux » les auteurs du massacre de la rédaction de *Charlie Hebdo*).

[69] CourEDH, 23 septembre 1998, *Lehideux et Isorni c. France*, req. n°24662/94.

[70] CourEDH, 15 janvier 2005, *Orban c. France*, req. n°20985/05.

[71] CourEDH, 22 février 2011, *Association nouvelle des Boulogne Boys c. France*, req. n° 6468/09 ; CEDH, 27 octobre 2016, *Les Authentiks et Supras Auteuil 91 c. France*, req. n° 4696/11 et 4703/11.

[72] CourEDH, 8 octobre 2020, *Ayoub et autres c. France*, req. n° 77400/14, 34532/15 et 34550/15 (les dirigeants de ces associations ont « abusé de leur liberté d'association, en tant qu'organisations radicales menaçant le processus politique démocratique, en contradiction avec les valeurs de tolérance, de paix sociale et de non-discrimination qui sous-tendent la Convention », § 138).

9.6 La jurisprudence

Le régime français de la liberté de la liberté d'expression est un régime législatif, comme le prévoit l'article 11 de la Déclaration de 1789. C'est la loi qui érige en délits certains abus de la liberté d'expression. C'est la loi qui créé des polices spéciales protégeant l'ordre public contre d'autres abus de cette même liberté (police du cinéma, police des réunions publiques, police des spectacles, police des publications destinées à la jeunesse…). L'apport de la jurisprudence, pour autant, est loin d'être négligeable, en droit administratif comme en droit pénal.

9.6.1 Police administrative générale

Le Conseil d'État a mobilisé la notion de dignité de la personne humaine pour faire évoluer la définition du discours de haine au-delà des hypothèses prévues par la loi. Il a en effet décidé que l'autorité administrative pouvait, même en l'absence de risque de troubles matériels à l'ordre public, interdire *ex ante* un discours attentatoire à la dignité. Il a ainsi admis l'interdiction d'un spectacle où il était hautement prévisible que des propos antisémites et négationnistes seraient proférés (affaire *Dieudonné*[73]), et il ne s'est pas opposé à l'interdiction de la conférence publique d'un imam salafiste « théoricien » de l'infériorité des femmes.[74] Mais ce type de décision reste très rare. Pour prononcer à titre préventif une mesure d'interdiction, l'autorité administrative doit en effet établir que le risque d'atteinte à la dignité humaine se réalisera de manière presque certaine, et résultera de propos qui, par ailleurs, tombent sous le coup de la loi pénale.[75] Ce sera évidemment le cas d'un banquet organisé en hommage au négationniste Robert Faurisson,[76] puisqu'il n'existe aucun doute sur la teneur des propos qui seront échangés lors de ce banquet, ni sur leur qualification pénale.

L'invocation du respect de la dignité humaine pour prévenir ou faire cesser des discours de haine est donc d'un maniement très encadré. Elle n'en séduit pas moins de nombreux requérants, qui se tournent vers le juge administratif pour obtenir, au nom du respect de la dignité, l'interdiction de tel ou tel acte expressif qu'ils jugent raciste,[77] ou sexiste.[78] Devant le Conseil d'État (soucieux de ne pas alimenter l'appétit de censure qui émane de la société civile), ils échouent systématiquement.

---

[73] CE, ord. ref., 9 janvier 2014, *Société Les Productions de la Plume et M. D.,* n° 374508.

[74] CE, ord. ref., 4 mars 2023, *Madame C.,* n° 471871.

[75] V. exprimant un doute sur chacun de ces deux points et suspendant l'interdiction d'un concert de rap décidé par le maire, CE, ord. ref., 17 mars 2023, *Commune de Rennes,* n° 472161.

[76] TA Clermont-Ferrand, ord. ref., 24 janvier 2020, *M. F. et M. D.*, n° 2000155.

[77] CE, ord. ref. 11 décembre 2014, *Centre Dumas-Pouchkine* (à propos du spectacle *Exhibit B.);* CE, ord. ref., 16 avril 2015, *Société Grasse Boulange* (à propos de la vente de pâtisseries « têtes de nègres ») ; TA Lille, ord. ref., 9 mai 2018, *Conseil représentatif des associations noires de France,* n°1802009 (bal « nuit des Noirs » à Dunkerque).

[78] CE, ord. ref., 1er septembre 2017, *Commune de Dannemarie*, n° 413607 (panneaux « sexy » implantés par la commune à l'occasion de la journée des droits des femmes) ; CAA Marseille, 18

La Cour de cassation, de son côté, a solennellement énoncé que si l'atteinte à la dignité peut être prise en compte dans l'exercice de mise en balance des intérêts en présence, elle ne saurait constituer un fondement autonome des restrictions à la liberté d'expression.[79]

9.6.2 *Droit pénal*

La définition du discours de haine en droit pénal - de manière plus surprenante puisque dans cette matière les textes sont, en principe, d'interprétation stricte - évolue, elle aussi, sous l'impulsion de la jurisprudence. Le cas le plus connu (et le plus problématique) concerne l'article 24 al. 7 de la loi du 29 juillet 1881 sur la liberté de la presse (« provocation à la discrimination, à la haine ou à la violence à l'égard d'une personne ou d'un groupe de personnes à raison de leur origine ou de leur appartenance ou de leur non-appartenance à une ethnie, une nation, une race ou une religion déterminée »).

Depuis l'origine, la chambre criminelle de la Cour de cassation hésite entre plusieurs approches de ce délit. Elle pose parfois que l'infraction est caractérisée lorsque le discours litigieux est « propre à susciter un sentiment d'hostilité ou de rejet » envers un groupe déterminé.[80] Il suffit alors que le propos *tende,* ou soit *de nature à* susciter un tel sentiment, à condition qu'il atteigne une certaine intensité (variable selon les circonstances), et que les membres du groupe considérés soient mis en cause à raison de caractéristiques protégées par la loi (le degré de protection semblant, lui aussi, varier selon le type de caractéristiques en cause). Mais à d'autres reprises, la Cour exige davantage, en approuvant des relaxes fondées sur l'absence « d'exhortation ou de provocation caractérisée»,[81] ou « d'incitation manifeste, d'instigation ou d'exhortation».[82] Dans cette seconde perspective, le propos n'est condamnable que si son auteur a délibérément *appelé* à la discrimination ou la violence, l'appel devant présenter un degré suffisant de précision. Ainsi, lorsqu'un maire diffuse des photos de classe en guise de preuve du « grand remplacement » des élèves blancs par des élèves d'une autre couleur, il doit être relaxé car la teneur de son propos « restait trop floue et imprécise pour contenir le moindre appel, même implicite, à la discrimination, la haine ou la violence ».[83] L'hypothèse de l'exhortation

---

janvier 2021, *Osez le féminisme ! et Mouvement citoyennes maintenant*, n° 19MA00274 (affiches parodiques créées par la commune pour critiquer la politique ferroviaire de l'État).

[79] Cass. ass. plénière, 25 octobre 2019, n° 17-86.605.

[80] Par ex. Cass. crim. 1er février 2017, n° 15-84.511, approuvant la cour d'appel d'avoir retenu que « les limites du droit à la libre expression ont été dépassées, les propos tenus suscitant un sentiment d'hostilité ou de rejet envers un groupe de personnes déterminées » (Rom présentés par un maire comme des voleurs et des incendiaires).

[81] Cass. crim, 28 janvier 1992, n° 91-81.778 (tract intitulé « Non à l'islamisation de Saint-Nazaire »).

[82] Cass., crim., 7 décembre 1993, n° 92-81.091 (numéro de *Fluide glacial* tournant en dérision des religieuses catholiques).

[83] Cass., crim., 4 juin 2019, n° 18-82.742.

« implicite » (qui ne simplifie pas les choses…) a en revanche été admise, quelques semaines plus tard, pour le tweet « trop de Noirs dans l'équipe de France. Trop de juifs à la télé ! ».[84]

Cette oscillation entre plusieurs définitions du délit de provocation raciale a été relevée par la Cour européenne des droits de l'homme, qui a estimé qu'elle ne contrevenait pas aux exigences d'accessibilité et de prévisibilité requises par l'article 10 § 2 de la Convention.[85] Cette appréciation généreuse (ou laxiste ?) s'appuie notamment sur le *satisfecit* que la Cour de cassation a délivré à sa propre jurisprudence: les termes de l'article 24 al. 7 « sont suffisamment clairs et précis pour que l'interprétation de ce texte, qui entre dans l'office du juge pénal, puisse se faire sans risque d'arbitraire » (Sect. 9.1.1).

Gwénaële Calvès is Professor of Public Law at the University of Cergy-Pontoise, France. Her research focuses on free expression, non-discrimination, and *laïcité*. Her recent books include *Envoyer les racistes en prison ? Le procès des insulteurs de Christiane Taubira*, L.G.D.J., 2015 ; *Territoires disputés de la laïcité. 44 questions (plus ou moins) épineuses*, P.U.F., 2018, ; *La laïcité*, La Découverte, 2022 et *La discrimination positive*, P.U.F., 5th ed., 2024. Along with philosopher Charles Girard, Calvès is currently preparing a collection of scholarly analyses entitled *Grandes décisions de la liberté d'expression en Europe.*

---

[84] Cass., crim., 15 octobre 2019, n° 18-85.365.

[85] Cour EDH, *Zemmour c. France*, 20 décembre 2022, n° 63539/19, § 13 à 15 et 42 à 44 ; *Sanchez c. France* [gde ch], 15 mai 2023, n° 45581/15, § 44 et 129.

Chapter 10
Germany

Brian Valerius

Contents

B. Valerius (✉)
University of Passau, Passau, Germany
e-mail: brian.valerius@uni-passau.de

E. Heinze (ed.), *Criminalising Hate Speech*,
https://doi.org/10.1007/978-94-6265-650-5_10

Abstract This chapter summarises the legal situation regarding hateful expression in Germany. Such statements are also covered by freedom of expression. However, this does not mean that hate speech is not punishable in Germany in view of the rights of those affected. Increasingly, social network providers are also involved in the fight against hate speech. International conventions, although signed by Germany, are at best of minor importance in dealing with hate speech. Also the impact of European legal instruments on national criminal law is still rather limited. Instead, legislation in Germany primarily reacts to current events and social developments. Sometimes reference is made to the special historical responsibility that Germany has due to the crimes of the National Socialist reign of violence and arbitrariness.

Keyword Freedom of expression · Hate speech · German Basic Law · German Criminal Code · Incitement of masses · Network Enforcement Act · Social media

10.1 National Constitutional Law

To outline the significance of constitutional law for legislation, administration and for the courts with regard to hateful expression, first the relevant legal provisions in the German constitution, the Basic Law ('Grundgesetz'),[1] must be briefly summarised. The fundamental right of freedom of expression is enshrined in Article 5 (1) sentence 1 of the Basic Law. According to this, everyone has the 'right freely to express and disseminate his opinions in speech, writing and pictures'. However, according to Article 5 (2) of the Basic Law, freedom of expression 'shall find [its] limits in the provisions of general laws, in provisions for the protection of young persons and in the right to personal honour'. Thus, even the Basic Law does not guarantee unlimited freedom of expression, which can rather be restricted under certain expressly named circumstances. This is referred to as a so-called qualified statutory reservation ('qualifizierter Gesetzesvorbehalt').

The fact that the Basic Law provides limits to freedom of expression does not mean, however, that freedom of opinion is accorded only minor value. Rather, the Federal Constitutional Court has expressly stated that 'the fundamental right to freedom of expression ... as the most direct expression of the human personality in society [is] one of the noblest human rights of all' and that it is 'for a liberal-democratic state order ... absolutely constitutive, because it uniquely enables the constant intellectual debate, the battle of opinions, which is its life force'.[2] Freedom of opinion is important not least in relation to public authority, since fundamental

---

[1] An English translation of the Basic Law is available at https://www.gesetze-im-internet.de/englisch_gg/ (this and all other web sites in this report were last accessed on 12.7.2021).

[2] BVerfG 15.1.1958, *BVerfGE* 7, 198, 208—*Lüth*.

rights in Germany are primarily understood as defensive rights of the citizen against the state. Their function is therefore to ward off interference by the state on the guaranteed freedoms (so-called *status negativus*).

Of the triad of restrictions in Article 5 (2) of the Basic Law, the first-mentioned 'general laws' are the most important.[3] A law can only be described as 'general' in this sense if it is not directed against freedom of opinion per se or against the expression of a particular opinion, but seeks to protect a legal interest (such as honour or public peace).[4] Criminal offences, especially from the German Criminal Code ('Strafgesetzbuch'), are also to be regarded as 'general laws' in this meaning.[5] In each case, however, the legal interest concerned has to be protected in general, i.e. not only against violations through expressions of opinion, but also against impairments in other ways.[6] Accordingly, a regulation restricting opinions would be illegitimate if it is not formulated in a sufficiently open manner and is instead a priori directed only against certain convictions, attitudes or ideologies.[7]

In other words, special law is prohibited ('Sonderrechtsverbot') for all laws restricting opinion (see also Sect. 10.10 below on the controversial Section 130 (4) of the German Criminal Code).[8] These considerations do not only apply to the restrictions of 'general laws', but equally to the other restrictions standardised in Article 5 (2) of the Basic Law ('protection of young persons and the right to personal honour') as well as to provisions for the protection of other legal interests.[9] Article 5 (2) of the Basic Law thus expresses that freedom of expression is basically independent of the content of the statements in question. Whether a statement appears valuable or worthless or right or wrong, whether it is justified emotionally or rationally, is therefore irrelevant to the scope of protection of freedom of opinion.[10] Rather, polemical and hurtful expressions are also covered by freedom of expression.[11]

To limit freedom of expression, it is therefore already inherent in the Basic Law itself to assume conflicting interests, indeed to conflicts involving fundamental rights

---

[3] Schemmer 2021, Article 5 para 98.

[4] BVerfG 15.1.1958, *BVerfGE* 7, 198, 209–210—*Lüth*; BVerfG 10.10.1995, *BVerfGE* 93, 266, 291—'Soldaten sind Mörder'; BVerfG 23.6.2004, *BVerfGE* 111, 147, 155—Inhaltsbezogenes Versammlungsverbot; BVerfG 4.11.2009, *BVerfGE* 124, 300, 321–322—*Wunsiedel*.

[5] Specifically on the offence of incitement of masses (Section 130 of the German Criminal Code) BVerfG 6.9.2000, *NJW* 2001, 61, 62; BVerfG 12.11.2002, *NJW* 2003, 660, 661; BVerfG 23.6.2004, *BVerfGE* 111, 147, 155—Inhaltsbezogenes Versammlungsverbot; specifically on Section 130 (3) of the German Criminal Code BVerfG 22.6.2018, *NJW* 2018, 2861, 2862. For the offence of 'insult' according to Section 185 of the German Criminal Code see BVerfG 10.10.1995, *BVerfGE* 93, 266, 291—'Soldaten sind Mörder'; BVerfG 12.5.2009, *NJW* 2009, 3016, 3017.

[6] BVerfG 23.6.2004, *BVerfGE* 111, 147, 155—Inhaltsbezogenes Versammlungsverbot; BVerfG 4.11.2009, *BVerfGE* 124, 300, 322—*Wunsiedel*.

[7] BVerfG 4.11.2009, *BVerfGE* 124, 300, 323—*Wunsiedel*.

[8] BVerfG 4.11.2009, *BVerfGE* 124, 300, 326–327—*Wunsiedel*.

[9] BVerfG 4.11.2009, *BVerfGE* 124, 300, 327—*Wunsiedel*.

[10] BVerfG 22.6.1982, *BVerfGE* 61, 1, 7—CSU als 'NPD Europas'.

[11] BVerfG 10.10.1995, *BVerfGE* 93, 266, 289—'Soldaten sind Mörder'; BVerfG 19.5.2020, *NJW* 2020, 2622, 2623; BVerfG 19.5.2020, *NJW* 2020, 2629, 2629.

or other values of constitutional rank. There is a reciprocal interaction ('Wechselwirkung') such that the general laws may set limits to freedom of opinion, but must themselves be restricted in their effect of limiting the fundamental right.[12] However, the spillover effect of freedom of expression and its value-setting significance in a free democratic state must be taken into account not only in the enactment of laws restricting opinion, but also in their interpretation.[13] Consequently, conflicting interests must be weighed against each other both in the making of law and in the application of law. The conflict of interests must be resolved by means of practical concordance, i.e. by balancing the conflicting rights as gently as possible.[14]

10.1.1 Freedom of Expression and Hateful Expression

In the case of hateful expression, the provisions of the Basic Law must also be taken into account in order to determine the scope of freedom of expression and to weigh up the conflicting interests. As an example, one may refer to the legislature's justification for the incrimination of 'incitement of masses', which is the prime example of a criminal offence in Germany intended to combat hate crime, including hateful expression (in addition, please see Sect. 10.2 on national statutory or administrative law).

With the Sixth Criminal Law Amendment Act of 30 June 1960,[15] 'incitement of masses' was criminalised in Section 130 of the German Criminal Code. According to this original draft, it was punishable to violate the human dignity of others by inciting hatred against sections of the population (No. 1), by calling for violent or arbitrary measures against them (No. 2) or by insulting, maliciously maligning or defaming them (No. 3). However, this had to be done in a manner likely to cause a breach of the peace.[16] This offence thus entails a violation of human dignity, which stands as the highest value of the German constitution.[17]

Similarly, Section 130 of the German Criminal Code was explicitly described in the explanatory memorandum as 'an offence against humanity'.[18] In addition, through the requirement of being suitable for causing a disturbance of the public peace, the legal peace within society as a fundamental interest was ultimately sought

---

[12] BVerfG 15.1.1958, *BVerfGE* 7, 198, 208–209—*Lüth*; BVerfG 13.1.1982, *BVerfGE* 59, 231, 265—freier Rundfunkmitarbeiter.

[13] BVerfG 15.1.1958, *BVerfGE* 7, 198, 208–209—*Lüth*; BVerfG 11.5.1976, *BVerfGE* 42, 143, 150—*Deutschland-Magazin.*

[14] BVerfG 11.5.1976, *BVerfGE* 42, 143, 152—*Deutschland-Magazin.*

[15] BGBl. I, S. 478.

[16] An English translation of the German Criminal Code is available at http://www.gesetze-im-internet.de/englisch_stgb/.

[17] Article 1 (1) sentence 1 of the Basic Law: 'Human dignity shall be inviolable.'

[18] BT-Drs. III/1746, 3.

as an object of protection.[19] This objective was also expressed by the legislature on a later occasion. For example, in the explanatory memorandum to the Act Amending the Criminal Code, the Code of Criminal Procedure and Other Laws (Crime Control Act) of 28 October 1994,[20] which in particular made the denial of the Holocaust a punishable offence in Section 130 (3) of the German Criminal Code, it is explicitly stated that 'the provision is intended to prevent the political climate from being poisoned by the trivialisation of the National Socialist reign of violence and terror'.[21]

Current amendments to the law also proceed in a similar 'two-track' manner to refer both to the individual interest of the person affected by 'hate speech' and to the effects of such expression on society as a whole. For example, the explanatory memorandum of the Act to Combat Right-Wing Extremism and Hate Crime of 30 March 2021[22] states that the 'increasing roughening of communication ... not only attacks and calls into question the general right of personality of the person concerned, but also the political discourse in the democratic and pluralistic social order'.[23] The memorandum also points to the danger 'that people completely withdraw from public political debate. This endangers the free exchange of opinions on the internet and ultimately the freedom of expression. Being able to express one's own opinion freely and openly, and to exchange opinions about it, is an essential pillar of a democratic pluralistic society, which the state has to defend with the means at its disposal'.[24] This ultimately refers to a *de facto* endangerment of freedom of expression if it were to be granted without legal restrictions and if hateful statements remained unpunished.

The legislature usually limits itself to referring to the human dignity or the general right of personality of the person affected by a hateful statement,[25] and to a general legal interest of public peace or open public debate. The courts proceed in a similar manner by referring to the human dignity of the person affected in order to punish the author of a hateful statement. For example, in the case of the offences of insults under Sections 185 et seqq. of the German Criminal Code, freedom of expression is generally limited if a statement turns out to be mere defamatory criticism, i.e. the focus is not on dealing with the matter at hand, but on the mere defamation of the person concerned.[26] Likewise, freedom of expression always recedes if a statement violates someone else's human dignity, i.e. denies the victim the core of his or her personality that constitutes human dignity.[27] In the same way the 'incitement of

---

[19] Krauß 2021, Entstehungsgeschichte.

[20] BGBl. I, 3186.

[21] BT-Drs. 12/8588, 8.

[22] BGBl. I, 441. Among other things, the law amended the offences of defamation under Sections 185 et seq. of the German Criminal Code as well as the offence of Threatening commission of serious criminal offence under Section 241, in some cases not insignificantly.

[23] BT-Drs. 19/17741, 1.

[24] BT-Drs. 19/17741, 1.

[25] The general right of personality is also anchored in Article 1 (1) of the Basic Law (human dignity) in addition to Article 2 (1) (general freedom of action).

[26] See e.g. BVerfG 19.5.2020, *NJW* 2020, 2622, 2624, on the insult of a judge in an internet blog.

[27] BVerfG 19.5.2020, *NJW* NJW 2020, 2622, 2625.

masses' in Section 130 of the German Criminal Code does not need any balancing of interests if the human dignity of the person concerned is violated.[28]

In all other cases, the significance of freedom of expression must be weighed against the importance of the legal interest affected by the expression of opinion on a case-by-case basis.[29] The conflicting legal interests are, in the case of insults, honour, which is also mentioned in Article 5 (2) of the Basic Law, and, in the case of incitement of masses under Section 130 of the Criminal Code, human dignity and the public peace, which the Federal Constitutional Court interprets as a guarantee of peacefulness.[30] Thus, it is only intended to protect against the external effects of expressions, which, according to their content, are recognisably designed to endanger legal interests.[31]

It can be noted—not surprisingly due to the described interaction of freedom of expression and conflicting interests—that both the legislature and the courts focus on the protected interests of the specific provision when dealing with restrictions on freedom of expression. However, the consequence of this orientation is that other legal interests not protected by the respective norm are not considered in the balancing process. This applies not only to the right to non-discrimination and the freedom of association in Article 9 (1) of the Basic Law,[32] which are not usually referred to in detail in the discussion about 'hate speech'. This does not mean, however, that the legislature would fail to recognise the discriminatory character of such statements.

The lack of explicit reference may also be due to the fact that the right to non-discrimination in Germany is not formulated as a right of the individual in Article 3 (3) sentence 1 of the Basic Law, but as a principle of equal treatment or a prohibition of discrimination. Fundamental rights of equality are usually only examined after fundamental rights of freedom, so that in the event of a violation of a fundamental right of freedom, it is at least factually unnecessary to deal with a violation of equality.[33] This is all the more true because in the discussion about hateful expression, reference is usually made to human dignity as the highest value of the Constitution.

So that the right to non-discrimination is also included in the consideration of how far freedom of expression can be restricted, a general anti-discrimination offence would have to be enacted that elevates this very right to an object of protection. In a similar way, when it comes to the question of how far freedom of arts can be restricted by the criminal provision of Section 166 of the German Criminal Code (Revilement of religious faiths and religious and ideological communities), which does not protect freedom of faith, but at least refers to religions and ideologies, reference is sometimes

---

[28] BVerfG 12.11.2002, *NJW* 2003, 660, 662.

[29] BVerfG 12.11.2002, *NJW* 2003, 660, 662.

[30] BVerfG 22.6.2018, *NJW* 2018, 2861, 2862.

[31] BVerfG 22.6.2018, *NJW* 2018, 2861, 2862.

[32] 'All Germans shall have the right to form societies and other associations.'

[33] Kischel 2021, Article 3 para 5.

made to the freedom of faith and conscience guaranteed in Article 4 (1) of the Basic Law.[34]

A new offence of inciting insult in Section 192a of the German Criminal Code enacted by the Act Amending the Criminal Code—Improving Criminal Law Protection Against So-Called Enemy Lists, Making the Distribution and Possession of Instructions for the Sexual Abuse of Children a Criminal Offence, and Improving the Fight against Inciting Content and Combating Propaganda Materials and Symbols of Unconstitutional and Terrorist Organisations—of 2021[35]—is venturing somewhat in the direction of a general anti-discrimination offence. The norm is a reaction in particular to the increasing open anti-Semitism in Germany[36] and covers content that insults, maliciously maligns or defames a group defined by its national, racial, religious or ethnic origin, its ideology, its disability or its sexual orientation, or an individual because of his or her membership in one of these groups and is therefore tantamount to a violation of human dignity.

It is now a punishable offence for these inciting contents to reach a member of the mentioned groups. A specific criminal offence was needed for this, since, due to the restriction of such behaviour to the perpetrator and the recipient, it lacks the likelihood of disturbing the public peace and thus the criminal offence of incitement of masses (Section 130 of the German Criminal Code) is not fulfilled.[37] The legal interest of the provision is considered to be the honour of the recipient, whose suitability for restricting freedom of expression is also explicitly addressed in the explanatory memorandum.[38] However, it is also stated that the content in question 'affects the right of those concerned to participate in social and political life on equal terms',[39] and thus the explanatory memorandum refers to the right to non-discrimination.

10.2 National Statutory and Administrative Law

10.2.1 Administrative Agencies

In Germany, as far as can be seen, no administrative agency has played an important role in the legal handling of hate speech. This is because hate speech can be prosecuted in Germany under certain circumstances and therefore the public prosecutors and the courts are primary responsible for combating hateful expressions. This task is therefore not assigned to the administrative authorities, at least not primarily.

---

[34] 'Freedom of faith and of conscience and freedom to profess a religious or philosophical creed shall be inviolable.' See e.g. OVG Koblenz 2.12.1996, *NJW* 1997, 1174, 1175.

[35] BGBl. I

[36] BT-Drs. 19/31115, 8.

[37] BT-Drs. 19/31115, 14.

[38] BT-Drs. 19/31115, 15.

[39] BT-Drs. 19/31115, 14.

Although there is a Federal Anti-Discrimination Agency, its objective is to protect against discrimination in general and not specifically against hateful expressions. In addition, its tasks are essentially limited to counselling, public relations work, conducting scientific research and submitting reports to the German Bundestag every four years.[40] For example, the third joint report to the German Bundestag in 2017 was generally dedicated to discrimination in Germany. However, the report, which was over 500 pages long, only dealt with the development of hate crime in passing.[41]

10.2.2 Criminal Laws Applied to Hateful Expression

The most significant legal and administrative regulations applied to hateful expression in Germany are criminal provisions. Currently, the most important criminal offence to combat hateful expression is 'incitement of masses' according to Section 130 of the German Criminal Code. According to its latest draft, it is punishable under Section 130 (1) of the German Criminal Code to incite hatred against a national, racial, religious group or a group defined by their ethnic origin, against sections of the population or individuals on account of their belonging to one of the aforementioned groups or sections of the population, or to call for violent or arbitrary measures against them (No. 1) or to violate the human dignity of others by insulting, maliciously maligning or defaming one of the aforementioned groups, sections of the population or individuals on account of their belonging to one of the aforementioned groups or sections of the population (No. 2) in a manner which is suitable for causing a disturbance of the public peace. A current special effort to fight hate crime is the new criminal offence of inciting insult in Section 192a of the German Criminal Code, as discussed in Sect. 10.1, although it is remarkable that the words 'hate crime', 'hate speech' or even the motive 'hate' are not mentioned at any point in the explanatory memorandum.[42]

In addition, there are many criminal provisions that were not enacted specifically to combat hateful expression, but only cover such matters among other things. These include the offences of insult under Sections 185 et seq. of the German Criminal Code, coercion (Section 240 of the German Criminal Code) and threatening commission of serious criminal offence (Section 241 of the German Criminal Code), the dissemination of propaganda material and the use of symbols of unconstitutional

---

[40] https://www.antidiskriminierungsstelle.de/EN/about-us/our-tasks/our-tasks-node.html.

[41] See in particular p. 169 of the report 'Discrimination in Germany', available at https://www.antidiskriminierungsstelle.de/SharedDocs/Downloads/DE/publikationen/BT_Bericht/gemeinsamer_bericht_dritter_2017.pdf?__blob=publicationFile&v=17. Key results in English are published at https://www.antidiskriminierungsstelle.de/SharedDocs/downloads/EN/publikationen/Zusammenfassung_en_Dritter_Bericht_an_den_BT_2017.pdf?__blob=publicationFile&v=2.

[42] Cf. however the press release of the Federal Ministry of Justice and Consumer Protection of 12.5.2021, available at https://www.bmjv.de/SharedDocs/Pressemitteilungen/DE/2021/0512_verhetzende_Beleidigung.html, in which the Federal Minister of Justice Christine Lambrecht speaks of 'hate messages' in this context.

organisations (Sections 86, 86a of the German Criminal Code),[43] public incitement to commit offences (Section 111 of the German Criminal Code) and offences relating to religion and ideology (Sections 166 et seq. of the German Criminal Code).

As already mentioned above in Sect. 10.1, the Act to Combat Right-Wing Extremism and Hate Crime of 30 March 2021[44] amended, among other things, the offences of insults under Sections 185 et seq. of the German Criminal Code as well as threatening commission of serious criminal offence under Section 241 of the German Criminal Code, in some cases significantly. However, the amendments did not take into account the characteristics of hate crime at all, neither the (e.g. discriminatory) content nor the (e.g. hateful) motivation of the perpetrator. Since then, for example, a qualified insult exists if it is expressed 'publicly'. In this way, however, all defamatory statements on the (freely accessible) internet are covered, without specifically hateful expressions being sanctioned more severely.[45]

Freedom of opinion must also be considered when interpreting these criminal provisions. In this respect, reference may again be made to the discussion in Sect. 10.1. Furthermore, freedom of opinion must be taken into account in the interpretation of any given statement. Thus, in the case of an ambiguous statement, the courts may only assume one—punishable—possibility of interpretation if they rule out all other—non-punishable—variants of interpretation with plausible reasons.[46]

The fact that a statement is made out of hatred can likewise be taken into account in assessing legal consequences. This applies to every criminal offence, i.e. also to those penal provisions that neither specifically nor factually serve to combat hateful expressions. According to Section 46 (2) sentence 2 of the Criminal Code, the numerous circumstances that the courts have to consider in sentencing include 'the offender's motives and objectives, in particular including racist, xenophobic or other motives evidencing contempt for humanity'. The explicit enumeration of the motives 'racist, xenophobic, antisemitic or other motives evidencing contempt for humanity' was only introduced in 2015 by the Act to Implement Recommendations of the NSU Investigation Committee of the German Bundestag of 12 June 2015,[47] to guide prosecutorial authorities and courts that are confronted with these hate-driven motives.[48] Through the aforementioned Act to Combat Right-Wing Extremism and Hate Crime, the attribute 'antisemitic' was finally added. However, there was already agreement beforehand that such motives could be considered in sentencing to the disadvantage of the perpetrator.[49] Therefore even the federal government attributed 'primarily symbolic character' to this amendment of the law.[50]

---

43 See e.g. Sotiriadis 2014, pp. 261, 264.

44 BGBl. I, 441.

45 See Valerius 2020, pp. 666, 689.

46 BVerfG 10.10.1995, *BVerfGE* 93, 266, 295 f. —'Soldaten sind Mörder'; BVerfG 12.11.2002, *NJW* 2003, 660, 661.

47 BGBl. I, 925.

48 Cf. BT-Drs. 17/8131, 4.

49 Keiser 2010, pp. 46, 48; see also BT-Drs. 17/3124, 8 and BT-Drs. 18/3007, 14.

50 BT-Drs. 17/9345, 7.

Since August 2015, the public prosecutor's offices have also been explicitly encouraged in the Guidelines for Criminal Proceedings and Administrative Fines ('Richtlinien für das Strafverfahren und das Bußgeldverfahren') to extend investigations to 'racist, xenophobic or other motives evidencing contempt for humanity' if there is evidence to that effect, as these can be relevant for determining legal consequences (No. 15 para 5). The characteristic 'antisemitic' has not yet been added to the list. These guidelines are administrative regulations that address the public prosecutor's office in particular to ensure that criminal proceedings are handled as uniformly as possible. For judges, however, these guidelines are not binding.

10.2.3 Non-criminal Laws Applied to Hateful Expression

In addition to criminal provisions a second, non-criminal law approach is being pursued to combat hateful expression. This approach reflects the fact that hateful statements are becoming increasingly widespread, not least in social media. On 1 October 2017, the Law to Improve Law Enforcement in Social Networks (Network Enforcement Act; 'Netzwerkdurchsetzungsgesetz', NetzDG) came into force.[51] Its aim is, among other things, to effectively combat and prosecute hate crime as a 'major threat to peaceful coexistence in a free, open and democratic society'.[52]

The Network Enforcement Act obliges providers of social networks to remove unlawful content immediately, i.e. usually within seven days of becoming aware of it, or to block access to it (Section 3 (2) no. 3 NetzDG). If the unlawfulness is obvious, i.e. its determination does not require an in-depth examination,[53] the time limit is only 24 hours (Section 3 (2) no. 2 NetzDG). The already mentioned Act to Combat Right-Wing Extremism and Hate Crime also introduced a reporting obligation in Section 3a NetzDG, which came into force on 1 February 2022. Since then the providers of social networks are obliged to transmit content to the Federal Criminal Police Office, among other things, if there are concrete signs of the commission of listed criminal offences to enable the prosecution of these offences. The listed criminal offences include, among others, Sections 86, 86a, 130 and 241 of the German Criminal Code and thus also norms that are regularly committed by hateful expression.

---

[51] BGBl. I, 3352.

[52] BT-Drs. 18/12356, 1.

[53] BT-Drs. 18/12356, 22.

10.3 International Covenant on Civil and Political Rights (ICCPR)

10.3.1 Concluding Observations on Hateful Expression

The Federal Republic of Germany signed the International Covenant on Civil and Political Rights (ICCPR) of 16 December 1966 in 1968 and ratified it by law on 15 November 1973.[54] The Covenant entered into force in Germany on 23 March 1976,[55] albeit initially without Article 41 on state complaints, the entry into force of which followed on 28 March 1979.[56]

The most recent Concluding Observations (on the sixth periodic report of Germany) of the United Nations Human Rights Committee (UNHRC) were published in 2012. This report addressed the phenomenon of 'hate speech' as follows:

> 17. While noting the various measures taken by the State party to combat racism, the Committee is concerned at the persistence of racially-motivated incidents against members of the Jewish and Sinti and Roma communities as well as Germans of foreign origin and asylum seekers in the State party. The Committee is concerned about the persistent discrimination faced by members of the Sinti and Roma communities regarding access to housing, education, employment and health care (Articles 2, 18, 20, and 26). The State party should take concrete measures to increase the effectiveness of its legislation and to investigate all allegations of racially-motivated acts and to prosecute and punish those responsible. The State party should also strengthen its efforts to integrate members of the Sinti and Roma communities in Germany by firmly promoting their access to education, housing, employment and health care. The State party should further pursue its awareness-raising campaigns and promote tolerance between communities.
>
> 18. The Committee is concerned at continued allegations of hate speech and racist propaganda on the Internet including from right-wing extremism, despite awareness-raising efforts and judicial measures taken on the basis of Sections 86 and 130 of its Criminal Code (Articles 2, 18, and 26). The State party should take the necessary steps to effectively prohibit and prevent hate speech and racist propaganda in particular through the Internet. It should increase its awareness at federal and at Länder levels with regard to racist propaganda and speech, in particular from extreme right-wing associations or groups.

The Concluding Observations (on the seventh periodic report of Germany) are currently still pending. Germany's report (due on 30 July 2019, initially even in 2018) was not received by the UNHRC until March 2020. According to point 7 of the list of topics for the report,[57] the phenomenon of 'hate speech' is also addressed. The report

---

[54] BGBl. II, 1533.

[55] BGBl. II, 1068.

[56] BGBl. II, 1218.

[57] 'In connection with the previous concluding observations (paras 17–18), please report on the steps taken to respond to the reports of hate speech, including in the media, on the Internet and in politics, racist and xenophobic acts, including racially motivated crimes, against people of African descent, Sinti and Roma, Muslims, asylum seekers, refugees and immigrants, as well as manifestations of anti-Semitism, including physical attacks and desecration of cemeteries.'

mainly lists extra-legal measures that have been taken in recent years and, among other things, summarises the (already in the comments on question 1 mentioned) Act to Improve Enforcement of the law in Social Networks, which aims to ensure the rapid removal of hate speech.

10.3.2 Individual Complaints Procedure

The (first) Optional Protocol to the ICCPR of 19 December 1966, providing for individual complaints, was not initially acceded to by the Federal Republic of Germany in order to avoid conflicts of jurisdiction with the organs of the legal protection system of the European Convention on Human Rights (ECHR).[58] Accession to the Optional Protocol therefore took place only by Act of 21 December 1992,[59] but with the reservation, inter alia, with regard to Article 5 (2) (a) of the Optional Protocol, that the UNHRC does not consider any communications from an individual already examined under another procedure of international investigation or settlement. The Optional Protocol entered into force for Germany on 25 November 1993.[60] This reservation explains why only few individual complaints are generally made to the UNHRC. Of the communications published in this regard, as far as can be seen, not even one has involved hateful expression.

10.3.3 Application of ICCPR to Hateful Expression

With regard to offences of speech on the Internet, some changes were made by the 60th Criminal Law Amendment Act (modernisation of the definition of written communications and other terms as well as extension of criminal liability under Sections 86, 86a, 111 and 130 of the Criminal Code in the case of acts abroad) of 30 November 2000.[61] In the case of the paragraphs mentioned in the title of the law, the amendments aimed in particular to apply German criminal law even if corresponding content is disseminated on the internet from abroad, and thus also made accessible to the public in Germany.[62] However, the legislature was merely reacting to a change in the case law of the Federal Court of Justice. Neither the ICCPR nor the latest Concluding Observations were mentioned in the explanatory

[58] Cf. also Article 62 ECHR in its originally version, meanwhile Article 55 ECHR, according to which the High Contracting Parties to the ECHR will not, except by special agreement, avail themselves of treaties, conventions or declarations in force between them for the purpose of submitting, by way of petition, a dispute arising out of the interpretation or application of this Convention to a means of settlement other than those provided for in this Convention.

[59] BGBl. II, 1246.

[60] BGBl. 1994 II, 311.

[61] BGBl. I, 2600.

[62] See BT-Drs. 19/19859, 22–24.

memorandum. Otherwise the legislature does not refer to the ICCPR when fighting hate speech.

According to the new case law of the Federal Court of Justice, the offence of using symbols of unconstitutional organisations (Section 86a of the German Criminal Code) could not be applied to a case in which the accused uploaded pictures of swastikas to YouTube from the neighbouring Czech Republic. After all, Section 86a of the German Criminal Code is a criminal offence that already criminalises a generally dangerous activity as such, without requiring a factual outcome in the form of a concrete danger or a violation of the protected legal interest. Such abstract endangering offences ('abstrakte Gefährdungsdelikte') therefore did not have a place of impact that could justify the applicability of German criminal law.[63] Accordingly, only the place of activity is decisive, which in the case described was abroad. The fact that the uploaded content could be accessed in Germany was also not sufficient to establish the domestic connection necessary for the applicability of German criminal law.[64]

10.3.4 Reservations or Declarations that Specifically Relate to Hateful Expression

As mentioned above, Germany has declared reservations to both the ICCPR and the Optional Protocol. However, these reservations do not relate specifically to hateful expression.

Reservations to ICCPR:

1. Articles 19, 21 and 22 in conjunction with Article 2 (1) of the Covenant shall be applied within the scope of Article 16 of the Convention of 4 November 1950 for the Protection of Human Rights and Fundamental Freedoms.
2. Article 14 (3) (d) of the Covenant shall be applied in such manner that it is for the court to decide whether an accused person held in custody has to appear in person at the hearing before the court of review ('Revisionsgericht').
3. Article 14 (5) of the Covenant shall be applied in such manner that: (a) A further appeal does not have to be instituted in all cases solely on the grounds the accused person having been acquitted by the lower court-was convicted for the first time in the proceedings concerned by the appellate court. (b) In the case of criminal offences of minor gravity the review by a higher tribunal of a decision not imposing imprisonment does not have to be admitted in all cases.
4. Article 15 (1) of the Covenant shall be applied in such manner that when provision is made by law for the imposition of a lighter penalty the hitherto applicable law may for certain exceptional categories of cases remain applicable to criminal offences committed before the law was amended.

---

[63] BGH 19.8.2014, *NStZ* 2015, 81, 82. Cf. also BGH 3.5.2016, *NStZ* 2017, 146, 147, on the potential endangering offence of incitement of masses (Section 130 of the German Criminal Code) on the occasion of a speech held in Switzerland in which the Holocaust was denied.

[64] BGH 19.8.2014, *NStZ* 2015, 81, 82.

Reservations to the Optional Protocol to the ICCPR:

The Federal Republic of Germany formulates a reservation concerning article 5 para 2 (a) to the effect that the competence of the Committee shall not apply to communications (a) which have already been considered under another procedure of international investigation or settlement, or (b) by means of which a violation of rights is reprimanded having its origin in events occurring prior to the entry into force of the Optional Protocol for the Federal Republic of Germany (c) by means of which a violation of article 26 of the [said Covenant] is reprimanded, if and insofar as the reprimanded violation refers to rights other than those guaranteed under the aforementioned Covenant.

10.4 International Convention on the Elimination of All Forms of Racial Discrimination (ICERD)

10.4.1 Concluding Observations on Hateful Expression for Germany

Thes Federal Republic of Germany signed the International Convention on the Elimination of All Forms of Racial Discrimination (ICERD) of 7 March 1966 on 10 February 1967 and ratified it by law on 9 May 1969 without submitting any reservations or interpretive declarations, either in general or specifically in relation to hateful expression.[65] The Convention entered into force in Germany on 15 June 1969.[66]

The most recent Concluding Observations (on the combined nineteenth to twenty-second periodic reports of Germany) date back to 2015 and explicitly addressed the phenomenon of 'hate speech' in section 10.9 ('Hate speech and incitement to racial discrimination'). Among other things, the Committee recommended that Germany should:

(a) Increase its efforts and use all possible means to counter and stem the tide of racism, in particular by strongly condemning all racist statements by political leaders, public authorities and public figures, including through the institution of criminal proceedings; (b) Institute a comprehensive strategy, including mandatory training, to enhance the understanding of police, prosecutors and judges of the notion of racial discrimination and the way to combat it, and to ensure that any act that may contain racist motives is investigated effectively and that, where appropriate, perpetrators of such acts are charged and punished; (c) Implement appropriate measures to combat the proliferation of acts and manifestations of racism on the Internet, including by blocking websites devoted to inciting racial discrimination and hatred.

Section 10.10 of the concluding observations on 'Institutional shortcomings in investigating racially motivated acts' also dealt with hateful expression in passing. In this respect, the Committee urged the State Party, among other things,

(b) ... (i) to include provisions in the Police Service Regulations and the Guidelines for Criminal and Summary Proceedings imposing an explicit duty to investigate and document any racist or other discriminatory motives, in parallel to

[65] BGBl. II, 961.

[66] BGBl. II, 2211.

the legislative change to Section 46 of the Penal Code; (ii) to improve the State party's data collection system for statistics on complaints of hate crimes, including by officially requiring all law enforcement agencies to record all such instances and transmit statistics thereon to the federal authorities, disaggregated by mother tongue, language commonly spoken or other indicators of ethnic diversity, and regularly publicize such information; (iii) to ensure that all acts committed against groups requiring protection under the Convention are investigated through the racial discrimination lens with a focus on the victim and with systematic collection of data on indicators of racial discrimination, including the name of the victim and other intersectional criteria, such as gender and religion.

Moreover the 'Sarrazin case', which was the subject of an individual complaints procedure (see Sect. 10.4.2), was referred under section 19 ('individual communications') to remind 'the State party of the need for effective responses to racist hate speech in accordance with the Committee's general recommendation No. 35 [... on combating racist hate speech]'.

Germany did not submit its combined 23rd–26th state report (due on 15 June 2018) until April 2020. In this report, the fight against 'hate crime' in general and 'hate speech' in particular is addressed at various points, taking into account the corresponding recommendations of the last concluding observations. The 'priority issues' were to expand the statistical recording of hate crime and to take resolute action against racially motivated criminal offences.

Regarding 'hate speech', reference was made, among other things, to the aforementioned Network Enforcement Act, which obliges social network providers to delete or block unlawful content, in particular hate speech. In its report, however, Germany also emphasised that the Network Enforcement Act does not mandate any new forms of interference with the right of freedom of expression but is limited to criminal content. In this respect, the Network Enforcement Act should only ensure that networks take swift and rigorous action to meet their existing legal obligations. It was also mentioned in the report that the fight against 'hate speech' remains a central objective of the federal government.

10.4.2 Individual Complaints Procedure

On 30 August 2001, Germany declared to the Secretary-General of the United Nations, in accordance with ICERD Article 14, that it would recognize the competence of the Committee to receive and consider communications from individuals or groups of individuals within its jurisdiction claiming to be victims of a violation by Germany of any of the rights set forth in the Convention.[67] However, Communications to the Committee on the Elimination of Racial Discrimination are rare.

---

[67] BGBl. II, 1278.

In the UN's online database, there are only two communications from the years 2006 (38/2006) and 2013 (48/2010), although these involved discriminatory as well as hateful statements. The first case (Communication 38/2006) concerned a letter to the editor of the legal newspaper *The Criminalist* written by the vice-chairman of the Bavarian section of the BDK and Detective Superintendent of the Criminal Inspection of the city of Fürth. The author considered it certain, despite the lack of statistics, that Sinti and Roma kept the authorities disproportionately busy in view of their small group size. Among other things, he asked:

> 'Who, for example, commits nationwide thefts largely against old people? Who pretends to be a police officer to steal the scarce savings of pensioners which were hidden for the funeral in the kitchen cupboard or in the laundry locker? Who shows disabled and blind persons tablecloths and opens the door to accomplices? What about the trick with the glass of water and the paper trick? [...]
>
> Is it really a prejudice when citizens complain about the fact that Sinti drive up with a Mercedes in front of the social welfare office? Is it not true that hardly any Roma works regularly and pays social insurance? Why does this group separate itself in such a way and for example inter-marries without the registry office? Why are fathers of Sinti children not named to the youth welfare office?....'[68]

Preliminary proceedings initiated for incitement of masses (Criminal Code Section 130) were dropped.[69] However, the official was suspended from duty because generalised negative statements about social groups were unacceptable. The Committee found that the refusal to initiate preliminary proceedings was neither arbitrary nor amounted to denial of justice and stated that the facts do not disclose a violation of Articles 4 (a) and 6 of the Convention.

The second case (Communication 48/2010) concerned Thilo Sarrazin, a former Berlin finance senator and, at the time of the statement, a member of the supervisory board of the German Central Bank. Sarrazin had made derogatory and discriminatory remarks in an interview about what he called the lower classes of the population, who were not productive, lived on welfare, and would have to disappear over time to create a city of the elite. A large group of Arabs and Turks could not be expected to develop either. Among other things, they were said to be largely unwilling to integrate and failing to finish school, yet characterised by a higher birth rate and maintaining a collectivist mentality that was aggressive and outdated.

The public prosecutor's office discontinued preliminary proceedings for incitement of masses under Section 130 and for insult under Section 185 of the German Criminal Code for legal reasons. In their view, no criminal conduct was apparent,

---

[68] The quotation is from Communication No. 38/2006, 3–4, available at https://adsdatabase.ohchr.org/IssueLibrary/CERD_Communication_38_2006_Zentralrat%20Deutscher%20Sinti%20und%20Roma%20v.%20Germany.pdf.

[69] For the final decision in the non-successful action enforcement proceedings, see OLG Brandenburg 15.5.2006, *BeckRS* 2006, 19259, which rejected criminal liability for incitement of masses (Section 130 of the German Criminal Code) and stated in this regard, among other things: 'The defendant also uses existing prejudices against the applicants' ethnic group in an intolerable and shameful manner; however, he does evidentially not demonstrably use these stereotypes to incite hatred ...'.

also regarding freedom of expression. Rather, the statements in question were a contribution to a public discussion.

The Committee considered that the absence of an effective investigation into the statements in question amounted to a violation of Articles 2 (1) (d), 4 and 6 of the Convention:

> While acknowledging the importance of freedom of expression, the Committee considers that Mr. Sarrazin's statements amounted to dissemination of ideas based upon racial superiority or hatred and contained elements of incitement to racial discrimination in accordance with article 4, para (a), of the Convention. By concentrating on the fact that Mr. Sarrazin's statements did not amount to incitement of racial hatred and were not capable of disturbing the public peace, the State party failed in its duty to carry out an effective investigation into whether or not Mr. Sarrazin's statements amounted to dissemination of ideas based upon racial superiority or hatred. The Committee further considers that the criterion of disturbance of the public peace, which is taken into consideration in the evaluation if statements reach the threshold of dissemination of ideas based upon racial superiority or hatred, does not adequately translate into domestic legislation the State party's obligation under article 2, para 1 (d), in particular as neither article 2, para 1 (d), nor article 4 contain such a criterion.

10.4.3 Application of ICERD to Hateful Expression

After the Sarrazin case, the 49th Criminal Law Amendment Act of 21 January 2015[70] amended, among other things, the offence of incitement of masses under Section 130 of the German Criminal Code. However, according to the subtitle of the law, this was due to the implementation of European guidelines on sexual criminal law. It was also intended as a reaction to the increasing dissemination of incitement to hatred in broadcasting, telemedia and the internet.[71] However, neither the Convention nor the above-mentioned individual complaints procedure were mentioned in the explanatory memorandum. The criterion of public peace which was criticised by the Committee in the Sarrazin case have also remained unchanged.

Moreover, legislation refers to the ICERD only rarely and in passing. This was the case, for example, in the explanatory memorandum to the Act on the Implementation of Recommendations of the NSU Investigation Committee of the German Bundestag of 12 June 2015,[72] which explicitly added 'in particular including racist, xenophobic or other motives evidencing contempt for humanity' as factors for determining the penalty in Section 46 (2) sentence 2 of the German Criminal Code. Here it was pointed out that the 'explicit naming of racist motives ... corresponds to the recommendations of several international bodies concerned with combating racism and xenophobia'. In this context, reference was also made to the concluding observations of the Committee on the Elimination of Racial Discrimination (CERD) of

[70] BGBl. I, 10.
[71] Cf. BT-Drs. 18/2601, 16.
[72] BGBl. I, 925.

the United Nations on the 16th–18th State Reports of Germany.[73] Furthermore, in order to explain the term 'racist' or 'race' in more detail, it was stated that legal texts on human rights protection against racism, such as the ICERD, understand this term in a sociological sense.[74]

10.5 Regional Law and Organisations

German law has been influenced primarily by Europe, namely by legal instruments of the Council of Europe (see Sect. 5.2) and especially the European Union (see Sect. 5.3). However, the effects on criminal law are still rather small, despite the growing importance of European guidelines. This applies not least to the Council of Europe, a traditional association under international law in the sense that its member states have not transferred any legislative powers to it and therefore its legal acts (above all recommendations and conventions) are not strictly binding. The Council of Europe has no power to enact directly effective legislation over its member states.

By contrast, the European Union (EU) is an association to which Member States have transferred some of their traditionally sovereign powers. The European Union can enact law in certain areas defined in the Treaty on the Functioning of the European Union (TFEU), e.g. by means of regulations directly applicable in the Member States (Article 288 (2) TFEU) and by means of directives (Article 288 (3) TFEU). Member States must first implement these in order for them to become effective, but they are legally binding.

The European Union is authorised to adopt directives in the areas of criminal law to combat serious crimes with a cross-border dimension (Article 83 (1) TFEU). According to Article 83 (2) TFEU, this includes 'terrorism, trafficking in human beings and sexual exploitation of women and children, illicit drug trafficking, illicit arms trafficking, money laundering, corruption, counterfeiting of means of payment, computer crime and organised crime'. In the opinion of the German Federal Constitutional Court, however, this enabling provision must be interpreted in a restrictive manner and the member states must be left substantial leeway in shaping the law.[75] After all, custodial sentences and fines seriously interfere with the fundamental rights of citizens and therefore require sufficient democratic legitimation.[76]

---

[73] BT-Drs. 18/3007, 14; cf. also the statement of the Federal Government on the draft of the Act to Amend the Criminal Code—inclusion of inhumane motives as special circumstances in the sentencing process; BT-Drs. 17/9345, 7.

[74] BT-Drs. 18/3007, 14.

[75] BVerfG 30.6.2009, *BVerfGE* 123, 267, 412—*Lissabon.*

[76] BVerfG 30.6.2009, *BVerfGE* 123, 267, 360—*Lissabon.*

10.5.1 Legal Instruments of the Council of Europe

The Council of Europe first dealt with hate speech in its Recommendation on Combating Hate Speech of 30 October 1997. According to this understanding 'hate speech' is construed as 'covering all forms of expression which spread, incite, promote or justify racial hatred, xenophobia, anti-Semitism or other forms of hatred based on intolerance, including: intolerance expressed by aggressive nationalism and ethnocentrism, discrimination and hostility against minorities, migrants and people of immigrant origin'. In combating such expression, recourse to criminal sanctions is not ruled out. In addition, the member states were already advised about the dissemination of such statements in the new media and the resulting need to adapt legal measures.

Of major importance, however, was the Additional Protocol to the Convention on Cybercrime concerning the criminalisation of acts of a racist and xenophobic nature committed through computer systems of 28 January 2003,[77] which was intended to fight such propaganda, especially on the Internet. The Convention on Cybercrime of 23 November 2001[78] itself did not yet consider this concern, as a criminal prohibition of such expressions failed in particular due to the resistance of the USA with its high regard for freedom of expression.[79] The Additional Protocol provided that signatory states would prosecute certain acts of racism and xenophobia. The Protocol specifically mentions the dissemination of racist and xenophobic material through computer systems (Article 3), racist and xenophobic motivated threat (Article 4) and insult (Article 5), as well as denial, gross minimisation, approval or justification of genocide or crimes against humanity (Article 6).

Thus far, two rulings of the European Court of Human Rights (ECtHR) in cases brought against Germany have dealt with hate speech.[80] The case of *Annen v. Germany*[81] concerned an individual against whom a court injunction had been issued. According to the injunction, the applicant had to refrain from distributing leaflets in the immediate vicinity of a day clinic that performed abortions. The leaflets mentioned abortion doctors by name and claimed that illegal abortions were being performed in the clinic. In addition, the complainant was no longer allowed to include the names and addresses of the doctors concerned in a list of 'abortion doctors' on a website.

[77] ETS 189. Germany signed the Additional Protocol on 28.1.2003 and approved it by Act of 16.3.2011 (BGBl. II, 290).

[78] ETS 185.

[79] The USA—although not a member of the Council of Europe—participated in the drafting of the Convention, as did Canada, Japan and South Africa, in order to take into account the transnational character of the Internet.

[80] In addition to the two decisions below, the *Garaudy v. France* case should be mentioned. The ECtHR ruled that there is a category of historical facts, including the Holocaust, whose denial or questioning under Article 17 ECHR was not protected by Article 10 ECHR (ECtHR 24.6.2003, *NJW* 2004, 3691, 3692–3693—*Garaudy v. France*).

[81] ECtHR 26.11.2015, *NJW* 2016, 1867—*Annen v. Germany.*

The ECtHR considered the injunction issued by the courts to be an interference with the right to freedom of expression guaranteed by Article 10 ECHR, which was not justified by the protection of the doctors' reputation under the right to respect for private life protected by Article 8 ECHR. In particular, it should be noted that the complainant's conduct did not contradict the German legal situation and that he was participating in a very controversial debate of public interest.

The ECtHR considered Article 10 ECHR to have been violated because the German courts did not address specific elements related to the applicant's Internet site, but mainly referred to their conclusions concerning the leaflet. The Court evaluated the injunction as follows:

> Defamatory and other types of clearly unlawful speech, including hate speech and speech inciting violence, can be disseminated as never before, worldwide, in a matter of seconds, and sometimes remain persistently available online. Bearing in mind the need to protect the values underlying the Convention, and considering that the rights under Articles 10 and 8 of the Convention deserve equal respect, a balance must be struck that retains the essence of both rights. Thus, while the Court acknowledges that important benefits can be derived from the Internet in the exercise of freedom of expression, it is also mindful that liability for defamatory or other types of unlawful speech must, in principle, be retained and constitute an effective remedy for violations of personality rights.'

In the case *Nix v. Germany*,[82] the applicant challenged a conviction for using symbols of unconstitutional organisations (under Criminal Code Section 86a). He was accused of having disseminated a picture of the former NSDAP official Heinrich Himmler in SS uniform on his internet blog, bearing the badge of the NSDAP with a swastika on the breast pocket and a swastika bracelet, both symbols of an unconstitutional organisation under Criminal Code Section 86a.

In the view of the ECtHR, the interference with freedom of expression by the conviction of the applicant was necessary in a democratic society within the meaning of Article 10 (2) ECHR and thus justified. The ECtHR reiterated the historical experience of Germany and noted that the provision in question was intended to establish a so-called 'communicative taboo'. The conviction was not precluded by the fact that the applicant wanted to criticise National Socialism with his blog post and to protest against the discrimination of children with a migrant background. After all, the topic could also be discussed if one distanced oneself clearly from the objectives of Nazi ideology. This very distancing was lacking in the case at hand, even if the Court accepted that the applicant did not intend to spread totalitarian propaganda, to incite violence, or to utter hate speech, and that his expression had not resulted in intimidation.

10.5.2 Legal Instruments of the European Union

The European Union focuses mostly on economic cooperation and a common internal market for its member states, as implied by its origin as successor to the European

[82] Summarized in *MMR-Aktuell* 2018, 405392.

Economic Community. It is true that the European Union increasingly sees itself as a community of values and that the Charter of Fundamental Rights, which enshrines fundamental and human rights for the European Union, came into force in 2009 at the same time as the Treaty of Lisbon. However, the European Union is not *primarily* concerned with human rights.

In the context of 'hate speech', one should refer in particularly to Council Framework Decision 2008/913/JHA of 28 November 2008 on combating certain forms and expressions of racism and xenophobia by means of criminal law.[83] According to Article 1 (1) (c) of the Framework Decision, Member States shall criminalise 'publicly condoning, denying or grossly trivialising crimes of genocide, crimes against humanity and war crimes ... directed against a group of persons or a member of such a group defined by reference to race, colour, religion, descent or national or ethnic origin when the conduct is carried out in a manner likely to incite to violence or hatred against such a group or a member of such a group'. The Framework Decision also had in mind—see, for example, the jurisdiction provision in Article 9 (2) of the Framework Decision—the dissemination of corresponding content through an information system.

10.5.3 Implications on Germany's Laws or Policies on Hate Speech

Of the legal instruments mentioned, the recommendation of the European Council from 1997 had no obvious implications on Germany's laws.[84] However, both the Additional Protocol to the Council of Europe Convention on Cybercrime and the

---

[83] ABl. EU L 328, 55. Furthermore, Article 22 (3) sentence 1 of Directive 2012/29/EU of the European Parliament and of the Council of 25.10.2012 establishing minimum standards on the rights, support and protection of victims of crime, and replacing Council Framework Decision 2001/220/JHA refers to hate crime. According to this directive, victims who have suffered a crime committed with a bias or discriminatory motive which could, in particular, be related to their personal characteristics, shall be paid particular attention in the context of the individual assessment to prevent, inter alia, secondary victimisation. The requirements of the Directive were implemented by the Act to Strengthen Victims' Rights in Criminal Proceedings (3rd Victims' Rights Reform Act) of 21.12.2015 (BGBl. I, 2525). In the explanatory memorandum to the Act, which, inter alia, established a legal right of the aggrieved person to free psychosocial assistance in legal proceedings in Section 406g (3) of the German Code of Criminal Procedure, reference was also made to victims of prejudice-motivated violence and other hate crimes (BT-Drs. 18/4621, 32).

[84] Reference to the definition of 'Hate Speech' in the Recommendation was only made in the publication of the Scientific Services of the German Bundestag 'Treatment of 'Hate Speech' before 2015. YouTube, Face-book and Twitter', available at https://www.bundestag.de/resource/blob/662038/5f3bf16925be9219381d2a69eb56fc7d/WD-10-045-19-pdf-data.pdf; in this definition, however, 'Hate Speech' is understood rather less as speech motivated by hate than as speech to incite hate. The Scientific Services are an information centre of the German Bundestag and are intended to support and advise members of parliament in the exercise of their mandate by researching and analysing information, but do not reflect the view of the German Bundestag as Germany's legislative body.

Framework Decision 2008/913/JHA were implemented by law of 16 March 2011,[85] as indicated in its title ('Law on the Implementation of Council Framework Decision 2008/913/JHA of 28 November 2008 on combating certain forms and expressions of racism and xenophobia by means of criminal law and implementing the Additional Protocol of 28 January 2003 to the Council of Europe Convention on Cybercrime of 23 November 2001, concerning the criminalisation of acts of a racist and xenophobic nature committed through computer systems').

Moreover, the modifications were marginal and limited to the clarification that the national, racial, religious groups or groups defined by their ethnic origin mentioned in the European legal documents are also to be regarded as sections of the population within the meaning of Section 130 (1) and (2) of the German Criminal Code. In addition, Section 130 (1) and (2) was expanded in accordance with the European guidelines. The offences, including incitement to hatred and incitement to violent or arbitrary measures, are now also punishable if they are directed against individuals who are the target of the offence because they belong to one of the aforementioned groups or sections of the population.[86]

The legislature did not consider further amendments necessary because the German legal situation already complied with the other requirements of the Framework Decision.[87] It is unclear whether these two decisions of the ECtHR have had any impact on German law or policy. However, this would also be surprising, since 'hate speech' was only mentioned incidentally and the facts of the case did not constitute a prime example of statements that are commonly referred to as hateful expression.

10.6 Comparative National Law

10.6.1 References to Foreign Jurisdictions

The German legislature has not expressly referred to other national jurisdictions to orientate itself on their legal system, nor has it expressly rejected them as an alternative approach. This is at least the case with the legislative materials cited in this national report, which are likely to include the most important documents on combating hate crime in general and hateful expression in particular.

One can only guess at the reasons for this lack of comparative law references. It could be due to the fact that the described amendments to the law usually only

[85] BGBl. I, 418.

[86] BT-Drs. 17/3124, 6.

[87] BT-Drs. 17/3124, 6–9. For example, in the explanatory memorandum of the Act to Implement Recommendations of the NSU Committee of Inquiry of the German Bundestag of 30.10.2014, which explicitly added 'in particular including racist, xenophobic or other motives evidencing contempt for humanity' of the perpetrator as sentencing factors to Section 46 (2) sentence 2 of the German Criminal Code, pointed out that the explicit naming of racist motives would correspond to Article 4 of the Framework Decision; BT-Drs. 18/3007, 14.

concerned individual issues. Moreover, these issues arose on the basis of concrete situations—some of them of a factual nature, such as particular events, some of a legal nature, such as court rulings or European guidelines to be implemented. Alternatively, they concerned specific types of conduct, e.g. the new criminal offence of inciting insults (Criminal Code Section 192a), which are not covered by the provision of incitement of masses (Section 130) because they are limited to a two-person relationship between the perpetrator and the recipient. Accordingly, the legislature did not act to fully satisfy a recognised need for reform detached from a concrete case and to solve existing problems on thorough considerations which, among other things, also consult the legal situation in other states. Moreover, the German criminal lawmakers in general rarely refer to other national jurisdictions. The fact that this did not happen in the fight against hate crime is not a particularity but corresponds to the generally reluctant recourse to comparative law.[88]

Comments on comparative law by the legislature are limited to a passage in the explanatory memorandum of the Federal Government's draft of the 60th Criminal Law Amendment Act (modernisation of the definition of written communications and other terms as well as extension of criminal liability under Sections 86, 86a, 111 and 130 of the Criminal Code in the case of acts abroad) of 30 November 2000.[89] This Act extended the German criminal jurisdiction in Section 5 no. 5a lit. b of the German Criminal Code—irrespective of the law that is applicable at the place where the offence was committed—to certain acts of incitement of masses committed abroad under Section 130, provided that the inciting content is perceptibly disseminated in Germany or made accessible to the public in Germany in a manner likely to disturb the public peace, and the offender is a German national or has his or her livelihood in Germany. According to the explanatory memorandum, the inciting content must have the following effect:

> [P]rimarily acts are covered which are directed against persons who are in Germany. Without this criterion, on the other hand, a US–American living in Germany, for example, who during his holiday in the USA posts inciting content within the meaning of Section 130 (2) no. 1 of German Criminal Code on the internet that can also be accessed in Germany, but which refers to a group living only in the USA—for example, an Indian tribe—would also be liable to prosecution under German law (whereas he would presumably be exempt from prosecution in the USA).[90]

This reference is limited to a brief—and not even conclusively researched ('presumably be exempt from prosecution')—description of the punishability of expressing inciting content in a state known for its extensive guarantee of freedom

---

[88] In contrast, the Scientific Services of the German Bundestag referred to the legal situation in US federal law, in Canada and in Great Britain in their publication on the concept of hate crime, available at https://www.bundestag.de/resource/blob/192374/0d97067cfb4091dd3ccadcba87a1470c/hasskriminalitaet-data.pdf. Similarly the Services referred to the legal situation in the UK, France and the USA on the publication 'Treatment of 'Hate Speech' before 2015. YouTube, Face-book and Twitter', available at https://www.bundestag.de/resource/blob/662038/5f3bf16925be9219381d2a69eb56fc7d/WD-10-045-19-pdf-data.pdf.

[89] BGBl. I, 2600.

[90] BT-Drs. 19/19859, 46.

of expression. Furthermore, no conclusions are drawn for Germany's own approach to combating hate crime. Instead, the comment is intended only to counter concerns that Germany's criminal jurisdiction is being extended too far to foreign offences and that the principle of non-interference under international law is thus being given too little consideration.

10.6.2 References of National Courts to the Law of Other National Jurisdictions

Such concerns have indeed been expressed in Germany, not least by the courts. In the past, the courts tended to apply German criminal law quite willingly to speech acts made abroad if the statements as such are—often differently than at the place of the offence—punishable in Germany. This can be exemplified by the *Toeben* case of the Federal Court of Justice of 12 December 2000.[91] Toeben, an Australian citizen, was convicted of incitement of masses under Section 130 (3) of the German Criminal Code because he denied the Holocaust on an English website, although he had uploaded his statements from Australia to a server also located in Australia.

Since the content was freely accessible and could be read in Germany, the Federal Court of Justice considered the statements to be likely to disturb public peace in Germany also because of their special reference to the Holocaust and thus to Germany. This likelihood also established the place of impact in Germany, so that German criminal law was applicable.[92] This ruling was widely criticised in the academic literature, not least because of its consequences. The main criticism was that such a broadly understood place of impact could justify a universal jurisdiction of German judicial authorities for all expression on the internet, as long as the content could be accessed in Germany and was (maybe even exclusively) punishable under German law.[93]

From this point of view, comparative legal statements would certainly be desirable, especially in rulings that deal with the applicability of national criminal law to cross-border situations, such as hateful expression in a freely accessible communication service on the internet. However, neither in the *Toeben* case nor in the later, more restrictive rulings already cited[94] does the Federal Court of Justice look at the case law or the legal system in other states in order to gain insights or suggestions for the assessment of the German legal situation. On this occasion, the legal situation at the place where the offence was committed, namely in Switzerland, is only mentioned once. However, this only happened because the applicability of German criminal law in the specific case required the punishability at the place of the offence in

[91] BGH 12.12.2000, *BGHSt* 46, 212—*Toeben.*

[92] BGH 12.12.2000, *BGHSt* 46, 212, 221—*Toeben.*

[93] See only Hilgendorf 1997, pp. 1873, 1878.

[94] BGH 19.8.2014, *NStZ* 2015, 81; BGH 3.5.2016, *NStZ* 2017, 146.

accordance with Section 7 (2) no. 1 of the German Criminal Code.[95] Otherwise, no further conclusions were drawn from the discussion of Swiss law.

In general, the courts only rarely consider other national jurisdictions and thus only occasionally refer to a legal comparison. This applies not least to the non-constitutional courts, which focus on the interpretation of the relevant (national) provisions due to their task of deciding on concrete facts. In the case of the Federal Constitutional Court, if for example the unconstitutionality of provisions such as criminal offences is to be ruled on and thus more general and fundamental considerations detached from the individual case may be necessary, a comparative law approach may be applied somewhat more frequently.

For example, in deciding whether the offence of sexual intercourse between siblings (Criminal Code Section 173 (2) sentence 2) was compatible with the Basic Law, the Federal Constitutional Court commissioned an expert opinion from the Max Planck Institute for Foreign and International Criminal Law, which analysed the respective legal situation in twenty states from the Anglo-American, continental European and other non-European legal spheres. The Federal Constitutional Court pointed out that in 13 of the states examined, consensual sexual intercourse between adult siblings was punishable, and on the other hand, it noted that foreign constitutional courts had also confirmed the prohibition of incest as constitutional.[96] However, it is not known whether this view beyond national borders also contributed to the Federal Constitutional Court confirming the constitutionality of the criminal prohibition of incest between siblings by a vote of 7 to 1. This ruling alone does not confirm that the Federal Constitutional Court is receptive to comparative legal considerations. In any event, there are no comparative legal statements in the decisions of the Federal Constitutional Court on offences of expression in general or hateful expression in particular.

10.7 Judicial Rulings

There is neither complete agreement in Germany on the definition of 'hate crime' in general nor on the concept of 'hateful expression' in particular.[97] According to the most common view, and contrary to the first impression of the term '*hate* crime', it is less important that the perpetrator acts out of hatred as the motive for the act. Rather, it is decisive for the classification of an offence as hate crime that the act is directed against victims whom the perpetrator has chosen only because of their membership of a social group he rejects.[98]

---

[95] BGH 3.5.2016, *NStZ* 2017, 146, 147–148.

[96] BVerfG 26.2.2008, *BVerfGE* 120, 224, 230–232—Geschwisterinzest.

[97] In summary Valerius 2020, pp. 666, 667–668 and 678–679.

[98] This is the definition of the Scientific Services of the German Bundestag, 'Current term: hate crime', available at https://www.bundestag.de/resource/blob/192374/0d97067cfb4091dd3ccadcba87a1470c/hasskriminalitaet-data.pdf; cf. also the draft bill of the Federal Council to amend the

The motive for the offence thus appears to be the prejudices of the offender against certain sections of the population, which do not necessarily have to turn into hatred.[99] Similarly, when assessing an expression as 'hateful', the decisive criterion is that belonging to a certain population group is the reason for the perpetrator to verbally disparage or attack the group as a whole or one of its members.[100] The courts have not made any obvious contribution to the development of these definitions. This is probably because they concentrate on the definition and interpretation of the relevant elements of the offence as well as the assessment of the actual case. But the criteria that are crucial for hate crime or hate speech have hardly been taken into account in the formulation of the relevant criminal offences.

For example, the offence of incitement of masses under Criminal Code Section 130 lists some groups and sections of the population, namely 'national, racial, religious or defined by their ethnic origin', against which the inciting behaviour must be directed. However, the law does not refer to the prejudice-related motive of the offence. Likewise, the characteristic 'hatred' is mentioned in the Criminal Code not as a motivation of the perpetrator, but as one of the alternative modalities of the offence of 'incitement of masses', which can also be committed by 'inciting hatred'. In this context, the courts understand 'hatred' as 'an intensified hostile attitude against the concerned parts of the population that goes beyond mere rejection and contempt'.[101]

The task of distinguishing hateful expression from other statements therefore does not arise for the courts, or at least not with regard to the conditions for criminal liability. For example, when assessing cases under the offence of incitement of masses, the courts concentrate on whether the group of people affected can be classified as a 'national, racial, religious group or a group defined by their ethnic origin' or as a 'section(s) of the population' as set forth under Criminal Code Section 130 (1), rendering the perpetrator's motivation is irrelevant. Furthermore, the question often arises whether the prosecuted act has an inciting content or whether other interpretations that are not punishable are also plausible. In addition, the courts must often consider whether the act in question is likely to disturb the peace.

With respect to legal consequences, the courts might have to distinguish hateful expression from other types of statements. Finally, 'racist, xenophobic or other motives evidencing contempt for humanity' as well as such objectives of the perpetrator are explicitly mentioned in Criminal Code Section 46 (2) sentence 2 and must

---

Criminal Code—inclusion of motives evidencing contempt for humanity as special circumstances for sentencing, BT-Drs. 17/9345, 1, or the nationwide case figures 'Politically Motivated Crime in 2020', p. 7, available at https://www.bmi.bund.de/SharedDocs/downloads/DE/veroeffentlichungen/2021/05/pmk-2020-bundesweite-fallzahlen.pdf: 'Hate crime is crime that is motivated by group-related prejudices.'

[99] See Sotiriadis 2014, pp. 261, 264.

[100] Summing up the discussion about the term 'hate speech': Scientific Services of the German Bundestag 'Treatment of 'Hate Speech' before 2015. YouTube, Face-book and Twitter', available at https://www.bundestag.de/resource/blob/662038/5f3bf16925be9219381d2a69eb56fc7d/WD-10-045-19-pdf-data.pdf. In detail on the motivation of the perpetrator von Karsten Krupna (2010), pp. 30 et seq.

[101] BGH 15.3.1994, *BGHSt* 40, 97, 102—Leugnung des Holocaust.

be considered when sentencing. However, the courts have not yet dealt more closely with hateful expression and so have not contributed to its definition.[102]

Because of this concentration on considering the particular cases based on the specified elements of the offence, the courts have not adopted definitions of hate crime or hateful expression proposed by third parties. Only in some civil law rulings was indirect reference made to the understandings of third parties, namely to the guidelines of video platforms or to the community standards of social media. If a user violates these guidelines, so that his or her published content is deleted or his or her user account is blocked, the courts must consider whether the content in question is to be classified as hateful, for example.[103] However, the definitions of the providers are not checked for their appropriateness nor are these definitions used as a basis for later rulings as a generally accepted definition. The decisions are usually limited to reviewing the legal validity of such guidelines and standards of the providers and to assessing the content in question according to these guidelines.

10.8 Additional Information on International Law and Organisations

10.8.1 Impact of Other Human Rights Treaties

The Convention on the Prevention and Punishment of the Crime of Genocide (Genocide Convention) of 9 December 1948 was acceded to by the Federal Republic of Germany by law of 9 August 1954.[104] The Convention entered into force in Germany on 22 February 1955.[105] Its implementation in Germany initially led to the enactment of a criminal offence of genocide in Section 220a of the German Criminal Code (now Section 6 of the Code of Crimes against International Law; 'Völkerstrafgesetzbuch'), without at first being relevant for combating hateful expression.

However, this provision was referred almost 40 years later by the Act Amending the Criminal Code, the Code of Criminal Procedure and Other Laws (Crime Control Act) of 28 October 1994.[106] Since then, the criminal offence of incitement of masses in Section 130 (3) of the Criminal Code punishes with imprisonment of up to five years or a fine 'whoever ... approves of, denies or downplays an act committed under

[102] So far, the Federal Court of Justice has only criticised if the Court of First Instance has not included an obvious xenophobic motivation in the sentencing, emphasising that such an attitude of the offender is only relevant for the sentencing if it is expressed in the concrete act; BGH 20.8.2020, *BeckRS* 2020, 23538 paras 14–15.

[103] See e.g. KG 22.3.2019, *NJW-RR* 2019, 1260; OLG Dresden 11.12.2019, *NJW-RR* 2020, 426; OLG Hamm 15.9.2020, *K&R* 2020, 841; OLG München 7.1.2020, *MMR* 2021, 79; LG Bremen 20.6.2019, *MMR* 2020, 426.

[104] BGBl. II, 729.

[105] BGBl. II, 210.

[106] BGBl. I, 3186.

the rule of National Socialism of the kind indicated in Section 220a (1) of the German Criminal Code [currently Section 6 (1) of the Code of Crimes against International Law] in a manner which is suitable for causing a disturbance of the public peace'.

This was intended to make the denial of Holocaust (the so-called 'Auschwitz lie'; 'Auschwitzlüge') a punishable offence. However, the concrete reason for this amendment was a wave of hatred and violence against foreign citizens and asylum seekers at the beginning of the 1990s, which resulted, among other things, in right-wing extremist motivated arson attacks on houses in Mölln and Solingen, which were inhabited by residents of Turkish descent. The Convention on the Prevention and Punishment of the Crime of Genocide, which had been in force for more than 40 years at that time, probably played no role in this respect. At least the Genocide Convention is not mentioned in the explanatory memorandum to the law.[107]

The Convention on the Elimination of All Forms of Discrimination against Women of 18 December 1979 was signed by (the Federal Republic of) Germany on 17 July 1980. Ratification was made by law of 25 April 1985;[108] the Convention entered into force for Germany on 9 August 1985.[109] The Optional Protocol of 6 October 1999 was approved by Germany by law of 3 December 2001;[110] it entered into force in Germany on 15 April 2002.[111] As far as can be seen, however, the Convention has not affected German legislation on hate speech, even though the legislature noted in the explanatory memorandum of the Act to Combat Right-Wing Extremism and Hate Crime of 30 March 2021[112] that women are particularly affected by hate crime and hate speech.[113]

10.8.2 Impact of Other Monitoring Bodies or Major NGOs

Interventions by other monitoring bodies have not had any major impact on legislation or policy in Germany with regard to hate speech. Only in the explanatory memorandum of the aforementioned Act on the Implementation of Recommendations of the NSU Committee of Inquiry of the German Bundestag of 12 June 2015,[114] which explicitly added 'in particular including racist, xenophobic or other motives evidencing contempt for humanity' of the perpetrator as sentencing factors under Criminal Code Section 46 (2) sentence 2, was reference made to the corresponding 'recommendations of several international bodies concerned with

[107] See BT-Drs. 12/8588; as well as earlier draft laws to criminalise the so-called Auschwitz lie (BT-Drs. 9/2090 and BT-Drs. 10/1286).

[108] BGBl. II, 647.

[109] BGBl. II, 1234.

[110] BGBl. II, 1237.

[111] BGBl. II, 1197.

[112] BGBl. I, 441.

[113] BT-Drs. 19/17741, 15 and 32.

[114] BGBl. I, 925.

combating racism and xenophobia'. These included not only the concluding observations of the Committee on the Elimination of Racial Discrimination (CERD) of the United Nations on the 16th to 18th State Reports of Germany (see Sect. 10.4),[115] but also the report of the Special Rapporteur of the United Nations on Racism, Githu Muigai, on his visit to Germany of 22 February 2010, as well as the report of the European Commission against Racism and Intolerance (ECRI) of the Council of Europe on Germany in the fifth monitoring cycle of 25 February 2014.

Interventions by leading non-governmental organisations are also unlikely to have had a significant impact on legislation and policy in combating hate speech. As indicated above, recent legislation to combat hate speech has tended to be reactive and always driven by actual events or legal occasions rather than addressing the phenomenon in a thorough and well considered manner. Amnesty International's assessment that 'no comprehensive strategy to combat hate crime ... has been developed either at federal or state level'[116] can therefore be confirmed.

Likewise, the report by Human Rights Watch for Germany for the year 2020[117] states: 'Racism, antisemitism, and Islamophobia, including violent hate crimes, remained a concern.' Among other things, reference was made to the (sixth) report of the aforementioned European Commission against Racism and Intolerance (ECRI) of 10 December 2019,[118] according to which 'the police do not sufficiently co-operate with civil society to detect and register hate crimes, resulting in under-reporting of such offenses'.

According to my own cautious assessment, these criticisms could well be true, but they would probably not be an observation that describes the situation in Germany alone. Rather, as reports at the 37th Conference on Comparative Law of the Comparative Law Society ('Gesellschaft für Rechtsvergleichung') in Greifswald in September 2019 showed,[119] this is also likely to apply to other states for different reasons. However, ECRI's assessment that 'German public discourse has become increasingly xenophobic in recent years, and that hate speech has become more common'[120] is even more worrying. I am afraid, however, that this assessment is entirely correct.

---

115 BT-Drs. 18/3007, 14.

116 Amnesty 2020.

117 Available at https://www.hrw.org/world-report/2021/country-chapters/germany.

118 ECRI 2020.

119 Published in issue 3 of the 132nd volume [2020] of the *Zeitschrift für die gesamte Strafrechtswissenschaft*; see in particular on the reality of prosecuting hate crimes in the USA, Eisenberg 2020, p. 644, 649–654 and in Poland, Kremens 2020, pp. 596, 603–608.

120 ECRI 2020, p. 18.

10.9 National Popular Culture

I am not aware of any empirical studies that have examined the handling of hateful expression in the media or in the school system in more detail. My impressions are therefore based only on my own experiences, i.e., from the media I usually frequent and from my relatives, friends and acquaintances. These experiences are, of course, subjective. Moreover, since I am of both German and Korean descent, I am likely to be more sensitive to the issue of hateful expression and my answers may well differ from the prevailing opinion in Germany. Even the colleagues from Germany who are participating in the World Congress may well have a different view of the situation in Germany.

In Germany the topic of 'hate crime' has become more important in recent years. The mass media and educational institutions, as well as the population generally, have also increasingly understand hateful expression as a challenge for society as a whole. This development is probably due in part to the killing of the district president of Kassel, Walter Lübcke, who was shot dead in June 2019 by a perpetrator with contacts to the right-wing extremist scene.[121] The reason for the act was Lübcke's commitment to refugees during the refugee crisis (so-called 'Flüchtlingswelle').

The fact that Lübcke became the target of the crime was due to a video recording of an event in October 2015, at which he defended planned refugee shelters with clear words against public criticisms. This recording was distributed widely in right-wing communication services on the internet, often accompanied by comments calling for violence and murder. Lübcke's contact details, including his private address, were also published in these online groups. Depending on how the term is understood, the murder of Walter Lübcke might not even be classified as a 'hate crime' because it was not directed against a member of a population group against which the perpetrator, who was accused in his conviction of having a racist, nationalistic attitude and hatred of foreigners, was prejudiced. However, a distinctive connection to the phenomenon of hate crime cannot be denied because of the motive of Lübcke's refugee policy, for which the perpetrator attacked him. These events have shown the effects of hateful expression on the internet and how uncontrollable and far-reaching such statements can be.

The handling of hateful expression in the German media and educational institutions is certainly in need of improvement at times. However, it does not seem to me that there are any fundamental deficits. Thus I could not claim that social media have an unusually high influence on law and politics. Admittedly, the importance of social media is growing constantly, and we can also eagerly await the extent to which upcoming election campaigns for the German Bundestag will take place on

[121] The killing of Walter Lübcke is certainly not the only crime in recent years that can be seen as an expression of hate crime and has become the subject of public attention. One example is the attack in Halle (Saale) in October 2019, when a right-wing extremist perpetrator tried to enter a synagogue at gunpoint on Yom Kippur, the highest Jewish holiday, and kill the people gathered there. When this failed, the attacker shot at people outside the synagogue, killing two people before he could be arrested.

the internet and what statements will be made. However, it is not (yet) the standard in Germany, for example, for leading politicians to use social media daily and primarily to make questionable, sometimes even hateful statements. The role of social media is certainly viewed critically regarding the roughening of political debate, a reduction of content to buzzwords, the increasing spread of misinformation, and its importance in the dissemination of hateful expression. In sum, I would not attribute an excessive influence on law and politics in Germany to social media, but perhaps this assessment already expresses the classification of social media as a standard means of communication.

10.9.1 Depictions of Hateful Expression in Media

Most mass media agencies in Germany seem to have understood the significance of hateful expression and are critical of hesitant or inadequate developments in the fight against hate crime. Of course, there are also media in Germany that underrate the significance of hateful expression or fall back on it themselves. Unfortunately, there are also channels that address only certain groups of the population, such as right-wing extremist circles, and even welcome hateful expression or at least want to defend it as an exercise of freedom of expression. Regardless of whether such channels are professional in the sense of critically independent and carefully researching media, their reach and professional presentation should not be underestimated.

Whether the majority of the population are already aware of the dangers posed by hateful expression seems questionable to me, even after the aforementioned events of 2019. Many internet users have already encountered 'hate speech' and are thus well aware of the phenomenon, and the vast majority are also appalled by it.[122] However, according to surveys, the increasing discussion about so-called political correctness in public debate, i.e. the effort to avoid speech that could offend and disparage certain groups of the population, such as women, homosexuals, or people of non-white skin colour, is increasingly leading to the impression that people are no longer allowed to express their opinions freely.[123]

These concerns do not necessarily refer to 'hate speech'. However, the sensitive topics mentioned in the surveys are those that concern groups such as refugees, Muslims, Jews, homosexuals, women, and others[124] who are among the likely victims of 'hate speech'. In my impression, this development seems to lead to a situation

[122] See e.g. the results report of a survey conducted on behalf of the Media Authority of North Rhine-Westphalia 2020

[123] According to a survey conducted by the Allensbach Institute for Public Opinion Research in 2021, 44 % of respondents believe they are no longer able to freely express their own opinions in Germany. Only one percentage point more (45 %) believe that they are still able to express their opinions freely; https://www.zeit.de/kultur/2021-06/meinungsfreiheit-deutschland-allensbach-umfrage-gefuehle/komplettansicht.

[124] See e.g. the 2019 survey by the Allensbach Institute for Public Opinion Research 2019, Appendix Table A 1.

in which the discussion of 'hate speech' is often no longer about dealing with its contents and dangers, but about the question of whether such statements are or should be covered by freedom of expression.

10.9.2 Primary Education

I am the father of two school-age children. My impressions, however, cannot be used as a representative example for all schools in Germany, because the school system in Germany is the responsibility of the federal states. The textbooks sometimes strive for diversity and, for example, also depict students with a migration background. Sometimes, however, these books still contain expressions and associations that can no longer be described as socially acceptable, so, there is room for improvement. I don't know if 'hate speech' is discussed in class, at least I didn't notice it in my children's first years at school. However, hopefully schools will take a clear stand against 'hate speech' if this should be necessary due to current events.

10.9.3 Higher Education Institutions

I would describe higher educational institutions in Germany, e.g. universities, in a similar way. I do not assume that university administrations deny, downplay, or approve of 'hateful expression' or the dangers associated with it. To the contrary, there is currently an increasing emphasis on more tolerant language, and universities are certainly aware of the power of language.

10.10 Germany's History During the Nazi Regime

Due to the Holocaust, for which the Nazi regime was responsible, and which claimed the lives of around six million Jews during the Second World War, Germany has a special historical and painful background, which also affects the way hate crime and hateful expression are dealt with and is referred to in the explanatory memoranda of thematically relevant laws. For example, the extension of the grounds for sentencing in Criminal Code Section 46 (2) sentence 2 to include antisemitic motives of the perpetrator was justified by the special historical responsibility that Germany has because of the crimes of the National Socialist reign of violence and arbitrariness.[125]

The courts also sometimes refer to this historical background. For example, in the *Toeben* decision mentioned above (see Sect. 10.6), the Federal Court of Justice stated that the prosecuted act of Holocaust denial on a freely accessible website concerned

125 BT-Drs. 19/17741, 19.

a weighty domestic legal interest which, moreover, had a special reference to the territory of Germany and the violation of which the offence of incitement of masses was intended to prevent.[126] Thus, 'the offence of utterance under Section 130 (1) of the German Criminal Code ...—because of Germany's special history—seeks to counteract the setting in motion of a momentum of its own that has historically been proven to be dangerous' and 'the offence of denial under Section 130 (3) of the German Criminal Code ... has a special reference to the Federal Republic of Germany because of the uniqueness of the crimes committed against the Jews under National Socialism'.[127] In conclusion, the Federal Court of Justice considered Germany's appalling history to be a legitimising factor under international law in order to apply German criminal law also to acts of Holocaust denial committed abroad.

In the so-called Wunsiedel ruling,[128] the Federal Constitutional Court also justified the constitutionality of Criminal Code Section 130 (4) by referring to Germany's history. Since 1 April 2005, Section 130 (4) has made it a punishable offence to disturb the public peace publicly or in a meeting in a manner which violates the dignity of the victims by approving of, glorifying or justifying National Socialist tyranny and arbitrary rule. The Federal Constitutional Court has stated that this criminal provision only covers statements of opinion that express a certain attitude towards National Socialism, and that the legislature was thus reacting to concrete political opinions that were judged to be particularly dangerous in the public debate.[129]

Accordingly, the provision is not a general law, but a special law that is specifically intended to prevent such violations of legal interests that result from the approval of the National Socialist rule of violence and terror. Nevertheless, the Federal Constitutional Court considered the provision to be constitutional.[130] After all,

> [I]n view of the injustice and horror that elude general categories, which the National Socialist rule brought upon Europe and large parts of the world, and the emergence of the Federal Republic of Germany understood as a counter-draft to this ... Article 5 (1) and (2) of the Basic Law for provisions that set limits to the propagandistic approval of the National Socialist regime in the years between 1933 and 1945 are immanent an exception to the prohibition of the special right for opinion-related laws.[131]

The fact that incitement of masses, as a prime example of a criminal offence in the fight against hate crime, is associated with this historical background may have contributed to another German peculiarity concerning the statistical recording of hate crime.[132] In Germany, hate crime is still statistically recorded only as a subset of so-called 'politically motivated crime'. This term covers not only hate crime,

---

[126] BGH 12.12.2000, *BGHSt* 46, 212, 224—*Toeben.*

[127] BGH 12.12.2000, *BGHSt* 46, 212, 224—*Toeben.*

[128] BVerfG 4.11.2009, *BVerfGE* 124, 300—*Wunsiedel.*

[129] BVerfG 4.11.2009, *BVerfGE* 124, 300, 326—*Wunsiedel.*

[130] BVerfG 4.11.2009, *BVerfGE* 124, 300, 326—*Wunsiedel.*

[131] BVerfG 4.11.2009, *BVerfGE* 124, 300, 327 f.—*Wunsiedel.*

[132] Detailed on the police recording of hate crime *Glet*, Sozialkonstruktion und strafrechtliche Verfolgung von Hasskriminalität in Deutschland, 2011, S. 79 ff.

but also, among other things, common dangerous crimes such as arson or explosive offences, which are intended to influence the democratic decision-making process or are directed against the free democratic basic order, the existence and security of the federal government or a state.[133] Nevertheless, since hate crime always has a political, primarily right-wing extremist background, this approach arguably neglects the criminological specifics of hate crime.[134]

10.11 Addendum on Germany by Hilf. Doz. Dr. Selman DURSUN[135]

Bericht über die Entscheidung „Soldaten sind Mörder": Meinungsfreiheit und Ehrschutzdelikte[136]

Dieser Bericht handelt von dem Beschluss des Bundesverfassungsgerichts (Erster Senat) vom 10. Oktober 1995 zum Verhältnis von Meinungsfreiheit und Ehrenschutz bei Kollektivurteilen über Soldaten. Als Leitsatz ist die „Soldaten sind Mörder"-Entscheidung genannt (Fundstelle in der Entscheidungssammlung: BVerfGE 93, 266).

I. *Vorbemerkungen zur Aussage „Soldaten sind Mörder"*

Vor den Erläuterungen zur Entscheidung möchte ich kurz auf die Aussage „Soldaten sind Mörder" eingehen, damit man das Leitsatz und auch die Entscheidung besser verstehen kann. Der Ausdruck „Soldaten sind Mörder" ist ein Zitat, das auf eine Glosse des deutschen Journalisten und Schriftstellers Kurt Tucholsky zurückgeht und das 1931 in einer Zeitschrift veröffentlicht wurde. Unter einem Pseudonym hat er geschrieben:

> „Da gab es vier Jahre lang ganze Quadratmeilen Landes, auf denen war der Mord obligatorisch, während er eine halbe Stunde davon entfernt ebenso streng verboten war. Sagte ich: Mord? Natürlich Mord. Soldaten sind Mörder."

Der verantwortliche Redakteur der Zeitschrift wurde daraufhin 1932 wegen „Beleidigung der Reichswehr" angeklagt, jedoch freigesprochen mit der Begründung, dass keine konkreten Personen gemeint gewesen seien und eine unbestimmte Gesamtheit nicht beleidigt werden könne.

---

[133] See the Federal Government's answer in BT-Drucks. 17/1928 S. 4 to a Minor Question (BT-Drucks. 17/1630).

[134] Glet 2011, p. 90; Valerius 2020, pp. 666, 669.

[135] Lehrstuhl für Straf- und Strafverfahrensrecht an der juristischen Fakultät der Universität Istanbul.

[136] Dieser Text wurde im Rahmen des Projekts zur Übersetzung von Leitentscheidungen des Bundesverfassungsgerichts (Die Einführung der Verfassungsbeschwerde in der Türkei: Erste Erfahrungen, weitere Perspektive) vorbereitet und beim Workshop an der Frei Universität Berlin (20.-21. Juni 2014) vorgetragen.

In den folgenden Jahrzehnten wurde der Satz zu einer Parole von Pazifisten und Antimilitaristen. Auch in der Geschichte Deutschlands war diese Aussage Anlass für verschiedene Gerichtsverfahren bis hin zur vorhandenen Entscheidung des Bundesverfassungsgerichts, sowie den sogenannten „Soldatenurteilen" (Freispruch-Urteile) von Frankfurter Gerichten. In dem Fall der Frankfurter Soldatenurteile hatte sich ein Arzt und ehemaliger Sanitätsoffiziersanwärter bei einer Podiumsdiskussion 1984 gegenüber einem anwesenden Jugendoffizier folgendermaßen geäußert: „Jeder Soldat ist ein potentieller Mörder—auch Sie, Herr W. In der Bundeswehr gibt es einen Drill zum Morden."

Andererseits wurde als Reaktion auf den Freispruch 1932 ein besonderer „Ehrenschutz für Soldaten" durch eine neue Vorschrift (§ 134a) im Strafgesetzbuch festgeschrieben. Der § 134a StGB wurde 1946 abgeschafft. Auch als Reaktion auf die Urteile des Bundesverfassungsgerichts, die Gegenstand meines Berichts sind, wurde ein Gesetzesentwurf zum Ehrenschutz der Bundeswehr vorbereitet, aber abgelehnt[137].

Jetzt möchte ich direkt über die Entscheidung des Bundesverfassungsgerichts sprechen. Dabei werde ich dem System der Entscheidung folgen. Die etwa 50 Seitige Entscheidung enthält eine kurze Einleitung, die Entscheidungsformel, eine umfassende Begründung sowie eine abweichende Meinung.

II. *Einleitung*

Zu Beginn der Entscheidung werden die *Beschwerdeführer* und die jeweiligen strafgerichtlichen *Verurteilungen* wegen Beleidigung der Bundeswehr und einzelner Soldaten durch Äußerungen wie „Soldaten sind Mörder" oder „Soldaten sind potentielle Mörder" festgestellt.

Es gibt 4 Beschwerdeführer (Herrn F, E, S und Frau K) sowie 4 letztinstanzliche Strafgerichtsurteile der Revisionsinstanz (Oberlandesgericht). Dazu kommen die Urteile der ersten Instanz (Amtsgericht) und der zweiten Instanz/Berufungsinstanz (Landgericht)[138].

III. *Entscheidungsformel*

Gemäß der Entscheidungsformel hätten alle 4 Urteilen die Beschwerdeführer in ihrem Grundrecht aus Artikel 5 Absatz 1 Satz 1 des Grundgesetzes[139] verletzt. Die Entscheidungen wurden aufgehoben und die Sachen wurden an die zuständigen Strafgerichte (Amtsgericht oder Landgericht) zurückverwiesen. Auch wurde entschieden, dass die Länder (Bayern und Rheinland-Pfalz) den Beschwerdeführern die notwendigen Auslagen erstatten mussten.

---

137 Siehe für detaillierte Informationen *de.wikipedia.org*, Artikel für „Soldaten sind Mörder" und „Kurt Tucholsky". Siehe auch *Gounalakis*, „Soldaten sind Mörder", NJW, 1996, 481 ff.

138 Das heißt, in dem Fall sind die Verfassungsbeschwerden *eigentlich* gegen 12 Urteilen, die in Freistaat Bayern (drei Gruppen) und Rheinland-Pfalz (eine Gruppe) abgegeben wurden.

139 „Jeder hat das Recht, seine Meinung in Wort, Schrift und Bild frei zu äußern und zu verbreiten und sich aus allgemein zugänglichen Quellen ungehindert zu unterrichten."

IV. *Gründe*

Freilich ist die Begründung das wichtigste und umfassendste Stück der Entscheidung. Die Gründe wurden in drei Teilen dargelegt.

A. *Zusammenfassung der Sachverhalte, Verurteilungen und Verfassungsbeschwerden*

Im ersten Teil wurden für jedes der vier Urteile die *Sachverhalte*, die *Verurteilungen* (erste-, zweite- und Revisionsinstanz) und die *Verfassungsbeschwerden* (inklusive der Antworten/Auffassungen der Länder zu den Beschwerden) in vier Untertiteln zusammengefasst (fast 20 Seiten).

Die *Sachverhalte* sind kurz wie folgt:

1. Zeigen und Befestigen eines Transparents, das die englische (falsche) Übersetzung von „Ein Soldat ist ein Mörder" sowie „A Soldier is a Murder" (Ein Soldat ist ein Mord) enthält, als Protest gegen NATO-Herbstmanöver, durch einen 30-Jährigen Student, der anerkannter Kriegsdienstverweigerer ist.
2. Verteilen und Befestigen eines Flugblatts, das die Frage „Sind Soldaten potentielle Mörder?" und die bejahenden Antworten dafür enthält, von einem Oberstudienrat, der auch anerkannter Kriegsdienstverweigerer ist.
3. Veröffentlichung eines Leserbriefs in der Zeitung, der den Satz „Alle Soldaten sind potentielle Mörder!" enthält und aus Anlass des Freispruchs des Arztes Dr. A. im „Frankfurter Soldatenprozess" geschrieben wurde.
4. Hochhalten eines Transparents vor dem Informationsstand der Bundeswehr in einer Ausstellung, auf dem der Satz „Soldaten sind potentielle MÖRDER" steht, durch demonstrierende Kriegsdienstverweigerer, darunter auch die Beschwerdeführerin.

Alle Beschwerdeführer wurden wegen Beleidigung der Bundeswehr und einzelner Soldaten durch die eben genannten Äußerungen verurteilt. In *den Urteilen* haben die Gerichte sich der Rechtsauffassung des Bundesgerichtshofs (BGHSt 36, 83) angeschlossen, dass die Beleidigung aktiver Bundeswehrsoldaten unter der Kollektivbezeichnung „Soldaten" dann möglich sei, wenn ein Unwerturteil mit einem eindeutig allen Soldaten zuzuordnenden Kriterium verbunden sei und die weitergehende Bezeichnung (alle Soldaten schlechthin) auch den engeren, klar abgrenzbaren und überschaubaren Kreis der aktiven Soldaten der Bundeswehr mit umfasse. Die Äußerungen seien auch nicht durch die Wahrnehmung berechtigter Interessen (§ 193 StGB) in Verbindung mit Article 5 Abs. 1 Satz 1 GG gerechtfertigt. Sie seien als eine unzulässige Schmähkritik zu werten, weil nicht die Auseinandersetzung in der Sache, sondern die Herabsetzung des Ansehens der Soldaten und damit deren Diffamierung im Vordergrund stehen.

Mit ihren *Verfassungsbeschwerden* haben die Beschwerdeführer eine Verletzung ihrer Grundrechte und grundrechtsgleichen Rechte aus Article 5 Abs. 1 (Meinungsfreiheit), Article 103 Abs. 2 (Bestimmtheitsgebot) und Article 2 Abs. 1 GG in Verbindung mit dem Rechtsstaatsprinzip gerügt. Ihre wichtigsten Rügen sind kurz wie folgt:

- Alle Soldaten schlechthin stellten keine beleidigungsfähige Personenmehrheit dar. Die insoweit erforderliche Individualisierung liege nicht vor, da alle Soldaten einen deutlich umgrenzten Kreis von Einzelpersonen bildeten. Dieser Personenkreis sei nicht überschaubar, so dass sich eine eventuelle Beleidigung in diesem großen Personenkreis verliere. Die Äußerungen wollen nichts anderes besagen, als dass alle Soldaten der Welt - ohne Bezug auf eine bestimmte Armee - potentielle Mörder seien. Gerade der Hinweis auf die Äußerung Kurt Tucholskys zeige dies, da sich auch diese Äußerung auf alle Soldaten aller Armeen des Ersten Weltkrieges bezogen habe.
- Die Einordnung der beanstandeten Äußerung als Schmähkritik sei willkürlich und erfolge durch eine nur formelhafte, nicht auf den konkreten Fall bezogene Begründung.
- (Bestimmtheitsgebot) § 185 StGB beschreibe nicht ein bestimmtes Verhalten, sondern stelle auf den außerrechtlichen Begriff der Beleidigung ab. Es bestehe aber kein gesellschaftlicher Konsens, was unter einer Beleidigung zu verstehen sei.

Nach Auffassung des Bayerischen Staatsministeriums der Justiz sind die Verfassungsbeschwerden zulässig, aber nicht begründet.

- Es sei in der Rechtsprechung anerkannt, dass die Beleidigung von Einzelpersonen unter einer Kollektivbezeichnung möglich sei. Jedenfalls sei das Erfordernis einer abgrenzbaren Personenmehrheit bei den am Manöver beteiligten Soldaten erfüllt. Die Beleidigungsfähigkeit der aktiven Soldaten der Bundeswehr unter einer Kollektivbezeichnung sowie die Beleidigungsfähigkeit der Bundeswehr als Institution, seien nicht zu beanstanden.
- Die Gleichsetzung der Soldaten der Bundeswehr mit Mördern stelle eine schwerwiegende Ehrverletzung dar. Der Beschwerdeführer habe sein Anliegen auch mit einer auf die objektive Geschehen bezogene Formulierung wie „Krieg ist Mord“ verfolgen können. Der von ihm gewählte Weg überschreite den Bereich des nach Article 5 GG Zulässigen und sei als Schmähkritik an den Soldaten zu werten. Entsprechendes gelte im Verhältnis zur Bundeswehr als Institution.
- Der Begriff der Beleidigung werde zwar in § 185 StGB nicht näher umschrieben, er habe aber durch die Rechtsprechung des Bundesgerichtshofs und des Bundesverfassungsgerichts feste Konturen erhalten und werde allgemein als die Kundgabe der Missachtung, Geringschätzung oder Nichtachtung definiert.

B. *Zulässigkeit der Verfassungsbeschwerden*

Im zweiten Teil hat das Bundesverfassungsgericht die Zulässigkeit der Verfassungsbeschwerden geprüft und im Wesentlichen als zulässig befunden.

C. *Prüfung der Begründetheit*

Im dritten und letzten Abschnitt hat das Bundesverfassungsgericht die zulässigen Verfassungsbeschwerden auf ihre Begründetheit geprüft (mehr 20 Seiten). Die Gründe wurden in 6 Teilen erläutert.

1. Zusammenfassung der Gründe

Hier wurde zuerst der Schutzumfang von Article 5 GG mit Zitierung der betreffenden Rechtsprechungen dargelegt und dann die Fälle bewertet. Demgemäß liegen die Äußerungen im Schutzbereich des Grundrechts auf Meinungsfreiheit, weil die Beschwerdeführer mit ihren Äußerungen, Soldaten seien Mörder oder potentielle Mörder, nicht über bestimmten Soldaten behauptet haben, diese hätten in der Vergangenheit einen Mord begangen. Sie haben vielmehr ein Urteil über Soldaten und über den Soldatenberuf zum Ausdruck gebracht, der unter Umständen zum Töten anderer Menschen zwingt. Vom Vorliegen eines Werturteils, nicht einer Tatsachenbehauptung, sind auch die Strafgerichte ausgegangen.

Das Gericht hat betont, dass das Grundrecht auf Meinungsfreiheit allerdings nicht vorbehaltlos gewährleistet ist. Nach Article 5 Abs. 2 GG findet es seine Schranken vielmehr an den Vorschriften der allgemeinen Gesetze, den gesetzlichen Bestimmungen zum Schutz der Jugend und dem Recht der persönlichen Ehre. Dazu gehört auch § 185 StGB, der den angegriffenen Entscheidungen zugrunde liegt. Um die Verurteilung tragen zu können, muss die Vorschrift jedoch ihrerseits mit dem Grundgesetz übereinstimmen und überdies in verfassungsmäßiger Weise ausgelegt und angewandt werden.

2. Verfassungsmäßigkeit von § 185 StGB

Nach der Entscheidung sei § 185 StGB mit Articles 5 und 103 GG vereinbar, weil die Vorschrift in erster Linie die persönliche Ehre schütze und diese vor allem durch Meinungsäußerungen verletzt werden könne. Deswegen sei sie in Article 5 Abs. 2 GG ausdrücklich als rechtfertigender Grund für Einschränkungen der Meinungsfreiheit anerkannt.

Der Begriff der Beleidigung hätte jedenfalls durch die über hundertjährige und im wesentlichen einhellige Rechtsprechung einen hinreichend klaren Inhalt erlangt, der den Gerichten ausreichende Vorgaben für die Anwendung an die Hand gebe und den Normadressaten deutlich mache, wann sie mit einer Bestrafung wegen Beleidigung zu rechnen hätten. § 185 StGB sei daher auch nicht zu unbestimmt und verstoße damit nicht gegen Article 103 Abs. 2 GG. Soweit es zur Kollektivbeleidigung noch ungeklärte Streitfragen gebe, werde dadurch die Bestimmtheit der Norm nicht berührt.

3. Auslegungs- und Anwendungsmethode von § 185 StGB

Obwohl die Auslegung und Anwendung der Strafgesetze die Sache der Strafgerichte sei, sei bei Gesetzen, die die Meinungsfreiheit beschränken nach ständiger Rechtsprechung des Bundesverfassungsgerichts das eingeschränkte Grundrecht zu beachten.

Auf der Stufe der Normauslegung erfordere Article 5 Abs. 1 Satz 1 GG eine im Rahmen der Tatbestandsmerkmale der betreffenden Gesetze vorzunehmende *Abwägung* zwischen der Bedeutung einerseits der Meinungsfreiheit und andererseits des Rechtsguts, in dessen Interesse sie eingeschränkt worden ist. Damit sei eine Interpretation von § 185 StGB unvereinbar, die den Begriff der Beleidigung so weit ausdehne, dass er die Erfordernisse des Ehren- oder Institutionenschutzes überschreite oder für die Berücksichtigung der Meinungsfreiheit keinen Raum mehr lasse.

Wenn sich die Äußerung weder als Angriff auf die Menschenwürde noch als Formalbeleidigung oder Schmähung einstufen lasse, so komme es für die Abwägung auf die Schwere der Beeinträchtigung der betroffenen Rechtsgüter an und die Meinungsfreiheit müsse regelmäßig hinter dem Ehrenschutz zurücktreten.

Wegen seines die Meinungsfreiheit verdrängenden Effekts hätte das Bundesverfassungsgericht den in der Fachgerichtsbarkeit entwickelten Begriff der Schmähkritik jedoch eng definiert. Danach mache auch eine überzogene oder gar ausfällige Kritik eine Äußerung für sich genommen noch nicht zur Schmähung. Hinzutreten müsse vielmehr, dass bei der Äußerung nicht mehr die Auseinandersetzung in der Sache, sondern die Diffamierung der Person im Vordergrund stehe. Sie müsse, jenseits auch von polemischer und überspitzter Kritik, in der persönlichen Herabsetzung bestehen.

4. Bewertung der Auslegungs- und Anwendungsmethode der angegriffenen Entscheidungen

Nach dem Bundesverfassungsgericht seien die angegriffenen Entscheidungen den eben erwähnten Anforderungen nicht voll gerecht worden. Es bestünden keinen verfassungsrechtlichen Bedenken, dass die Gerichte bei der Abwägung zwischen Meinungsfreiheit und Ehrenschutz dem Ehrenschutz ohne weiteres den Vorzug geben, wenn in der umstrittenen Äußerung kein Beitrag zur Auseinandersetzung in der Sache liege, sondern die Diffamierung der Person im Vordergrund stehe. Das entspreche der Rechtsprechung des Bundesverfassungsgerichts zur Schmähkritik. Voraussetzung sei aber, dass es sich bei der fraglichen Äußerung wirklich um Schmähkritik handele. Merkmal der Schmähung sei die, das sachliche Anliegen völlig in den Hintergrund drängende, persönliche Kränkung. Den Beschwerdeführern sei es indessen erkennbar um eine Auseinandersetzung in der Sache gegangen, und zwar um die Frage, ob Krieg und Kriegsdienst und die damit verbundene Tötung von Menschen sittlich gerechtfertigt seien oder nicht.

Es sei nicht ausgeschlossen, dass auch bei herabsetzenden Äußerungen über große Kollektive die Diffamierung der ihnen angehörenden Personen im Vordergrund stehe. Das gelte insbesondere dann, wenn die Äußerungen an ethnische, rassische, körperliche oder geistige Merkmale anknüpfen, aus denen die Minderwertigkeit einer ganzen Personengruppe und damit zugleich jedes einzelnen Angehörigen abgeleitet werde. In der Regel würden aber nur Äußerungen über bestimmte Personen oder Personenvereinigungen als Schmähkritik in Betracht kommen. Nur in diesem Sinn sei der Begriff auch bisher in der Rechtsprechung des Bundesverfassungsgerichts und des Bundesgerichtshofs verwendet worden.

5. Die Mängel in jeden einzelnen Entscheidungen

Das Bundesverfassungsgericht hat ferner die Unvollständigkeiten in Teilen der angegriffenen Entscheidungen gerügt. Im ersten Verfahren hätte etwa das Amtsgericht sich die konkrete Abwägung zwischen Meinungsfreiheit und Ehrenschutz versperrt, die in Fällen, in denen weder eine Formalbeleidigung noch eine Schmähkritik vorliegt, stets erforderlich sei.

Im zweiten Verfahren sei die Wahrnehmung berechtigter Interessen dem Beschwerdeführer mit der Behauptung abgesprochen worden, dass sein Text die Menschenwürde herabsetze und die Grenze von der scharfen Kritik zur polemischen Diffamierung überschreite. Für beides fehle es an einer Begründung. Damit hätte sich das Gericht der Notwendigkeit einer Abwägung zwischen Meinungsfreiheit und Ehrenschutz entzogen. Für die weitere Annahme, dass die Äußerung nicht nur die einzelnen Soldaten, sondern die Bundeswehr im Ganzen beleidige, hätte sich das Gericht auf den Hinweis beschränkt, dass die Beleidigungsfähigkeit der Bundeswehr anerkannt sei. Es hätte aber weder dargelegt, inwiefern diese tatsächlich beleidigt worden sei, noch ausgeführt, warum die Herabsetzung ihres Ansehens schwerer wiege als die Beeinträchtigung der Meinungsfreiheit.

Ähnliche Kritiken an den anderen Verfahren finden sich auch in der Entscheidung.

6. Ergebnis

Nach dem Bundesverfassungsgericht sei in keinem der vier Fälle auszuschließen, dass die Gerichte, wenn sie naheliegende anderweitige Deutungsmöglichkeiten der Äußerungen erwogen, den Unterschied zwischen einer herabsetzenden Äußerung über alle Soldaten der Welt und die Soldaten der Bundeswehr beachtet und den Begriff der Schmähkritik verfassungskonform verwendet hätten, zu anderen Ergebnissen gekommen wären. Die angegriffenen Entscheidungen müssten daher aufgehoben und die Sachen zurückverwiesen werden. Damit würden jedoch weder die Beschwerdeführer freigesprochen noch Kränkungen einzelner Soldaten oder der Angehörigen bestimmter Streitkräfte durch Äußerungen wie „Soldaten sind Mörder“ für zulässig erklärt. Vielmehr müssten die jeweiligen Äußerungen unter Beachtung der dargelegten Anforderungen aus Article 5 Abs. 1 Satz 1 GG erneut gewürdigt werden.

Die Entscheidung ist hinsichtlich der Verfassungsbeschwerden zu (1), (3) und (4) mit fünf zu drei Stimmen, hinsichtlich der Verfassungsbeschwerde zu (2) im Ergebnis einstimmig ergangen.

V. *Abweichende Meinung*

Nach der abweichenden Meinung der Richterin Dr. Haas sei das Grundrecht der Beschwerdeführer aus Article 5 Abs. 1 GG nicht verletzt. Die Freiheit der Meinungsäußerung finde ihre Schranke im Recht der persönlichen Ehre. Ich möchte nur einige Argumente von ihr zitieren:

- „...Die Aufklärung und Würdigung des Sachverhalts obliegt den Fachgerichten. Das Bundesverfassungsgericht geht in ständiger Rechtsprechung davon aus, dass gerichtliche Entscheidungen im Verfahren der Verfassungsbeschwerde nur in engen Grenzen nachgeprüft werden können, dass insbesondere die Feststellung und Würdigung des Tatbestandes, aber auch die Auslegung einfachen Rechts und seine Anwendung auf den einzelnen Fall allein Sache der dafür allgemein zuständigen Gerichte und seiner Nachprüfung entzogen sind...“ / „...Ob der

Fachrichter den Sinn einer mehrdeutigen Äußerung in jeder Hinsicht zutreffend gedeutet hat, ist hingegen keine Frage des Verfassungsrechts. Die Auffassung der Senatsmehrheit, dass das Bundesverfassungsgericht gleichwohl prüfen kann, ob alle von ihm als denkbar erkannten Deutungsmöglichkeiten vom Fachgericht ebenfalls erwogen worden sind, teile ich daher nicht."

- „Für die Deutung des Begriffs ‚Mörder' ist schließlich auch unerheblich, was der Äußernde sagen wollte, solange dies keinen Ausdruck in der Äußerung gefunden hat. In Frage steht zunächst nur, was er tatsächlich gesagt hat; entscheidend ist der objektive Sinn, wie die Äußerung für den Durchschnittsbetrachter in der Lage des Äußerungsempfängers im Zeitpunkt der Aufnahme zu verstehen war. Deshalb kann die mögliche Absicht der Beschwerdeführer, durch die Wortwahl bei den Betroffenen das Bewusstsein persönlicher Verantwortlichkeit zu wecken, entgegen der Auffassung der Senatsmehrheit (…) die Sinnhaftigkeit der Äußerung nicht beeinflussen; denn an Inhalt und Sinn des gewählten Wortes ändert dies nichts…"
- „Auf der Grundlage des von ihnen festgestellten Sachverhalts, wonach die ehrverletzende Äußerung sich ausdrücklich oder aus dem Gesamtzusammenhang ersichtlich auf Soldaten der Bundeswehr bezog, konnten die Gerichte auch bejahen, dass die Soldaten der Bundeswehr und damit jeder einzelne Angehörige der Streitkräfte Adressat der Äußerung war. Inwieweit den Ausführungen der Senatsmehrheit zur Kollektivbeleidigung gefolgt werden kann, kann hier dahinstehen…"
- „…Eine Rechtsordnung, die junge Männer zum Waffendienst verpflichtet und von ihnen Gehorsam verlangt, muss denjenigen, die diesen Pflichten genügen, Schutz gewähren, wenn sie wegen dieses Soldatendienstes geschmäht und öffentlich als Mörder bezeichnet werden. Dabei geht es nicht um die Konstruktion einer besonderen ‚Soldatenehre'. Es geht um die schlichte Selbstverständlichkeit, dass die Verfassung, will sie ihre Glaubwürdigkeit nicht verlieren, diejenigen nicht schutzlos stellen darf, die ihre Gebote befolgen und (ausschließlich) gerade deshalb angegriffen werden. Die Wechselbeziehung zwischen Schutz und Gehorsam gehört zu den elementaren Grundsätzen einer Rechtsordnung. Dies kann und darf nicht unberücksichtigt bleiben."

References

Allensbach Institute for Public Opinion Research (2019) Survey. https://www.ifd-allensbach.de/fileadmin/user_upload/FAZ_Mai2019_Meinungsfreiheit.pdf.

Amnesty Deutschland (2020) Amnesty Report Deutschland. https://www.amnesty.de/informieren/amnesty-report/deutschland-2020.

Antidiskriminierungsstelle (2017) Discrimination in Germany. https://www.antidiskriminierungsstelle.de/SharedDocs/Downloads/DE/publikationen/BT_Bericht/gemeinsamer_bericht_dritter_2017.pdf?__blob=publicationFile&v=17.

Eisenberg AK (2020) Den Hass kriminalisieren: Rechtsgrundlagen und Vollzugsdelikte bei der strafrechtlichen Verfolgung von Hassdelikten in den Vereinigten Staaten. Zeitschrift für die gesamte Strafrechtswissenschaft: 644–665.

European Commission against Racism and Intolerance (ECRI) (2020) ECRI Report on Germany (sixth monitoring cycle). https://rm.coe.int/ecri-report-on-germany-sixth-monitoring-cycle-/16809ce4be.

Federal Ministry of Justice and Consumer Protection (2021) Press release 0512. https://www.bmjv.de/SharedDocs/Pressemitteilungen/DE/2021/0512_verhetzende_Beleidigung.html.

Glet Z (2011) Sozialkonstruktion und strafrechtliche Verfolgung von Hasskriminalität in Deutschland. Duncker & Humblot, Berlin.

Hilgendorf E (1997) Überlegungen zur strafrechtlichen Interpretation des Ubiquitätsprinzips im Zeitalter des Internet. Neue juristische Wochenschrift: 1873–1878.

Keiser C (2010) Unerlässliches zur Verteidigung der Rechtsordnung gegen so genannte Hasskriminalität. Zeitschrift für Rechtspolitik: 46–49.

Kischel U (2021) Kommentierung des Art. 3 GG. In: Beck'scher Online-Kommentar Grundgesetz, 47th edn. C.H. Beck, München.

Krauß M (2021) Kommentierung des § 130 StGB. In: Leipziger Kommentar. Strafgesetzbuch, 13th edn. de Gruyter, Berlin.

Kremens K (2020) Hasskriminalität in Polen. Zeitschrift für die gesamte Strafrechtswissenschaft: 596–615.

Krupna K (2010) Das Konzept der 'Hate Crimes' in Deutschland. Peter Lang, Bern.

Media Authority of North Rhine-Westphalia [Landesanstalt für Medien Nordrhein-Westfalen] (2020) Hate speech. https://www.medienanstalt-nrw.de/fileadmin/user_upload/NeueWebsite_0120/Themen/Hass/forsa_LFMNRW_Hassrede2020_Ergebnisbericht.pdf.

Schemmer F (2021) Kommentierung des Art. 5 GG. In: Beck'scher Online-Kommentar Grundgesetz (edit. 15.5.2021). C.H. Beck, München.

Sotiriadis G (2014) Brauchen wir sanktionsrechtliche Normen, damit Hate Crimes von der Strafjustiz angemessen beurteilt werden? Kritische Justiz: 261–275.

Valerius B (2020) Hasskriminalität – Vergleichende Analyse unter Einschluss der deutschen Rechtslage. Zeitschrift für die gesamte Strafrechtswissenschaft: 666–689.

Brian Valerius received his Doctorate from the University of Würzburg in 2004, where he habilitated in 2009. In 2011, he was appointed to the University of Bayreuth, where he held the Chair of Criminal Law, Criminal Procedure Law and Medical Criminal Law. Since October 2022, he holds the Chair of Artificial Intelligence in Criminal Law at the University of Passau. In his research and teaching, he focuses on the challenges associated with digitalisation and artificial intelligence in particular. He also specialises in medical criminal law and international and intercultural issues.

Chapter 11
Greece

George Karavokyris

Contents

Abstract Greek law currently criminalizes the provocation of, or incitement to, "acts of violence" or "hatred" against specified groups or persons. The law also penalizes the "denial" or "trivialization" of crimes of genocide, crimes against humanity, and war crimes recognized by international bodies. In these respects, Greece is broadly aligned with the continental conception of freedom of expression, bonding civil society to the State and restricting speech that is patently incompatible with the universal concept of human dignity and autonomy or with the principle of equality. The legislation has rarely been enforced but limitations on speech have often drawn public attention. The national legislature has recently taken significant steps which may signify the final turn of Greek democracy to the militant model.

Keyword Public incitement of violence · Denial of genocide · Racism · Homophobia · Hate speech by religious leaders · Ban on political parties

G. Karavokyris (✉)
University of Thessaloniki, Thessaloniki, Greece
e-mail: gkaravok@law.auth.gr

E. Heinze (ed.), *Criminalising Hate Speech*,
https://doi.org/10.1007/978-94-6265-650-5_11

11.1 National Constitutional Law

11.1.1 Constitutional Framework

According to Article 14 of the Greek Constitution,

"1. Every person may express and propagate his thoughts orally, in writing and through the press in compliance with the laws of the State. 2. The press is free. Censorship and all other preventive measures are prohibited. 3. The seizure of newspapers and other publications before or after circulation is prohibited. Seizure by order of the public prosecutor shall be allowed exceptionally after circulation and in case of: a) an offence against the Christian or any other known religion, b) an insult against the person of the President of the Republic c) a publication which discloses information on the composition, equipment and set-up of the armed forces or the fortifications of the country, or which aims at the violent overthrow of the regime or is directed against the territorial integrity of the State d) an obscene publication which is obviously offensive to public decency, in the cases stipulated by law. 4. In all the cases specified under the preceding paragraph, the public prosecutor must, within twenty-four hours from the seizure, submit the case to the judicial council which, within the next twenty-four hours, must rule whether the seizure is to be maintained or lifted; otherwise it shall be lifted ipso jure. An appeal may be lodged with the Court of Appeals and the Supreme Civil and Criminal Court by the publisher of the newspaper or other printed matter seized and by the public prosecutor. 5. Every person offended by an inaccurate publication or broadcast has the right to reply, and the information medium has a corresponding obligation for full and immediate redress. Every person offended by an insulting or defamatory publication or broadcast has also the right to reply, and the information medium has a corresponding obligation to immediately publish or transmit the reply. The manner in which the right to reply is exercised and in which full and immediate redress is assured or publication and transmission of the reply is made, shall be specified by law. 6. After at least three convictions within five years for the criminal acts defined under paragraph 3, the court shall order the definitive ban or the temporary suspension of the publication of the paper and, in severe cases, shall prohibit the convicted person from practicing the profession of journalist as specified by law. The ban or suspension of publication shall be effective as of the date the court order becomes irrevocable 7. Matters relating to the civil and criminal liability of the press and of the other information media and to the expeditious trial of relevant cases, shall be specified by law 8. The conditions and qualifications requisite for the practice of the profession of journalist shall be specified by law 9. The ownership status, the financial situation and the means of financing of information media must be made known as specified by law. The measures and restrictions necessary for fully ensuring transparency and plurality in information shall be specified by law. The concentration of the control of more than one information media of the same type or of different types is prohibited. More specifically, concentration of more than one electronic information media of the same type is prohibited, as specified by law. The capacity of owner, partner, major shareholder or managing director of an information media enterprise, is incompatible with the capacity of owner, partner, major shareholder or managing director of an enterprise that undertakes towards the Public Administration or towards a legal entity of the wider public sector to perform works or to supply goods or services. The prohibition of the previous section extends also over all types of intermediary persons, such as spouses, relatives, financially dependent persons or companies. The specific regulations, the sanctions, which may extend to the point of revocation of the license of a radio or television station and to the point of prohibition of the conclusion or to the annulment of the pertinent contract, as well as the means of control and the guarantees for the prevention of infringements of the previous sections, shall be determined by law".

The abovementioned constitutional provision empowers the legislature, and possibly the courts, to impose restrictions on the freedom of expression, whenever another constitutional right or rule is being violated or compromised. The right to freedom of expression has been common in all Greek constitutions (Article 10 of the Constitution of 1844, Article 14 of the C. of 1864 and 1911, Article 16 of the C. of 1925 and 1927 and Article 14 of the C. of 1952). The difference in the exact phrasing of the Constitution of 1975 has been the replacement of the word "publishes" by the words "express" and "propagate".[1]

Furthermore, Article 15 of the Greek Constitution stipulates that "1. Protective provisions for the press are not applicable to films, sound recordings, radio, television or any other similar medium for the transmission of speech or images. Radio and television shall be under the direct control of the State. The control and imposition of administrative sanctions are under the exclusive competence of the NCRTV, which is an independent authority, as specified by law. 2. Radio and television shall be under the direct control of the State. The control and imposition of administrative sanctions belong to the exclusive competence of the National Radio and Television Council, which is an independent authority, as specified by law. The direct control of the State, which may also assume the form of a prior permission status, shall aim at the objective and on equal terms transmission of information and news reports, as well as of works of literature and art, at ensuring the quality level of programs mandated by the social mission of radio and television and by the cultural development of the Country, as well as at the respect of the value of the human being and the protection of childhood and youth.

Matters relating to the mandatory and free of charge transmission of the workings of the Parliament and of its committees, as well as of the electoral campaign messages of the political parties by radio and television, shall be specified by law".

According to Article 16 par.1 of the Constitution,

"1. Art and science, research and teaching shall be free and their development and promotion shall be an obligation of the State. Academic freedom and freedom of teaching shall not exempt anyone from his duty of allegiance to the Constitution".

Article 5A of the Constitution stipulates that,

---

[1] Markopoulos 2017, p. 314.

"1. All persons have the right to information, as specified by law. Restrictions to this right may be imposed by law only insofar as they are absolutely necessary and justified for reasons of national security, of combating crime or of protecting rights and interests of third parties.

All persons have the right to participate in the Information Society. Facilitation of access to electronically transmitted information, as well as of the production, exchange and diffusion thereof, constitutes an obligation of the State, always in observance of the guarantees of Articles 9, 9A and 19".

Finally, according to Article 29 par.1 of the Constitution,

"1. Greek citizens possessing the right to vote may freely found and join political parties, the organization and activity of which must serve the free functioning of democratic government.

Citizens who have not yet acquired the right to vote may participate in youth sections of parties".

B. Fundamental principles

The Greek Constitution of 1975 follows the fall of the dictatorship of the colonels (1967-1974) and guarantees the transition to democracy. Thus, the constituents had adopted, more or less, a liberal conception of the freedom of expression, particularly regarding political ideas and beliefs. On the other hand, revisiting the parliamentary archives and the debates on freedom of press reveals the will of the Assembly not only to protect pluralism and freedom of journalists, but also society from abuses of the right. To sum it up, a certain ambivalence seems to emerge towards a freedom which is the cornerstone of democracy, essentially associated with public sovereignty and general will.[2]

Freedom of expression turns out to be a "mixed" right, being recognized both as an individual and political freedom. As a civil right, freedom of expression refers mostly to the concept of negative liberty, meaning the absence of obstacles, barriers or constraints imposed by the State. Moreover, the Article 14 par. 1 of the Greek Constitution, stipulates the clause of "general reserve" in favor of the law, understating that no specific or special law should target directly and bound the right to freedom of expression. For this reason, any law that aims in particular to restrict the expression and the propagation of an idea, opinion or information is contrary to the Constitution. The right to freedom of speech acquires also the status of a "positive" liberty, founding the obligation of the State to provide and promote the major institutional conditions of communication and information of the citizens, according to the Article 5A of the Constitution.

The abovementioned constitutional provisions set without doubt a solid normative ground for the protection of freedom of expression. Nevertheless, whenever a major issue of restricting the right arises, as in the case of the anti-racist legislation (Law N. 4285/2014, Government Gazette A/191), the conflict between two dominant and mainstream 'for the limits of freedom of speech' concepts resurfaces. The liberal/libertarian theory advances ethical and political tolerance and the free movement

[2] Tassopoulos 2023a, b. Article 14. Freedom of expression and freedom of press, p. 9

of ideas. On the contrary, the more moderate/protectionist/paternalistic approach implies the direct or implicit intervention of the legislator so as to protect basic freedoms and values and guide public opinion. The former refers to the American pragmatism and the famous First Amendment doctrine, where the absolute freedom of expression reflects in principle the strong suspicion of State authority and the trust to the free "marketplace of ideas", while the latter stems from the European concept of Rule of Law (in French theory «légicentrisme»), bonding civil society to the State and restricting speech that is frontally incompatible with the universal content of human dignity/autonomy or with the principle of equality.[3] In this view, hate speech is undermining free speech and therefore its prohibition should be not considered as a restriction but as a service to our freedom. Hate speech may silence persons or groups that are being attacked and prevent their consideration and comprehension[4]. Jeremy Waldron has argued that hate speech violates the "social" dignity of the victim, meaning its "basic entitlement to be regarded as a member of society in good standing, as someone whose membership of a minority group does not disqualify him or her from ordinary social interaction".[5]

The political and constitutional debate in Greece flourishes on the same controversial ground. Advocates of freedom of expression denounce the criminalization of speech and the policing of ideas, in particular legislation on negationism and banalization of certain crimes and genocides or the Holocaust. Yet, for the legislator, the imperial necessity of confronting the racist phenomenon and discourse in a democratic society justifies harsh limitations on the freedom of expression, especially when no major difference separates the effects between words and actions.[6]

Following the roots of modern liberalism, freedom of expression is strongly attached to the tolerance of the most shocking ideals and arguments, under the condition that the speech respects the famous "harm principle".[7] Even the wrong or irrational opinions and ideas can contribute in exploring and coming up with the best answer to crucial questions and the so-called "hard cases" of the public sphere. For the United States Supreme Court, "under the First Amendment, there is no such thing as a false idea".[8] Moreover, freedom of expression is based on personal autonomy and the democratic principle: only the well-informed individual can become a responsible citizen, developing his or her personality by serving the common good and general interest. On an institutional level, pluralism of ideas and expressions embraces and legitimizes political decisions that are most beneficial to the public interest. Public consultation and deliberation, the most substantial components of parliamentary representative democracy, depend on the political value of

[3] Stuart Mill 1998, p. 21. See the recent work of Tourkochoriti 2021. Also, Morange 2009. Heinze 2022.

[4] Papadopoulou 2020a, b. Kiviorg 2017, p.102. See also L. Papadopoulou 2022.

[5] Papadopoulou 2020a, b, p. 103. Waldron 2012, p. 9 ff.

[6] Tourkohoriti 2018.

[7] Feinberg 1986.

[8] Supreme Court, *Gertz v. Robert Welch*, 1974, https://supreme.justia.com/cases/federal/us/418/323/.

argumentation and rationalize general will and the majority principle.[9] However, defining in concreto what constitutes exactly a "harm" for the society and individual freedoms remains an interpretative challenge for identifying the -often obscure- limits of speech: in the European context, legislation against hate speech belongs to our common constitutional tradition and to the core values of European Convention of Human Rights[10] and EU law.[11] In any case, a tolerant democracy shall regard its enemies as simple opponents by preserving the liberal distinction between speech and action.[12]

11.2 National Statutory or Administrative Law

The Greek Parliament has amended Law No. 927/1979 on Combating Race Discrimination, so as to comply with European Union rules regarding hate speech and denial of genocide. (Law No. 4285/2014, adjusting to EU Council Framework Decision 2008/913/JHA of 28 November 2008 on Combating Certain Forms and Expressions of Racism and Xenophobia by Means of Criminal Law (2008 O.J. (L 328) 55.) More specifically, Law 4285/2014 stipulates.

11.2.1 Public Incitement of Violence or Hate Speech

Anyone, who publicly incites, provokes, or stirs, either orally or through the press, the Internet, or any other means, acts of violence or hatred against a person or group of persons or a member of such a group defined by reference to race, colour, religion, descent or national or ethnic origin, sexual orientation, gender identity, or disability, in a manner that endangers the public order and exposes the life, physical integrity, and freedom of persons defined above to danger, will be punished by imprisonment of from three months to three years and a fine of €5,000 to €20,000 (Law No. 4285/ 2014, art. 1 par. 11.1).

---

[9] Urbinati 2006.

[10] Haarcher 2007. Lina Papadopoulou underlines "that States enjoy a margin of appreciation and are free to take into consideration the specific characteristics of each society; nevertheless, the use of this margin is subject to examination by the European Court of Human Rights. More specifically, concerning limitations on free speech: 'tolerance and respect for the equal dignity of all human beings constitute the foundations of a democratic, pluralistic society. That being so, as a matter of principle it may be considered necessary in certain democratic societies to sanction or even prevent all forms of expression which spread, incite, promote or justify hatred based on intolerance ..., provided that any 'formalities', 'conditions', 'restrictions' or 'penalties' imposed are proportionate to the legitimate aim pursued' (Erbakan v Turkey, App no 59405/00 (ECHR, 6 Jul 2006), [56]" See Papadopoulou 2020a, b, p. 101.

[11] https://commission.europa.eu/strategy-and-policy/policies/justice-and-fundamental-rights/combatting-discrimination/racism-and-xenophobia/combating-hate-speech-and-hate-crime_en.

[12] Tourkochoriti 2013a, b.

If the conduct described above results in the commission of a crime, then it will be punishable by imprisonment of at least six months and a fine of €15,000 to €30,000. When the court imposes one year of imprisonment, it may also impose deprivation of political rights for a period of one to five years. (art. 1 par. 11.1 & 11.3.)

Public officials or employees who engage in the conduct described above are subject to harsher punishments. They face imprisonment of six months to three years and fines of €10,000 to €25,000. If additional acts are committed by such officials, the term of imprisonment will be at least one year, and the fine will range from €25,000 to €50,000. (art. 1 par. 11.5.)

11.2.2 Public Endorsement or Denial of Certain Crimes

Anyone who intentionally, either orally, through the press, online, or by any other means or methods, condones, trivializes, or denies the existence or seriousness of the crimes of genocide, war crimes, crimes against humanity, the Holocaust, or Nazi crimes, when those crimes have been established by international court decisions or the Greek Parliament, if this conduct is directed against a group of persons or a member of such a group defined by race, color, religion, descent, national or ethnic origin, sexual orientation, or gender identity and in a manner that is likely to incite hatred or violence or is of a threatening or insulting nature against such a group or one of its members, will be punished by the punishments indicated above (art. 2).[13]

The criminalization of provocation/agitation to "acts of violence" or "hatred" against specific groups/persons and the "denial" or "trivialization" of crimes of genocide, crimes against humanity and war crimes recognized by international bodies seems broadly aligned with the continental conception of freedom of expression, in other words with subjecting individual freedom to the (moral) norm of universalization.[14] Furthermore, the law enforces a flexible –not to say loose and uncertain-relation between words and actions, under the general estimation of the potential danger to public order. The same applies for the crimes of denialism or nullification of recognised genocides and war crimes. The latter falls under the scope of the law if expressed «in a manner that endangers» the public order and constitutional rights of life, physical integrity and freedom. However, apart from defining harm, the identity of the victim becomes a key factor for applying the restriction of speech. Anti-racist legislation regulates insults against groups and not only specific persons and therefore overcomes the (liberal/libertarian) criterion of individualization. Some scholars argue that the abstraction of the rule and the grouping of victims may result in recognizing "victimless crimes" or "imaginary crimes" that mediate the conflict of ideas, which always involves an indefinite number of persons.[15] On the other hand,

---

[13] https://www.loc.gov/item/global-legal-monitor/2014-09-24/greece-new-law-criminalizes-denial-of-genocide-hate-speech-and-other-acts-of-racism/).

[14] Karavokyris 2011, p. 599.

[15] From a philosophical standpoint see the work of Ogien 2007.

it is reasonably argued that hate speech is always public and directed to one or more individuals perceived as a group, based on certain characteristics (such as religion, ethnicity, nationality, gender identity). Thus, there is a major difference between defamation and abuse and hate speech which is not directed at a specific person but derives from hatred based on a the perceived group characteristics of the victim.[16]

The law has been criticized for his vague provisions, making possible for the authentic interpreter –the courts- to extensively restrict freedom of speech and eventually penalize harmful and provocative ideas rather than focusing on concrete actions, which are in fact harmful to society. Regarding the prohibition of denialism, plausible objections had been raised on its overall compliance with the freedom of research and academic freedom (Article 16 par.1 of the Constitution). Although the necessity of these laws, in order to symbolically condemn the banalization of extreme and unhuman atrocities, they can have dangerous unintended consequences for freedom of speech, leading to imposing an official version of the truth. Hence, they can possibly drain public debate by censoring critical contributions by historians and intellectuals.[17] Nonetheless, the rise of Golden Dawn neo-Nazi party in Greece during the recent financial crisis and the racist discourse and action in the Greek public sphere have socially and politically consolidated the need to impose limits on political antidemocratic discourse and the violent manifestations of xenophobia and racism.[18]

Last but not least, the Code of Ethics for Members of the Greek Parliament (Article 2 and paragraph 1 of Article 8) stipulates their obligation to contribute to the prevention of hate speech against persons on the base of their racial or ethnic origin, religious or political beliefs, sex, age, disability or sexual orientation.[19]

11.2.3 Acts Committed via Internet and the Media

Article 3 of Law 927/1979 provides: "When the acts of the previous articles are performed via internet or other means of communication, the Greek Territory is also considered as a place of execution, if that access to the specific means is provided in its territory, regardless of their place of establishment." In a joint statement (2022), Humanists International and the Humanist Union of Greece (HUG), invited Greece to address racism and hate crime. According to the statement, hate speech against minorities is extensive online and in the media, and remains unpunished, particularly when performed by influential institutions and individuals[20].

---

[16] Papadopoulou 2020a, b, pp. 100–101.

[17] Tourkochoriti 2-18.

[18] https://www.reuters.com/article/us-greece-racism-idUSKBN1H41VF.

[19] https://www.hellenicparliament.gr/UserFiles/f3c70a23-7696-49db-9148-f24dce6a27c8/kodikas-deonto_1.pdf (in Greek).

[20] https://humanists.international/2022/03/in-greece-those-who-challenge-hateful-rhetoric-face-reprisals-say-humanists-at-un/.

The European Commission against Racism and Intolerance (ECRI) 2022 report indicates that Greece has ratified the Additional Protocol to the Council of Europe Convention on Cybercrime, concerning the criminalisation of acts of a racist and xenophobic nature committed through computer systems (25 January 2017, put into force on 1 May 2017). According to the report, the statistics of the Hellenic Police show 51 hate speech incidents in 2020, 34 of which were online. The corresponding numbers were 92 (38 online) in 2019, 63 (39 online) in 2018, 88 (48 online) in 2017 and 29 (15 online) in 2016. Moreover, Article 8 of Law 4779/2021 instructs the audio-visual media services to not contain incitement to violence or hate against individuals or a group of people, which is defined by race characteristics, colour, national or ethnic origin, descent, religion, disability, sexual orientation, gender identity or sex characteristics. ECRI also has observed that a police website through which hate speech and hate crime incidents can be reported was created. Finally, a Cybercrime Division of the Hellenic Police is also taking action against hate speech online.[21]

The Greek Council of Radio television (an administrative independent authority) has –for the first time- issued a decision punishing media for the broadcasting of hate speech during a sports broadcasting. The host referred to a famous basket ball player as 'negro' and 'ape'. The broadcasting company was held responsible for the host's actions and was obliged to pay administrative fines and shut down the channel for 24 hours (decision No. 155/2018). The Council underlined that the broadcasting company has: a) violated its legal obligation to broadcast quality programmes, b) offended the person's value and personality, and c) allowed derogatory comments and the use expressive means which are capable of promoting discrimination on the basis of race.[22]

11.2.4 Gender Equality and Gender Base Violence

New legislation about gender equality and combatting gender base violence has been introduced in Greek legal order. The Law 4604/2019 on Substantive Gender Equality, Preventing and Combating Gender-Based Violence establishes a national mechanism for gender equality. Its aim is to design and implement policies for the promotion of equal treatment between men and women, as well as to address and monitor discrimination based on gender and sexual orientation.[23]

However, according to the 2022 report of the European Institute for Gender Equality with 53.4 out of 100 points, Greece ranks last in the EU on the Gender Equality Index, scoring 15.2 points below the EU's score. Since 2010, Greece's score has increased by 4.8 points, but its ranking has remained the same as other countries

---

[21] https://rm.coe.int/ecri-first-report-on-greece-adopted-on-28-june-2022-published-on-22-se/1680a818bf.

[22] http://fra.europa.eu/en/databases/anti-muslim-hatred/node/6889.

[23] https://isotita.gr/en/law-4604-2019-substantive-gender-equality-preventing-combating-gender-based-violence/.

have progressed more rapidly. Since 2019, Greece's score has slightly increased by 0.9 points, mainly due to improvements in the domains of power and health.[24] In fact, the domain of power has seen the most improvement of all since 2010 (15.3 points). Women in the EU hold more nowadays more decision-making positions in significant political, economic and social institutions. In Greece, the score in this domain has increased compared to 2010 (6.5 points). Still, gender inequalities are strongly effective in this domain, in which Greece ranks second to last.[25]

11.2.5 Blasphemy Laws

Abolition of "blasphemy laws": Article 198 of the Greek Penal Code stipulated that "1. One who publicly and maliciously and by any means blasphemes God shall be punished by imprisonment for not more than two years; 2. Anyone, except as described in par.1, who displays publicly with blasphemy a lack of respect for things divine, is punished with up to 3 months in prison. Article 199 declared similar provisions against anyone who "blasphemes the Greek Orthodox Church or any other religion tolerable in Greece", imprisonable for up to two years. These controversial provisions were suppressed in 2019.[26]

Article 3 of the Greek Constitution stipulates solemnly that the Eastern Orthodox Church is recognized as the "prevailing" religion in Greece. Even if the exact normative power of such a declarative provision is contested, it is a fact that, given its official status, the Orthodox Church enjoys State benefits, including financial support. The salaries of the Clergy are assured by the State and education in Orthodox Christianity is mandatory in all public schools, except for non orthodox students. In addition, the Orthodox Church is exempted from the administrative burdens that other religions face, for instance when it comes to licenses for construction of religious sites. The Council of Europe's Venice Commission has highlighted that "the solid historical links between the Eastern Orthodox Christianity and the emergence of the Greek nation, are used in order to justify a high level of interference of the church in the State affairs, in all different levels".[27] Many scholars have argued that prosecutions for blasphemy under Penal Code Articles 198 and 199 were related to the social and political influence of the Orthodox Church.[28] Abolishing the blasphemy laws has

---

[24] https://eige.europa.eu/gender-equality-index/2022/country/EL.

[25] https://www.eliamep.gr/en/publication/in-focus-η-ισότητα-γυναικών-και-ανδρών-στην-ε/.

[26] https://end-blasphemy-laws.org/countries/europe/greece/. See also Papadopoulou 2020a, b p. XXX and Papadopoulou XXX, pp. 847–864.

[27] https://www.refworld.org/docid/4d5a700bc.html.

[28] Among the famous in Greek courts cases of blasphemy has been the ban of American director Martin Scorsese's film The Last Temptation of Christ. Orthodox Christians held demonstrations outside cinemas and forced the authorities to initiate legal measures. Athens Court of First Instance stated that "protection of religious feelings is imperative because they are moral-social values...worthy of protection ... . Religion is not a purely personal affair ... but the foundation of the State, a vector of spiritual civilization." Another famous case has been the charge with blasphemy

been a constant petition of humanist groups. The legislation was frequently used to overturn religious criticism by art creators, members of LGBT rights groups, advertising campaigns, and social media influencers.[29] Still, according to Article 14 of the Constitution, newspapers and other print media can still be seized if they offend Christianity or any other "known religion," or "public decency." The Parliamentary Assembly of the Council of Europe has concluded that: "blasphemy, as an insult to a religion, should not be deemed a criminal offence…'and that in a democratic society, religious groups must tolerate, as must other groups, critical public statements and debate about their activities, teachings and beliefs, provided that such criticism does not amount to intentional and gratuitous insults or hate speech and does not constitute incitement to disturb the peace or to violence and discrimination against adherents of a particular religion. Public debate, dialogue and improved communication skills of religious groups and the media should be used in order to lower sensitivity when it exceeds reasonable levels".[30]

11.2.6 No Hate Speech Movement

No Hate Speech Movement (2019): the Greek Ministry of Education, Research and Religious Affairs has supported the No Hate Speech Movement, a youth campaign led by the Council of Europe Youth Department seeking to mobilize young people to combat hate speech and promote human rights online.[31]

The National Council against Racism and Intolerance (NCRI) was established by Law 4356/2015 as a collective advisory body and comes under the General Secretariat for Human Rights of the Ministry of Justice (lministerial decision 10.03.2016). The

of the author M. Androulakis and his publisher T. Kastaniotis for the novel M to the Power of N and its references to the sexual desires of Jesus Christ. The Thessaloniki Court of First Instance imposed an interim injunction on the distribution of the novel, effective in the northern provinces of Greece and justified as a means of "preventing outbreaks of violence". Finally the ban was lifted and the Court of First Instance in Athens underlined that the content of the book was not a "malicious insult" against "religion as such". Another case was built on the accusation of Austrian cartoonist Gerhard Haderer with blasphemy under for his satirical book The Life of Jesus, which depicted Christ as a heavy-drinking, marijuana-smoking hippie. The Greek Court found him guilty of malicious blasphemy and imposed a six-month suspended prison sentence, along with an injunction on distribution of the book. Finally, the Appellate Court of Athens acquitted him of all charges on the grounds that the humorous quality of the book precluded it from being malicious. See for the abovementioned cases and the legal framework on blasphemy https://www.refworld.org/docid/4d5a700bc.html. Also Tsakyrakis 2011.

[29] https://end-blasphemy-laws.org/2019/06/greece-quietly-drops-blasphemy-laws-new-criminal-code/.

[30] Council of Europe, Parliamentary Assembly, Recommendation 1805 (2007), Blasphemy, religious insults and hate speech against persons on grounds of their religion, Text adopted by the Assembly on 29 Jun 2007 (27th Sitting), http://assembly.coe.int/nw/xml/XRef/Xref-XML2HTML-en.asp?fileid=17569&lang=en. See Papadopoulou XXXX, p. 114.

[31] https://hackinghate.eu/news/hate-speech-in-greece-legal-and-educational-measures-against-the-rhetoric-of-hatred/.

National Action Plan against Racism and Intolerance is supported by the European Commission's "Rights, Equality and Citizenship"(REC) programme (2016-2020). The National Council against Racism and Intolerance consists of representatives of the ministries involved, the National Commission for Human Rights, the UN High Commissioner for Refugees, the Racist Violence Incident Registration Network, the National Confederation of Persons with Disabilities, the Ombudsman and other important civil society organizations. One of its main responsibilities is to develop a comprehensive strategy against racism, intolerance and racist crimes.[32]

The European Commission has sent in June 2021 a letter of formal notice to Greece as the national laws do not fully or accurately transpose EU rules on combating racism and xenophobia by means of criminal law (Council Framework Decision 2008/913/JHA). According to the Commission "The Greek legal system criminalizes hate speech only when public incitement to violence or hatred endangers public order or poses a threat to life, freedom or physical integrity of persons".[33]

11.3 International Convention on the Elimination of All Forms of Racial Discrimination (ICERD)

Greece has ratified the International Convention on the Elimination of All Forms of Racial Discrimination. According to the The National Action Plan against Racism and Intolerance (2020-2023) of the Greek Ministry of Justice:

> "In 2016, the UN Committee on the Elimination of Racial Discrimination published its Concluding Observations on the 20th to 22nd periodic reports of Greece. The committee 's experts identified the complicated situation in Greece, which was characterized by the economic recession and the humanitarian crisis, which was exacerbated by the rise of racism throughout Europe. Inter alia, the Commission called on Greece to:
>
> - Prevent, combat and effectively punish racist hate speech and hate crimes
> - Strengthen education on the identification, recording, prevention and control of hate crimes, hate speech and bias motives, in particular for the judiciary, police, prosecutors and labour inspectorate, and improve coordination between these institutions
> - Organize intensive campaigns across the country, in collaboration with national human rights bodies and civil society actors
>
> -Adopt concrete measures, in consultation with stakeholders, so as to increase allegations of racist hate crimes, ensuring that the reporting mechanism is transparent and accessible and finding ways for victims to have more trust in the police and the justice system. According to ECRI, there is a continuation of racist violence cases against immigrants, refugees and asylum seekers. In addition, ECRI notes that hate speech is particularly prevalent on the Internet and in the media. It states, inter alia, that discrimination against LGBTQI + individuals as well as crimes with a homophobic/transphobic motive, such as physical violence and verbal harassment, as well as homophobic / transphobic speech are quite widespread in Greece. The ECRI has drafted a broad list of recommendations to Greece in order to

[32] https://ministryofjustice.gr/English/?p=785.

[33] https://ec.europa.eu/newsroom/just/items/713873.

address these phenomena, such as the development of a national strategy to combat discrimination and homophobia/transphobia, which includes educational institutions. In addition, it is suggested that teachers be encouraged and supported to help victims of bullying in the school environment"[34] and also Committee on the Elimination of Racial Discrimination - Concluding observations on the twentieth to twenty-second periodic reports of Greece, Adopted by the Committee at its ninetieth session (2-26 August 2016).[35]

Greece has also ratified the International Covenant on Civil and Political Rights (ICCPR) and follows its observations. In the 2017 Concluding Observations no direct reference was made to hateful expression.

On the field, during January-December 2022, Racist Violence Recording Network[36] recorded, through interviews with victims, 74 incidents of racist violence. According to the annual report of 2022:

"In 33 incidents, migrants, refugees or asylum-seekers were targeted due to their national origin, religion or color. In one of these incidents, a person was targeted both due to national origin as well as sexual orientation and gender identity. In 1 incident, the target was Roma Greek citizens (ethnic origin). In 2 incidents, a mosque and a Holocaust memorial were targeted. In 38 incidents, the targets were LGBTQI+ individuals as well as human rights defenders, due to their connection with the LGBTQI+ people/persons. In this context, RVRN has recorded incidents of domestic violence, as well as intra-school or intra-university attacks, targeting LGBTQI+ people. In 22 incidents, the victims stated that they have experienced racist violence in the past. In 39 incidents the attack was carried out by a group, while in 28 incidents only one perpetrator was reported. Regarding the perpetrators' profile, according to the victims: In 41 incidents, there were civilians involved. In 15 incidents, the perpetrators were law enforcement officials. Based on the victims' testimony, almost half of these incidents took place near the country's borders. In 7 incidents, the perpetrators were public servants. In 2 incidents, the perpetrators were employers in agricultural works. In 6 incidents, the perpetrators were identified by the victims as members of racist violence groups. In 3 incidents, the perpetrators were identified as mixed groups of citizens and members of racist violence groups. Regarding the victims' access to complaints mechanisms: In the majority of incidents (44), the victims said that they would not take further action. Main factors seem to be the fear for secondary victimization or re-victimization. Fourteen (14) incidents had been reported to the police at the time they were recorded by RVRN. Criminal procedures were initiated for 5 incidents. In 4 incidents, the victims said that they had not reported the incident to the police but intended to do so. The above shows that underreporting of incidents of racist violence continued as a trend for one more year.

RVRN stresses the need for the State to take immediate action to address secondary victimization, and violence in general, so that victims and targeted communities can

[34] https://moj.gov.gr/wp-content/uploads/2021/03/NAPRI-en.pdf, p. 9.

[35] https://tbinternet.ohchr.org/_layouts/15/treatybodyexternal/Download.aspx?symbolno=CERD/C/GRC/20-22&Lang=en).

[36] https://www.nchr.gr/en/racist-violence-recording-network.html.

have more trust in the authorities. In addition, the competent authorities should prioritize the creation of an effective support and protection system for victims of racist violence. Based on the RVRN findings for 2022, the key trends are the following: Existence of racism against refugees/migrants and LGBTQI+ individuals in the context of managing their daily lives (i.e. incidents of racist violence and/or racist behaviors during the daily activities of the victims, e.g. in public transportation, in the neighborhood etc. These incidents are usually of low intensity and their perpetrators are individuals.) Occurrence of incidents of organized racist violence, although to a limited extent, against refugees/migrants and LGBTQI+ individuals. Targeting of human rights defenders, within Greek territory, especially those operating at the borders".[37]

11.4 European Law and the ECHR Greek Cases

Greece is a member of the Council of Europe and the ECHR impact is of great significance for Greek laws and policies. The European Commission again Racism and Intolerance (ECRI) monitors problems of racism, xenophobia, anti-Semitism, intolerance and discrimination in the member states. Based on its findings, ECRI published General Policy Recommendation No.15 on combating hate speech providing guidelines to the member states on how to deal with this problem.[38]

The 2022 report of ECRI underlines that the Greek authorities shall establish a system for monitoring the hate speech offenses, including these that are online incidents, based on the expertise of various organizations (State authorities such as the police, NGO, self-regulatory bodies and human rights institutions etc.). The Commission recognizes that actions have been taken by the State authorities in order to contain hate speech and recommends that "that the Greek authorities launch public awareness campaigns against hate speech, in which the dangers posed by hate speech are underlined and the falsity and unacceptability of its foundations stressed, involving responsible political and religious leaders engaging in counter-speech" (…) Regarding hate-motive violence, the ECRI 2022 report mentions that "according to data reported by the Greek authorities to the OSCE/ODIHR, there were 164 cases of hate crime reported by the police in 2018; 128 in 2017 and 40 in 2016. In 2018, hate crimes motivated by racism and xenophobia numbered 78; bias against Roma and Sinti 2; antisemitism 8; bias against Muslims 6; bias against Christians 6; bias against members of other religions or beliefs 3; and bias against sexual orientation or gender identity 30.39 The number of cases prosecuted in relation to reported incidents was low,40 and the cases which resulted in a sentence much lower, at four in 2018; six in 2017 and two in 2016 (…) The Racist Violence Recording Network (RVRN),41 for

[37] https://www.nchr.gr/en/news/1594-presentation-of-the-annual-report-for-2022-racist-violence-recording-network.html.

[38] https://rm.coe.int/ecri-general-policy-recommendation-no-15-on-combating-hate-speech/16808b5b01.

the period from 2016 to 2020, recorded a total of 521 incidents of racist violence. In 148 incidents the targets were refugees, asylum-seekers or migrants, persons working with them or accommodation centers. In seven incidents, the targets were Greek citizens on grounds of ethnic origin or color, while in 28 incidents, the attacks took place on the ground of religion. In 131 incidents, the targets were LGBTI individuals and human rights defenders due to their association with LGBTI communities".[39]

The European Court of Human Rights has addressed racist violence in the cases of *Sakir v. Greece* (application no. 48475/09) and *Gjikondi and others v. Greece* (application no. 17249/10). The Sakir case concerns the violation by the authorities of their obligation to conduct an effective investigation into a violent attack against an immigrant. In particular, the authorities failed to investigate the racist motive of the attack (breach of the procedural part of Article 3 of the ECHR). Precisely, the case concerned an assault against Rafi Sakir in 2009 in the center of Athens which led to his hospitalization, and also the conditions in which he was detained in a police station after his release from hospital. The Court underlined that the police had not requested from the hospital whether Mr Sakir's state of health allowed him to be placed in detention. Despite medical instructions, there had been failings in the manner in which the applicants medical condition and state of vulnerability were taken into account. The Court also found a violation of Article 13 of the Convention due to the lack of an effective remedy to complain about the conditions of detention. Furthermore, the Court spotted deficiencies in the investigation conducted after the assault, as far as the gathering of evidence and the questioning of witnesses were concerned. In particular, it queried the authorities' failure to clarify whether or not A.S.'s statement was truthful, taking into consideration the circumstances. Finally, the authorities had failed to assess the case in the view of the racist incidents which frequently took place in Athens.[40] The case of Gjikondi and others concerned the murder of a foreigner and the failure to investigate the possible racist motives.[41] The Court considered that the authorities failed to carry out an effective investigation into the fatal assault, committed by an unidentified person in 2004. The authorities, according to the Court, had not handled the case with the necessary diligence, had failed to involve the applicants to the extent required in the relevant investigation, and had not examined a possible racist motive (procedural violation of Article 2).[42]

---

[39] https://rm.coe.int/ecri-first-report-on-greece-adopted-on-28-june-2022-published-on-22-se/1680a818bf.

[40] https://www.coe.int/en/web/impact-convention-human-rights/-/hate-crime-laws-strengthened-after-police-failed-to-properly-investigate-A-racist-attack.

[41] https://moj.gov.gr/wp-content/uploads/2021/03/NAPRI-en.pdf, p. 11.

[42] https://greekhelsinki.wordpress.com/tag/gjikondi-and-others/.

11.5 Judicial Rulings—The Limited Effect of Anti-racist Law

The "Richter case" was the first to address hate speech in the Framework Decision on Racism and Xenophobia (the Law 4285/2014 which introduced the Framework Decision to the Greek legal order). The Criminal Court had the opportunity to explore the limits of academic freedom in relation with the "hate speech" issue and more specifically the denial of crimes against humanity. Legal proceedings were enacted against Heinz Richter, a German historian, Professor at the University of Mannheim, for his controversial book on the battle of Crete. The University of Crete decided to honour the 75-year-old former professor of Greek and Cypriot modern history at the University of Mannheim by awarding him an honorary doctorate. His 2011 book "Operation Mercury: The Invasion of Crete," was found offensive by his critics, focusing on the demythification of the resistance on the island during WWII. Richter was accused to have demeaned the Cretan resistance, naming it "dirty." He was charged by the prosecutor with "denial of defamatory nature of the Nazi crimes committed against the Cretan people." It was the first time that an individual had been charged under anti-racism legislation introduced in Greece.[43]

The first instance criminal court of Rethymno in Crete (dec. 2383/2015) stated that the law was unconstitutional for violating freedom of expression and academic freedom. For the Court, the law could be held constitutional only to the extent that it concerns speech that is threatening, defamatory or can provoke hatred. The Court underlined that Article 2 of the Law No 4285/2014 is "contrary to freedom of expression and academic freedom to the extent that it habilitates the parliamentary majority to act as a body of scientific knowledge on historical facts".[44]

According to the Court, "scientific bodies are not formed by the current parliamentary majorities and governments, but by researchers and academics. The latter, however, are not obliged to adjust their opinions to that of the parliamentary majority". In this sense, "the recognition that public authorities can legislate and impose historical truths and events and prohibit alternative interpretations of specific historical events inevitably leads many different groups to seek to use the power of law in order to protect their own versions from any dispute". Therefore, "the reference of art. 2 of Law 4285/2014 to "decisions of the Parliament" excessively restricts the freedom of expression and information, regarding issues of historical interest, and in particular infringes the scientific and academic freedom…". As in theory was firmly put, "enacting legislation that commemorates a genocide that took place in the past and legislation that criminalises the denial of crimes against humanity can have pernicious unintended consequences for important freedoms. Although these laws are the result of collective disapproval of certain historical atrocities, they can lead down the slippery slope of threatening freedom of speech. Extreme caution is needed to control the irrational elements within collective consciousness in a way that

[43] https://www.ekathimerini.com/society/204196/history-on-trial/.

[44] Tourkochoriti 2018.

is compatible with the protection of important liberties such as academic freedom. Our collective search for meaning within our various communities should be open and allow for expressing interpretations of historical facts that might seem idiosyncratic or even offensive and disturbing to the collective narratives of a community in its search for self-understanding”.[45]

In 2018, the Greek Orthodox Bishop of Kalavryta, was charged for the crime of public incitement to violence or hatred under Article 1 of Law 4285/2014 (Anti-racist Law), in connection with Article 196 of the Greek Criminal Code, providing an aggravated sentence for religious leaders. Amvrosios (the Bishop) had written posts on homosexuality, urging his readers to «Spit on them! Jeer at them! Blacken their names!», adding that “They are mentally disturbed! Unfortunately, they are three times worse and more dangerous than those in the madhouses». The First Instance Criminal Court of Aigio has acquitted him but the prosecutor of the Court of Misdemeanours in Aigio appealed the decision. On January 28, 2019 the bishop was found guilty by the three-member Misdeanor Court in Aigio of incitement to hatred and abuse of religious office and sentenced to 7 months imprisonment (on a probation term).[46]

The Supreme Court (dec. 858/2020) upheld this decision for the part concerning the violation of the anti-racist law and annulled the conviction for the abuse of religious office. Specifically, the Court underscored that “the accused did not simply express his opinion on the occasion. His speech had "threatening" content, within the meaning of Article 1 of 927/1979 as amended and now in force with art. 1 Law 4285/2014, as it aimed at identifying distinctively the persons belonging to the group of homosexuals in an objectively appropriate way to instill terror and anxiety in its members…”. Furthermore, “his speech was able to result to the immediate and imminent danger of disrupting peace and social order and the rights of homosexuals, being excommunicated by a minister of the Church whose view, due to his status, has high prestige and influence, especially among the numerous believers of the orthodox Christian religion, which is the official in our country and of the vast majority of its inhabitants”.[47]

Ruling on this case, the European Court of Human Rights has found in the Lenis v. Greece decision that the applicant attempted to deflect Article 10 (freedom of expression) from its real purpose by using it for ends which were clearly contrary to the values of the Convention. Consequently, according to Article 17 (prohibition of abuse of rights), the Court underlined that the application was incompatible ratione materiae with the Convention and rejected it.[48]

---

[45] Ibid.

[46] https://apnews.com/article/d740b45c3fd64979946a1d796d68b8c9.

[47] http://www.areiospagos.gr/nomologia/apofaseis_DISPLAY.asp?cd=MM8X2SENB1Z5BP1 0XPW156841DB4JS&apof=858_2020&info=%D0%CF%C9%CD%C9%CA%C5%D3%20-% 20%20%D3%D4 (in Greek).

[48] ECtHR, 27 June 2023, Lenis v. Greece.

11.6 Ban of Political Parties Electoral Rights: A Change of Paradigm

According to Article 29 par.1 of the Constitution, "the organization and activity" of political parties "must serve the free functioning of democratic government". This provision has been interpreted throughout the last five decades as a moral or "pedagogical" direction for the legislator, meaning that no prohibition of a political party could be enacted in relation to political activities or beliefs.[49] Greece has not until now adopted a militant conception of democracy for two reasons:

> "The first has to do with the bitter cold war experience of the ban against the Communist Party. Introduced in the aftermath of the Civil War, Law 509/ 1947 ordered the dissolution of every political party, association or organization that aimed 'to directly or indirectly act on ideas whose goal was to overthrow through violent means the form of government, the current social system or to remove part of the land's territory'. On the basis of this law, the Greek Communist Party was continuously banned until 1974. The second reason that made the Third Greek democracy resistant to party bans is the memory of the military junta's dissolution of all political parties in 1967 (retrospectively legalized by Emergency Law 575, 27 September 1968). In addition, the Colonels' 1968 constitution had established a puppet Constitutional Court, which would be responsible for the 'continuous supervision' of political parties [Article 58(4)] and could outlaw them even if their actions were nonviolent and formally legal, which substantially lowered the threshold for prosecution. Thus, after the military dictatorship's collapse in 1974, laws and practices regarding party dissolution were tainted with the memory of anti-communism and dictatorial oppression in Greece".[50]

Hence, the major legal effect of the constitutional provision has been the review of the Supreme Court on the party's charter. A formal declaration of conformity with the democratic principles is sufficient for the party to be founded as an association and furthermore to participate in the elections. In other words, the party simply provides the Court with a formal statement of compliance with the Article 29 par.1 -in fact repeating its wording- and no substantial oversight on the parties concrete actions were undertaken.[51] The interpretation of Article 29 par.1 has been challenged over the years and mostly after the rise of the Golden Dawn neo-Nazi party, members of which have been convicted for the murder of antifa activist and musician Pavlos Fyssas and for being a criminal organization.[52] However, their trial is a penal one and the exercise of their political rights has never been compromised, given that the Greek Constitution stipulates in Article 51 par.3 that "The law cannot abridge the right to vote except in cases where a minimum age has not been attained or in cases of legal incapacity or as a result of irrevocable criminal conviction for certain felonies". On the other hand, scholars argued that banning a party from elections is a legitimate interpretation option for Article 29 par.1 because the obligation of the party to serve the free functioning of a democratic government should not be deprived totally from

---

[49] Karavokyris 2023, p. 1.

[50] Malkopoulou 2021, pp. 177–201.

[51] Karavokyris 2023, p. 12.

[52] Tourkochoriti 2013a, b.

its normative status.[53] Thus, the legislator has recently taken significant steps which may signify the final turn of Greek democracy to the militant model.[54]

Article 92 of law 4804/2021 bans parties whose leader, secretary general, board members, or legal representatives have been convicted for certain offenses against the State from participating in elections. Recent legislative amendments in the electoral law have stipulated that a party may not participate in the parliamentary elections if "the party's President, General Secretary, Managing Committee members, representative, and actual leadership have been convicted at any instance for [participating and managing a criminal organization]". Additionally, a political party's organization and activity must serve "the free functioning of democratic government" and this condition "may only be determined by reference to the conviction at any instance of the party's candidates or founding members or former Presidents for [crimes that include participating and managing a criminal organization]". Based on these legal grounds the Greek Court of Cassation (Areios Pagos) has refused to certify the participation of the Hellenes National Party, which was founded on 4 June 2020 by I. Kasidiaris, the former press representative and MP of the neo-Nazi Golden Dawn party. On 2 May 2023, Areios Pagos excluded the party from the Greek parliamentary elections of 21 May.

The constitutional debate on the abovementioned legislation and amendments was rather rich and intense as many scholars highlighted the (new) social and political necessity to adopt a more militant conception of democracy against the neo-Nazi parties. At the same time, serious objections were raised in the name of the political and democratic freedoms which a democracy should recognize even for its enemies.[55] Nevertheless, the government claimed that the new legislative framework is not contrary to the Constitution for two main reasons: first, there is no ban per se of the political party in terms of a legal entity but only a serious limitation on the exercise of its political freedom (the right to participate to the elections). Given the fact that the parties actions violate the fundamental principles, the legislation avoids targeting ideas and remains compatible with the harm principle and with the proportionality principle.[56] Secondly, while a party run by a convicted in the first-degree criminal cannot participate in the elections, the individual can still run for office as an independent candidate, in accordance with Article 51(3) of the Constitution. Areios Pagos defended that Hellenes National Party constitutes a threat to liberal democracy by confirming its status as Golden Dawn's political successor. It highlighted the instances in which Kasidiaris used hate speech and incited his followers

[53] Anthopoulos and Garypidis 2015, pp. 653–672.

[54] Samartzis and Vadivoulis 2023.

[55] Areios Pagos held in 2014 that Golden Dawn could participate in the EU elections, given the fact that "in the absence of final conviction and the concomitant deprivation of political rights, it is not possible to deprive the person in question of the right to run for office and to undermine the legal status and institutional activity of the political party, within the Constitution's normative framework, according to Article 29(1) of the Constitution regarding the free functioning of democratic government" (A1 Civil Division Chamber, decision 65 of 8 May 2014). See Samartzis and Vadivoulis 2023.

[56] Karavokyris 2023, p.12 ff.

to violence against minority groups and political opponents. It also emphasized the undisputable acts of violence that matched these incitements.[57] Furthermore, the new legislation appears to comply with the ECHR standards and decisions on the possibility to impose harsh limitations on political parties based on their concrete opposition to the fundamental values of a democratic society.[58]

Ultimately, Kasidiaris attempted to run as an independent candidate in the second Greek general elections that took place on June 25. In this way he tried to avoid the legislation on the ban of political parties claiming that these provisions do not apply on a coalition of independent candidates throughout the country (under the name "Hellenes").[59] The Supreme Court blocked against the participation of the "Hellenes", ruling that the coalition of candidates in multiple electoral districts of Greece is a de facto political party which tries illegally to bypass the limitations of the law and therefore commits an evident abuse of its political rights. To justify this normative consideration the Court has again accomplished a substantial assessment on the political actions of Kasidiaris and other members of the independent coalition, repeating essentially the previous judgement for the May elections.[60]

References

AnthopoulosCh, Garypidis N (2015) The Emergence of the Golden Dawn Party: Political and Constitutional Implications. Diritto pubblico comparato ed europeo, Rivista trimestrale 3:653–672.

Feinberg J (1986) Harm to Self: The Moral Limits of the Criminal Law. Oxford University Press.

Haarcher G (2007) Liberté d'expression, blasphème, racisme: essai d'analyse philosophique et comparée. Working papers du Centre Perelman de philosophie du droit, n. 2007/1. http://www.philodroit.be.

Heinze E (2022) The Most Human Right. Why Free Speech Is Everything. MIT Press.

Karavokyris G (2011) Freedom of Speech as a Freedom of Offense [in Greek]. Journal of Administrative Law 4.

Karavokyris G (2023) Article 29. Political Parties. In: Vlachopoulos S, Contiades X, Tassopoulos I (eds) Constitution. Commentary [in Greek]. https://www.syntagmawatch.gr/my-constitution/arthro-29/.

Kiviorg M (ed) (2017) Securitisation of Religious Freedom: Religion and Limits of State Control, European Consortium for Church and State Research, Proceedings of the XXIXth Annual Conference Tallinn, 16-18 November 2017. https://ssrn.com/abstract=3952388.

Malkopoulou A (2021) Greece: A Procedural Defence of Democracy against the Golden Dawn. European Constitutional Law Review 17:177–201. https://www.cambridge.org/core/services/

[57] Samartzis and Vadivoulis 2023.

[58] For instance, ECtHR 13 February 2003 [GC], Case No. 41340/98, No. 41342/98, No. 41343/98, No. 41344/98, Refah Partisi (The Welfare Party) and others v Turkey. ECtHR justified the ban in terms of the party's endorsement of violence and its aim to establish the application of a legal system (sharia) fundamentally contrary to many freedoms guaranteed by the European Convention on Human Rights.

[59] https://www.ekathimerini.com/news/1211857/kasidiaris-will-try-to-bypass-election-ban-by-running-as-an-independent/.

[60] Tassopoulos 2023a, b, pp. 411–418. Karavokyris 2023, p. 20 ff.

aop-cambridge-core/content/view/7960B84331A30FFF34FDDE3A051B439F/S1574019621000146a.pdf/greece-a-procedural-defence-of-democracy-against-the-golden-dawn.pdf.
Markopoulos N (2017) Article 14. In: Spyropoulos P, Contiades X, Anthopoulos Ch, Gerapetritis G (eds). Constitution. Commentary [in Greek]. Sakkoulas,
Morange J (2009) La liberté d'expression. Bruylant, Bruxelles.
Ogien R (2007) L'éthique aujourd'hui. Maximalistes et minimalistes. Folio, Essais, Gallimard, Paris.
Papadopoulou L (2020) Prohibitions of Religiously Loaded Speech: (How) Can Advocacy for Allowing Blasphemy be Reconciled with Supporting the Prohibition of Hate Speech? In: Staat – Religion – Recht. Festschrift für Gerhard Robbers zum 70, Kerstin von der Decken, Angelika Günzel. Geburtstag (dir). Nomos, Baden-Baden.
Papadopoulou L (2020) Hate Speech and Autonomy of Religious Communities (October 29, 2020). Hate speech and autonomy of religious Communities by Lina Triantafyllia Papadopoulou :: SSRN
Papadopoulou L (2022), Hate speech and religion. A constitutional evaluation. Kallipos, 2022, https://doi.org/10.57713/kallipos-308.
Samartzis A, Vadivoulis N (2023) Greece's Ambivalent Turn to Militant Democracy. VerfBlog. https://verfassungsblog.de/greeces-ambivalent-turn-to-militant-democracy/.
Stuart Mill J (1998) On Liberty. In: Gray J (ed). Oxford University Press.
Tassopoulos I (2023) The Decision 8/2023 of the Supreme Court and the Constant Interpretation and Application of Article 29§1 of the Constitution against Neofascism [in Greek]. e-POLITEIA 7:411–418. https://www.epoliteia.gr/wp-content/uploads/2023/07/TEYXOS-7-INTERACTIVE.pdf.
Tassopoulos I (2023) Article 14. Freedom of Expression and Freedom of Press. In: Vlachopoulos S, Contiades X, Tassopoulos I (eds). Constitution. Commentary [in Greek]. Electronic and open access edition https://www.syntagmawatch.gr/my-onstitution/arthro-14/.
Tourkochoriti I (2013) Bans of Political Parties and the Case of Golden Dawn's Right Wing Extremism in Greece. VerfBlog, 2013/10/31, https://verfassungsblog.de/bans-of-political-parties-and-the-case-of-golden-dawns-right-wing-extremism-in-greece/.
Tourkochoriti I (2013) Bans of Political Parties and the Case of Golden Dawn's Right Wing Extremism in Greece. VerfBlog. https://verfassungsblog.de/bans-of-political-parties-and-the-case-of-golden-dawns-right-wing-extremism-in-greece/.
Tourkochoriti I (2021) Freedom of Expression: The Revolutionary Roots of American and French Legal Thought. Cambridge University Press.
Tourkohoriti I (2018) Memory Politics and Academic Freedom: Some Recent Controversies in Greece. VerfBlog, https://verfassungsblog.de/memory-politics-and-academic-freedom-some-recent-controversies-in-greece.
Tsakyrakis S (2011) Religion against Art [in Greek]. Polis.
Urbinati N (2006) Representative Democracy: Principles and Genealogy. University of Chicago Press, Chicago, Ill.
Waldron J (2012) The Harm in Hate Speech. Harvard University Press, Cambridge, MA.

George Karavokyris studied law at the Aristotle University of Thessaloniki. He received his Master (2001) and his PhD (2008, with distinction) from the Law School of the University Paris II (Panthéon-Assas). His doctoral thesis is entitled *Personal Autonomy in French Public Law* (Bruylant, 2013, in French). Karavokyris is an Assistant Professor of Constitutional Law at the Faculty of Law of the Aristotle University of Thessaloniki. He is currently also a counsellor of the President of the Greek Republic on constitutional matters and member of the Scientific Committee of the Hellenic Parliament Foundation for Parliamentarism and Democracy.

Chapter 12
Italy

Paolo Caroli

Contents

Abstract This chapter outlines the legal framework—both supranational and domestic—that underpins and limits the criminalisation of hate speech within the Italian legal system. It begins by examining the constitutional, international, and European constraints before delving into the criminal legislation in force. The scope of the chapter extends beyond specific hate crimes that explicitly include hatred in the description of the offence. It also explores how 'traditional offences' are applied by the judiciary to address hate speech, taking into account both practical interpretations and existing gaps in the response through criminal law with particular reference to homotransphobic speech.

Keyword Anti-LGBTQ+ speech · Penalties for hate speech · Law and social media · Racism

---

P. Caroli (✉)
Faculty of Law, University of Turin, Turin, Italy
e-mail: paolo.caroli@unito.it

E. Heinze (ed.), *Criminalising Hate Speech*,
https://doi.org/10.1007/978-94-6265-650-5_12

12.1 National Constitutional Law

Article 21 para 1 of the Italian Constitution of 1948 states that "Everyone has the right to freely express their thoughts in speech, writing, or any other form of communication". Paragraphs 2 and 3 add: "The press may not be subjected to any authorisations or censorship. Seizure may be permitted only by reasoned judicial order and only for offences expressly determined by the law on the press or in case of violation of the obligation to identify the persons responsible for such offences." Paragraph 6 only provides one possible reason for limiting free speech: "Publications, performances, and other exhibits offensive to public morality shall be prohibited. Prevention and enforcement relating to such violations shall be established by law."

The principle of freedom of the press has been cited by the Constitutional Court to affirm the partial non-constitutionality of the crime of defamation in relation to journalists with specific reference to sanctions of imprisonment. As a result, journalists who are found guilty of defamation can be sentenced to imprisonment only in cases of exceptional gravity, which may include hate speech and incitement to violence (cf. Constitutional Court, Order 132/2020, Decision 150/2021).

In addition to the right to free speech, it is important to mention the principle of equality under Article 3 of the Constitution. Paragraph 1 refers to so-called *formal equality*: "All citizens shall have equal social dignity and shall be equal before the law, without distinction of gender, race, language, religion, political opinion, personal and social conditions." However, para 2 refers to so-called *substantial equality*: "It shall be the duty of the Republic to remove those obstacles of an economic or social nature which constrain the freedom and equality of citizens, thereby impeding the full development of the human person and the effective participation of all workers in the political, economic and social organisation of the country."

The Court of Cassation (the highest Court) has affirmed that criminal norms against racial discrimination can be justified both on the basis of Article 117 of the Constitution (which binds the legislators to the obligations deriving from international law) and of the principle of equality *ex* Article 3 of the Constitution (Cass., I, 23024/01, Cass., V, 31655/01, Cass. II, 37581/08). In 2018 the norms criminalizing racial discrimination, previously placed outside the Criminal Code (in the so-called *Mancino* Law), were moved into the Criminal Code (at Articles 604bis and 604ter) in a newly created section, which was called "Crimes against equality".

The principle of freedom of scientific research has been applied (Cass., I, 2058/12) by affirming that the criteria to limit that principle are to be found in the relationship between content and form and in the proportion between the fact and the tone of the criticism. A very important principle is Article 2 of the Constitution: "The Republic shall recognise and protect the inviolable rights of the person, both as an individual and in the social groups where human personality is expressed. The Republic expects that the fundamental duties of political, economic and social solidarity be fulfilled." The jurisprudence and part of the scholarship derive from this article the principle of protection of the human dignity. Anti-discrimination criminal norms were originally interpreted as to protect public order (Cass., I 3791/1993), however the interpretation of the protected legal interest radically changed in the most recent years and it seems now to be accepted in the jurisprudence that anti-discrimination norms are aimed to protect human dignity and are therefore justified under Article 2 of the Constitution (see in particular the precedent Cass. III, n. 13234/2007). This interpretation allows a major limitation of free speech.

This principle is now evoked by civil society and part of the scholarship in order to support an extension of anti-discriminatory norms, in order to include the motivations based on sex, gender, sexual orientation, gender identity and disability (see *infra*). Article 2 can also be seen as the source of the right to dignity and reputation, which justifies the crime of defamation. The Tribunal of Turin applied this crime to Dr. De Mari, who publicly affirmed that homosexuals are sick and paedophiles; the Court linked the concept of "dignity and reputation" not to the homosexuals as such (which would be impossible, since the norm requires a specific victim), but to the LGBTQ+ organisations as representatives of the homosexuals (Trib. Turin, VI, 5009/2018).

It is also necessary to recall the twelfth transitory and final provision of the Italian Constitution, which prohibits the reorganization of the National Fascist Party ("It shall be forbidden to reorganise, under any form whatsoever, the dissolved Fascist party"). This was the basis for the introduction of a law which prohibits the public use of fascist symbols and gestures (so-called *Scelba* Law, Law 20 of June 1952, No. 645).

Lastly, but probably most importantly, it has to be recalled the pivotal decision in relation to speech crimes in general: the decision of the Constitutional Court n. 65 of 1970 in relation to the inchoate offence of Article 414 of the Criminal Code: "apologia di reati" (apology of crimes, i.e. glorification of criminal acts). The Court affirmed that the use of criminal law at this very early stage (basically to criminalize the mere public speech, without any physical act following) is only admissible when, given the specific concrete context, the public speech can be seen as an "indirect incitement" to the commission of crimes. This basic principle is still applied to all speech crimes and led, for instance, to excluding the criminal relevance in case of use of fascist symbols and gestures, when the context is considered to be merely commemorative, without a concrete danger of reconstitution of the Fascist party (Cass., I, 11038/2017; Cass., I, 8108/2018; c.f. Cass., S.U, 16153/2024).

12.2 National Statutory and Administrative Law

Under Italian criminal law, there is no general hate crime that covers all forms of hate speech basing the criminality of the conduct on its hate motive. The only crime where a hateful motive is included in the legal description of the offence is Article 604 bis of the Criminal Code (*Propaganda and incitement to crime on grounds of racial, ethnic and religious discrimination*), which is limited to racial, ethnic, national and religious hate speech, and in the case of propaganda to racial or ethnic hate speech.

This Article punishes anyone who propagates ideas based on racial or ethnic superiority or hatred, or who commits or incites others to commit acts of discrimination on racial, ethnic, national or religious grounds. It also applies to anyone who, in any way, commits or incites others to commit violence or acts of provocation to violence for racial, ethnic, national or religious reasons. Article 604 ter of the Criminal Code also provides for an aggravating circumstance, which can influence sentencing, when a crime (e.g., defamation) is committed for purposes of discrimination or ethnic, national, racial or religious hatred, or in order to facilitate the activity of organizations, associations, movements or groups that have the same purposes.

In certain cases, some forms of hate speech could be punished under the crimes of Articles 4 and 5 of the *Scelba* Law (Law 645/1952), which refer to the public exaltation of fascism or the use of fascist symbols and gestures, including slogans. The crime under Article 2 of the Law Decree 122/1993 (converted into law by Law 205/1993, *Mancino* Law) could be relevant too. This punishes anyone who, in public meetings, performs external demonstrations or flaunts emblems or symbols proper or usual of organizations, associations, movements or groups whose purposes include inciting hatred or racial discrimination.

To some forms of hate speech, "traditional" speech crimes such as "diffamazione" (defamation, Criminal Code Article 595), can be applicable. This crime punishes anyone who, by communicating with various people, harms somebody's reputation in their absence. This crime is aggravated when it is committed through the media, including social media. On the contrary, if the person is present, this represents an "ingiuria" (insult, Criminal Code Article 594). This offence, which punished anyone who offends the honour or decorum of a person in their presence, since 2016 is not a crime anymore, but it is punished with a civil law fee. Lastly, the more serious crime of "calunnia" (slander, Criminal Code Article 368) needs to be considered. This crime comes into play when someone accuses somebody of having committed a crime, knowing that the accusation is false.

There are some specific criminal offences against the dignity of some public figures, such as the President of the Republic (Article 278 of the Criminal Code, punished with imprisonment from 1 to 5 years). Blasphemous curses and outrageous acts towards the dead are punished with a fine.

Beyond criminal law, hate speech can have consequences on the basis of labour law. One example is the *Taormina* Case, which also involved the European Court of Justice (ECJ). On July 2013 Mr. Taormina, a famous lawyer and former member of the Italian parliament, made strong remarks during a radio interview declaring that he would never hire a gay lawyer in his law firm. Following this outburst, the Italian LGBTQ+ association Rete Lenford brought a legal action before the Tribunal of Bergamo, claiming that those statements constituted a direct discrimination prohibited by Legislative Decree no. 216/2003, which implemented the Directive 2000/78/EC on equal treatment in employment and occupation.

The Tribunal of Bergamo ruled in favour of Rete Lenford, condemned Mr. Taormina to the payment of € 10.000,00 and ordered the publication of the ruling on a national newspaper at his expense. Mr. Taormina consequently filed an appeal against this decision, which the Court of Appeal of Brescia upheld. He then filed an appeal to the Court of Cassation, which requested a preliminary ruling to the ECJ on the application of the Directive 2000/78/CE for a case of discrimination on the ground of sexual orientation and access to work. In 2020 the ECJ Grand Chamber ruled that Taormina's remarks did indeed constitute discrimination, as they fell into the scope of "conditions for access to employment … or to occupation" described in the directive.

12.3 International Covenant on Civil and Political Rights (ICCPR)

Italy is a party to the ICCPR and has consented to individual complaints procedures. The most recent concluding observations were issued in 2017 (VI reporting cycle. As for hateful expression, it is interesting to refer to some of those observations in part C:

Anti-discrimination legislation

8. The Committee is concerned that Article 3 of the Constitution does not contain a comprehensive list of prohibited grounds of discrimination and that existing anti-discrimination legislation addresses only some grounds of discrimination, in limited spheres (Articles 2 and 26).

9. The State party should take all measures necessary, including the adoption of comprehensive anti-discrimination legislation, to ensure that its legal framework: (a) provides full and effective protection against discrimination in all spheres, including in the private sphere, and prohibits direct and indirect discrimination; (b) comprehensively addresses all grounds of discrimination, including colour, national origin, citizenship, birth, disability, age, sexual orientation and gender identity and any other status; and (c) provides for effective remedies in cases of violations, including in cases of multiple and intersectional discrimination.

Discrimination on the grounds of sexual orientation and gender identity

10. […] It is also concerned […]about the prevalence of discrimination and hate speech against lesbian, gay, bisexual, transgender and intersex persons (Articles 2, 23-24 and 26).

11. The State […] should also intensify its efforts to combat discrimination, hate speech and hate crimes against lesbian, gay, bisexual, transgender and intersex persons. Hate speech and racial discrimination

12. The Committee is concerned about reports of persistent stigmatization, stereotyping, and racist discourse against Roma, Sinti and Camminanti communities and non-citizens, exacerbated by the media and public officials at the local level. It is also concerned that the aggravating circumstances in Law No. 205/1993 (*Mancino* Law) on hate crimes [later moved under Article 604 ter of the Criminal Code] are applied only when a racist motive appears to be the sole motivation but not when there are mixed motives (Articles 2 and 26).

13. The State party should: (a) strengthen its efforts to eradicate stigmatization, stereotyping and racist discourse against Roma, Sinti and Camminanti communities and non-citizens, including by conducting awareness-raising campaigns to promote tolerance and respect for diversity; (b) review Law No. 205/1993 with a view to giving effect to aggravating circumstances to all hate crimes; and (c) ensure that all cases of racially motivated violence are systematically investigated, that perpetrators are prosecuted and punished and that appropriate compensation is awarded to the victims.

At the same time, the UN-HRC also advocates free speech:

> Criminalization of defamation
>
> 38. The Committee is concerned that some forms of expression, including defamation, libel and blasphemy, remain criminal offences and can be punished with imprisonment and that Article 13 of the press law and Article 595 of the Criminal Code impose harsher punishments for defaming public officials, including the Head of State. It is also concerned about the high number of journalists reportedly convicted of libel (Article 19).
>
> 39. The State party should decriminalize blasphemy. It should also consider the complete decriminalization of defamation and libel and, in any case, it should restrict the application of criminal law to the most serious of cases. It should also revise its legislation, including Article 13 of the press law and Article 595 of the Criminal Code, with a view to bringing it into conformity with its obligations under the Covenant, taking into account the Committee's general comment No. 34 (2011) on the freedoms of opinion and expression. Furthermore, it should ensure that such lawsuits are not used as tools to curtail freedom of expression beyond the narrow restrictions permitted by Article 19 of the Covenant.

12.4 International Convention on the Elimination of All Forms of Racial Discrimination (ICERD)

Italy is a state party to ICERD and has consented to individual complaint procedures. In 2017 (XIX-XX periodic reporting period) the UN-CERD issued concluding observations, including the following observations:

> Anti-discrimination legislation
>
> 6. The Committee takes note of the general equality provision set out in Article 3 of the constitution and the assurance provided by the State party delegation that the provisions of Article 1 of the Convention have been transposed in its entirety into its domestic legislation. However, the Committee remains concerned at the lack of clarity regarding the specific legislation and the provisions which prohibit racial discrimination, in accordance with Article 1 of the Convention, in particular with regard to the prohibition of discrimination on the basis of colour and national or ethnic origin, and regardless of whether discrimination was a consequence of "purpose or effect" (Article 1).
>
> 7. The Committee recommends that the State party adopt the necessary measures to ensure that its domestic anti-discrimination legislation prohibits all forms of discrimination in accordance with Article 1 of the Convention, including on the basis of colour and national or ethnic origin, as well as discrimination caused by intent or negative impact. It recalls that legislative guarantees against racial discrimination should apply to non-citizens, regardless of their immigration status, as underlined in the Committee's general recommendation No. 30 (2004) on discrimination against non-citizens. The Committee requests that the State party provide, in its next periodic report, further clarification on the legislative framework and the exact wording of the legal provisions which prohibit all forms of racial discrimination in accordance with Article 1 of the Convention.
>
> Disaggregated statistical data
>
> 8. While noting the recent efforts made by the State party to improve its data collection of criminal offences committed on the basis of racist motives, the Committee reiterates its previous concern regarding the lack of detailed data on the racial and ethnic composition of the State party. [...]
>
> Racist hate speech

14. While noting the initiation of judicial proceedings against some local politicians for the dissemination of ideas based on racial superiority or hatred, the Committee is concerned that the provisions in the constitution providing immunity for members of parliament for the opinions that they express in the exercise of their functions may prevent them from also being held accountable. It expresses particular concern at the prevalence of racist discourse, stigmatization and negative stereotypes in political debates, which are directed against migrants, Muslims, people of African descent and Roma, Sinti and Camminanti communities and which are also perpetrated by the media. The Committee expresses further concern regarding (a) the instances of racist hate speech on the Internet, including the increasing number of Facebook groups that promote and incite hatred against non-citizens; and (b) the lack of data regarding the prosecution of the individuals responsible and the remedies provided to victims (Articles 2 and 4). 15. Taking into account the Committee's general recommendation No. 35 (2013) on combating racist hate speech, the Committee recommends that the State party:

(a) Ensure that all individuals, including politicians at all levels, are held accountable and are sanctioned for the dissemination of ideas based on racial superiority or hatred and other violations of Article 4 of the Convention, including by lifting parliamentary immunity for racist hate speech in conformity with general recommendation No. 7 (1985) relating to the implementation of Article 4;

(b) Ensure that victims of racist hate speech are provided with effective remedies;

(c) Establish a coherent data collection mechanism to record systematically incidents of racist hate speech, the application of relevant legislation, penalties imposed on the perpetrators and remedies provided to the victims;

(d) Condemn unequivocally at the highest political level the dissemination of hate speech and hateful ideas and engage in promoting a culture of tolerance and respect;

(e) Ensure that the prohibition of racist hate speech extends to the Internet, and ratify the Additional Protocol to the Convention on Cybercrime concerning the criminalisation of acts of a racist and xenophobic nature committed through computer systems;

(f) Encourage public and private media to adopt and abide by codes of professional ethics and press codes that incorporate respect for the principles of the Convention and other fundamental human rights standards, including avoidance of stereotyping and unnecessary referral to race, religion and other group characteristics in a manner that may promote intolerance;

(g) Ensure the prohibition of, promotion or incitement to, racial discrimination by public authorities or public institutions at both national and local levels in accordance with Article 4(c) of the Convention;

(h) Use the platforms of public office to encourage the means of eliminating barriers between races and to discourage policies that tend to strengthen racial division, in accordance with Article 2(1)(e) of the Convention."

The twenty-first periodic report submitted by Italy under Article 9 of the Convention, of 6 march 2019, underlines the strategic role of the National Strategy the National Office Against Racial Discrimination (hereinafter UNAR) on the theme of the hate speech on the web, through the activity of the Observatory on Media and the Internet which, by extending the monitoring already carried on traditional media, aims to research, monitor and analyse on a daily basis.

Italy's adherence to ICERD is the reason why the country criminalized racist propaganda/incitement to hatred in the first place, back in 1975 (as previously said, since 2018 this offence is now within the Criminal Code). The international obligations arising from the Convention have been mentioned as one of the reasons legitimizing the limitations to free speech (Cass., I, 23034/2001). The Convention is also one of the sources which is referred to by the jurisprudence (alongside EU Directive 2000/43/CE) in order to define the concept of "discrimination".

12.5 European Law

Italy is a member of the Council of Europe. Even if the Strasbourg case law on hate speech did not involve Italy directly, Italy is indirectly affected by that case law. In particular, the case law on historical denialism (see in particular the *Perinçek* decision) can be seen as one of the reasons while the Italian aggravating circumstance for historical denialism, introduced in 2016, refers to "the Shoah", on one hand, and to the crimes of genocide, crimes against humanity and war crimes as defined in the Rome Statute of the ICC, on the other.

As for the EU, the *Taormina* case (ECJ – GC, 23 April 2020, Case C-507/18) (see *supra*) deserves attention. In June 2021 the Italian Prime Minister, Mario Draghi, was among the 17 EU leaders who published a joint letter vowing to "continue fighting against discrimination towards the LGBTI community," a day after the EU Commission said it would take legal steps against Hungary's new anti-LGBTQ+ legislation.

Regarding EU legislation, the Council Framework Decision 2008/913/JHA of the EU of 28 November 2008 "on combating certain forms and expressions of racism and xenophobia by means of criminal law" is also important. The Italian Law of 16 July 2016, No. 115 implemented the Council Framework Decision by providing for a specific criminalisation of denialism through the addition of a new para 3 bis to the (then) Article 3 of the Law 13 October 1975 No. 654 (so-called *Mancino* Law, now Article 604 bis of the Criminal Code).

Italy has joined the countries that sanction practices of historical denialism with an *ad hoc* provision. The Italian legislature has chosen a particular implementation method, unique in the EU landscape, opting not for an autonomous typical offence but for an aggravating circumstance of the crime, then referred to under Article 3 of the *Mancino* Law. Consequently, it is hard to believe that this aggravating circumstance also extends to what, in the German scholarship, is defined as simple denialism (*einfache* or *bloße Auschwitzlüge*), which differs from qualified denialism (*qualifizierte Auschwitzlüge*) in that it consists of mere denialism, not qualified by the incitement to violence or intolerance.

In a case prior to the introduction of the aggravating circumstance, a school teacher was accused of racist propaganda and found not guilty. The judge ascertained that he did deny the Holocaust to the class, but "with completely aseptic methods, without using terms indicative of the superiority of the Aryan people or of hatred towards the Jewish people" (Trib. Rome, VI, 3 December 2013). It is difficult to believe that the aggravating circumstance would have made any difference in such a case.

Under Italian law a requirement of minimal public relevance is implicit in the structure of the typical conduct of the main offence, on which the aggravating circumstance is embedded. The additional requirement of the "concrete danger of diffusion" is also required. In identifying the categories of crimes whose denialism is punished, the Law includes, on the one hand, a historically identified and circumscribed element (literally "the Shoah"), and on the other, a regulatory element (international crimes "as these are defined" by the Rome Statute of the ICC).

Within the EU it is also important to mention Directive 2010/13/UE and the Directive 2018/1808. Regarding soft law, in 2016 the EU Commission together with Facebook, Twitter and YouTube ("the IT companies") unveiled a code of conduct that includes a series of commitments to combat the spread of illegal hate speech online in Europe. In the future, an important impact will probably come from the European Media Freedom Act, the Digital Services Act and the AI Act.

12.6 Comparative National Law

Reference to comparative national law has been particularly relevant, especially in the media and public discussion with reference to the proposed reform of Article 604-bis of the Criminal Code (racial discrimination), which is currently limited to discrimination (through violence, propaganda, incitement to hatred) to racial, religious, ethnic or national motivation. A proposed bill (so-called *Zan* bill, see *infra*) aimed at extending it to motivation based on sex, gender, sexual orientation, gender identity and disability. In particular the public debate highlighted the fact that most of the other EU Countries, such as Sweden, Spain, France, and Germany, have already reached similar solutions, thanks to legislative or judicial initiatives.

12.7 Judicial Rulings

Judicial rulings have been essential for the interpretation and evolution of hate speech. A trademark case is the so-called *Tosi* case (see the following decisions: Trib. Verona, 2203/2004, C. App. Venezia, 30.01.2007, Cass., III, n. 13234/2007). This case in particular affirmed that the concept of hate speech goes beyond that of racist speech. In the light of human dignity, hate speech cannot be limited to outdated racist theories based on biology. On the contrary, it should include "Implicit racism [...] and neo-racism [...]—understood in the two forms of racism—universalist (heterophobic)—based on the denial of the common identity and therefore, on the contempt for particular cultural forms according to certain scales of values and—[...] differentialist (heterophile)—founded on the denial of common humanity and, therefore, on the absoluteness of the identity and of the racial, ethnic, cultural, national differences of the group" (Trib. Verona, 2203/2004).

In another case, the Court of Cassation also affirms, in relation to the sentence "go away from here, dirty n**er",[1] that this should be punished as racist speech regardless of whether the perpetrator reacted on the emotional thrust of an unfair behaviour of the victim. The Court excludes the need for "a subjective analysis of the perpetrator's motivation", since there is discrimination by virtue of the same "disavowal of equality, or in the affirmation of the social or legal inferiority of others" (Cass., V, 9381/2006, prior to that also Cass., V, 19378/2005, later also Cass., V, 38217/2008, Cass., V, 7859/2017; Cass., V, 32028/2018; Cass., V, 14200/2018; Cass., V, 13530/2017; Cass., V, 43488/2015; Cass., F., 3887/2015 Cass., V, 30525/2013; Cass., V, 22570/2010; Cass., V, 38597/2009; Cass. V, 49694/2009). Yet a different jurisprudence exists as well (for instance Cass., V, n. 44295/2005), which excludes the racial discrimination when ethnic/racial/religious hate represents just one of the internal motivations of the perpetrators. Nonetheless, this jurisprudence did not prevail.

In other decisions, the Court of Cassation also defined the boundaries between hate speech and free political critique (cf. Cass., V, 7859/2017; Cass., 59/2018). In one decision, the Court of Cassation also qualified as hate speech the emission of guttural sounds, as a typical reference to the howling of monkeys, towards black athletes during a sporting event (Cass., III, 12351/2013).

There is a contrast within the jurisprudence on the hate speech on social media in regard to sentencing. The issue is the following: a post can be published quickly and read by millions of people without any need for a further active propagandistic intervention of the author of the post; should this be considered as a mitigating factor in the sentencing? In favour Trib. Padova, 844/2011 ("it was written quickly"); against Trib. Livorno, n. 38912/2012 (motivating that, precisely because the author chose to post a sentence on social media, he must have been aware of the potential high number of readers).

Italy has not introduced a specific hate crime or aggravating circumstance in cases of homophobia or transphobia. As mentioned, both Article 604 bis and ter of the Criminal Code are limited to hatred against racial, ethnic, national and religious groups. Since these two articles provide for such a specific list it is considered that this cannot be extended by the jurisprudence, but only by the legislator (*contra* Trib. Trieste, 2 December 2011; Trib. Milan, 20 October 2022). Nonetheless, in many cases conduct remains punishable under "traditional" hate crimes (diffamazione, ingiuria, calunnia...) when the criminality is not specifically focused on the hateful motive. Defamation (Article 595 of the Criminal Code) is one of the most relevant. For example, defamation is committed by anyone who publicly discloses a person's homosexuality in order to denigrate them (Trib. Milan, IV, 9393/2018). It also constitutes defamation to call a person on Facebook a "disgusting f****t" (Cass., V, 19359/2021).[2] In one case, a senator was found guilty, and not covered by the constitutional right of political criticism connected to his function, because he qualified the activities of an LGBTQIA+ association at a school, aimed at countering homophobic bullying

---

[1] Quotation from case on https://dejure.it/ (in Italian); Translation by the author.

[2] Quotation from case on https://dejure.it/ (in Italian); Translation by the author.

and providing information on the prevention of sexually transmitted diseases, as a form of solicitation of minors (Cass., V, 25759/2022).

In a recent case, a group of people were convicted in relation to a Facebook post with the picture of a man participating at the local gay pride and wearing angel wings. The author of the post and those who commented made fun of the man portrayed in the picture by calling him a chicken or commenting with a picture of the *Diagnostic and Statistical Manual of Mental Disorders* (Trib. Siena, 645/2020).

There are two contrasting views in the jurisprudence regarding the criminal liability of individuals who use insults and offensive language as a reaction against someone else's homophobia. In one case, two girls were found guilty of defamation against the staff of a beach resort. The girls had both commented on a public Facebook post of a boy, who had been victim of an episode of homophobia at that resort. In order to show support for the boy, the two girls used aggressive and offensive language towards members of the staff. The judges did not find that the previous episode of homophobia could be seen as justification (Trib. Ascoli Piceno, 440/2020).

However, in other cases judges have decided not to penalize individuals who commented with insults on the post of a politician who was calling homosexuals "genetic aberrations" (G.I.P. Busto Arsizio, Order 24 February 2015), or individuals who, on Instagram, insulted an influencer who expressed the hope that Hitler would come back to get rid of the local Pride march, which had caused her to be stuck in the traffic (Prosecutor of Milan, request for filing, 18 October 2019). Meanwhile, the jurisprudence considers that even LGBTQIA+ people can be found guilty of homophobic defamation, as in the case of a lesbian who used the slur "lesbian whore" against another woman whom she discovered having an affair with her girlfriend: Cass., V, 30545/2021.

Also notable is a case involving the neighbour of a gay couple who repeatedly addressed them with homophobic speech and writings. This conduct forced the couple to move out, and the court found the perpetrator guilty of the crime of stalking under Criminal Code Article 660. Even if "traditional" speech crimes cover many cases of homo and transphobic speech, this has consequences in terms of proportionality of the sanctions. Compared to racist, national or religious hate speech—where Articles 604 bis or ter can be applied—the sanctions for homo-transphobic speech are much lower.

In one case, the non-applicability of Article 604 bis to homophobia has a more radical consequence: the lack of a criminal law remedy and therefore the legitimacy of the conduct. This is the case of pure homophobic propaganda, i.e. where hate speech is not directed to one or more specific individuals but to the group as whole (gay people, the homosexuals…). The judiciary has tried to overcome this lack of legislation in *Taormina* by referring to labour law as well as the *De Mari* cases. De Mari in her online blog accused "the LGBT movement" of "spreading paedophilia." The Tribunal of Turin found her guilty of defamation, identifying the local LGBT association as a representative of the LGBT movement and therefore a concrete and identifiable victim of the defamation (Trib. Turin, 5009/2018 and Court of Appeal Turin, 14 June 2022). Nevertheless, even with that logical leap, the judges had to admit that other sentences, which did not mention the movement, had to go unpunished in the absence of a crime of homo- transphobic propaganda (an example: "if we allow today that homosexuality is not considered a disorder of nature, then tomorrow paedophilia could be considered the same").

12.8 Additional Observations

Ten years after its signature, Italy has not yet ratified yet the Additional Protocol to the Convention on Cybercrime, concerning the criminalisation of acts of a racist and xenophobic nature committed through computer systems. In addition, an international law debate arose in June 2021 amid the debate on the so called *Zan* bill, a proposed bill which aimed at extending Article 604 bis of the Criminal Code (*Propaganda and incitement to crime on the grounds of racial, ethnic and religious discrimination*) to motives based on sex, gender, sexual orientation, gender identity and disability. The bill was approved by the Chamber of Deputies on the 4 November 2020 and (as of the end of July 2021) but later dismissed by the Senate of the Republic on 27 October 2021. The debate related to the possibility that the Italian Parliament could not adopt such a bill because of a limitation imposed by an international treaty with the Holy See, the so-called Lateran Pacts. Based on an interpretation provided by the Holy See, this international obligation, on the basis of the Italian Constitution, would prevail over the legislative power of the Parliament.

With an unprecedented intervention in the history of the Italian State, the Holy See, acting officially as a State and not as a Church, took a drastic position on the issue. The Secretary for Relations with States, Archbishop Paul Richard Gallagher, delivered a formal diplomatic note to the Italian Embassy to the Holy See on 17 June 2021,[3] expressing concern about the text under debate, affirming that the proposed criminalisation of homophobic speech could result in a limitation of the Church's free speech, particularly considering that some parts of the Bible "consider sexual differences in an anthropological perspective, which for the Catholic Church is not disposable, since it is derived from God's Revelation".

The Holy See considers that the proposed bill could constitute a violation of the international obligations for the Italian State deriving from the Agreement of Revision of the Lateran Pacts (also called "second Concordat"), which was signed in 1984 (while the original Lateran Pacts, or Concordat, between Italy and the Holy See were signed in 1929). The diplomatic note reads:

> …the Secretariat of State notes that some contents of the legislative initiative - particularly in the part which establishes the criminalization of discriminatory conduct for reasons 'based on sex, gender, sexual orientation, gender identity' - would have the effect of negatively impacting the freedoms guaranteed to the Catholic Church and its faithful by the existing Concordat regime. Various expressions of Sacred Scripture, of ecclesial Tradition, and of

[3] The text can be found here: https://www.vaticannews.va/it/vaticano/news/2021-06/testo-integrale-nota-verbale-segreteria-stato-ddl-zan.html.

> the authentic Magisterium of the Popes and Bishops, consider, with multiple effects, sexual difference, according to an anthropological perspective that the Catholic Church does not believe can be changed because it stems from divine Revelation itself. This prospect is in fact guaranteed by the Agreement between the Holy See and the Italian Republic for the revision of the Lateran Concordat, signed on 18 February 1984. Specifically, in Article 2, para 1, it is stated that 'the Italian Republic accords the Catholic Church full freedom to carry out his pastoral, educational and charitable mission, of evangelization and sanctification. In particular, freedom of organization, of public exercise of worship, of exercise of the magisterium and of the spiritual ministry as well as of jurisdiction in ecclesiastical matters is guaranteed to the Church'. In Article 2, para 3, it is further stated that 'Catholics and their associations and organizations are guaranteed full freedom of assembly and expression of thought by word, writing and any other means of dissemination.
> The Secretariat of State therefore hopes that the Italian Party will be able to take due consideration of the aforementioned arguments and find a different version of the legislative text, continuing to guarantee compliance with the Lateran Pacts, which for almost a century have regulated relations between the State and the Church and to which the same Republican Constitution reserves a special mention.

This unprecedented diplomatic action gave rise to enormous mediatic debate on the possible limitations to free speech in Italy. On June 23, the Italian Prime Minister, Mario Draghi, addressed the Parliament on this issue, without discussing the merits of the diplomatic note. However, he stressed that Italy is "a secular state, not a confessional state and therefore the Parliament is certainly free to debate and legislate. (...) Moreover, our legal system contains the guarantees to ensure that laws always respect constitutional principles and international commitments, including the Concordat with the Church, both before and after the adoption of the law". He also quoted a decision of the Constitutional Court of the year 1989, according to which "secularism does not mean indifference of the State to the religious phenomenon, but rather protection of pluralism and cultural diversity."

12.9 NGO Activity

The increasing data on hate speech against LGBT+ people in Italy has been highlighted, among others, in the 2016 report of the European Commission against Racism and Intolerance (ECRI) and in the 2013 EU LGBT survey of the EU Agency for Fundamental Rights. An invitation, although not specifically to Italy, to act against LGBTI hate speech comes also from the European Parliament resolution of 18 December 2019 on public discrimination and hate speech against LGBTI people, including LGBTI free zones. An important NGO monitoring initiative came from Amnesty International and its "Barometro dell'odio" (Hate Barometer) project, which began in 2018, monitoring hate speech in political posts and declarations relation to political elections and describing the targeted groups.

12.10 National Popular Culture

In recent years, hate speech on social media has been the object of intense debate within Italian society and media, especially thanks to the activism of some notorious women who have been targeted with gender-based hate speech. Particularly, it should be mentioned that Laura Boldrini, former spokesperson to UNHCR and former President of the Chamber of Deputies in Italy, and the novelist Michela Murgia, who was targeted both as woman and because of her weight. NGOs, awareness groups and legal counselling group (such as #odiareticosta) have been funded. Amnesty International funded the "Barometro dell'odio" (Hate Barometer), monitoring hate speech in political posts and declarations relation to political elections.

A prominent figure in order to raise awareness on hate speech has been Senator Liliana Segre. Italian Jewish, Auschwitz survivor, Senator Segre obtained that the Parliament established an Extraordinary commission for combating the phenomena of intolerance, racism, anti-Semitism and incitement to hatred and violence. In April 2021, Segre herself was elected president of the new commission. In 2019, Senator Segre quantified to receive about 200 hateful posts per day.

Recently there has been growing activism, particularly among celebrities, in support to the so-called Zan Bill, raising awareness in relation to homophobic and transphobic hate speech and hate crimes. For the first time, a very important role has been played by Instagram influencers, particularly the fashion blogger Chiara Ferragni and her husband Fedez. In the days after the dismissal of the Bill (27 October 2021) many public and crowded protests have been taking place in several Italian cities.

Paolo Caroli is Lecturer of Criminal Law in the Faculty of Law at the University of Turin, Italy. Much of his work focuses on the interlacements of historical memory and criminal law, and on the limitations to free speech. He was Alexander von Humboldt Fellow (University of Hamburg—Humboldt University of Berlin), Post-Doc Researcher (University of Bologna—M.E.L.A. Project) and Post-Doc Lecturer (University of Trento). He is author of the monographs *Transitional Justice in Italy and the Crimes of Fascism and Nazism* (Routledge 2022), *Il potere di non punire: Uno studio sull'amnistia Togliatti* (Esi 2020).

Chapter 13
The Netherlands

Tom Herrenberg

Contents

Abstract In the Netherlands, hate speech is banned by various provisions in the criminal code, including articles 137c (prohibiting group defamation) and 137d (prohibiting incitement to discrimination, hatred, or violence). Public controversies over the limits of provocative expression erupt every now and then, in particular when the prosecuted individual is a highly visible member of society (for example, Member of Parliament Geert Wilders). Due to the direct effect and precedence of international law in the Dutch legal system, international and regional bodies, notably the European Court of Human Rights, play a significant role in case law on hateful or discriminatory expression.

Keyword Hate speech legislation · Anti-LGBTQ+ speech · Anti-religious speech · Hate speech by public officials · Hate speech and international law · Hate speech and the European Court of Human Rights

T. Herrenberg (✉)
Faculty of Law, Open Universiteit, Heerlen, The Netherlands
e-mail: tom.herrenberg@ou.nl

E. Heinze (ed.), *Criminalising Hate Speech*,
https://doi.org/10.1007/978-94-6265-650-5_13

13.1 National Constitutional Law

In the Netherlands, constitutional provisions are not directly applied to hateful expression. Although the Dutch Constitution contains a non-discrimination/equal treatment provision (Article 1 of the Constitution),[1] this provision does not directly apply to speech.[2] Instead, in cases of hateful expression, various provisions in criminal law (e.g. the group defamation ban) or private law (e.g. tort law) provide the legal framework to evaluate such expression. That being said, equality and non-discrimination considerations do play a role in legislation against hateful expression, as the bans on group defamation and hate speech are designed to combat discrimination.[3]

Moreover, religious freedom, protected by Article 6 of the Dutch Constitution, plays an indirect role in case law on hateful expression. Dutch law grants more leeway to expression in a number of contexts, namely artistic expression, expression that is directly related to someone's religious conviction, and statements that contribute to or serve a public debate.[4] Article 6 of the Dutch Constitution is sometimes explicitly mentioned in authoritative opinions on hateful expression. For example, the Netherlands Public Prosecution Service ('Openbaar Ministerie') referenced this constitutional provision in its decision of March 2020 not to prosecute the translators of the 'Nashville Statement', a statement of evangelical Christians regarding human sexuality.[5] Another example stems from a case decided by the Dutch Supreme Court in 2001, in which the defendant had compared homosexuality to theft. The Advocate General at the Supreme Court stated in his advisory opinion: 'Also more orthodox believers, whether this concerns the Jewish tradition, the Christian factions, Islam or believers from other households, have on the basis of Article 6 of the Dutch Constitution a strong right to propagate and promulgate their faith in any way.'[6]

---

[1] 'All persons in the Netherlands shall be treated equally in equal circumstances. Discrimination on the grounds of religion, belief, political opinion, race or sex or on any other grounds whatsoever shall not be permitted.' ('Allen die zich in Nederland bevinden, worden in gelijke gevallen gelijk behandeld. Discriminatie wegens godsdienst, levensovertuiging, politieke gezindheid, ras, geslacht of op welke grond dan ook, is niet toegestaan.')

[2] Cf. van Noorloos 2014, p. 68.

[3] The Dutch Government has stated that these bans are 'intended to prevent discrimination against certain groups. (...) Defamation [can] create a negative image of a particular group, which can lead to discrimination and social deprivation of those who belong to this group.' See Second Chamber, 1988–1989, Parliamentary Paper No 20239 (5), p. 6 ('Zij zijn bedoeld om discriminatie van bepaalde groepen tegen te gaan. (...) [D]oor belediging [kan] een negatief beeld van een bepaalde groep ontstaan, wat kan leiden tot discriminatie en maatschappelijke achterstelling van degenen die tot deze groep behoren.')

[4] See for example, Dutch Supreme Court, 29 March 2016, ECLI:NL:HR:2016:511.

[5] Netherlands Public Prosecution Service, 'Beoordeling strafbaarheid Nashvilleverklaring', p. 6.

[6] Advisory opinion of advocate general Machielse to the case of Dutch Supreme Court, 9 January 2001, ECLI:NL:PHR:2001:AA9367 ('Ook meer orthodoxe gelovigen, of dit nu de Joodse traditie, de christelijke facties, de Islam of gelovigen van anderen huize betreft, hebben op grond van artikel 6 GW een sterk recht om hun geloof—op enigerlei wijze—uit te dragen en te verkondigen').

13.1.1 National Statutory and Administrative Law

Various provisions in statutory law are applied to hateful expression. The Dutch Criminal Code (DCC) contains multiple provisions specifically tailored to discriminatory or hateful expression, including a group defamation ban ('groepsbelediging', Article 137c DCC), a ban on incitement to hatred, discrimination or violence ('haatzaaien', Article 137d DCC), and a ban on the distribution of material that defames groups or incites to hatred, discrimination, or violence (Article 137e DCC). On top of this, general provisions, such as the prohibition on individual defamation or the ban on incitement to commit a criminal offence ('opruiing', Article 131 DCC) may be applied to hateful or discriminatory expression.[7] The hateful or discriminatory aspect may constitute an aggravating factor in such a case. Moreover, private (tort) law ('onrechtmatige daad', Article 6:162 of the Dutch Civil Code) may also be applied to hateful expression.[8]

The Netherlands Public Prosecution Service is equipped with prosecuting violations of the criminal law. It maintains, since 1998, an internal National Discrimination Expertise Centre ('Landelijke Expertise Centrum Discriminatie'). The objective of this centre is to 'optimize the enforcement of criminal law in the field of discrimination, i.e. positioning, advising, policy-making, investigation, prosecution and reporting.'[9] Other bodies, such as the Dutch Ombudsman—who investigates complaints of citizens regarding the functioning of the government—and the Netherlands Institute for Human Rights ('College voor de Rechten van de Mens') are also involved in combatting discriminatory or hateful expression.

---

[7] For example, the ban against incitement to commit a criminal offence was applied in a 2020 case in which the victim had livestreamed on her Facebook page a demonstration against the controversial figure Black Pete ('Zwarte Piet'), a helper of Saint Nicholas ('Sinterklaas'). The victim in this case received thousands of largely negative comments under her livestream, including comments of a violent and discriminatory nature. Eighteen people were convicted on the basis of incitement. For an example, see Court of Amsterdam, 2 November 2020, ECLI:NL:RBAMS:2020:5288.

[8] See for example the case against MP Thierry Baudet for posts comparing Covid-19 measures with the Holocaust. See BBC, Dutch MP ordered to delete Covid Holocaust social media posts, 16 December 2021. Court case: Amsterdam Court of Appeal, 23 May 2023, ECLI:NL:GHAMS:2023:1139.

[9] See Netherlands Public Prosecution Service, Landelijke Expertise Centrum Discriminatie (LECD).

13.1.2 Blasphemy and Hate Speech

On 1 March 2014, the Dutch anti-blasphemy law of 1932 was effectively repealed (although it was dormant since the 1960s).[10] In December 2013, amidst the parliamentary debate on the bill to repeal the blasphemy ban, a motion was adopted in which the Government was asked to examine whether a possible amendment of the provisions on group defamation and hate speech could be useful to ensure sufficient protection for citizens against seriously felt insults of their religion and religious experience.[11] After a study on behalf of the Ministry of Security and Justice's Research and Data Centre ('Wetenschappelijk Onderzoek- en Datacentrum'),[12] the Government concluded that no new restrictions on free expression should be adopted after the blasphemy ban had been repealed. The Government argued that the criminal law offers sufficient protection against discriminatory statements on the basis of religion, while by extending that protection, free expression possibly be jeopardized.[13]

13.1.3 Denialism

In December 2023, the Dutch Government proposed a law that seeks to criminalize condoning, denying or grossly trivializing genocides, crimes against humanity, or war crimes.[14] This law stems from a notice by the European Commission of June 2021, stating that the Dutch legal system fails to accurately transpose EU rules, namely the Council Framework Decision 2008/913/JHA on combating racism and

---

[10] See, generally, P. Cliteur & T. Herrenberg, 'On the Life and Times of the Dutch Blasphemy Law (1932–2014),' in: P. Cliteur & T. Herrenberg (eds.), *The Fall and Rise of Blasphemy Law*, Leiden: Leiden University Press 2016, p. 71–109.

[11] Senate, 2013–2014, Parliamentary Paper No 32203 (E).

[12] L.A. van Noorloos, *Strafbaarstelling van 'belediging van geloof' Een onderzoek naar mogelijke aanpassing van de uitingsdelicten in het Wetboek van Strafrecht, mede in het licht van internationale verdragsverplichtingen*, Den Haag: Boom Lemma uitgevers 2014. Until November 2023, the centre was named the Research and Documentation Centre (*Wetenschappelijk Onderzoek- en Documentatiecentrum*).

[13] Senate, 2013–2014, Parliamentary Paper No 32203 (F), p. 2 (*Brief inzake uitvoering van motie van lid Schrijver c.s. over de bescherming van godsdienstige gevoelens (32 203, E)—Voorstel van Wet van de leden Schouw en De Wit tot wijziging van het Wetboek van Strafrecht in verband met het laten vervallen van het verbod op godslastering*).

[14] Second Chamber, 2023–2024, Parliamentary Paper No 36491 (2).

xenophobia by means of criminal law.[15] The proposed law is aimed at the conversion into Dutch law of Articles 1 (c)[16] and (d)[17] of the Framework Decision.

Although Holocaust denial is under certain circumstances punishable under the existing group defamation provision,[18] the European Commission holds the position that there is no correct and complete transposition of the aforementioned Framework Decision provision, as the text of Article 137c of the Dutch Criminal Code does not explicitly refer to those specific behaviors mentioned in Articles 1 (c) and (d) of the Framework Decision.[19] Hence, the Government seeks to alter Article 137c by adding a clause that holds that group defamation can consist of publicly condoning, denying or grossly trivializing the international crimes.

13.2 International Covenant on Civil and Political Rights (ICCPR)

The Netherlands ratified the International Covenant on Civil and Political Rights (ICCPR) on 11 December 1978,[20] it entered into force on 11 March 1979.[21] The UN Human Rights Committee has issued Concluding Observations for the Netherlands commenting specifically on hateful expression. In its Concluding observations on the fifth periodic report of the Netherlands (2019) the Committee expressed concern 'at the persistent racist hate speech used against migrants, refugees, Muslims, Jews and other ethnic and religious minorities in the Netherlands by politicians and high-level public officials, through social media and at public events, such as football matches. It is also concerned that hate speech has not only led to significant harm

[15] Second Chamber, 2023–2024, Parliamentary Paper No 36491 (3), p. 1; 'Commission calls on Greece, the Netherlands and Lithuania to fully transpose EU law criminalising hate speech and hate crimes', 9 June 2021, https://ec.europa.eu/newsroom/just/items/713873.

[16] 'publicly condoning, denying or grossly trivialising crimes of genocide, crimes against humanity and war crimes as defined in Articles 6–8 of the Statute of the International Criminal Court, directed against a group of persons or a member of such a group defined by reference to race, colour, religion, descent or national or ethnic origin when the conduct is carried out in a manner likely to incite to violence or hatred against such a group or a member of such a group.'

[17] 'publicly condoning, denying or grossly trivialising the crimes defined in Article 6 of the Charter of the International Military Tribunal appended to the London Agreement of 8 August 1945, directed against a group of persons or a member of such a group defined by reference to race, colour, religion, descent or national or ethnic origin when the conduct is carried out in a manner likely to incite to violence or hatred against such a group or a member of such a group.'

[18] See for example, Court of Midden-Nederland, 23 September 2016, ECLI:NL:RBMNE:2016:5142; Arnhem Court of Appeal, 19 August 2010, ECLI:NL:GHARN:2010:BN4204.

[19] Second Chamber, 2023–2024, Parliamentary Paper No 36491 (3), p. 3–4.

[20] Treaty Series (*Tractatenblad*) (1978) no. 177, p. 31.

[21] Ibid., p. 40.

to the rights or reputations of persons and groups of persons subjected to it, but has also contributed to a growing climate of intolerance and to hate crimes.'[22]

The UN Human Rights Committee submitted that the Netherlands 'should strengthen its efforts, through both law enforcement and awareness-raising activities, to combat racial discrimination, hate speech and incitement to discrimination or violence on racial, ethnic or religious grounds, in accordance with Articles 19 and 20 of the Covenant and the Committee's general comment No. 34 (2011) on the freedoms of opinion and expression.'[23] Moreover, the Netherlands was a party to the case *Rabbae, A.B.S and N.A. v The Netherlands*, which came before the UN Human Rights Committee.[24] In this case the complainants claimed that the acquittal of Dutch MP Wilders in his first trial (which ended in 2011), over charges of group defamation and incitement to hatred and discrimination, was contrary to Article 20 (2) of the ICCPR.[25]

The Human Rights Committee concluded however that the Netherlands had 'taken the necessary and proportionate measures to "prohibit" statements made in violation of Article 20 (2) and to guarantee the right of the authors to an effective remedy in order to protect them against the consequences of such statements. The obligation under Article 20 (2), however, does not extend to an obligation for the State party to ensure that a person who is charged with incitement to discrimination, hostility or violence will invariably be convicted by an independent and impartial court of law. The Committee therefore cannot conclude that the State party violated Article 2 (3), read in conjunction with Articles 26 and 20 (2) of the Covenant.'[26]

ICCPR Article 20 requires that any propaganda for war shall be prohibited by law, and that any advocacy of national, racial or religious hatred that constitutes incitement to discrimination, hostility or violence shall be prohibited by law. This is implemented by Article 137d (1) of the Dutch Criminal Code.[27] This article states that 'Any person who publicly, either verbally, in writing or by way of images, incites to hatred or discrimination against persons, or violence against persons or their property because of their race, religion or philosophy of life, their sex, their hetero- or homosexual orientation or their physical, mental or intellectual disability, shall be liable to a term of imprisonment not exceeding two years or a fine of the fourth category.'

---

[22] UN Human Rights Committee, Concluding observations on the fifth periodic report of the Netherlands (2019), CCPR/C/NLD/CO/5CCPR/C/NLD/CO/5, para 15.

[23] Ibid., para 16.

[24] *Rabbae, A.B.S and N.A. v The Netherlands*, Views, CCPR/C/117/D/2124/2011.

[25] Ibid., at para 3.1.

[26] Ibid., at para 10.7.

[27] See the State's observations in *Rabbae, A.B.S and N.A. v The Netherlands*, Views, CCPR/C/117/D/2124/2011CCPR/C/117/D/2124/2011 at paras 6.5, 10.5.

13.3 International Convention on the Elimination of All Forms of Racial Discrimination (ICERD)

In its Observation of16 November 2021, the UN Committee on the Elimination of Racial Discrimination (UN-CERD) noted 'the efforts by the State party to combat racist hate speech, including through the appointment of a national coordinator on anti-discrimination and antiracism and of a national coordinator on antisemitism.' The Committee further observed that:

> It takes note of the establishment of [the office for complaints of online discrimination *Meldpunt Internet Discriminatie* or MiND], which has concluded agreements to improve cooperation with social media companies. The Committee is, however, concerned that: (a) People protected under the Convention, including but not limited to people of African descent, Asian people and people of Asian descent, members of Jewish and Muslim communities and migrants, continue to be victims of hate speech and hate crimes; (b) A high number of expressions of hate speech remain online for a period of weeks, months or years unless they are reported to MiND; (c) The political debate on immigration has been polarized and has led to aggravated forms of racial discrimination (Article 4).'[28]

The Committee recommended that the Netherlands should:

> … take measures to increase awareness of the prohibition of hate speech, including on the Internet, among the population, in particular among potential victims of hate speech, as well as of remedies available to them, including through MiND. It also recommends that the State party: (a) Establish that MiND can proactively and ex officio identify and request the removal of discriminatory online content; (b) Ensure the availability of MiND in other languages, in addition to Dutch; (c) Ensure effective implementation of agreements concluded between social media companies and MiND, and evaluate their impact on the propagation of racist stereotypes and discriminatory attitudes; (d) Distance itself from political discourse on immigration that leads to racial discrimination and ensure that expressions of hate speech by politicians are thoroughly investigated and properly sanctioned.'[29]

In addition, the Committee expressed concern over the fact 'that cases of racist abuse in football have risen in the State party over the past years.'[30] The Committee made recommendations for expressions of racism in the football context, including 'robust and meaningful education programmes to tackle racial stereotyping and discrimination within the football community and all segments of society directly or indirectly involved with the problem.'[31] In an earlier Concluding observation, from 2015, the Committee had expressed concern 'about incidents of racist and xenophobic hate speech emanating from a number of extremist political parties and politicians.' The report continued:

[28] Committee on the Elimination of Racial Discrimination, Concluding observations on the combined twenty-second to twenty-fourth periodic reports of the Kingdom of the Netherlands (2021), CERD/C/NLD/CO/22-24, para 11.

[29] Ibid., para 12.

[30] Ibid., para 13.

[31] Ibid., para 14.

> [The Committee] is also concerned about the prevalence of racist discourse in the media and the increase in racist statements and threats on the Internet. The Committee is particularly concerned about the sharp increase in discrimination against members of Jewish and Muslim communities, including the reported increase in verbal abuse, harassment and physical violence against Jewish and Muslim persons. The Committee notes with concern that anti-Semitic and racist chants are commonplace in football stadiums. While noting the explanation given by the delegation, the Committee remains concerned that the approach of the courts to determining whether an insulting statement amounts to hate speech under the Convention may make adequate prosecution of such statements unnecessarily difficult (Articles 2, 4 and 5).'[32]

Commenting specifically on the cultural practice of 'Black Pete', a holiday traditionally celebrated in the Netherlands prior to Christmas including what is now widely viewed as a racist gollywog character, the Committee observed:

> While the Committee understands that the tradition of Sinterklaas and Zwarte Piet (Black Pete) is enjoyed by many persons in Dutch society, it notes with concern that the character of Black Pete is sometimes portrayed in a manner that reflects negative stereotypes of people of African descent and is experienced by many people of African descent as a vestige of slavery, which is injurious to the dignity and self-esteem of children and adults of African descent. The Committee is concerned about the discriminatory effect of such portrayals, which may convey a conception at odds with the Convention. It is also concerned at reports that citizens seeking to peacefully protest against such portrayals have been denied authorization to conduct such protests at a meaningful time and place and have been subjected to violent attacks and other forms of intimidation, which have not been adequately investigated (Articles 2, 5 and 7).'[33]

In the case of *L.K. v. the Netherlands* (1991), threats of violence were publicly made by a group of people against a Moroccan citizen (L.K.) in the Netherlands. While visiting a house together with a friend (A.B.) for which a lease had been offered to L.K. and his family, some 20 people had gathered outside the house. 'During the visit, the author heard several of them both say and shout: "No more foreigners". Others intimated to him that if he were to accept the house, they would set fire to it and damage his car.'[34] After visiting the Municipal Housing Office and asking an official to accompany L.K. and A.B. to the street, 'several inhabitants told the official that they could not accept the author as their neighbour, due to a presumed rule that no more than 5% of the street's inhabitants should be foreigners. Told that no such rule existed, street residents drafted a petition, which noted that the author could not be accepted and recommended that another house be allocated to his family.'[35]

The author filed a complaint with the police, alleging that he had been the victim of articles 137c and 137d of the Criminal Code. Ultimately, the public prosecutor 'informed the author that the matter had not been registered as a criminal case with

---

[32] Committee on the Elimination of Racial Discrimination, Concluding observations on the combined nineteenth to twenty-first periodic reports of the Netherlands (2015), CERD/C/NLD/CO/19-21, para 11.

[33] Ibid., para 17.

[34] Committee on the Elimination of Racial Discrimination, *L.K. v. the Netherlands*, CERD/C/390, pp. 24–30, para 2.1.

[35] Ibid.

his office, because it was not certain that a criminal offence had taken place.'[36] Subsequently, L.K.'s counsel requested the Court of Appeal of Amsterdam to order the prosecution—a so-called 'Article 12 procedure', named after Article 12 of the Code of Criminal Procedure—for racial discrimination.[37] The Court of Appeal dismissed the author's request.[38] After a request to the Prosecutor-General at the Supreme Court to declare the decision of the Court of Appeal invalid was rejected,[39] L.K. ultimately asked the Minister of Justice 'to order the prosecutor to initiate proceedings in the case.' However, the 'Minister replied that he could not grant the request, as the Court of Appeal had fully reviewed the case.'[40]

L.K. complained that the authorities had not properly examined 'all the relevant facts of the case or at least did not formulate a motivated decision in respect of his complaint' and that 'the police investigation was neither thorough nor complete.' L.K. also complained about other issues, for example that 'the decision of the prosecutor not to institute criminal proceedings remained unmotivated.'[41] The Committee sided with L.K. and found that 'the remarks and threats made (…) constituted incitement to racial discrimination and to acts of violence against persons of another colour or ethnic origin, contrary to Article 4 (a) of the International Convention on the Elimination of All Forms of Racial Discrimination, and that the investigation into these incidents by the police and prosecution authorities was incomplete.'[42] 'When threats of racial violence are made, and especially when they are made in public and by a group, it is incumbent upon the State to investigate with due diligence and expedition. In the instant case, the State party failed to do this' according to the Committee.[43]

The current legal regime of regulating hateful expression is strongly influenced by the ICERD. In 1971, as a result of the ICERD, the prohibition on incitement to hatred or discrimination (Article 137d) was added to the Dutch Criminal Code. The Dutch Criminal Code had no provision against incitement to discrimination or hatred prior to this. This provision was intended to 'banish from the public sphere, expressions that threaten the elementary rights of people belonging to a specific group.'[44]

In addition, a new ban on group defamation was adopted in 1971, replacing the old 1934 ban (the Article number remained the same, 137c).[45] The government submitted that Articles 137c and 137d were important in order to 'emphasize a standard of tolerance in an ideologically and religiously diverse Dutch society.'[46] Although the

[36] Ibid., para 2.5.
[37] Ibid.
[38] Ibid., para 2.7.
[39] Ibid., para 2.8.
[40] Ibid.
[41] Ibid., para 3.2.
[42] Ibid., para 6.3.
[43] Ibid., para 6.6.
[44] Second Chamber, 1967–1968, Parliamentary Paper No 9724 (3), p. 5.
[45] Bulletin of Acts and Decrees (*Staatsblad*) 1971, no. 96.
[46] Senate, 1970–1971, Parliamentary Paper No 9724 (22a), p. 4.

ICERD does not require state parties to adopt a group defamation ban, the Dutch government was of the opinion that it would fail its duties regarding the implementation of the ICERD if a provision against group defamation would be left out of the criminal code. Besides this international law rationale, there was a felt need for a ban on group defamation because of Dutch society 'becoming increasingly composed of different ethnic and ideological groups.'[47] The new group defamation ban, which was drafted 'in the context of possible intercommunal conflicts in society,'[48] sought to 'banish from the public sphere, expressions that seriously harm the honor of people belonging to specific groups.'[49]

Whilst 'hatred' was not given a legal definition by the government,[50] the term 'discrimination' was defined in Article 90 quater of the Dutch Criminal Code as 'any distinction, exclusion, restriction or preference which has the purpose or possible effect of nullifying or impairing the recognition, enjoyment or exercise, on an equal footing, of human rights and fundamental freedoms in the political, economic, social, cultural or any other field of public life.' Moreover, the ICERD has played a role in interpreting the term 'race' in Articles 137c and 137d. During the parliamentary debate on Articles 137c and 137d in 1969, the government submitted that the definition in Article 1(1) CERD should function as a guide line in interpreting the term 'race' in Articles 137c and 137d.[51]

This issue was prevalent during the second criminal case (2014–2021) against Dutch politician Geert Wilders of the right-wing Party for Freeom (*Partij voor de Vrijheid*). In this case, Wilders had asked his audience at a political rally whether they wanted 'more or fewer Moroccans' in the Netherlands. The judges in Wilders's trial had to examine whether or not Articles 137c and 137d could be applied to the facts of the case as these two provisions are concerned with offensive or hateful expression about *race*, and as such, it had to be established whether or not 'Moroccans' are a race for the purpose of the law. The court concluded that the way Wilders had used the term 'Moroccans,' namely by singling that specific group of people out on the basis of their shared origin, falls within the scope of the ICERD's clause about 'descent, or national or ethnic origin.' According to the court, the term 'national or ethnic origin' refers to 'persons who have ties to a nation state or territory because they are from that state or region, and who share a history, traditions, a culture and/or a language.' The court was of the opinion that 'virtually all of these aspects can be found in the Moroccan community in the Netherlands.' That being the case, it established that 'Moroccans' are a 'race' for the purposes of Article 137c and 137d, while the court

[47] Second Chamber, 1969–1970, Parliamentary Paper No 9724 (6), p. 4.

[48] Ibid., p. 3.

[49] Second Chamber, 1967–1968, Parliamentary Paper No 9724 (3)Parliamentary Paper No 9724 (3), p. 5.

[50] It has been described by judges as 'an extreme emotion of deep aversion and hostility' ('een extreme emotie van diepe afkeer en vijandigheid').

[51] Second Chamber, 1969-1970, Parliamentary Paper No 9724 (6), pp. 3–4.

acknowledged that the legal definition of 'race' is 'much broader than is typical in common parlance and academia.'[52]

13.3.1 Council of Europe

The Netherlands is a member of the Council of Europe. The Netherlands ratified the European Convention on Human Rights (ECHR) on 31 August 1954.[53] Due to the fact that provisions of treaties or resolutions by international institutions that are binding on all persons take precedence over national laws,[54] case law from the European Court on Human Rights is a major source of law. In determining whether provocative expression may be illegal, Dutch courts devote ample attention to case law European Court on Human Rights.[55]

13.3.1.1 Judicial Rulings

Judges apply a 'three-part test' to examine expression under the group defamation and hate speech bans of articles 137c and 137d DCC.[56] Under this three-part test, initially developed in case law on group defamation but also applicable to incitement to hatred or discrimination,[57] a court first looks at the content of an utterance. Is the utterance, examined in its context, in itself insulting? Insulting ('beledigen') has been understood as 'casting someone in an unfavorable light' and 'assaulting him in his

---

[52] District court of The Hague 9 December 2016, ECLI:NL:RBDHA:2016:15014 (para 5.4.2).

[53] https://www.coe.int/en/web/conventions/full-list/-/conventions/treaty/005/signatures?p_auth=U6CfaEGg. It entered into force on the same day.

[54] Cf. Articles 93–94 of the Dutch Constitution.

[55] See, for example, the decision by the The Hague Court of Appeal in the second Wilders case. The Court of Appeal examined the limits on free expression in light of Article 10 ECHR, and in doing so referred to ECtHR 16 July 2009, nr. 15615/07 (*Féret vs. Belgium*); ECtHR 28 February 2017, nr. 45416/16 (*Le Pen vs. France*); ECtHR 6 July 2006, nr. 59405/00 (*Erbakan vs. Turkey*). ECtHR 19 July 2018, nr. 64659/11 and 24133/13 (*Makraduli vs. The former Yugoslav Republic of Macedonia*); ECtHR 7 November 2007, nr. 12697/03 (*Mamère vs. France*); ECtHR 7 December 1976, nr. 5493/72 (*Handyside vs. United Kingdom*); ECtHR 23 April 1992, nr. 11798/85 (*Castells vs. Spain*); ECtHR 23 June 2016, nr. 20261/12 (*Baka vs. Hungary*); ECtHR 15 October 2015, nr. 27510/08 (*Perinçek vs. Switzerland*); ECtHR 20 October 2015, nr. 25239/13 (*M'Bala M'Bala vs. France*); ECtHR 23 September 1994, nr. 15890/89 (*Jersild vs. Denmark*); ECtHR 15 March 2012, nrs. 4149/04 en 41029/04 (*Aksu vs. Turkey*); ECtHR 25 October 2018, nr. 38450/12 (*E.S. vs. Austria*); ECtHR 3 October 2019, nr. 55225/14 (*Pastörs vs. Germany*); ECtHR 16 July 2009, nr. 15615/07 (*Féret vs. Belgium*); ECtHR 10 July 2008, nr. 15948/03 (*Soulas et autres vs France*).

[56] See also T. Herrenberg, 'Van Nashville tot Staphorst: Over homoseksualiteit, genderidentiteit, en de uitingsvrijheid van orthodoxe gelovigen', *Nederlands Juristenblad* (2019), p. 1796–1801; T. Herrenberg, 'Een overzicht van groepsbelediging en aanzetten tot haat of discriminatie', in: T. Herrenberg (ed.), De grenzen van het publieke debat: Over verdraagzaamheid en de vrijheid van meningsuiting in de democratische samenleving, Den Haag: Boom Juridisch 2019, p. 17–46.

[57] See Dutch Supreme Court 16 December 2014, NJ 2015/108.

honour and good name'.[58] If a certain utterance is considered insulting, judges turn to step two of the test, which considers the broader context in which the utterance was made. Dutch law acknowledges a number of specific contexts in which people have more leeway to express opinions, namely artistic expression, expression that is directly related to a religious conviction, and expression that contributes to or serves a public debate.[59] Third, in case the broader context nullifies the insulting nature of an utterance, courts have to decide whether the utterance is nonetheless 'unnecessarily offensive' ('onnodig grievend'). If the court considers the utterance as 'unnecessarily offensive' the defendant fails the test anyways, notwithstanding the presence of a sphere in which one is allowed to say more (e.g. a public debate or artistic expression). In the literature the term 'unnecessarily offensive' has been interpreted as 'a mismatch between the degree of insult and the degree to which a contribution has been made to the social debate'.[60] Examples of utterances that have been labelled 'unnecessarily offensive' include the accusation that Jews have made up or exaggerated the Holocaust,[61] referring to people as cockroaches or rats,[62] scum,[63] and the use of 'dirty faggots' for homosexuals.[64]

References

van Noorloos M (2014) Strafbaarstelling van 'belediging van geloof.' Een onderzoek naar mogelijke aanpassing van de uitingsdelicten in het Wetboek van Strafrecht, mede in het licht van internationale verdragsverplichtingen. Boom Lemma uitgevers, Den Haag.

van Noorloos LA (2015) De Hoge Raad over de vrijheid van meningsuiting van politici. Tijdschrift Praktijkwijzer Strafrecht: Issue no. 12; p. 98–102.

Tom Herrenberg is assistant professor of constitutional law and legal theory at the Open Universiteit (Netherlands). He holds degrees from Maastricht University (LLB, LLM) and Leiden University (LLM, PhD), and was a visiting researcher at the University of Oxford. He has edited several volumes on free expression and is a co-editor of the *Oxford Handbook of Hate Speech* (forthcoming 2025).

[58] Dutch Supreme Court 29 March 2016, ECLI:NL:HR:2016:511.

[59] Dutch Supreme Court 29 March 2016, ECLI:NL:HR:2016:511.

[60] van Noorloos 2015, para 2.

[61] District court of Overijssel 24 December 2014, ECLI:NL:RBOVE:2014:6877.

[62] Amsterdam Court of Appeal 11 October 2010, ECLI:NL:GHAMS:2010:BO0041.

[63] Amsterdam Court of Appeal 23 November 2009, ECLI:NL:GHAMS:2009:BK4139.

[64] Amsterdam Court of Appeal 17 November 2006, ECLI:NL:GHAMS:2006:AZ3011.

Chapter 14
New Zealand

Ursula Cheer

Contents

Abstract In New Zealand, reforms to measures criminalising hate speech have been debated and reviewed since 2019, without agreement on government action

---

U. Cheer (✉)
University of Canterbury, Christchurch, New Zealand
e-mail: ursula.cheer@canterbury.ac.nz

E. Heinze (ed.), *Criminalising Hate Speech*,
https://doi.org/10.1007/978-94-6265-650-5_14

being achieved. Public controversies erupted around the prominent case of *Wall v Fairfax* [2018] 2 NZLR 471. Mass media have played an important role reporting on the attack on two mosques by a lone gunman in Christchurch in 2019, and on the Royal Commission that investigated the incident and New Zealand's hate speech laws afterwards. Within the general population, public opinion sharply disagrees about bans on hate speech, polarising around the safety of religious and other diverse groups and the need to protect freedom of expression. Currently no new hate speech laws are proposed.

Keyword Racism · Law and broadcast media · Hate speech legislation · Hate speech and international law · Hate speech and freedom of expression

14.1 Background

14.1.1 True Hate Speech Provisions

New Zealand has a variety of laws relevant to hate speech. The most prominent could be described as true hate speech provisions and are found in the Human Rights Act 1993. These are limited racial disharmony provisions which specifically require an element of hate motivation.

The first provision is Section 131 of the Human Rights Act 1993 which establishes a criminal offence of publishing or broadcasting threatening, abusive or insulting statements, these statements being intended and likely to excite hostility or ill will against, or bring into contempt or ridicule any group of persons in New Zealand on the ground of the colour, race or ethnic or national origins of that group of persons. The offence is punishable by up to three months imprisonment or a fine not exceeding $7,000. The Attorney-General must consent to any prosecution. The offence has only been prosecuted once. It does not include religion or sexual orientation as a ground and is only focussed on race, and on speech directed at groups, not individuals.

The second provision is Section 61 of the Human Rights Act, which makes it civilly unlawful to publish or broadcast threatening, abusive or insulting matter likely to excite hostility against or bring into contempt any group of persons in or who may be coming to New Zealand on the ground of the colour, race or ethnic or national origins of that group. No intention is required—the words simply have to be likely to excite hostility against the group or bring it into contempt. Complaints based on this racial disharmony provision may be made to the Race Relations Conciliator, whose office is part of the Human Rights Commission. The remedies are not punitive, but if the matter is not settled through conciliation, it can be referred to the Human Rights Review Tribunal. Among other remedies the Tribunal may uphold the complaint, issue a declaration that the Human Rights Act has been breached, award damages or make a restraining order. Damages may be significant, covering pecuniary loss,

loss of benefit, and humiliation, loss of dignity and injury to feelings. The media are exempt from liability for accurately reporting the remarks of others, under s 61(2).

There are only three decisions applying Sections 131 and 61 of the Human Rights Act (and equivalent provisions in earlier legislation). A lone criminal prosecution under what is now s 131 resulted in the Court of Appeal decision in *King-Ansell v Police.*[1] The appellant had printed 9000 copies of a pamphlet which targeted Jewish people and the Court concluded that Jews in New Zealand were a group with common ethnic origins within the meaning of the provision.

The civil provision arose in two decisions. In *Proceedings Commissioner v Archer,*[2] the Complaints Review Tribunal (now the Human Rights Review Tribunal) applied an ordinary reasonable person test to a broadcast which contained stereotypes about Japanese and Chinese people. The other decision is a key decision of the High Court, *Wall v Fairfax New Zealand Ltd,*[3] which did not uphold an appeal about a complaint and is discussed further below.[4] These racial disharmony provisions were reviewed from 2020–2023 and are now under further review by the New Zealand Law Commission.[5]

14.1.2 Sentencing Provisions

The Sentencing Act 2002 provides that aggravating factors may be taken into account to increase a sentence for a criminal offence.[6] The fact that an offender committed an offence partly or wholly because of hostility towards a group of persons who have an enduring common characteristic such as race, colour, nationality, religion, gender identity, sexual orientation, age, or disability, is one such factor. The provision survived a Bill of Rights analysis by the Court of Appeal in *Philip Neville Arps v New Zealand Police,*[7] discussed below.

14.1.3 Other Relevant Forms of Regulation

Threats. Section 307A of the Crimes Act 1961 deals broadly with threats of harm to people or property. It has been used to deal with serious bomb threats and the like,

[1] *King-Ansell v Police* [1979] 2 NZLR 531 (CA).

[2] *Proceedings Commissioner v Archer* (1996) 3 HRNZ 123 (CRT).

[3] *Wall v Fairfax New Zealand Ltd* [2018] NZHC 104, [2018] 2 NZLR 471.

[4] See paras 14.2 and 14.6.

[5] See Press Release, Prime Minister, Rt Hon Chris Hipkins, 8 February 2023, 'Government takes new direction with policy refocus'; McClure 2023.

[6] Sentencing Act 2002, s. 9(1)(h).

[7] *Philip Neville Arps v New Zealand Police* [2019] NZCA 592.

for example in *Police v Joseph*.[8] However, as that case demonstrates, the provision can also have impact on protest speech.

Public order offences. The Summary Offences Act 1981 contains a number of offences against public order which may impact on hate speech, for example, behaving in an insulting manner in a public place likely in the circumstances to cause violence against persons or property to start or continue; and behaving in a disorderly manner. These offences are minor and only attract minor penalties. The offending must take place in (or within hearing of) a public place and only physical locations are covered by the definition.

Incitement. Under ss 66 and 311 of the Crimes Act 1961 it is wrongful to "incite, counsel or procure" any person to commit an offence, whether or not the offence is eventually committed.

The Films, Videos and Publications Classification Act 1993. This legislation establishes a censorship regime under which 'objectionable' publications can be banned or subject to a restricted classification. The definition of "objectionable" in Section 3(3) includes where the publication represents (whether directly or by implication) that members of any particular class of the public are inherently inferior to other members of the public by reason of any characteristic of members of that class, because of a characteristic that is a prohibited ground of discrimination under Section 21(1) of the Human Rights Act. This provision covers representations of inferiority and does not require any incitement element.

Online communication. Specific liability for online communication arises under the Harmful Digital Communications Act 2015 (HDCA), which contains a criminal offence and a civil complaints process. The HDCA sets out ten communication principles. According to Principle 10: "A digital communication should not denigrate an individual by reason of his or her colour, race, ethnic or national origins, religion, gender, sexual orientation, or disability." Thus the protected characteristics in the HDCA include religion, gender, sexual orientation and disability as well as colour, race, ethnic or national origins.

The Broadcasting Act 1989. Broadcasters are required to maintain standards that are consistent with good taste and decency and to ensure that controversial issues of public importance are discussed in a balanced way. Broadcasting standards include discrimination and denigration. Persons must not be portrayed in a manner that encourages denigration of, or discrimination against, sections of the community on account of sex, race, age, disability or occupation status or as a consequence of legitimate expression of religious, cultural or political beliefs. The legislation establishes a complaints process following broadcast to the Broadcasting Standards Authority, with appeal rights to the High Court.[9]

---

[8] *Police v Joseph* [2013] DCR 482.

[9] See Broadcasting Act 1989, s 4(1) and Broadcasting Standards Authority.

Repealed offences. New Zealand has removed old offences like blasphemy and sedition from the law.

14.2 National Constitutional Law

14.2.1 New Zealand Bill of Rights Act 1990

Constitutional law has been applied in New Zealand to hateful expression in important legislative, administrative, and case law. The most significant law is the New Zealand Bill of Rights Act 1990 (NZBORA). Although it has ordinary law status, the rights contained within the NZBORA reflect those contained in international rights instruments, and the statute itself has *de facto* constitutional importance.[10] It contains a form of freedom of expression in Section 14 which provides:

> Everyone has the right to freedom of expression, including the freedom to seek, receive, and impart information and opinions of any kind in any form.

The rights in this statute are not absolute and there are many laws which limit freedom of speech, those described at 1. above among them. Under s 5 of NZBORA, the right to freedom of expression may be '*subject only to such reasonable limits prescribed by law as can be demonstrably justified in a free and democratic society.*'[11] There is therefore considerable scope for argument and controversy as to whether hate speech offences or other forms or regulation are 'reasonable limits' when it comes to the right to freedom of expression.

14.2.2 Interpretation of Racial Disharmony Provisions in the Human Rights Act 1993

In 2017 the Human Rights Tribunal in *Wall v Fairfax New Zealand Ltd*[12] refused to find that two cartoons published by newspapers, which the parties accepted were objectively offensive because they were racist, breached s 61 of the Human Rights Act 1993 which provides civil sanctions for published racist remarks. On appeal, s 61 was considered for the first time by the High Court in 2018 in *Wall v Fairfax New Zealand Ltd*[13] and its ambit was construed narrowly to ensure consistency with freedom of expression. In determining whether the cartoons breached the racial disharmony provision, the Court interpreted the provision by referencing the New

[10] Dr Caroline Morris, *New Zealand Hate Speech Report*, 1.

[11] See *Wall v Fairfax* [2018] NZHC 104, [2018] 2 NZLR 471, at [172].

[12] *Wall v Fairfax New Zealand Ltd* [2017] NZHRRT 17.

[13] *Wall v Fairfax New Zealand Ltd* [2018] NZHC 104, [2018] 2 NZLR 471.

Zealand Bill of Rights Act,[14] and concluded that it seeks to stop relatively serious examples of expression which inspire enmity, extreme ill-will or are likely to result in a group being despised. Thus, s 61 has been found to only sanction publications at the serious end of the spectrum.

14.2.3 Protest by Flag Burning

Expression in the form of protests that challenge public order has received attention in prominent flag burning cases where freedom of expression has prevailed. These cases involve deliberate insults being directed at those using public places. In *Hopkinson v Police*[15] the appellant was protesting in Parliament grounds and attached a New Zealand flag upside down to a pole, doused it in kerosene and lit it. The flag was destroyed in a fireball. The appellant was convicted of destroying the New Zealand flag with the intention of dishonouring it under s 11(1)(b) of the Flags, Emblems, and Names Protection Act 1981, which provides:

> S 11. Offences involving New Zealand Flag—
>
> (1) Every person commits an offence against this Act who,—
>
> … (b) In or within view of any public place, uses, displays, destroys, or damages the New Zealand Flag in any manner with the intention of dishonouring it.

The Court considered whether the conduct of the appellant fell within the natural meaning of the statute, then asked whether there was prima facie inconsistency with NZBORA and moved to determine whether the limit imposed was a justifiable one. On a natural and ordinary meaning the provision was not a justified limit on freedom of speech, therefore NZBORA required the Court to attempt to read it consistently with the rights protected. This was possible because the word "dishonour" could be read as requiring "vilification" of the flag. Applying this interpretation, the conduct of the appellant did not amount to vilifying the flag.[16]

A similar outcome was the result in *R v Morse*[17] where the appellant had been convicted for offensive behaviour under the Summary Offences Act for flag burning. Morse set fire to the New Zealand flag behind, but within view of people assembled at the Wellington Cenotaph for a dawn service on Anzac Day 2007, to protest against New Zealand military involvement in Afghanistan and other foreign conflicts. Whereas the Court of Appeal considered that treating the burning of the flag as offensive behaviour did not prevent the appellant from exercising her right of freedom of speech, but only limited the means of expression that may be used on particular occasions and this was seen as an appropriate limit on the right to freedom of expression

[14] *Wall v Fairfax New Zealand Ltd* [2018] NZHC 104, [2018] 2 NZLR 471, [38]–[43].

[15] *Hopkinson v Police* [2004] 3 NZLR 704.

[16] *Hopkinson v Police* [2004] 3 NZLR 704, [81].

[17] *R v Morse* [2011] NZSC 45, 34 TCL 17.

under s 14 NZBORA, the Supreme Court did not agree. To be offensive, the expressive conduct had to interfere with the use of a public place by others to an extent that went beyond what a democratic society is expected to tolerate. Tolerance of the expressive behaviour of others is expected of the public using public space because of the value placed on freedom of expression in New Zealand.[18] Because the effect of the appellant's actions on public order had not been assessed, her conviction was set aside.

14.2.4 Disorder

Brooker v Police[19] was one of the first New Zealand Supreme Court decisions where the Court attempted to grapple with the constitutional impact of freedom of expression as embodied in 14 of NZBORA on the interpretation of a minor offence of disorder. Mr Brooker protested outside the house of a female police officer, Ms Croft, because he believed she had abused police powers in relation to him. The protest took place at 9.20 am, and consisted of playing a guitar, singing in a normal voice and displaying a placard with messages such as 'Freedom from unreasonable search and seizure'.

Mr Brooker was originally arrested for loitering with intent to intimidate,[20] but the charge was substituted in the lower court with behaving in a disorderly manner.[21] The split in the Supreme Court reflected the complexities presented by the case. The majority of Elias CJ, and Blanchard and Tipping JJ allowed the appeal and set aside the conviction, largely because primacy was given to freedom of expression.

14.2.5 Trespass Law

Police v Beggs & Ors[22] involved reconciliation by the High Court of NZBORA and the Trespass Act 1980. Here the Court held that the powers of the Speaker of the House to control protestors on Parliament grounds by using powers in the Trespass Act had to be exercised consistently with the rights in NZBORA. Limits could be placed on the rights in the Bill so long as they were reasonable, and what is reasonable depends on the circumstances. Relevant considerations in this case could include whether the assembly was unreasonably prolonged; the rights and freedoms of others using Parliament grounds; the rights of the occupier and those whose business or duties take them to Parliament; the size and duration of the assembly in relation to the interests of

[18] See Elias CJ in *R v Morse* [2011] NZSC 45, 34 TCL 17, at [40].

[19] *Brooker v Police* [2007] 3 NZLR 91.

[20] Section 21(1)(d) Summary Offences Act 1981.

[21] Under s 4(1)(a) of the Summary Offences Act 1981.

[22] *Police v Beggs & Ors*: [1999] 3 NZLR 615.

protesters; the content of what was being expressed; the interests of national security; public order, and the protection of public health. The Speaker had to act in good faith, within the purpose of the power, and reasonably, with due regard to the wishes of others present, but so as to effectively manage and control the property.

14.2.6 Offensive Display and the Resource Management Act 1991—Displaying a Swastika

Under s. 17 of the Resource Management Act 1991, there is a duty to avoid, remedy, or mitigate adverse affects on the environment. An enforcement order or abatement notice may be made under the Act to require a person to cease anything that is or is likely to be noxious, dangerous, offensive, or objectionable to such an extent that it has or is likely to have an adverse effect on the environment. The definition of 'environment' is very wide and includes people and communities, all natural and physical resources, social, economic, aesthetic and cultural conditions.[23]

In *Zdrahal v Wellington CC*[24] the High Court examined the requirement that other enactments must be construed consistently with the rights and freedoms in NZBORA, but subject to reasonable limits demonstrably justified in a free and democratic society, and applied this to the display on the outside of a residential home of a swastika. The Court found that the objective of the Resource Management Act 1991 required that precedence should be given to the protection of the environment over the right to express opinions and beliefs which were offensive or objectionable and adversely affected the environment. Therefore the slight restriction on the appellant by an abatement notice was outweighed by the protection of the environment and the enjoyment by people of their surroundings, unimpaired by the offensive and objectionable display.[25]

14.2.7 Censorship of Objectionable Material

Relationship between freedom of expression and New Zealand's censorship legislation. The case of *Living Word Distributors Ltd v Human Rights Action Group (Wellington)*[26] examined the relationship between freedom of expression and New Zealand's censorship legislation. The Court of Appeal overturned a decision of the High Court banning as objectionable two videos discussing the rights of homosexuals in an extremely negative context. The Court had to consider the effect of s 3(3)(e) of the Films, Videos and Publications Classification Act 1993 (FVPC Act)

---

[23] Resource Management Act 1991, s 2.

[24] *Zdrahal v Wellington CC* [1995] 1 NZLR 700.

[25] *Zdrahal v Wellington CC* [1995] 1 NZLR 700, 710–711.

[26] *Living Word Distributors Ltd v Human Rights Action Group (Wellington)* [2000] 3 NZLR 570.

which provides that material which "represents (whether directly or by implication) that members of any particular class of the public are inherently inferior to other members of the public by reason of any characteristic of members of that class, being a characteristic that is a prohibited ground of discrimination specified in s 21(1) of the Human Rights Act 1993" and whether this trumped freedom of expression which was required to be taken into account.

The Court held that there was no clash of rights values because the section did not create a special stand-alone topic for censorship which could embrace the videos. It merely pointed to factors that may be given weight in the censorship process. However, freedom of expression was to be given full weight in assessing whether the videos were likely to injure the public good. This meant the right to be free from discrimination set out in s 19 NZBORA was not directly applicable and therefore there was no conflict between ss 14 and 19 of NZBORA. The judgment emphasises the importance of freedom of expression in the process of censorship, and gives a rather vague place to values underlying human rights in relevant cases. This part of the decision caused some concern from human rights activists, who then saw little purpose for the inclusion of s 3(3)(e) in the FVPC Act.

14.2.8 Classification of Extremist Material Under Censorship Laws

Online terrorist manifesto. On 15 March 2019, a lone terrorist carried out a series of terrible shootings on two mosques in Christchurch, New Zealand in which 51 people died and many were injured. Two days after the Mosque shootings, the Chief Censor called in a text file for examination[27] and on 23 March classified it as objectionable. The decision[28] deals with a publication that was a 74 page text file attributed to the Christchurch gunman. The file is in a number of parts made up of various materials, including an image of the *sonnenrad* or *black sun*, a pagan European symbol co-opted by the Nazis; the text of Dylan Thomas' 1947 poem *Do not go gentle into that good night*; a two page introduction to 'replacement theory', motivated by falling 'European' birth rates and an increase in immigration of non-Europeans; a Q and A dealing with motives, reasoning and ideology; a modified version of Rudyard Kipling's *The Beginnings,* (an anti-German poem from WWI circulated by far-right groups) a 43 page polemic of the author's thoughts and beliefs opening with a quote from Sir Oswald Mosely, and William Ernest Henley's poem *Invictus,* followed by a final appeal by the writer, and a concluding rallying cry.

---

[27] The Chief Censor has authority to call in a publication for examination under section 13(3) of the Films, Videos and Publications Classification Act 1993, which allows classification if there are concerns that the publication might be harmful to the public. In such cases, no written submissions need be called for.

[28] OFLC 1900149.000: *The Great Replacement (subtitle: Towards a New Society/We March Ever Forwards),* 23 March 2019.

The manifesto passed through a required censorship subject matter gateway because it dealt with crime, cruelty and violence and put forward written justification for undertaking violent terrorist attacks and murdering unarmed members of the public—including children.[29] The decision also noted that specific statements in the text expressed criminal intent. The manifesto promoted violence, cruelty, murder and terrorism as heroic and aspirational, and was found to be injurious to the public good because it:

- Included unambiguous calls for acts of terrorist violence;
- Included information about possible terrorist targets in New Zealand;
- Provided some information on the means and method for terrorist attacks;
- Created a false sense of urgency by characterising the presence of non-white New Zealand residents as an invasion;
- Dehumanised and demonised non-white New Zealanders as "invaders"—justifying violent action to remove them;
- Exhorted readers to violence and murder by misrepresenting these actions as part of a grand historical struggle;
- Attempted to show that the disaffected and vulnerable can find meaning through violence; and
- Used specific cues and references to create a sense of community and connection with those who are already susceptible to the writer's violent, extremist views.[30]

However, the decision did not find the manifesto promoted or supported the idea that members of any racial or ethnic group are inferior, because it in fact contained grudging admiration of non-white races said to have higher fertility, greater social cohesion and greater religious devotion and therefore were a clear and present threat to white Europeans.

The decision made a distinction between mere hate speech, and dangerous speech, the latter of which was said to have a speaker with the status and genuine influence over his or her intended audience; an audience that is particularly susceptible to messages that promote violence; a social or historical context in which certain groups are primed for violence; a medium or way of disseminating a message that has broad reach and influence amongst the intended audience (for example, wide distribution to an established online community); and a message that characterises an identified group of people as dehumanised and threatening, necessitating the use of violence as a form of 'self-defence.' Because the content and context of the document fitted all of these criteria, it was characterised by the Chief Censor as posing a genuine and identifiable danger to society. That danger required banning the document, which, although a limit on freedom of expression, was stated to be justified in terms of NZBORA.

---

[29] *Living Word Distributors Ltd v Human Rights Action Group (Wellington)* [2000] 3 NZLR 570 (CA).

[30] OFLC 1900149.000: *The Great Replacement (subtitle: Towards a New Society/We March Ever Forwards,* 23 March 2019, 9.

The finding that the manifesto was hate speech and objectionable because it was dangerous speech suggests that there were concerns about attempting to ban the manifesto based on hate speech characteristics alone, and whether that would survive an NZBORA analysis. Finding the publication to be dangerous speech made strong links between speech and actual harms rather than mere offensiveness, and appeared more supportable.

Video livestream. The Christchurch Mosque shooter also livestreamed the murders as he carried out the attack. At nearly 17 minutes long, the video footage captured on a helmet cam recorded the gunman as he got in his car and drove to one mosque, recorded the killings, at a distance and close range, he carried out there, and recorded his analysis of his performance throughout. The video was live-streamed on Facebook and on other websites. That livestream became available online immediately and the video was also classified by the Chief Censor[31] following the calling in of the video file. It was classified as objectionable within a day.[32]

Because the video depicted real mass murder, it passed through the subject matter threshold for censorship because it showed extreme violence and cruelty. Unlike the manifesto decision, this classification decision found the video could be simply deemed objectionable because it supported and promoted the activities in it—it was more than mere depiction of what happened, because it instead recorded, shared and was intended to glorify the shootings, and contained no element of denunciation.[33]

However, the Chief Censor also found that the same result could be reached under the lesser provisions in the FVPC Act, by taking contextual matters into account and giving them appropriate weight.[34] Here the things that carried weight were the manner in which the shooter carried out the shootings, the instructional monologue which accompanied them, the use of references to extremist memes and symbols, in particular, on the guns, the first person presentation facilitated by the captured helmet footage which meant viewers felt part of each moment and act, the shooter referring to the victims as 'targets' throughout, many of the victims were identifiable, the graphic and brutal content, instructional elements, and the video was made to share. Banning as objectionable was stated to be a demonstrably justified limit on freedom of expression due to the high likelihood of significant injuries to the public good arising directly from the video's continued availability.

The banning of the manifesto polarised media and others in a debate about freedom of expression.[35] Ultimately, both classification decisions survived an independent review process with little difficulty.[36]

---

31 OFLC 1900148.000, Christchurch Mosque Attack Livestream, 18 March 2019.

32 See Classification Office News 18 March 2019, 'Christchurch Mosque Attack Livestream classification decision.'

33 Films, Videos and Publications Classification Act 1993, s 3(2).

34 Films, Videos and Publications Classification Act 1993, s 3(3)(d).

35 See Classification Office News, 9 December 2020, 'Classification Response to the March 2019 Christchurch terrorist attack;' *RNZ Mediawatch*, 7 April 2019, 'Manifesto ban divides media.'

36 See Application by Brian Johnston of Christchurch for a review of the publication entitled: *Christchurch Mosque Attack Livestream*, 14 June 2019; Application by The Kiwi Party (Incorporated) for a review of the publication titled: *The Great Replacement*, 12 August 2019.

Sentencing for distribution of objectionable publication. In 2019, Philip Arps was convicted of two offences of distributing the live-stream video of the Christchurch mosque shooter under s 124(1) of the Films, Videos and Publications Classification Act 1993 and sentenced to 21 months' imprisonment. The sentence was determined applying s 9(1)(h) of the Sentencing Act 2002 which allows an uplift for aggravation arising from the fact the crime was a hate crime. The Court of Appeal upheld the provision and found it survived an NZBORA challenge because legislating against hate speech was an important objective and giving effect to this through recognising a specific aggravating factor in sentencing is rationally connected to such an objective.[37]

14.3 National Statutory or Administrative Law

National statutory or administrative laws have been applied to hateful expression. Some examples are described below.

14.3.1 Jurisdiction of the Broadcasting Standards Authority (BSA)

BSA decisions have to be subjected to a Bill of Rights analysis. Although such an approach can be implied from the context of any decision, the decision will much better withstand scrutiny if this is overt. The Authority, under its then Chair, Judge Bill Hastings,[38] developed an approach in which the matter of freedom of expression is always the starting point. The BSA recognises the value of freedom of expression and refers to classic freedom of expression arguments including the need for the public to be informed and engaged in New Zealand society. The Authority deals with complaints by weighing the value of the relevant programme and the broadcaster's right to freedom of expression against the level of actual or potential harm that might be caused by the broadcast. However, it notes that the law and common sense require the BSA to be cautious before restricting freedom of expression, and that NZBORA states this should only occur when it is 'demonstrably justified in a free and democratic society'.[39]

---

[37] *Philip Neville Arps v New Zealand Police* [2019] NZCA 592.

[38] See BSA *Annual Report* (2019) at 4–5.

[39] See Broadcasting Standards Codebook, Introduction, Freedom of Expression.

14.3.2 Media Coverage of the Mosque Attacks

In August 2019, the BSA released its first decisions on complaints about New Zealand broadcast coverage of the 15 March mosque attacks.[40] In making these decisions, the Authority acknowledged the differing perspectives and experiences that may need to be balanced in such circumstances. First was the impact these events have had on New Zealanders, particularly on the family and friends of victims and the wider Muslim community. Against this was the critical role media play in reporting during crisis events and the unprecedented circumstances facing New Zealand broadcasters at this time. The Authority Chair emphasised the need for broadcasters to exercise a high level of care and discretion in their broadcast coverage. For these complaints, the BSA considered whether harm could be caused to audiences generally, both in Christchurch and around New Zealand. The BSA weighed this potential harm against the right to freedom of expression, which covers both the right of the broadcaster to impart ideas and information, and the audience's right to receive information.

The Authority upheld one complaint, about use of extensive extracts from the shooter's livestream video on *Sky News New Zealand*.[41] Sky NZ broadcasts *Sky News Australia* in New Zealand as *Sky News New Zealand* on Sky NZ's pay television platform. *Sky News New Zealand* is a foreign pass-through news channel, and there is actually no corporate connection between the two entities. However, as the pay television host in New Zealand, Sky NZ is the broadcaster with responsibilities under the New Zealand Pay Television Code of Broadcasting Practice. Sky NZ broadcast a number of extracts from the livestream video (and the manifesto) over about five hours, some of which had warnings, but some did not.

News and current affairs programming is not subject to classification under the Pay Television Code. However the BSA noted that disturbing or alarming material in news and current affairs should nevertheless be justified in the public interest and carry audience advisories where appropriate. This means broadcasters must use judgment and discretion when deciding the degree of graphic material to be used in news programmes. SKY NZ had limited editorial control over the content that was broadcast and limited options as to the action it could take in response to any potential breach. It could not direct the presenters or edit content selected within the broadcast. However, the BSA said it did have the option to cut the channel from the platform (even though this would have commercial implications), or to work with *Sky News Australia* to change the feed, which apparently was the action that was subsequently taken at the instigation of *Sky News Australia*.

Ultimately, the BSA found that the degree of potential harm that could be caused to audiences through the broadcast of the clips was greater than the public interest in the clips themselves. The clips as broadcast had potential to promote and glorify the alleged attacker and his message and to cause significant distress to members of the public, and particularly to the family and friends of victims and the wider Muslim community in New Zealand. The content of the clips also had the potential

---

[40] See para 14.2.

[41] *UJ v Sky Network Television Ltd* BSA 2019-030, 19 August 2019.

to incite or encourage violence. The BSA also thought the broadcast of the clips, in the context of the attacks, had the potential to promote serious antisocial and illegal behaviour in the form of violent terrorist activity. There was a risk that susceptible viewers may have been encouraged by what they had seen.

While the Authority acknowledged Sky NZ's limited editorial control over the programme, it found overall that the clips as broadcast were highly disturbing and should not have been aired. Therefore, despite strong denunciation of the attacks throughout the five-and-a-half hours of Sky NZ coverage, the violence and law and order standards were breached. Despite being edited, the clips broadcast were highly disturbing and distressing, and further provided a voice and platform for the alleged attacker and his messages. The level of public interest in the detailed depictions of violence shown in these clips was not proportionate to the high level of harm that could be caused to viewers, particularly the family and friends of victims and members of the Muslim community. The Authority upheld the complaint and ordered the broadcaster, Sky NZ, to pay $4,000 in costs to the Crown.

In contrast to this decision are complaints against "One News" on TVNZ, NZ's state tv broadcaster, which were not upheld.[42] These complaints arose from coverage by "One News" which featured a very brief extract from the livestream video, as well as footage of identifiable victims, some with visible injuries, as they were being taken into hospital. Following the attacks, "One News" at 6.00 pm twice broadcast an edited clip taken from the alleged shooter's 17-minute livestream video. The clip showed a man's hands holding a weapon and reaching for two weapons in the open boot of his car. White writing on the weapons was not legible and the man's face could not be seen. A complaint was made that the broadcast was in breach of the good taste and decency and violence standards. The Authority thought TVNZ had a duty to provide viewers with information about the attacks, making challenging editorial decisions in unprecedented circumstances. It exercised judgment and discretion in deciding the degree of graphic detail to be included in the programme, and broadcast appropriate audience advisories. TVNZ's use of the footage in this case met a "test of necessity"—it showed only what was necessary to give the public a sufficiently comprehensive account of what had occurred.

14.3.3 Discrimination

Broadcasters should not encourage discrimination against, or denigration of, any section of the community on account of sex, sexual orientation, race, age, disability, occupational status or as a consequence of legitimate expression of religion, culture or political belief.[43] "Discrimination" is defined as encouraging the different treatment

[42] *NT v Television New Zealand* BSA 2019-028, 19 August 2019.

[43] See BSA Codebook, Standard 4.

of the members of a particular section of the community, to their detriment. "Denigration" is defined as devaluing the reputation of a particular section of the community.[44] The standard does not apply to individuals or organisations. A high level of condemnation is required and statements that are simply critical of a particular group, and offend people or are rude are unlikely to breach the standard. The requirements of NZBORA compel this. Nonetheless, comments that reinforce negative stereotypes may reach the threshold.[45]

BSA decisions have given prominence to the issue of "hate speech", and these illustrate when the level of denigration is sufficient. Celebrity broadcaster Paul Holmes made comments about the United Nations and its Secretary-General Kofi Annan on his private radio breakfast show, referring to him as a "cheeky darkie" five times. The Radio Network received numerous complaints and responded internally by various means. The host also broadcast a radio apology and a voluntary apology on his evening current affairs television programme. The BSA received 10 complaints and agreed that the comments were a serious breach of programme standards.[46] It considered that whether or not the comments were intentionally racist did not matter; they supported a racist view of the world, which the host had later stated in his apology he abhorred. Thus, intention is irrelevant to this standard. The BSA then considered whether the Radio Network's actions were sufficient and concluded that they were swift, comprehensive and reflected the seriousness of the complaints. It therefore declined to uphold complaints that insufficient action had been taken.

In the same programme, the host had interviewed a journalist about the dominance of women in journalism. At one point, Holmes put the question: "Is it, do you think, making our journalism ignorant and bitchy do you think?" He later asked: "At certain times of the month do the newspapers get particularly judgmental?" These comments were also the subject of a complaint alleging denigration of or discrimination on account of gender. This complaint was rejected by the BSA, which noted that a high level of denigration is required to constitute a breach.[47] The Authority found the comments had been made during an exchange between the host and an interviewee and were clearly intended to be provocative.

Four days after Holmes' radio comments, a programme broadcast by Triangle Television between 3.00 pm and 4.00 pm on a Monday included a lecture titled: "Challenges Facing Muslims in the New Millennium". The lecture was delivered by a Brother Abdullah Hakim Quick, who stated that AIDS is caused by the "filthy practices" of homosexuals, that homosexuals are dropping dead from AIDS and "want to take us all down with them", that the Islamic position on homosexuality is "death", that homosexuals are "sick" and "not natural", and that "Muslims are going to have to take a stand [against homosexuals] and it's not enough to call names". This broadcast

---

[44] Ibid., Guideline 4.1.

[45] Ibid., Guidelines 4.2, 4.3 and Commentary.

[46] *Smith v The Radio Network Ltd* BSA 2003-174-183, 19 December 2003.

[47] Ibid.

was found by the BSA to unlawfully encourage discrimination and denigration.[48] The Authority considered the statements to be "hate speech"; in particular, those advocating death and taking a stand were seen as an incitement to violence.

In a prominent recent decision, two complaints were upheld about private radio host Heather du Plessis-Allan's use of the term "leeches" to describe the Pacific Islands. The BSA found that her dismissive tone and deliberate choice of language suggested a high level of condemnation towards the Pacific Islands. The term "leeches" went beyond being critical of Pacific nations or being a genuine expression of political opinion. It was highly inflammatory and could have been interpreted by listeners that Pasifika people provide no value to New Zealand.[49]

Note also that case law has contributed to defining or clarifying the problem of hateful expression in New Zealand.[50]

14.4 International Covenant on Civil and Political Rights (ICCPR)

New Zealand became a party to ICCPR on 28 December 1978. When ratifying the *ICCPR*, New Zealand entered a reservation to Article 20, stating:

> The Government of New Zealand, having legislated in the areas of the advocacy of national and racial hatred and the exciting of hostility or ill will against any group of persons, and having regard to the right of freedom of speech, reserves the right not to introduce further legislation with regard to Article 20.

In *Mendelssohn v Attorney-General*,[51] the Court examined the rights protecting religious freedom in NZBORA (ss 13, 14, 15, 17 and 20) and held the Bill did not impose positive duties on the state in any relevant sense to protect religious freedom. The Court also examined New Zealand's international obligations, and noted that Article 18 of the ICCPR protects freedom of religion, but primarily affirms a freedom from state interference. In the Court's view, Article 20 unambiguously requires protective action in favour of religion, but only in limited extreme situations. The Court of Appeal identified the relevant legislation referred to in New Zealand's reservation as including the racial disharmony provisions in the Human Rights Act, and the crime of blasphemous libel. The latter was removed from national legislation in 2019. The former have been referred for review by the Law Commission.[52]

---

[48] *Clayton v Triangle Television Ltd* BSA 2004-001, 26 February 2004. Standard 6 and Guideline 6g of the then Free-to-Air TV Code.

[49] *Day & Moss v NZME Radio Ltd* BSA 2018-090, 2 April 2019.

[50] See the discussion of *Wall v Fairfax New Zealand Ltd* [2018] NZHC 104, [2018] 2 NZLR 471 at para 14.6.

[51] [1999] 2 NZLR 268 (CA).

[52] See lawcom.govt.nz; Law Commission Projects: Legal Responses to Hate.

New Zealand consented to the individual complaints process of the ICCPR.[53] New Zealand ratified the Optional Protocol to the ICCPR on 26 May 1989.

14.5 International Convention on the Elimination of All Forms of Racial Discrimination (ICERD)

New Zealand ratified the International Convention on the Elimination of All Forms of Racial Discrimination on 22 November 1972. It gave effect to the ratification domestically by passing the Race Relations Act 1971. That Act mirrored the ICERD and did not provide for religion as a protected characteristic. Section 25 of that Act introduced an offence of inciting racial disharmony (which is now Section 131 of the Human Rights Act 1993). Section 25 was designed to address Article 4 of ICERD. Prohibiting racial disharmony rather than racial hatred was chosen because Article 4 only requires States to prohibit "incitement to racial discrimination". It was thought that Courts could not be expected to measure hatred and it was necessary to ensure an appropriate balance with freedom of speech.

Civil liability was introduced in Section 9A of the Race Relations Act by the Human Rights Commission Act 1977. Section 9A was repealed in 1989 but was effectively re-enacted as Section 61 of the Human Rights Act.

New Zealand has not accepted the jurisdiction of the UN Human Rights Committee to hear individual complaints under ICERD.[54]

The 2014 Universal Periodic Review addressed hate speech, recommending that the New Zealand government "continue combatting and condemning racism and hate speech used by politicians and the expression of racism in the media, in particular discriminatory language and hate speech and the dissemination of racist ideas and languages".[55] This recommendation was accepted by the New Zealand government.[56]

In CERD/C/NZL/CO/21-22, 22 September 2017, the Committee on the Elimination of Racial Discrimination made the following Concluding observation on the combined twenty-first and twenty-second periodic reports of New Zealand:[57]

> Racist hate speech and hate crimes [...]. The Committee is concerned that while the State party's legislation criminalizes incitement of racial disharmony and allows race-related hostility to constitute an aggravating factor in sentencing, there were no prosecutions

---

[53] Declaration 28 December 1978.

[54] Dr Caroline Morris, *New Zealand Hate Speech Report*, 4.

[55] Human Rights Council, *Report of the Working Group on the Universal Periodic Review: New Zealand*, UN Doc A/HRC/26/3 (7 April 2014) at [122.100].

[56] Human Rights Council, *Report of the Working Group on the Universal Periodic Review: New Zealand*—Addendum Views on conclusions and/or recommendations, voluntary commitments and replies presented by the State under review, UN Doc A/HRC/26/3/Add.1 (26 May 2014) at [15].

[57] CERD/C/NZL/CO/21, International Convention on the Elimination of All Forms of Racial Discrimination, 22 September 2017, at 2–3.

> for incitement of racial disharmony during the reporting period. The Committee is also concerned by the lack of comprehensive statistics relating to prosecutions, convictions and sanctions related to racist hate speech. The Committee notes with interest the State party's current efforts to address CERD/C/NZL/CO/21-22 3 those gaps, but is concerned that existing legislation may be inadequate to effectively combat acts of racial hatred (Articles 2 and 4).
>
> [...] Recalling its general recommendation No. 35 (2013) on combating racist hate speech, the Committee recommends that the State party: (a) Review the adequacy of current legislation in addressing and sanctioning racist hate speech and incitement to racial hatred, and ensure that the legislative framework conforms to Article 4 of the Convention; (b) Ensure that all incidents of racist hate crimes and racist hate speech are investigated and prosecuted, that the perpetrators are sanctioned and that victims are compensated; (c) Set as a government priority the collection of reliable and comprehensive statistics, disaggregated by the ethnicity of the victims, concerning investigations, prosecutions, convictions and sanctions for racist hate speech and incitement to racial hatred, and provide such data in the next periodic report.

The Universal Periodic Review of New Zealand in 2019 included several recommendations relating to combatting racism, discrimination, xenophobia and hate crime.[58] These recommendations were all accepted by the New Zealand government.[59] They included recommendations that the government:

> Continue efforts to combat racial discrimination and hate speech and promote diversity and tolerance (Recommendation 44); and
>
> Develop and implement a national plan of action against racial discrimination, xenophobia and hate crime (Recommendation 48).[60]

The report of the Royal Commission into the terrorist attack on Christchurch masjidain on 15 March 2019 was presented to Parliament on 8 December 2020.[61] The Royal Commission found that the wording of the existing racial disharmony criminal provision in the Human Rights Act (s 131), did not provide a clear standard or understanding of the type of behaviour that should be criminalised. It recommended focusing the provision on the concept of stirring up or provoking hatred of a particular group, thus:

> Every person commits an offence and is liable on conviction to imprisonment for a term not exceeding three years who:
>
> With intent to stir up, maintain or normalise hatred against any group of persons in New Zealand on the ground of the colour, race, or ethnic or national origins or religion of that group of persons; and

---

[58] Human Rights Council, *Report of the Working Group on the Universal Periodic Review: New Zealand,* UN Doc A/HRC/41/4 (1 April 2019) at [122.44]-[122.48].

[59] Human Rights Council, Report of the Working Group on the Universal Periodic Review: New Zealand—Addendum Views on conclusions and/or recommendations, voluntary commitments and replies presented by the State under review, UN Doc A/HRC/41/4/Add.1 (17 June 2019) at [17]: (Recommendations 44–48).

[60] See Whakamauāhara 2021.

[61] See Report of Royal Commission of Inquiry into the terrorist attack on Christchurch mosques on 15 March 2019: Hate speech and hate crime related legislation, 26 November 2020.

> Says or otherwise publishes or communicates, any words or material that explicitly or implicitly call for violence against or is otherwise, threatening, abusive or insulting to such group of persons.

The Commission expressed the view that a plain and strong term such as hatred would help provide a better indication of the extreme dislike or disgust required for criminal sanction. It did not recommend the inclusion of protection for forms of exempted speech as set out in s 29J of the Public Order Act 1986 (UK), preferring instead a high threshold for liability which it thought would be established by its restrictive definition of the offence.[62]

In 2021, in a proactive release,[63] the Minister of Justice sought an agreement in principle from Cabinet to the following proposals:

> Replace the existing criminal provision with a new criminal offence for intending to stir up, maintain or normalise hatred, against all groups protected by s 21 of the Human Rights Act, through threatening, abusive or insulting communications, including inciting violence, made by any means;
>
> Include the grounds of stirring up, maintaining or normalising hatred, against all groups protected by s 21 of the Human Rights Act, in the civil provision currently dealing with inciting racial disharmony, alongside the existing grounds;
>
> Insert the criminal offence for incitement into the Crimes Act 1961, rather than the Human Rights Act, to reflect the seriousness of the behaviour;
>
> Extend the legal protections under the civil and criminal provisions to a wider range of groups, by extending the protections to all groups listed as protected from discrimination under s 21 of the Human Rights Act;
>
> Amend the prohibited grounds of discrimination in s 21 to include a separate ground of 'gender' which includes gender identity and gender expression, and amend the ground of sex to explicitly include sex characteristics or intersex status.

These proposals went further than the recommendations in the Royal Commission report and were not the subject of consultation. They were not well received, particularly by those with concerns about the need to protect freedom of expression.[64] After 19,000 submissions were received on the six proposals, the government announced in late 2022 that it would make one change only to address incitement towards religious communities, by adding religious belief to the grounds for incitement set out in ss 61 and 131 of the Human Rights Act. It would also ask the Law Commission to undertake an independent and first principles review of legal responses to hate-motivated offending, and of hate speech.[65] Accordingly, a Human Rights (Incitement on Ground of Religious Belief) Amendment Bill was introduced, but in February 2023, the Prime Minister announced it was to be withdrawn and not progressed that

---

[62] Ibid., at p. 31.

[63] Ministry of Justice, Proposed changes to the incitement provisions in the Human Rights Act 1993, 13 April 2021.

[64] See e.g., Bryce Edwards, *RNZ Comment*, 'The confusing and concerning hate speech reforms,' 30 June 2021.

[65] See Press Release, Minister of Justice, Hon Kiritapu Allan, 19 November 2022, 'Human Rights Act enhanced to protect religious communities.'

term, while the matter was to be referred to the Law Commission for guidance on 'a difficult and highly contested area of law in totality'. In an election year, the government was 'doing too much too fast, and (needed) to focus on the cost of living.'[66] This announcement was also not well received.[67] Law Commission work on the project has yet to begin.[68]

14.6 Comparative Law

New Zealand courts can have regard to the ECHR, to which New Zealand is not a party, for the purpose of interpretive guidance.[69] In additional, national lawmakers and courts have cited the law of other national jurisdictions regarding hateful expression in important ways.

Case law. The High Court in *Wall v Fairfax New Zealand*[70]construed the ambit of New Zealand's civil racial disharmony provision[71] narrowly to ensure consistency with freedom of expression. The Court interpreted the provision by referencing NZBORA and held that it is not sufficient for written matter or words to be threatening, abusive or insulting alone. The Court emphasized that the test in the provision is a two-stage test that recognises using threatening, abusive or insulting language does not automatically result in a likelihood of exciting hostility against or bringing into contempt the group of persons about whom the language is used. Therefore there is a requirement of a causal link between the two parts. The High Court quoted a Canadian court that put it this way: 'Hate speech is not aimed at discouraging repugnant or offensive ideas. ...It does not target the ideas, but their mode of expression in public and the effect this mode of expression may have.'[72] The Court concluded that it seeks to stop relatively serious examples of expression which inspire enmity, extreme ill-will or are likely to result in a group being despised. Thus, s 61 only sanctions publications at the serious end of the spectrum.

Statute law. In the companion paper to its Report,[73] the Royal Commission referred to Sections 28-32 of the Crime and Disorder Act 1998 (UK) as a desirable model for New Zealand to replicate to create new hate-motivated offences for offensive

---

66 See Press Release, Prime Minister, Rt Hon Chris Hipkins, 8 February 2023, 'Government takes new direction with policy refocus.'

67 See McClure 2023.

68 See Law Commission Projects, Legal Responses to Hate.

69 *Wall v Fairfax* [2018] NZHC 104, [2018] 2 NZLR 471, at [15].

70 *Wall v Fairfax* [2018] NZHC 104, [2018] 2 NZLR 471.

71 Section 61, Human Rights Act 1993.

72 *Saskatchewan Human Rights Commission v Whatcott* 2013 SCC 11, [2013] 1 SCR 467 at [51].

73 'Hate speech and hate crime related legislation,' 26 November 2020, Companion paper to *Report of the Royal Commission into the Terrorist Attack on Christchurch Masjidain on 15 March 2019* (at pp. 15–17).

behaviour and language, assault, wilful damage and intimidation that correspond with existing offences in the NZ Summary Offences Act, and hate-motivated offences for assaults, arson and intentional damage that correspond with existing offences in the NZ Crimes Act 1961. It recommended the creation of these hate motivated offences in addition to the creation of the proposed new criminal hate speech offence detailed at 5 above.[74]

14.7 Popular Culture

14.7.1 Cartoons in Print Media

There have been high profile controversies about hateful expression in New Zealand's media. In February 2006, the New Zealand commercial print media became involved in an international controversy over what many Muslims considered were blasphemous caricatures of the Prophet Mohammad that had been published previously by a Danish newspaper. Wellington's *Dominion Post* and *The Press* in Christchurch joined a number of European newspapers in reprinting the Danish cartoons.

Amidst threats of blasphemy action, the Human Rights Commission hosted a meeting between interest groups, which resulted in the release of a statement. The parties affirmed without dissent the importance of freedom of the media, but also noted that such freedom is not absolute and comes with responsibilities. Those responsibilities included sensitivity to diverse cultures and beliefs, and recognition of the diversity within cultures and beliefs; responsibility to inform the community about diverse cultures and beliefs; and the provision of dialogue and channels of communication between the media and faith communities. Nonetheless, the meeting acknowledged that the media has to make difficult calls on such issues on a daily basis and these need to be considered in an international context of conflict, and accepted that the media which published the cartoons did not set out to insult or offend, only to inform. Those media apologised for the offence caused, but did not resile from the decision to publish based on the context at that time. The two newspapers also gave an undertaking not to publish the cartoons again.

14.7.2 Terrorist Attack on Mosques

The most significant and impactful event relating to hate speech in New Zealand has been the attack on two mosques by a lone gunman that took place in Christchurch on Friday 15 March 2019. New Zealand has had few mass shooting events, but this was the worst in modern history. Fifty-one people died as a result of gunshot

[74] Ibid., at p. 40.

wounds suffered at the two masjidain that day. The oldest victim was 77 years old and the youngest three years old. Another 40 people suffered gunshot injuries, many of which have been catastrophically life changing. Some families suffered multiple tragedies with more than one person killed or injured. The Australian gunman, a far-right terrorist who live-streamed the massacre and also posted online a bizarre manifesto justifying his actions, was arrested, pleaded guilty and was sentenced to life imprisonment with no parole.

A Royal Commission of Inquiry was established to investigate the event and its report was presented to Parliament on 8 December 2020. That report led directly to a review of New Zealand's hate speech criminal offences which did not result in any change and is discussed above.[75] Following the attack on 15 March 2019, the country's Muslim population has become vocal and politicised and the general population has become deeply sensitized to the problem of hate speech directed at Muslims and hate speech in general. The Royal Commission recommended changes to the education system as well as to hate speech laws. There is increasing support for the introduction of a compulsory new educational course for high school students: One proposed example is a Civics and Technology course containing the following teaching and learning:

- Rights and responsibilities in liberal, democratic societies.
- The nature of human rights.
- What it is to be a citizen and what responsibilities go with that.
- Technology, digital literacy, digital freedom and responsibilities.
- Religious studies, being the study of all main religions of the world.
- The nature of equality, and recognition and respect for diversity.

The Government continues to work on all-of-government response to the Royal Commission report under the leadership of a Lead Coordination Minister, Hon Andrew Little.[76]

14.7.3 Renaissance of Māori Culture

In recent years, Māori, who are tangata whenua, the indigenous people of New Zealand, have been leading a re-invigoration of their culture, including increasing mainstreaming of Te reo Māori, the Māori language, which is an official New Zealand language. Te reo is now increasingly used in the education system at primary, secondary and tertiary levels, and in media.

State broadcasters have engaged with te reo more than the private media sector. Radio New Zealand, the commercial-free state radio station, makes the greatest use

---

[75] See para 14.5.

[76] See New Zealand Parliament Hansard Debates, Oral Question to Minister, Question No. 8, 16 March 2021: Government's response to the Royal Commission of Inquiry into the terrorist attack on Christchurch masjidain report.

of te reo.[77] This has attracted a high level of complaint from some members of its audience, which tends to be in an older age group. TVNZ, the state television broadcaster, has also increased its use of te reo in mainstream programming. In 2021, the Broadcasting Standards Authority determined that using te reo Māori on air is not in breach of the country's broadcasting standards. The Authority directed broadcasters to respond to complaints by indicating that it is not a breach of standards.[78]

The private print media have also responded to the challenge of racism by examining past media practices. For example, Stuff.co, New Zealand's largest independent media organisation, is undertaking 'Our Truth, Tā Mātou Pono', which is a project investigating the history of racism. Part one focused on *Stuff* and its newspapers, and how they portrayed Māori.[79]

Initiatives impacting on the education system include the launch of a teacher-focused 'Unteach Racism' campaign[80] and a government directive establishing a new curriculum for the teaching of history to teach the history of all peoples living in NZ.[81] Teaching of the new content began in 2023. In May 2021, the Council for Legal Education passed resolutions requiring the teaching of Te Ao Māori concepts, particularly tikanga Māori, in each of the core law subjects within the Bachelor of Laws and Bachelor of Laws with Honours degree at New Zealand universities.[82] Teaching of new content and new courses are to begin in 2025.

14.7.4 Effects of Covid Pandemic

Unfortunately in spite of the advances noted above, the 2020 Covid pandemic apparently caused an increase in anti-Asian speech in New Zealand. For example, in May 2020, New Zealand's Race Relations Commissioner referenced many reports of Chinese and Asian people in New Zealand experiencing racism and xenophobia because of COVID-19.[83] The Human Rights Commission also reported that in 2020, there was a rise in racist and xenophobic language, as well as stigmatisation of Chinese and Asian communities. Netsafe, the private agency with responsibility for monitoring harmful online communications under the Harmful Digital Communications Act confirmed that it had observed a significant increase in reports of hate speech.[84]

---

[77] See Radio New Zealand Collection: Te Reo Māori on RNZ.

[78] BSA Media release: BSA draws a line under complaints about te reo 9 March 2021.

[79] Our Truth: Tā Mātou Pono, the Press' bias has failed Māori, 30 November 2020: Stuff.co.nz.

[80] Human Rights Commission and Teaching Council of Aotearoa New Zealand: Unteach Racism: Unteach Racism website: https://www.unteachracism.nz/.

[81] .Ministry of Education, Changes in education, the New Zealand Curriculum 2023.

[82] See Council for Legal Education website: https://nzcle.org.nz/.

[83] See Human Rights Commission News, 17 February 2021, 'COVID-19 fuelling discrimination against Tangata Whenue and Chinese communities.'

[84] Netsafe Lab 2020.

14.8 Conclusion

In the years 2020–2023, New Zealand stumbled and paused proposed changes to its hate speech laws. Expectations of the review of hate speech regulation were high, probably too high. The New Zealand Government has since acknowledged that its goal of reforming hate speech law is too complex and polarising to be successfully achieved in the time available before the 2023 election. Hence, the matter has been referred to the New Zealand Law Commission, though that work has yet to begin. It is apparent that the review needs to encompass wider reforms that include the education system, and any changes to the criminal law must be properly resourced and operationalised by police and prosecuting authorities, otherwise the hopes of minorities, the government and civil society for wide cultural change are unlikely to be realised and democracy will suffer. In particular, significant work remains to be done reconciling proposed changes to the criminal law with NZBORA and our still developing constitutional law that has so far accorded high value to freedom of expression.

References

Edwards B (2021) RNZ Comment. The Confusing and Concerning Hate Speech Reforms. https://www.rnz.co.nz/news/on-the-inside/445877/bryce-edwards-the-confusing-and-concerning-hate-speech-reforms

Human Rights Commission News (2021) COVID-19 Fuelling Discrimination against Tangata Whenue and Chinese Communities. https://tikatangata.org.nz/news/covid-19-fueling-discrimination-against-tangata-whenua-and-chinese-communities

McClure T (2023) New Zealand Government under Fire after Shelving Christchurch Hate Speech Reforms. The Guardian. https://www.theguardian.com/world/2023/feb/09/new-zealand-government-under-fire-after-shelving-christchurch-hate-speech-reforms

Netsafe Lab (2020) Covid-19 Online Harm Insights. https://netsafe.org.nz/covid19/

Our Truth: Tā Mātou Pono, the Press' Bias Has Failed Māori. (2020) https://interactives.stuff.co.nz/2021/02/our-truth-history-aotearoa-new-zealand/about-our-truth/

Whakamauāhara K (2021) Hate Speech. An overview of the current legal framework. Human Rights Commission.

Ursula Cheer is Professor of Law, University of Canterbury, New Zealand, specialising in media law. She is the author of *Burrows and Cheer: Media Law in New Zealand* (8th ed, 2021, LexisNexis) and also a contributing author in *Todd on Torts*, Thomson Reuters (2023, 9th ed, S Todd ed), on defamation and privacy. Cheer is a member of the editorial committee of the *Journal of Media Law* (Hart Publishers, UK) and a member of the editorial committee and international contributing editor of the *Media & Arts Law Review* (MALR) (LexisNexis Butterworths) CMCL, Melbourne Law School, Melbourne, Australia.

Chapter 15
Poland

Jan Kulesza and Joanna Kulesza

Contents

Abstract In Poland, the constitutional guarantee of freedom of expression, as enshrined in Article 54, is frequently invoked in legal proceedings concerning the limits of free speech. Polish statutory law does not explicitly define "hate speech," but relevant provisions within the civil and criminal codes address this issue by balancing individual speech rights with the protection of others. Notably, Articles 256, 257, and 196 of the Polish Criminal Code impose penalties for inciting hatred and offending religious feelings, thereby setting legal boundaries on speech. These measures have sparked debates on their application and implications within Polish society.

Keywords Polish Constitutional Law · Hate Speech Legislation · Freedom of Expression · Criminal Code of Poland · Religious Offense · Penalties for Hate Speech

J. Kulesza (✉)
University of Lodz, Lodz, Poland
e-mail: jkulesza@wpia.uni.lodz.pl

J. Kulesza
Lodz Cyber Hub Research Center, University of Lodz, Lodz, Poland
e-mail: joanna_kulesza@wpia.uni.lodz.pl

E. Heinze (ed.), *Criminalising Hate Speech*,
https://doi.org/10.1007/978-94-6265-650-5_15

15.1 National Constitutional Law

Article 54 of the Polish Constitution provides for a freedom of expression guarantee in para 1: "The freedom to express opinions, to acquire and to disseminate information shall be ensured to everyone."[1] This provision is referenced whenever the limits of free expression are set by courts of all instances, including leading Polish caselaw (see Section 7), while, as noted below, the definition of "hate speech" is not of direct relevance in Polish case law.

15.2 National Statutory and Administrative Law

Hate speech is not directly referenced in Polish statutory law, however specific provisions of civil and criminal codes are applied to assess the limits of individual free speech and balance it with the protection of others' rights. A key statutory safeguard is included in Article 256 of the Polish Criminal Code, which in the section on "Offenses against public order" reads:

> Whoever publicly propagates a fascist or other totalitarian political system or incites to hatred based on national, ethnic, racial, political or religious affiliation or lack of religious affiliation, is subject to a fine, the penalty of limitation of liberty or the penalty of deprivation of liberty for up to 2 years.

Article 196 of the Polish Criminal Code, as with other types of offenses, does not limit the content of the incriminating communication, does not censor it, and does not subject it to evaluation. The provisions of the article indicate a causative activity (i.e. the perpetrator is to "offend" religious feelings of others, rather than insult them, for example). Offending ("insulting feelings") is not the activity of the perpetrator but the result of his activities. For this offense to be committed, it must be demonstrated that at least two individuals felt harmed by having their religious feelings offended, thus narrowing the scope of criminality of the act.

Having said this, it should be noted that it is not difficult to find such two people in Poland. The offending effect is indisputable; that is, you cannot convince someone that they have not been offended, should not feel offended, or are exaggerating. There is no objectivity in this respect (justification by circumstances, as in Article 148, para 4 or Article 190, para 1 of the Polish Criminal Code), and it is therefore not possible to examine whether another follower, tolerant, not devotional, would also feel offended. While "objectionable" as a causative act, it is strongly objectified to social assessment.

In addition, Article 257 penalizes discrimination and public insults:

> Whoever publicly insults a group of people or an individual person because of their national, ethnic, racial, political or religious affiliation or lack of religious affiliation, or violates the

[1] Official translation available on the website of Sejm, lower chamber of Polish Parliament, https://www.sejm.gov.pl/prawo/konst/angielski/kon1.htm.

> personal inviolability of another person due to such reasons, is subject to the penalty of deprivation of liberty for up to 3 years.

The Criminal Code sets limits for free speech also in Article 196 and its blasphemy clause:

> Whoever offends the religious feelings of others, publicly insulting the subject of religious worship or a place intended for public performance of religious rites, is subject to a fine, the penalty of restriction of liberty or the penalty of deprivation of liberty for up to 2 years.[2]

When applying these laws, Article 53 on the principles of imposing penal measures must be taken into consideration. It reads:

> Section 1. The court imposes the punishment according to its own discretion, within the limits prescribed by a statute, observing that its onerousness does not exceed the degree of fault, taking into account the degree of social harmfulness of the act and taking into consideration preventive and educational aims it is to achieve with regard to the sentenced person, as well as the need to develop legal awareness of the society.

Paragraph 2 refers to the perpetrator's motive and manner of conduct, which must be considered particularly when involving discriminatory motives:

> Section 2. While imposing a penalty, the court takes into account especially the perpetrator's motivation and manner of conduct, particularly in case of the commission of a crime against a person who is helpless due to age or health condition, commission of the crime in complicity with a minor, the type and degree of the violation of the perpetrator's duties, the type and the extent of negative consequences of the crime, the characteristics and personal conditions of the perpetrator, the perpetrator's way of life prior to the commission of the crime and his behaviour after the commission of the crime, especially his efforts to redress the damage or to satisfy public sense of justice in any other form, as well as the harmed party's conduct.

Complementarily, Article 23 or the Polish Civil Code (PCC) protects personal rights by referencing the protection of personal interests:

> Personal interests of a human being, such as in particular health, freedom, dignity, freedom of conscience, surname or pseudonym, image, confidentiality of correspondence, inviolability of home as well as scientific, artistic, inventive and reasoning activities shall be protected by the civil law regardless of the protection provided for by other provisions.

Article 24 PCC provides for comprehensive means of protection, including means of preventive nature:

> [A] person whose personal interests are jeopardized by another person's action [has the right to] demand that the action be abandoned, unless it is not illegal. In the case of actual violation, he may also demand that the person who committed the violation perform acts necessary to remove its consequences, in particular that the latter make a statement of a relevant content and in a relevant form. [Moreover,] on the basis of the principles provided for by the Code he may also demand pecuniary compensation or a payment of an adequate amount of money for a specified community purpose". [As per para 2 thereof] if, as a result of a of personal interests damage to the property was inflicted, the injured party may demand it to be redressed on the basis of general principles.

---

[2] Unofficial English translations by sip.lex.pl.

These are the fundamental provisions applied by Polish courts and administrative bodies to define limits for freedom of expression and to deny protection to expression beyond these limits, including hate speech, in accordance with the ECtHR margin of appreciation doctrine. On numerous occasions the Ombudsman, of the Office of the Polish Commissioner for Human Rights, has urged the government and other national bodies to advance legislation and enforcement on combating hate speech as per international standards, guidelines and targeted recommendations.[3]

15.3 International Covenant on Civil and Political Rights (ICCPR)

Poland ratified the International Covenant on Civil and Political Rights on June 18, 1997, and since February 7, 1992, it has also been bound by the provisions of the Optional Protocol to the International Covenant on Civil and Political Rights, introducing the possibility of submitting individual complaints about violation of the rights guaranteed by this Covenant. Among the few complaints filed against Poland, none of them addressed hate speech. Polish legislators, officials, or courts strongly prioritize references to national laws, possibly complementing these with relevant EU law and/or ECtHR case law.

The 2017 National report for Poland covered national implementation of norms preventing racism, xenophobia and hate crimes, combatting racist crimes. These focused on Ministry of the Interior and Administration (MIA) setting up a unit responsible for the monitoring of events that could constitute hate crimes. Their report noted:

> In view of the need to ensure a more comprehensive sourcing of data on hate crimes, a new system was put in place in 2015 to compile hate crime data, which is now shared by the police and the MIA and covers all proceedings opened in cases of hate crimes. The new data registration tool supports the collection of detailed information about the specifics of events and the activity of the police. The police understand the need to intensify the fight against online hate crimes. Some of the local police departments have established task forces responsible for the work or special investigative groups.

The report covered a detailed analysis of criminal law framework on preventing hate speech. Focus was placed on Article 53 Section 2 of the CC, noted above:

[3] For a summary of these efforts, see: "Activities of the Commissioner for Human Rights Adam Bodnar on hate speech as of: September 5, 2019". In Polish, available at: https://bip.brpo.gov.pl/sites/default/files/Mowa%20nienawi%c5%9bci%20wrzesien%202019.pdf. See also the letter to the Prime Minister on the need to implement the EU Council 2000/43/EC implementing the principle of equal treatment between persons irrespective of on racial or ethnic origin (Journal of Laws UE.L.2000.180.22) on its 20th anniversary with specific recommendations for Poland. In Polish, available at: https://bip.brpo.gov.pl/sites/default/files/Wyst%c4%85pienie%20do%20Prezesa%20Rady%20Ministr%c3%b3w%20ws.%20mowy%20nienawi%c5%9bci,%2030.06.2020.pdf.

Article 53 of the CC applies to all crimes defined in the Code, including among other things battery and slander. The foregoing provisions are general and do not specify or restrict the motivation which the court must take into account.

This is particularly important in today's fast-changing reality where new social trends emerge, including discriminatory trends. This ensures that any such motivation will always be considered by the court and that it will not require time-consuming legislative amendments at each time.

The crime defined in Article 212 of the CC includes among other things libel against an individual or a group, attributed with behaviour or qualities which may denigrate them among the general public or expose them to a loss of trust required in a given position, profession or activity.

Furthermore, libel in the mass media is a qualified form of the crime. Hence, if a person resorts to libel in order to denigrate a person or a community on grounds of ethnicity, nationality or race, this is penalised. In turn, insult, which is penalised under Article 216 of the CC, is an offence against human dignity understood as the individual's subjective sense of self-worth. In that case, the insulted person may claim protection under Article 216 of the CC.[4]

15.4 International Convention on the Elimination of All Forms of Racial Discrimination (ICERD)

Poland has been party to the ICERD since 1968 and consented to individual complaints procedures in 1998. As noted above, Polish legislators, officials, or courts prioritize references to national laws, possibly complementing these with relevant EU law and/or ECtHR case law. There are no substantial, direct references to ICCPR to report in this section.

UN-CERD issued Concluding Observations of Poland in 2019.[5] Among the positive aspects, the CERD named the fact that had Poland ratified the Additional Protocol to the Convention on Cybercrime, concerning the criminalization of acts of a racist and xenophobic nature committed through computer systems, on 20 February 2015. The Committee also recognized "the creation of the interministerial team for preventing the promotion of fascism and other totalitarian systems and crimes of incitement to hatred based on national, ethnic, racial or religious differences or for reason of lack of any religious denomination, in 2018" as well as "the establishment of the Office of the National Police Headquarters for Combating Cybercrime and the appointment of coordinators for combating hate crimes in cyberspace, in 2016."

With regard to racist hate speech and hate crimes and with regard to Articles 256 and 257 of the Criminal Code, the Committee expressed its "deep concern" that "colour" and "descent" as grounds for inciting hatred are missing from this definition as well as due to the fact that "by the prevalence of racist hate speech

---

[4] Polish Penal Code, Article 216.

[5] UN-CERD, "Concluding observations on the combined twenty-second to twenty-fourth periodic reports of Poland", 2019 available at: http://docstore.ohchr.org/SelfServices/FilesHandler.ashx?enc=6QkG1d%2FPPRiCAqhKb7yhsrvH7CU4hlDYCm%2FQk5dWFUfg2vXGNFWBc%2F6mIf5L63ad9qagFzKbnoRg4hVGBvPlLWxPs6a0BBfjqZhmokVVF4K6a0frSbYkWuX67gLK4wD%2BBx0GhA%2Bk21PL2UH2cCZT3A%3D%3D.

against minority groups, in particular Muslims, Roma, Ukrainians, people of African and Asian descent, Jews and migrants, refugees and asylum seekers' Poland allows for speech" which "fuels hatred and intolerance and incites violence towards such groups."[6]

Moreover, it expressed concern that "leading public figures, including politicians and media officials, are frequently the source of such offensive statements or fail in their responsibility to strongly denounce hate speech" as well as over the fact that "the Criminal Code still does not contain a provision expressly establishing racist motives of a crime as an aggravating circumstance (Articles 4 and 6)." Issuing this 2019 report, CERD referenced its general recommendations No. 15 from 1993 on Article 4 of the Convention and No. 35 on combating racist hate speech and noted that to comply with its international obligations Poland needs to:

> Ensure that the definition of hate speech enshrined in the Criminal Code is fully in line with Article 4 of the Convention and that it includes all grounds of discrimination recognized in Article 1 of the Convention and recommendation No . R 97 (20) of the Committee of Ministers of the Council of Europe;
>
> Take all necessary measures to firmly combat racist hate speech and incitement to violence, including on the Internet, and publicly condemn and distance itself from racist hate speech by public figures, including politicians and media officials;
>
> Intensify its public campaigns to combat hate speech, incitement to hatred and hate crimes, to address prejudices and negative sentiments towards national and ethnic minorities, migrants, refugees and asylum seekers, and to promote tolerance and understanding towards these groups;
>
> Send strong messages to journalists and broadcasters that they have a responsibility to avoid the use of hate speech and stereotypes in describing minority communities, take action against websites promoting racial hatred and, particularly in the context of election campaigns, closely scrutinize broadcasters with respect to content that incites hatred or strengthens xenophobic attitudes;
>
> Amend Article 53 (2) of its Criminal Code, specifically making a racist motive of a crime an aggravating circumstance and allowing for enhanced punishment to combat the occurrence of such acts."[7]

CERD also observed that the prohibition in Article 13 of the Constitution prohibits the operation of "political parties and other organizations … whose programmes or activities sanction racial or national hatred." The Committee expressed concern "that the participation in such organizations is not yet prohibited by law" and was "alarmed by the continuing existence and open operation of organizations that promote racial hatred in the State party, in particular those that openly espouse affinity with the ideology and publicly display the symbols of Nazism, fascism or totalitarianism (Article 4)."[8] As a result of the report, the Committee "urged" Poland to:

Ensure effective enforcement of the laws declaring illegal parties or organizations which promote or incite racial discrimination, such as the National Movement, the

[6] Ibid., para 15 (b).

[7] Ibid., para 16.

[8] Ibid., para 17.

National Radical Camp, All-Polish Youth, Falanga, Szturmowcy, Niklot, the National and Social Congress, Autonomous Nationalists, Pride and Modernity Association, and the local chapter of Blood and Honour"; and "amend the Criminal Code to make participation in such organizations a punishable offence, in line with Article 4 (b) of the Convention and general recommendation No. 35".[9]

The Committee further urged Poland to improve its effort to ensure effective prosecution of racially motivated crimes, and expressed "concern" about "the extremely low percentage of offences of hate speech and hate crimes that are reported, despite the recorded increase in the incidence of such crimes" as well as "the fact that some of the reported racially motivated crimes remain unregistered and not investigated as such".[10] Moreover, the Committee highlighted the need to attend to the "increased number of preparatory proceedings and indictments of perpetrators of racist crimes" which "did not result in a significant increase in the number of convictions" as well as "the lack of detailed information on investigations and prosecutions of, and convictions for, racist hate speech and hate crimes, especially those committed by public figures and politicians (Articles 4, 6 and 7)."[11] It noted that "in line with general recommendation No. 31 (2005) on the prevention of racial discrimination in the administration and functioning of the criminal justice system, a low number of complaints may signify the existence of barriers to victims accessing their rights, such as a lack of trust among victims in the State party's justice institutions and authorities".[12] This observation was complemented by a detailed list of recommended measures.[13]

15.5 European Law

The safeguards in the European Union Charter apply in Poland, however there have been no complaints with the ECJ on its Article 11 and hate speech. Poland is also a party to the European Convention on Human Rights and individual complaints are filed with the European Court on Human rights. Cases referencing hate speech, although inconclusive, include:

- Hösl-Daum and Others v. Poland, 7 October 2014 (decision on admissibility), where the applicants were charged with insulting the Polish nation and inciting hatred on a national background. The applicants alleged a violation of their rights to freedom of expression on account of their conviction for disseminating posters in German, depicting the atrocities committed after World War II against Germans by Poles and Czechs. The Court declared the application inadmissible

[9] Ibid., para 18.
[10] Ibid., para 19.
[11] Ibid.
[12] Ibid., para 20.
[13] Ibid.

for non-exhaustion remedies. It found that as a result of a failure to file a constitutional complaint concerning the challenged provisions of the Criminal Code, the applicants did not exhaust measures provided for by Polish law.
- W.P. and Others v. Poland (no. 42264/98), decision on the admissibility of 2 September 2004 (on the refusal by the Polish authorities to allow creating an association with a statute covering anti-Semitic statements—The Court ruled that the applicants could not enjoy the protection provided for by Article 11 (freedom of assembly and association) of the Convention).

15.6 Judicial Rulings

The issue of courts defining “hate” as the core of hate speech does not appear in civil jurisprudence. Civil courts only analyze the infringement of personal rights, according to the criteria of Article 23 of the Civil Code. Courts avoid examining the broader context of hate speech directed against individuals by declining to recognize it as a specific ground for standing trial. Generalized statements about groups are not treated as referring to specific individuals and their claims for the protection of personal rights are rejected at the stage of examining the right to file a complaint.

In the jurisprudence of criminal courts, the problem of expressing hatred appears only in the context of the courts examining the fulfilment of the criteria of a crime under Article 256 of the Penal Code. In this respect, both the courts and academia developed an interpretation of the characteristics used by the legislator. The case law did not contribute to the definition or explanation of the problem of hate speech. When deciding on specific cases, courts interpret Article 256 of the Penal Code containing the phrase “incites to hatred” on the basis of national, ethnic, racial, religious differences or due to non-denominationality. In this context “incitement to hate” is defined as follows:

> Incitement to hatred (...) boils down to this type of statements that evoke feelings of strong aversion, anger, lack of acceptance, even hostility towards individual people or entire social or religious groups, or due to the form of expression, maintain and intensify such negative attitudes and thus emphasize the privilege and superiority of a specific nation, ethnic group, race or religion.[14]

In the judgment of the Court of Appeal in Katowice of 24 September 2013 (II AKa 301/13—OSACat 2013 No. 4, item 14—the official collection of decisions of the court of appeal) the court observed:

> The concept of inciting hatred on the basis of racial differences should be treated as public exhortation of other people to feel and perpetuate negative emotions, aversion and hostility

[14] Decision of the Supreme Court of 5 February 2007, ref. no. IV KK 406/06 OSNwSK 2007 No. 1, item 367. The same understanding of “inciting to hatred” was repeated in the judgment of the Supreme Court of 8 February 2019, IV KK 38/18, published at www.sn.pl in the official electronic collection of judgments of the Supreme Court. There are no official English or French translations of Polish caselaw, these are authors’ own translations of direct quotes from respective court decisions published in Polish in official, online databases.

> towards representatives of a different race, and for the implementation of the offense specified in Article 256 Section 1 of the Criminal Code is not necessary as a result of persuading other recipients to the views presented by the perpetrator, although this should be the motivation behind his behavior in the incriminated place and time.

Similarly, according to the judgment of the Court of Appeal in Wrocław of 5 July 2018:

> The phrase "incites to hatred" within the meaning of Article 256 Section 1 of the Penal Code means summoning, encouraging, inciting a feeling of strong aversion, hostility towards someone. It is not enough to evoke feelings of disapproval, antipathy, prejudice, dislike.[15]

Also the decision of the Supreme Court of September 1, 2011 (case V CC 98/11) includes similar observations:

> The causative activity of "inciting to hatred" is associated with the desire to arouse in third parties the strongest negative emotion (similar to "hostility") towards a specific nationality, ethnic group or race. It is by no means about evoking feelings of disapproval, dislike, prejudice, dislike.

In some judgments, the courts indicate a broader context of hate speech than that resulting from Article 256 of the Penal Code, and so the judgment of the Supreme Court of February 8, 2019 (IV KK 38/18—published at www.sn.pl in the electronic collection of judgments of the Supreme Court) notes that:

> The crime under Article 256 Section 1 of the Penal Code falls within the area defined as hate speech. This term is commonly understood as statements and images that reproach, mock and degrade groups and individuals for reasons completely or partially beyond their control, as well as belonging to other natural social groups, where natural groups are those that are not chosen, participation in some is determined biologically (sex, skin color), in other socially, such as ethnicity, religion, language.

Jan Kulesza Ph.D., habil., associate professor of criminal law at the University of Lodz, is recognized for his extensive academic contributions and organizational achievements. Holding a doctorate in law, he leads numerous research projects and is a well-recognised author. Jan's expertise extends to legal commentary and serving as an expert for various projects and publications.

Joanna Kulesza Ph.D., assistant professor of international law and director of Lodz Cyber Hub research center at the University of Lodz, holds prominent roles in global cybersecurity initiatives. She chairs various committees, advises international organisations, and leads multiple research projects on cybersecurity and human rights. Joanna is a prolific author in international law and technology.

---

[15] Case II AKa 200/18 published at www.orzeczenia.ms.gov.pl, the official portal of Polish courts' judgments operated by the Ministry of Justice.

Chapter 16
Romania

Florin Streteanu and Cristina Tomuleț

Contents

Abstract The problem of hateful expression in Romania is a recurrent one and is based on deep-seated prejudices of the Romanian society. Those prejudices are reflected in the discrepancy between the 'legal' realm – composed of the applicable national laws and international treaties – and the 'real' realm – which is made up of numerous incidents amounting to hate speech and the passive reaction of the Romanian authorities when confronted with them. Thus, the report on Romania aims at highlighting the fact that simply adopting laws and ratifying international treaties is useless in the absence of a change of mindset towards truly believing in the equality of all people.

Keywords Hate speech legislation · Hate speech by public officials · Racism · Anti-LGBTQ+ speech · Ineffective criminal investigation regarding hate speech

F. Streteanu · C. Tomuleț (✉)
Faculty of Law, Department of Public Law, University of Cluj-Napoca, Cluj-Napoca, Romania
e-mail: cristina.tomulet@law.ubbcluj.ro

F. Streteanu
e-mail: florin.streteanu@law.ubbcluj.ro

E. Heinze (ed.), *Criminalising Hate Speech*,
https://doi.org/10.1007/978-94-6265-650-5_16

16.1 National Constitutional Law

In practice, the Constitutional Court of Romania has most often the opportunity to interpret and apply constitutional provisions, including those relating to hateful expression. However, given the fact that this court has a jurisdiction limited in principle to verifying in the abstract the compatibility of statutory law with the Constitution, it does not have the opportunity to apply the constitutional provisions to specific instances of hateful expression. The Constitutional Court of Romania cannot examine judicial decisions in terms of their constitutionality, which is why it does not have the opportunity to apply the relevant constitutional provisions to hateful expressions. In terms of ordinary courts, even though they may sometimes mention constitutional provisions in their decisions, they mainly apply statutory or administrative laws.

16.2 National Statutory and Administrative Law

National statutory laws have been applied to hateful expression in Romania. In the field of civil law, the provision protecting the right to dignity (Article 72 of the Romanian Civil Code) can underlie civil judgments sanctioning hateful expressions and awarding damages to the victims. At the same time, in the Criminal Code there is a specific provision targeting hateful expression (Article 369), according to which incitement of the public by any means to violence, hatred or discrimination against a category of persons, based on discriminatory motives, shall be punishable by imprisonment for a term of 6 months to 3 years or a fine. Furthermore, there is a special administrative law (Government Ordinance No. 137/2000 on the prevention and punishment of all forms of discrimination), which is mainly applied by an administrative agency, The National Council for Combating Discrimination, which has the power to sanction hateful expression through administrative fines or warnings. This agency has played an important role in sanctioning discrimination, including in relation to hateful expression.

For example, in a famous decision (Judgment no. 168/2018), the NCCD sanctioned the President of Romania for using a certain expression during a press conference—"some criminals are making a desperate attempt to attack and discredit the National Anticorruption Directorate and the management of this directorate," when publicly discussing the fight against corruption. In this case, following a three-part test in the context of analyzing if the interference with the freedom of expression is justified, the Council held that the President exceeded the informative sphere, which is of interest to the public, by violating the dignity of the persons involved in judicial proceedings, as well as the presumption of innocence. Firstly, the NCCD examined if the interference with the freedom of expression is based on law. In this regard, it invoked the national provisions of the aforementioned Government Ordinance No. 137/2000 on the prevention and punishment of all forms of discrimination, considering they are sufficiently accessible and foreseeable, even though they protect values which are abstract. Secondly, the NCCD verified if the interference pursues a legitimate aim, considering that the aim in question is the protection of the dignity of all Romanian citizens, including those who are prosecuted and complain about the procedural abuses to which they are subjected. Thirdly, the NCCD examined the necessity of the interference, by reference to the following criteria: the objective pursued by the applicant when making the statements in question (even though the President wanted to inform the population about a subject of general interest in the context of attacks on the National Anticorruption Directorate, he used pejorative terms when referring to a category of persons), the context of the statements (information appeared in the media regarding the abuses committed by the NAD when prosecuting corruption offences, which is a subject of general interest), the language used by the President (which amounted to a violation of the presumption of innocence), the status of the President as a politician (even though the freedom of expression of politicians is broad, politicians cannot make comments leading to intolerance). However, the judgment of the Council was recently overturned by a court through a decision which remained final.

16.3 International Covenant on Civil and Political Rights (ICCPR)

Romania has been a party to the ICCPR since 1974, and consented to individual complaints procedures by accepting the Optional Protocol to the International Covenant on Civil and Political Rights in 1993. However, to date no individual complaints have raised matters of hateful expression. Human rights issues, including those relating to hateful expression, are generally addressed by Romania's legislators, officials, and courts by reference to the European Convention on Human Rights and the case-law of the European Court of Human Rights, and not with reference to other international instruments for the protection of human rights. Very rarely is the ICCPR mentioned by national actors in the context of the protection of human rights.

In its Concluding Observations regarding Romania dated 5 November 1993, the Committee expressed concern at the continuing problems in Romania regarding discrimination against persons belonging to minorities and, in particular, offences committed as a result of incitement to ethnic or religious intolerance. This situation was especially threatening to vulnerable groups, such as the Roma (gypsies). The Committee was concerned that the Government has not been sufficiently active in combating such discrimination or effectively countering incidents of violence committed against members of minority groups (para 9). At the same time, the Committee recommended that the Government take more active steps to combat racist and xenophobic attitudes and promote tolerance and understanding among the various ethnic, religious and national groups in Romania. In this connection, a positive approach should be taken to counter negative attitudes in the media which are likely to reinforce racist attitudes among the public, particularly in regard to the Roma.

In its Concluding Observations regarding Romania of 11 December 2017, the UN-HRC regretted the lack of information offered by Romania about the application of the provisions of the Covenant by domestic courts. Also, in its report of 11 December 2017, the Committee expressed its concerns regarding discrimination against lesbian, gay, bisexual, transgender and intersex persons, especially in employment and education, incidents of verbal and physical attacks against such persons and stereotypical attitudes and prejudice against them (para 15). At the same time, the Committee was concerned about incidents of hate speech against religious and national minorities, allegations of unequal treatment of national minorities and obstacles to their exercise of religious freedom, such as conducting burials in accordance with their faith and in some cases gaining access to burial (para 43). The Committee advised the state to enforce the prohibition of any advocacy of national, racial or religious hatred that constitutes incitement to discrimination, hostility or violence; take measures to promote tolerance and an environment inclusive of persons belonging to minorities, including with respect to their linguistic and cultural rights; and remove barriers to their exercise of religious freedom (para 44).

16.4 International Convention on the Elimination of All Forms of Racial Discrimination (ICERD)

Romania has been a party to ICERD since 1970 and consented to individual complaints procedures in 2003, however to date there have been no cases relating to hateful expression. As mentioned above, human rights issues, including those relating to hateful expression, are generally tackled by Romania's legislators, officials and courts by reference to the European Convention of Human Rights and the case-law of the European Court of Human Rights and not by reference to other international instruments for the protection of human rights.

Nevertheless, regarding UN-CERD's Concluding Observations for Romania, in its report of 22 September 1995, UN-CERD noted that the legal provisions prohibiting speech that encourages racism or incites violence are believed to be constructive (para 269). However, concern was expressed as to the continued prevalence of xenophobic attitudes and traditional prejudices in Romanian society against certain minorities, manifested in the appearance of extremist political parties and increasing acts of violence (para 270). At the same time, while it was noted that Romania's new legal framework prohibits manifestations of racism, including acts of violence, the propagation of racist speech, and discriminatory employment practices, the extent to which measures are being taken by the Government to translate the legal prohibition of such acts into effective prohibition is unclear. Once such acts occur, it is not evident what remedies are available to victims and whether and how it is ensured that the guilty parties are prosecuted in an adequate and timely manner. It is noted in this connection that with regard to violence on 20 September 1993, which resulted in the death of three members of the Roma and the destruction of the homes of 170 others, victims have yet to receive compensation or have their homes reconstructed (para 272).

In its report of 12 April 2001, UN-CERD expressed concern that the provisions of Romanian legislation making punishable acts of racial discrimination by individuals, are not in full conformity with the provisions of Article 2, para 1 (d), of the Convention. The fact that legislation contains no clear prohibition of organizations which promote and incite racial discrimination, within the meaning of Article 4 (b) of the Convention, was also found to be unsatisfactory (para 9). A further subject of concern was the persistence of xenophobic attitudes and prejudice against certain minorities within Romanian society, which manifest themselves on numerous occasions in various mass media (para 10). UN-CERD recommended that the State party adopt measures to include in legislation provisions which fully prohibit any act of racial discrimination by individuals, as provided for in Article 2, para 1 (d), of the Convention, and also any organization which promotes and incites racial discrimination, within the meaning of Article 4 (b) of the Convention (para 12).

At the same time, the Committee noted the limited number of cases of racial discrimination that have come before the organs administering justice. The Committee was of the opinion that the lack of more complaints and judicial decisions may indicate a lack of awareness of the existence of available legal remedies and of the protection against racial discrimination provided by the Convention. It suggested to the State party that it take measures to remedy that situation (para 13). Also, the Committee recommended that the State party take measures to prevent and punish racist practices in the mass media. In addition, adequate means should be found to ensure that the media constitute an instrument that helps to combat racial prejudice, particularly against the Roma, and fosters a climate of understanding and acceptance among the various groups which make up the country's population (para 14).

In its report of 13 September 2010, UN-CERD welcomed the adoption of a number of laws and ordinances aimed at preventing or combating discrimination, some of which are relevant to the problem of hateful expression, such as Ordinance No. 137/2000 on the prevention and sanctioning of all forms of discrimination, which provides the overall legal framework in this area, Emergency Ordinance No. 31/2002, prohibiting organizations and symbols of a fascist, racist or xenophobic nature and the glorification of those found guilty of committing crimes against peace and humanity, articles 317 and 247 of the Criminal Code, on incitement to discrimination and the abuse of authority on discriminatory grounds, Act No. 504/2002 on audio-visual media (as amended and supplemented by Act No. 402/2003), which prohibits the broadcasting of programmes containing any form of incitement to hatred on grounds of race, religion, nationality, gender or sexual orientation (para 4).

At the same time, UN-CERD noted that the State party's criminal legislation, particularly the Criminal Code, does not entirely cover the activities proscribed in Article 4 of the Convention. Recalling its general recommendations Nos. 1 (1972), 7 (1985) and 15 (1993), according to which Article 4 is of a preventive and mandatory nature, the Committee recommended that the State party include in the Criminal

Code, when it is next reformed, provisions that give full effect to Article 4 of the Convention (para 13). Also, the Committee was concerned at reports of the spread of racial stereotyping and hate speech aimed at persons belonging to minorities, particularly Roma, by certain publications, media outlets, political parties and certain politicians. The Committee recommended that the State party take effective measures to punish the publications, media outlets, political parties and politicians guilty of such behaviour. It also recommended that the State party take measures to promote tolerance among ethnic groups (para 16). The Committee was also concerned at the persistence of racism in sport, particularly football, as manifested in hate speech and racist incidents targeting certain minorities, including the Roma. The Committee recommended that the State party continue its efforts to combat racism in sport, particularly football. It also recommended that the State party use sport to promote a culture of tolerance and multicultural and ethnic diversity (para 17).

16.5 Council of Europe

Romania became a member of the Council of Europe in 1993 and ratified the European Convention on Human Rights in 1994. The case law of the European Court of Human Rights has a mandatory character in the national legal order according to the Constitution. Accordingly, the Parliament has grounds to change the existing laws or to amend them in order to avoid adverse judgments by the European Court.

Regarding relevant judgments of the European Court having actual or potential impact on Romania's laws and policies on hateful expression, the judgment *Association ACCEPT and Others v. Romania* (1 June 2021) is worth mentioning. The applicants were an association promoting the interests of lesbian, gay, bisexual and transgender people (LGBT) in Romania and five individuals. On 20 February 2013 the first applicant organised the public screening of a movie portraying a same-sex family on the premises of a public museum, which was attended, *inter alia,* by the other applicants. The event was interrupted by a group of about 50 people who entered the venue shouting homophobic remarks, insulting and threatening the participants. Some of the intruders displayed fascist and xenophobic signs and brandished the flag of a former Romanian far-right party which had been dissolved by court order for fascist propaganda. The event could no longer continue but was rescheduled and took place on a later date.

The investigation into the applicants' criminal complaint, for incitement to discrimination, abuse of office by restriction of rights and the use of fascist, racist or xenophobic symbols in public, was discontinued by the prosecutor and their challenges thereto were unsuccessful. From the perspective of Article 14 taken together with Article 8, the Court held that the applicants had suffered discrimination on grounds of their sexual orientation given that the authorities had failed to offer them adequate protection in respect of their dignity (and more broadly, their private life), and to effectively investigate the real nature of the homophobic abuse directed against them. As to the obligation to protect, the Court observed that a sufficient number of police officers had been present on the premises from the beginning of the incident, after having been informed by the first applicant of possible opposition to the event. At no point had the officers been overpowered by the intruders. Nor did they claim that they had been caught unprepared and thus lacked the proper equipment to intervene. Yet, they had not stopped the counter-demonstrators but had remained outside the room in which the incident occurred and largely refrained from intervening to de-escalate the situation and prevent the individual applicants from being bullied and insulted. This had been despite being aware of the views manifested by the intruders and having heard the contents of the slurs uttered by them.

This also seemed to indicate a certain bias against homosexuals, which had also permeated their subsequent reports on the incident; these contained no reference to the homophobic insults suffered by the individual applicants and described the incident in terms that completely disregarded any such manifestations of homophobia. Accordingly, the authorities had failed to correctly assess the risk incurred by the individual applicants at the hands of the intruders and to respond adequately in order to protect their dignity against homophobic attacks by a third party. As to the obligation to investigate, the authorities had deemed that the alleged threats or remarks had not reached the threshold required by the applicable law to constitute a criminal offence. The Court reiterated, however, that while being careful not to hold that each and every utterance of hate speech must, as such, attract criminal prosecution and criminal sanctions, comments that amounted to hate speech and incitement to violence, and were thus clearly unlawful on the face of things, might in principle require the States to take certain positive measures.

Likewise, inciting hatred did not necessarily amount to a call for an act of violence or other criminal acts. Attacks on people committed by insulting, holding up to ridicule or slandering specific groups of the population could be sufficient for the authorities to favour combating racist speech in the form of freedom of expression exercised in an irresponsible manner. At the same time, the language consistently used by the authorities in their reports about the incident and all involved, far from being neutral or accidental, suggested bias on their part against the individual applicants, which might be seen as indicating that the authorities had turned a blind eye to the homophobic overtones of the acts that had been perpetrated, thus jeopardising the accuracy and effectiveness of the domestic proceedings as a whole.

The Court emphasized that the necessity of conducting a meaningful inquiry into the possibility that discriminatory motives had lain behind the abuse was absolute, given the hostility against the LGBT community in the respondent State and in the light of the evidence that homophobic slurs had been uttered by the intruders during the incident. In the absence of such an inquiry, prejudice-motivated crimes would inevitably be treated on an equal footing with cases without such overtones, and the resultant indifference would be tantamount to official acquiescence, or even connivance in, hate crimes. In conclusion, the authorities had failed to discharge their positive obligation to investigate in an effective manner whether the verbal abuse directed towards the individual applicants constituted a criminal offence motivated by homophobia. In doing so, the authorities had shown their own bias towards members of the LGBT community.

This judgment seems to throw light on the same issue previously identified by the Court in the judgment of *M.C. and A.C. v. Romania* (12 April 2016). In 2006, the applicants participated in a Lesbian, Gay, Bisexual, Transgender and Intersex (LGBTI) rally in Bucharest. The march was accompanied by counter-demonstrations which, despite the police protection afforded to the participants, ended in several individuals being fined for disturbing the event. At the end of the march, the applicants were attacked by a group of individuals who also shouted homophobic insults. The subsequent criminal investigation was ultimately terminated in 2011 without the perpetrators of the attack having been identified. From the perspective of Article 14 in conjunction with Article 3, in the Court's view, the aim of the physical and verbal abuse the applicants had been subject to had probably been to frighten them so that they would desist from their public expression of support for the LGBTI community. The applicants' feelings of emotional distress must have been exacerbated by the fact that they had been attacked because they were exercising rights guaranteed by the Convention, namely, participating in an LGBTI rally.

Bearing in mind the reports prepared by several international bodies, including the Commissioner for Human Rights of the Council of Europe, the Court acknowledged that the LGBTI community in the respondent State found itself in a precarious situation, being subject to negative attitudes towards its members. Therefore, the treatment to which the applicants had been subjected reached the requisite threshold of severity to fall within the ambit of Article 3 read in conjunction with Article 14 of the Convention. As to the investigation of the incidents, the applicants had promptly lodged a criminal complaint and presented all the evidence at their disposal, evidence which they considered made it possible to identify at least some of the attackers. However, the authorities took no significant steps for a period of almost a year and, more than five years after the initial criminal complaint, they had not yet established the identity of the perpetrators. In addition, the Court observed several shortcomings in the investigation.

In particular, the authorities did not take into account the role played by possible homophobic motives behind the attack. This was indispensable given the hostility against the LGBTI community in the respondent State and in the light of the applicants' submissions that clearly homophobic hate speech had been uttered by the assailants during the incident. Without such a rigorous approach from the law-enforcement authorities, prejudice-motivated crimes would inevitably be treated on an equal footing with cases involving no such overtones, and the resultant indifference would be tantamount to official acquiescence, or even connivance, in hate crimes. Moreover, without a meaningful investigation, it would be difficult for the respondent State to implement measures aimed at improving the policing of similar peaceful demonstrations in the future, thus undermining public confidence in the State's anti-discrimination policy.

Regarding relevant documents adopted by organs belonging to the Council of Europe, the findings of the European Commission against Racism and Intolerance (ECRI) are insightful in terms of the problem of hateful expression in Romania. In its latest report from 3 April 2019, ECRI noted that racist statements by politicians, in particular at local level, continue to be a problem. Many sources have stated that as a result of political gains in local elections through anti-Roma rhetoric and more nationalistic discourse, the use of hate speech, including by mainstream political parties, has become commonplace. For example, a local councillor in Mahmudia stated that 'the best Gypsy is a dead Gypsy' (ActiveWatch, Annual Report on Hate Speech in Romania 2015–2016, p. 11), (para 23 of the Report).[1]

At the same time, reports suggested that derogatory public statements have often been expressed in the context of the longstanding tension persisting between the Hungarian national minority and the state authorities, mostly with political overtones arising from the discussion over demands for 'autonomy' and the use of Székler flag and symbols in public places. Recently, in January 2018, after a call for territorial autonomy by ethnic Hungarian parties, the then Romanian Prime Minister stated in a TV show that 'if they fly Székler flag on institutions in Széklerland, all those responsible over there will be flying next to it' (para 25 of the Report). Also, ECRI stated that civil society indicated that hateful language is prevalent in traditional and social media, mostly towards Roma, LGBT persons, the Hungarian minority, the Jewish community and Muslims (para 29 of the Report).

The ECRI also noted that sports events have continued to be a forum for incidents of hate speech. The Romanian Football Federation has imposed sanctions on several occasions and banned fans and players over racist behaviour during football matches (para 32 of the Report). Regarding the sanctions applied for hate speech, ECRI observed that as for criminal responses, hate speech is covered by the criminal offence of incitement to hatred (Article 369 of the Criminal Code). Several articles of GEO No. 31/2002 can also be used for hate speech incidents. However, the authorities informed ECRI that only two cases went to trial under Article 369 between 2014 and 2017 and only five under GEO No. 31/2002. ECRI was astonished that so few cases of hate speech have reached court. Despite its recommendation in its fourth report, ECRI regretted to note that the application of the provisions on incitement to hatred remains extremely limited, which in ECRI's view, sends a strong message to the public that hate speech is not a serious offence and can be engaged in with impunity (para 34 of the Report).

16.6 Judicial Rulings

Regarding the definition of hateful expression, it must be mentioned that the applicable anti-discrimination legislation does not explicitly define hate speech. Usually, courts implement the principles established by the European Court of Human Rights in this field without creating new definitions of hate speech. Having regard to the fact that the case law of the National Council for Combating Discrimination is the most relevant in this field, I will make a few observations regarding its approach in

[1] https://activewatch.ro/documents/179/Raport_anual_cu_privire_la_discursul_instigator_la_ura_2015_20161.pdf (activewatch.ro), in the Romanian language; translation by the authors.

handling the problem of hateful expression. First, as already mentioned, when tackling the problem of hate speech, the NCCD uses the three-part test, enshrined by the European Court when analyzing interferences with the freedom of expression. After verifying if the interference is prescribed by law and pursues a legitimate aim, the NCCD examines the necessity of the interference in a democratic society in light of the following criteria: the objective pursued by the persons who made the statements, the meaning of the statements, the context in which they were made and the status of the persons who made the statements. The approach presented can be found, for example, in Judgment no. 168/2018 of the NCCD (Hotarare-168-2018.pdf (cncd.ro)). At the same time, it is important to mention that the NCCD uses a factual approach by analyzing the specific statements linguistically and from the other perspectives mentioned earlier in order to ascertain their discriminatory nature, not focusing on creating theoretical definitions of hateful expression (see Judgments no. 4/2016, 164/2016, 288/2017, 356/2017).

Florin Streteanu is a Professor in Criminal law at the University of Cluj-Napoca (Romania) and a former dean of the Faculty of Law. He is also trainer at the National Institute of Magistracy in Bucharest and he was appointed as an *ad hoc* judge at the European Court of Human Rights. From 2006–2009 he was a member of the Commission established for drafting the new Romanian Criminal Code.

Cristina Tomulet is an assistant professor in the fields of constitutional and human rights law at Babeş-Bolyai University, in Cluj-Napoca, Romania. Her research interests revolve around legal interpretation, philosophy of law and human rights protection in post-communist states. Passionate about delving deep into difficult questions about law, her published papers show a yearning for finding an ideal of justice as a foundation for positive law. She has also recently published a book on criminal law interpretation, as a result of her Ph.D. studies.

Chapter 17
Russian Federation

Anastasiia Vorobiova

Contents

Abstract In the Russian Federation, measures for criminalising hate speech have been used in light of positive and negative obligations under global and regional human rights treaties. Yet they have also been abused as tools of oppression and persecution against national, ethnic, religious minorities, and persons viewed as political opponents for the current government. This chapter explores the perils of misusing hate speech legislation in the practice of the Russian Constitutional Court, Supreme Court, and domestic courts implementing local legislation. It traces the response of international and regional bodies to the undemocratic measures imposed by the Russian government in their purported struggle against extremism. Broad definitions of 'extremism' and 'religious and interracial hatred' within Russian legislation leave a wide margin of appreciation in restricting rights and freedoms of religious and ethnic minorities, LGBTQI+ community, dissidents and those opposing the current

The Author would like to express most immense gratitude to dr. Uladzislau Belavusau for assistance and inspiration in writing this chapter.

A. Vorobiova (✉)
Institute of Legal Sciences, Polish Academy of Sciences, Warsaw, Poland
e-mail: a.vorobiova@inp.pan.pl

E. Heinze (ed.), *Criminalising Hate Speech*,
https://doi.org/10.1007/978-94-6265-650-5_17

war against Ukraine, with a little or no prospect to challenge described legislation on international or regional levels.

Keywords Hate speech legislation · Anti-LGBTQ+ speech · Anti-religious speech · Yarovaya laws · Russia and ECtHR · Racial discrimination · Extremism

17.1 National Constitutional Law

17.1.1 General Constitutional Provisions

The 1993 Constitution of the Russian Federation is the first real Constitution in Russian history and is a reaction against the Russian past, the embodiment of the Russian experience, and the repository of Russian values and desires for its future.[1] The 1993 Constitution was indeed an aspirational document which secured a broad range of democratic values, supremacy of international law norms over national ones and a range of guarantees. However, given the authoritarian tendencies taking place in Russia since Putin's ascend to power, the Constitution was also accordingly amended to secure this authoritarian grip.[2] For example, the Constitutional Court of the Russian Federation (hereinafter—CCRF) was vested in deciding whether decisions by supranational bodies or international tribunal pertaining to Russia can be enforced, if they contradict the national Constitution or the tenets of public order. The amendments also included protecting the "institution of marriage as the union of a man and a woman", designating the Russian language as a "state-forming tool" and protecting the heroic memory of the "Fatherland's defendants" in the Second World War. The latter had become a literal "Chekhov's gun" in 2022 when Vladimir Putin announced the start of the so-called "Special Military Operation" (hereinafter—SMO) against Ukraine with the purported aim of "denazification"[3] and protecting the Russian-speaking population of Ukraine.[4] Overall, according to some Russian scholars, the 2020 amendments are contributing to securing the "national constitutional identity" which is threatened by outside influences, such as the ECtHR, which is disrespecting the "Russian traditional values".[5]

However, the new amendments have not touched the substantive parts of the rights and freedoms part of the Constitution, which has remained largely unchanged. Thus, Article 28 guarantees the "freedom of conscience, the freedom of religion, including

[1] Butler 2019.

[2] Law on amendment to Russian Federation Constitution, 14 March 2020. http://en.kremlin.ru/acts/news/62988.

[3] Georgesco 2022

[4] Ibid.

[5] The constitution of the Russian Federation and constitutional identity in the context of global changes, SHS Web of Conferences 108, 01003 (2021) https://www.shs-conferences.org/articles/shsconf/pdf/2021/19/shsconf_blf2021_01003.pdf.

the right to profess individually or together with others any religion or to profess no religion at all, to freely choose, possess and disseminate religious and other views and act according to them" and Article 29 safeguards the freedom of speech, the freedom of information and the freedom of mass communication.[6]

Article 29 also prohibits "propaganda or campaigning" intended "to incite social, racial, national, or religious hatred and strife." These prohibitions have been codified in the Russian Criminal code and are justified in the name of combatting extremism and hate speech but are more often used to prosecute political opponents or undesirable speech.[7] Strictly speaking, the Russian legal system does not have a direct analogue of the Anglo-American heading of "hate speech," with the closest analogues used being "incitement to hatred on the grounds of (…)" (*разжигание ненависти на […] почве*) or "propaganda of hatred" (*пропаганда ненависти*), although in the literature one can encounter occasional attempts to directly translate "hate speech" in comparative legal contexts as "yazyk vrazhdy", which resembles "language of hatred." The term "yazyk vrazhdy" is occasionally utilised in academic literature.[8]

17.1.2 Constitutional Court Case Law

The Constitutional Court of the Russian Federation (hereinafter—the CCRF) has a vast caseload on the constitutionality of the anti-extremism legislation. The CCRF judicial practice is mostly dedicated to the issue of whether the provisions of anti-extremism legislation are in conformity with the relevant Constitutional guarantees. In this regard, the petitioners were claiming that the provisions of this legislation were inconsistent with the following constitutional provisions: Articles 1 (Russia being a democratic state), 13 (ideological diversity), 15 (primacy of the Constitution), 18 (direct operation of the rights and freedoms), 28 (freedom of conscience and religion), 29 (freedom of thought and speech) and 55 (no law can cancel or derogate from human rights and freedoms which can be limited only to an extent necessary for the protection of the fundamental principles of the constitutional system, morality, health, the rights and lawful interests of other people, ensuring the defence of the country and security of the State). Insofar the CCRF held that article 282 of the Criminal Code did not lack clarity and stated that the law was formulated clearly and did not obstruct one's understanding of what constituted an illegal action and the liability such an action could result in.[9] That also concerned bans of certain materials of religious matters that have been recognised as "extremist" solely due to

---

[6] The Constitution of the Russian Federation, 1993 (last amended under the controversial referendum orchestrated by President Putin on 4 July 2020). https://www.refworld.org/docid/3ae6b59f4.html.

[7] Ibid. For a legal overview, see Мария Китайчик 2014.

[8] Особенности "языка вражды" или "риторики ненависти" в медиапространстве России и США https://www.hse.ru/edu/vkr/364643408.

[9] The Case of Anton Nossik, https://globalfreedomofexpression.columbia.edu/cases/the-case-of-anton-nossik/.

proclaiming the truth of the teachings set forth in it—along with the assertion that other teachings are false.[10]

The first group of cases concern the provision which allows banning dissemination of religious texts which promote the superiority of one religion over another, except for the Bible, Quran, Tanakh and Kanjur.[11] In 2011 Vladislav Kochemarov, who is also a follower of the Russian Scientology church, petitioned the CCRF to contest district court decision which recognised as extremist and confiscated several materials of the Church of Scientology's founder. The materials were found to be inciting religious discord and propaganda of superiority based on religious and social belonging. One of Kochemarov's key arguments is that the law lacked sufficient clarity in formulating what "extremism" is and therefore state authorities are given a discretion which is too wide in deciding which materials to ban on these grounds. The CCRF refused Kochemarov's argument and noted that the requirements of legal clarity and certainty "does not at all exclude the use of evaluative or generally accepted concepts (categories), the meaning of which should be accessible to perception and understandable to the subjects of the relevant legal relations or directly from the content specific regulation or from a system of regulations that are clearly interconnected, or by identifying a more complex relationship of legal prescriptions, including through clarifications given by courts on issues of their application".[12] In 2015 the CCRF on the same grounds refused to accept the complaints of the Jehovah's Witnesses aiming to overturn ban of brochure "Dobraya vest ot Boga"[13] and a Jehovah's Witnesses website[14] referring that such measures prescribed by the anti-extremism legislation are in line with the Russian Constitution.

In reverse, in 2017 a Jehovah's Witnesses follower Vladimir Sergienko challenged the constitutionality of the law, which allows banning certain sacred scriptures. Sergienko petitioned the local prosecutor's office to recognise as extremist the

[10] Определение Конституционного Суда РФ от 17.02.2015 N 347-О "Об отказе в принятии к рассмотрению жалобы гражданина Синицына Михаила Владимировича на нарушение его конституционных прав положениями пункта 1 статьи 1 Федерального закона "О противодействии экстремистской деятельности" https://www.consultant.ru/document/cons_doc_LAW_176719/.

[11] Федеральный закон от 25.07.2002 г. № 114-ФЗ "О противодействии экстремистской деятельности" http://www.kremlin.ru/acts/bank/18939.

[12] https://www.lawmix.ru/prof/96548.

[13] Ruling of the Constitutional Court of the Russian Federation of July 16, 2015 No. 1787-O "On the refusal to accept for consideration the complaint of the local religious organization of Jehovah's Witnesses in the city of Birobidzhan on violation of constitutional rights and freedoms by para 3 of Article 1 and Article 13 of the Federal Law "On Counteracting Extremist Activities". https://rulaws.ru/acts/Opredelenie-Konstitutsionnogo-Suda-RF-ot-16.07.2015-N-1787-O/.

[14] Ruling of the Constitutional Court of the Russian Federation of December 22, 2015 No. 3024-O "On the refusal to accept for consideration the complaint of the foreign organization "Watchtower Bible and Tract Society of New York, Inc." for violation of constitutional rights and freedoms by para 3 of Article 1 and Article 13 of the Federal Law "On Counteracting Extremist Activity", as well as para 2 of Part 5 of Article 15.1 of the Federal Law "On Information, Information Technologies and Information Protection" https://www.garant.ru/products/ipo/prime/doc/71214816/.

treatise of Joseph Volotsky "The Enlightener" (in original "Prosvetitel", late 15th–early 16th century) since it contains calls for discrimination and violence against religious and national identity, namely the anti-Jewish rhetoric. However, the prosecutor rejected Sergienko's application, as the "Enlightener" contains quotations from the Bible and thus cannot be recognised as being of an extremist character. The local courts also refused to accept the complaint on the prosecutor's refusal, as "the rights, freedoms and legitimate interests of the administrative plaintiff are not violated or otherwise affected" by the prosecutor's decision.

After that, Sergienko appealed to the CCRF, pointing out that exceptions provided within the anti-extremism legislation do not comply with Articles 2 and 29(2) of the Constitution as materials containing incitement to violence can omit being included in the list only due to inclusion of quotations from the protected materials. The CCRR also refused to consider Sergienko's complaint.[15]

The anti-extremist legislation was challenged not only on religious grounds. A blogger Anton Nossik was charged with incitement of hatred or enmity for publishing a blog post entitled "Wipe Syria from the Face of the Earth" where he compared Syria with Nazi Germany and welcomed bombing launched by the Russian government.[16] The charges were based on expert linguists' report from the Federal Security Service's (FSB) Institute of Criminology which qualified the article as "extremist statements."[17] The "Article 19" organisation has found this case as "symptomatic of a growing trend in Russia to abuse "incitement" provisions as well as legislation that targets content deemed "extremist" or "separatist"".[18] Nossik complained that the article's formulation allows holding a person accountable for the opinion expressed, using the vague concepts of "social group" and "motives of hatred or enmity", but the CCRF rejected his complaint.[19]

In all mentioned cases the CCRF's reasoning regarding the anti-extremism legislation is obviously flawed and is more understandable in regard to the current political situation. That is inter alia evident from the CCRF's double standards in treating the religious materials of non-Christian denominations such as Scientological materials in Kochemarov's case which were found to "promote the superiority of one religion" and the clear anti-Jewish statements in the "Enlightener" which were deemed not falling under the anti-extremism legislation. Rejection of Jehovah's Witnesses cases further indicates that the CCRF's understanding of the rights and freedoms within the Russian Constitution and how they interact with the anti-extremism legislation

[15] Ruling of the Constitutional Court of the Russian Federation of April 20, 2017 No. 906-O "On the refusal to accept for consideration the complaint of citizen Sergienko Vladimir Ivanovich about the violation of his constitutional rights by paragraph 3 of part 1 of Article 128 of the Code of Administrative Procedure of the Russian Federation and Article 3.1 of the Federal Law "On countering extremist activity" https://www.garant.ru/products/ipo/prime/doc/71579790/.

[16] Article 19 2016.

[17] Webb 2016.

[18] Article 19 2016.

[19] https://globalfreedomofexpression.columbia.edu/wp-content/uploads/2022/08/Const_Court_Kort_07.18.2017.pdf.

is quite specific, to put it mildly. Hence, the CCRF is not a suitable ground to challenge the vast amount of anti-extremism legislation which will be discussed in the following part of the chapter.

17.2 National Statutory and Administrative Law

The Russian commitment to fighting "extremism" dates to the terrorist attacks in Russia in the late 1990s and early 2000s. The 2002 Law "On Combatting Extremist Activity" ("O protivodeistvii ekstremizma") classified the following activities as "extremism": public advocacy of terrorism and the forcible overthrow of the government, promotion of social discord on the basis of religion, ethnicity, or race, and the promotion of one's superiority on the basis of one of these categories. Most "extremist" activities on the list were framed in terms of public statements or views rather than concrete actions taken in response to these beliefs. The law allowed for the criminalisation of any organisation and barring the publication and distribution of materials considered by the government to be contrary to this law, thus granting significant power to curtail any expression under the umbrella term of "extremism".[20]

The law received further amendments in the following years. The most significant of them relate to the so-called 2016 "Yarovaya Laws"[21] dramatically expanded anti-extremist enforcement and introduced heftier penalties for violators.[22] The two bills consist of the Federal Law "On Amendments to the Federal Law "On Combating Terrorism" and Certain Legislative Acts of the Russian Federation to establish additional measures to counter terrorism and ensure public safety"[23] and the Federal Law "On Amendments to the Criminal Code of the Russian Federation and the Criminal Procedure Code of the Russian Federation with regard to establishing additional measures to counter terrorism and ensure public security".[24] The first bill supplemented the Criminal Code with the new offence of "promoting extremist activity".[25]

---

[20] Baran and Knox 2019, p. 97.

[21] The amendments are commonly referred to as the "Yarovaya Law," after their key author, Irina Yarovaya, a leading member of the ruling "United Russia" party.

[22] Federal Law of 06.07.2016 No. 374-FZ "On the Introduction of Amendments to Federal Law 'On the Counteraction of Terrorism' and to Certain Legislative Acts of the Russian Federation with Regard to Establishing Additional Measures Designed to Counteract Terrorism and Promote Public Safety".

[23] Federal Law No. 374-FZ, "On Amendments to the Federal Law "On Combating Terrorism" and Certain Legislative Acts of the Russian Federation to establish additional measures to counter terrorism and ensure public safety".

[24] Federal Law No. 375-FZ, "On amendments to the Criminal Code of the Russian Federation and the Criminal Procedure Code of the Russian Federation with regard to establishing additional measures to counter terrorism and ensure public security".

[25] The Yarovaya Law: One Year After, 2017 https://analytica.digital.report/wp-content/uploads/2017/07/The-Yarovaya-Law.pdf.

The "Yarovaya Laws" impose new data retention obligations on communication services providers on the Internet and secure the provision of information to federal investigators and prosecutors.[26] Some researchers note that the primary aim of these amendments is to further restrict the flow of information which can criticise the current regime and undermine its stability.[27] The "Yarovaya Law" are thus inconsistent with the freedom of conscience, freedom of association, and other rights such as increasing penalties for vaguely defined "public justification of terrorism" online and banning proselytising, preaching, praying, or disseminating religious materials outside of officially recognised religious institutions.[28] Consequently, the non-Orthodox religious denominations label it as the "anti-missionary" law as it requires religious groups and missionaries to obtain government permission to operate and thus the ministry activity of non-registered churches is severely restricted.[29]

As for the judicial reviews of such restrictive measures, the Russian human rights organisations note that in domestic cases of extremism, judges heavily rely on the expert's conclusions, which may even substitute a thorough judicial assessment. Moreover, Russian courts mostly limit their assessment to checking whether the impugned statements meet the definition of the offence as set out in the law and if so, automatically impose a restriction on freedom of expression, which often involves disproportionate sanctions.[30] It can also be argued that some judicial decisions on the matter are not just falling short of legal reasoning but also pure common sense, such as the 2017 Supreme Court decision, which included Jehovah's Witnesses in the list of extremist organisations.[31] That decision resulted in numerous convictions of regular believers for simple things such as praying or storing religious literature in their homes (which was also included in the list of extremist materials), and the 2021 Supreme Court's clarification that mere worship and praying does not fall under the extremism had not lessened the number of such convictions.[32]

The Russian war against Ukraine had lead to even tighter restrictions on the freedom of information under the Yarovaya amendments. In March 2022 Tverskoy District Court of Moscow recognised activities of Meta Platforms Inc. as being of an extremist character for failing to take measures to block materials containing calls to carry out violence against citizens of the Russian Federation and change the foundations of the constitutional system. The Court also subsequently banned Meta's products, including social networks Facebook and Instagram.[33] The ban in

---

[26] https://gowlingwlg.com/en/insights-resources/articles/2016/yarovaya-law-russian-parliament-passes-package-of/.

[27] Tabachnik. https://cyber.haifa.ac.il/index.php/all-posts/yarovaya-law.

[28] Human Rights Watch 2016a, b.

[29] Yarovaya Law v. Religious Freedom https://missioneurasia.org/yarovaya-law-vs-religious-freedom/.

[30] Rights in extremis: Russia's anti-extremism practices from an international perspective. https://u.pcloud.link/publink/show?code=XZqg3HkZU9jKLdd0hGH23cIdIrhCO7BnNLhX.

[31] Human Rights Watch 2017.

[32] https://www.forum18.org/archive.php?article_id=2842.

[33] https://mos-gorsud.ru/rs/tverskoj/services/cases/civil/details/de7ea6a0-a3ab-11ec-8a7e-51b31fb55b35.

justified due to "intentional discriminatory and extremist manifestations in relation to the citizens of the Russian Federation, the Russian mass media, expressing an "alternative opinion" on the so-called "special military operation" carried out by the Russian Armed Forces".[34] The Appellate court decision upheld the ban.[35] In October 2022 Meta was included in the list of extremist organisations, albeit no sanctions follow for those users who continue using them via anonymisation tools.[36]

Hence, under Russian domestic law, provisions pertaining to the criminalisation of "extremist" speech are enshrined in several legislative acts, including the Law on Counteraction to Terrorism, the Law on Combating Extremist Activity, the Criminal Code and the Code of Administrative Offences.[37] Since their emergence in 2002 as an effort to combat terrorism, Russian anti-extremism laws have been expanded, and the legal notion of extremism now encompasses terrorism, separatism, hate speech, libel, insult of religious feelings and more.[38] These laws have been utilised by Russian authorities to neutralise threats to the country's "information safety", national sovereignty, political and social stability, and Constitutional order. At the same time, anti-extremism laws have considerably impacted online speech and have restricted citizens' freedom of expression.

17.2.1 Russian Federal Law "On Combating Extremist Activity"

The 2002 Russian Federal Law "On Combating Extremist Activity"[39] defines the prohibited acts as follows:

- forcible change in the foundations of the constitutional system and (or) violation of the territorial integrity of the Russian Federation (including the alienation of part of the territory of the Russian Federation), with the exception of the delimitation, demarcation, redemarcation of the State Border of the Russian Federation;
- public justification of terrorism and other terrorist activities;
- incitement of social, racial, national or religious hatred;
- propaganda of the exclusivity, superiority or inferiority of a person on the basis of his social, racial, national, religious or linguistic affiliation or attitude to religion;

34 https://mos-gorsud.ru/rs/tverskoj/services/cases/civil/details/de7ea6a0-a3ab-11ec-8a7e-51b31fb55b35.

35 Halpert 2022.

36 The Moscow Times 2022. 7.

37 Joanna Szymanska, Programme Officer, ECA (Article 19), Laurens Hueting, Legal Officer (Article 19), and Maria Kravchenko (SOVA Center) RUSSIA'S OVERUSE AND MISUSE OF ANTI-EXTREMISM LAWS, https://ehrac.org.uk/en_gb/blog/russias-overuse-and-misuse-of-anti-extremism-laws/?fbclid=IwAR2YdAdQ5CTBx4-LAecEc23DrhAsqVv1v9Sx1qQH62A6WLtSrnSuaQsldL8.

38 Sherstoboeva Pavlenko 2018), pp. 101–115.

39 Relevant as of July 2023.

- violation of the rights, freedoms and legitimate interests of a person and a citizen based on his social, racial, national, religious or linguistic affiliation or attitude to religion;
- preventing citizens from exercising their electoral rights and the right to participate in a referendum or violating the secrecy of voting, combined with violence or its threat;
- obstruction of the lawful activities of state bodies, local self-government bodies, election commissions, public and religious associations or other organisations, combined with violence or the threat of its use;
- commission of crimes motivated by political, ideological, racial, national or religious hatred or enmity, or motivated by hatred or enmity against any social group (specified in para 1e of Article 63 of the Russian Criminal Code);[40]
- use of Nazi paraphernalia or symbols, or paraphernalia or symbols confusingly similar to Nazi paraphernalia or symbols, or paraphernalia or symbols of extremist organisations, with the exception of such symbols in order to form a negative attitude towards the ideology of Nazism and extremism with no signs of propaganda or justification of Nazi and extremist ideology;
- public calls for the commission of these acts or the mass distribution of obviously extremist materials, as well as their production or storage;
- publicly and deliberately falsely accusing a person holding a public position in the Russian Federation or its constituent entities of committing the acts specified in this article during the performance of his official duties;
- organisation and preparation of these acts, as well as incitement to their implementation;
- financing of these acts or other assistance in their organisation, preparation and implementation, including through the provision of educational, editorial, material and technical base, telephone and other types of communication or the provision of information services.[41]

The law has been severely criticised for its vague formulations. The Venice Commission expressed the opinion that "to proclaim as extremist any religious teaching or proselytising activity aimed at proving that a certain worldview is a superior explanation of the universe" could "affect the freedom of conscience or religion of many persons" and can be easily abused. The Commission concluded that the "broad and imprecise wording" gives "too wide discretion in its interpretation and application, thus leading to arbitrariness" and carries "potential dangers to individuals and NGOs".[42]

---

[40] https://www.consultant.ru/document/cons_doc_LAW_10699/31577810105ef97a75f2f49154b1a1d3803ffe52/.

[41] http://www.kremlin.ru/acts/bank/18939.

[42] CDL-AD(2012)016-e. Opinion on the Federal Law on Combating Extremist Activity of the Russian Federation adopted by the Venice Commission at its 91st Plenary Session (Venice, 15-16 June 2012) https://www.venice.coe.int/webforms/documents/default.aspx?pdffile=CDL-AD(2012)016-e paras, 77–78.

In order to specify the provisions of the "anti-extremism law", a "Strategy for Countering Extremism in the Russian Federation until 2025" was developed and approved in 2014.[43] "Extremist ideology" in the Strategy is understood as a "set of views and ideas representing violent and other illegal actions as the main means of resolving political, racial, national, religious and social conflicts". The extremist threats are divided into external and internal. External threats are emanating from foreign agents, including states and non-governmental organisations, who aim at destabilising the situation in Russia and violating its unity and territorial integrity. Those include promoting the activities of international extremist and terrorist organisations, in particular the spread of extremist ideology and radicalism in society.[44]

Internal extremist threats emanate from organisations, associations and individuals of extremist character conducting activities to spread the ideology of violence and recruit Russian and foreign citizens.[45] Internal threats also include interethnic and territorial contradictions and conflicts in individual constituent entities of Russia and consequent separatist manifestations and incitement to their implementation.[46] Another extremist threat is the "deliberate distortion of history" and "revival of the ideas of Nazism and fascism" within foreign states. Interestingly, the desired outcomes of the strategy implementation are not only mitigation of extremist cases and threats but also forming "an atmosphere of intolerance towards extremist activities, rejection of extremist ideology", especially among youth and contribute to the development of the "spiritual and civic unity of the multinational people of the Russian Federation."[47]

Hence, the Strategy includes an educational component, which must teach the younger generation the state-proscribed version of what extremism is and how to combat it—and a pertinent educational module is now expected to be implemented in Russian universities.[48] However, given the very pervasive understanding of what constitutes extremism within the Russian legislation, this course will most likely become another tool to build allegiance to the government and instil narratives favourable to it.

---

[43] Информация Российской Федерации в связи с запросом Управления Верховного комиссара ООН по правам человека относительно выполнения положений резолюции 75/187 Генеральной Ассамблеи ООН «Борьба с нетерпимостью, формированием негативных стереотипных представлений, стигматизацией, дискриминацией, подстрекательством к насилию и насилием в отношении лиц на основе религии или убеждений» https://adsdatabase.ohchr.org/IssueLibrary/RUSSIA_Contribution%20to%20A_RES_75_187.pdf.

[44] Ibid., para 8.

[45] Ibid., para 9.

[46] Стратегия противодействия экстремизму в Российской Федерации до 2025 года" (утв. Президентом РФ 28.11.2014 N Пр-2753) https://www.consultant.ru/document/cons_doc_LAW_194160/c7ee7750b35ec02d1647c3c44f538e6a2af88ad3/.

[47] https://www.consultant.ru/document/cons_doc_LAW_194160/7df6E96cde0217dd99ef5E14D9E94bf22D63920E/.

[48] https://nerulife.ru/V-rossiyskikh-vuzakh-studentov-budut-uch/.

17.2.2 *Criminal Code of the Russian Federation*

Article 282.1

The Article 282 of the Russian Criminal Code criminalises actions aimed at inciting hatred or enmity, as well as at humiliating the dignity of a person or a group of persons on the grounds of sex, race, nationality, language, origin, attitude to religion, as well as membership in any social group. The act should be committed publicly (with the use of mass media or the Internet) after the perpetrator has been brought to administrative responsibility for a similar offence within one year. The notion of the "crimes of an extremist orientation" includes acts "committed for reasons of political, ideological, racial, national or religious hatred or enmity or for reasons of hatred or enmity against any social group".[49] According to the Chairman of the Russian Supreme Court, at least 606 persons were convicted for the commission of extremist crimes in 2021[50] and 693—in 2022.[51] According to analytics, 51 verdicts were given based on the Article 282 in 2022 (50 in 2021) and 42 based on the Article 354.1 (rehabilitation of Nazism), compared with 35 in 2021.[52]

The Supreme Court Decree ("postnanovlenie plenuma") clarifies that incitement of hatred or enmity includes statements that substantiate and (or) affirm the need for genocide, mass repressions, deportations, and other illicit actions against representatives of any nation, race, social or political group. Criticism of political organisations, ideological and religious associations, political, ideological, or religious beliefs, and national or religious customs should not in itself be considered falling under the auspice of this prohibition.[53] However, in reality, criticism of Russian government officials falls under the auspices of the Article 282.1, for example in the case of Igor Girkin (Strelkov) who has been detained in July 2023 for criticising the conduct of the so-called "Special military operation" (hereinafter—"SMO"), namely the poor management of Vladimir Putin and Russia's Defence Minister Sergei Shoigu. Notably, Girkin did not criticise the war itself, is a proponent of Ukraine's full destruction and subsequent occupation by Russia and had been convicted by the Hague Court for shooting down the MH-17 aircraft as a leader of a Russian guerrilla group in Donestk.[54] Despite these circumstances, he was labelled as a "political prisoner" by the Russian opposition, namely late Alexey Navalny, who called Girkin's

---

[49] "Уголовный кодекс Российской Федерации" от 13.06.1996 N 63-ФЗ (ред. от 10.07.2023) https://www.consultant.ru/document/cons_doc_LAW_10699/b99a4508e05471a407e532780d2c0c95471049d9/.

[50] Верховный суд разъяснил соотношение религиозных обрядов и экстремизма. https://www.rbc.ru/society/09/02/2022/6203ce6c9a794703fc69ca3e.

[51] В России в 2022 году более 1,5 тыс. человек осудили за терроризм и экстремизм, 14 February 2023. https://tass.ru/proisshestviya/17047161.

[52] Ibid.

[53] Supreme Court Decree as of 28 June 2011 No. 11 "On judicial practice in criminal cases on crimes of an extremist orientation". https://www.consultant.ru/document/cons_doc_LAW_115712/.

[54] Dutch News 2023.

arrest as being on a "ridiculous and obviously politically motivated charge".[55] Aside from the ridiculousness of calling a person convicted of shooting down the civil aircraft and murder of 298 persons on board a "political prisoner", this case clearly demonstrates that not only the government opposition can fall under the repression machine and the anti-extremism legislation is applied quite broadly.

Article 280.3.

The impugned provision was adopted on 18 March 2023 and criminalises public actions aimed at discrediting the use of the Russian Armed Forces. Basically, in casu "discreditation" means denying that the Russian army is protecting the interests of the Russian Federation and its citizens, maintaining international peace and security, including public calls to prevent the use of the Armed Forces of the Russian Federation for these purposes. The provision also covers criticising execution by state bodies of the Russian Federation of their powers outside their territory for these purposes, as well as the actions of volunteer formations, organisations or individuals in the performance of tasks assigned to the Armed Forces of the Russian Federation. To be brought under criminal liability, the perpetrator must have been brought to administrative responsibility for a similar act within one year. The maximum penalty is up to five years of imprisonment. It is known that a resident of Nalchik was charged on this ground for posting a video on Instagram which describes the Russian Army's atrocities in Chechnya and Ukraine.[56] An ex-teacher from the occupied Crimea was fined 100,000 rubles for the post where he accused the Russian Army of murdering Ukrainian people.[57] In 2022 he was fined under the Code of Administrative Offences and dismissed from his job at college for showing his students a video with the Ukrainian patriotic song "Bayraktar".[58]

Article 207.3

Article 207.3 prohibiting public dissemination of knowingly false information about the use of the Armed Forces of the Russian Federation was included in the Criminal Code in March 2022 as a reaction towards the anti-war speeches and statements, as well as the dissemination of information not from official Russian sources.[59]

According to the impugned provision, the following public dissemination under the guise of reliable messages of deliberately false information is criminalised. First, it concerns the messages which go "against the good image of the Russian Armed Forces". It is worth noting that according to the Russian legislator, the Russian Army during all operations "solely protects the interests of the Russian Federation" and

---

[55] Meduza 2023.

[56] https://ovd.news/express-news/2023/07/16/astra-na-zhitelya-nalchika-zaveli-ugolovnoe-delo-o-diskreditacii-armii-rf-iz.

[57] https://www.currenttime.tv/a/sud-belozerov/32330648.html.

[58] https://www.currenttime.tv/a/krym-uvolili-prepodavatelya-bespilotnik-bayraktar/32035292.html.

[59] Путин подписал поправки о наказании до 15 лет за «фейки» о действиях российской армии, 04.03.2022 shttps://ovd.news/express-news/2022/03/04/putin-podpisal-popravki-o-nakazanii-do-15-let-za-feyki-o-deystviyah.

maintains "international peace and security". Second, it concerns the same materials but in relation to the state bodies of the Russian Federation and the extraterritorial exercise of their powers for these purposes. And third, it covers the provision of assistance by volunteer formations, organisations, or individuals in the performance of the tasks assigned to the Russian Armed Forces. The sanction for such actions can rise to 1.5 mln rubles or deprivation of liberty for up to five years.[60]

Part 2(e) of the provision prescribes aggravated liability for the same act committed on the grounds of political, ideological, racial, national or religious hatred or enmity or on the grounds of hatred or enmity against any social group. The fine is risen up to 5 mln rubles, and imprisonment can last up to 10 years.[61]

There was a number of convictions on 207.3.2(e) of the Criminal Code. A media manager Ilya Krasilshchik was sentenced in absentia to 8 years in a penal colony[62] for publicly speaking about the destruction in Ukrainian cities and the death of civilians, including in Bucha.[63] Alexander Somryakov from Krasnodar was sentenced to 6 years in prison based on posts about the killings of civilians in Ukraine, such as a Russian attack on a maternity hospital and a drama theatre in Mariupol, and general "mass slaughter of civilians" in Ukraine.[64] A famed conductor Prokhor Protasov was sentenced in absentia to 5 years imprisonment due to his posts on VKontakte social network about the tragedy in Bucha and the missile attack on a shopping centre in Kremenchuk.[65] The prison sentence in mentioned cases was also accompanied by the prohibition to administer websites or publish on the internet for the period of 4–5 years.

The convictions were also made in relation to professional journalists. The RusNews journalist Maria Ponomarenko was sentenced to 6 years in prison because

---

[60] УК РФ Статья 207.3. Публичное распространение заведомо ложной информации об использовании Вооруженных Сил Российской Федерации, исполнении государственными органами Российской Федерации своих полномочий, оказании добровольческими формированиями, организациями или лицами содействия в выполнении задач, возложенных на Вооруженные Силы Российской Федерации https://www.consultant.ru/document/cons_doc_LAW_10699/11177828050e6cdd8d29ef24e9b6095aa05e2d89/.

[61] https://www.consultant.ru/document/cons_doc_LAW_10699/11177828050e6cdd8d29ef24e9b6095aa05e2d89/.

[62] Суд заочно приговорил медиаменеджера Илью Красильщика к 8 годам колонии за пост в инстаграме и интервью, 29 June 2023, https://zona.media/news/2023/06/29/krasil.

[63] Медиаменеджера Илью Красильщика заочно приговорили к восьми годам колонии, 29 June 2023, https://ovd.news/express-news/2023/06/29/mediamenedzhera-ilyu-krasilshchika-zaochno-prigovorili-k-vosmi-godam-kolonii.

[64] Краснодарцу утвердили шесть лет колонии по статье о «фейках»: он писал про Бучу и Мариуполь, 20 July 2023, https://ovd.news/express-news/2023/07/20/krasnodarcu-utverdili-shest-let-kolonii-po-state-o-feykah-pisal-pro-buchu-i.

[65] Дирижера Протасова заочно приговорили к 5 годам колонии из-за постов про Бучу, 29.06.2023, https://ovd.news/express-news/2023/06/29/dirizhera-protasova-zaochno-prigovorili-k-5-godam-kolonii-iz-za-postov-pro.

of a post about the destruction of the drama theatre in Mariupol and banned from journalism for five years.[66]

The public figure and publicist Vladimir Kara-Murza was sentenced to twenty five years on the charges of treason, spreading false information about the Russian army and managing an "undesirable organisation". The charges on the Article 207.3 were brought after Kara-Muraza's speech in the lower house of the Arizona Senate on 15 March 2022, where he accused the Russian army of using prohibited means and methods of warfare in Ukraine.[67] In August 2024 Kara-Murza was released from Russian prison after having been granted pardon from Putin. He was exchanged for Russian citizens arrested and convicted abroad on various charges, including assassinations and espionage.[68]

On 17 May 2022, the Basmanny District Court of Moscow arrested Ukrainian TV presenter Maria Efrosinina in absentia for Instagram publications about the Russian Army's activities in Ukraine. The court ruling noted that, if remaining undetained, a Ukrainian TV presenter "may continue to engage in criminal activity".[69]

The motives of political hatred and national hatred were also mentioned in the verdict in Krasnodar Krai. The convicted published information on his Facebook page about the Russian armed forces' losses of military equipment and personnel and criticised the Russian military during the Russia-Ukraine war. Such information was deemed by the court to be not only motivated by political hatred but also by national hatred towards Chechens, who take part in the so-called "SMO".[70]

17.2.3 Code of Administrative Offences

Article 20.3 of the Russian Code of Administrative Offences bans not only the propaganda of the symbols or attributes of Nazi or extremist organisations but also their public display. Other administrative offences that are or can be motivated by extremism are the intentional public desecration of religious or theological literature, objects of religious veneration, signs or emblems, ideological symbols, and paraphernalia (Article 5.26, part 2); abusing freedom of mass information (Article 13.15); organising the activity of a social or religious organisation against which a

---

[66] Журналистке Марии Пономаренко утвердили приговор — шесть лет колонии из-за поста о Мариуполе, 20.04.2023 https://ovd.news/express-news/2023/04/20/zhurnalistke-marii-ponomarenko-utverdili-prigovor-shest-let-kolonii-iz-za.

[67] BBC 2023.

[68] https://humanrightsfirst.org/library/vladimir-kara-murza-is-free-from-russian-prison/

[69] https://ovd.news/express-news/2023/05/18/V-moskve-sud-zaochno-arestoval-ukrainskuyu-televedushchuyu-po-state-O-feykah.

[70] https://www.sova-center.ru/en/xenophobia/reports-analyses/2023/03/D47033/.

decision on suspension of activities was entered (Article 20.28); and producing and distributing extremist materials (Article 20.29).[71]

Article 20.3.1

Article 20.3.1. covers "incitement of hatred or enmity, as well as humiliation of human dignity"—that includes actions aimed at inciting hatred or enmity, as well as at humiliating the dignity of a person or a group of persons on the grounds of sex, race, nationality, language, origin, attitude to religion, as well as membership in any social group, committed publicly, including using the mass media or information and telecommunication networks, including the Internet, if these actions do not contain a criminally punishable act. The sanctions entail the imposition of an administrative fine of up to twenty thousand roubles, compulsory labour up to one hundred hours, or administrative arrest for a term of up to fifteen days; for legal entities—from two hundred and fifty thousand to five hundred thousand rubles.[72]

In 2022, the SOVA Anti-Extremist Centre recorded 65 cases filed arbitrarily under Article 20.3.1 for incitement to hatred or enmity or humiliation of human dignity based on belonging to a particular group. 64 individuals were charged (one was punished twice, and one–three times) along with one legal entity. A fine was imposed in 39 cases, community service in 10 cases, arrest for a period of five to 15 days in 10 cases, three cases were closed, and the outcome of the remaining three is unknown. In most cases, inappropriate sanctions targeted internet users for their critical statements made at different points in time against the authorities and law enforcement agencies—some of them were related to coronavirus restrictions, and some—to recent events, including military operations in Ukraine.

In 33 cases, charges under Article 20.3.1 for inciting hatred or humiliation on the basis of belonging to a social group were based on harsh statements about representatives of law enforcement agencies that contained no calls for violence.[73] People are fined for the most minor offences—for example, in mid-June 2023, the pensioner and trade union activist Oleg Tyryshkin from Kemerovo was fined 10,000 rubles for posting unfavourable comments about the FSB officers in groups on VKontakte social media outlet.[74]

Article 20.3.3

The Article 20.3.3. covers acts described in relation to the Article 207.3 of the Criminal Code which lacks a criminal character and with less hefty penalties, prescribing only fines. According to the data analysed at the end of November 2022 by the

---

[71] See Кодекс об административных нарушениях Российской Федерации (Code of Administrative Offences of the Russian Federation, 2001) Legal Provisions on Fighting Extremism, Library of Congress. Accessible at: https://www.loc.gov/item/2016295693/.

[72] КоАП РФ Статья 20.3.1. Возбуждение ненависти либо вражды, а равно унижение человеческого достоинства, https://www.consultant.ru/document/cons_doc_LAW_34661/5488786953c91e4cfc6fce519cc71d4ddd707562/.

[73] https://www.sova-center.ru/en/misuse/reports-analyses/2023/05/d47038/#_Toc135301601.

[74] Неправомерный антиэкстремизм в июне 2023 года, https://www.sova-center.ru/misuse/publications/2023/07/d48379/?sphrase_id=1569679.

Russian outlet “Mediazona”, at least 5,159 cases have been launched on this charge. However, by analysing court statistics, “Mediazona” has determined that in every ninth case the court rules in favour of the accused and people avoid penalty.[75]

In late July 2022, the Ministry of Justice circulated guidelines to the regional authorities on how to conduct case qualification under 20.3.3 of the Administrative Code and 207.3 of the Criminal Code. As instructed by the Ministry of Justice, “discrediting” is to be understood as “deliberate actions aimed at undermining confidence in government bodies and diminishing their authority”. The analysed case should include statements on the use of the armed forces of the Russian Federation and provide grounds for their negative evaluation.[76]

According to the “Mediazona”, until June 2023 the total number of cases received by Russian courts under Article 20.3.3 since its acceptance reached 7,182. The cases include statements made offline and online, picketing, displaying posters, bearing inscriptions on clothes, painting graffiti on various buildings, distributing printed campaign materials, and chanting Ukrainian songs.[77] In September 2022, the Bakhchisaray District Court of the occupied Crimea found several Crimean Tatars guilty under Articles 20.3 and 20.3.3 for playing the song “Chervona Kalyna”. That was a battle song of the Organization of Ukrainian Nationalists (founded in 1929), whose activities are recognised as extremist and banned in Russia—and the song has become extremely popular in Ukraine in the aftermath of 2022 Russia’s invasion. The court also ruled that the song’s line “liberate our Ukrainian brothers from Moscow’s shackles” discredited Russian armed forces.[78]

In 2022, Oleg Orlov, one of the leaders of the Nobel Prize-winning “Memorial” organisation, was fined fined for discrediting the armed forces for holding a poster at the Read Square in Moscow that read “USSR 1945—the country that defeated fascism, Russia 2022—the country of fascism that won”. In March 2023, he was charged with discrediting the Russian army for giving a critical comment about Russia’s war in Ukraine to a French newspaper.[79] In February 2024 he was sentenced to 2.5 years imprisonment, but in August 2024 released on the same terms as Kara-Murza.[80]

---

[75] Eight to one. More than 500 «discrediting the armed forces» cases have been dismissed by court or returned to the police, 09.03.2023, https://en.ovdinfo.org/eight-one-more-500-cases-under-article-2033-administrative-code?_gl=1*kvx8iv*_ga*MTI2ODA4NTM5MC4xNjg5NjIxMTUx*_ga_J7DH9NKJ0R*MTY4OTYyMTE1MS4xLjAuMTY4OTYyMTE1MS42MC4wLjA.

[76] Вот за аргументы, а вот за факты: Минюст разъяснил следователям и судьям, в чем отличие мнений и утверждений о спецоперации, 02.08.2022, https://www.kommersant.ru/doc/5491522.

[77] Неправомерный антиэкстремизм в июне 2023 года, https://www.sova-center.ru/misuse/publications/2023/07/d48379/?sphrase_id=1569679.

[78] https://www.sova-center.ru/en/misuse/reports-analyses/2023/05/d47038/#_Toc135301601.

[79] https://verfassungsblog.de/weaponizing-russias-memory-law/.

[80] https://www.fidh.org/en/region/europe-central-asia/russia/russia-human-rights-defender-oleg-orlov-released

Article 20.3.4.

Article 20.3.4 stipulates punishment for calls for imposing or extending political or economic sanctions against the Russian Federation, citizens of the Russian Federation, or Russian legal entities. The punishment for the first such violation within a year took the form of a fine of 30 to 50 thousand rubles for citizens, from 100 to 200 thousand for officials, and from 300 to 500 thousand for legal entities.[81]

In 2022, SOVA Anti-Extremist Centre recorded five cases filed under Article 20.3.4 that sanctioned calling for sanctions against Russia, its organisations and citizens (in 2022 there have been no cases of prosecution under the related criminal Article 284.2 for repeated calls for sanctions). In March 2022 Vladislav Arinichev was fined 35 thousand rubles for a video in which he talked about imposing sanctions and in April Andrei Balin was fined 30 thousand rubles in Tolyatti for ten VKontakte posts with a proposition to impose sanctions against Vladimir Putin and Russia in general.[82]

17.2.4 Extremism and Historical Memory

According to already mentioned "Ant-extremism Strategy", another extremist threat in Russia's understanding is the "deliberate distortion of history" and "revival of the ideas of Nazism and fascism" within foreign states.[83] According to Francine Hirsch, Putin has already cemented the memory of the Second World War as a cornerstone of Russian state ideology, and fines and prison sentences for challenging the government-prescribed narratives are a culmination of a decade-long effort to impose total control over the past and the present.[84] The 2014 Law "Against the Rehabilitation of Nazism" effectively criminalises speech regarding Russian involvement in the war prior to 1941, particularly of the Molotov-Ribbentrop Pact and of the Soviet atrocities committed in Poland and the Baltics during that period of non-aggression between the 1939 pact and the 1941 Nazi invasion of the Soviet Union.[85] Specifically, the Article 354.1 of the Russian Criminal Code establishes the following:

> The denial of the facts established by the verdict of the International Military Tribunal for the trial and punishment of the main war criminals of the European Axis countries, the approval of the crimes established by the said verdict, as well as the dissemination of knowingly false information about the activities of the USSR during the Second World War, about veterans of the Great Patriotic War, committed publicly -

---

[81] https://www.sova-center.ru/en/misuse/reports-analyses/2023/05/d47038/#_Toc135301601.

[82] Ibid.

[83] https://www.consultant.ru/document/cons_doc_LAW_194160/7df6e96cde0217dd99ef5e14d9e94bf22d63920e/.

[84] https://www.lawfaremedia.org/article/putins-memory-laws-set-stage-his-war-ukraine?fbclid=IwAR0Z_Gef7_nH2BqVzsJk5Ls9OP0-8uXMIa0WjW5siDikjQomRLVHlUF_eJc.

[85] Talley, supra note 17.

> shall be punishable by a fine in the amount of up to three million rubles, or in the amount of the wage or salary, or any other income of the convicted person for a period of up to three years, or by compulsory labor for a term of up to three years, with the deprivation of the right to hold certain positions or engage in certain activities for a term of up to three years, or by deprivation of liberty. for the same period with deprivation of the right to hold certain positions or engage in certain activities for up to three years.[86]

Significant negative changes were made in April 2021, which strengthened criminal liability for publishing on the Internet the information covered under Article 354.1 of the Criminal Code and introduced criminal penalties for "insulting the memory" of veterans and slander against them, using a vague notion of "abasement of honour and dignity".[87] On 16 April 2022 the Russian Code of Administrative Offences was amended with the new Article 13.48 establishing administrative responsibility for equating the "goals, decisions and actions" of the leadership of the USSR and Nazi Germany and for "denying the decisive role of the Soviet people" in its defeat.[88]

The primary legal mechanism for censoring materials is the Federal List of Extremist Materials, which is maintained by the Ministry of Justice and according to FIDH, includes a number of prohibited materials of purely scientific value.[89] That concerns history materials which contradict the government-prescribed narratives, such as for example Raphael Lemkin's work on the Soviet genocide in Ukraine.[90]

The anti-Ukraine sentiment is persistent within Russia. Several Russian journalists, bloggers and activists were punished under the anti-extremist law for supporting the Ukrainian versions of history in what concerns the deportation of Crimean Tartars in 1944, the Holodomor, the evaluation of the activities of Ukrainian collaborationists in 1941-1945, and other sensitive issues between Russian and Ukrainian authorities. In June 2016, Vladimir Luzgin from Perm was found guilty under Article 354.1 for reposting on his social network page a text criticising Nazis and communists and denying Ukrainian Insurgent Army's collaboration with the Third Reich.[91] The events of the 20th century remain the central point in these informational wars, but ideological battles about history can sometimes go far back to the past, like the contradictory narratives about the early Russian state (Kievan Rus'), whose political continuity is vehemently contested between Russia and Ukraine.[92]

---

[86] УК РФ Статья 354.1. Реабилитация нацизма [Criminal Code Article 354.1. Rehabilitation of Nazism] (Consultant Plus), available at https://www.consultant.ru/document/cons_doc_LAW_10699/be763c1b6a1402144cabfe17a0e2d602d4bb7598/ (accessed 29 January 2023).

[87] https://tbinternet.ohchr.org/_layouts/15/treatybodyexternal/Download.aspx?symbolno=INT%2FCCPR%2FCSS%2FRUS%2F47733&Lang=en.

[88] https://www.sova-center.ru/en/misuse/reports-analyses/2023/05/d47038/#_Toc135301601.

[89] FIDH 2021.

[90] Russian court labels Raphael Lemkin, who coined the term "genocide", an extremist, 25/11/2015, https://euromaidanpress.com/2015/11/25/russian-court-labels-raphael-lemkin-who-coined-the-term-genocide-an-extremist/.

[91] https://ehrac.org.uk/en_gb/blog/russias-overuse-and-misuse-of-anti-extremism-laws/?fbclid=IwAR2YdAdQ5CTBx4-LAecEc23DrhAsqVv1V9Sx1qQH62A6WLtSrnSuaQsldL8.

[92] Antonov 2019.

Article 19 and SOVA Centre reiterate that legislation that criminalises or sanctions expression challenging historical facts and an official version of history concerning the crimes committed during the Second World War does not pursue a legitimate aim in imposing restrictions on freedom of expression. Moreover, it is poorly formulated and causes interference with the freedom to seek historical truth.[93] The war against Ukraine only worsened the situation. For example, a resident of Kransoyarsk was charged with spreading false information about the Russian army and exonerating Nazism for posting on social media that "Stalin was as much of an aggressor as Hitler" and that the Russian armed forces were killing civilians and destroying cities in Ukraine (by having referred to the bombing of the theatre in the besieged Mariupol in April 2022).[94]

The 2012 Law on Foreign Agents[95] did not directly intend to take issue with historical interpretations. Indirectly, this Law affected a few Russian non-profit organisations which promote principles that contradict the official conservative narratives: such as non-discrimination of LGBT, democracy, gender equality, and, unsurprisingly, several "Memorial" organisations that investigate the crimes of the Soviet regime, including the mass repressions. In 2014 the first "Memorial" organisation in Moscow was brought on the list of foreign agents by the Ministry of Justice, with this decision being confirmed by courts. This practice was followed in other regions of Russia.[96]

On 13 January 2022 the Supreme Court in Moscow has ordered the liquidation of Memorial.[97] On 28 February 2022, the Appeal Board of Russia's Supreme Court dismissed Memorial's appeal against the decision of the Supreme Court to liquidate the organisation and the decision was left unchanged.[98] Even though the formal ground for liquidating Memorial is incompliance with the "Foreign agents'" law, the real reason behind such actions is organisation's damage to the Russian regime's reputation by documenting Stalinist crimes and by monitoring present-day repression of the political opposition.[99] The repressions against "Memorial" activists continue even after its dissolution, such as a criminal case against a deputy chairman of "Memorial" Oleg Orlov was opened for "discreditation of the Russian Armed Forces"

[93] https://u.pcloud.link/publink/show?code=XZqg3HkZU9jKLdd0hGH23cIdIrhCO7BnNLhX.

[94] https://verfassungsblog.de/weaponizing-russias-memory-law/.

[95] Федеральны˘и закон (20.7.2012, No.121-ФЗ) "О внесении изменени˘и в отдельные законодательные акты Росси˘иско˘и Федерации в части регулирования деятельности некоммерческих организаци˘и, выполняющих функции иностранного агента" от [Federal Law "On Bringing Amendments in Particular Legislative Acts of the RF Concerning the Regulation of Activities of Non-Commercial Organizations that Carry out Functions of a Foreign Agent"].

[96] Antonov 2019.

[97] https://ipn.gov.pl/en/news/9191,The-Supreme-Court-in-Moscow-has-ordered-the-liquidation-of-Memorial-The-oldest-o.html.

[98] https://www.memo.ru/en-us/memorial/departments/intermemorial/news/690.

[99] https://sceeus.se/en/publications/liquidation-of-a-foreign-agent-the-historical-significance-of-the-dissolution-of-memorial/.

(Article 280.3(1) of the Criminal Code) in his article, "They wanted fascism. They got it".[100]

In June 2022 the ECHR issued a judgment in *Ecodefence and Others v. Russia,* based on a number of complaints by Russian NGOs recognised as entities performing the functions of a "foreign agent", which caused significant difficulties in their work, including further dissolution and bans. The ECtHR ruled creation of a special "foreign agent" status was not justified, not "necessary in a democratic society," and, therefore, Russia violated the applicant's right to freedom of assembly and association in the light of Article 10 on the right to freedom of expression.[101] Nevertheless, the pressure on NGOs and civil society has become even harder.

17.2.5 International Covenant on Civil and Political Rights (ICCPR)

Russia ratified the International Covenant on Civil and Political Rights in 1973. It further ratified the First Optional Protocol in 1991, thereby submitting to the individual complaints procedure. In the 2023 Concluding Observations on the Eighth Periodic Report for the Russian Federation, the Human Rights Committee expressed concern about manifestations of Islamophobia and anti-Semitism along with other racist and xenophobic acts, as well as the proliferation of extremist groups such as ultra-nationalist, racist, and neo-Nazi groups, and, moreover, the use of discriminatory language against national, ethnic, religious or other minorities.[102] The report also referred to discrimination, hate speech, and violence against lesbian, gay, bisexual and transgender (LGBT) individuals and activists as well as violations of their rights to freedom of expression and assembly.[103]

Regarding the individual complaint's procedure, there have been 34 complaints lodged against Russia for supposed violations of the ICCPR. In the case *Irina Fedotova v Russian Federation* (2012), the applicant, an openly lesbian woman, had displayed posters stating 'Homosexuality is normal' and 'I am proud of my homosexuality'. She was subsequently convicted by a Justice of the Peace for an administrative offence under Section 3.10 of the Ryazan Region Law concerning "public actions aimed at the propaganda of homosexuality" and fined 1,500 Russian Roubles.[104] The Committee found that this conviction and sentence violated Articles 19 (freedom of

[100] https://www.amnesty.org/en/latest/news/2023/06/russia-renowned-human-rights-defender-oleg-orlov-on-trial-for-discrediting-russian-army/.

[101] https://www.sova-center.ru/en/misuse/reports-analyses/2023/05/d47038/#_Toc135301601.

[102] United Nations Human Rights Committee 2015.

[103] Ibid.

[104] Equal Rights Trust, Irina Fedotova v Russian Federation case summary. https://www.equalrightstrust.org/ertdocumentbank/Case%20Summary%20Irina%20Fedotova%20v%20Russian%20Federation%20(HRC%20Communication)-%20Final.pdf?utm_conten.

expression) and 26 (equality before law) of the International Covenant on Civil and Political Rights (ICCPR).

In the latest reporting period, in the 2023 concluding observations, the Committee was concerned about manifestations of hate speech, particularly during electoral campaigns, by politicians and religious leaders, in particular against migrants, refugees, Roma, and lesbian, gay, bisexual and transgender persons. The especially deteriorate position of the LGBTQI community was observed, including as a result of the 2013 law banning the dissemination of "propaganda" on non-traditional sexual relations among minors and the subsequent ban on the "denial of family values" and the "promotion", among persons of all ages, of non-traditional sexual orientations. Lesbian, gay, bisexual and transgender persons are not recognised in the Criminal Code as a social group for the purpose of determining the aggravating circumstances of offences connected with violence and attacks and their persistent harassment (apart from the police, as will be discussed in the ECtHR section).

Russia was recommended to combat all forms of social stigmatisation, including hate speech against persons based on their sexual orientation or gender identity, including by providing adequate training for law enforcement officials, prosecutors and members of the judiciary; amending the Criminal Code to include lesbian, gay, bisexual and transgender persons as a group for the purpose of determining the aggravated circumstances of an offence; and raising awareness to promote respect for diversity among the general public. Russia was also recommended to repeal the 2013 law banning the dissemination of "propaganda" on non-traditional sexual relations among minors and any other legislation stigmatising or discriminating against lesbian, gay, bisexual, and transgender persons.[105]

As for the domestic measures, the Russian Human Rights Commissioner claimed that awareness-raising campaigns to promote respect for human rights and tolerance for diversity were conducted. In 2020 12 projects and 44 events were implemented, in 2021—twelve projects and 66 events (total coverage of more than 5 million people), and in the first eight months of 2022–21, projects and events were implemented, with over 50 events organised for various target audiences.[106] From 2017 to 2022 the Commissioner received 18 appeals concerning discrimination on the grounds of sexual orientation. Applicants were given explanations of the current legislation on 11 appeals, inspections were conducted on 7 appeals, and no violations of the rights of the applicants were found.[107] However, given the Russian government's recent focus on "traditional values" and promotion of families as a "union between man and women", the objectivity of such reviews is raising serious doubts.

---

[105] https://tbinternet.ohchr.org/_layouts/15/treatybodyexternal/Download.aspx?symbolno=CCPR%2FC%2FRUS%2FCO%2F8&Lang=en. para 13.

[106] Comments by the Commissioner for Human Rights in the Russian Federation on Compliance with the International Covenant on Civil and Political Rights by the Russian Federation. https://tbinternet.ohchr.org/_layouts/15/treatybodyexternal/Download.aspx?symbolno=INT%2FCCPR%2FNHS%2FRUS%2F50544&Lang=en.

[107] https://tbinternet.ohchr.org/_layouts/15/treatybodyexternal/Download.aspx?symbolno=INT%2FCCPR%2FNHS%2FRUS%2F50545&Lang=en.

Nevertheless, despite the government's assurances, civil society organisations remain critical of Russia's actions in implementing the recommendations. First, the government did not revise the Federal Law on "Combating Extremist Activity" which was criticised for its vague wording. Second, the regulations regarding the Federal List of Extremist Materials also have not changed."[108] The persecution of LGBTQI+ persons remain a blind spot for the government's attention. In May 2022 Russia's biggest LGBT+ group "Sphere" has been shut down.[109] December 2022, President Vladimir Putin signed into law a bill which significantly expands Russia's restrictions on 'gay propaganda'—referring to any material relating to the LGBTQI+ community.[110] According to the HRW assessment, this law is "one further step in representing LGBT+ rights as a foreign threat and a Trojan-horse 'enemy within'".[111] In April 2023 two young men were arrested on this law due to the content on their social media pages describing their life as a gay couple.[112] In November 2023, the Russian Supreme court labelled the "international LGBT movement" as an "extremist organisation" and banned its activities for allegedly "inciting social and religious discord".[113]

Under Russian procedural legislation, Committee decisions are not expressly mentioned as a ground for reopening cases at the domestic level. While ECtHR judgments were directly mentioned in Russian procedural legislation, this was changed by federal laws of 11 June 2022, which provide that only ECtHR judgments which became final before 15 March 2022 can be a ground for reopening cases. However, in the case of Committee decisions, there is case law of the Supreme and Constitutional Courts of Russia recognising the binding nature of recommendations of the Committees.[114] Moreover, complaints to the Human Rights Committee can potentially become the only remedy for those seeking redress in light of Russia's failed court system, but recent amendments which allow not enforcing decisions which contradict Russia's national laws make this remedy seem like a bleak hope for at least symbolic justice.

[108] https://tbinternet.ohchr.org/_layouts/15/treatybodyexternal/Download.aspx?symbolno=INT%2FCCPR%2FCSS%2FRUS%2F47733&Lang=en.

[109] https://www.humanium.org/en/russia-suppresses-an-organization-defending-lgbtqia-rights-across-russia/.

[110] https://www.ibanet.org/LGBTQI-rights-legislative-changes-worldwide-flux.

[111] Human Rights Watch 2023.

[112] The Moscow Times 2023.

[113] https://www.hrw.org/news/2023/11/30/russia-supreme-court-bans-lgbt-movement-extremist

[114] See Decision of the Constitutional Court of Russia of 28 June 2012 No 1248-O; Decision of the Supreme Court of Russia of 28 December 2012 No 55-O18-4; Decision of the Supreme Court of Russia of 24 July 2017 No 46-KG17-24.

17.3 International Convention on the Elimination of All Forms of Racial Discrimination (CERD)

Russia signed ICERD in 1966 and ratified the treaty in 1969. In 2023, the Committee on the Elimination of Racial Discrimination (hereinafter—UN-CERD) adopted its Concluding Observations which contained several provisions relevant to hateful expression. First, the Committee reiterated its previous recommendation to include a clear definition of direct and indirect forms of racial discrimination, which is currently absent within domestic legislation, contrary to the requirements of ICERD.[115]

Second, like the UN-HRC's 2015 Concluding Observations, UN-CERD expressed concern about the broad definition of extremist activity under Russian Federal Law and its potential to silence individuals arbitrarily, in particular, those belonging to groups vulnerable to discrimination, such as ethnic minorities, indigenous peoples or non-citizens.[116] In its response, the Russian delegation called such accusations unjustified, disrespectful to Russia's legal system and an attempt of the "collective West" to create a negative image for their country.[117]

The third and most important point is where UN-CERD noted the widespread hate crime and racist hate speech and the dissemination of negative stereotypes against Roma communities and other ethnic minorities, Indigenous Peoples, and migrants and widespread impunity for such offences. Moreover, racist hate speech is widely utilised by politicians, including members of the parliament, and public figures, including religious leaders, with no adequate reaction from the government to such actions. The UN-CERD recommended that Russia develop a system for filing complaints of incidents of hate crime and hate speech and ensure the system's accessibility and availability to vulnerable groups.[118] However, the Russian government notes that such remarks are inconsistent with reality, and the Committee is simply reluctant to see how many positive things are done for the well-being of indigenous people and "gypsies" (original language used).[119]

Regarding the individual complaints' procedure, there have been 2 cases lodged against Russia, but both were deemed inadmissible by the Committee.

In the 2023 concluding observations on Russia, in light of the ongoing armed conflict with Ukraine, the UN-CERD urged to adopt measures to monitor and combat racist hate speech, incitement to and promotion of racial hatred and discrimination,

---

[115] United Nations Committee on the Elimination of Racial Discrimination, Concluding observations on the twenty-fifth and twenty-sixth periodic reports of the Russian Federation, 2017. https://tbinternet.ohchr.org/_layouts/15/treatybodyexternal/Download.aspx?symbolno=CERD%2FC%2FRUS%2FCO%2F25-26&Lang=en.

[116] Ibid.

[117] https://tbinternet.ohchr.org/_layouts/15/treatybodyexternal/Download.aspx?symbolno=INT%2FCERD%2FCOB%2FRUS%2F52929&Lang=en.

[118] https://tbinternet.ohchr.org/_layouts/15/treatybodyexternal/Download.aspx?symbolno=CERD%2FC%2FRUS%2FCO%2F25-26&Lang=en.

[119] https://tbinternet.ohchr.org/_layouts/15/treatybodyexternal/Download.aspx?symbolno=INT%2FCERD%2FCOB%2FRUS%2F52929&Lang=en.

including on State-owned media and by State officials and public figures, targeted at ethnic Ukrainians.[120] The UN-CERD in 2017 Concluding Observations referred to the situation in Crimea and noted the administrative or legislative measures that discriminate against ethnic groups or indigenous peoples, including in relation to nationality and citizenship rights, the registration of religious communities and the operation of Crimean Tatar representative institutions and functioning of the Ukrainian language.[121]

The Committee gave a specific reference to the 2017 Order on provisional measures in Ukraine v. Russia case, which directly concerns the question of Russia's racial discrimination of Crimean Tatars and Ukrainians on the Russia-occupied peninsula. According to Ukraine, the Russian Federation has engaged in a sustained campaign of racial discrimination, carried out since 2014, against the Crimean Tatar and Ukrainian communities in Crimea.[122] Additionally, it was claimed that the Russian Federation violated its obligations under CERD by systematically discriminating against and mistreating the Crimean Tatars and ethnic Ukrainians in Crimea, suppressing the political and cultural expression of Crimean Tatar identity and banning the Mejlis (Crimean Tatars' representative body) on extremist grounds.[123] In 2024, the ICJ issued a final judgement on the case, concluding that there was insufficient evidence to prove that such treatment was based on the purely racial or ethnic grounds, but rather on political affiliation. Thus, there was no violation of CERD in regards to Crimean Tatars.[124] Nevertheless, such approach was severely criticised by judge Sebutinde in her dissenting opinion.[125]

To provide a background, prior to purported annexation, Crimea has 250 local mejlises with over two thousand people associated with them.[126] On 15 April 2016, Crimea's so-called prosecutor, Natalia Poklonskaya, banned the Mejlis, Crimean Tatars' representative body in Crimea, labelling it "an extremist organization" and consequently Russia-controlled Crimea's Supreme Court banned the Mejlis on 26 April 2016.[127] These measures were criticised and labelled unjustified by the CoE[128] and Human Rights Watch.[129]

In assessing the plausibility of claimed rights under CERD, Judge Crawford referred to the historical persecution of the Crimean Tatars and the role of the Mejlis

120 https://tbinternet.ohchr.org/_layouts/15/treatybodyexternal/Download.aspx?symbolno=CERD%2FC%2FRUS%2FCO%2F25-26&Lang=en.

121 Ibid.

122 https://www.icj-cij.org/sites/default/files/case-related/166/166-20191108-JUD-01-00-EN.pdf, para 130.

123 https://www.icj-cij.org/sites/default/files/case-related/166/166-20170419-ORD-01-00-EN.pdf, para 38.

124 https://www.icj-cij.org/sites/default/files/case-related/166/166-20240131-jud-01-00-en.pdf

125 https://www.icj-cij.org/sites/default/files/case-related/166/166-20240131-jud-01-06-en.pdf

126 OSCE 2013.

127 Knott 2016.

128 COE 2016.

129 Human Rights Watch 2016a, b.

in advancing and protecting the rights of the people it represents.[130] However, the situation of Crimean Tatars had only deteriorated. In 2023 the UN-CERD referred to the destruction of cultural heritage, restriction of civil and political rights and education provision in a native language, as well as forced conscription into the Russian army and urged Russia to stop such practices. However, given the Russian comments on the 2023 Concluding observation, the prospect of a reasonable dialogue on the matter remains bleak. Russia does not recognise Crimea to be "occupied" and calls a war against Ukraine a "humanitarian mission" aiming to protect the Russian-speaking population and stated that pertaining Committee's recommendations will not be implemented. The same concerns recommendations on Roma's discrimination, inter-ethnic conflicts, and dire position of indigenous peoples.[131]

17.4 Council of Europe

17.4.1 General Remarks

Strasbourg's influence can be seen in the Russian legal system as the Constitutional Court often cites the ECHR as an interpretative instrument and refers to it in its judgements. For example, in a 1999 case regarding freedom of religion, the Court referred to the ECtHR's 1993 judgement in *Kokkinakis v. Greece* case.[132]

However, after the ECtHR made a contentious ruling in 2011 that diverged from the opinion of the CCRF and essentially overruled a decision by the Russian Constitutional Court, thereby provoking a storm of protest from Russia's leading jurists and politicians,[133] relations have become turbulent when for the first time. The case concerns a military serviceman Konstantin Markin who was denied 3-year parental leave because only female military personnel were entitled to it, regardless of him being a single parent. The ECtHR ruled that the difference in treatment was not justified and thus constituted discrimination in combination with the breach of the right to private/family life.[134] Within the chamber judgement, the Court quite harshly criticised the CCRF's reasoning as being "unconvincing" and pointed to "gender prejudices" in the decision. Russian lawyers perceived the decision as showing disrespect for Russia's sovereignty and its legislature and interference in the internal affairs of Russia,[135] even though the Grand Chamber's judgement has significantly softened the wording. In 2013, Mr Markin petitioned for the reopening of procedures in his case because of the ECtHR's ruling, and CCRF ruled that district courts must reopen

[130] https://www.icj-cij.org/sites/default/files/case-related/166/166-20170419-ORD-01-05-EN.pdf.

[131] https://tbinternet.ohchr.org/_layouts/15/treatybodyexternal/Download.aspx?symbolno=INT%2FCERD%2FCOB%2FRUS%2F52929&Lang=en.

[132] Pomeranz 2012.

[133] Ibid.

[134] Markin v Russia.

[135] Huntley 2012.

proceedings in such cases, but if a decision cannot be enforced due to inconsistency with domestic law, CCRF must assess the constitutionality of such provisions.[136]

In 2015 the amended Constitutional Court Act granted the CCRF the right to rule that a decision of an international court cannot be enforced if it contradicts the Russian constitutional norms.[137] On 19 April 2016, the CCRF ruled for the first time that an ECtHR decision cannot be implemented in Russia because measures aimed at its implementation would contradict the Russian Constitution.[138] The 2020 amendments to the Russian Constitution introduced into Article 79 a provision stipulating that "decisions of interstate bodies" shall not be "subject to enforcement in the Russian Federation" if they are inconsistent with the Constitution.[139]

However, after 24 February 2022 and Russia's full-scale invasion of Ukraine, its further membership in the CoE was no longer possible. On 15 March 2022, the CoE Parliamentary Assembly unanimously agreed that Russia should be excluded from the organisation,[140] and on the same day the Russian Government announced its withdrawal from the CoE with a subsequent denunciation of the European Convention on Human Rights (hereinafter—ECHR).[141] The official withdrawal date was set to 16 September 2022. In June 2022 the Russian parliament adopted bills denouncing ECtHR's jurisdiction, which, in the words of the parliament speaker "has become an instrument of the political battle against our country in the hands of Western politicians."[142] Russia will also not execute judgements issued after 15 March 2022. On 23 February 2023 the Federal Law which terminates the validity of the CoE international treaties with regard to the Russian Federation, was adopted.[143]

On 22 March 2022, the ECtHR passed a resolution, reaffirming its jurisdiction over any applications filed prior to the official withdrawal date and re-starting consideration of current and pending cases against Russia. Moreover, the outcomes of these cases will continue to be legally binding for Russia. Overall, there were 17,450 cases pending against Russia at the time of withdrawal, including several inter-state cases brought by Ukraine, Georgia and the Netherlands.[144] 2,129 judgments and decisions were to be fully implemented by Russia and remain pending before the Committee of Ministers.[145]

---

[136] Levin and Schwarz 2015.

[137] https://www.osw.waw.pl/en/publikacje/analyses/2016-04-20/russia-has-refused-to-execute-european-court-human-rights-judgment.

[138] Russian Federation: Constitutional Court Allows Country to Ignore ECHR Rulings, 18 May 2015. https://www.loc.gov/item/global-legal-monitor/2016-05-18/russian-federation-constitutional-court-allows-country-to-ignore-echr-rulings/.

[139] Amnesty International 2020.

[140] CEO 2022.

[141] https://search.coe.int/cm/pages/result_details.aspx?objectid=0900001680a5d7d9.

[142] Aljazeera 2022.

[143] Federal Law On the Termination of International Treaties of the Council of Europe with Regard to the Russian Federation http://en.kremlin.ru/acts/news/70605.

[144] Leach 2022.

[145] https://www.coe.int/en/web/portal/-/russia-ceases-to-be-party-to-the-european-convention-on-human-rights.

Since March 2022, Russia has ceased communicating with both the ECtHR and the Committee of Ministers and has not provided information about the progress of execution of the ECtHR's judgments.[146] As poignantly observed by Courtney Hillebrecht, by adjudicating on cases concerning Russia's behaviour the ECtHR in a symbolic way can acknowledge the harms done, give a voice to victims and reassert its position as the "conscience of Europe."[147]

17.4.2 Relevant Case Law

In *Pavel Ivanov v. Russia* and *Stomakhin v. Russia* the applicants' convictions of public incitement to ethnic, racial and religious hatred through the use of the mass media (Article 282.1 of the Criminal Code) were both deemed to fall short of Article 10 protection. *Pavel Ivanov v. Russia* concerned pure anti-Semitic speech[148] and in *Atamanchuk v. Russia* the applicant unfavourably spoke about the "non-Slavic" residents of Kuban region.[149] The sanctions for the impugned speeches were also found in conformity with Article 10.

However, things get more complicated when politically sensitive issues come into play. In *Stomakhin v. Russia* the journalist received a five-year prison sentence and a three-year ban on professional activities for having published a newsletter that criticised the conduct of Russia's war in Chechnya. The articles were found to incite "hatred and enmity", including those which were levelled against the Russian government, such as calls to record atrocities committed by the Russian authorities in Chechnya and a request to abstain from the presidential elections. The ECtHR found that there was no "pressing social need" to convict the Applicant and the imposed penalty was inconsistent with Article 10 of the ECHR.[150] In *Savva Terentyev v. Russia* the applicant's online comments criticising police abuse resulted in a one-year suspended sentence for "publicly inciting hatred and enmity and humiliating the dignity" (Article 282.1 of the Criminal Code) of police officers on the grounds of their membership of a "social group". The ECtHR held that the Applicant's conviction was a disproportionate interference with his right to freedom of expression and the Russian laws regulating hate speech and incitement to violence

[146] Ausra Padskocimaite 2023.

[147] Hillebrecht 2022.

[148] Pavel Ivanov v. Russia, https://globalfreedomofexpression.columbia.edu/cases/pavel-ivanov-v-russia/.

[149] Atamanchuk v. Russia, https://globalfreedomofexpression.columbia.edu/cases/atamanchuk-v-russia/.

[150] Stomakhin v. Russia, https://globalfreedomofexpression.columbia.edu/cases/stomakhin-v-russia/.

lack sufficient clarity. These Russian laws, according to the ECtHR, allow "to prosecute for such offences becomes too broad and potentially subject to abuse through selective enforcement".[151]

In *Alekhina and Others v Russia,* the three members of the band Pussy Riot band were charged with "hooliganism motivated by religious hatred" (Article 213(2)) for chanting "Mother of God, Drive Putin away" in the Cathedral of Christ the Saviour in Moscow. The applicants were sentenced to a two-year prison sentence. The ECtHR ruled that there is insufficient evidence to discern "incitement to religious hatred" in the applicants' conduct and a two-year prison sentence was disproportionate to the legitimate aims pursued.[152]

In *Ibragim Ibgragimov and Others v. Russia* the Prosecutor of the Tatarstan Republic initiated criminal proceedings against members of the religious movement Nurculuk (Нурджулар) for distributing Said Nursi's books from the Risale-I Nur Collection. These individuals were charged with incitement of hatred or discord, as well as abasement of human dignity (Article 282 of the Criminal Code). The ECtHR unanimously concluded that Russia violated the right to freedom of expression by prohibiting the publication and distribution of religious books as there was no substantiated evidence indicating any harmful consequences resulting from individuals reading it. Additionally, the Court dismissed the government's objection to the case under Article 17 since the books promoted a moderate and non-violent understanding of Islam.[153]

In *Yefremov and Youth Human Rights group v Russia*, the first applicant (a head of the Youth Human Rights group) negatively spoke of the Russian Orthodox Church and the country's ruling party as "fooling people with fairy-tales about our good life while ranking in money". The applicant was subsequently charged under Article 282.1 with undermined the dignity of religious believers, added to the list of terrorists and extremists, and placed in a psychiatric ward. His association was subsequently dissolved. The ECtHR found that there had been a violation of Article 10 as the post could not incite violence, hatred or intolerance and that "merely because a remark may be perceived as offence or insulting by particular individuals or groups of individuals does not mean that it constitutes hate speech".[154]

The latest decision in *Taganrog LRO and Others v. Russia*[155] is harshly criticising Russian anti-extremism legislation. The case concerns various actions taken against Jehovah's Witnesses religious organisations in Russia, including already described amendments to anti-extremist legislation paving the way to the banning of their religious literature and international website and the eventual nationwide ban on

---

[151] Savva Terentyev v. Russia, https://globalfreedomofexpression.columbia.edu/cases/savva-terentyev-v-russia/, para 85.

[152] Mariya Alekhina and Others v. Russia—38004/12.

[153] Ibragim Ibgragimov and Others v. Russia, https://globalfreedomofexpression.columbia.edu/cases/ibragim-ibgragimov-and-others-v-russia/.

[154] Yefimov and Youth Human Rights Group v. Russia, https://globalfreedomofexpression.columbia.edu/cases/yefimov-and-youth-human-rights-group-v-russia/, para 44.

[155] Taganrog LRO and Others v. Russia, Application nos. 32401/10 and 19 others.

Jehovah's Witnesses religious organisations and the criminal prosecution of hundreds of individual believers.[156]

The ECtHR reiterated that the extremely broad definition of "extremist activities" which does not require any elements of violence or hatred opens the possibility of having individuals and organisations prosecuted on extremism charges for entirely peaceful forms of expression or worship. That broad definition of "extremism" not only led to arbitrary prosecutions but also prevented individuals or organisations from being able to anticipate that their conduct, even entirely devoid of hatred or animosity.[157] Accordingly, the ECtHR found the definitions of "extremism" and "extremist activities", as formulated and applied in practice by the Russian authorities, falling short of the lawfulness requirement. Moreover, there were no adequate and effective safeguards against an excessively broad interpretation of the concept of "extremism". Hence, the interference on the charge of "proclaiming superiority" was not "prescribed by law".[158]

Since the June 2022 judgment, the CoE Committee of Ministers has strongly urged Russia to reverse the 2017 Supreme Court decision that effectively banned the religious activities of Jehovah's Witnesses. The Committee has also called on Russia "to review the anti-extremism legislation declaring Jehovah['s] Witnesses['] organisations extremist ... ; to discontinue all criminal proceedings against Jehovah's Witnesses and to release those imprisoned, fully erase the consequences of their convictions, as well as to return the applicant's withheld property or pay compensation for it."[159] In a letter to Russia's Minister of Foreign Affairs dated 9 December 2022, the CoE Secretary General urged Russia to comply with recent judgments of the ECtHR,[160] however, there is no sign any change in Russia's attitude will follow.

References

Aljazeera (2022) Russian MPs Vote to Quit European Court of Human Rights. The Move Formalised the Broken Ties between Russia and the Council of Europe, of Which the ECHR is a Part. https://www.aljazeera.com/news/2022/6/7/russia-exits-european-court-of-human-rights-jurisdiction.

Amnesty (2020) Europe/Russia: Venice Commission Denounces Putin Constitutional Amendments Which Avoid Execution of ECtHR Rulings. https://www.amnesty.org/en/latest/news/2020/06/europerussia-venice-commission-denounces-putin-constitutional-amendments-which-avoid-execution-of-ecthr-rulings/.

---

[156] Council of Europe Urges Russia to Reverse Ban on Jehovah's Witnesses, 21 December 2022, https://www.jw.org/en/news/region/russia/Council-of-Europe-Urges-Russia-to-Reverse-Ban-on-Jehovahs-Witnesses/.

[157] Taganrog LRO and Others v. Russia, Application nos. 32401/10 and 19 others, 7 June 2022, para 158.

[158] Taganrog LRO and Others v. Russia, https://hudoc.echr.coe.int/eng?i=001-217535.

[159] Ibid., para 159.

[160] https://rm.coe.int/letter-for-the-attention-of-mr-sergey-lavrov-minister-for-foreign-affa/1680a956f6.

Amnesty (2023) Russia: Renowned Human Rights Defender Oleg Orlov on Trial for "Discrediting" Russian Army. https://www.amnesty.org/en/latest/news/2023/06/russia-renowned-human-rights-defender-oleg-orlov-on-trial-for-discrediting-russian-army/.

Antonov M (2019) Law and Memory Politics in Russia. https://www.nomos-elibrary.de/10.5771/0030-6444-2019-4-410.pdf.

Arnold A (2023) RUSSIA: Judges 'Ignore Completely' Amended Supreme Court Guidance on Extremism Law Application. https://www.forum18.org/archive.php?article_id=2842.

Article 19 (2016) Russia: Drop Charges against blogger Anton Nossik. https://www.article19.org/resources/%E2%80%A8russia-drop-charges-against-blogger-anton-nossik/.

Baran EB, Knox Z (2019) The 2002 Russian Anti-Extremism Law: An Introduction. Soviet & Post-Soviet Review 46:97.

Butler W (2019) Five Generations of Russian Constitutions: Russia as Part of the Western Legal Heritage. BRICS Law Journal 6(3):13–21. https://doi.org/10.21684/2412-2343-2019-6-3-13-21.

COE (2016) Crimea: Commissioner Urges a Reversal of the Ban on the Mejlis. https://www.coe.int/ca/web/portal/full-news/-/asset_publisher/y5xQt7QdunzT/content/crimea-commissioner-urges-a-reversal-of-the-ban-on-the-mejlis.

COE (2022) Consequences of the Russian Federation's Aggression against Ukraine. Opinion 300. https://pace.coe.int/en/files/29885/html.

COE (2022) https://www.coe.int/en/web/portal/-/russia-ceases-to-be-party-to-the-european-convention-on-human-rights.

Current Time TV (2023) https://www.currenttime.tv/a/sud-belozerov/32330648.html.

Digital Report Analytica (2017) The Yarovaya Law: One Year Afte. https://analytica.digital.report/wp-content/uploads/2017/07/The-Yarovaya-Law.pdf.

Dutch News (2023) Igor Girkin, Found Guilty of Downing MH17, Is Arrested in Russia. https://www.dutchnews.nl/2023/07/igor-girkin-found-guilty-of-downing-mh17-is-arrested-in-russia/.

Equal Rights Trust (2012) Irina Fedotova v Russian Federation case summary. https://www.equalrightstrust.org/ertdocumentbank/Case%20Summary%20Irina%20Fedotova%20v%20Russian%20Federation%20(HRC%20Communicatio)-%20Final.pdf?utm_conten.

FIDH (2021) Crimes Against History. https://www.fidh.org/IMG/pdf/russie-_pad-uk-web.pdf.

Georgesco F (2022) The Russian Myth of the Great Patriotic War and Its Manipulations. Le Monde. https://www.lemonde.fr/en/international/article/2022/05/03/the-russian-myth-of-the-great-patriotic-war-and-its-manipulations_5982273_4.html.

Gowling WLG (2016) Yarovaya Law: Russian Parliament passes package of laws on data retention obligations. https://gowlingwlg.com/en/insights-resources/articles/2016/yarovaya-law-russian-parliament-passes-package-of/.

Halpert M (2022) Russian Court Upholds Ban on Meta for 'Extremist' Activities. https://www.forbes.com/sites/madelinehalpert/2022/06/20/russian-court-upholds-ban-on-meta-for-extremist-activities/?sh=707c84552db3.

Hillebrecht C (2022) Rights at Risk: Russia's Withdrawal from the ECtHR. https://www.openglobalrights.org/rights-at-risk-russias-withdrawal-from-the-ecthr/.

https://tbinternet.ohchr.org/_layouts/15/treatybodyexternal/Download.aspx?symbolno=CCPR%2FC%2FRUS%2FCO%2F8&Lang=en.

Human Rights Watch (2016) Crimean Tatar Elected Body Banned in Russia. https://www.hrw.org/news/2016/09/29/crimean-tatar-elected-body-banned-russia.

Human Rights Watch (2016) Russia: 'Big Brother' Law Harms Security. https://www.hrw.org/news/2016/07/12/russia-big-brother-law-harms-security-rights.

Huntley S (2012) Konstantin Markin Threw a Military Court into a Dilemma: To Side with the ECHR or to Support the Constitutional Court of the Russian Federation. http://echrrussia.blogspot.com/2012/08/konstantin-markin-threw-military-court.html.

Kara-Murza V (2023) Russian Opposition Figure Jailed for 25 years. BBC. https://www.bbc.com/news/world-europe-65297003.

Knott E (2016) What the Banning of Crimean Tatars' Mejlis Means. https://www.atlanticcouncil.org/blogs/ukrainealert/what-the-banning-of-crimean-tatars-mejlis-means/.
Leach P (2022) A Time of Reckoning? Russia and the Council of Europe. https://strasbourgobservers.com/2022/03/17/a-time-of-reckoning-russia-and-the-council-of-europe/.
Levin I, Schwarz M (2015) At a Crossroads: Russia and the ECHR in the Aftermath of Markin. VerfBlog, 2015/1/30. https://verfassungsblog.de/crossroads-russia-echr-aftermath-markin-2/, https://doi.org/10.17176/20181005-150226-0.
Meduza (2023) Alexey Navalny Calls Igor Strelkov 'Political Prisoner'. https://meduza.io/en/news/2023/07/25/alexey-navalny-calls-igor-strelkov-political-prisoner.
OSCE (2013) The Integration of Formerly Deported People in Crimea, Ukraine: Needs Assessment. https://www.osce.org/files/f/documents/e/a/104309.pdf.
Padskocimaite A (2023) https://strasbourgobservers.com/2023/05/15/execution-of-the-ecthrs-judgments-against-russia-some-legal-and-political-aspects/.
Pomeranz WE (2012) Uneasy Partners: Russia and the European Court of Human Rights. https://corteidh.or.cr/tablas/r29628.pdf.
Russia: Court Bans Jehovah's Witnesses. Withdraw Lawsuit, Protect Religious Freedom. https://www.hrw.org/news/2017/04/20/russia-court-bans-jehovahs-witnesses.
Sherstoboeva E, Pavlenko V (2018) Freedom of Expression and Regulation of Extremism in Russia in the Context of the Council of Europe Standards. In: Internet Science. Cham, Springer International Publishing, pp 101–115.
Szymanska J (2019) Russia's Overuse and Misuse of Anti-Extremism Laws. https://ehrac.org.uk/en_gb/blog/russias-overuse-and-misuse-of-anti-extremism-laws/?fbclid=IwAR2YdAdQ5CTBx4-LAecEc23DrhAsqVv1v9Sx1qQH62A6WLtSrnSuaQsldL8.
Tabachnik A. The Yarovaya Law as an Example of Ill-conceived Legislation, Center for Cyber, Law and Policy (CCLP). https://cyber.haifa.ac.il/index.php/all-posts/yarovaya-law.
The Moscow Times (2022) Russia Adds Meta to List of 'Terrorist and Extremist' Orgs. https://www.themoscowtimes.com/2022/10/11/russia-adds-meta-to-list-of-terrorist-and-extremist-orgs-a79057.
United Nations Human Rights Committee (2015) Concluding Observations on the Seventh Periodic Report of the Russian Federation. http://docstore.ohchr.org/SelfServices/FilesHandler.ashx?enc=6QkG1d%2FPPRiCAqhKb7yhstWB5OJfDOQhMEkiX20XNhIfwS44vVjDCG9yOfCaGgJ%2B4aMVruPFpyUaMYJvfEOEBQCPHWJdUArBGlBJo5DzI4ZqOZa12FMGUZJqFSjwcIYP.
Webb I (2016) He Supported Bombing Syria a Little Too Eagerly, Now RuNet Pioneer Faces Prison. https://advox.globalvoices.org/2016/09/20/he-supported-bombing-syria-a-little-too-eagerly-now-runet-pioneer-faces-prison/.

Anastasiia Vorobiova is a research assistant at the Institute of Legal Sciences, Polish Academy of Sciences, employed as a part of the MEMOCRACY project. Her current work is focused on the misuse of historical memory in Russia and its relevant implications within international human rights law, with a particular emphasis on education rights. Her research interests include international human rights law, humanitarian law and international criminal law. Ms Vorobiova holds an LLM degree in International Human Rights Law from Lund University, Sweden.

Chapter 18
Serbia

Darko Dimovski and Filip Mirić

Contents

Abstract The regulation of hate speech in Serbia can best be understood through the country's normative mechanisms. Particularly important are the mechanisms of constitutional law, statutory and administrative law, and criminal law, along with relevant international legal instruments. Although Serbia has a solid normative framework for combatting hate speech, the main obstacle is its timely application. Equally important are questions of judicial practice, which shed light on the translation of these normative frameworks into practice.

18.1 National Constitutional Law

"Hate speech" may generally be defined as expression that contains messages of hatred or intolerance towards a racial, national, ethnic or religious group or its members. More recently, the term has also included goal-oriented speech producing hatred and intolerance towards gender and sexual orientation, national and social origin, and different political and other opinions. The targets of hate speech are individuals or groups who are considered (by the speaker) to be inferior on the basis of

D. Dimovski (✉)
Faculty of Law, University of Niš, Niš, Serbia
e-mail: darko@prafak.ni.ac.rs

F. Mirić
Faculty of Law, University of Niš, Niš, Serbia
e-mail: filip@prafak.ni.ac.rs

E. Heinze (ed.), *Criminalising Hate Speech*,
https://doi.org/10.1007/978-94-6265-650-5_18

some characteristics that are either innate or a constituent part of their identity (e.g. race, ethnicity, sexual orientation, etc.). In this context, the question arises as to how we should treat hate speech in relation to freedom of speech.[1]

Freedom of speech is a universal human right, but it is not absolute and has some restrictions. In that sense, the legislation of Serbia does not differ from other developed countries and states parties to relevant international agreements. At the international level, the Republic of Serbia has ratified a number of international treaties, such as the International Covenant on Civil and Political Rights, and the European Convention on Human Rights, all of which include free speech rights. At the national level, Article 46 of the Serbian Constitution guarantees freedom of thought and expression as well as the freedom to seek, receive, and impart information and ideas through speech, writing, art, or in some other manner. However, Article 46 (2) states that freedom of expression may be restricted by the law if it is necessary to protect the rights and reputation of others, to preserve the authority and impartiality of the court, and to protect public health, morals in a democratic society, and national security of the Republic of Serbia.

The 2006 Serbian Constitution guarantees the equality of citizens and prohibits discrimination. Article 1 specifies that the Republic of Serbia is a state of the Serbian people and of all the citizens who live in its territory, based on the rule of law and social justice, principles of civil democracy, human and minority rights and freedoms, and commitment to European principles and values.[2]

Article 5 proclaims the freedom to form political parties, and prohibits the activities of political parties which are aimed at violently overthrowing the constitutional system, violating the guaranteed human or minority rights, and inciting racial, national or religious hatred. Article 14 proclaims that the Republic of Serbia shall protect the rights of national minorities and guarantee special protection to national minorities for the purpose of ensuring their full equality and preserving their identity. Article 15 proclaims gender equality and prescribes that the State shall guarantee the equality of women and men, and develop a policy of equal opportunities.

Article 18 provides for the direct implementation of the human and minority rights guaranteed by the Constitution. The Constitution guarantees and directly implements human and minority rights guaranteed by generally accepted rules of international law, ratified international treaties and laws. The law may prescribe the manner of exercising these rights only if it is explicitly stipulated in the Constitution, or if it is necessary for the exercise of a specific right rights due to its nature, whereby the law may not under any circumstances affect the substance of the guaranteed right. The provisions on human and minority rights are to be interpreted to the benefit of promoting the values of a democratic society, in accordance with applicable international standards on human and minority rights, as well as the practice of international institutions monitoring their implementation.

---

[1] Dimovski 2020.

[2] The Constitution of the Republic of Serbia, "*Official Gazette of the Republic of Serbia*" no. 98/2006, English translation available at http://www.ustavni.sud.rs/page/view/en-GB/235-100028/constitution.

Article 21 prohibits discrimination on any ground, declaring that that all citizens are equal before by the Constitution and the law. Thus everyone has the right to equal legal protection, without any direct or indirect discrimination on the basis of race, sex, nationality, social origin, birth, religion, political or other beliefs, property status, culture, language, age, and physical disability or mental impairment. The Constitution also stipulates that special measures (of affirmative action), which may be introduced to achieve full equality of individuals or groups in a substantially unequal position as compared to other citizens, shall not be considered to be discriminatory. Article 22 guarantees judicial protection to individuals whose human and minority rights have been violated or denied, and envisages the right to have recourse to relevant international institutions in order to protect their constitutionally guaranteed rights and freedoms.

Article 43 guarantees freedom of thought, conscience, belief and religion, as well as the right to stand by one's belief or religion or to change it by choice. Moreover, no one is obliged to publicly declare his or her religious and other beliefs. Everyone is free to express one's religion or belief in worship, by performing religious rites, attending a religious service or teaching, either individually or in community with others, as well as to present one's religious beliefs in private or in public. The freedom of expressing one's religion or beliefs may be restricted by law only if it is necessary in a democratic society, for the purpose of protecting human lives and health, the moral norms of the democratic societies, the rights and freedoms guaranteed by the Constitution, public security and public order, or for the purpose of preventing the incitement of religious, national or racial hatred.

Pursuant to Article 44, churches and religious communities are equal and separate from the state. They can independently organize their internal structure, manage religious matters, perform religious rites in public, establish and manage religious schools, social and charity institutions, in accordance with the law. The Constitutional Court may ban a religious community only if its actions endanger the right to life, the right to mental and physical health, children's rights, the right to personal and family integrity, the right to property, public security and public order, or if it incites and encourages religious, national or racial intolerance.

Article 46 guarantees freedom of thought and expression, as well as the freedom to seek, receive and impart information and ideas in oral or written form, through art or in some other manner. Freedom of expression may be restricted by the law, if it is necessary to protect the rights and reputation of others, preserve the authority and impartiality of the court, and protect public health, morals of a democratic society, and national security of the Republic of Serbia.

Article 48 promotes diversity and observance of differences through measures in education, culture and public information. The Republic of Serbia encourages understanding, recognition and respect for differences arising from specific ethnic, cultural, linguistic or religious identity of its citizens. Under Article 49, any incitement and encouragement of racial, national, religious or other inequality, hatred and intolerance is prohibited and punishable in accordance with the law.

Article 50 proclaims the freedom of the media, stipulating that everyone is entitled to establish a media outlet (a newspapers, TV and radio station, and other means of public information) without prior approval, in the manner prescribed by the law. The media in Serbia shall not be subject to censorship but the competent court may prevent dissemination of information and ideas through the media only if it is necessary in a democratic society in order to prevent the incitement of violent overthrowing of the constitutional system established by the Constitution or violation of the territorial integrity of the Republic of Serbia, to prevent the propagation of war or incitement to direct violence, or to prevent advocacy of racial, national or religious hatred, which entices discrimination, hostility or violence. The law also regulates the exercise of the right to correct false, incomplete or inaccurately imparted information resulting in a violation of one's rights or interests, as well as the right to respond to published information.

Article 55 guarantees the freedom of association. Political, union and other associations may be established without prior approval, in compliance with the law. Secret and paramilitary associations are prohibited. The Constitutional Court may prohibit the association whose activities are aimed at inciting a violent overthrowing of the constitutional order, violating the guaranteed human or minority rights, or inciting racial, national or religious hatred.

Article 76 explicitly prohibits discrimination against national minorities, whose members are guaranteed equality before the law and equal legal protection. Any discrimination on the grounds of affiliation to a national minority is prohibited but the State may introduce specific regulations and affirmative action measures to ensure full equality of minority members and eliminate unfavourable effects that may affect their living conditions.

Article 81 of the Constitution proclaims the obligation to develop the spirit of tolerance in the area of education, culture and information. Thus, the State shall encourage the spirit of tolerance and intercultural dialogue, and undertake effective measures to promote mutual respect, understanding and cooperation among all people living in its territory, regardless of their ethnic, cultural, linguistic or religious identity.

18.2 National Statutory and Administrative Law

Serbian legislation regulates freedom of speech and prohibits hate speech in a number of separate legislative acts, such as the Anti-Discrimination Act, the Broadcasting Act, the Advertising Act, the Public Information Act, the Electronic Media Act, and the Criminal Code.

Anti-Discrimination Act. This is one of the basic legislative acts which regulates the right to equality and non-discrimination in Serbia. It was adopted on 3 March 2009.[3] It has an extensive scope of application, including both State authorities and non-state actors, and prohibits both direct and indirect discrimination on the

[3] The Act on the Prohibition of Discrimination (hereafter: the Anti-discrimination Act), *The Official Gazette of the RS*, no. 22/2009. Articles 28–40 started being applied as of 1st January 2010; English

grounds of race, skin colour, ancestors, citizenship, national affiliation, ethnic origin, language, religious or political beliefs, gender, gender identity, sexual orientation, financial position, birth, genetic characteristics, health, disability, marital and family status, previous convictions, age, appearance, membership in political, trade union and other organisations, and other personal characteristics.

Article 4 states that everybody has to respect the principle of equality, and observe the prohibition of discrimination, hate speech and disturbing and humiliating treatment (Article 5). Article 11 explicitly prohibits hate speech, i.e. expressing ideas, information and opinions inciting discrimination, hatred or violence against an individual or a group of persons on account of their personal characteristics, in public organs and other publications, in gatherings and places accessible to the public, by writing and displaying messages or symbols, and in other ways. Article 15 envisages that everybody who has been subjected to discriminatory conduct has the right to initiate civil or administrative proceedings before relevant judicial authorities. Given that the Act also established the Commissioner for the Protection of Equality, as an independent state body (Article 1), Article 35 stipulates that anyone who has been discriminated against is entitled to file a complaint with the Commissioner for the Protection of Equality, who is obliged to review the submitted evidence and provide opinion and recommendations (Article 39).

The Commissioner for Protection of Equality has a specific role in the Serbian anti-discrimination system. Under Article 33 of the Anti-Discrimination Act, the Commissioner:

1. shall receive and review complaints pertaining to violations of provisions of this Act, provide opinions and recommendations in specific cases, and issue relevant measures (in accordance with Article 40 of this Act);
2. shall provide information to the person lodging a complaint and the possibility of initiating court or some other proceedings for the purpose of protection, or recommend reconciliation (in accordance with Article 38 of this Act);
3. shall file charges (in compliance with Article 43 of this Act) pertaining to violations of rights guaranteed by this Act, in his/her own name and on behalf of the discriminated person, unless court proceedings have already been initiated or terminated by passing an enforceable decision;
4. shall submit misdemeanour notices on account of violations of rights guaranteed in this Act;
5. shall submit an annual report and special reports to the National Assembly about the situation concerning the protection of equality;
6. shall warn the public of the most frequent, typical and severe cases of discrimination;
7. shall monitor the implementation of laws and other regulations, initiate the passing or amending of regulations for the purpose of implementing and developing protection against discrimination, and provide opinions concerning the

translation available at https://www.legislationline.org/download/id/5671/file/Serbia_Law_Prohibition_Discrimination_en.pdf.

provisions of draft laws and other regulations pertaining to the prohibition of discrimination;
8. shall establish and maintain cooperation with bodies authorised to ensure equality and the protection of human rights on the territory of an autonomous province or a local government;
9. shall recommend measures to public administration organs and other persons aimed at ensuring equality (Article 33 of the Anti-discrimination Act).

The Broadcasting Act. Article 21 of this Act envisages the suppression of hate speech.[4] The National Broadcasting Agency, as an autonomous organisation in charge of ensuring the efficient implementation and improvement of the broadcasting policy in Serbia, in a manner befitting a democratic society (Article 6), is to ensure that the broadcasters' programs do not contain information that promotes or incites discrimination, hatred or violence against individuals or a group of individuals on the grounds of their political affiliation, race, religion, nationality, ethnicity, gender, or sexual orientation. If broadcasters act contrary to this prohibition, the Agency may impose specified sanctions, regardless of other legal remedies which are at the disposal of the injured party. Pursuant to Article 17 of this Act, the Agency may issue a reprimand and a warning to the broadcaster. The Agency may also temporarily or permanently revoke the broadcaster's broadcasting license. It may initiate proceedings against a broadcaster or its officials if any act, or failure to act, bears the character of a punishable offence.

The Advertising Act. Freedom of advertising is based on equal rights and obligations of legal entities and natural persons involved, in accordance with the law, regulations, fair business practices, professional ethics and other forms of self-regulation (Article 4).[5] Article 6 of this Act refers to the principle of social responsibility, which implies that advertisement shall not give rise to hatred or intolerance, contain insulting or humiliating statements, misuse trust and relations of dependence, inexperience, ignorance and superstition of advertisement recipients. Article 8 sets forth the principle of non-discrimination, specifying that advertising may not, directly or indirectly, encourage discrimination on any grounds, especially on the grounds of race, color, sex, nationality, ethnicity, social origin, birth, religion, political or other opinion, property, culture, language, age, mental or physical disability. Article 9 envisages the prohibition of discrimination against advertisers, thus it is prohibited to reject advertising or broadcasting an advertisement on the basis of racial, national, or ethnic affiliation, gender or other personal characteristics of the person requesting the publication, or on the basis of unjustifiable difference or unequal treatment, exclusion, restriction or preference of another advertiser.

---

[4] The Broadcasting Act, Official Gazette of the RS, No. 42/2002, English translation available at https://www.ilo.org/dyn/natlex/docs/ELECTRONIC/85339/95499/F464515368/SRB 85339%20English.pdf.

[5] The Ad*vertising Act*, Official Gazette of the Republic of Serbia, No. 6/2016, English translation available at https://untobaccocontrol.org/impldb/wp-content/uploads/serbia_2018_annex-2_law_on_advertising.pdf.

The Public Information Act. The right to public information entails the freedom of thought and expression, the freedom to gather, investigate, publish and disseminate ideas and information, the freedom to print and distribute newspapers, the freedom to produce and broadcast radio/television programs, the freedom to receive ideas, information and opinions, the freedom to establish legal persons dealing with public information (Article 1).[6] It extends to special categories of persons, such as national minorities and ethnic communities (who are entitled to use their own languages and nurture their cultural identities), as well as handicapped persons and other individuals with special needs (Article 5). Article 17 prescribes a ban on dissemination of information aimed at inciting a violent overthrow of the constitutional order, undermining the territorial integrity, inciting violence, hostility, or racial, ethnic or religious hatred. Article 38 explicitly prohibits hate speech, thus it is prohibited to publish ideas, information and opinions that incite discrimination, hatred or violence against an individual or a group of individuals on grounds of their race, religion, nationality, ethnicity, gender or sexual orientation, regardless of whether a criminal offence has been committed by such publication.

The Electronic Media Act. Article 51 of this Act explicitly prohibits hate speech. Thus the Regulatory authority for electronic media (the Regulator) must ensure that the content of the media service provider does not contain information which overtly or covertly encourages discrimination, hatred or violence based on race, colour, ancestry, citizenship, national origin, language, religion or political beliefs, sex, gender identity, sexual orientation, economic status, birth, genetic characteristics, health status, disability, marital and family status, criminal record, age, looks, membership in political, trade union and other organizations, and other actual or presumed personal characteristics.[7]

The Serbian Criminal Code. The Criminal Code sets forth a number of criminal offenses containing elements of discrimination, intolerance, incitement to violence, hate speech and hate crime. These include the violation of equality (Article 128),[8] the violation of the right to use language and writing (Article 129), the violation of the right to expression of national or ethnic affiliation (Article 130), the violation of freedom of religion and belief (Article 131), the violation of the reputation of people of particular racial, religious, national and ethnic affiliation (Article 174), instigating national, racial and religious hatred and intolerance (Article 317), violent conduct during sports event or public gathering (Article 344a), organizing and inciting the commission of genocide and war crimes (Article 375), and racial and other forms of discrimination (Article 387).[9]

---

[6] The Public Information Act, Official Gazette RS, No. 43/2003, 61/2005, 71/2009, 89/2010; English translation available at https://www.legislationline.org/download/id/5479/file/Serbia_law_on_public_information_2003_en.pdf.

[7] The Electronic Media Act, Official Gazette of the RS, No. 83/2014, 6/*2016;* English translation available at http://www.anem.org.rs/download/files/cms/attach?id=508.

[8] It should also be noted that disability is included as one of elements of violation of equality (Article 128) to improve the protection of people with disabilities against discrimination and hate crime.

[9] The Criminal Code of the Republic of Serbia, Official Gazette RS, Nos. 85/2005, 88/2005 (Corrigendum), 107/2005 (Corrigendum), 72/2009, 111/09, 121/2012, 104/2013, 108/2014, 94/2016 and

Finally, we can say that there is no possibility to convict the perpetrator of hate crime or hate speech by interpreting specific provisions of certain criminal offenses.

18.3 International Covenant on Civil and Political Rights (ICCPR)

The ICCPR was ratified by the former Yugoslavia in 1971 and Serbia as a successor of Yugoslavia is also a State Party. Serbia ratified Protocols 1 and 2 without any reservation. As to individual complaints, from 2006 the institution of the constitutional complaint was established in Serbia. An individual can go to the Serbian Constitutional Court in pursuit of his or her human rights. One can launch a constitutional complaint without the help of a professional lawyer and it is tax free. After the Constitutional Court the petitioner may also lodge a complaint with to the European Court for Human Rights (ECtHR). Serbia counts among the top ten countries in Europe by the number of complaints applied to the European court.

The Constitutional Court has thus far issued no judgements regarding the hate speech, but only for insults, nor has there been any complaint about hate speech to the ECtHR. However, there has been one case of a person who was a member of the religious Hare Krishna group in one small town. He complained to some domestic agencies that he had been victimized by unknown citizens because of his unconventional dress and behavior. When the aggression did not stop and he complained to the ECtHR, which concluded that the investigation and other efforts of the domestic police and other agencies were had been inadequate to stop the aggression and hate crime. This was the only case of any crime connected with the hate brought before the ECtHR. Otherwise, as mentioned, there was one case of a hate crime against a LGBT person, which was discussed in the national courts and the perpetrator of that crime was convicted.

The UN Human Rights Committee published Concluding Observations for Serbia in 2017, finding in part as follows:

> While the Committee acknowledges the strategy for prevention and protection from discrimination, it remains concerned about: (a) the lack of, or delays in, the practical implementation of the strategy; (b) the non-recognition of indirect discrimination in the current anti-discrimination law; (c) the lack of information on civil proceedings and the limited number of criminal proceedings brought forward on the basis of discrimination; and (d) the State party's failure to collect disaggregated data on ethnic and racial minorities (articles 2-3 and 26-27).
>
> The State party should: (a) take concrete measures to ensure that the action plan for implementing the strategy for prevention and protection from discrimination is carried out in a timely and effective manner; (b) ensure that the planned amendments to the anti-discrimination law adequately address indirect discrimination as a form of discrimination; (c) increase the capacity of the Commissioner for the Protection of Equality to bring claims under

---

35/2019; English translation available at https://www.mpravde.gov.rs/files/Criminal%20%20%20Code_2019.pdf.

the anti-discrimination law; (d) strengthen judicial enforcement of the anti-discrimination law through criminal and civil proceedings, including by training judges, law enforcement officials and lawyers regarding non-discrimination; and (f) collect data and develop tools that will allow the State party to assess and ensure the effective enjoyment by racial and ethnic minorities of all human rights and fundamental freedoms and make use of such data for planning and evaluation purposes.

Hate crimes. The Committee is concerned that, despite the State party's efforts to prevent offences motivated by hatred, hate crimes, particularly against Roma, continue to be a serious problem in the State party. While noting the amendments to article 54 (a) of the Criminal Code introducing aggravating circumstances for crimes committed by individuals.

The State party should: (a) increase its efforts to promote tolerance for persons belonging to ethnic, national, racial, religious and other minorities, including persons belonging to the Roma community; and (b) effectively implement article 54 (a) of the Criminal Code, including by ensuring that hate crimes are identified and promptly investigated, that alleged perpetrators are prosecuted and, if convicted, that they are punished with appropriate sanctions.

18.4 International Convention on the Elimination of All Forms of Racial Discrimination (ICERD)

The former Yugolavia had signed and ratified the ICERD in 1966 and 1967. Serbia, together with Montenegro, became a State Party to ICERD in 2001. Upon succession the Government of the Federal Republic of Yugoslavia recognized the competence of the Committee on the Elimination of Racial Discrimination (UN-CERD) to receive and consider complaints submitted by individuals and groups alleging violations of rights guaranteed under the International Convention on the Elimination of All Forms of Racial Discrimination.

18.5 Council of Europe (COE)

In its report on Serbia (fifth monitoring cycle) published on 16 March 2017, the European Commission against Racism and Intolerance (ECRI) recommended that the Serbian Parliament and Government adopt codes of conduct to prohibit hate speech, and to provide for suspension of mandate and other sanctions for breach of their provisions, and to establish effective reporting channels. The Serbian authorities informed ECRI that the rights and obligations of the Members of Parliament (MP) are regulated by the Constitution, different pieces of legislation and the Rules of Procedure of the National Assembly. Articles 107 and 109 of the Rules of Procedure prohibit the use of insulting expressions (cf. § 18b of ECRI's General Policy Recommendation (GPR) No. 7) and its Article 108 provides the President of the National Assembly with the power to issue a warning to MPs, bar them from speaking and exclude them from a session. In such a case, a fine would be deducted from the MP's salary according to Article 114 of the Rules of Procedure.

In 2017, the rules of procedure were further amended with the aim of preventing MPs from resorting to hate speech when commenting on court decisions. This covers court decisions taken in the framework of war crime trials, and the denial of such crimes (cf. § 18e of GPR No. 7). According to the authorities, additional work is under way to implement ECRI's recommendation and to further strengthen the prohibition of hate speech in the Rules of Procedure of the National Assembly. The Serbian Commissioner for the Protection of Equality (Commissioner) informed ECRI that she had addressed a recommendation to the National Assembly to amend the Rules of Procedure with a view to ensuring the respect of the prohibition of discrimination as enshrined in the Constitution and the law, and that disciplinary penalties should be introduced for those failing to adhere to the prohibition of discrimination.

In June 2019, the Commissioner decided that a statement by a MP from the city of Nis had violated Article 20 of the Law on Prohibition of Discrimination on the ground of gender. With regard to the second part of the recommendation on the adoption of a code of conduct by the Serbian Government, the Commissioner refers to the Code of Conduct for Civil Servants of 2008. Article 13 states that a civil servant shall abide by the principle of equality and refrain from granting privileges on the ground of a client's characteristics and personal traits and shall in particular take due care to show respect to client's dignity when interacting with persons with disabilities and special needs.

ECRI further regretted that no progress had been made with regard to the adoption of rules by the Serbian Government that would prohibit the use of hate speech by its members and contain sanctions for the breach of its provisions and effective reporting channels (cf. § 6a of ECRI's GPR No. 15 on Combating hate speech). With regard to the prohibition of hate speech in the Serbian Parliament's Rules of Procedure, ECRI takes positive note of the progress made with regard to the denial of war crimes. At the same time, it underlines that these rules need further strengthening and that they should contain a coherent and appropriate prohibition of hate speech (cf. § 6a of GPR No. 15 and the different forms of hate speech listed in § 18a to f of ECRI's GPR No. 7). ECRI concluded that this recommendation had been partly implemented.

In its 2017 report, the ECRI further recommended that the authorities give high priority to hiring a proportionate number of Roma and members of other minorities to the civil service and ensure that they benefit from equally stable working conditions as other civil servants. The Serbian authorities informed ECRI that the Action Plan for the Realisation of the Rights of National Minorities contains one chapter with 21 activities that aim to achieve adequate representation of members of national minorities in the public sector and public enterprises. They comprise activities in view of:

(i) facilitating the economic recovery, ECRI furthermore notes that the Serbian Government and its Office for Human and Minority Rights recently adopted the IHRA Working Definition of Antisemitism. In this respect ECRI refers to its ongoing work on the revision of its General Policy Recommendation No.

9 on the fight against antisemitism. 6 development of underdeveloped regions, which are traditionally inhabited by national minorities;

(ii) attracting investment in these areas;

(iii) improving the employability and encouraging employment of members of national minorities by implementing active employment measures, and

(iv) encouraging foreign investment in these areas.

Without giving concrete figures, the government informed ECRI that Roma have been hired as pedagogical assistants, health mediators and coordinators for Roma issues. The Ministry of Interior continued to organise workshops in which it prepared Roma to succeed in the competitions that are organised for the recruitment of police officers. Among the employees of public utility companies in Novi Sad, 121 have declared that they are Roma. This figure could be higher as Serbia does not oblige national minorities to declare their ethnic belonging, in line with ECRI's recommendations. In Nis, another 166 employees of such companies declared themselves to be Roma, and in Belgrade 27 others did so. Furthermore, among the employees of the local self-government bodies in the Autonomous Province of Vojvodina, 609 (8,99%) belong to the Hungarian minority and their number increases.

According to data of the National Employment Service, 9 007 members of national minorities took part in active employment measures in 2018. In Belgrade, 102 Roma attended training for starting a business and 50 of them received funds to do so. The Commissioner for the Protection of Equality informed ECRI that its office hired one young Roma professional following an internship programme that two Roma participants had completed. The Protector of Citizens informed ECRI that, according to a survey carried out by his institution, only ten Roma men and two Roma women are members of local assemblies and only 26 Roma men and 13 Roma women were employed in the administration of the participating 143 local self-government units. These figures show, according to the report, the continued exclusion of Roma as well as the non-existence or non-application of adequate instruments and institutional frameworks for their participation at all levels of local administration.

The 2019 EU report on Serbia calls on the authorities to ensure a consistent implementation of legislation regarding national minorities, including Roma, leading to a tangible improvement in the effective exercise of their rights across the country. ECRI regrets to note that the number of Roma and members of other minorities employed in the public sector of Serbia remains far from being proportionate and that the progress made with the implementation of this recommendation remains narrow. Furthermore, ECRI did not receive any information regarding the question of whether they benefit from equally stable working conditions as other civil servants. Given the described improvements, it concludes that this recommendation has been partly implemented.

According to a COE report about hate speech in Serbia during the COVID crisis:

> The media have powerful impact on Serbian society and a corresponding responsibility in addressing hate speech. Media representatives should not only refrain from using hate speech but also emphasize and promote positive and value-driven arguments about members of vulnerable groups, thus contributing to breaking predominant stereotypes and prejudices.

> The legal framework in place does not appear to be effective - it is necessary for the media community to establish a system of collective self-regulation based on agreed codes of conducts and mechanisms to deal with complaints of hate speech. This has been underlined in today's presentation of the new "Report on the use of hate speech in Serbian media" prepared under the joint European Union/Council of Europe action "Promotion of diversity and equality in Serbia".[10]

18.6 Judicial Practice

The Serbian judicial system allows leeway for enhancing the role of domestic courts and developing the judicial practice of domestic courts on the subject matter of hate speech. The critics of hate speech legislation claim that the existing legal provisions are insufficient and ineffective. The Anti-discrimination Act[11] provides the definition of hate speech, which *de facto* defines endangered groups that may be subject to discrimination, on account of race, religion, nation, ethnic group, sex or sexual orientation. However, the process of deciding whether a specific conduct or utterance constitutes hate speech rests on whether such an act may be qualified as incitement to intolerance and discrimination. As this question is still unresolved at the international level, it is unrealistic to expect from domestic law to specify the requirements in each individual case.

In the Republic of Serbia, the Public Prosecution Office and the competent courts play the key role in cases involving hate speech. The hate speech protection mechanism may be instituted in two separate sets of proceedings: criminal proceedings and litigation proceedings. The Anti-discrimination Act contains key provisions on active legitimacy (legal standing) for filing a criminal complaint or a civil action, and thus initiating legal proceedings in hate speech cases.[12]

In civil litigation proceedings, the injured party may file a claim (motion) asking the court to prohibit the acts which are found to be discriminatory, to prohibit the ongoing discriminatory acts or recurrence of such acts, to confirm the commission of discriminatory acts against the complainant or another person, to remedy the detrimental consequences of discriminatory acts, to award pecuniary and non-pecuniary damages, to render and publish the final judgment. The Civil Procedure Act[13] prescribes legal rules applicable in urgent proceedings (in pending cases).

---

[10] Authors are thankful for former Constitutional Court of Serbia Judge Jovan Ćirić's contribution and prof. dr Eric Heinze who kindly sent us edited version of Judge Ćiric's Report from 2021.

[11] The Anti-discrimination Act, Official Gazette of the RS, No 22/2009.

[12] Article 11 of the Anti-discrimination Act: "It is forbidden to express ideas, information and opinions inciting discrimination, hatred or violence against an individual or a group of persons on account of his/her or their personal characteristics, in public bodies and other publications, in gatherings and places accessible to the public, by writing out and displaying messages or symbols, and in other ways".

[13] The Civil Procedure Act, Official Gazette of the RS, No. 72/2011, 49/2013-CC decision, 74/2013-CC decision S, 55/2014, 87/2018, 18/2020.

During the examination and assessment of hate speech cases, it is necessary to establish and assess all circumstances under which they occur, or which could be taken into account as incitement of violence, intimidation, hostility or discrimination. [14] This is closely related to the very nature of speech, particularly given that linguists clearly note that there is no universal agreement on the kind of speech which may be considered offensive.[15]

The cases from judicial practice serve as an indicator of actual efficiency of enacted legislation in addressing hate speech. Beside their legal dimension, judicial decisions can also have a cultural and (sometimes) political dimension. In Serbia, the worrisome fact is that the prosecutorial investigations and final judgments on hate speech cases are still quite rare. The small number of existing judicial decisions is no more than "a dead letter on paper". While there is still a relatively small number of judicial proceedings against those who have been accused of committing an act of hate speech, another fact of paramount concern is that these judicial proceedings often involve various representatives of the political authorities.

The judicial practice (case law) of national courts also shows that international norms are applied sporadically. In Concluding observations on periodic reports of Serbia (2017)[16], the UN Committee on the Elimination of Racial Discrimination (UN-CERD) expressed concerns about Serbia's lack of available, comprehensive statistical data about investigations, prosecutions and convictions of hate speech on racial grounds (item 13). The UN-CERD urged Serbia to strengthen its measures, to contribute to effective identification and investigation, and to ensure punishment for all forms of hate speech (items 13-14).

The proof that Serbia does not have comprehensive statistical data on hate speech is shown in the Strategy for Prevention and Protection against Discrimination (2013).[17] The accessible data from various sources (the Commissioner for the Protection of Equality, the Ombudsman/Protector of Citizens, the Public Prosecution Office, the Ministry of Interior Affairs, etc.) indicate that hate speech is still relatively frequent, although the number of recorded offences has been declining in recent years. According to the prosecution statistical data of the Public Prosecution Office, a total of 216 persons were charged with hate speech in the period from January 2011 to May 2016. In 211 cases, charges were raised on the basis of Article 317 of the Criminal Code[18] (Instigating national, racial and religious hatred and intolerance), 3 charges were based on Article 387 (Racial and other discrimination), and 2 charges

---

[14] ECRI General Policy Recommendation No. 15 on Combating Hate Speech.

[15] Jay and Janschewitz 2008, pp. 267–288.

[16] UN Committee on the Elimination of Racial Discrimination: Concluding observations on the combined second to firth periodic reports of Serbia, CERD/C/SRB/CO/2-5, dated 1 December 2017. http://docstore.ohchr.org/SelfServices/FilesHandler.ashx?enc=6QkG1d%2FPPRiCAqhKb7yhslztXd5Nnh5GF9yFH9jwvil9B8B11%2FuXciI8LTQu0fJ4OYldltZ8n4OMBwTQDg7SZF6eFXhi1q9YdxBd%2BRQfdDSZnBiSnXOW3tWQbHMJqen0.

[17] Strategy for Prevention and Protection against Discrimination 2013, Official Gazette of the RS. 60/2013.

[18] The Criminal Code, Official Gazette of the RS, no. 85/2005, 88/2005-corr., 107/2005-corr., 72/2009, 111/2009, 121/2012, 104/2013, 108/2014, 94/2016, 35/2019.

were based on Article 174 (Violation of one's reputation due to racial, religious, national, ethnic, and other affiliation).

Out of the total number of cases, 207 charges were based on national or ethnic origin, 5 charges were based only on religious affiliation,[19] one charge was related to nationality and one charge was related to sexual orientation. In most of these cases, the targeted individuals were Roma, lesbians, gay, bisexual or transgender (LGBT) persons. The bill of indictment was raised against 106 offenders, and 42 offenders were convicted. In additional 138 cases, criminal charges were raised for the commission of high-tech crimes: 20 cases of racism-related crimes and 118 cases of homophobic/transphobic violence. In these case, 20 offenders were prosecuted under Article 138 (Endangering safety of another), three persons were prosecuted under Article 317, and one person was prosecuted under Article 387 of the CL.[20]

However, criminal investigation, prosecution, conviction and sanctions for hate speech often do not ensure adequate protection to victims, particularly in cases involving hate speech, threats and attacks against members of the LGBT community. There are cases where official investigation has never been instituted. In year, the Public Prosecution Office recorded two hate crimes committed against LGBT people and procecuted under Article 138 of the CC. There is still a lack of centralized database which would provide official data on hate crimes. State authorities should clearly demonstrate political commitment to promoting the rights of LGBT and stronger support in terms of improving their social inclusion. State authorities have to ensure a safe environment for LGBT people and high representatives of the state should set a role model of behavior when it comes to improving general public attitudes towards the LGBT community.

In Serbian judicial practice, there are a few examples of judicial decisions on hate speech, some of which involve politicians. An example of a disparaging statement, which received much publicity in Serbia after the LGBT Pride Parade in 2016, was the statement of the then Prime Minister (and later President) Aleksandar Vučić, who said that he would rather attend the wedding of the former Defence Minister's son than join the Pride Parade.[21] There is no judicial decision about this case of hate speech.

The fact that judicial authorities do not always recognize hate speech against the LGBT population may be illustrated by the judicial proceedings in the discrimination case involving a politician Dragan Marković Palma, leader of the political party "United Serbia." In 2011, the Citizens' Association "Gay-Straight Alliance" (GSA) filed a criminal complaint against Marković under the Anti-discrimination Act for his derogatory statement about the LGBT population. Markovic said that he and his party are "against any gathering where homosexuals demonstrate in the streets of

[19] It is also important to emphasize that 22 cases registered as hate speech related to national or ethnic origin also related to religious affiliation. A total of 27 cases were registered as hate speech based on religious affiliation; Muslims were targeted in 12 cases; Catholics in 7 cases, Jehovah's witnesses in 5 cases, and Jews in 3 cases.

[20] ECRI 2017, p. 17.

[21] Newpaper Danas 2016.

Belgrade and present something that is a disease as something normal." In November 2011, the First basic Court in Belgrade found that the politician had violated the sexual minorities', and he was issued a court order prohibiting him to repeat the discriminatory statement. Upon the defendant's appeal (based on procedural flaws), in September 2012, the Appellate Court in Belgrade reversed the first-instance court decision and remanded the case for a retrial. In the retrial, the First Basic Court in Belgrade rejected the GSA complaint as ill-founded. In the explanation of the verdict, the court stated that although Mr. Marković's statement contains signs of discriminatory behavior, it is not sufficient to qualify the disputed statement by the court as an act of discrimination.[22]

In September 2009, the Republic Prosecution Office submitted a request (motion) to the Constitutional Court of Serbia to ban the Citizens' Association "Patriotic Movement *Obraz*" for activities involving multiple violations of human and minority rights, hate speech against sexual minorities, and inciting racial, national and religious hatred. In 2012, the Constitutional Court prohibited the work of this association on the aforesaid grounds and ordered that it shall be deleted from the Register of associations kept by the Business Registers Agency.[23]

In 2011, the Higher Court in Belgrade issued the first judgment on hate speech on the basis of Article 11 of the Anti-discrimination Act. In July 2009, the GSA filed a criminal complaint against the daily newspaper *Press* for failing to remove discriminatory comments against the LGBT population posted on the newspaper's website portal *Press online*.[24] The court held that the readers' comments constituted direct hate speech against the LGBT population. The newspaper website was found to have violated the rights of LGBT people and discriminated them by allowing these comments to be published. The court imposed the provisional measure, ordering the newspaper to remove the controversial comments and to publish the court judgment in its entirety.Upon the defendant's appeal, the decision was confirmed by the Court of Appeals in February 2012.[25]

In 2011, the GSA filed a discrimination lawsuit against a politician Nebojša Bakarec for his text published in the Vidovdan Magazine (online) in September 2011. In October 2012, the first-instance court held that his speech constituted an aggravated form of discrimination against the LGBT population.[26] Of equal importance is the first judgment related to hate speech on the Internet, where the defendant S.Vladičić was convicted in March 2012 for endangering safety of the LGBT population by posting comments on a Facebook group."[27](Blagojevič, 2016: 91–92).

---

[22] Portal Mondo 2013.

[23] Judgment of the Constitutional Court of Serbia V PU 249/2009, dated 12.06.2012.. http://www.ustavni.sud.rs/page/predmet/sr-Latn-CS/8221/?NOLAYOUT=1_ Accessed 3 April 2021.

[24] Gay-Straight Alliance website 2011.

[25] Gay-Straight Alliance website 2012.

[26] Newspaper Blic 2012a. g.

[27] Newspaper Blic 2012b. _ Blagojević 2016, pp. 81–95; University of Niš, http://casopisi.junis.ni.ac.rs/index.php/FULawPol/article/view/1747/1174.

These judgments are important because they were the first judgments of this kind in Serbia. But, even when there are final court decisions, the penalties largely remain minimal. The lack of adequate judicial response in hate crime cases has been criticized by the members of Serbian civil society organizations, such as the Lawyers' Committee for Human Rights (YUKOM).[28]

In conclusion, Serbia has a solid legal framework for combatting hate speech crimes. The main problem is disagreement between normative act and reality, hence the lack of judgments against perpetrators of hate speech crime.

References

Blagojević A (2016) The Normative Framework of Hate Speech in Serbia and Serbian Media. FACTA UNIVERSITATIS: Law and Politics 14(1):81–95.

Dimovski D (2020) Zločin mržnje [Hate Crime]. Niš: Centar za publikacije Pravnog fakulteta Univerziteta u Nišu.

ECRI (2017) ECRI report on Serbia (fifth monitoring cycle). Council of Europe, Strasbourg. https://www.anti.media/uploads/main/content-pages/srb-cbc-v-2017-021-srp.pdf.

Gay-Straight Alliance website (2011) Prva presuda zbog vorova mr\nje proti LGBT populacije [The first judgment for hate speech against LGBT people. Beograd. https://gsa.org.rs/2011/06/prva-presuda-zbog-govora-mrznje-protiv-lgbt-populacije-presuda-dnevnim-novinama-press-po-tuzbi-gej-strejt-alijanse/.

Gay-Straight Alliance website (2012) Apelacioni sud sud potvrdio da se govor mržnje prema LGBT osobama ne može pravdati slobodom govora i informisanja [Court of Appeals confirmed that hate speech against LGBT people cannot be justified by freedom of speech and information], Beograd. Accessed 3 April 2021. https://gsa.org.rs/2012/02/apelacioni-sud-potvrdio-da-se-govor-mrznje-prema-lgbt-osobama-ne-moze-pravdati-slobodom-govora-i-informisanja/.

Jay TB, Janschewitz K (2008) Pragmatičnost psovanja. Revija za istraživanje pristojnosti: jezik, ponašanje, kultura. In: Rokša-Zubčević A, Bender S, Vojvodić J (eds) Medijska regulatorna tijela i govor mržnje autori. Vijeće Europe, pp 267–288.

Newpaper Danas (2016) Vučić: Pre bih na svadbu sina Bate Gašića nego na paradu [Vučić: I'd rather go to Gašićson's wedding than to Pride Parade]. https://www.danas.rs/politika/vucic-pre-bih-na-svadbu-sina-bate-gasica-nego-na-paradu/. Accessed 3 April 2021.

Newspaper Blic (2012a) Presuda Nebojši Bakarecu za diskriminaciju LGBT populacije postala pravosnažna [Judgment issued to Nebojsa Bakarec for discrimination against LGBT is final]. http://www.blic.rs/vesti/politika/presuda-nebojsi-bakarecu-za-diskriminaciju-lgbt-populacije-postalapravosnazna/cbnfr9g.

Newspaper Blic [2012b] Presuda zbog govora mržnje na internetu [First judgment for hate speech on the Internet]. http://www.blic.rs/vesti/hronika/presuda-zbog-govora-mrznje-na-internetu/lg3etnr.

Portal Mondo (2013) Palma oslobođen optužbi za diskriminaciju [Palma's discriminarion charges dropped]. https://mondo.rs/Info/Drustvo/a631981/Palma-oslobodjen-optuzbi-za-diskriminaciju.html. Accessed 3 April 2021.

YUCOM (2017) Izveštaj o radu YUCOM 2016/2017 [Report of YUCOM activities 2016/2017]. https://www.yucom.org.rs/wp-content/uploads/2017/11/YUCOM-izvestaj-o-radu-2016-17.-20-godina-YUCOM-a.pdf. Accessed 3 April 2021.

[28] YUCOM 2017.

Darko Dimovski is Professor in the field of criminal law at the Faculty of Law, University of Niš. He is currently a president of the NGO Judicial Research Center. Professor Dimovski was a visiting lecturer in Serbia and abroad in the area of Criminology, as well as in European human rights law, developing a wide network in many academic and research institutions and exchanging knowledge and experience with colleagues from different universities.

Filip Mirić (LL.D) graduated from the Faculty of Law, University of Niš. He received a doctorate in 2014 at the same faculty, defending with special mention doctoral dissertation "Contemporary conceptions of the phenomenology and etiology of juvenile delinquency". Filip Mirić obtained the scientific title of Research Associate in 2019 and 2024. He has published over 140 scientific and professional articles. He is co-author and author of various monographs in field of criminal law, juvenile delinquency and sports law and a textbooks in field of adapted physical activities. He is employed at the Faculty of Law, University of Niš, at the Post Graduate Studies Services.

Chapter 19
Switzerland

Luc Gonin

Contents

Abstract La question des interactions entre liberté d'expression et incitation à la haine se pose également en Suisse. La présente contribution offre une analyse juridique de la problématique, en tenant compte autant des droits subjectifs concernés, des bases légales applicables que de la jurisprudence rendue en la matière. Cet article prend également en considération la démocratie semi-directe, très étendue en Suisse, dans le cadre son analyse. Les propos n'engagent que l'auteur, à l'exclusion de tout employeur passé ou présent.

Keywords Law and social media · Law and print media · Hate speech litigation · Policing hate speech · Hate speech and freedom of expression

L. Gonin (✉)
Département de droit public, Université de Fribourg, Geneva and Neuchâtel, Switzerland
e-mail: luc.gonin@unifr.ch

E. Heinze (ed.), *Criminalising Hate Speech*,
https://doi.org/10.1007/978-94-6265-650-5_19

19.1 Introduction

Le discours de haine ne connaît pas de frontières. Il peut apparaître aussi bien sur le continent européen, par exemple en Suisse, que sur d'autres continents. L'Histoire a souligné à quel point ce discours ne s'en prend pas uniquement à la dignité de chacune et de chacun, mais peut participer–à terme–à la commission des pires exactions. Il s'agit dès lors de sanctionner ces discours qui s'en prennent à l'Homme lui-même.

En même temps, la liberté d'expression est une des grandes conquêtes de la Modernité politique. Elle est aussi bien protégée sur le plan international que sur le plan national. Il s'agit dès lors de faire interagir interdiction du discours haineux et liberté d'expression, dont personne ne saurait cependant abuser.

Le présent rapport analyse la situation en Suisse. Il définira, dans un premier temps, le contexte général de la problématique pour la Confédération, en s'arrêtant en particulier sur la liberté d'expression et ses limites. Dans un deuxième temps, il se penchera de façon approfondie sur l'article 261bis du Code pénal (CP) suisse du 21 décembre 1937.[1] C'est ce dernier, en effet, qui se trouve aux premières loges à l'heure de réprimer pénalement le discours de haine. L'analyse portera en particulier sur la disposition elle-même, ses origines et son évolution, ainsi que sur ses interactions avec le fédéralisme, la Suisse étant un Etat fédéral. Le présent rapport examinera, également, la jurisprudence rendue en lien avec l'article 261bis CP. Celle-ci vient concrétiser juridiquement l'étendue exacte, en droit suisse, de l'interdiction du discours de haine.

Dans un troisième temps, notre analyse s'arrêtera sur les interactions entre discours de haine et démocratie semi-directe telle qu'existant au sein de la Confédération helvétique. L'ordre constitutionnel suisse permet, en effet et notamment, un droit très large de modification de la Constitution par des initiatives populaires. Le présent rapport se terminera par une brève prise de position personnelle.

19.2 Contexte Général

En Suisse, la condamnation du discours de haine s'inscrit dans une certaine tradition politique, celle de l'Etat libéral et démocratique, dont les origines philosophiques sont à rechercher, notamment, dans les Lumières.[2] Le libéralisme politique doit beaucoup, en particulier mais pas uniquement, à Locke et à Montesquieu, tandis que l'élément démocratique a été mis en exergue par Rousseau entre autres, né à Genève et venu se réfugier par la suite sur les terres de l'ancienne Confédération suisse.[3]

---

[1] Recueil systématique suisse (ci-après: RS) 311.0.

[2] Sur les principes structurels de la Suisse, dont le principe démocratique, cf. not. Tschannen 2016, pp. 81ss.

[3] Sur la notion d'Etat libéral, cf. not. Haller et al. 2020, N 85ss.

19.2.1 La Liberté D'expression

Une reconnaissance large sur le plan international et national. Le libéralisme politique a notamment conduit à la reconnaissance juridique de la liberté d'expression, que ce soit sur un plan international, que ce soit sur un plan national. Ainsi, au niveau interétatique, l'article 10 de la Convention européenne des droits de l'homme (CEDH),[4] mais aussi l'article 19 al. 2 du Pacte international relatif aux droits civils et politiques du 16 décembre 1966 (Pacte II de l'ONU),[5] ou encore l'article 5 let. d) ch. viii de la Convention internationale sur l'élimination de toutes les formes de discrimination raciale du 21 décembre 1965[6] protègent de façon explicite cette liberté (CERD). Au niveau national, cette liberté est ancrée à l'article 16 du texte constitutionnel (Cst.) lui-même,[7] ainsi que, souvent, sur un plan constitutionnel cantonal.[8]

L'absence d'un droit absolu à la liberté d'expression, et à d'autres libertés. Cette liberté d'expression, quoiqu'inscrite dans le tissu normatif contemporain de la Suisse, n'est cependant pas absolue. Ainsi et à titre purement exemplatif, l'article 10 § 2 de la CEDH stipule que :

> L'exercice de ces libertés comportant des devoirs et des responsabilités *peut être soumis à certaines formalités, conditions, restrictions ou sanctions prévues par la loi*, qui constituent des mesures nécessaires, dans une société démocratique, à la sécurité nationale, à l'intégrité territoriale ou à la sûreté publique, à la défense de l'ordre et à la prévention du crime, à la protection de la santé ou de la morale, à la protection de la réputation ou des droits d'autrui, pour empêcher la divulgation d'informations confidentielles ou pour garantir l'autorité et l'impartialité du pouvoir judiciaire.[9]

---

[4] Convention de sauvegarde des droits de l'homme et des libertés fondamentales du 4 novembre 1950, RS 0.101, article 10. Le § 1er de cet article se lit comme suit: « *Toute personne a droit à la liberté d'expression.* Ce droit comprend la liberté d'opinion et la liberté de recevoir ou de communiquer des informations ou des idées *sans qu'il puisse y avoir ingérence d'autorités publiques et sans considération de frontière.* Le présent article n'empêche pas les Etats de soumettre les entreprises de radiodiffusion, de cinéma ou de télévision à un régime d'autorisations » (emphases ajoutées).

[5] RS 0.103.2.

[6] RS 0.104.

[7] L'art. 16 de la Constitution fédérale du 18 avril 1999 (Cst.; RS 101) se lit comme suit: « (1) La liberté d'opinion et la liberté d'information sont garanties. (2) Toute personne a le droit de former, d'exprimer et de répandre librement son opinion. (3) Toute personne a le droit de recevoir librement des informations, de se les procurer aux sources généralement accessibles et de les diffuser ».

[8] Cf. p. ex. article 17 al. 1 de la Constitution du canton de Berne du 6 juin 1993 (RS 131.212), l'art. 11 al. 1 let. l) de la Constitution du canton de Bâle-Ville du 23 mars 2005 (RS 131.222.1; par renvoi au droit supérieur) ou encore l'art. 19 al. 1 de la Constitution du canton de Fribourg du 16 mai 2004 (RS 131.219).

[9] Emphase ajoutée. L'art. 36 Cst., qui va dans le même sens, détermine pour sa part que: « (1) Toute restriction d'un droit fondamental doit être *fondée sur une base légale.* Les restrictions graves doivent être prévues par une loi. Les cas de danger sérieux, direct et imminent sont réservés. (2) Toute restriction d'un droit fondamental doit être justifiée *par un intérêt public* ou par la protection d'un droit fondamental d'autrui. (3) Toute restriction d'un droit fondamental doit être *proportionnée au but visé.* (4) *L'essence des droits fondamentaux est inviolable* » (emphases ajoutées).

Ainsi, aussi importante soit-elle dans l'émergence d'une société démocratique et dans sa survie, la liberté d'expression peut être restreinte, notamment pour lutter contre les discours de haine. Ceux-ci remettent en effet en cause la réputation et les droits d'autrui, voire peuvent conduire à des atteintes à l'ordre public ou, selon leur contenu exact, à des agissements criminels à l'encontre de minorités.[10]

Il en va de même, par exemple, pour la liberté de réunion et d'association,[11] ainsi que pour la liberté de pensée, de conscience et de religion.[12] Si ces libertés sont également importantes pour l'émergence d'une liberté effective au sein d'un territoire et de sa survie, le cadre conventstitutionnel[13] en vigueur prévoit lui-même, pour la liberté de réunion et d'association, qu'elle peut faire l'objet de restrictions prévues dans la loi, nécessaires dans une société démocratique et qui ont *inter alia* pour objectif de protéger les « droits et libertés d'autrui » ou de participer « à la défense de l'ordre et à la prévention du crime ».[14] Des restrictions similaires sont possibles en lien avec la liberté de pensée, de conscience et de religion.[15] Ces restrictions concrétisent le principe selon lequel « la liberté consiste à pouvoir faire tout ce qui ne nuit pas à autrui ».[16]

Au-delà de ces limites posées par diverses libertés de façon explicite, il faut relever qu'il ne saurait être fait, par un individu, un usage abusif, notamment, de la liberté d'expression. Celui-ci est notamment exclu par l'article 17 CEDH.[17]

La protection, en miroir, de la dignité humaine et l'interdiction de la discrimination. Il sied de relever que si la liberté d'expression, tout comme d'autres libertés, est reconnue sur un plan constitutionnel et international, le cadre normatif en vigueur

---

[10] Cf. not., dans ce contexte, l'arrêt *Gündüz c. Turquie* de la CourEDH qui précise que: « Par ailleurs, nul doute que *des expressions concrètes constituant un discours de haine*, comme la Cour l'a noté dans l'affaire Jersild c. Danemark ..., pouvant être insultantes pour des individus ou des groupes, *ne bénéficient pas de la protection de l'article 10* de la Convention » (*Gündüz c. Turquie*, n° 35071/97, § 41, 4 décembre 2003; emphases ajoutées). Cf. également sur l'exclusion des discours de haine, à titre exemplatif, Gonin 2018, pp. 591–641, N 89ss.

[11] Celle-ci est notamment protégée par l'art. 11 CEDH.

[12] Celle-ci est notamment protégée par l'art. 9 CEDH.

[13] Par droit conventstitutionnel, l'on comprend les normes matériellement constitutionnelles d'un ordre juridique déterminé qui appartiennent cependant, d'un point de vue technique, au droit international. Il s'agit donc d'un terme combinant l'idée de *droit conven*tionnel (dérivant d'une convention internationale) à celle de droit con*stitutionnel*. On peut notamment songer, dans ce contexte, aux droits subjectifs protégés sur le plan international.

[14] Article 11 § 2 CEDH.

[15] Cf. article 9 § 2 CEDH.

[16] Article 4 de la Déclaration des Droits de l'Homme et du Citoyen de 1789.

[17] Cet article se lit comme suit: « Aucune des dispositions de la présente Convention ne peut être interprétée comme impliquant pour un Etat, un groupement ou un individu, *un droit quelconque de se livrer à une activité ou d'accomplir un acte visant à la destruction des droits ou libertés reconnus dans la présente Convention* ou à des limitations plus amples de ces droits et libertés que celles prévues à ladite Convention » (emphase ajoutée).

protège, « en miroir » en quelque sorte, la dignité humaine[18] et interdit la discrimination, notamment fondée sur l'origine, la race ou les convictions religieuses ou philosophiques.[19] La tenue de discours de haine forme, par essence en quelque sorte, un acte délibérément discriminatoire qui, très souvent, se fonde sur l'origine, la race ou les convictions d'un individu ou d'un groupe d'individus.

19.2.2 La Problématique de la Protection Judiciaire

Une évolution importante. La reconnaissance de droits et de libertés est une évolution importante en direction de l'émergence, et de la survie, d'un Etat libéral et démocratique. La reconnaissance d'une protection judiciaire effective est le pas suivant dans cette direction. Les libertés mentionnées au préalable, au premier rang desquels l'on retrouve la liberté d'expression, bénéficient d'une telle protection.

Tribunal fédéral. Sur le plan national, une violation–notamment–de la liberté d'expression peut être invoquée devant le Tribunal fédéral, la plus haute instance judiciaire nationale, par exemple par le biais d'un recours en matière pénale.[20] Dans ce contexte, le recours peut aussi bien être formé pour violation du droit fédéral, du droit international ou de droits constitutionnels cantonaux.[21] Selon les précisions indiquées au préalable, la liberté d'expression ne sera cependant pas protégée par la Haute Cour lorsque la teneur des propos contestés « est de nature à attiser la violence et la haine, excédant ainsi ce qui est tolérable [même] dans le débat politique ».[22]

Cour européenne des droits de l'homme. Sur le plan international, la CEDH est protégée par la Cour européenne des droits de l'homme (CourEDH), qui est notamment en droit de statuer sur des recours qui portent sur des décisions rendues par les autorités judiciaires suisses.[23] Dans sa jurisprudence et comme on l'a brièvement relevé, la CourEDH a cependant clairement exclu qu'un discours de haine, ou portant sur des faits historiques manifestement établis, puisse être protégé par l'article 10 CEDH. Soulignons à titre complémentaire que, toujours au niveau du Conseil de l'Europe et comme pour d'autres nations, la situation en Suisse est analysée régulièrement, sur un plan non-judiciaire, par la Commission européenne contre le racisme et l'intolérance.[24]

---

[18] Cf. not. article 7 Cst. Cette disposition « ouvre » par ailleurs le catalogue des droits fondamentaux de la Constitution fédérale.

[19] Cf. not. article 8 al. 2 Cst., ainsi que l'art. 14 CEDH. Cf. également article 1 al. 1 CERD pour ce qui est spécifiquement de la discrimination raciale.

[20] Cf. article 78 ss de la Loi sur le Tribunal fédéral du 17 juin 2005 (RS 173.110; ci-après: LTF).

[21] Cf. article 95, resp. let. (a), (b) et (c), LTF.

[22] Arrêt du Tribunal fédéral (ci-après: ATF) 137 IV 313, consid. 3.3.3.

[23] En lien avec la Suisse, ce sont les requêtes individuelles auprès de la CourEDH (article 34 CEDH) qui se trouvent clairement en première ligne. Les conditions de recevabilité pour un recours auprès de la CourEDH sont, pour leur part, réglées à l'art. 35 CEDH.

[24] Ci-après: ECRI. Cf. not. le Rapport de l'ECRI sur la Suisse (sixième cycle de monitoring) du 10 décembre 2019.

Pacte II de l'ONU. En lien avec le Pacte II de l'ONU, la Suisse a, comme les autres Etats parties, l'obligation de soumettre tous les quatre ans un rapport présentant les mesures prises et les progrès réalisés.[25] Elle n'a par contre pas ratifié le premier Protocole facultatif au Pacte II de l'ONU, qui donne la compétence au Comité des droits de l'homme de se prononcer sur cas concrets dans lesquels des personnes estiment être victimes d'une violation dudit Pacte par un Etat.[26] Dès lors, il n'existe pas de protection judiciaire devant ledit Comité pour les litiges ayant trait à la Suisse. Signalons par ailleurs que, d'un point de vue pratique, l'article 19 du Pacte II de l'ONU fait l'objet de développements nettement moins développés que, par exemple, l'article 16 Cst. ou, sur un plan international, l'article 10 CEDH, dans la jurisprudence du Tribunal fédéral.[27]

Convention sur l'élimination de toutes les formes de discrimination raciale. En lien avec la CERD, à laquelle la Suisse a adhéré le 29 novembre 1994, la Confédération helvétique soumet régulièrement des rapports périodiques, potentiellement combinés.[28] La Suisse a par ailleurs reconnu la procédure de communication individuelle, telle que prévue à l'article 14 CERD, le 19 juin 2003.[29] Nonobstant, la jurisprudence relative à la Suisse demeure très limitée vu que seuls deux cas sont listés sur le site officiel de l'ONU à ce sujet.[30]

Impact des ONG. Sur le plan de la société civile, la problématique du respect des droits de l'homme, et de la lutte contre le racisme et les discours de haine, est suivie de près par diverses ONG, parfois actives dans d'autres pays également. Parmi les organisations impliquées dans cette lutte contre le racisme et les discours de haine, on

---

[25] Cf. not. le Quatrième rapport périodique du Gouvernement suisse au Comité des droits de l'homme des Nations Unies, du 7 juillet 2016. Sur la discrimination raciale et le racisme en général, cf. not. §§ 54ss dudit Rapport. Sur le discours de haine, cf. en part. § 58. Cf. également les Observations finales du Comité des droits de l'homme concernant le quatrième rapport périodique de la Suisse du 22 août 2017 (not. §§ 20s., qui concernent spécifiquement le discours de haine).

[26] Cf. Office fédéral de la Justice (ci-après: OFJ) > Etat & Citoyen > Droits de l'homme > Pactes relatifs aux droits de l'homme, www.bj.admin.ch (consulté le 19.06.2023).

[27] Cf., à titre purement exemplatif, l'ATF 136 I 332, consid. 3.1. à 3.2.2. Cf. également ATF 131 IV 23, consid. 3.1.

[28] Le Département fédéral de l'Intérieur est compétent, en Suisse, pour ces rapports, la Confédération helvétique ayant déposé un Dixième, onzième et douzième rapports périodiques combinés le 30 novembre 2018 au Comité de l'ONU pour l'élimination de la discrimination raciale.

[29] Cf. not., sur la question, le Message relatif à la reconnaissance de la compétence du Comité pour l'élimination de la discrimination raciale (CERD) pour recevoir et examiner des communications au sens de l'art. 14 de la Convention internationale de 1965 sur l'élimination de toutes les formes de discrimination raciale (Feuille fédérale [ci-après: FF] 2001 5649ss). Cf. également le site de la Commission fédérale contre le racisme > Bases juridiques > Droit international public > Procédure de communication individuelle, https://www.ekr.admin.ch, consulté le 09.08.2021.

[30] Cf. UN Treaty Body Database > Reporting Status for Switzerland > Acceptance of individual complaints procedures for Switzerland > CERD, Article 14, https://tbinternet.ohchr.org/SitePages/Home.aspx, consulté le 09.08.2021. Les deux opinions dont il est question concluent par ailleurs à l'absence de violation de la CERD par la Suisse (CERD/C/84/D/50/2012 et CERD/C/91/D/53/2013).

retrouve notamment Amnesty International.[31] Le site humanrights.ch, pour sa part, donne accès à un « Réseau de centres de conseil pour les victimes du racisme », celui-ci rassemblant « 24 services spécialisés, issus de toute la Suisse [qui] proposent des consultations en cas de discrimination raciale ».[32] Les actions de ces organisations, ainsi que d'autres, font régulièrement l'objet d'une couverture médiatique. A l'instar d'autres associations ou regroupements, elles possèdent des « relais » au sein des instances politiques cantonales ou fédérales du pays pour défendre leur cause. Leurs activités participent ainsi véritablement au débat public, plusieurs de ces ONG offrant par ailleurs un soutien juridique aux victimes potentielles de violation de droits de l'homme, comme par exemple les personnes victimes de discours de haine.

19.2.3 L'art. 261bis CP

Texte actuel de la norme. Le contexte général posé, il convient de souligner que, face aux évolutions sociétales et eu égard à ses obligations internationales, la Suisse a adopté une disposition pénale consacrée spécifiquement à la discrimination et à l'incitation à la haine: l'article 261bis CP. Depuis sa modification le 14 décembre 2018, entrée en vigueur le 1er juillet 2020,[33] l'article 261bis CP stipule que:

Quiconque, publiquement, incite à la haine ou à la discrimination envers une personne ou un groupe de personnes en raison de leur appartenance raciale, ethnique ou religieuse ou de leur orientation sexuelle,

quiconque, publiquement, propage une idéologie visant à rabaisser ou à dénigrer de façon systématique cette personne ou ce groupe de personnes,

quiconque, dans le même dessein, organise ou encourage des actions de propagande ou y prend part,

quiconque publiquement, par la parole, l'écriture, l'image, le geste, par des voies de fait ou de toute autre manière, abaisse ou discrimine d'une façon qui porte atteinte à la dignité humaine une personne ou un groupe de personnes en raison de leur appartenance raciale, ethnique ou religieuse ou de leur orientation sexuelle ou qui, pour la même raison, nie, minimise grossièrement ou cherche à justifier un génocide ou d'autres crimes contre l'humanité,

quiconque refuse à une personne ou à un groupe de personnes, en raison de leur appartenance raciale, ethnique ou religieuse ou de leur orientation sexuelle, une prestation destinée à l'usage public,

---

[31] La Section suisse d'Amnesty International peut compter sur le soutien de plus de 40'000 membres et environ 85'000 donateurs et donatrices; elle compte par ailleurs une septantaine d'employés (cf. site officiel d'Amnesty International suisse > Faits et chiffres, www.amnesty.ch, consulté le 10.08.2021).

[32] Cf. le site de Humanrights.ch > Réseau de centres de conseil pour les victimes du racisme, www.humanrights.ch, consulté le 10.08.2021.

[33] L'article reproduit dans le corps du texte est donc celui en vigueur (depuis le 1er juillet 2020), selon le ch. I 1 de la Loi fédérale du 14.12.2018 (Discrimination et incitation à la haine en raison de l'orientation sexuelle; Recueil officiel [ci-après: RO] 2020 1609; FF 2018 3897 et 5327).

est puni d'une peine privative de liberté de trois ans au plus ou d'une peine pécuniaire.

19.2.4 *Origines*

Cette disposition, qui est entrée en vigueur dans sa version originale au 1er janvier 1995,[34] tisse des liens étroits avec la CERD. Ainsi, dans un message officiel du 2 mars 1992, le Conseil fédéral, pouvoir exécutif de la Suisse, relève à ce sujet que:

> La Convention interdit la discrimination raciale et oblige les Etats parties à prendre différentes mesures destinées à combattre et à prévenir celle-ci. Elle exige notamment que certains actes de discrimination raciale soient sanctionnés par des dispositions pénales. *Pour tenir compte de ces exigences, le Conseil fédéral propose d'introduire dans le code pénal et le code pénal militaire une disposition qui rendra désormais punissables* la propagande raciste, les atteintes racistes à la dignité humaine et le refus, pour des motifs racistes, d'un bien ou service offerts publiquement.[35]

Il faut signaler, dans ce contexte, qu'à l'inverse de la situation depuis le 1er juillet 2020, la communauté homosexuelle, en tant que groupe, ne bénéficiait pas de la protection de l'article 261bis CP dans sa version originale. Ainsi, dans un arrêt 6B_361/2010, du 1er novembre 2010, le Tribunal fédéral a relevé que:

> 4.4.1 L'article 261bis CP a été adopté en exécution des obligations contractées par la Suisse en adhérant à la Convention internationale du 21 décembre 1965 sur l'élimination de toutes les formes de discrimination raciale (…), qui vise toute distinction, exclusion, restriction ou préférence fondée sur la race, la couleur, l'ascendance ou l'origine nationale ou ethnique (article 1). Si, comme le soutiennent les recourants, l'article 261bis CP sanctionne également la discrimination fondée sur l'appartenance religieuse, respectivement la religion, ce critère a été retenu parce qu'il ne sortait pas du cadre d'une répression pénale fondée sur la discrimination raciale. On doit, en effet, considérer le lien existant fréquemment entre l'origine ethnique, voire nationale, et la religion. Ce critère était en outre conforme aux recommandations du Conseil de l'Europe et n'avait été abandonné, dans le texte de la Convention, que pour des raisons politiques liées au conflit au Proche-Orient … *En revanche, d'autres caractères, tels que le sexe, les tendances sexuelles ou les convictions idéologiques n'ont pas été retenus, à dessein, parce que l'on se serait trop écarté du but de la révision du Code pénal qui était de satisfaire aux obligations internationales de la Suisse* et parce qu'une norme générale sur la discrimination n'aurait pas eu sa place dans le contexte des délits contre la paix publique ….[36]

Le Tribunal fédéral poursuit son raisonnement en soulignant que:

> (…) [E]n introduisant cette disposition [= article 261bis CP], le législateur *n'envisageait pas une extension* illimitée de la répression pénale *à tous les actes de discrimination ou*

[34] Cf. RO 1994 2887.

[35] Message du Conseil fédéral concernant l'adhésion de la Suisse à la Convention internationale de 1965 sur l'élimination de toutes les formes de discrimination raciale et la révision y relative du droit pénal, du 2 mars 1992 (FF 1992 III 265, 266; emphase ajoutée).

[36] Arrêt du Tribunal fédéral (ci-après: TF) 6B_361/2010, 01.11.2010, consid. 4.4.1 (emphase ajoutée).

d'atteinte à des groupes ou des collectivités. Cela confirme aussi qu'à ses yeux l'adoption d'une norme spécifique protégeant la paix publique, et non seulement des intérêts privés, était nécessaire pour réprimer les atteintes collectives ...[37]

19.2.5 La Modification du 14 Décembre 2018

Intervention parlementaire « Lutter contre les discriminations basées sur l'orientation sexuelle » (n° 13.407). Peu heureux de la situation sous l'empire de l'article 261bis CP dans sa version originale, et trois ans après l'arrêt précité du Tribunal fédéral, le Conseiller national Reynard, membre de l'Assemblée fédérale, a déposé une initiative populaire intitulée « Lutter contre les discriminations basées sur l'orientation sexuelle » (n° 13.407). Celle-ci avait pour objectif « de compléter la disposition existante du Code pénal luttant contre la discrimination raciale, afin de l'étendre à la discrimination basée sur l'orientation sexuelle ».[38] Le parlementaire était en effet d'avis que: « Alors que notre Constitution interdit la discrimination fondée sur le mode de vie (article 8 al. 2), un vide juridique existe dans la répression des incitations à la haine basées sur l'orientation sexuelle des individus ».[39]

Travaux préparatoires. Si la Commission des affaires juridiques du Conseil national, chambre basse de l'Assemblée fédérale, a décidé de donner suite à cette intervention parlementaire, la même Commission du Conseil des Etats, chambre haute de l'Assemblée fédérale, a, dans premier temps, refusé de lui donner suite. Après confirmation du traitement par le Conseil national en plénum, le Conseil des Etats a également décidé de lui donner suite.[40] Ensuite, dans un avis du 3 août 2018 du Conseil fédéral à ce sujet, le pouvoir exécutif a certes reconnu que l'orientation sexuelle pouvait conduire à des discours ou actes haineux, mais a refusé d'étendre la protection de l'article 261bis CP à la thématique de « l'identité de genre ».[41]

Plus spécifiquement: les débats parlementaires. Les débats parlementaires ont été nourris en lien avec cet amendement de l'article 261bis CP, tant au sein du Conseil national qu'au sein du Conseil des Etats. Si la Commission des affaires juridiques du Conseil national accepte d'intégrer autant l'interdiction d'incitation à la haine en raison de l'orientation sexuelle que de l'identité de genre, celle du Conseil des

[37] Arrêt du TF 6B_361/2010, 01.11.2010, consid. 4.4.1 (emphase ajoutée).

[38] Intervention parlementaire n° 13.407, partie « Développement ». Cf. également Bigler 2019, p. 5.

[39] Intervention parlementaire n° 13.407, partie « Développement ».

[40] Cf. Bigler 2019, p. 5.

[41] Cf. Avis du Conseil fédéral relatif au rapport de la Commission des affaires juridiques du Conseil national du 3 mai 2018 portant sur l'initiative parlementaire « Lutter contre les discriminations basées sur l'orientation sexuelle » (FF 2018 I 5327, 5331). Dans ce contexte, le Conseil fédéral relève en lien avec l'identité de genre que: « *Il convient en tout cas de renoncer à compléter les art. 261bis CP et 171c CPM avec un critère vague dont la portée n'est pas suffisamment prévisible.* Si le projet se limitait à l'ajout du critère de l'orientation sexuelle, tel que proposé par l'initiative, il tiendrait mieux compte de l'exigence de précision de la loi pénale et présenterait moins de difficultés de mise en œuvre » (FF 2018 I 5327, 5331; emphase ajoutée).

Etats suit le Conseil fédéral et exclut la seconde composante.[42] La problématique du champ d'application concret de la loi revue et corrigée occupe, ainsi, une part importante des débats. Au niveau des plénums, le Conseil national rejoint, après débats, la solution retenue par le Conseil des Etats et rejette ainsi une extension à l'identité de genre.[43]

Les conditions de réalisation de l'article 261bis CP en matière d'incitation à la haine. Quant aux conditions de réalisation de l'article 261bis CP en matière d'incitation à la haine, il convient de signaler qu'elles sont au nombre de trois. En premier lieu, il doit y avoir commission d'un acte réprimé, par exemple par la propagation d'une idéologie ayant pour objectif de rabaisser ou de dénigrer de façon systématique. En deuxième lieu, il faut que cet acte réprimé porte sur une personne ou un groupe de personnes bénéficiant de la protection de l'article 261bis CP. Enfin et en troisième lieu, il faut que cet acte réprimé ait lieu dans la sphère publique, et non dans la sphère privée.[44]

19.2.6 Autres Questions en Lien avec l'art. 261bis CP

Fédéralisme et article 261bis CP. La Suisse est marquée par le principe du fédéralisme et son influence est notamment marquée au niveau de la structure judiciaire du pays.[45] Nonobstant, tous les cantons ont l'obligation d'appliquer le droit fédéral, et donc le Code pénal, le principe de la primauté du droit fédéral s'appliquant par ailleurs en Suisse.[46] De plus et comme il ressort du développement précédent, un Tribunal fédéral a été institué sur le plan national, siégeant principalement à Lausanne. Celui-ci est tenu, comme les autres autorités, d'appliquer et la loi, et le droit international.[47] La Loi sur le tribunal fédéral prévoit explicitement un recours en matière pénale.[48] Celui-ci est en particulier « recevable contre les décisions prises par les autorités cantonales de dernière instance »,[49] les cantons ayant l'obligation d'« institue[r] des tribunaux supérieurs comme autorités cantonales de dernière instance ».[50] Ceux-ci statuent, notamment, sur de potentielles violations de l'article 261bis CP.

---

[42] Cf. également Uhrmeister (2020), pp. 1381–1390, N 23 (avec divers renvois).

[43] Cf. également, sur les débats parlementaires, Bigler 2019, p. 7.

[44] Pour plus de détails sur les éléments constitutifs de l'infraction, cf. not. Corboz (2010), pp. 372ss.

[45] Cf. not. l'art. 123 al. 2 Cst., qui précise que « l'organisation judiciaire et l'administration de la justice ainsi que l'exécution des peines et des mesures en matière de droit pénal *sont du ressort des cantons*, sauf disposition contraire de la loi » (emphase ajoutée). Plus généralement, sur le fédéralisme suisse, cf. p. ex. Gonin (2021), pp. 381ss.

[46] Cf. not. art. 46 al. 1er Cst., ainsi qu'art. 49 Cst.

[47] Explicite à ce sujet: article 190 Cst. Sur cette disposition, cf. not. Martenet (2021), pp. 3445–3467, N 1ss.

[48] Cf. article 78 ss LTF.

[49] Article 80 al. 1er LTF.

[50] Article 80 al. 2 LTF.

19.2.7 Interactions de l'art. 261bis CP avec les Droits et Libertés

Comme relevé précédemment, l'article 261bis CP vient en quelque sorte protéger, d'un point de vue pénal, la dignité humaine et sanctionner certaines formes spécifiques de discrimination publique. Cet article du Code pénal doit, on l'a signalé, être lu en lien avec la liberté d'expression. Celle-ci n'est cependant pas absolue et peut–et doit–être restreinte selon le cadre normatif lorsqu'elle constitue un simple prétexte à une incitation à la haine par le biais, par exemple, de discours.

L'article 261bis CP interagit toutefois aussi avec la liberté religieuse *lato sensu*. La liberté de pensée, de conscience et de religion ne saurait cependant conduire à des incitations à la haine à l'encontre de fidèles d'autres communautés religieuses ou de pensée, ou à l'égard de personnes considérées comme « mécréantes ». Une personne, rétribuée ou non, n'est pas en droit de parler « sous le couvert d'une divinité » quelconque, ou alors sous le couvert d'une conviction de l'absence de toute forme de divinité, pour objectivement inciter à la haine. Une société libérale et démocratique–et l'Etat qui l'accompagne–obéissent à des règles devant par essence être déterminées par la sphère laïque, sous peine de crucifier pareille société sur le bois d'une « intolérance sacrée ».[51] Ainsi, sous peine de régression vers un âge que l'on espère à jamais révolu dans la sphère occidentale, la conviction religieuse–et plus encore la règle religieuse–doivent céder le pas à la règle étatique en la matière.

En pratique, le juge sera cependant confronté à des pesées d'intérêt potentiellement délicates. La liberté d'expression est en effet, lorsqu'elle n'est pas un alibi cachant des intentions pénalement prohibées, un pilier d'une société libérale et démocratique.[52] De plus, le droit pénal ne saurait se muer en un outil de censure de toute conviction s'éloignant des conceptions « main stream » à un moment x d'une société déterminée y. Comme l'Histoire l'enseigne, ainsi le veulent l'émergence et la survie d'une société libérale. Par ailleurs, la lutte contre l'esclavagisme, au Royaume-Uni, aux Etats-Unis et ailleurs, la remise en cause de l'apartheid en Afrique du sud, et bien d'autres causes nobles favorisant l'émergence de sociétés moins divisées et « injustes » furent le fait de personnes–dans un premier temps manifestement minoritaires–qui défendaient des opinions personnelles avec conviction, et parfois passion, remettant en cause–à tout le moins de façon figurée–des élites spécifiques ainsi que des conceptions spécifiques de leur période, parfois sur la base de convictions religieuses.

L'article 261bis CP tisse, également, des liens avec les libertés d'association et de réunion. Dans ce contexte, cette disposition pénale influencera en particulier–eu égard à ses conditions de réalisation–les réunions publiques potentiellement organisées par de telles associations, ainsi que leurs publications destinées au public. Dans

[51] L'Etat libéral et démocratique s'est en effet, comme on le sait, développé grâce à une séparation effective des pouvoirs temporel et spirituel, chacun d'entre eux « gouvernant » un domaine spécifique et de nature différente.

[52] Sur la question, délicate, des rapports entre liberté religieuse et liberté d'expression, avec de nombreux renvois à la jurisprudence, cf. not. Gonin (2018), pp. 533–589, N 186 ss.

ce contexte et malgré l'importance de la liberté d'expression également pour ces associations, il sied de relever que ces véritables poumons de la société civile ne sont en droit de faire circuler dans le corps social des discours de haine, véritables poisons pour la survie d'une société propice au développement de chacune et de chacun.

19.2.8 Impact du Droit Comparé?

Comme on l'a signalé au préalable, l'interdiction pénale du discours incitant à la haine découle en premier lieu de l'adoption par la Suisse de la CERD. Dans ce contexte, on l'a signalé, la maturation des esprits et des solutions législatives concrètement retenues sur le plan pénal a pris un certain temps, et même un temps certain.

Ainsi, plutôt que les solutions normatives retenues par d'autres Etats, c'est le contexte international qui a conduit la Suisse à adapter son cadre législatif interne. Cet impact du droit international passe, aussi, par l'interdiction du discours de haine par la CourEDH, de même que par l'analyse régulière de l'évolution de la situation en Suisse par des organismes internationaux, notamment au sein du Conseil de l'Europe et de l'ONU.

Il semble donc, en premier lieu, se dessiner une forme d'interaction entre sphère internationale et sphère nationale, plutôt qu'entre ordres normatifs interagissant sur un plan horizontal. Il n'en demeure pas moins que la Suisse, petit Etat niché au cœur d'un grand continent et parlant la langue de la France, de l'Allemagne, de l'Autriche, du Liechtenstein et de l'Italie, ses voisins directs, observe avec attention–et se nourrit– des solutions retenues par-delà ses frontières. A l'heure d'une médiatisation intense des rapports sociaux et des débats sociétaux, qui favorise également la circulation des solutions juridiques, les parlementaires ont l'opportunité, régulièrement, de réfléchir à la pertinence, ou non, des solutions en vigueur sur un plan national.[53]

Rôle, en particulier, de la Commission fédérale contre le racisme. Sur le plan fédéral, il existe une Commission fédérale contre le racisme.[54] Celle-ci « tient à jour une importante base de données très utile sur les discours et les crimes de haine ».[55] Il existe aussi, sur un plan cantonal, un réseau de centres qui conseillent les personnes victimes de racisme.[56]

Autres dispositions topiques. D'autres dispositions, notamment pénales, protègent la personne humaine de propos touchant à sa personne. On retrouve en particulier

---

[53] Pour une réflexion de fond sur la circulation juridique des idées, cf. not. Le Quinio (2011).

[54] Instituée en 1995 par le Conseil fédéral, cette Commission forme une commission extraparlementaire et indépendante. Dotée d'un secrétariat, elle comprend une quinzaine de membres qui sont des experts actifs dans le domaine du racisme.

[55] Rapport de l'ECRI sur la Suisse (sixième cycle de monitoring) adopté le 10 décembre 2019 et publié le 19 mars 2020, p. 7. Cf. également Commission fédérale contre le racisme > Recueil de cas juridiques (www.ekr.admin.ch, consulté le 03.08.2021).

[56] Rapport de l'ECRI sur la Suisse (sixième cycle de monitoring) adopté le 10 décembre 2019 et publié le 19 mars 2020, p. 7. Cf. également Commission fédérale contre le racisme > Réseau de centres de conseil pour les victimes du racisme (www.ekr.admin.ch, consulté le 03.08.2021).

l'article 173 CP, qui protège contre la diffamation; l'article 174 CP, qui condamne pénalement la calomnie, l'article 175 CP étant pour sa part spécifiquement consacré à la diffamation ou à la calomnie contre un mort. Comme cela ressort du développement ci-dessus, le Code pénal militaire sanctionne, lui aussi, l'incitation à la haine au sens strict du terme. D'un point de vue du droit privé, les article 28ss du Code civil suisse protègent la personnalité[57]. Ainsi, l'article 28 al. 1 CC stipule explicitement que: « Celui qui subit une atteinte illicite à sa personnalité peut agir en justice pour sa protection contre toute personne qui y participe ».

19.2.9 Jurisprudence et Article 261bis CP

Le droit, de par sa nature même, prête à interprétation.[58] Il en va de même pour l'article 261bis CP qui recourt à des termes ou expressions relativement indéterminées, à l'instar de « incitation », « haine », « discrimination », « race » ou « ethnie ». Les exemples jurisprudentiels qui suivent soulignent, dès lors, le poids, certain, de la jurisprudence dans la concrétisation effective de la disposition pénale examinée.

19.2.10 Arrêts Choisis en Lien avec l'art. 261bis CP

Au niveau du champ d'application matériel de l'article 261bis CP, le Tribunal fédéral a notamment pu, dans une affaire en lien avec l'initiative populaire visant à modifier la Constitution et cherchant à lutter contre « l'immigration de masse », se pencher sur des affiches affirmant que « Kosovaren schlitzen Schweizer auf ! », que l'on peut traduire librement par « Les Kosovars poignardent les Suisses ! ».[59]

Le Tribunal fédéral a considéré que cette affirmation, affichée dans les rues, tombait sous le couperet de l'article 261bis CP. Il a aussi précisé, dans ce contexte, que cette phrase « incitait » à la haine contre les Kosovars.[60] Dans le même contexte, la Haute Cour a souligné qu'il n'était pas nécessaire qu'une personne incite explicitement à la haine pour potentiellement tomber sous le coup de l'article 261bis CP.[61] Il suffit, souligne la Haute Cour, que « ses déclarations créent une atmosphère propice à la haine ou à la discrimination ».[62]

---

[57] RS 210 (ci-après: CC).

[58] Sur les méthodes d'interprétation utilisées par le Tribunal fédéral, cf. p. ex. ATF 143 I 109, consid. 6.

[59] Cf. ATF 143 IV 193.

[60] ATF 143 IV 193, consid. 4.3.

[61] ATF 143 IV 193, consid. 4.3.

[62] Dans la version originale: «*Es genügt, wenn er durch seine Äusserungen eine Stimmung schafft, in welcher Hass oder Diskriminierung gedeihen*» (ATF 143 IV 193, consid. 4.3.). Cf. également, déjà, ATF 123 IV 202, consid. 3.b).

Dans un autre arrêt, de 2017, le Tribunal fédéral a souligné que, selon les circonstances, le recours à un geste potentiellement polysémique, à l'instar de la « quenelle », pouvait conduire à une condamnation en raison de l'article 261bis CP. Dans le cas d'espèce, la quenelle litigieuse avait été faite devant la synagogue, à Genève.[63]

Plus spécifiquement en lien avec la négation du génocide, en l'occurrence arménien, le Tribunal fédéral a estimé en 2007 qu'un orateur, M. Perinçek, avait violé l'article 261bis CP par ses propos tenus lors de divers meetings.[64] Cette personne avait notamment affirmé que « les allégations de "génocide arménien" sont un mensonge international ».[65] Cette affaire avait fait relativement grand bruit puisque la condamnation prononcée par la Suisse à l'encontre de M. Perinçek a été, en fin de compte, renversée par la Grande Chambre de la CourEDH.[66]

Pour ce qui est, autre thématique importante, de la nature publique de l'incitation à la haine, ou à la discrimination, le Tribunal fédéral a précisé le cadre légal, notamment par le biais d'un ATF 133 IV 308. Eu égard à l'importance des biens juridiques protégés, dont la dignité humaine, le Tribunal fédéral a relevé dans cette affaire qu'il convenait désormais de faire une interprétation large de l'adverbe « publiquement » et, corollairement, une interprétation restrictive de l'adjectif « privé ».

Ainsi, le Tribunal fédéral définit, dans cette affaire, que: « Sont privés les expressions et les comportements dans le cercle de la famille et entre amis, ou dans un environnement caractérisé par des relations personnelles ou une confiance particulière ».[67] Il faut cependant, précise le Tribunal fédéral, que la discrimination raciale (ou l'incitation à la haine) apparaisse clairement comme un acte de discrimination raciale (ou d'incitation à la haine) aux yeux d'un tiers moyen non prévenu au vu des circonstances.[68]

De même, dans une autre affaire, le Tribunal fédéral a déterminé que, lorsque 40 à 50 skinheads qui n'avaient pas de liens particuliers de confiance entre eux et qui appartenaient à différents groupuscules se réunissaient, les propos tenus dans une telle réunion, dont l'accès était contrôlé, pouvaient, eux aussi, tomber sous le coup de l'article 261bis CP.[69]

---

[63] Cf. arrêt du TF 6B_734/2016, 18.07.2017, consid. 3.1ss.

[64] Cf. Arrêt du TF 6B_398/2007, du 12.12.2007, not. consid. 3.1ss.

[65] *Perinçek c. Suisse* [GC], no. 27510/08, du 15 octobre 2015, § 13.

[66] Cf. *Perinçek c. Suisse* [GC], no. 27510/08, du 15 octobre 2015, §§ 226-282 (constat de violation de l'art. 10 CEDH).

[67] ATF 133 IV 308, consid. 8.3. Dans la version originale, en allemand: « Privat sind Äusserungen und Verhaltensweisen im Familien- und Freundeskreis oder sonst in einem durch persönliche Beziehungen oder besonderes Vertrauen geprägten Umfeld ».

[68] Cf. ATF 133 IV 308, consid. 8.4. Sur la question de la nature publique de l'infraction, cf. également Corboz (2010), p. 375s.

[69] Explicite à ce sujet: ATF 130 IV 120, consid. 6.

19.2.11 Eléments Statistiques en Lien Avec l'application de l'art. 261bis CP

D'un point de vue quantitatif, et comme indiqué ci-dessus, la Commission fédérale contre le racisme tient à jour une base de données contenant des résumés d'arrêts, d'ordonnances pénales, d'ordonnances de classement et de non-entrées en matière qui portent sur l'article 261bis CP. Selon une étude mandatée par cette Commission, entre 1995 et 2019, « la banque de données a enregistré 935 cas, dont 63 % se sont terminés par une condamnation, et 37% par un acquittement, le classement de la procédure ou une ordonnance de non-entrée en matière ».[70]

Toujours selon la même étude, parue en 2021, la grande majorité des cas (plus de 490) concerne la discrimination–ou rabaissement–par racisme.[71] Les cas d'incitation à la haine, au sens étroit du terme, ou à la discrimination suivent avec 150 cas, la diffusion d'idéologies racistes ayant été dénoncées dans 130 cas.[72] La négation d'un génocide (2e partie de l'al. 4 de l'article 261bis CP) est également un sujet récurrent puisqu'il constitue le grief de près de 90 cas.[73]

Pour ce qui est des victimes de discours de haine, ou dénigrants, l'on retrouve en première place les personnes de confession juive (avec 265 cas).[74] Il ressort par ailleurs de l'analyse judiciaire précitée qu'ils étaient suivis des « étrangers », au sens large du terme (avec 217 cas),[75] et des « Noirs » (avec 188 cas).[76] D'un point de vue spatial, les actes litigieux sont la plupart du temps, même dans une ère dite numérique, commis dans un lieu public (324 cas). Les actes répréhensibles s'élèvent à 260 cas sur les réseaux sociaux et les médias (papier ou en ligne).[77]

---

[70] V. Leimgruber (pour la CFR), La norme pénale antiraciste dans la pratique judiciaire–Analyse de la jurisprudence relative à l'art. 261bis CP de 1995 à 2019, CFR, Berne 2021, p. 11.

[71] V. Leimgruber (pour la CFR), La norme pénale antiraciste dans la pratique judiciaire–Analyse de la jurisprudence relative à l'art. 261bis CP de 1995 à 2019, CFR, Berne 2021, p. 11.

[72] V. Leimgruber (pour la CFR), La norme pénale antiraciste dans la pratique judiciaire–Analyse de la jurisprudence relative à l'art. 261bis CP de 1995 à 2019, CFR, Berne 2021, p. 11.

[73] L'analyse judiciaire souligne encore que « l'organisation d'actions de propagande (al. 3) et le refus de fournir des prestations destinées au public (al. 5) font [pour leur part] chacun l'objet d'un peu plus de 20 cas » (Leimgruber 2021, p. 11).

[74] Cf. not. ATF 123 IV 202. Cf. également arrêt non publié du TF 6S.614/2001, 18.03.2002, consid. 4., et arrêt du TF 6B_1100/2014, 14.10.2015, consid. 3.1ss.

[75] Ainsi, les instances judiciaires suisses ont eu à se pencher, à titre exemplatif, sur les propos suivants, publiés sur Facebook: « J'organise une *Kristallnacht*. Qui est partant pour aller bruler du muzz? » (sic). La personne condamnée avait publié, le même jour, le commentaire suivant: « J'ai mon P226 qui doit bientôt arriver + le calibre 12 » (ATF 143 IV 380, Faits). Cf. également arrêt du TF 6B_644/2020, 14.10.2020 (cet arrêt concernait la communauté musulmane et impliquait un politicien connu au niveau national).

[76] Leimgruber 2021, p. 11. Ces chiffres doivent cependant être relativisés en ce sens qu'un grand nombre d'affaires ne précise pas explicitement qui sont les personnes ou les groupes visés.

[77] Ibid., p. 11.

19.3 Démocratie Semi-Directe et Condamnation du Discours de Haine

La Suisse a opté pour un régime politique combinant des éléments de démocratie représentative (existence d'un pouvoir législatif bicaméral) avec des éléments de démocratie (semi-)directe (not. existence d'une initiative populaire permettant d'amender directement la Constitution et d'un référendum facultatif contre les lois).[78] Si ces spécificités ne rendent pas le débat politique omniprésent, il n'en demeure pas moins que les échanges de vue sur des questions politiques sont nombreux, que ce soit dans les cafés, les médias ou plus généralement au sein de la société civile.[79]

Dans ce contexte, il sied en outre de relever que, déjà avant l'apparition du Covid, face à un monde en pleine mutation (en lien notamment avec la transnationalisation de l'économie et des échanges sociaux, le multiculturalisme, ou encore le réchauffement climatique), les positions politiques défendues divergent fortement, également au sein du microcosme helvétique. Ainsi, si certains embrassent cette ouverture en la considérant comme source de nombreuses opportunités, d'autres la craignent et préfèrent avoir une attitude plus conservatrice, sans jugement de valeur de notre part.[80] Les votations étant, dans la pratique, fréquemment serrées–les principales villes du pays ayant une tendance plus marquée à l'ouverture et les campagnes en général une attitude un peu plus dubitative–, les débats font, à l'occasion, rage. La coexistence de trois régions linguistiques principales (germanophone, francophone et italophone) vient encore complexifier la donne.

De plus, il convient de mettre en exergue que, par le biais de l'initiative populaire visant à amender la Constitution, les sujets débattus peuvent avoir une implication marquée sur des groupes de personne déterminés. A titre exemplatif, l'initiative contre l'immigration de masse, par ailleurs adoptée par le souverain en 2014, concernait directement les ressortissants étrangers, la Suisse étant un pays marqué par une forte immigration ces dernières années.[81] Il en va de même des deux initiatives pour le renvoi des criminels étrangers, la première d'entre elles étant, elle aussi, adoptée en 2010 grâce au double soutien du peuple et des cantons.[82] A titre exemplatif, les initiatives pour l'interdiction de la construction de minarets, de même que celles contre l'interdiction de se dissimuler le visage, concernant en particulier le port de la burka,

---

[78] Cf. resp. article 138s. Cst. et art. 140, al. 1 not. let. a), Cst.

[79] En Suisse, il y a en pratique plusieurs votations fédérales par année, sans compter les votations communales et/ou cantonales.

[80] Concrètement, le spectre politique suisse va ainsi, désormais, d'une fraction parlementaire verte à gauche, relativement importante, à un parti politique dénommé l'« Union démocratique du centre », qui se trouve néanmoins à la droite de l'échiquier politique. Ce second parti est le plus important au sein du Conseil national, la Chambre basse du pouvoir législatif.

[81] Cette initiative populaire a concrètement modifié la Constitution, y introduisant un nouvel article 121a dont l'al. 2 détermine notamment que : « Le nombre des autorisations délivrées pour le séjour des étrangers en Suisse est limité par des plafonds et des contingents annuels ».

[82] Son ancrage constitutionnel, depuis le 28 novembre 2010, se situe à l'art. 121, al. 3 à 6, Cst. La seconde initiative portant sur les « criminels étrangers » a, pour sa part, été refusée en votation le 28 février 2016 (cf. not. FF 2016 3557).

toutes deux acceptées en votation populaire,[83] concernaient pour leur part directement, ou en tout cas indirectement pour la seconde, les personnes de confession musulmane.[84] Cette thématique des interactions entre « l'étranger » et la Constitution, ne date cependant d'hier puisque la première initiative populaire adoptée par le souverain avait pour but d'interdire l'abattage rituel d'animaux, le 20 août 1893.[85] Cette initiative avait pu entre autres pu bénéficier des tendances antisémites au sein de la population.

Ces points précisés, il faut signaler que si les échanges de vue se retrouvent au cœur du processus–et d'une société–démocratiques, et que si la liberté d'expression joue un rôle particulier en la matière, il n'en demeure pas moins que l'ordre politique suisse doit, aussi en l'espèce, respecter les normes pénales en vigueur et donc aussi l'article 261bis CP. En effet, un processus politique ne saurait, lui aussi, en aucun cas servir de prétexte à l'incitation à la haine.

Un tel processus peut–et doit–cependant pouvoir permettre à chacune et à chacun, selon la formule consacrée, de la CourEDH d'exprimer–aussi–les opinions qui heurtent ou choquent. Strasbourg a en effet mis en exergue, en 1976 déjà, que:

> « [La liberté d'expression] vaut non seulement pour les "informations" ou "idées" accueillies avec faveur ou considérées comme inoffensives ou indifférentes, mais *aussi pour celles qui heurtent, choquent ou inquiètent l'Etat ou une fraction quelconque de la population. Ainsi le veulent le pluralisme, la tolérance et l'esprit d'ouverture sans lesquels il n'est pas de "société démocratique"* ».[86]

A défaut, si les positions minoritaires sont censurées, la démocratie court le risque d'être réduite à une coquille « vide de sens ». Il convient donc, paradoxalement, de protéger certaines minorités politiques, quoiqu'elles dérangent potentiellement des franges de la population, contre les potentielles « sensibilités excessives » d'autres minorités, politiques ou non. On l'aura saisi: le système politique suisse exige ainsi, pour pouvoir fonctionner, un système éducatif de qualité, donnant les outils pour saisir les grandes questions contemporaines, pour suivre–de façon critique–les débats y relatifs.

---

[83] La première d'entre elles a été adoptée le 29 novembre 2009; la seconde a été adoptée relativement récemment, le 23 mars 2021.

[84] La première a introduit dans la Constitution, l'art. 72 al. 3 qui se lit comme suit: « La construction de minarets est interdite ». A son sujet, cf. not. Martenet et Zandirad (2021), pp. 1602–1627, N 61ss. La seconde, pour sa part, a fait naître l'art. 10*a* Cst., dont l'al. 1er a la teneur suivante: « Nul ne peut se dissimuler le visage dans l'espace public, ni dans les lieux accessibles au public ou dans lesquels sont fournies des prestations ordinairement accessibles par tout un chacun; l'interdiction n'est pas applicable dans les lieux de culte ». Sur cette disposition récente, cf. not. Zandirad (2021), pp. 433–453, N 1ss.

[85] Cf. not. Külling (2021).

[86] *Handyside c. Royaume-Uni* [GC], no. 5493/72, du 7 décembre 1976, § 49 (emphase ajoutée). Cf. not., à ce sujet, Cottier (2021), pp. 577–596, N 46. La prof. Hertig, pour sa part, parle de la liberté d'expression, au sens large du terme, comme d'un « konstituierendes Element einer demokratischen, offenen Gesellschaft » (Hertig (2015), pp. 356–372, N 4).

19.4 Prise de Position Personnelle

Le développement ci-dessus souligne qu'une fois de plus, la société suisse n'est pas exception au sein de l'Occident, et bien au-delà: la haine–et son incitation–sont aussi une question qui se pose dans ce pays. Il s'agit donc, pour l'ordre constitutionnel suisse et les autorités qui le font vivre, l'appliquent et le protègent, de parvenir à un équilibre délicat entre liberté d'expression d'une part, dont on ne saurait abuser, et condamnation pénale de certains propos.

Par conséquent, si la critique doit être tolérée, puisqu'elle est au cœur de toute société véritablement démocratique, elle ne saurait se muer en haine de l'autre. Dans ce contexte, il faut relever que la situation au sein de la Confédération helvétique est d'autant plus intéressante que l'actualité politique n'est pas déterminée uniquement par l'agenda et les partis politiques, ni par les médias, mais également par des initiatives populaires émanant de la société civile elle-même.

De fait, la démocratie telle que vécue en Suisse est par essence exigeante, aussi pour les libertés. L'interdiction pénale de l'incitation à la haine forme un des garde-fous se dressant sur la route des dérives les plus sévères. Si son utilisation doit demeurer proportionnée, elle doit, à notre sens, être « intolérante » avec celui, ou celle, qui propage de véritables discours haineux. Si le lecteur nous concède une métaphore pour terminer le présent rapport national, une démocratie « qui fonctionne » est un peu comme une forêt de pins, en plein été torride; la haine, c'est la flamme que l'on dépose à ses pieds, ignorant si le feu prendra, et jusqu'où. A notre sens, il serait orgueilleux de croire que les arbres suisses résistent mieux à l'incendie que les arbres « étrangers ».

References

Bigle O (2019) La révision de l'article 261bis CP du 14 décembre 2018 – Avis de droit. Etude NVB, Neuchâtel.

Corboz B (2010) Les infractions en droit suisse–Volume II, 3e édition. Stämpfli, Berne.

Cottier B (2021) Article 16. ', In : Martenet V, Dubey J (édit) Commentaire romand de la Constitution fédérale. Helbing, Bâle, pp. 577–596.

Gonin L (2018) Article 9. In : Gonin L, Bigler O (édit) Commentaire pratique de la CEDH–Article 1 à 18. Lexis Nexis et Stämpfli, Paris et Berne, pp. 533–589.

Gonin L (2021) Droit constitutionnel suisse. Schulthess, Zurich et Genève.

Haller W, Koelz A, Gächter Th (2020) Allgemeines Staatsrecht – Eine juristische Einführung in die allgemeine Staatslehre, 6e édition. Schulthess, Zurich, Bâle et Genève.

Hertig M (2015) Article 16. In : Waldmann B, Belser EM, Epiney A (édit) Basler Kommentar der Bundesverfassung. Helbing, Bâle, pp. 356–372.

Külling F (2021) Abattage rituel. In : Dictionnaire historique de la Suisse (DHS). www.hls-dhs-dss.ch. Consulté le 20.08.2021.

Le Quinio A (2011) Recherche sur la circulation des solutions juridiques – Le recours au droit comparé par les juridictions constitutionnelles, thèse. Fondation Varenne, Paris.

Leimgruber V (pour la CFR) (2021) La norme pénale antiraciste dans la pratique judiciaire–Analyse de la jurisprudence relative à l'article 261bis CP de 1995 à 2019. CFR, Berne.

Martenet V, Zandirad D (2021) Article 72. In : Martenet V, Dubey J (édit) Commentaire romand de la Constitution fédérale. Helbing, Bâle, pp. 1602–1627.
Martenet V (2021) Article 190. In : Martenet V, Dubey J (édit) Commentaire romand de la Constitution fédérale. Helbing, Bâle, pp. 3445–3467.
Tschannen P (2016) Staatsrecht der Schweizerischen Eidgenossenschaft, 4e édition. Stämpfli, Berne.
Uhrmeister P (2020) Article 261bis. In: Graf DK (édit) StGB – Annotierter Kommentar. Stämpfli, Berne, pp. 1381–1390.
Zandirad D (2021) Article 10a. In : Martenet V, Dubey J (édit) Commentaire romand de la Constitution fédérale. Helbing, Bâle, pp. 433–453.

Luc Gonin studied law in Switzerland (Geneva, Bern and Neuchâtel), in Paris II (Panthéon-Assas) and in New York (Columbia Law School). His doctoral thesis examined the concept of the State, followed by post-doctoral work on human rights in practice. Gonin has taught at the Universities of Fribourg, Geneva and Neuchâtel. He is the author of a Practical Commentary on the ECHR (Lexis Nexis and Stämpfli, 2018, with Olivier Bigler) and a Summary of Swiss constitutional law (Schulthess, 2021). He has worked for four different departments within the Swiss federal administration.

Chapter 20
United Kingdom

Chara Bakalis

Contents

Abstract The United Kingdom has a complex array of statutes which can be used to tackle online hate speech. However, these laws were not designed with the internet in mind, and as such, they are unwieldy and difficult to use against perpetrators of online hate. In recent years, the focus of policy makers has shifted towards holding platforms accountable for the material they host, and the Online Safety Act 2023 has been enacted accordingly. In parallel to this, fears about the impact of online hate speech have manifested themselves in social media controversies, such as that surrounding 'cancel culture'. These discussions have little to do with the law itself, and are linked to broader concerns about the coarsening of public debate and the polarisation of views on social media.

Keyword Online hate speech · Responsibility of social media companies · Cancel culture · Digital hate · Cyberhate

C. Bakalis (✉)
School of Law and Social Sciences, Oxford Brookes University, Oxford, United Kingdom
e-mail: cbakalis@brookes.ac.uk

E. Heinze (ed.), *Criminalising Hate Speech*,
https://doi.org/10.1007/978-94-6265-650-5_20

20.1 National Constitutional Law

The United Kingdom does not have a written constitution. Nevertheless, civil liberties have always formed an intrinsic part of UK common law, including freedom of speech (see, e.g., *Attorney General v Guardian Newspapers* (1990) 1 AC 109). In 1998, Parliament enacted the Human Rights Act 1998. This Act has effectively incorporated the European Convention on Human Rights (ECHR) into UK Law and has put into statutory footing the requirement for judges to interpret UK law so that it is consistent with ECHR jurisprudence. The Human Rights Act 1998 does not give freedom of speech a constitutional basis as such, but it does allow the Courts to declare a statute incompatible with freedom of expression.

The ECHR does not contain a positive obligation on Member States to enact hate speech legislation, but Article 10 on freedom of expression allows for limits under certain circumstances, and as such, hate speech legislation has been found by the European Court of Human Rights (ECtHR) to be compatible with Article 10 (see for example Glimmerveen and Hagenbeek v the Netherlands application nos 8348/78 and 8406/78 (1979)). More recent ECtHR jurisprudence suggests that in some cases hate speech and hate crime legislation are positively required under the Convention in order to protect other Convention Rights. I go into this in more detail in Sect. 20.5 below.

20.2 National Statutory or Administrative Law

It is important to note at the outset that the UK is made up of England, Wales, Scotland and Northern Ireland. Whilst these nations share some laws, there are also some differences which will be highlighted below, although the emphasis will be on the law of England and Wales.

20.2.1 Stirring Up Hatred Offenses

The most important stirring up hatred offences are the incitement offences under Part III of the Public Order Act 1986 (POA 1986) which apply to England and Wales (and did apply to Scotland until April 2021). These constitute the most direct form of 'hate speech' provisions. POA 1986 Part III creates a series of offences concerned with words or behaviour, or dissemination or possession (with a view to dissemination) of material that is intended to stir up racial hatred or hatred on grounds of religion or sexual orientation. Whilst the offences originally applied only to race, religion and sexual orientation have been added in subsequent iterations, though with slightly less protection than that afforded to race because of concerns relating to freedom of speech (see POA 1986, Part 3A).

As a result of these piecemeal changes to the stirring up offences, we now have two sets of offences. Those relating to racial hatred involve: (a) threatening, abusive or insulting words, or material (b) intended or likely to stir up racial hatred. The narrower offences relating to sexual orientation and religion involve: (a) threatening words or material (b) intended to stir up hatred.

For offences relating to religion and sexual orientation, there are additional 'freedom of speech' clauses (s. 29J and s. 29JA), which limit the application of these offences. For example, the freedom of speech clause in relation to sexual orientation makes it clear that 'any discussion or criticism of sexual practices or the urging of persons to refrain from such conduct' or any criticism of same-sex marriage is not in and of itself conduct falling under the offence. In relation to religion, the freedom of speech clause makes it clear that there is protection for the 'discussion, criticism or expressions of antipathy, dislike, ridicule, insult or abuse of particular religions or the beliefs or practices of their adherents, or of any other belief system or the beliefs or practices of its adherents, or proselytising or urging adherents of a different religion or belief system to cease practising their religion or belief system'. Arguably these freedom of speech clauses do nothing more than to reiterate the position under Article 10 of the ECHR. Nevertheless, those clauses were deemed to be important to reassure the public that speech of this nature was not illegal.

In Northern Ireland, Part III of the Public Order (Northern Ireland) Act 1987 (POA 1987) creates several offences relating to the stirring up of hatred or of arousal of fear. These are very similar, but not identical to the POA 1986 Part III Offences. One notable difference is that they apply to a wider category of protected characteristics, as they cover disability as well as race, religion and sexual orientation.

In Scotland, the new Hate Crime and Public Order (Scotland) Act 2021 modifies the POA 1986 Part III offences to include a broader range of protected characteristics and has made changes to material parts of the offence, such as including a defence of reasonableness. Finally, there is also an offence related to racialist changing under the Football (Offences) Act 1991, which under s. 3(1) makes it an offence to 'engage or take part in chanting of an indecent or racialist nature at a designated football match'. This offence applies to England and Wales. Similar provisions used to exist in Scotland, but were repealed in 2018 over fears that the law was excessive and contravened free speech.

20.2.2 Other Speech Offences

Whilst the stirring up offences are the main sources of hate speech offences, there are other ways in which speech that is hateful can be criminalised, albeit less directly. In England and Wales, there are offences under the Public Order Act 1986 under s. 4, 4A and s. 5 which make it unlawful to use words in particular contexts which are 'threatening', 'abusive' or insulting. These offences do not directly punish 'hate', but there are aggravated versions of these offences under the Crime and Disorder Act 1998, meaning that if hostility towards race or religion was demonstrated during the commission of these offences, then the offence is aggravated and the maximum penalty is higher than for the non-aggravated version of the offence. If the hostility relates to sexual orientation, transgender or disability, then the general hate crime sentencing provisions apply which allow the hostility to be taken into account at sentencing, but the maximum penalty stays the same.

In addition, we have two communications offences which can be used to deal with speech that appears online. These are s. 127(1) of the Communications Act 2003, applicable to the whole of the UK, and s. 1 of the Malicious Communications Act 1988, which applies to England and Wales only. As with POA 1986 s. 4, 4A and s. 5, these offences do not directly criminalise hate speech as no 'hate' element needs to be present for the commission of these offences. Instead, these offences require speech to be 'grossly offensive,' 'indecent,' or 'obscene'. However, under general sentencing provisions relating to hate crime, if these offences are committed and any hostility towards race, religion, sexual orientation, transgender or disability can be taken into account, but the maximum penalty remains the same.

It is clear from these developments that the regulation of hate speech in the UK is extremely complex. Yet in reality, as far as the stirring up offences are concerned, there are very few prosecutions—fewer than five most years, and often none at all. This fact can be interpreted in different ways. For some, this is an indication that fears over the Draconian nature of the laws are exaggerated, and the law is sufficiently narrow to preserve free speech. For others, the lack of prosecutions suggests that the stirring up offences are not wide enough to offer any real protection to victims. For those who oppose hate speech laws entirely, the lack of prosecutions suggests that these are unnecessary laws which are purely symbolic in nature and should be repealed because of lack of use. It is impossible to know to what extent the stirring up offences have a deterrent effect, and are therefore successful in terms of setting standards for public debate, and this is why prosecutions seem largely unnecessary. Equally, it is not possible to determine the extent to which these laws may cause ordinary citizens to feel constrained in what they can say thereby stifling or 'chilling' free speech.

20.2.3 Reform and Online Hate Speech

In recent years, the topics of hate speech and hate crime have been high up on the political agenda in the UK. There have been law reform consultations in England and Wales, Scotland and Northern Ireland in the past four years. The Scottish reform proposals have progressed furthest, with the new Hate Crime and Public Order (Scotland) Act 2021 becoming law in April 2021, and which was partly based on a report undertaken by Lord Bracadale. Judge Marrinan published his proposals for Northern Irish reform at the end of 2020, but have yet to be taken on board by the Northern Irish Assembly. Meanwhile, the Law Commission for England & Wales published a report in 2021 outlining a number of reform proposals for hate crime law which have largely been ignored by the government.

These proposals have been comprehensive, but from the point of view of hate speech a couple of issues are worth highlighting. First, the discussions have centred around whether the protected characteristics for hate speech offences should be extended to gender, transgender, disability, age, or other characteristics. A second question is whether the so-called 'dwelling' defence should be refined. Currently, under s. 18(2) there is a defence if the words used were 'displayed, by a person inside a dwelling and are not heard or seen except by other persons in that or another dwelling.' The purpose of this defence is to give people protection for speech uttered in their homes; but in the internet age, this defence can effectively give protection to anyone who posts material from their own home and therefore could render the offences as useless for the vast majority of material published online. This highlights the problem with trying to use existing offences in the online sphere which were originally created for use in an analogue world. One option would be to remove this defence entirely from the law. However, doing so would open up the possibility of criminalising speech that individuals may engage in with friends and family, so to speak, around the dinner table. The Law Commission and Judge Marrinan have tried to reconcile these two approaches by proposing that the 'dwelling' defence be replaced with one which gives protection to 'private conversations', thus protecting 'private' speech irrespective of where it takes place whilst still ensuring that speech posted on the internet is no longer given immunity if posted from a 'dwelling'.

This leads us neatly to a broader debate, namely, how to deal with online hate speech in general, and whether a more desirable approach would be to focus on the responsibility of social media companies for the material they host online, rather than on criminalising individual perpetrators for speech they have posted. To this end, the UK Parliament has passed the Online Safety Act 2023 which imposes duties on internet companies to protect their users - particularly children - from online harms. The Act has appointed Ofcom as the new online regulator, with the power to impose fines on internet companies if they do not comply with their duties under the Act. The Act has yet to come into effect, so it is too soon to determine whether it will make a difference to victims. Over the coming years, it will be important for lawyers and academics to scrutinise in fine detail how the regulator will operate in order to ensure that an appropriate balance is struck between freedom of expression on the one hand, and the need to protect victims of hate speech on the other.

20.3 International Covenant on Civil and Political Rights (ICCPR)

The United Kingdom is a party to the ICCPR and has not entered any reservations in relation to it. However, UK law does not fully comply with ICCPR requirements in that some forms of advocacy of hatred such as incitement to discrimination are not unlawful under UK law.

20.4 International Convention on the Elimination of All Forms of Racial Discrimination (ICERD)

The UK ratified ICERD in 1969. However, there has been ongoing debate about the UK's interpretation of Article 4(a). The UK's formal interpretation of Article 4(a) which was submitted as a interpretative declaration upon ratification (Reservation and Interpretative Statement of the United Kingdon, 11 October 1966) is that legislation is only needed insofar as this is compatible with freedom of expression and opinion, and the right to assembly and association, and only insofar as religion and belief are not covered by Article 4(a). In this respect, UK law does not fully comply with ICERD requirements.

For example, ICERD requires the dissemination of ideas based on racial superiority or hatred to be made unlawful, whereas under UK law, such dissemination is only unlawful if the ideas stir up hatred in the way required under the stirring up offences (discussed above); ICERD requires all incitement to racial hatred to be unlawful whereas under UK law it is only unlawful in limited circumstances; finally, ICERD requires the assisting and financing of racist activities to be unlawful whereas under UK law this is only unlawful if the underlying activities are themselves criminal. In 2016, in its most recent review of the UK, the Committee on Elimination of Discrimination reiterated its recommendation that the UK withdraw its interpretative declaration on Article 4 (Committee on the Elimination of Racial Discrimination, 'Consideration of Reports Submitted by State Parties under Article 9 of the Convention', 2003, CERD/C/63/CO/1110, December, 2003.

20.5 Council of Europe

The UK is a Member State of the Council of Europe and a signatory to the ECHR. The UK Human Rights Act 1998 requires courts to interpret UK legislation so that it is compatible with the rulings of the European Court of Human Rights, and if it is not possible to do so, the Supreme Court can make a declaration of incompatibility. However, due to the constitutional set-up in the UK, the Supreme Court cannot actually strike down legislation for being incompatible with the Convention.

The most important right in this context is Article 10 freedom of expression, which states the following:

> Everyone has the right to freedom of expression. This right shall include freedom to hold opinions and to receive and impart information and ideas...
>
> The exercise of these freedoms ... may be subject to such formalities, conditions, restrictions or penalties as are prescribed by law and are necessary in a democratic society, in the interests of national security, territorial integrity or public safety, for the prevention of disorder or crime, for the protection of health or morals, for the protection of the reputation or rights of others...

The right to freedom of expression is therefore not an absolute right, and laws can be created limiting citizens' freedom of expression so long as the law fulfils certain criteria and is 'necessary in a democratic society'. There is a rich body of ECrtHR case law which deals specifically with hate speech laws. Various types of hate speech laws have been found to be legitimate in a number of cases such as those relating to ethnic hate (Pavel Ivanov v Russia, Application no. 35222/04 (2007), racial hate (Glimmerveen and Hagenbeek v the Netherlands application nos 8348/78 and 8406/78 (1979)), and religious hate (Norwood v UK Application no. 23131/03 (2004)). Protection has also been given, albeit to a lesser extent to homophobic hate (Vejdeland and Others v Sweden application no. 1813/07 (2012)) incitement to ethnic hatred (Balsytė-Lideikienė v. Lithuania Application no. 72596/01 (2008)) and incitement to racial discrimination or hatred (Jersild v. Denmark, 298 Eur. Ct. H.R. (ser A) (1994)).

There is no positive obligation on states to have hate speech laws, but a couple of recent cases (Aksu v Turkey [2012] (App. Nos. 4149/04 and 41029/04) and Karaahmed v Bulgaria [2015] (App. No. 30587/13) suggest that the ECrtHR does impose such an obligation on states where such laws are necessary to protect other Convention rights (namely Article 8, respect for private life; and Article 9, freedom of religion). Moreover, whilst the principles of ECrtHR jurisprudence applies equally to all Member States, it is worth highlighting that a couple of important ECrtHR cases dealing with the general principles of how Article 10 operates in relation to hate speech laws deal specifically with cases brought against the UK, and as such, these are of particular interest to UK judges.

For example, many years ago, the case of *Handyside v UK*, 24 Eur. Ct. H.R (ser A) (1976) set out a classic explanation of the parameters of Article 10 and in particular makes it clear that Article 10 protects ideas that 'offend, shock or disturb'. A few decades later, in *Norwood v UK* Application no. 23131/03 (2004), the applicant had displayed a British National Party poster in his window which depicted New York's Twin Towers on fire during the terrorist attacks of 11 September 2001, with the accompanying words: 'Islam out of Britain—Protect the British People'. He was charged with a s. 5 Public Order Act 1988 offence and argued that this breached his Article 10 right to freedom of speech. However, the ECrtHR used Article 17 to say that this was not 'speech' protected by Article 10 as the words undermined the underlying values of the Convention.

20.6 Judicial Rulings

The common law nature of UK law means that judicial interpretation of case law is very important. There is some clarification from the case law about the meaning of hateful expression, but not a huge amount. This is largely because few cases have gone to court prosecuting the stirring up offences, so our understanding of most of the terms come from accompanying explanatory notes to the statute. However, some case law is useful here. For example, while not directly about the stirring up offences, the case of *Cakmak* [2002] EWCA Crim 500 has confirmed that the test to be applied, when deciding whether words or behaviour are threatening, is a question of fact to be decided by the jury using an objective test based on whether the reasonable person would perceive the words were threatening rather than on whether the defendant believed s/he was making threatening comments or if any perceived victim did or would have believed them to be threatening. *Brutus v Cozens* [1973] AC 854, [1972] 3 WLR 521 and *DPP v Clarke* (1991) 94 Cr App R 359 stated that the words need to be given their ordinary meaning, and the jury need to take into account the impact that the words or behaviour would have on an ordinary reasonable person.

In terms of what is meant by racial hatred, the definition is outlined in other pieces of legislation (such as the Equality Act 2010), but cases such as *White* [2001] EWCA Crim 216 have held that the definition given to 'racial group' should be non-technical and broad, and should be interpreted as it would normally be understood in everyday language.

20.7 Popular Culture

A prominent topic in recent years has been so-called 'cancel culture'. This started predominantly as an online phenomenon but has trickled down to live settings as part of what is commonly referred to as the 'culture wars' in the UK. These manifest as what we can loosely see as the conflict between the 'woke' left and the 'alt' right. Free speech is central to this culture war. 'Cancel culture' or 'call-out' culture is a modern form of ostracism whereby someone is publicly rejected and expelled from a social or even professional group for saying something that the group disagrees with.

A prominent example of this was the response to the author JK Rowling's comments about trans women which many felt were transphobic. The response to her comments were furious and created a media and Twitter storm. Rowling was labelled a TERF (trans-exclusionary radical feminist), and openly criticised by a number of the *Harry Potter* film cast as well as by the Robert F Kennedy Institution which had hitherto awarded her a human rights prize. Online cancel culture has offline implications, and has been blamed for the 'no platforming' of prominent feminists such as Germaine Greer from UK universities. This typically involves seeking to annul events featuring guest speakers at universities because of their views. In the past, no-platforming has generally focussed on racist or far-rights speakers, but in recent years, much emphasis has been on feminist speakers who question some of the policies recommended by pro-trans groups. This has been seen as a danger to free speech by the UK government and the Higher Education (Freedom of Speech) Act 2023 has been enacted which allows speakers to be compensated if they are no-platformed, and imposes fines on any universities or student unions with no-platforming policies

The public debate on this topic frames the issue as one relating to freedom of speech, and in particular the alt right have used the existence of cancel culture to attack the existence of hate speech laws. They claim this as evidence of a free speech crisis, and highlight the 'chilling effect' of hate speech laws. However, from a legal perspective, there is very little here to do with hate speech laws or their implementation. Cancel culture is about the social ostracism of the individual rather than about criminalising them. The issue is really about how social norms are changing and how these are spread and enforced via the internet. It also feeds into broader concerns about the coarsening of public debate, the binary nature of political and social discussions online, and intolerance of the views of others.

In fact, cancel culture is just as prevalent (if not more so) in the US where there are no laws banning hate speech as a general matter. Even in the UK, where hate speech laws do exist, the stirring up offences are still rarely prosecuted and there is no evidence that this is likely to change. In fact, there is evidence that the courts will continue to view the preservation of free speech as paramount. In January 2019, there was a high-profile incident relating to Harry Miller, a man who, in a Tweet, questioned whether trans women are in fact women. His tweets were reported to the police, and he was visited by a police officer in his home to discuss his comments. He sought judicial review of this decision and the court found in his favour saying that the police's actions were a 'disproportionate interference' with his right to freedom of expression. Concerns surrounding the legal implementation of hate speech laws may therefore be exaggerated. Nevertheless, cancel culture as a social phenomenon is troubling and will likely have a chilling effect on how people behave on the internet for fear of what will happen if they make or post controversial statements.

Chara Bakalis is a Reader in Law at Oxford Brookes University in the UK. She has a particular expertise in the criminalisation of online hate speech. Her work has been cited extensively in a number of law reform projects relating to hate crime both in the UK and internationally.

Chapter 21
Short Country Report–Criminalising Hate Speech: Egypt

Ahmed Elkahwagy

Contents

Abstract The prohibition of hateful expression in Egypt was historically used as a tool to protect the interests of the Egyptian State, by linking the crime to the criteria of disturbance of the public peace. With different UN treaty bodies reviewing the Egyptian Law, it looks like some official efforts have been deployed to give effect to international norms, as the 2014 Constitution in its equality clause has considered incitement of hatred a crime to be punished by Law, but the current legal framework relating to hateful expression remains fragmented and incomplete.

Keyword History of hate speech · Constitutional obligation to criminalise hate speech · Disturbance of public peace · Hate speech as protection of the State

21.1 National Constitutional and Criminal Law

According to Article 53 of the 2014 Egyptian Constitution, "discrimination and *incitement to hate* are crimes punishable by law. The state shall take all necessary measures to eliminate all forms of discrimination, and the law shall regulate the establishment of an independent commission for this purpose." (emphasis added) The Egyptian legislature has yet to expressly criminalize incitement to hate under this constitutional provision. However, in 2006, Article 176 of the Penal Code was

A. Elkahwagy (✉)
Alexandria University, Alexandria, Egypt
e-mail: kahwaji_ahmad1@hotmail.com

E. Heinze (ed.), *Criminalising Hate Speech*,
https://doi.org/10.1007/978-94-6265-650-5_21

amended, and the word 'hate' was replaced with the word 'discriminate'. Article 98-a-bis criminalizes inciting hatred or disdain towards the State or "the basic principles on which stands the socialist system of rule in the State".

Otherwise constitutional law has never been applied to hateful expression *per se*. However, constitutional provisions relating to religious freedom has been applied by different Egyptian courts, as testified by the case of Bahai faith. Bahais lived in Egypt as a tolerated community for decades until the promulgation of Law 263 of 1960 which dissolved Bahai spiritual assemblies and institutions. While this law did not criminalize adherence to the Bahai faith, it has opened the door for security agencies to subject Baha'is in Egypt to harassment, discrimination and detentions in violation of the Constitution and international human rights law. (cf. www.eipr.org)

The Supreme Court of Egypt considered the constitutional validity of the 1960 Law in 1975. The Court established a distinction between freedom of religion and freedom of religious expression (Supreme Court, case no. 7, judicial year 2). Based on that distinction, it ruled that the Bahai faith was not entitled to the same protection as the three recognized monotheistic religions (Islam, Christianity, Judaism), as the Public Order decrees that the expression of the Bahai faith be in the hearts and not in public.

However, after a protracted legal case in 2009 (Supreme Administrative Court, case no. 10831, judicial year 54, 16 March 2009), the Bahai finally secured the right to an identification card. The Court found that the current legal framework violates article 46 of the then-applicable 1971 Constitution, guaranteeing freedom of faith and freedom of religious expression. Nevertheless, as their faith remains unrecognized by the State, Bahai are obliged to put a dash in the space instead of their religious affiliation, since identifying Bahai faith in ID documents would amount to a recognition of the Bahai faith which violates the Public Order that guarantees exclusive protection for monotheistic religions (cf. www.justice.gov).

21.2 International Covenant on Civil and Political Rights (ICCPR)

Egypt ratified the ICCPR on 14 January 1982, but has not consented to individual complaints procedures. The UN Human Rights Committee (UN-HRC), in its consideration of the third and fourth periodic reports of Egypt (CCPR/C/EGY/2001/3), issued the following Concluding Observations (CCPR/CO/76/EGY, 28 November 2002).

"The Committee is deeply concerned at the State party's failure to take action following the publication of some very violent articles against the Jews in the Egyptian press, which in fact constitute advocacy of *racial and religious hatred* and incitement to discrimination, hostility and violence. The State party must take whatever action is necessary to punish such acts by ensuring respect for article 20, paragraph 2, of the Covenant." (para 18, emphasis added)

Currently there is no precedent for Egypt's legislators, officials, or courts applying the ICCPR to situations involving hateful expression.

21.3 International Convention on the Elimination of All Forms of Racial Discrimination (ICERD)

Egypt ratified ICERD on 1 May 1967, but has not consented to individual complaints procedures. The UN Committee on the Elimination of Racial Discrimination (UN-CERD), in its consideration of the thirteenth, fourteenth, fifteenth and sixteenth periodic reports of Egypt (CERD/C/384/Add.3), has issued the following Concluding Observations (U.N. Doc. A/56/18, paras 278–297 [2001]):

"The Committee remains concerned that the legislation of the State party does not seem to respond fully to the requirements of article 4 of the Convention, specifically article 4 (a), which requires States parties to declare as an offence punishable by law all dissemination of ideas based on racial superiority or *hatred*, incitement to racial discrimination, as well as all acts of violence or incitement to such acts against any race or group of persons of another colour or ethnic origin." (para 287, emphasis added)

Currently there is no precedent for Egypt's legislators, officials, or courts applying the ICERD to situations involving hateful expression. However, Egypt has replied to the UN-CERD observations relating to hateful expression in its seventeenth to twenty-second periodic reports (CERD/C/EGY/17–22, 15 April 2014) as follows:

> Chapter 3 of the new Constitution on rights and freedoms provides in article 53, as detailed in part I of this report, for the equality of citizens before the law, prohibits discrimination on any grounds, treats discrimination and *incitement to hatred* as a criminal offence punishable by law, requires the State to take the necessary measures for the elimination of all forms of discrimination and further provides for the establishment of an independent commission for that purpose. [...] In the light of the above, the necessary legislative amendments are being made in order to criminalize all forms of discrimination and *incitement to hatred*, lay down appropriate penalties and establish an independent commission to combat discrimination, as provided for in the new Constitution.

Furthermore, the Human Rights National Council has commented on the above-mentioned UN-CERD report in 2015 and has observed that "Egyptian law is still devoid of any provisions that make ethnic or racial motives an aggravating circumstance for the actions prohibited under Paragraph (a) of Article 4 of the ICERD." Thus, the Council recommended that "all necessary measures be taken to ensure the promulgation of a law prohibiting discrimination and *incitement to hatred* and the establishment of an independent commission in accordance with the provisions of Article (53) of the Constitution."

The UN-CERD has reviewed Egypt's recent efforts in its concluding considerations on the 17–22 periodic reports (CERD/C/EGY/CO/17–22, 6 January 2016). It expressed some concerns regarding the amendment of Article 176 of the Criminal Code making racial discrimination an offense:

> The Committee regrets that this offence is provided for only in the limited context of the media and is linked to the existence of a breach of the peace. The Committee reaffirms its concern that the law of the State party does not prohibit the dissemination of ideas based on racial superiority or *hatred* or the establishment of racist organizations.

21.4 Regional Law and Organisations

Egypt is a party to the African Charter on Human and Peoples' Rights since 1984. No known rulings or findings of the African Commission has been revealed that have actually or potentially affected Egypt's laws or policies on hateful expression.

21.5 Judicial Rulings

The body of Egyptian judicial rulings relating to hateful expressions dates to the 1940s and the 1950s. The rulings coincide with a period of political turmoil in Egypt, with popular voices calling for the abolition of feudalism and the imprisonment of capitalists. Back then, the applicable text of the Penal Code relating to hateful expression was article 176. It read as follows:

> Whoever incites, by any of the aforementioned methods, to *hate or contempt* a group or groups of people, if such incitement is likely to disturb the public peace, shall be punished by imprisonment for a period not exceeding one year and a fine of no less than twenty pounds and not exceeding one hundred pounds, or either of these two penalties.

The Cassation Court, the highest judicial body in Egypt, in its criminal division, has issued several rulings applying article 176 of the Penal Code:

- Two journalists were accused of inciting hatred of capitalists in their articles (Cassation Court [criminal], case no. 43, judicial year 17, 21 January 1947)
- A person was accused of spreading communist ideas that calls for the revolution of the Proletariat and "calls for the hatred of capitalists seen as traitors" (Cassation Court [criminal], case no. 1394, judicial year 20, 17 April 1951)
- Another journalist was convicted for publicly inciting hatred against the group of agricultural landowners "by using words and expressions that describes landowners as feudal tyrants who oppress the peasants and force them to cultivate the land" (Cassation Court [criminal], case no. 440, judicial year 22, 12 April 1954)

After the 1952 revolution that brought a political regime sympathetic to the socialist cause, the judicial rulings relating to hateful expression did not know the same relevance. A search of the judicial database of the Cassation Court did not bring any occurrences of the application of article 176 of the Penal Code.

21.6 Additional Observations

Henry Maina describes African laws and jurisprudence related to incitement of hatred as 'a patchwork', 'uneven and inconsistent', 'the interpretation and legal reasoning deployed often appears vague, ad hoc and possibly lacking in conceptual discipline or rigour'. (Henry Maina, *The prohibition of incitement to hatred in Africa: Comparative review and proposal for a threshold*, A study prepared for the regional expert meeting on Article 20, Organized by the Office of the High Commissioner for Human Rights, Nairobi, April 6–7, 2011).

Although Henry Maina did not analyse Egyptian Law, his statements apply nonetheless to the Egyptian legal framework regarding hateful which is very fragmented. In addition to the constitutional and criminal provisions noted above, it is worth observing, for example:

Civil Society Law provisions: Another prohibition of incitement to hatred is the result of combination of Articles 15 and 95 of the 2019 Law no. 149 regulating civil work activities. In Article 15, associations are prohibited from calling for discrimination between citizens and of exercising "any activity inciting discrimination or *hatred*". Article 95 penalises the violation of the prohibition with a hefty fine of up to a million Egyptian pounds.

Sports Law provisions: The Egyptian legislator has sometimes taken a venue-specific approach to criminalizing hateful expression. Law no. 71 of 2017 considers a crime the act of inciting hatred or discrimination during Sports activities. It is the only occurrence in Egyptian Law where hateful expression is explicitly mentioned as a crime against individuals and not the State.

It is obvious from this national survey that the prohibition of hateful expression was historically used as a tool to protect the interests of the Egyptian State. With different UN treaty bodies reviewing the Egyptian Law, it looks like some official efforts have been deployed to give effect to international norms, but the current legal framework relating to hateful expression remains fragmented and incomplete.

Ahmed Elkahwagy is Associate Professor of Criminal Law, Alexandria University, Egypt. He obtained his Ph.D in 2019 from the University of Poitiers, entitled The application of international treaties by the domestic criminal judge in Egypt, the United States and France. Poitiers Bar First Prize 2021, Special Mention of the AHJUCAF Prize 2021. Elkahwagy currently serves as Executive Director of the journal Al-Hoqouq for Legal and Economic Studies (published by the Faculty of Law of Alexandria University) and Executive Director of the Alexandria Center for Arbitration and Legal Services.

Chapter 22
Short Country Report—Criminalising Hate Speech: Montenegro

Velimir Rakočević

Contents

Abstract In Montenegro, hate speech has escalated into violence and hostility and it is mostly present in media content. The most frequent victims are women, members of the Roma community, LGBT persons and persons with disabilities. The state is obliged to apply provisions related to the prohibition of hate speech, which are defined in the Criminal Code and other acts in accordance with international standards and ECtHR jurisprudence. The state's response to hate speech did not produce the expected results. The reactions of the public to hate speech, which are often not the consequent and condemning, are worrying. The state must suppress hate speech more effectively with the help of international institutions.

Keywords Hatred · Violence · Sexism · Homophobia

22.1 National Constitutional Law

Article 7, Article 8 and Article 53 of Constitution, Official Gazette of Montenegro, number 1/2007 and 38/2013-amendments I-XVI.

V. Rakočević (✉)
Faculty of Law, University of Montenegro, Podgorica, Montenegro
e-mail: Velimir@gmail.com

E. Heinze (ed.), *Criminalising Hate Speech*,
https://doi.org/10.1007/978-94-6265-650-5_22

22.2 National Statutory or Administrative Law

The Ombudsman: The first basic group of jobs-the area of justice, public administration and general competencies, the second main group of jobs -the area of protection against abuse, security and the national preventive mechanism for protection against torture, the third basic group of jobs-the are area of children's rights, youth and social protection, fourth basic group of tasks-area of protection against discrimination, vulnerable groups and gender equality -Institutional mechanisms for protection against discrimination.

22.3 International Covenant on Civil and Political Rights (ICCPR)

The High Court in Podgorica sentenced A.H. to 10 months in prision, because by posting on his facebook profile, he incited hatred towards members of Serbian nationality.

22.4 International Convention on the Elimination of All Forms of Racial Discrimination (ICERD)

During 2020, the Higher State Prosecutor's Office in Podgorica opened cases against 46 persons for the criminal offense of inciting national, racial and religious hatred, and in all cases all necessary measures and actions were taken to establish the existence of elements of this criminal offense. With comprehensive analysis of collected information and evidence, the Prosecutor's Office filed indictments against 4 persons with the High Court in Podgorica, while in relation to 7 persons cases were transferred to the jurisdiction of basic state prosecutor's offices, and in relation to 34 persons decisions on rejection of criminal charges were made, because they did not find that there is a grounded suspicion that the reported persons committed that criminal offense, while 1 case is in the reconnaissance phase.

In all cases in which decisions on rejection of criminal charges were made, of which the applicants of criminal charges were informed at the same time, with the instruction that they have the right to file a complaint against the decisions cases, and in all 3 cases the complaints were rejected as unfounded, which indicates that the prosecution made a correct and lawful decision, and in 2 cases prosecution was undertaken after the decision to reject the criminal complaint where the court ruled that there was no place for charges. In relation to the 4 persons against whom the indictment was filed, the proceedings were terminated before the High Court in Podgorica with convictions and in 3 cases the prosecutor filed an appeal against the decision on the sentence.

Having in mind the number of criminal charges for those criminal offenses in 2020, in relation to the number of criminal charges for this criminal offense in 2019 where there were charges against 6 persons, and in 2018 only against 2 persons, this clearly indicates conclusion that the number of criminal charges for this criminal offense has significantly increased in 2020, and which cases were approached by the prosecution with great care and detailed analysis of all collected information and data obtained during the investigation, and were also applied in making the decision and the standards and case law of the European Court of Human Rights, all with the aim of making a correct and lawful decision.

In 2021, the Higher State Prosecutor's Office in Podgorica opened cases against 6 persons, for the criminal offense of inciting national, racial and religious hatred, and on these cases it was decided that an indictment was filed against 1 person and the trial is ongoing, against 4 persons were issued decisions on the rejection of the criminal report, while 1 case is in the investigation phase.

22.5 Council of Europe

The European Commission against Racism and Intolerance (ECRI) is an independent monitoring body which provides member States with concrete and practical advice on how to tackle problems of racism and intolerance in their country.

Velimir Rakočević is a Professor at the Faculty of Law, University of Montenegro, Podgorica, Montenegro.

Chapter 23
Short Country Report—Criminalising Hate Speech: North Macedonia

Nikola Tupancheski and Boban Misoski

Contents

Abstract In the Republic of North Macedonia, measures for criminalizing hate speech have been accepted within the provisions of several specific offenses within the Criminal Code. However, the Criminal Code does not specifically contain the offence of "hate speech," nor does it specify a legal definition. Important steps regarding prevention of hate speech and all sorts of discrimination were undertaken with the enactment of the Law on Prevention of Discrimination. This law contains provisions where specific types of discrimination are defined, and specific administrative activities are undertaken in prevention of discrimination including hate speech. State Commission for Prevention of Discrimination, that is a state's body established under the Law on Prevention of Discrimination, has performed a significant role into raising the awareness regarding prevention of the discrimination, but also undertook important activities into prevention of the discrimination in specific cases.

Keywords Hate speech legislation · Penalties for hate speech · Discrimination

N. Tupancheski · B. Misoski (✉)
Faculty of Law Iustinianus Primus, University of Ss. Cyril and Methodius, Skopje, Republic of North Macedonia
e-mail: b.misoski@pf.ukim.edu.mk

E. Heinze (ed.), *Criminalising Hate Speech*,
https://doi.org/10.1007/978-94-6265-650-5_23

23.1 National Constitutional Law

In 1991 the Republic of North Macedonia adopted a constitution, which includes many human rights including non-discrimination rights. These rights have been further developed within national law. Some key articles are as follows:

> Article 9 presents the first and most general constitutional provision providing that all citizens in North Macedonia are equal in all rights, regardless of gender, race, nationality, social background, religious beliefs, etc. Article 9 is the first constitutional step in regard to anti-discrimination rights and represents one of the most important provisions in the Constitution.
>
> Article 16 guarantees freedom of speech and of the press.
>
> Article 19 defines freedom of religion and religious gatherings, and separates the secular character of the state from religious institutions.
>
> Article 20 sets forth fundamental rights such as freedom of association and the creation of organisations that allow people to express their political, economic, cultural, and other views. It also forbids the creation of military and paramilitary formations.
>
> Under Article 29, non-citizens in North Macedonia have rights in the Constitution and under statutory laws and international conventions. In this article the state also grants rights for asylum seekers and non-nationals from countries that persecute them for their democratic or political views or actions. Extradition is authorised only on the basis of international conventions or through the institution of reciprocity.
>
> Article 50 protects all rights including anti-discriminatory ones and the right of every citizen to judicial protection. It sets the bases for protection of all constitutional rights before the Constitutional Court as well as the judicial protection of legislative rights in from of a court. The citizen has the right to be familiarized with his human rights and freedoms, as well as the right to actively contribute to their promotion and protection.
>
> Article 51 requires that all laws must be in accordance with the Constitution. In itself this is not an anti-discrimination provision, however it applies the supremacy of the Constitution and all its guarantees.

23.2 National Statutory and Administrative Law

Regarding hate speech, numerous laws have evolved to further shape the Constitution, particularly in relation to non-discrimination laws. There is no specific crime in the Criminal Code that covers hate speech in detail, or provides any definition of hate speech. Instead, the regulation of hate speech arises from several laws:

- Article 179: "those who, intending to ridicule, shall publicly mock the Macedonian people and the communities that live in the country, shall be punished with a fine".
- Article 319: "A person who by force, mistreatment, endangering the security, ridicule of the national, ethnic or religious symbols, by igniting or in another manner destroying a flag of the Republic of Macedonia or flags of other countries, damaging other people's objects, by desecration of monuments, graves,

or in some other manner causes or excites discord and intolerance based on sex, race, skin color, gender, membership in a marginalized group, ethnicity, language, citizenship, social origin, religion or religious persuasion or other kinds of persuasions, education, political affiliation, family or marital condition, property status, health condition or any other basis envisaged by law or by a ratified international agreement, shall be punished with imprisonment of one to five years".

- Article 394-d: "(1) The person who through a computer system spreads resist and xenophobic written material, images or other representation of an idea or theory that assists, promotes or encourages hatred, discrimination or violence against any person or group based on their sex, race, skin color, gender, membership in a marginalized group, ethnicity, language, citizenship, social origins, religion or religious persuasion, other types of persuasion, education, political affiliation, personal or social status, metal or physical disability, age, family or marital condition, property status, health condition or any other base envisaged with the law or ratifies international agreement, shall be punished with imprisonment of one to five years.

  (2) The punishment referred to in paragraph (1) from the present Article shall apply to the person that commits the act through other means of public information.

  (3) The person who shall perpetrate the criminal act referred to in paragraphs (1) and (2) from the present Article, by abusing their position or authorization or if those actions resulted in disorder, and violence against people or significant property damage, they shall be punished with imprisonment of one to ten years".

- Article 407-a: "(1) The person that shall deny, minimize, approve or justify the criminal activities defined in Articles 403 to 407 by using public information system shall be given a prison sentence of 1 to 5 years.

  (2) If the denying, minimizing, approval or justification has been performed to stimulate hatred, discrimination or violence against some person or group of persons because of their race, skin color, nationality, ethnicity, religion or persuasion, mental or physical difficulty, sex, gender identity, sexual orientation and political persuasion, the perpetrator shall be punished with imprisonment of at least four years."

- Article 417, paragraph 3: "a person who spreads ideas about the superiority of one race above another, or who advocates racial hate, or instigates racial discrimination, shall be punished with imprisonment of six months to three years".

  In 2019, the national Parliament passed a "Law for prevention and protection against discrimination", which set the cornerstone for the country's struggle against discrimination. This law aims to define discrimination and its forms, and creates a commission for the prevention and protection against discrimination. This is an independent state financed body and has the exclusive authority to work in the frame of the law itself, as well as to monitor the progress of its implementation. This law defines the freedom of religion in the articles:

- Article 3 explains the freedom of religion publicly or privately.
- Article 4 forbids discrimination against religion
- Article 5 defines the freedom of any religious institution to internal organisation.

23.3 International Covenant on Civil and Political Rights (ICCPR)

Regarding Concluding observations on hateful expression, the ICCPR has issued for North Macedonia, the following:

- Optional Protocol to the International Covenant on Civil and Political Rights ratified 18th of January 1994.

  Regarding individual complaints procedures, there are few that can be singled out.

- Optional Protocol to the International Covenant on Civil and Political Rights ratified 18th of January 1994.

23.4 International Convention on the Elimination of All Forms of Racial Discrimination (ICERD)

Regarding Concluding observations on hateful expression, the ICCPR has issued for North Macedonia, the following:

- A concluding observation of the committee on the elimination of Racial Discrimination. This concluding observation was issued twice. Once on 13th of June 1997 and also on 15th of October 2007.
- Concluding comments of the Committee on the Elimination of Discrimination against Women: Regarding individual complaints procedures, there are few that can be singled out.

- Individual complaints procedure under the International Convention on the Elimination of All Forms of Racial Discrimination, which was accepted on the 22nd of December 1999.

23.5 Council of Europe

Regarding the Council of Europe, North Macedonia has ratified few treaties on the matter of hateful expression and anti-discrimination:

- Council of Europe Convention on preventing and combating violence against women and domestic violence, ratified on 1st of August 2014.
- Additional Protocol to the Convention on Cybercrime, concerning the criminalisation of acts of a racist and xenophobic nature committed through computer systems, ratified on the 1st of March 2006.
- Framework Convention for the Protection of National Minorities, ratified on the 1st of February 1998

23.6 Judicial Rulings

In North Macedonia, case law does not set binding precedent but it does hold authority, and is sometimes taken into account by the legislative branch.

Nikola Tupanceski is a Professor of Criminal Law, with strong educational, scientific and research activities, with longtime experience in organizing conferences, seminars, trainings and workshops. He has participated in national and regional conferences as a keynote speaker or panelist. With extensive experience in legislative activities (such as drafting laws and by-laws) and experience in writing expert analysis on various topics in the field of criminal law, especially financial crimes, organized crime, corruption and white collar crimes. He is author of three university text-books and has authored or co-authored scientific articles published in national and international peer-reviewed renowned journals.

Boban Misoski is Professor in Criminal Procedure Law at Faculty of Law Iustinianus Primus at the University Ss. Cyril and Methodius in Skopje, which also awarded his 2013 PhD thesis *Bail as a measure for successful conveyance of the Criminal Procedure*. Misoski has published four co-authored textbooks and more than 50 scholarly articles. His primary research filed includes Effective and Efficient Criminal Procedure, Confiscation and Social Re-use of Confiscated Assets, Juvenile Justice, Illegal Firearms. In addition to research in Germany, USA and UK, he has worked at the Ministry of Justice's work group drafting the Law on Criminal Procedure and is Head of the Ministry of Justice's work group for new law on Management of Confiscated Assets.

[illegible] Terms of [illegible]

[illegible] Council of [illegible]

- [illegible] and [illegible]
- Additional [illegible]
  [illegible] on the [illegible]
- [illegible] of February 1998 [illegible]

[illegible]

Chapter 24
Short Country Report—Criminalising Hate Speech: United States of America

Alexander Tsesis

Contents

24.1 National Constitutional Law

The United States Supreme Court has interpreted the Free Speech Clause of the First Amendment to limit the effectiveness of international covenants containing restrictions on speech. In ratifying conventions, the United States has included codicils qualifying its signatory status as only extending to those provisions that do not require violation of constitutional clauses, especially the Free Speech Clause of the First Amendment. Its reservations, limit the effectiveness of other signatories to pursue and/or punish the expression of racism, hatred, incitement, and ethnocentrism emanating from the United States. Specific reservations are discussed below.

A. Tsesis (✉)
Florida State University College of Law, Tallahassee, United States of America
e-mail: alexanderTsesis@gmail.com

E. Heinze (ed.), *Criminalising Hate Speech*,
https://doi.org/10.1007/978-94-6265-650-5_24

24.2 National Statutory and Administrative Law

The United States is a federal system. The treaties that the executive signs and that are later passed by the advice and consent of the Senate become supreme law of the land. Nevertheless, states retain the right to pass sovereign legislation that does not conflict with the national plenary powers. That is, federal treaties pre-empt state law. Because the power of the President to enter and the Senate to consent to a Treaty is plenary, and they are supreme law and binding on state governments.[1] Most importantly, in this context, each state must follow the terms of treaties, covenants, and charters, including any added reservations.

24.3 International Covenant on Civil and Political Rights (ICCPR)

In the United States, prior to an international covenant being treated with as much force of law as domestic legislation, the Senate must give its advice and consent to the instrument consistent with common law. This is especially the case with common law constitutionalism, by which is meant judicial interpretation of constitutional principles. Most relevant for purposes of this report are Supreme Court decisions protecting the use of even offensive language targeting a protected group, such as gays and lesbians. Snyder v. Phelps, 562 U.S. 443 (2011).

The United States became a party to the ICCPR at the time of ratification in 1992. Cf. Sosa v. Alvarez–Machain, 542 U.S. 692, 734–35 (2004). The Covenant then became the law throughout the United States pursuant to the Supremacy Clause of the Constitution; however, the United States adopted several reservations to it. While as a matter of international law the ICCPR binds the United States, America regards the Covenant not to be self-executing, thereby creating no obligation on federal courts to enforce it absent prior enactment of a federal statute.[2] Igartua v. United States, 626 F.3d 592, 605 (1st Cir. 2010). In light of U.S. Supreme Court precedents and the libertarian free speech culture, it is highly unlikely that federal legislation would be enacted to enforce the ICCPR's required prohibitions against hateful expressions. In the fleetingly small likelihood that such legislation would be passed it would not survive judicial scrutiny under the prevailing jurisprudence. The U.S. Supreme Court

[1] The Supremacy Clause, Art. VI, cl. 2, reads: "This Constitution, and the Laws of the United States which shall be made in Pursuance thereof; and all Treaties made, or which shall be made, under the Authority of the United States, shall be the supreme Law of the Land; and the Judges in every State shall be bound thereby, any Thing in the Constitution or Laws of any State to the Contrary notwithstanding."

[2] Treaties in the United States can either be self-executing or executory. A self-executing treaty "is one that operates of itself without the aid of legislation." U.S. v. Lindh, 212 F.Supp.2d 541, 554 n. 20 (E.D.Va.2002), whereas an executory treaty requires action by Congress to be effective to file claims in U.S. district courts.

prohibits the use of viewpoint-selective discrimination in the formulation of speech codes. *See* R.A.V. v. St. Paul, 505 U.S. 377 (1992).

Under current circumstances any such legislation would be especially unlikely because the United States Senate has set out reservations to American obligations under the ICCPR that reject the enforcement of Article 20's prohibition against "national, racial or religious hatred that constitutes incitement to discrimination, hostility or violence." Such regulation, the United States Senate, in keeping with Supreme Court precedent, is regarded as an infringement on the rights of free speech and association under the First Amendment of the U.S. Constitution. 138 Cong. Rec. 8070–71; Igartua-De La Rosa v. United States, 417 F.3d 145, 174 n.42 (1st Cir. 2005). Due to this fact, the rare American cases that mention the ICCPR refer to the reservations but, in compliance with federal law, refuse to apply the Covenant . In one case, a Court of Appeals mentioned European nations that had adopted the ICCPR without deposing any such reservations. Yahoo! Inc. v. La Ligue Contre Le Racisme Et L'Antisemitisme, 433 F.3d 1199, 1227 (9th Cir. 2006). Neither has Congress passed implementing legislation to grant federal courts jurisdiction to adjudicate matters against state actors (42 U.S.C. sec. 1983) for allegedly violating the ICCPR. Ciaprazi v. Goord, GLS/, 2005 WL 3531464, at *15 (N.D.N.Y. Dec. 22, 2005).U.S. federal court cases that recognize subject matter jurisdiction to hear and adjudicate cases under ICCPR, nevertheless are restrained by the country's reservation on hate speech. For example, the Fifth Circuit Court of Appeals has found that the U.S. reservation on ICCPR Article 6(5) was a valid exercise of treaty power and restricted subject matter jurisdiction. Beazley v. Johnson, 242 F.3d 248, 264 (5th Cir. 2001).

As mentioned, the ICCPR treaty is not self-executing. 138 Cong. Rec. S4783–84 (daily ed. Apr. 2, 1992); United States ex rel. Perez v. Warden, 286 F.3d 1059, 1063 (8th Cir.2002). It therefore requires legislative action to create enforceable rights. Whitney v. Robertson, 124 U.S. 190 (1888). Furthermore, the ICCPR will not allow individual relief for persons praying for a private right of action because of religious and moral grounds. Ruhaak v. Comm'r, 422 F. App'x 530, 532 (7th Cir. 2011). Moreover, absent federal statute no habeas corpus relief is available to petitioner. Habeas relief is not available for a violation of the ICCPR because it is not self-executing. Leinenbach v. Williamson, 152 F. App'x 197, 199 (3d Cir. 2005); Bannerman v. Snyder, 325 F.3d 722, 724 (6th Cir. 2003). Another line of cases relies on the plain language of the ICCPR about its jurisdictional reach to find that the United States is not obligated under the Covenant to provide relief for alleged violations committed outside its borders. See United States v. Duarte-Acero, 296 F.3d 1277, 1283 (11th Cir. 2002).

24.4 International Convention on the Elimination of All Forms of Racial Discrimination (ICERD)

The United States ratified of the Convention on the Elimination of All Forms of Racial Discrimination in 1994, almost three decades after having signed it in 1966. Even then, the country's ratification was accompanied with substantial reservations that the treaty was not self-executing. U.S. Reservations, Declarations, and Understandings, International Convention on the Elimination of All Forms of Racial Discrimination, § III, 140 Cong. Rec. S7634–02 (June 24, 1994). Sarei v. Rio Tinto, PLC, 671 F.3d 736, 768 (9th Cir. 2011), cert. granted, judgment vacated, 569 U.S. 945 (2013). Therefore, legislative action by Congress is required to create causes of action tied to the international obligation.

Upon the 1994 ratification, the United States included a short statement, "That the Constitution and laws of the United States contain extensive protections of individual freedom of speech, expression and association. Accordingly, the United States does not accept any obligation under this Convention, in particular under Articles 4 and 7, to restrict those rights, through the adoption of legislation or any other measures, to the extent that they are protected by the Constitution and laws of the United States." Text - Resolution of Ratification: Senate Consideration of Treaty Document 95-18, sec. 1, https://www.congress.gov/treaty-document/95th-congress/18/resolution-text?r=14&s=1; see also 138 Cong. Rec. 4783, at Reservation I(1), Understanding III(2) (1992) (ratified); see also 140 Cong. Rec. 7634, at Reservation I(1) (1994) (ratified). Such reservations are consistent with United States constitutional and international practices such as those cited in the above discussion of the ICCPR. Hate speech remains a protected category in the United States, where Supreme Court libertarian doctrine limits legislative initiatives on hateful expressions and rhetoric.

The reservation prevents operation in the United States of Article 4 of CERD, which calls on signatories to "adopt immediate and positive measures designed to eradicate all incitement to, or acts of, such discrimination, . . . all dissemination of ideas based on racial superiority or hatred, incitement to racial discrimination, as well as all acts of violence or incitement to such acts." At the time of its adoption, the U.S. delegate "emphasized that her delegation had been able to support the text only on the understanding that ... article IV did not impose on a State Party the obligation to take any action impairing the right to freedom of speech and freedom of association." U.N. GAOR, 20th Sess., 1318th mtg. at 152, ¶ 59, U.N. Doc. A/C.3/SR.1318 (Oct. 25, 1965). The concern in the United States is primarily with the CERD's restrictions on speech. Particularly, the concern is with ambiguity of what constitutes "racial superiority or hatred, incitement of racial discrimination," and many forms of protected expressive conduct that this language might prohibited. Neither are those terms narrowly tailored. American jurists are more concerned than their European counterparts about Article 4's potential to erode the marketplace of ideas.

24.5 Judicial Rulings

The few judicial opinions all mention U.S. reservation providing no substantive interpretation about the ICCPR or CERD.

Alexander Tsesis is the D'Alemberte Chair in Constitutional Law at Florida State University. He is General Editor of the Cambridge Studies on Civil Rights and Civil Liberties and the Oxford Theoretical Foundations in Law. His most book is *Free Speech in the Balance* (Cambridge University Press 2020). His previous books include *Constitutional Ethos* (Oxford University Press 2017) and *The Thirteenth Amendment and American Freedom* (New York University Press 2004). His articles on free speech, constitutional interpretation, and civil rights have appeared in journals such as *Columbia Law Review*, *Cornell Law Review*, *Northwestern University Law Review*, and *Southern California Law Review*.

MIX
Papier aus verantwortungsvollen Quellen
Paper from responsible sources
FSC® C105338

If you have any concerns about our products,
you can contact us on
ProductSafety@springernature.com

In case Publisher is established outside the EU,
the EU authorized representative is:
Springer Nature Customer Service Center GmbH
Europaplatz 3, 69115 Heidelberg, Germany

Printed by Libri Plureos GmbH
in Hamburg, Germany